SOX BID CURSE FAREWELL

• THE 2004 BOSTON RED SOX •

Edited by Bill Nowlin

Associate editors Len Levin and Carl Riechers

Society for American Baseball Research, Inc.

Sox Bid Curse Farewell
The 2004 Boston Red Sox
Edited by Bill Nowlin
Associate editors Len Levin and Carl Riechers

Design: Gilly Rosenthol

All photographs in this book were provided courtesy of the Boston Red Sox, unless otherwise noted.

Back cover photo of Keith Foulke's championship ring is by Bill Nowlin.
Back cover photo of "The Curse is Over" is courtesy of Major League Baseball.

Front cover photograph: Julie Cordeiro, courtesy of the Boston Red Sox. The photograph shows Orlando Cabrera's teammates greeting him as he approaches home plate, having just hit a walkoff 12th-inning home run to beat the Baltimore Orioles on September 22, 2004.

ISBN 978-1-960819-19-2 (paperback)
ISBN 978-1-960819-18-5 (ebook)
Library of Congress Control Number: 2024902760

Copyright © 2024 Society for American Baseball Research, Inc.
All rights reserved. Reproduction in whole or in part without permission is prohibited.

Cronkite School at ASU
555 N. Central Ave. #416
Phoenix, AZ 85004
Phone: (602) 496-1460
Web: www.sabr.org
Facebook: Society for American Baseball Research
Twitter: @SABR

SOX BID CURSE FAREWELL

• THE 2004 BOSTON RED SOX •

To Chris —
Go Sox! It was a long wait.
Bill Nowlin

*This book is dedicated to the memory of
Tim Wakefield (1966-2023)*

CONTENTS

- 7 **Curse Reversed** by Joanne Hulbert
- 9 **Editor's Introduction** by Bill Nowlin

THE PLAYERS

- 11 **TERRY ADAMS** by Jason Scheller
- 15 **ABE ALVAREZ** by Bob LeMoine
- 19 **JIMMY ANDERSON** by Ralph Caola
- 23 **BRONSON ARROYO** by Greg D. Tranter
- 28 **PEDRO ASTACIO** by Gregory H. Wolf
- 33 **MARK BELLHORN** by Jason Scheller
- 38 **JAMIE BROWN** by Bob LeMoine
- 42 **ELLIS BURKS** by Robert Brustad
- 49 **ORLANDO CABRERA** by Tony S. Oliver
- 55 **FRANK CASTILLO** by Luca Rossi
- 58 **CÉSAR CRESPO** by Tony S. Oliver
- 61 **JOHNNY DAMON** by Mark S. Sternman
- 67 **BRIAN DAUBACH** by Karl Cicitto
- 73 **LENNY DINARDO** by Scott Melesky
- 77 **ANDY DOMINIQUE** by Bob LeMoine
- 81 **ALAN EMBREE** by Bill Nowlin
- 85 **KEITH FOULKE** by Keley Russo and Karen DeLuca Stephens
- 91 **NOMAR GARCIAPARRA** by Ralph Caola
- 97 **RICKY GUTIERREZ** by Malcolm Allen
- 103 **ADAM HYZDU** by George "Skip" Tuetken
- 108 **BOBBY JONES** by Budd Bailey
- 112 **GABE KAPLER** by Donna L. Halper
- 118 **BYUNG-HYUN KIM** by Robert P. Nash
- 123 **CURTIS LESKANIC** by Jesse Asbury
- 127 **DEREK LOWE** by Bill Nowlin
- 131 **MARK MALASKA** by John Vorperian
- 135 **ANASTACIO MARTÍNEZ** by Eric Conrad and Mark Morowczynski
- 138 **PEDRO MARTÍNEZ** by Norm King
- 144 **ANGEL "SANDY" MARTÍNEZ** by Eric Conrad and Mark Morowczynski
- 147 **DAVE MCCARTY** by Jeff English
- 152 **RAMIRO MENDOZA** by Nick Malian
- 156 **DOUG MIENTKIEWICZ** by Ryan Palencer and Bill Nowlin
- 160 **KEVIN MILLAR** by Karen DeLuca Stephens and Keley Russo
- 166 **DOUG MIRABELLI** by Matt Perry
- 170 **BILL MUELLER** by Kevin Bley
- 175 **MIKE MYERS** by Robert Emerson
- 178 **JOE NELSON** by Bob Webster
- 182 **TROT NIXON** by Tim Peeler
- 187 **DAVID ORTIZ** by Bill Nowlin
- 195 **BRANDON PUFFER** by Bill Nowlin
- 201 **MANNY RAMÍREZ** by Bill Nowlin
- 206 **POKEY REESE** by Bob LeMoine
- 212 **DAVE ROBERTS** by Richard Bogovich
- 219 **CURT SCHILLING** by Bill Nowlin
- 225 **PHIL SEIBEL** by Greg D. Tranter
- 229 **EARL SNYDER** by Budd Bailey
- 233 **MIKE TIMLIN** by Bill Nowlin
- 239 **JASON VARITEK** by Chad Hagan
- 243 **TIM WAKEFIELD** by Bill Nowlin
- 249 **SCOTT WILLIAMSON** by Mark Schremmer
- 253 **KEVIN YOUKILIS** by Dave Dionisio

MANAGER

260 **TERRY FRANCONA** by Robert Emerson

COACHING STAFF

265 **INO GUERRERO** by Bill Pruden
268 **BILL HASELMAN** by David Moore
274 **RON "PAPA JACK" JACKSON** by Tony Oliver
281 **LYNN JONES** by Paul Hofmann
287 **DANA LEVANGIE** by Saul Wisnia
292 **BRAD MILLS** by Will Hyland
296 **EUCLIDES "EUKY" ROJAS** by Tony S. Oliver
302 **DAVE SVEUM** by Bill Pruden
306 **DAVE WALLACE** by Bill Pruden

OTHER

310 **How the 2004 Red Sox Team was Put Together** by Bill Nowlin
312 **Red Sox Reserves in the Playoffs** by Bill Nowlin
313 **The View From Above the Crowds** by Bill Ballou
316 **Down on the Farm: The Story of the 2004 Sarasota Red Sox** by Christopher Chavis
318 **A Yankee Fan's Perspective on the 2004 American League Championship Series** by Jeb Stewart
320 **Graveyard visit in October 2004**
321 **The Red Sox and the Yankees: Father and Son** by Paul Semendinger
323 **The Trophy Tour: Touch 'Em All Across Red Sox Nation** by Cecilia M. Tan
327 **Kathryn Gemme Finally Saw the Red Sox Win the World Series, at Age 109** by Bill Nowlin
330 **Significant games from the 2004 season**
333 **CONTRIBUTORS**

RED SOX MEMORIES

Larry Baldassaro 8	Scott Melesky 200
Fr. Gerald Beirne 8	Tom Nahigian 27
Charlie Bevis 80	Eric T. Poulin 248
Mike Bresciani 22	José Ramírez 174
Walt Cherniak 137	Alexander Reardon 66
Kit Crissey 32	Victor Son 66
Anne Enos 130	David Southwick 143
M (New York) Frank 32	Mark Stangl 273
Norm Ginsberg 165	Karen DeLuca Stephens 72
Belt High Hallisey 259	Mark Sternman 174
Donna Halper 200	John Tierney 111
Barry Halpern 48	Richard Dixie Tourangeau ... 57
Joanne Hulbert 122	Skip Tuetken 232
Evan Katz 41	Ed Wheatley 177
Seamus Kearney 155	

CURSE REVERSED

BY JOANNE HULBERT

Eighty-six years. Decades of near-misses and long-shot losses that kept a World Series win out of reach of the Boston Red Sox. Years turned into decades and – occasionally – a near-miss tantalized the team and fans. What could possibly have been the reason for all the misfortune? Waiting until next year became an old, tired phrase that kept the Old Town Team looking forward but also sometimes glancing back, looking for reasons why this disappointing record kept on growing. Was it Frazee? Was it the Yankees? Inept managing? Or were the fans not rooting loud enough? Blame must be placed somewhere, or on someone. After all the excuses and theories faded away, all eyes turned toward Babe Ruth and the Curse of the Bambino. How, when, and why did the Boston Red Sox end up with this ethereal, poetic, and commercially lucrative explanation?

On January 5, 1920, a day of infamy for Boston's baseball fans, Babe Ruth signed with the New York Yankees for the money and then some (two years at $10,000 per year with bonuses of $10,000 a year and $5,000 for signing), and he wanted $20,000 from Harry Frazee for signing a contract with Miller Huggins which was to come from the Boston club.[1] That is what we know about the history that would ultimately set into motion the seeds planted for a curse upon the Boston Red Sox. Seventy years would pass by before the curse was revealed as the cause of Boston's baseballic misfortune. All the usual suspects, Harry Frazee, Jacob Ruppert – and even the Bambino, Babe Ruth himself – none would live long enough to see how 86 years of Red Sox World Series drought would end.

In the days following the 1920 announcement, Boston newspapers did their best to defuse anxiety over Babe Ruth's exit from Boston. Arthur Duffey wrote: "Why all this hubbub over the sale of Babe Ruth to the New York Yankees? Is the price worth the candle? Boston baseball fans are a pretty sensible lot and why wouldn't it be a good idea to reserve judgment over the Ruth sale for a while until things really have had time to shape themselves? This is not the first time that Boston fans have been thrown a bit into the air with the sale of one of their star players, but in any of the former cases, did it work to the disadvantage of the Boston Club? Of course, it is going to be tough to see the champion fence buster disport in another uniform next season, but after the first storm of criticism has blown away I wouldn't be surprised that if the sale of Ruth to the New York Yankees would prove one of the best things that could happen [to] the Boston Red Sox."[2]

History tells a different tale about Babe Ruth and his celebrated baseball career in New York. When the Babe returned to Fenway Park in the 1920 season, the headline proclaimed: "Babe Ruth Is Here to Make Boston's Holiday Complete." Burt Whitman wrote, "He came into his own as a Red Sox and Hub fans always will keep their enthusiasm for him and his long-distance smashes."[3] No hard feelings, just "welcome back."

As time went on, seasons came and went along with new hope that "this is the year!" The Red Sox counted up near-misses, miscalculations, optimistic predictions, and lost opportunities, and not even the greatest hitter who ever lived could single-handedly rescue the entire franchise. The misfortune of the Red Sox inspired writers to compare the team in terms reminiscent of a Greek tragedy. In the *Saturday Evening Post* in 1946, *Boston Globe* writer Harold Kaese asked a simple question that was year after year repeated: "What's the Matter with the Red Sox?"[4]

In 1986, as Boston went down to defeat in the seventh game of the World Series at the hands of the New York Mets, *New York Times* writer George Vecsey blamed the Bambino in his column titled "Babe Ruth Curse Strikes Again." He wrote: "All the ghosts and demons and curses of the past 68 years continued to haunt the Boston Red Sox last night."[5]

In 1990 the cause of decades of Red Sox misfortune was settled. Simply stated, the sale of Babe Ruth to the Yankees was the punishment endured by Boston for that colossal, disastrous decision. The person who unveiled the news was Dan Shaughnessy of the *Boston Globe*, who said he was informed of this curse by a woman whose grandfather had proclaimed, "Boston will not win a World Series because Babe Ruth was sold to the Yankees. It's the Curse of the Bambino."[6]

Despite all their efforts, must the Boston Red Sox endure some sort of punishment for a ruthless mistake made in 1920? Red Sox fans immediately embraced The Curse that explained away decades of misfortune. Newspapers devoted lines, paragraphs, stories, and The Curse was celebrated in books, including children's literature.[7]

With new ownership and management changes, the 2003 season instilled hope that the Red Sox' fortunes might improve. The gut-wrenching loss to the Yankees in that year's ALCS only confirmed the awful suspicion that the Red Sox were indeed cursed, and something must be done about it.

In 2004, as the Red Sox advanced up the American League East standings, whispers rose to shouts that this might be the year that The Curse would be broken. There were visitations to the Bambino's gravesite where curse-breaking offerings were left. Signs appeared around New England – "Reverse the Curse!" – and as if fans could sing a curse away, songs rang out in Fenway Park – "Dirty Water" – and a twenty-first-century version of an old tune, "Tessie," by the Dropkick Murphys debuted in June 2004. The original song had been adapted and sung by the Royal Rooters at the first World Series back in 1903 and some of the losing Pittsburgh Pirates said it had rattled them, perhaps causing them to lose the World Series.

Had the Boston Red Sox won the World Series in 2004 because they vanquished The Curse of the Bambino? Or did the Babe finally let it go, giving a tip of his hat to Boston after the thrilling ALCS series against New York? There is another possibility. After Boston's victory in the 1918 World Series, there appeared a curious headline and story about the end of the final game: "Tessie! Where was the Old 'Gal' at Fenway?" wrote H.W. Lanigan in the *Boston American*. "Where was 'Tessie?' Forsooth, there wasn't any music at all. President Frazee planned to have music, but so great was the demand for grandstand seats that he was forced to sell the space he had allotted for the band. Curses!"[8]

Ed Martin, baseball writer for the *Boston Globe*, wrote, "The crowd did not come up to expectations. While there was no material evidence of the presence of 'Tessie,' she must have been there in spirit. It is the first time that any Boston club has been in a series that "Tessie" has not been heard from good and proper."[9] Tragically, Martin died of influenza less than a month after writing the lament.

The Dropkick Murphys, the Celtic punk band from Quincy, Massachusetts, played the new-and-improved "Tessie" live at Fenway Park on July 24, 2004. That also happened to be the same day Red Sox catcher Jason Varitek and New York Yankees star Alex Rodriguez conducted a mitt-a-mano brawl. It was the same game where Bill Mueller hit a game-winning walk-off home run to spoil Mariano Rivera's perfect save streak, as well. The ghost of Babe Ruth must have been impressed.

"To this day, the Red Sox have never won a World Series without 'Tessie,'" said Dr. Charles Steinberg, once a Fenway Park man-of-all-jobs. "The Red Sox had it in their first five world championships from 1903 to 1918, and we brought it back in 2004. It's been part of Fenway Park's musical culture."[10]

Was the curse about the Babe? Or had the curse been about Tessie all along? "Tessie" disappeared after 1918 and reappeared in 2004. In 2016 the Tessie mascot joined Wally, and they roam Fenway Park at game time, amusing the fans and perhaps serving another purpose. "Hell hath no fury like a woman scorned," wrote William Congreve in *The Mourning Bride*, published in 1697. To be on the safe side, "Tessie" continues being seen at Fenway Park, just in case, and is heard throughout the park after every Red Sox win.

NOTES

1. "Babe Ruth to Get $45,000," *Boston Post*, January 7, 1920: 1.
2. Arthur Duffey, "Sports Comment," *Boston Post*, January 7, 1920: 11.
3. Burt Whitman, "Babe Ruth Is Here to Make Boston's Holiday Complete," *Boston Herald*, April 19, 1920: 7.
4. Dan Shaughnessy, *At Fenway* (New York: Crown. 1996), 94. Al Hirshberg wrote a book by that title: *What's the Matter with the Red Sox?* (New York: Dodd, Mead and Company, 1973).
5. George Vecsey, "Babe Ruth Curse Strikes Again," *New York Times*, October 28, 1986.
6. Shaughnessy, 94.
7. For instance, see Dan Shaughnessy and C.F. Payne, *The Legend of the Curse of the Bambino* (New York: Simon & Schuster/Paula Wiseman Books, 2005).
8. Ty Waterman and Mel Springer, *The Year the Red Sox Won the World Series* (Boston: Northeastern University Press, 1999), 244.
9. Edward F. Martin, "Wonderful Support When Babe Wobbles," *Boston Globe*, September 10, 1918: 6.
10. "'Tessie' and the Dropkick Murphys, a Red Sox History," www.oursportscentral.com, December 21, 2022. https://www.oursportscentral.com/services/releases/tessie-and-the-dropkick-murphys-a-red-sox-history/n-5908671.

A RED SOX MEMORY

For me, a Sox fan since the late 1940s, the 2004 season was a mix of disbelief, sheer joy, and a tinge of regret. When the Sox wrapped up their historic comeback from a 3-games-to-none deficit to beat the Yankees in the ALCS, I leapt out of my recliner and cheered loudly. But then, when the final out of the World Series was recorded, I sat in that same chair speechless, and with tears streaming down my cheeks, as I thought about those fans, like my parents, who did not live long enough to share that magical moment.

LARRY BALDASSARO

A RED SOX MEMORY

Leaving Fenway Park after David Ortiz's home run finished the Angels, we were intercepted by Providence's WJAR-TV sports reporter Frank Carpano, who asked, "Who do I want the Sox to play next – the Twins or the Yankees?" Of course I shouted, "The Twins!" (dreading the Yankees).

And we got home in time to see it all on the news.

Renteria rolled one back to Foulke, who tossed it to Mientkiewicz, and the Red Sox were now at last WORLD CHAMPIONS! But the four of us watching, deep fans and longtime sufferers, simply watched in silence. Amazingly, not a word was spoken. A few sips of champagne, and we went home. Just another game. Go figure!

FR. GERALD BEIRNE

EDITOR'S INTRODUCTION

BY BILL NOWLIN

This book began as a project of the Boston Chapter of SABR, but as the 20th anniversary of the 2004 Red Sox season approached, it was adopted by the national organization and we are pleased to have it presented as a SABR publication. At the beginning of 2024, SABR published its 100th book in the SABR Digital Library.

This book is free to all SABR members. One of the real benefits of SABR membership is free access to all of SABR's publications in digital form – books and journals – a value that is many times greater than the cost of membership.

Each SABR book is written by SABR members and edited by SABR members. It is another benefit of membership – the opportunity to contribute to SABR publications. A typical SABR book is the collective work of 35 or more authors and editors. This book contains contributions by 68 SABR members.

As lead editor of this book, I feel I should "apologize" for one thing. My name shows up as author of an inordinate number of the biographies and other articles contained herein. Normally, SABR's lead editor will try to limit any one member to no more than two or three contributions, in order to offer the opportunity to become involved to as many members as possible. In the case of the 2004 Red Sox, I had already written eight of the player biographies in the years before we decided to undertake a book on this team. That still left 53 other bios for others to write. There are 41 other SABR members who have contributed by writing a biography for this book.

Another SABR "team book" might have also included biographies of the broadcasters, team executives, and a ballpark bio as well. There were already so many bios of players, the manager, and the 10 coaches that it was decided not to add more – so that we could include a few other features as well, such as the 28 "memories" – appreciations of the 2004 season, and what the season meant to these many other SABR members.

Winning the World Series for the first time in 86 years was something that resonated throughout New England and "Red Sox Nation" beyond, and tapped into the strong sentiments that many people have in often rooting for the underdog. Once the Red Sox had been eliminated in 2005 and the Chicago White Sox were in that year's World Series, a healthy portion of Red Sox Nation started rooting for White Sox fans to enjoy what we just had – and their wait had been two years longer – 88 years. I think it's safe to say that most Red Sox fans had always seen ourselves as kindred spirits with Chicago Cubs fans. They had an even longer wait – 108 years! – but in 2016 Cubs fans got to experience the thrill of the ultimate victory.

In terms of long waits, I hope readers will enjoy the story of Kathryn Gemme, who finally saw the Red Sox win it all when she herself was 109 years old.

I will indulge myself by adding one other thing here. Scouring some old emails, I found something I wrote before the 2004 season got underway. I emailed it to myself on March 23, 2004, at 10:44 P.M. Here is the email. (Yes, sometimes my emails to myself have footnotes.)

How to Help the Red Sox Win the World Series

After 86 seasons without a World Championship, Red Sox fans are burdened with bitterness, cynicism, and curses. Maybe it's time to try a different approach.

Last season, when several Red Sox players celebrated after clinching the American League "wild card," a certain segment of Red Sox Nation came down on them. After the September 25 game, five players (Gabe Kapler, Derek Lowe, Lou Merloni, Kevin Millar, and Todd Walker) all jogged from the park down Yawkey Way to the Baseball Tavern on Boylston Street, wearing wild card T-shirts over their street clothes. At the Tavern, they were "high-fiving and embracing delighted patrons." One of those patrons described them as "drenched in sweat, champagne and beer."[1] The *Boston Globe* ran a photo by Jim Davis showing Tim Wakefield spraying fans behind the dugout with champagne. An accompanying story said that principal owner John W. Henry poured some champagne for fans, and he and team chairman Tom Werner joined the fans in a toast.[2]

I'd been at the game with my young son and left right afterwards, so I missed all this. When I learned about the celebration, I wished I'd been there at the Baseball Tavern. I gave the players a lot of credit for actually mingling with real people and including them in their celebration.

The next day, though, the players were chastised for going "over the top" and there was a general feeling that they shouldn't have celebrated so much when there were still more games that had to be won. And besides, it was said, this wasn't the pennant; it was just the wild card.

"For people to be concerned about how much people celebrate something is ridiculous," said Kevin Millar to a *Globe* reporter. "This team had fought through 159 games to get to that point. You know what? I don't think we celebrated enough."

Millar went on to ask, "Who wrote the script for celebrations? What it is? Clinch wild card, no beers? Clinch Division Series, 4 to 9 beers? Clinch LCS, 6 to 9 beers? Win World Series? No limit? I never had more fun in my life, running down Yawkey Way in my spikes with Derek and Todd and heading into that tavern.... We were there ten minutes. I wish we could have stayed four hours."[3]

Winning the wild card earned the Sox a slot in the Division Series. Only four teams reach that stage; the others are eliminated. Personally, my own reaction was that maybe if the players got in the habit of celebrating a little more, they'd find that they liked it and go for more. And, after all, if the last eight generations of Red Sox players had waited for the final celebration, they'd still be waiting.

It seemed that a good part of New England was down on the players for having too much fun, while we were all busy worrying that something was sure to go wrong soon and that we were all just waiting to find out what it was going to be this time. Well, we found that out in the ALCS. There was Pedro accepting congratulatory hugs in the Red Sox dugout after closing out the seventh – something that would never happen if he were still in the game. Oops, he soon got asked to put his game face back on and go pitch the eighth.

At the same time the season was winding down, I was busy over at the Boston Public Library researching the 1904 season. Boston's American League team had won the first World's Championship in 1903 and they won the pennant again in 1904. In '04, though, John McGraw and the New York Giants declined to meet the A.L. champs in a World Series so Boston retained their status as the undefeated "world beaters."

The regular season ended on October 10 that year. Without an opportunity to play the National League pennant winner, a testimonial evening was planned for the players at the Boston Theatre on the afternoon of the 13th. Mayor Collins attended, as did Governor Bates and, of course, many of the Royal Rooters, the Bosox Club of their day.

The ballplayers were introduced one at a time, with Candy LaChance first up. "He was given three hearty cheers and it was several minutes before the noise subsided." The champions, "dressed in the ordinary attire of mankind, blushed like schoolboys when presented to the audience."[4] Each player went home with $100.00.

Sentiments expressed at the post-pennant banquet hosted by John I. Taylor indicated that the Boston ballplayers "were unanimously of the opinion that their best work was brought out by an intelligent and fair-minded baseball public and just treatment by the press."[5]

If that's what it takes, a fan might wonder a century later, is there any hope in Boston?

Right after the post-celebration flap last September, Todd Walker muttered, "No matter what happens around here, somebody will have something negative to say."[6] Is that really the message we want to convey to Red Sox players? Don't get too happy about winning?

Some will remember Elizabeth "Lib" Dooley, for decades a Red Sox season ticket holder. She had name cards printed up, characterizing herself "a friend of the Red Sox." I respected her greatly. She was very knowledgeable about the team, and aware of its weaknesses, but would not speak ill of the Sox. Maybe more of us should emulate her example. It's fun to be cynical. We can share our wisdom with a snicker. We can cringe, anticipating the final fall. Maybe Lib Dooley was on to something, too.

Shall we try it? No more "Yankees Suck" chants when the Sox score five runs in the third inning of an early May game against Kansas City. Let's become more "fair-minded" and even more intelligent a baseball public than we already are. If the press – or talk radio – start getting cynical on us, let's sing the praises of our boys.

Rah rah, team! Go team go!

We've tried dredging ponds for pianos Babe Ruth drowned. Paul Giorgio burned a Yankees cap in the thin air on Mt. Everest. Laurie Cabot has thrown her spells, and Father Guido Sarducci splashed something like holy water on the Fenway façade. We've tried just about everything else. What have we got to lose? Let's try for just treatment by the press. And talk radio. Those players who celebrated had to feel deflated, to have fans come down on them for celebrating victory. Let's shoot for something different. No more demoralization. Go team go! This could be The Year.

—end

Indeed, it *was* the year. And Red Sox fans have been fortunate in the years that followed 2004. It's a feeling we hope that fans of other teams will enjoy from time to time as the years unfold.

Meanwhile, we hope all will find things to enjoy in this book celebrating the 2004 Red Sox team.

—Bill Nowlin

NOTES

1. Bob Hohler, "That's the ticket," *Boston Globe*, September 26, 2003: E1, E6.
2. Gordon Edes, "Excitement overflowing in all corners," *Boston Globe*, September 26, 2003: E1, E6.
3. Bob Ryan, "Martinez makes short work of Rays," *Boston Globe*, September 27, 2003: E6.
4. *Boston Record*, October 14, 1904.
5. *Boston Journal*, October 14, 1904.
6. Ryan.

TERRY ADAMS

BY JASON SCHELLER

"Don't ever get comfortable, because the game has a way of humbling you."
– Terry Adams[1]

A relief pitcher most of his career, Terry Adams won his first and only World Series with the Boston Red Sox in 2004. Standing 6-feet-3-inches tall and weighing 225 pounds, the fiery right-hander was an imposing presence on the mound.[2] In 11 seasons he spent time with many storied franchises including the Chicago Cubs (1995-1999), Los Angeles Dodgers (2000-2001), Philadelphia Phillies (2002-2003 and 2005), Toronto Blue Jays (2004), and Boston Red Sox (2004). He finished his career with the Indianapolis Indians, the Pittsburgh Pirates Triple-A affiliate in the International League (2005-2006).

With the Red Sox in 2004, Adams earned the distinction of being the only Red Sox pitcher on the postseason roster not to play a game in the ALDS, ALCS, or World Series but to earn a ring.

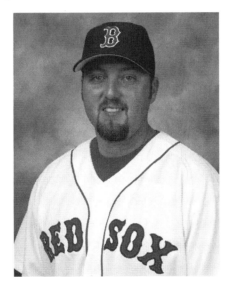

Terry Wayne Adams was born on March 6, 1973, in Mobile, Alabama, to Terry and Peggy Adams. Terry Adams Sr. was a route salesman for a grocery distributor and Peggy worked as an assistant broker for Merrill Lynch. Growing up, young Terry was a fan of the Chicago Cubs. "I would run home from the bus to catch the end of the day games on WGN," he said. "I loved Ryne Sandberg, Mark Grace, and Shawon Dunston."[3] In high school Adams played football, baseball, and basketball at Mary G. Montgomery High School in Semmes, Alabama. "I excelled in baseball," Adams said. During his senior season in 1991, Adams hurled his way to a 12-2 record with a 1.17 earned-run average. He was named the Alabama High School Player of the Year and subsequently the Gatorade Player of the Year for the effort.[4] "My high-school career was fun," Adams said. "We finished 10th in the country according to *USA Today* in 1991."

High-school senior Adams was selected in the fourth round of the 1991 amateur draft by the Chicago Cubs. His rookie season was spent with the Huntington Cubs of the Appalachian League. His career got off to an inauspicious start: an abysmal 0-9 record with a 5.77 ERA. His record of nine losses was enough to lead the Appalachian League that season.

In 1992 Adams moved up to the Peoria Chiefs of the Class-A Midwest League. In Peoria he looked to improve on his slow start as a rookie and did just that. Through 157 innings pitched, he amassed a 4.41 ERA with 96 strikeouts. He hurled three complete games, one of them a shutout.

Adams's pitching at Peoria propelled him to the Daytona Cubs of the advanced Class-A Florida State League in 1993. In the first half of the season, he posted a 3-5 record and a 4.97 ERA in 70⅔ innings. Arthroscopic surgery on his right shoulder caused him to miss the second half of the 1993 season and he spent time on the disabled list from June 21 to September 21.

After a successful surgery, Adams found himself in the starting rotation for Daytona in 1994. However, after a 1-5 start over his first seven games with a horrendous 6.32 ERA, he was converted to a reliever and finished the season with a 4.38 ERA and seven saves.

In 1995 Adams moved up, beginning the season with the Orlando Cubs of the Double-A Southern League before being moved up again to the Iowa Cubs of the Triple-A American Association. While with Orlando, he appeared in 37 games and put together a respectable 1.43 ERA over 37⅔ innings pitched, recording 19 saves. With Iowa he had five saves in seven games, with a stellar 0.00 ERA.

Adams made his major-league debut with the Cubs on August 10, 1995, in a Wrigley Field doubleheader against the San Diego Padres. Adams pitched two-thirds of an inning and gave up one hit in the first game, which the Cubs lost, 3-2. He was called on again in the second game, pitching one inning, striking out one and walking one in the Cubs' 12-5 victory.[5] Of his debut, Adams said, "I don't recall how I felt, but I'm sure I was a bundle of nerves. I remember closing the first game and then in the locker room they told me to suit up again, so I ended up finishing both games of a doubleheader."[6]

On August 14, 1995, the Cubs had a historic game as Sammy Sosa hit what was widely reported as the 10,000th home run in Cubs history. Adams got the last three outs of the game to record his first major-league save in the Cubs' 5-4 victory over the Los Angeles Dodgers.[7] Against the Dodgers on September 13, Adams earned his first major-league victory, pitching a scoreless top of the 13th inning in a walk-off 7-6 victory over Los Angeles.[8]

In 1996, his first full year with the Chicago Cubs, Adams had a banner season. He pitched 101 innings in relief, making him the third Cubs rookie to pitch at least 100 relief innings alongside Willie Hernández (103 in 1977) and Chuck McElroy (101 1/3) in 1991).[9] He pitched in 69 games and finished the season with four saves and a 2.94 ERA.

In 1997 Adams pitched in 74 games and had 18 saves in 22 opportunities. In 13 games from April 13 to May 11, he hurled 18 2/3 consecutive scoreless innings, the longest streak by a Cubs reliever since Les Lancaster pitched 30 2/3 innings in 1989. Adams finished the season with a 2-9 record and a 4.62 ERA.

In 1998 Rod Beck signed as a free agent with the Cubs and became the closer, collecting 51 saves. As as result, Adams's production fell off; he recorded just one save in 72 2/3 innings pitched. He finished the season with a 7-7 record and a 4.33 ERA.

In 1999 Adams rebounded, despite multiple trips to the disabled list, recording 13 saves in 18 tries. Through 65 innings pitched he had 6-3 record and a 4.02 ERA. But after the season the Cubs traded Adams, Chad Ricketts, and minor-league pitcher Brian Stephenson to the Los Angeles Dodgers for right-handed pitcher Ismael Valdéz and second baseman Eric Young Sr. "Giving up Terry Adams was a very tough thing to do because he has a chance to be one of the best relievers in the game," Cubs GM Ed Lynch lamented. "But in Ismael Valdéz, we've got a very consistent performer, and Eric Young is a very exciting player who we think will make a difference for our offense in the leadoff role."[10]

In 2000 Adams led the Dodgers pitchers with 66 appearances. He got his first save for the Dodgers in his first appearance of the season, at Montreal on April 3. On May 16, after a three-hit rally by the Cubs at Wrigley Field, he was part of what could have been the largest mass suspension resulting from one brawl in baseball history had it not been for Paul Beeson, baseball's chief operating officer. Frank Robinson, then baseball's vice president of on-field operations, handed down suspensions totaling 89 games to 16 players and issued $77,000 in fines for a scuffle between a fan and Dodgers catcher Chad Kreuter after Kreuter was struck by the fan, who then stole his cap. Beeston overturned the suspensions of 11 of the 16 players and one of the three coaches involved in the melee. Adams's suspension of three games was reduced to zero.[11] Adams finished the season with a 6-9 record and a 3.52 ERA. In 84 1/3 innings pitched he recorded two saves in seven opportunities.

In 2001 Adams began the season in the bullpen before being moved to the starting rotation after injuries sidelined Andy Ashby, Kevin Brown, and Darren Dreifort.[12] He did not allow a run in his first six appearances of the season. The streak ended on April 17 when Barry Bonds deposited an Adams pitch into San Francisco Bay for his 500th career home run.[13] Adams pitched a career-high 166 1/3 innings and finished the season with a 12-8 record. He made 22 starts and led the NL that year in the fewest home runs allowed per nine innings pitched (0.487) and was third in the NL in Fielding Independent Pitching (3.09). His 12 victories were second on the Dodgers team.[14]

Despite a career year, Adams was released by the Dodgers after the season. The Dodgers said they released him to free up salary space but refused to comment beyond that. However, Adams believed the Dodgers had cost him millions of dollars by spreading rumors about his elbow.[15] Whatever the case, Adams signed with the Philadelphia Phillies on January 15, 2002. He said of his time with the Dodgers, "I loved playing for the Dodgers and Jim Tracy and Jim Colburn. They treated me well." He added, "My number one goal is to stay healthy and prove that I can be effective."[16]

The Phillies signed Adams to an incentive-laden one-year, $2.7 million contract with the option of two additional years totaling $19.5 million. Noting that Adams had made 22 starts in 2001, Phillies GM Ed Wade said, "Our guys have always liked Terry's arm. They've always thought he had the stuff to be a quality closer. The Dodgers, and Terry, struck gold when they moved him into the rotation."[17] Adams was expected to be the third starter in the rotation that year behind Robert Person and Vicente Padilla. However, after posting a 4-7 record and a 5.00 ERA, Adams was replaced in the rotation by Brett Meyers.[18] He pitched in 46 games, of which 19 were starts. He finished the season with a 7-9 record and a 4.35 ERA over 136 2/3 innings pitched.

In 2003 Adams returned to the Phillies as a set-up man. He led the pitching staff in games pitched with 66. He posted a 1-4 record with a 2.65 ERA, the lowest of his career. He was taken out of the lineup for the remainder of the season on September 12, 2003, with loose bodies in his right elbow. He underwent arthroscopic surgery on September 27, 2003, in Birmingham, Alabama, bringing his season to a close. The Phillies released him on October 27 and he signed with the Toronto Blue Jays on January 7, 2004.

The 2004 season was Adams's first in the American League. With Toronto, he posted a 4-4 record with a 3.98 ERA and three saves before being traded to the Red Sox for Double-A third baseman John Hattig on July 24. At the time of the trade Adams led all Toronto pitchers with 42 appearances. "I had a good feeling I'd be traded by the Blue Jays," Adams said in his interview with the author. "We weren't contenders and I had pitched as a closer and in a set-up role mostly. I was excited to be traded to Boston." Adams said that even though he was excited for the trade he had no idea what his role with the Red Sox would be. "I was fine with whatever role I was given," he said. "I just wanted to be part of a winner and I was late in my career."

The Red Sox assumed $1.7 million of Adams's contract and brought him in to help strengthen the bullpen for the playoff run. Red Sox GM Theo Epstein said, "We're hurting. We've got a lot of guys who have thrown a lot of innings lately."[19] Epstein went on to say, "We've been asking a lot of our relievers. You can only ask them to go to the well so many times in July and August if you expect them still to be healthy in September and October." Manager Terry Francona echoed Epstein's sentiments, saying, "Adams is a professional reliever who can help so we don't go through our relievers and hurt them."[20]

Adams appeared in 19 games for the Red Sox in 2004. His last appearance was two innings of relief against the Baltimore Orioles on Sunday, October 3, the last game of the regular season. Adams made the postseason roster for the Red Sox, but did not play in the Division Series, Championship Series, or World Series.[21] "Yeah I was on the roster," Adams said. "I was told prior to the playoffs I would be used as an insurance to any reliever who may get hurt or injured. I traveled with the team and did get a ring. I was proud to do what was asked of me."

On October 29, just two days after the Red Sox brought Boston its first World Series championship in 86 years, they released Adams. He signed with the Phillies on January 11, 2005. Adams struggled mightily with Philadelphia, posting a 12.83 ERA in 16 appearances. He also pitched in 14 games for the Triple-A Scranton/Wilkes Barre Red Barons but was released by the Phillies on May 24. In January 2006, he signed a minor-league contract with the Pittsburgh Pirates Triple-A affiliate, the Indianapolis Indians of the International League.[22] He made 48 appearances that season and finished with a 4.26 ERA. On October 15, 2006, Adams was released and retired from baseball.

Asked to summarize his career in his own words, Adams said, "I'm very proud of my career. I never expected to be so successful and play so long. I had amazing teammates and played for the best franchises and fan bases." He lamented missing out on certain aspects of the game, saying, "I wished I would have taken it all in more and played longer. I ran out of gas and my arm just didn't hold my velocity after my elbow surgery. I wish I could've played at a high level for longer."

After baseball, "Life is different now and sometimes not so easy as baseball was," Adams said. "When you retire it's a huge change." His high school jersey (#21) was retired in 1995 in Semmes, Alabama. Adams was made an honorary sheriff's deputy and given the key to the city of Mobile, Alabama in 1996. He has led a quiet life after baseball. He married his wife Sheila in 2013 and they have two children, Noah age 9 and Anistyn age 7 in 2023. After retiring from baseball, he has spent time coaching T-ball, coaching pitching, and coaching travel baseball.

In 2023 he was coaching baseball at St. Paul's Episcopal School in Mobile, Alabama; his children attend the school. He said that aside from coaching, his duties as a cheer and dance Dad with his daughter kept him busy. In 2009 Adams was inducted into the Mobile, Alabama Sports Hall of Fame, which also includes such names as Hank Aaron, Satchel Paige, Willie McCovey, and Ozzie Smith. Of the honor Adams said, "It's not just being associated with great players from this area, but some guys who are in Cooperstown, too. I'm very proud to have that association and I'm very honored."[23] Reflecting on his time in baseball he said, "I miss those days. The competition and the clubhouse were fun. I'm glad I was able to be a part of such a great game and brotherhood."

SOURCES

In addition to the sources cited in the Notes, the author consulted Baseball-Reference.com, Retrosheet.org, baseballalmanac.com, Stats Crew, and the Terry Adams player file at the National Baseball Hall of Fame.

Thanks to Terry Adams, Sarah Coffin of the Boston Red Sox, and Rachel Wells at the National Baseball Hall of Fame, as well as Greg Fowler, Joe Johnston, Pat Scheller, and Holly Scheller for their support.

NOTES

1. Sapna Pathak, "Twenty Questions with Terry Adams," https://www.milb.com/news/gcs-102919, accessed September 3, 2023.
2. Several standard online baseball websites provide Adams's weight as 180 pounds. In an October 2023 email to the author, Adams stated that he never weighed 180 pounds and asked that his weight be given as 225 pounds – which is the same weight cited in the *2004 Red Sox Post-Season Media Guide* (p. 31).
3. Terry Adams, email interview with author, September 26, 2023. Unless indicated, all otherwise unattributed quotations from Adams come from this interview.
4. Gatorade Player of the Year: https://playeroftheyear.gatorade.com/winner/terry-adams/20609, accessed September 3, 2023.
5. "Scoreboard," *Galveston Daily News*, August 11, 1995: 18.
6. Sapna Pathak, "Twenty Questions with Terry Adams." The games were actually finished by other pitchers.
7. Bob Nightengale, "Dodgers Run Out of Magic in End," *Los Angeles Times*, August 15, 1995: C1.
8. "Chicago Beats Dodgers After Blowing Lead," *Greenwood* (South Carolina) *Index-Journal*, September 14, 1995: 16.
9. MLB.com, Terry Adams statistics: https://www.mlb.com/player/terry-adams-110067.
10. Chuck Johnson, "Dodgers Trade Pricey Pair," *USA Today*, December 13, 1999.
11. Jason Reid, "12 Dodgers Get Pardon on Appeal," *Los Angeles Times*, June 30, 2000: 1.
12. Rob Maaddi, "Adams Signs With Phillies," *Midland* (Texas) *Daily News*, January 14, 2002. https://www.ourmidland.com/news/article/Adams-Signs-With-Phillies-7076513.php, accessed September 11, 2023.
13. "This Date in Baseball – Barry Bonds Hits His 500th Home Run," *USA Today*, April 16, 2023. https://www.usatoday.com/story/sports/mlb/2023/04/16/this-date-in-baseball-barry-bonds-hits-500th-home-run/70119456007/, accessed September 11, 2023.
14. Bill Shaikin, "Adams Joins Phillies' Rotation," *Los Angeles Times*, January 16, 2002: D9.
15. Bob Brookover, "Adams Bolsters Case – and Stays Angry," *Philadelphia Inquirer*, March 21, 2002.
16. Brookover.
17. Maaddi.
18. "Phillies, Adams Agree to a One-Year Deal," *Pocono Record* (Stroudsburg, Pennsylvania), February 10, 2003.

19 Bob Hohler, "Adams Acquired from Jays," *Boston Globe*, July 25, 2004: D7.
20 Bob Hohler, "Adams Acquired from Jays," *Boston Globe*, July 25, 2004: D7.
21 ESPN Terry Adams gamelog, https://www.espn.com/mlb/player/gamelog/_/id/3318/year/2004/category/pitching, accessed September 11, 2023.
22 "Scoreboard," *Indiana* (Pennsylvania) *Gazette*, January 22, 2006: 24.
23 Paul Cloos, "Terry Adams Honored by Upcoming Mobile Sports Hall of Fame Induction," *Press-Register*, (Mobile, Alabama), April 29, 2009. https://www.al.com/press-register-sports/2009/04/terry_adams_honored_by_upcomin.html, accessed October 15, 2023.

2004 banner being installed at Fenway. Photo by Bill Nowlin.

ABE ALVAREZ

BY BOB LEMOINE

*"You look out and you're in a big-league park, you're on a big-league field, you're going to pitch.
It's a hundred emotions going through you."*
Abe Alvarez, on his major-league debut with the 2004 Boston Red Sox[1]

Abe Alvarez pitched four games in the major leagues, including his debut for the 2004 Boston Red Sox. The 21-year-old lefty spent just half a season at the Double-A level before being thrown into the heat of a pennant race. The Red Sox were desperate for a pitcher and optimistic about the young crooked-hat, bushy-haired pitcher who threw so soft that a Red Sox scout said, "[Y]ou can catch him with a napkin."[2] The Long Beach State phenom had dominated the college ranks the year before with his solid control and pinpoint location. Alvarez had a meteoric rise from short-season Class A to the major leagues in one year. *Baseball America* listed Alvarez as the top Red Sox pitching prospect, ahead of such notables as Jon Lester and Jonathan Papelbon.[3] He spent his entire career (2004-2006) with the Red Sox and received a World Series ring.

Alvarez rose from poverty to top pitching prospect, only to watch other prospects supersede him. His experiences with the highs and lows of the game prepared him for coaching at the college level. "Baseball really doesn't need a guy like him," ESPN's Brian Triplett wrote. "It needs one on every team."[4]

Abraham Alvarez was born on October 17, 1982, in Maywood, California, mere minutes south of Los Angeles. His parents, Alex and Mercedes (Olivares) Alvarez, had emigrated from Mexico. Alex often had trouble finding employment to provide for his family, which included Abe's brother and sister. Mercedes was a cosmetologist. Spotlights from police helicopters and sirens were a normal occurrence in their neighborhood, as was the presence of gangs. Their home was broken into often. "I didn't really understand," Abe said. "My parents didn't make it a big deal. [Robbers] didn't take much because there wasn't much that we had. My parents kept us safe, and that's all that pretty much mattered." Alex found work when Abe was 7, and moved the family to Fontana, 50 miles from Maywood.[5]

Alex, a basketball player in Mexico, encouraged his sons to play baseball. Abe, around 5 years old, played in the T-ball Peanut League in the Bella South Gate area of Los Angeles County, then later Little League.[6] As a youngster he checked out library books about Sandy Koufax. But the current Dodger lefty star grabbed his attention. "I was just five or six at the time," Alvarez remembered. "Fernando Valenzuela was my first athletic idol." His dad would take him to Dodger Stadium after Sunday Mass if Valenzuela was pitching.[7] Valenzuela looked to the sky as he delivered the ball to the plate. Alvarez had only one good eye.

"I was born with a birth defect in my left eye, and I don't have very good vision in it," he said in 2003. His mother tried prescription drops to no avail. "Being a left-hander, it doesn't bother me because I can focus with my right eye. But if I was right-handed, I think it would be a problem for me."[8] "If I close my good eye," he explained another time, "it's a blur. If things are close, *maybe* I can read them. I can see colors, but the vision is bad."[9] It was one more obstacle in his childhood.

Abe started wearing glasses around age 8 and faced childhood bullying since the lens for his left eye was much thicker than that for the right. "It affected me socially as a kid a lot," Alvarez said. An optometrist recommended that Alvarez wear a patch on his right eye when not in school to strengthen the vision in his left eye. "So every Halloween for about six years I was a pirate," he joked. Alvarez switched to wearing a single contact lens late in his high-school years.[10] Tilting his cap helped balance out the lighting for his good eye, and he could peek at a runner at first from the stretch without craning his neck. It worked, and he was a successful pitcher at A.B. Miller High School in Fontana. He credited his father for his confidence.

"My dad has always been there telling me not to give up," Alvarez said. "Much of my confidence comes from him because he believes in me. He is always pushing me and his confidence in me gives me confidence in myself."[11] Alex had never finished beyond seventh grade, so the discussion of college rarely came up at home. Neither his older brother nor younger sister attended college. Abe played in the Area Code Baseball program with future major leaguer Chad Cordero. College recruiters were watching.[12] He drew more attention striking out 16 batters in six innings for the Colton Night Hawks in the USABF World Series, a tournament for 16- to 18-year-olds.[13] During his sophomore year of high school, his coach took him to a baseball camp at Arizona State University. Alvarez decided to attend Long Beach State because of its proximity.

Alvarez pitched just three innings as a freshman. "We had a lot of older guys on our staff," he said. "I think it was good for me to sit and watch how the older guys did it." He received extra training in Alaska that summer. "I think pitching in Alaska really helped me. I'm just glad they didn't rush me at Long Beach."[14] The extra work was beneficial. He finished his sophomore season 12-3 (2.72 ERA), walked only 27 while striking out 89 in 102⅔ innings, and was Big West Pitcher of the Year.[15]

Alvarez followed with an 11-2 junior season (2.35 ERA). His 23-5 combined record (2.56 ERA) is the most for any Long Beach State University left-hander and he shared the 2003 Big West Pitcher of the Year Award with teammate Jered Weaver. The two were a powerful one-two punch (25-6 combined) along with their freshman shortstop, Troy Tulowitzki. Alvarez led the top-ranked 49ers into their first NCAA home regional playoff game against Pepperdine. He allowed one run on four hits for a 6-1 victory.[16]

Alvarez pitched for Team USA in the summer of 2002, appearing in the World University Championship. He allowed only an unearned run in 1⅓ innings. His valuable relief work helped Team USA win the Haarlem Baseball Week Tournament in the Netherlands.[17]

Jim Woodward of the Boston Red Sox scouted Alvarez. His bad left eye became an issue for the first time. "MLB sent one of their guys in," Alvarez recalled. "He said, 'Your vision in your left eye is really bad. I don't get how you're able to pitch.'"[18] Alvarez learned he was legally blind, with 20:16 vision in the eye. It may have cost Alvarez a first-round selection in the June 2003 amateur draft. The Red Sox selected him in the second round (49th overall) with a $700,000 signing bonus.[19]

The Red Sox assigned Alvarez to short-season Class-A Lowell (Massachusetts) of the New York-Penn League. With his high number of innings at Long Beach State, the Red Sox were cautious with the 20-year-old's workload. Alvarez started nine games but was limited to 19 innings. He struck out 19, walked 2, and was unscored upon. "They made me understand," Alvarez said. "I got used to it and I know it was good for me."[20]

The Red Sox promoted Alvarez in 2004 to Double-A Portland (Maine) of the Eastern League. "My favorite city in minor-league baseball," Alvarez remembered. "It was like a college town."[21]

"It's a big jump, no doubt. We could have sent him to Sarasota (Advanced A level)," confessed Red Sox farm director Ben Cherington. "We felt that challenging him was the right thing to do." Alvarez struggled, allowing five runs in his first start, but settled down and allowed only five runs in his next four starts. His fastball was not overpowering (85-88 mph) and he relied on location, control, and mixing pitches. "He's a very mature kid who has a good idea about pitching," Cherington said.[22]

The Red Sox were desperate for a starting pitcher in game one of a doubleheader with the Baltimore Orioles on July 22. They were struggling at 51-42, eight games behind the New York Yankees, after being just one game behind at the start of June. "I think we've had a couple of instances recently where we've gotten behind in a game and have become semi-lifeless," said outfielder Gabe Kapler. "I think it's important that we show a little amount of tenacity right now."[23] The Red Sox hoped Alvarez could bring the team that tenacity and summoned him from Portland. He was 8-6 (3.53 ERA) in 19 starts with an 82/24 strikeout-to-walk ratio in 99⅓ innings. Opponents were batting .261 against Alvarez. He learned of the promotion two days before it happened.[24]

"You're going to the big leagues," manager Ron Johnson told him. "I started shaking," Alvarez said. "I didn't sleep that night."[25] "Really, I thought more about my dad, what he did and what he worked for, everything he pushed for me to get this opportunity."[26] Alvarez was chosen partly because the Orioles struggled against left-handers at the time (10-21 vs. left-handed starters, batting .245 vs. .296 against righties).[27] To make room on the roster, left-hander Jimmy Anderson (6.00 ERA in six innings) was designated for assignment. Anderson had thrown his last pitch while Alvarez prepared to throw his first.

"With a bushel of curly black hair jutting out from under a hat turned to the side," wrote Paul Doyle in the *Hartford Courant*, "Abe Alvarez strode to the mound with the urgency of someone approaching the ceremonial first pitch. Alvarez looked more like a college kid in the bleachers than a major league pitcher dropped into the pennant race by a desperate team."[28] At 21 years and 9 months old, the young Alvarez stepped into the heat of a pennant race.

Alvarez fell behind early. He walked leadoff hitter Brian Roberts, who stole second and scampered home on Melvin Mora's double to right. Miguel Tejada launched a home run into the Monster seats in left, and the Orioles led, 3-0. Mora later homered. Alvarez gutted out five innings, allowing eight hits, five earned runs, five walks and two strikeouts. The Red Sox fell, 8-3. "We all think that he has a bright future. Maybe not quite yet, here," said manager Terry Francona. "He kept his composure and actually kept us in the game."[29]

"It was kind of like a welcome-to-the-big-leagues type of deal," Alvarez said honestly. "That was a big inning just for me being out there for the first time." While the outcome was not what he wanted, he found the positive. "I'm glad that they have a lot of confidence in me, and I am moving up quick. Hopefully, I will be able to stick around, or come back quicker."[30] But Alvarez would have just a cup of coffee, or as Mark Murphy wrote in the *Boston Herald*, "There was no time to add the cream and sugar."[31] Alvarez was optioned back to Portland to make room for the recently acquired infielder Ricky Gutierrez. Alvarez finished 10-9 for Portland with a 3.66 ERA and 1.22 WHIP. He was 1-2 in August despite a splendid 2.14 ERA, holding batters to a .167 average.[32] The Red Sox turned their season around in memorable fashion, winning their first World Series in 86 years and everyone on the team, including Alvarez, received a ring.

Alvarez spent most of 2005 with Triple-A Pawtucket of the International League. He was 11-6 with a 4.85 ERA (1.20 WHIP) in 26 starts. In June he threw a seven-inning, one-hit shutout against Richmond.[33] In July he was briefly recalled to Boston but never made an appearance. He was recalled again on August 28 and had back-to-back relief appearances, throwing a scoreless inning against the Tigers, and then getting pounded for four runs by Tampa Bay. He was back in Pawtucket on August 30.[34]

Alvarez returned to Pawtucket in 2006 with a cutter added to his pitching repertoire. "I think it's a big part of my success," he said. "With a cutter, I'm able to come inside to righties instead of always using my change-up."[35] He was a stellar 5-0 with a 2.18 ERA and lefties batted a weak .167 against him. Alvarez was recalled to Boston in May. "My confidence is high," he said. "This is a challenge I look forward to take on."[36]

The Red Sox were in Philadelphia. Alvarez relieved Lenny DiNardo in the third with runners at first and second and the Red Sox trailing, 4-1. He got out of the inning unscathed and pitched a scoreless fourth. In the fifth, Ryan Howard smashed a changeup for his 14th home run to deep left. Alvarez didn't record an out in the sixth, allowing a double to Jimmy Rollins, a single to Chase Utley, and a home run in the center-field bushes by Bobby Abreu. Alvarez walked off a major-league field for the final time in a 10-5 loss. David Riske was activated and Alvarez was back in Pawtucket.[37]

Alvarez went 1-9 with a 7.58 ERA upon returning to Pawtucket. He finished 6-9 (5.64 ERA, 1.49 WHIP). Staying mentally focused was the majority of the problem. "You know you had a shot and you come back down and you're thinking the wrong things," he said. "That's why you go out there and give up eight runs in three innings (vs. Columbus), because your head's not in the game. I talked to (Red Sox mental skills coach) Bob Tewksbury, and people can tell you things, but you are the one who has to make the adjustments."[38] In August he fractured his ankle in an off-field accident and missed the remainder of the season.[39]

Alvarez was placed on the 60-day disabled list and removed from the 40-man roster. He was no longer a top pitching prospect but accepted the Red Sox' invitation to spring training in 2007 as a nonroster invitee. Alvarez, now 24, was surrounded by youngsters. "I pitched with a lot of these (younger guys in camp)," he said. "I came up faster, but they're catching up to me on the fast track. And now I have to get over the hump."[40] He pitched for Pawtucket the entire season, going 5-8 (4.77 ERA, 1.47 WHIP) with 16 starts in 25 appearances. He was released in May 2008 after 13 appearances and a 6.46 ERA (1.76 WHIP).

"It was awesome to be on the fast track," Alvarez said in 2010, "and to go from Low A to Double A and then get a chance to start in the majors. Then I had a good first year at Triple A. But I felt in that second year there that I had missed a step in my development."[41] "I would put a lot of blame on myself," he said. "It's a business, it's your career. What are you trying to do to get better? I felt pretty good in who I was, but at the same time I didn't realize who was coming behind me. I probably would have benefited even more from going to high A and learning."[42]

Alvarez signed with the Camden (New Jersey) Riversharks of the independent Atlantic League. He pitched one game and was traded to the Long Island Ducks. He went 7-4 in 31 appearances, then spent the winter pitching for the Lobos de Arecibo of the Puerto Rican Winter League.

Alvarez went overseas to pitch for Palfinger Reggio Emilia in the Italian Baseball League in 2009. He finished 3-8 with a 2.96 ERA. "It was still fun," he said, playing on the weekends and sightseeing during the week. "The fields were nice, and I loved traveling in Italy."[43] Abe went home and married Natalie Casas, an elementary school teacher. They had two children, Isabella and Benjamin.

In 2010 Alvarez served as a volunteer undergraduate assistant coach at Long Beach State which provided free tuition while he attained a bachelor's degree in history. "I promised my mom I would finish college," he said. "First one in my family."[44] In 2011, he became the baseball coach at Cerritos High School. He moved on to St. Bernard High School, where he coached, taught, and served as dean of students. Alvarez led St. Bernard to its first league title in 30 years. In 2017 he earned a master's in secondary education from Loyola Marymount University. In 2018 Alvarez joined the Nevada State baseball program as a volunteer and was promoted to a paid assistant in 2019. In 2021 he led the Wolfpack to the Mountain West championship and on to the NCAA Regionals. In 2022 Alvarez became the pitching coach at Brigham Young University.[45]

"My dream was to play in the major leagues, and I achieved that," Alvarez said. "But I learned it's hard to stay there. I knew coaching was something I've always to do."[46]

SOURCES

College statistics were taken from the baseballcube.com.

Besides sources listed in the Notes, the author consulted Baseball-reference.com, Familysearch.org, Findagrave.com, and Retrosheet.org.

NOTES

1. Abe Alvarez interview on Brett Lorin's "Too Tall Sports Podcast," Season 1, Episode 29, November 19, 2020. Retrieved June 24, 2022. youtube.com/watch?v=Yn9Cx_fUYhc. Hereafter listed as "Podcast."
2. Gordon Edes, "Alvarez Is Back in Business," *Boston Globe*, May 20, 2006: E5.
3. Cited by Michael Silverman, "Baseball – Team Won't Split Hairs With Lefty Alvarez," *Boston Herald*, March 16, 2004: 84.
4. Brian Triplett, "Gangbanger? Try Modest Abe," ESPN. Retrieved June 25, 2022. espn.com/mlb/news/story?id=1873839.
5. Triplett.

6   Podcast; Doug Krikorian, "Alvarez in Good Form for D'Bags," *Long-Beach Press Telegram*, May 8, 2003: B1.

7   "Alvarez in Good Form"; Janis Carr, "Alvarez Usually Finds Way to Win. The Long Beach State ace Is 22-4 the Past Two Years," *Orange County Register* (Santa Ana, California), May 27, 2003. Retrieved June 20, 2022. Infoweb-newsbankcom.hpld.idm.oclc.org/apps/news/document-view?p=NewsBank&docref=news/0FB85941DA9630F8.

8   Krikorian, "Alvarez in Good Form."

9   Dana Oppedisano, "A Reason for Alvarez's Appearance," *Naples* (Florida) *Daily News*, March 7, 2005: 6C.

10 Podcast.

11 Carr, "Alvarez Usually Finds Way to Win."

12 Podcast.

13 "Rangers Off to 2-0 Start at Series," *San Luis Obispo* (California) *Tribune*, August 5, 2000: C2.

14 Krikorian, "Alvarez in Good Form."

15 James Lee, "Relief Effort," *Los Angeles Times*, August 1, 2002: A8.

16 "Baseball Program Picks Its All-Time Greats." Long Beach State University. Retrieved June 21, 2022. longbeachstate.com/sports/2018/8/1/_trads_alltime_base_html.aspx; Eric Stephens, "Two Aces, One Tough Team," *Los Angeles Times*, May 30, 2003: D15; Eric Stephens, "Long Beach Works Fast," *Los Angeles Times*, May 31, 2003: D13; Darrell Moody, "Three Players See Action in College Baseball Playoffs," *Sacramento Bee*, June 6, 2002: 47.

17 Lee, "Relief Effort."

18 J.P. Hoornstra, "Abe Alvarez Hits the Mark," *Long Beach Press-Telegram*, May 23, 2012. Retrieved June 20, 2022. presstelegram.com/2012/05/23/abe-alvarez-hits-the-mark/.

19 Pete Marshall, "Cordero, Alvarez, Begin Quest for MLB Glory," *Inland Valley Daily Bulletin* (Ontario, California), June 27, 2003: 3.

20 Kevin Thomas, "Sox Hope Alvarez Is What's Left," *Portland* (Maine) *Press Herald*, May 9, 2004: 1D.

21 Podcast.

22 "Sox Hope Alvarez Is What's Left."

23 Bob Hohler, "Home Sickness," *Boston Globe*, July 22, 2004: E1.

24 Bob Hohler, "Gutierrez Acquired After Reese Lands on DL," *Boston Globe*, July 22, 2004: E3.

25 Kevin Thomas, "Keeping His Cool on the Hot Seat," *Portland Press Herald*, July 23, 2004: D1.

26 Podcast.

27 Bob Hohler, "Like Night and Day," *Boston Globe*, July 23, 2004: E7.

28 Paul Doyle, "Salvage Job for Wake – Orioles Rough Up Alvarez," *Hartford Courant*, July 23, 2004: C1.

29 Mark Murphy, "O's Rock Rookie – Alvarez Takes Loss in MLB Debut," *Boston Herald*, July 23, 2004: 124.

30 "O's Rock Rookie.".

31 "O's Rock Rookie."

32 Bob Hohler, "Only a Few Will Realize Big Dreams," *Boston Globe*, August 29, 2004: F11.

33 Joe McDonald, "Alvarez of PawSox Stays on Fast Track by 1-Hitting Braves," *Providence Journal*, June 7, 2005: C5.

34 Jeff Horrigan, "Alvarez Is Ready to Go," *Boston Herald*, July 3, 2005: B11; Tony Massarotti, "Vazquez a Surprise Cut," *Boston Herald*, July 4, 2005: 58; Jeff Horrigan, "Remlinger Doesn't Make Cut," *Boston Herald*, August 29, 2005: 98; Jeff Horrigan, "Red Sox Notebook – Wells Called to MLB Office," *Boston Herald*, August 31, 2005: 88.

35 Karen Guregian, "On Call When Need to Re-arm – Four Top Prospects Working to Be Ready," *Boston Herald*, May 14, 2006: B16.

36 Michael Silverman, "Red Sox Notebook: Honest, Abe Up – Lefty Called from Pawtucket," *Boston Herald*, May 20, 2006: 48; Edes, "Alvarez Is Back in Business."

37 Gordon Edes, "Sox Absorb Blows," *Boston Globe*, May 22, 2006: D6.

38 Steven Krasner, "Alvarez Out to Show Sox He's Not So Forgettable," *Providence Journal*, February 15, 2007: C1.

39 Gordon Edes, "Hinske's Versatility a Big Plus," *Boston Globe*, August 18, 2006: C6.

40 "Alvarez Out to Show Sox He's Not So Forgettable."

41 Bob Keisser, "Back to Basics – Former Pitcher Is Back at LBSU to Get an Education, Both in Class and on the Field," *Long-Beach Press Telegram*, March 24, 2010: 1B.

42 Podcast.

43 Hoornstra, "Abe Alvarez Hits the Mark."

44 Hoornstra, "Abe Alvarez Hits the Mark."

45 "Abe Alvarez," Nevada Wolf Pack Coaches. Retrieved June 19, 2022. nevadawolfpack.com/sports/baseball/roster/coaches/abe-alvarez/2016; Chris Murray, "Abe Alvarez Promoted to Full-Time Assistant for Nevada Baseball," Nevada SportsNet. Retrieved June 19, 2022. nevadasportsnet.com/news/reporters/abe-alvarez-promoted-to-full-time-assistant-for-nevada-baseball; "Abe Alvarez," BYU Baseball. Retrieved February 28, 2023. byucougars.com/staff/baseball/1300431/abe-alvarez.

46 "High School Baseball – Alvarez Named Coach at St. Bernard," *Inland Valley Daily Bulletin*, September 11, 2013: 2; "Abe Alvarez," *Nevada Baseball 2020 Media Guide*, 43. Retrieved June 24, 2022. s3.amazonaws.com/sidearm.sites/nevadawolfpack.com/documents/2020/2/18/BaseballMediaGuide_2020_ALTTEXT.pdf.

JIMMY ANDERSON

BY RALPH CAOLA

Born on January 22, 1976, in Portsmouth, Virginia, Jimmy Anderson became a star pitcher at Western Branch High School. As a senior, the left-hander was "practically unhittable"[1] with an ERA of 0.11, and was named Virginia High School Player of the Year.[2] In the major leagues Anderson compiled a career record of 25-47 (.347) and an ERA of 5.42. He pitched for the Pittsburgh Pirates, then briefly for the Cincinnati Reds and Chicago Cubs, before a monthlong stint with the Boston Red Sox during their championship season of 2004.

Anderson's father, Jimmy, Sr., influenced his son's development. Junior said, "He was pretty much my coach until pro ball. He pretty much taught me everything I know."[3] Senior, a former Norfolk shipyard general foreman,[4] recalled, "We have a pitching rubber and a home plate in the yard. If I had a dollar for every pitch Jimmy has thrown to me I'd be a millionaire."[5]

As a high-school sophomore in 1992, Anderson threw a no-hitter and a one-hitter in consecutive games.[6] Overall, he notched six victories to go with his district-leading ERA of 0.88, and, as a bonus, hit four home runs.[7]

In 1993 Anderson, with a perfect 10-0 regular-season record, was chosen All-Southeastern District most valuable player. The junior had a sparkling 0.79 ERA, struck out 116 batters in 63 innings and walked only 18, leading the Bruins to an undefeated district season.[8] But Anderson was not only a terrific pitcher. Robin Brinkley of the *Virginian-Pilot* called Anderson "one of the best hitters in the district."[9]

In 1994 Anderson was even better, somehow improving his ERA to a microscopic 0.11.[10] He struck out 22 batters in one game,[11] again went undefeated (8-0) in the regular season and was voted the district's most valuable player.[12] Overall, in his junior and senior seasons, Anderson struck out nearly two batters per *inning*. Possessing pinpoint control, he walked fewer than two per nine innings. About his dominating high school career, Anderson said, "I matured early. I probably could have been in pro ball then."[13]

A superb athlete, Anderson averaged more than 20 points per game as a sophomore on the junior varsity basketball team and shot in the high 70s in golf. But skipped practices kept him off varsity basketball and got him expelled from the golf squad.[14] Anderson explained, "The basketball team had a summer camp that conflicted with an important baseball showcase event in Cincinnati, Ohio. The basketball coach told me I had a decision to make." It didn't take Anderson long. He said, "I played basketball for fun, but I was going to possibly get drafted for baseball." As for golf, Anderson admitted he "lost interest."[15]

In June 1994 Anderson was selected by the Pittsburgh Pirates in the ninth round of the amateur draft, although scouts had told him he might be taken as early as the first round and no later than the third.[16]

The Pirates sent Anderson to the Gulf Coast Rookie League, where he went 5-1 (1.60 ERA). In 1995 Anderson advanced to the Augusta GreenJackets of the low Class-A Sally League, posting a record of 4-2 (1.53 ERA). Later the Pirates promoted Anderson to the Lynchburg Hillcats of the High-A Carolina League, where things got tougher. In 52⅓ innings pitched, Anderson went 1-5 (4.13 ERA).

In 1996, Anderson did better in the High-A league, with an ERA of 1.93 in 65⅓ innings. Consequently, he was promoted to the Carolina Mudcats of the Double-A Southern League (Raleigh, North Carolina), and again did well, going 8-3 (3.34 ERA).

Anderson started the 1997 season at the same level, pitched to a 1.46 ERA, and was moved up to the Calgary Cannons of the Triple-A Pacific Coast League. There he began a disturbing trend of wildness, walking 5.6 batters per nine innings. His ERA was 5.68, which doesn't look impressive, but was only 6 percent higher than league average (5.36).[17] The trying season was made worse on August 10, when Anderson received news that his father, only 44 years old, had died of a massive heart attack.[18]

Anderson spent all of 1998 with the Nashville Sounds, the Pirates' new Triple-A affiliate. His poor control continued (5.2 walks per 9 innings), leading to a record of 9-10 (5.02 ERA).

Anderson was back with the Sounds for the first three months of the 1999 season, where he was terrific, achieving a record of 11-1 (3.86 ERA).[19] His control improved, as he walked only 2.8 batters per nine innings. The reason, said Nashville manager Trent Jewett, "He's 100 percent different this year because he's confident. If a pitcher has any doubts, he tends to pitch around the bats. Now he believes he belongs at this level."[20]

His outstanding performance earned Anderson a promotion to Pittsburgh, and he made his debut for the Pirates on July 4, 1999, at Pittsburgh's Three Rivers Stadium. He said it was the biggest thrill of his career. "My Dad was the first person I thought of. It was what we worked so hard for."[21] Anderson recalled the weather that day. "Hot as fire," he said. "It was, like, 120 out on the turf."[22] He gave up three hits and a walk, but no runs, while working the seventh and eighth innings of a 4-3 loss to the Milwaukee Brewers.

Anderson was sent back to Nashville, but was recalled on July 31. He started three games at the end of August with mixed results. In September, he pitched five games in relief – all Pirates losses.

In 2000 Anderson won the first start in which he got a decision, then lost his next five. The fifth came on June 14, when he walked five in four innings. The next day, the Pirates demoted him, again to work on his control.[23] He showed improvement, in a small sample, walking only four in 13 innings. Upon returning, Anderson went 2-0 in July, but in his final 11 starts went 2-6 (6.14 ERA).[24] Both wins came against the Los Angeles Dodgers. In one, Anderson pitched eight shutout innings; in the other, he threw a complete game in which he yielded only one run.

After his first two starts of 2001, Anderson had an ERA of 6.97. In his next three, he won twice and reduced his ERA to 2.76. But from May through August, he went 4-15 with an ERA of 6.46. He turned things around in his final six starts, going 3-1 with a 2.49 ERA. His overall record was 9-17 (5.10 ERA).

In 2002 Anderson got the decision in each of his first 14 starts, going 6-8 (4.61 ERA). The last was a complete-game five-hit win over Cincinnati. The rest of the way, he went 2-5 (6.67 ERA). Anderson lost his job as a starter in mid-August after giving up eight hits and five runs in three innings in a 9-5 loss to the Cardinals. In his final three outings, he gave up eight earned runs in four innings and consequently pitched only once in the month of September. Pirates manager Lloyd McClendon said, "[Jimmy] just has to be consistent in what he's trying to accomplish. Hopefully … his workout regimen, workout habits, pitching habits will be such that it will allow him to become a better pitcher, a more consistent pitcher."[25] The Pirates released Anderson on December 16.

In the three years from 2000 through 2002, Anderson was one of the least effective starting pitchers in the majors, ranking third from the bottom in both ERA (5.24) and winning percentage (.349).[26] In his last season with the Pirates, he struck out the fewest batters per nine innings (3.0) and had the second-lowest strikeout-to-walk ratio (0.75). Perhaps nibbling too much, he surrendered 4.0 walks per nine innings.

Yes, Anderson lost 41 games in his three full seasons as a starter with the Bucs, but a manager has to be confident enough to give a pitcher the opportunities to lose that many games. Anderson started 85 games over that span, more than any Pirates pitcher. In fact, he never missed a start nor spent a day on the injured list in his professional career.[27]

On January 15, 2003, Anderson signed with the Cincinnati Reds. In two stints with the Reds, separated by a trip to Triple-A Louisville, he recorded one win against five losses and an 8.84 ERA. On June 26 Anderson surrendered 11 earned runs on 15 hits in five innings. He was released a week later and never started another game in the majors. He signed with the San Francisco Giants, but pitched only in the minors, and was released on August 21.

Since being drafted in 1994, Anderson had gained significant weight. He weighed 180 pounds on signing,[28] but by 2003, had increased to 240. Over the winter, Anderson decided to get in better shape, lost 30 pounds, and in 2004 spring training with the Cubs had a 2.14 ERA, sixth-best in baseball.[29]

After beginning 2004 at Triple-A Iowa, Anderson was summoned to Chicago in late May.[30] In his first six appearances, Anderson pitched only 5⅔ innings. But on June 14 against the Houston Astros, he recorded a four-inning save, an event that 20 years later would be quite rare. With the Cubs ahead 5-0 in the sixth inning, starter Mark Prior surrendered a leadoff double. Anderson came in and stranded the runner. Although he allowed two singles in the seventh, he avoided any scoring with the help of a double play, and in the eighth retired in order the estimable trio of Lance Berkman, Jeff Kent, and Jeff Bagwell. In the bottom of the ninth, after the Cubs had extended their lead to 7-0, Anderson allowed two runs before sealing the victory.[31]

Although Anderson had pitched well in five of his seven outings for the Cubs, on June 23 he cleared waivers and was sent back to Iowa. On July 2 the Cubs traded him to the Red Sox for minor-league right-hander Andy Shipman.

Anderson knew a few of his new teammates, particularly Bronson Arroyo, with whom Anderson played in Pittsburgh and throughout the Pirates' minor-league system. Sox fans will remember Arroyo as the pitcher from whom Álex Rodríguez slapped the ball in Game Six of the 2004 League Championship Series against the New York Yankees. What initially looked like a disastrous play for the Red Sox was subsequently corrected, with A-Rod called out for interference and Yankees runners returning to their bases.

In Anderson's first appearance for the Sox, July 4 against Atlanta, Boston led 4-1 after four innings. But in the bottom of the fifth, Red Sox starter Derek Lowe allowed seven of the first eight batters to score and left the game trailing 8-4. Anderson relieved Lowe with one out and the bases empty and gave up a walk, double, and triple as the Braves extended their lead to 10-4, the final score.

Two days later, with the Red Sox thrashing Oakland 11-0, Anderson pitched a scoreless eighth and ninth to preserve the win.

On July 15 Anderson needed only nine pitches to stymie the Anaheim Angels in the seventh inning. Unfortunately for the Red sox, they were down 8-1. Ramiro Mendoza pitched a one-two-three eighth, but the Red Sox were unable to cut into the Angels' lead.

On July 17 Anderson relieved Joe Nelson in the bottom of the sixth with the bases loaded, one out, and the Angels ahead 5-1. Anderson threw a wild pitch, allowing one run, and gave up a two-run single to Garret Anderson, making the score 8-1. Red Sox manager Terry Francona let his pitcher start the seventh, but after Anderson retired the first two batters, he walked the next two and was relieved by Mendoza. The Red Sox lost 8-3.

On July 21, with the Orioles leading 8-4, Anderson entered in the ninth and gave up two doubles and a single before recording an out. The two resulting runs and a homer by Boston's Trot Nixon made the final score 10-5.

Eleven days later, Anderson was released and never pitched another major-league game. In his brief stay with Boston, he had no decisions and an ERA of 6.00. Though he wasn't with the Red Sox for their entire run, Anderson received a World Series ring commemorating his contribution. He called the Sox a tight-knit group of "great guys."[32]

Thereafter, Anderson bounced around the minors with affiliates of the Cubs, Minnesota Twins, Tampa Bay Devil Rays, Houston Astros, and Florida Marlins. In 2006, just after his first child was born, and "miserable" in Albuquerque, New Mexico, Anderson retired.[33]

Subsequently, he went to work with Bob McKinney, a former Pirates scout who helped sign Anderson to his first contract. At McKinney Baseball, Anderson gave private pitching lessons to players from 7 years old to college age. He also coached a 17-and-under team that played tournaments in a showcase league. Anderson estimated that 97 percent of the players he coached went on to play college ball, including Chris Taylor, who became a main cog on the World Series Champion Los Angeles Dodgers in 2020.[34] Anderson said, "I love helping the kids get into college and get better. It's my favorite thing."[35]

From 1998 to 2001, Mark McGwire, Sammy Sosa, and Barry Bonds established the six highest single-season home-run totals. It was the pinnacle of the steroids era, which continued at least until penalties were instituted in 2005, and so covered Anderson's entire career. Anderson said he was fully aware that players were using. "Players are, with each other, pretty honest," he said. "You kind of know what's going on. Plus, you could just look at somebody and tell."[36]

Anderson accumulated just under six years of major-league service time, and naturally wishes he had gotten 10 years, which would have guaranteed a healthier pension – about $150,000 per year.[37] So he holds some bitterness from having played against guys who were juicing. "I wonder what would've happened if maybe it was a more level playing field, if I could've maybe got that 10 years or maybe get to that contract where I [would be] set family-wise," he said. "That part does aggravate me."[38]

As of 2023, Anderson seemed happy with his life after pro ball. He remained busy with pitching lessons, but because he made his own schedule, still had plenty of time for family and hobbies. Anderson and his wife, Sarah, lived in Portsmouth, Virginia. They have two daughters, Jordyn, who played soccer at Randolph College in Lynchburg, Virginia and Jenna, a basketball player at Portsmouth Christian. His mother, Florence, lived only minutes away. Anderson's favorite pastimes were fantasy football and golf. In 2022 he walked away with a championship in fantasy football and had his golf handicap down to five–an all-time low.[39]

SOURCES

In addition to the sources cited in the Notes, the author consulted Baseball-Reference.com.

NOTES

1. Rich Radford, "Baseball Draft '94: Jimmy Anderson," *Norfolk* Virginia) *Virginian-Pilot*, June 2, 1994: C1.
2. Robin Brinkley, "Western Branch Still Looks Like No. 1," *Norfolk Virginian-Pilot*, May 29, 1994: D13.
3. Paul Meyer, "Dad in His Thoughts as Anderson Debuts," *Pittsburgh Post-Gazette*, July 5, 1999: B-7.
4. Tom Robinson, "Anderson Mourns Father Who Pushed Him So Hard," *Norfolk Virginian-Pilot*, September 13, 1997: C1.
5. Robin Brinkley, "W. Branch's Anderson Has All the Right Pitches," *Norfolk Virginian-Pilot*, April 27, 1993: C1.
6. "W. Branch's Anderson Has All the Right Pitches."
7. Bill Leffler and Ed Miller, "14-Player All-Star Squad Features Six Juniors," *Norfolk Virginian-Pilot*, June 3, 1992: 14.
8. Jim Leffler, "Manor, Churchland Players on All-District," *Norfolk Virginian-Pilot*, June 4, 1993: 26.
9. Brinkley, "Western Branch Still Looks Like No. 1."
10. Bill Leffler and John Gordon, "All-Southern District Baseball," *Norfolk Virginian-Pilot*, June 24, 1994: 18.
11. Paul White, "A Super Year for Area Schools, Individuals," *Norfolk Virginian-Pilot*, June 19, 1994: C12.
12. Leffler and Gordon, "All-Southern District Baseball."
13. Phone interview with Jimmy Anderson, October 30, 2023. Hereafter, Anderson interview.
14. Brinkley, "W. Branch's Anderson Has All the Right Pitches."
15. Email from Anderson, November 9, 2023.
16. Rich Radford, "Baseball Draft '94: Jimmy Anderson," *Norfolk Virginian-Pilot*, June 2, 1994: C1.
17. While Anderson pitched in the Pacific Coast League, the league average ERA was about 5.00.
18. Robinson, "Anderson Mourns Father Who Pushed Him So Hard,"
19. Paul Meyer, "Anderson Is Called Up to Help Ailing Bullpen," *Pittsburgh Post-Gazette*, July 4, 1999: D6.
20. Paul Meyer, "Anderson Shows Control," *Pittsburgh Post-Gazette*, July 4, 1999: D-6.
21. Meyer, "Dad in His Thoughts as Anderson Debuts," *Pittsburgh Post-Gazette*, July 5, 1999: B-7.
22. David Hall, "Bonus Coverage: Jimmy Anderson," *PilotOnline.com*, July 24, 2013 (last accessed May 19, 2023). https://www.pilotonline.com/sports/norfolk-tides/article_da864ee7-883a-5ffc-be24-7a4872cc6fff.html.
23. Alan Robinson (Associated Press), "Injury Apparently Didn't Ruin Loiselle's Career," *Tyrone* (Pennsylvania) *Daily Herald*, June 16, 2000: 4.
24. While Anderson pitched in the National League, the league average ERA was about 4.50.
25. Robert Dvorchak, "Pirates Report – Notebook," *Pittsburgh Post-Gazette*, September 21, 2002: B-5.

26 Pitchers who started at least 60 percent of their games and had at least 50 decisions.
27 Anderson interview.
28 Rich Radford, "Baseball Draft '94: Jimmy Anderson."
29 Tom Robinson, "Anderson Lost Weight and Added Confidence," *Norfolk Virginian-Pilot,* April 7, 2004: C-3.
30 Paul Sullivan, "Muscle Tear Will Shelve Wellemeyer," *Chicago Tribune,* May 28, 2004: 4-5.
31 Paul Sullivan, "Cubs Ace Notches First Win," *Chicago Tribune,* June 15, 2004: 4-1.
32 Anderson interview.
33 David Hall, "Bonus Coverage: Jimmy Anderson," *PilotOnline.com*, July 24, 2013, Updated August 4, 2019 (last accessed June 24, 2023). https://www.pilotonline.com/2013/07/24/whatever-happened-to-jimmy-anderson-2/.
34 Anderson interview.
35 David Hall, "Bonus Coverage: Jimmy Anderson," *PilotOnline.com*, July 24, 2013, Updated August 4, 2019 (last accessed June 24, 2023) https://www.pilotonline.com/2013/07/24/whatever-happened-to-jimmy-anderson-2/.
36 David Hall, "Bonus Coverage: Jimmy Anderson."
37 David Hall, "Bonus Coverage: Jimmy Anderson."
38 David Hall, "Bonus Coverage: Jimmy Anderson."
39 Anderson interview.

A RED SOX MEMORY

As a child, I was fortunate to spend a lot of time with my grandfather. Gramps, a baseball fan, was born in 1906. He remembered the 1918 World Series. Every time we were together, we talked baseball. He used to tease me by saying, "The Red Flops will never win a championship!"

Despite some close calls in the '70s and '80s, I began to think my grandfather might be correct.

Fast-forward to 2004. When Mientkiewicz secured the last out of the 2004 World Series, my family went crazy. I quickly thought of my grandfather (he passed away in the early 1980s). I know that wherever he was, he was laughing hysterically.

The next morning, on my way to work, I decided to visit his grave at the Hopedale cemetery. Driving onto the grounds, I noticed there were three or four cars at the site. It was readily apparent why they were there. One guy had placed a Red Sox pennant on a tombstone. Another guy was walking around in a Red Sox jacket and hat. Doubtful that he had even slept.

I planned to leave my Red Sox hat on my grandfather's grave. However, as I was getting out of my car, another vehicle pulled up and parked in front of me. It had a Yankees bumper sticker on the rear fender. I had no idea why he was there. I changed my mind and decided not to leave the Sox hat on the grave. Those Yankee fans are everywhere, and you can't trust any of them.

In 2023, Mike Bresciani placed a cap on the gravestone of grandfather Jim McGrath.
Photo by Mike Bresciani.

MIKE BRESCIANI

BRONSON ARROYO

BY GREG D. TRANTER

Bronson Arroyo played 16 years of major-league baseball and helped the Boston Red Sox end the Curse of the Bambino with the 2004 World Series championship. His controversial tag of Álex Rodríguez in Game Six of the ALCS, when the umpires reversed their original call, spurred the Red Sox on to a victory. Boston closed out the series with a win over the Yankees in Game Seven. Arroyo later pitched for Cincinnati, and 108 of his 148 career victories were for the Reds.

Bronson Anthony Arroyo was born on February 24, 1977, in Key West, Florida, to Gus and Julie (Dopp) Arroyo, one of two children. (He has an older sister, Serenity.) He was named after the actor Charles Bronson. Arroyo's father, who came to the US from Havana, worked in the roofing business with his father until they sold the business in 1986, then invested in real estate. The family moved to Brooksville, Florida, when Bronson was a youngster. As a 14-year-old, he played for the Northeast Pensacola team that won the Dixie League state title and was runner-up in the Dixie Boys (13- and 14-year-olds) World Series.[1] He was 1-1 in World Series games that he pitched.

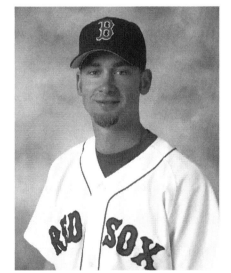

Arroyo starred in baseball and basketball at Hernando High School in Brooksville, Florida. As a sophomore he made the *Tampa Bay Times* All-North Suncoast all-star team as a second baseman. He hit .265 with 21 runs scored and was considered an outstanding defensive player for the district champions. He also was a starting guard on the varsity basketball team as a sophomore.

During the summer of 1993, Arroyo, at 16, pitched the Hernando Dixie-Majors to the summer-league state baseball championship. He pitched six innings in relief, giving up one run and striking out 11 to win the title game. "He's the best player to come through Hernando County in a long time – 15, 20 years," Hernando coach Tim Sims said.[2] "From a mental standpoint in his approach to the game he's years ahead of a 16-year-old. He's more like a junior or senior in college, or a second-year pro player.[3] Hernando was defeated in the ages 15-18 Dixie League World Series, but Arroyo recorded the team's only victory.[4]

Arroyo suffered from tendinitis in his arm during much of his junior year, so his pitching was limited. He still managed to play shortstop, hit .380, and drive in 24 runs and make the *Tampa Bay Times* All-North Suncoast team as an infielder. His pitching line was 4-3 with a 1.08 ERA. Hernando finished 24-9 and repeated as Class 3A-District 7 champions, despite losing seven starters from the previous year – including two pitchers who were drafted. "At the start of the season, I don't think anyone on the team thought we'd be in this position," Arroyo said. "The second half of the season, we've just played together as a team. That's why we've won."[5] Hernando went on to win one more game in the district tournament, a two-hit shutout by Arroyo, before its season ended with a loss. Arroyo also continued to play basketball and was Hernando's leading scorer as a junior, averaging 15.4 points per game.

In the fall of his senior year Arroyo signed a letter of intent to play baseball at the University of South Florida, where he would concentrate on pitching. The first Hernando player to sign with a Division 1 baseball school, he was highly recruited by such baseball powers as Florida, Georgia Tech, Georgia Southern, and Mississippi State. Arroyo finished his high-school basketball career as one of the leading scorers in school history. He averaged 16.2 points per game and was named to the All-North Suncoast first team.

As a senior Arroyo for the third year in a row was named to the All-North Suncoast first team. He was voted the District Class 4A Player of the Year and was named to the all-state first team by the *Tampa Bay Times*. He finished his senior season with a 10-3 record, a 0.44 ERA and 131 strikeouts in 80 innings. He batted .308 from the leadoff spot for the 26-8 district champions, who lost in the semifinals of the state tournament.

Arroyo was selected by the Pittsburgh Pirates in the third round of the 1995 amateur draft. His high school coach, Sims, said of Arroyo, "Mentally, he's prepared to play in the big leagues, he's blessed with good size and he's got such a fluid motion that he makes it look easy. As far as his potential, I think no one around here is as good."[6] "I wanted to go with the Pirates all along," Arroyo said. "I've known the Pittsburgh scout since I was in ninth grade and he's always been straight with me. I've got a good impression of the organization just from my contacts with him."[7] He was at the barbershop getting his hair cut when the Pirates called. When he returned home, his dad told him he had been drafted by Pittsburgh.

Arroyo decided to forgo college and signed his professional contract the day he was drafted. "We had an amount in mind and they more than exceeded that amount with their first offer,"

Gus Arroyo said. "He would have been a fool to pass up that kind of opportunity, we took it right away."[8]

Arroyo reported to the Bradenton Pirates of the Rookie Gulf Coast League, two days following his high-school graduation. He made his minor-league debut, pitching one inning and striking out two. He finished his first season of professional baseball with a 5-4 record and a 4.26 ERA in 61⅓ innings. "I have a lot of work ahead of me. It's going to take a while," said the 18-year-old hurler. "I realize I have to be patient. I also know anything could happen in the future. There is no guarantee and I never expected one. I just want to give it my best shot and if it's in the cards, well, great."[9]

With Augusta of the low Class-A Sally League in 1996, Arroyo began learning how to pitch and about the wear and tear on his arm. "I'm learning that you can't just go out and try to strike everybody out," he said. "You have to work on getting people to pop up, ground out, and concentrate more on saving your arm. It's a long season."[10] With Augusta he posted an 8-6 record with a 3.52 ERA. (In his debut on April 5, he allowed just one hit in six innings.)

During spring training in 1997, Arroyo was asked by a reporter if he had fantasized about playing professional baseball as a kid. "I would have bet my life on it when I was 6 years old," he said. "I always knew I'd play pro ball. I never thought about doing anything else."[11]

With Lynchburg of the advanced Class-A Carolina League in 1997, Arroyo was 12-4 with a 3.31 ERA and helped lead the team to the league title. He pitched 166 innings, his highest season total in the minor leagues. In the playoffs he was 2-0 with a sparkling 0.52 ERA. Arroyo was selected to the midseason all-star team.

Arroyo continued his progression through the Pirates' minor-league system in 1998, playing for the Double-A Carolina Mudcats (Raleigh, North Carolina). He finished with a 9-8 mark and his ERA ballooned to 5.46. Despite that, the Pirates remained high on the youngster. "He's really developing on a good course," said Mudcats manager Jeff Banister. "The way he's advancing, he has a good chance to pitch in the big leagues someday in the near future."[12] Pittsburgh sent Arroyo to the Arizona Instructional league for two months that fall to further his development. He finished with a 2-4 record and a 6.51 ERA.

Arroyo was back in Double A in 1999 with the Altoona Curve. He put together his best minor-league season with a 15-4 record, tied for the Eastern League lead in wins, and a 3.65 ERA. He won eight of his first nine starts. Arroyo was promoted to Triple-A Nashville on August 20 and made three starts, losing two with one no-decision.

Arroyo began the 2000 season in Nashville and was 8-2 with a 3.65 ERA. The call he had been waiting and hoping for came, when he was informed by Sounds manager Richie Hebner on Sunday afternoon June 11, about an hour before he was scheduled to pitch. "Richie said, 'Stop, you're pitching against the Braves on Tuesday,'" Arroyo said. "I said, 'Sweet!'"[13]

Arroyo had never attended a big-league game until he made his debut at Pittsburgh's Three Rivers Stadium on June 12, 2000. But it wasn't as a pitcher. A decent hitter in the minor leagues, Arroyo batted for pitcher Scott Sauerbeck in the bottom of the sixth inning. He ran the count to 3-and-2 against Braves pitcher Bruce Chen, and then hit a groundball back to the mound.

Arroyo made his pitching debut the next night, June 13, against the Braves. He pitched five innings, allowed five runs and 10 hits, and got a no-decision as the Pirates rallied for a 7-6 10th-inning victory. Arroyo lost three starts before getting his first major-league victory on July 22 against the Philadelphia Phillies at Three Rivers Stadium. He surrendered two hits over seven scoreless innings. "I think I appreciate (the win) more because I didn't win in my first or second outing," Arroyo said. "I had to claw my way to get a win. If it had happened in my first outing, I probably wouldn't appreciate it so much."[14] His second win came six days later, on July 28 in a 16-5 Pirates romp over San Diego. Arroyo allowed three earned runs in six innings and collected his first major-league hit, a double off Matt Clement. During his time with the Pirates, he made 20 big-league appearances – 12 starts and 8 relief appearances – while compiling a 2-6 record and a 6.40 ERA.

That fall Arroyo married his high-school sweetheart, Aimee Faught. They had dated since 1994 and were engaged in 1998. They divorced in 2008.

Arroyo made the Pirates' Opening Day roster for the 2001 season. "Breaking camp with the team, it will be a little different experience than it was last year," he said. "With us opening the new ballpark (PNC Park), I think it will not be overwhelming, but kind of like, 'Wow, it's coming together.'"[15] He won his first start of the season, on April 7 at Houston, 5-3. He bounced between Pittsburgh and Nashville throughout the season. Arroyo made 24 appearances for the Pirates, 13 starts, and pitched his first complete game on October 2, a 10-1 win over the New York Yankees. He was 5-7 with the Pirates and made nine starts in Nashville, finishing with a 6-2 record. After the season he played winter ball in Puerto Rico with Santurce and had a strong season.[16]

Arroyo's 2002 season was similar to 2001 except that he spent more time with Nashville than with Pittsburgh. He was disappointed that he did not make the Pirates' Opening Day roster. "After the season I had in winter ball, I thought I definitely would make the team," he said.[17] In his eighth season in the Pittsburgh organization, he was 8-6 in Nashville with a career minor-league-low ERA of 2.96 in 22 games. With the Pirates he appeared in nine games with a 2-1 record, highlighted by a 4-1 victory over future Hall of Famer Tom Glavine of the Braves on August 29.

Pittsburgh surprisingly placed Arroyo on waivers after the season and the Red Sox claimed him on February 4, 2003. After signing pitcher Jeff Suppan, the Pirates felt they could do without Arroyo. "At this point in time we're just not convinced by his performance," general manager Dave Littlefield said of Arroyo. "He just falls off the list as far as our priorities."[18]

Arroyo was out to prove that the Pirates made a mistake. In his first year in the Boston organization, he was named the Red Sox Minor League Player of the Year. He went 12-6 with a 3.43 ERA in 24 starts for Triple-A Pawtucket and was second in the International League in strikeouts with 155 in 149⅔ innings. On August 10 he pitched the fourth perfect game in the 120-year history of the International League, a 7-0 win over Buffalo. He struck out nine in the victory. "I didn't feel especially great in the bullpen," Arroyo said afterward. "But after you get through three or four innings of easy work and you haven't thrown many pitches you kind of keep rolling and rolling."[19]

Twelve days later Arroyo was called up to the Red Sox in the heat of the pennant race. He pitched in six games in relief with no won-lost record but a good 2.08 ERA. He recorded his first major-league save in his Red Sox debut. He relieved Pedro Martínez on August 25 against Seattle and pitched three scoreless innings, allowing two hits. Arroyo was on Boston's 2003 postseason roster. He did not pitch in the Red Sox' Division Series win over Oakland, but appeared three times against the Yankees in the ALCS, pitching 3⅓ and allowing one run.

In 2004 for the first time, Arroyo spent the entire season in the big leagues. He became a dependable fifth starter, making 29 starts in his 32 appearances. Arroyo finished with a 10-9 record and a 4.03 ERA. He was at his best down the stretch, going 5-0 in his last nine starts with a 3.78 ERA, all Red Sox wins. He led the major leagues with 20 hit batsmen, tying the Red Sox record set by Howard Ehmke in 1923.

On July 19 against the Seattle Mariners, Arroyo recorded 11 consecutive outs via strikeout in innings three through seven. (Seattle won the game in extra innings.) Five days later, on July 24, Arroyo triggered a bench-clearing brawl with the Yankees. In the top of the third inning with Boston trailing 3-0, he beaned Álex Rodríguez and then, in an effort to restrain the Yankee star, Jason Varitek pushed his catcher's mitt into Rodríguez's face and a melee ensued. New York went ahead of Boston, 9-4, but the Red Sox clawed their way back and Bill Mueller hit a walk-off two-run homer in the bottom of the ninth off Mariano Rivera. That 11-10 win provided confidence to the team, especially later in the year in the playoff rematch with New York.

Arroyo also played an important role in the postseason that began with a start in Game Three of the Division Series in Anaheim against the Angels. He pitched six innings while allowing two runs and three hits with seven strikeouts. Arroyo left the game with the Red Sox leading 6-1 and the crowd gave the right-hander a standing ovation. "Unbelievable. You can't describe it," he said. "Walking off the field, knowing you've earned the respect of the fans and your teammates."[20] The Angels rallied to tie the score, only to have David Ortiz win the game with a walk-off two run homer for Boston in the bottom of the 10th inning.

Arroyo started Game Three of the ALCS against the Yankees but did not pitch well. He gave up six runs in two-plus innings and was tagged for home runs by Hideki Matsui and Rodríguez. The Red Sox tied the game, 6-6, in the bottom of the third to get Arroyo off the hook, but they went on to lose the game 19-8 and trail in the series three games to none. He pitched a scoreless 10th inning of Game Five in the Red Sox' come-from-behind 14-inning 5-4 victory, won on Ortiz's game-winning single.

Arroyo was the center of controversy in Game Six of the ALCS in Yankee Stadium. Boston was leading 4-2 in the bottom of the eighth and the Yankees had Derek Jeter on first with one out and Arroyo pitching to Rodríguez. Rodríguez hit a groundball down the first-base line that Arroyo fielded. Arroyo went to tag Rodríguez but the Yankee third baseman slapped Arroyo's glove. The ball bounded out of the glove and rolled into right field with Jeter scoring from first and Rodríguez getting to second. Initially the umpires ruled Rodríguez safe. Arroyo and Red Sox first baseman Doug Mientkiewicz argued with first-base umpire Randy Marsh, claiming interference. Boston manager Terry Francona joined the fray to argue the call. The six-man umpire crew stepped aside to discuss the ruling. Finally, the umpires reversed the call and ruled that Rodríguez had interfered and was out. He stood at second base in disbelief while Jeter was returned to first base. The 56,128 fans in Yankee Stadium booed relentlessly and threw baseballs and other objects onto the field. After a 10-minute delay to restore order, Arroyo induced Gary Sheffield to pop to catcher Jason Varitek to end the threat. The Red Sox retired New York in the ninth inning with no damage and held on for a 4-2 victory.

"I didn't know what the rule was," Arroyo said after the game. "I wasn't sure what they were going to do. I was just putting the tag on him and he just chopped me across the arm. It was pretty obvious to me."[21] Umpire Marsh after the game said, "I did not see Alex wave at him and knock the ball out. In that situation (plate umpire) Joe West could see it clearly. He was the man who really helped us out. He had the best shot. He was sure of it."[22]

Arroyo relieved Tim Wakefield in the fourth inning of Game One of the World Series at Fenway Park on October 23 with the Red Sox leading 7-5. There was a runner on first with two outs. After surrendering a single, Arroyo forced Albert Pujols to ground out and end the inning. Arroyo pitched a perfect fifth inning with two strikeouts. In the sixth he allowed back-to-back run-scoring doubles to Edgar Rentería and Larry Walker as the Cardinals tied the game, 7-7. The Red Sox continued to hit and went on to an 11-9 victory.

Arroyo made one more appearance in the World Series, relieving Derek Lowe in the bottom of the eighth inning of Game Four with Boston leading 3-0. He prompted Roger Cedeño to pop out to second baseman Mark Bellhorn and then walked Reggie Sanders. Francona replaced Arroyo with Alan Embree. Embree retired the Cardinals and Keith Foulke set St. Louis down in the ninth and the Red Sox had their first World Series championship in 86 years. Arroyo, reflecting on his first full big-league season, said, "I wanted to prove I could pitch in this league and I think I accomplished all that. Winning the World Series was a bonus."[23]

Arroyo was back with Boston in 2005 and posted a 14-10 record. He led the team with 20 quality starts and established personal career highs in wins (14), starts (32), and innings pitched (205⅓). He won nine consecutive decisions, five from 2004 and four in 2005, before losing to Toronto on May 25.

After the season Arroyo signed a new three-year contract with Boston, securing his spot on the club, or so he thought. Two months later, on March 20, he was traded to the Cincinnati Reds for outfielder Wily Mo Peña. "I don't know if there's a moment in my life that's probably been lower than the phone call Theo Epstein (Red Sox general manager) gave me," Arroyo recalled years later. "I was three years in, you win a World Series in such a special place in Boston, I was really entrenched there. I was looking forward to doing that for six or seven years. For him to pull the plug on me was completely unexpected. It was a huge downer."[24]

Arroyo became a stalwart of the Reds' pitching staff for the next eight years, chalking up 108 wins in 279 starts. It took him a little while to adapt to Cincinnati, but once he did, it was home. "I feel very fortunate that I got off to a good start to have people enjoy me and love me right out of the gate," Arroyo said years later. "It started feeling like a place that I could be for a very long time. It felt like it was my speed. It didn't feel like the town was too large to get your hands gripped around it. It was just a real hometown feel for me and it happened relatively quickly."[25]

In 2006 Arroyo was an All-Star for the first time and was voted the winner of the Johnny Vander Meer Award as the Reds' Most Outstanding Pitcher and the Joe Nuxhall Good Guy Award. He had a 14-11 record and led the majors with 240⅓ innings pitched. In February 2007 he signed a three-year contract extension and he re-upped again with Cincinnati in 2010 which kept him with the club though the 2013 season.

Arroyo was the Reds' most reliable pitcher. In all eight seasons with Cincinnati, he made at least 32 starts and pitched over 200 innings except for one season when he pitched 199. Six times he had double-digit wins and in both of the two seasons he fell short he recorded nine. Arroyo had a high of 17 wins in 2010, twice he had 15 victories (2008, 2009), and twice 14 (2006, 2013). He led the team in starts seven times and innings pitched six times. From 2006 to 2013 he was among the major-league leaders in wins, starts, and innings pitched. He won the Vander Meer Award three times (2006, 2009, 2010) and the Joe Nuxhall Award four times (2006, 2009, 2011, 2012). Arroyo was only the second Reds pitcher to win a Rawlings Gold Glove Award for fielding excellence when he won it in 2010.

Arroyo helped lead the Reds to three playoff appearances, in 2010, 2012, and 2013, the franchise's only playoff seasons between 1996 and 2019. He was the Reds' leader in wins in 2010 and tied for the team lead in 2013.

Arroyo started Game Two of the 2010 ALDS against the Phillies at Citizens Bank Park on October 8. He pitched 5⅓ innings, allowing one earned run on four hits. His defense, with back-to-back errors in the fifth inning, cost him two unearned runs. He left the game with a 4-2 lead, but the bullpen could not hold it as Philadelphia rallied for a 7-4 victory.

In the 2012 ALDS, Arroyo started and won Game Two over San Francisco, 9-0. He allowed just one hit and one walk in seven innings. However, the Reds lost the five-game series, dropping the final three games at home.

After the 2013 season, Arroyo opted for free agency and signed with the Arizona Diamondbacks. He spent one season in Arizona where he made 14 starts and finished with a 7-4 record for the last-place Diamondbacks. Arroyo injured his arm in June and required Tommy John surgery. He sat out the rest of the 2014 season and all of 2015. He bounced around via a few trades and signed as a free agent twice, and at the age of 40 returned to the big leagues with the Reds in 2017, which was his final season. He made 14 starts and finished with a 3-6 record and a 7.35 ERA.

That was the end of the line for Arroyo after 16 major-league seasons and a 22-year professional baseball career. His final major-league statistics include 148 wins, 137 losses. with a 4.28 ERA. Arroyo dots the Reds all-time list in a few categories. He is sixth in strikeouts (1,157), seventh in starts (279) and 16th in wins (108).

Before ending his baseball career, Arroyo had a budding music career. He began playing the guitar when he was in Double A in 1999. While in Boston in 2004-05 he performed in the Hot Stove, Cool Music Show at the Paradise Rock Club to raise money for the Jimmy Fund, the Red Sox' charity to fight cancer in children. He released a music CD, *Covering the Bases*, in 2005. The record debuted at No. 1 in Boston and several other cities across New England.[26] After being traded to Cincinnati, Arroyo performed in concert with the Screaming Mimes to raise $35,000 for the Reds Community Fund in 2006. In addition, from 2006 to 2013 he performed at Redsfest each year. In 2020 he collaborated with classical pianist Harrison Sheckler to create a recording of "Take Me Out to the Ball Game." He returned to Boston in 2021 to play the Hot Stove, Cool Music Show.

Arroyo married Nicole McNees in 2021 and as of 2023 the couple resided in the Cincinnati area.

Arroyo was elected to the Cincinnati Reds Hall of Fame on October 26, 2022, and was enshrined in the summer of 2023, becoming the 82nd Reds player so honored. "It's something you work for your whole life," he said upon hearing he had been elected. "You just want to play in the major leagues. You have no idea if you're going to play long enough to leave your mark in any way, shape, or form. One of the things you don't think about as a player a lot of times is sticking with the same team long enough to build up these types of numbers to be in their hall of fame."[27]

Arroyo and his band '04 released an album, *Some Might Say*, on February 16, 2023. It was the first album for which he wrote all the music.

SOURCES

In addition to the sources cited in the Notes, the author consulted Ancestry.com, Baseball-Reference.com, Retrosheet.org, AZcentral.com, the *Boston Red Sox Media Guides* for 2004 and 2005, and the *Cincinnati Reds 2013 Media Guide*.

NOTES

1 Staff reports, "Northeast Pensacola reaches Dixie Boys World Series," *Pensacola News Journal*, August 16, 1991: Section C-1.

2 Tim Buckley, "Arroyo Shines for Dixie Team," *Tampa Bay Times* (St. Petersburg), August 6, 1993: 4.

3 "Arroyo Shines for Dixie Team."

4 Tim Buckley, "Hernando Boys Set Sights on World Series," *Tampa Bay Times*, July 31, 1993: 1.

5 Gregg Doyel, "Hernando Seeks More Surprises," *Tampa Tribune*, May 10, 1994: 4-Hernando.

6 Scott Danahy, "Arroyo Calm While Pitching Up a Storm," *Tampa Tribune*, June 3, 1995: 6-Citrus.

7 Thomas White, "Majors Come Calling on Hernando Pitcher," *Tampa Bay Times*, June 2, 1995: 1.

8 Scott Danahy, "USF Loses Arroyo to Lure of Pro Game," *Tampa Tribune*, June 6, 1995: 5-North Tampa.

9 Thomas White, "Arroyo Nostalgic, but Happy with Present," *Tampa Bay Times*, August 10, 1995: 4.

10 Mike Readling, "Arroyo Working on Fooling Hitters and Saving His Arm," *Tampa Bay Times*, July 18, 1996: 4.

11 Rick Gershman, "At Home on the Mound," *Tampa Bay Times*, March 30, 1997: 1.

12 Pete Young, "Arroyo Beating Numbers Game," *Tampa Bay Times*, September 3, 1998: 4.

13 Brant James, "Hernando Native Steps Up to the Big Leagues," *Tampa Bay Times*, June 13, 2000: 1.

14 Paul Meyer, "Arroyo Sparkles in 2-1 Victory," *Pittsburgh Post-Gazette*, July 23, 2000: D-6.

15 Brant James, "Pirates' Arroyo Is in 'The Show,'" *Tampa Bay Times*, April 1, 2001: 6.

16 Associated Press, "Pirates finally ready to Play," *Latrobe Bulletin*, February 26, 2002: 8.

17 Brant James, "Back to Nashville … Again," *Tampa Bay Times*, March 31, 2002: 4.

18 Robert Dvorchak, "Paper Pirates Are Improved," *Pittsburgh Post-Gazette*, February 1, 2003: C-2.

19 Associated Press, "PawSox's Arroyo Perfect," *Lewiston* (Maine) *Sun-Journal*, August 11, 2003: C3.

20 John Powers, "Emotions Bubbling Over for Arroyo," *Boston Globe*, October 9, 2004: E3.

21 Peter May, "A-Rod a Bigger Villain in One Swipe," *Boston Globe*, October 20, 2004: D2.

22 "A-Rod a Bigger Villain in One Swipe."

23 John Schwarb, "Arroyo, Red Sox Prove Their Worth, *Tampa Bay Times*, December 12, 2004: 4.

24 Bobby Nightengale, "From Reluctance, Cincinnati Became Home for Arroyo," *Louisville Courier-Journal*, October 30, 2022: B8.

25 "From reluctance, Cincinnati Became Home for Arroyo:" B8.

26 *2013 Cincinnati Reds Media Guide*, 54.

27 Bobby Nightengale, "Arroyo Voted into Reds Hall of Fame," *Cincinnati Enquirer*, October 28, 2022: C3.

A RED SOX MEMORY

I have loved baseball for as long as I can remember. When I was 10 years old in 1972, I watched the Red Sox finish second to the Detroit Tigers, a half-game out. In 1974 the Red Sox collapsed as they went 11-18 in September. In 1975 Jim Rice and Fred Lynn joined the Red Sox and they won the AL East and the AL pennant but lost to a great Cincinnati Reds team in a hard-fought World Series. In 1977 and 1978, they were so close yet so far. The years went by, 1986 another World Series loss, this time to the New York Mets. 1988, 1990, 1995, 1998, 1999 – all playoff losses. In 2003 they went as far as they could, but an Aaron Boone homer ended their season.

A pastor friend introduced me to a beautiful young lady and I went to the West Coast during a week in September 2004 to meet her. Our relationship developed and we married in May of 2006. I felt that after the Red Sox won, I could move along with my life. I had seen the Celtics, Bruins, and Patriots win and now it was the Red Sox' turn. I moved to Chicago in May of 2005 and worked for Acta Publications, the publisher of the *Bill James Handbook*. The Red Sox won again in 2007 under Terry Francona, under John Farrell in 2013, and under Alex Cora in 2018.

TOM NAHIGIAN

PEDRO ASTACIO

BY GREGORY H. WOLF

Right-hander Pedro Astacio made national news by tossing a shutout and fanning 10 in his major-league debut and proceeded to record four shutouts in just 11 starts as a midseason call-up for the Los Angeles Dodgers in 1992. Never the superstar his meteoric rise might have suggested, Astacio eventually developed into a sturdy, and sometimes spectacular, innings-eater. Traded to the Colorado Rockies in late 1997, Astacio proved a pitcher could have success hurling half his games in the mile-high hitters' paradise Coors Field. "I didn't put doubts in my mind (about pitching in Coors)," said Astacio, who twice led the league in home runs allowed with the Rockies. "Just get the ball, go to the mound, make some good pitches and see what happens."[1] In parts of five seasons in Denver, Astacio won 53 games (which ranked sixth in franchise history as of 2017) despite a 5.43 ERA, and his 17-win, 210-strikeout campaign in 1999 still ranks among the best single seasons in Rockies' history. "He's the pitcher who mentally has not been affected by pitching in Colorado," said one GM. "Pedro has always tended to throw strikes. He's aggressive with his stuff and trusts his stuff is good enough."[2] Astacio's teammates were equally impressed with his dogged determination. "He was a battler," said teammate Todd Helton. "He wouldn't back down. He could give up three early runs and you'd never know it."[3]

Pedro Julio (Pura) Astacio was born on November 28, 1968, in Hato Mayor, in the eastern Dominican Republic. He grew up on a rural farm between Hato Mayor and coastal San Pedro de Macoris, where his father, Fulgencio, planted crops and tended to livestock on about 100 acres. Astacio's mother died when he was 8, leaving his father the sole provider for his six children (three boys and three girls). Like almost all boys on the baseball-crazed island, Pedro loved baseball. According to one story, he learned to pitch by using an old tractor tire as a strike zone.[4] By the time Astacio was a student at Pilar Rondon High School, he was on the radar of big-league scouts. On November 21, 1987, 19-year-old Astacio signed with legendary Los Angeles Dodgers scout Ralph Avila and Elvio Jiménez.

Astacio's first taste of professional baseball came a few months later when he donned the uniform of the Tigres de Licey in Santo Domingo in the Dominican Winter League. Though he hurled only one game, he'd return to that club to pitch occasionally for the next eight seasons (through 1995-1996), compiling a 13-10 record.[5] In the spring of 1988 Astacio arrived in Campo Las Palmas, at the Dodgers visionary baseball academy Avila founded the year before.[6] That camp would serve as a model for almost all other big-league teams and produced dozens of major leaguers, among them Pedro and Ramón Martínez, Raúl Mondesi, and José Offerman, but Pedro was the first protégé to reach the majors. Astacio's 4-2 record with 2.08 ERA in the Dominican Summer League earned him a promotion to the Dodgers farm system in 1989.

Over the next three years Astacio progressed through the Dodgers system. He earned All-Star honors in the Rookie Gulf Coast League in 1989 and two years later had advanced to the Double-A San Antonio Missions in the Texas League. Though he struggled (4-11, 4.78 ERA) facing more experienced hitters in the Texas League, the Dodgers were impressed enough to invite him to spring training in 1992.

Photo courtesy of the National Baseball Hall of Fame.

The 23-year-old Astacio surprised the coaching staff by going 2-2 with a 1.42 ERA in the Grapefruit League.[7] Nonetheless, he began the 1992 season with Triple-A Albuquerque, where he was converted into a reliever. Astacio struggled in his new role, yet a series of events conspired to lead to his unexpected promotion to the Dodgers. Following the riots that had engulfed Los Angeles from April 29 to May 4 after four police officers were acquitted of using excessive force against Rodney King, the Dodgers were forced to play four doubleheaders in six days in early July. Desperately needing pitching, the club called up Astacio as an emergency starter. In what was described as the "finest debut in franchise history," Astacio tossed a five-hit shutout and fanned 10 (a new team record for debuts) to beat the Philadelphia Phillies, 2-0, in the second game of a twin bill on July 3.[8] "It was hard to believe what I was seeing," said teammate Brett Butler. "[H]e's toying with major-league hitters.[9] Astacio exhibited the kind of enthusiasm and raw emotion that would define his career – on and off the diamond – by jumping around after strikeouts and openly celebrating.

Astacio's roller-coaster ride was in its infancy. He was returned to Albuquerque after his next start, five days later, then recalled a month later to replace the injured Tom Candiotti. He tossed another shutout in three starts, and despite an eye-popping 1.42 ERA (six earned runs in 38 innings) was demoted again. Back with the Dodgers in September, Astacio was the feel-good story in the Dodgers' otherwise forgettable season and worst record in the majors. Astacio finished with a 5-5 slate, including four shutouts in 11 starts, and a 1.98 ERA in 82 innings.

Standing 6-feet-2 and weighing about 175 pounds, Astacio had a "good, lean power pitcher's body with a long trunk," according to one scout.[10] Indeed, Astacio was primarily a fastball pitcher with a bullwhip-like delivery that created late ball movement. Astacio struggled with mechanics his entire career. One scout described them as "poor [because] he hyperextends his elbow which throws off his command" and added "[h]e also arches his head, tightening his back, further contributing to his inconsistent command."[11] Astacio also had a big overhand curve and a changeup, and was never shy to challenge pitchers inside as evidenced by twice leading the league in hit batsmen.

Astacio's rookie success surprised everyone, yet the Dodgers were careful to temper their expectations in 1993. Slated for the fifth spot in the rotation after a productive spring, Astacio struggled early in the campaign. "It's his command," said skipper Tom Lasorda. "He's not getting the ball where he wants to or where he's supposed to."[12] By the end of July Astacio's 4.74 ERA (easily the highest on the staff) threatened his role in the starting rotation. In almost a repeat performance from a year earlier, Astacio caught fire, going 7-3 and posting a 1.82 ERA in 74⅓ innings over the last two months of the season. "He's not flying off the handle anymore and making dumb pitches," said catcher Mike Piazza of Astacio's transformation. "He realizes that every pitch has a purpose."[13] Called the "ace of the staff" by sportswriter Gordon Verrell, Astacio fashioned consecutive shutouts in September as part of a career-best 21⅓ scoreless innings. While the Dodgers split their 162 games to finish in fourth place in the NL West, Astacio led the steam with 14 victories and was the only starter with a winning record, while his 186⅓ innings were just short of the 200-inning barrier his mound mates Orel Hershiser, Ramón Martínez, Candiotti, and Kevin Gross all surpassed.

During Astacio's remaining tenure with the Dodgers, the right-hander flashed the brilliance that many experts had expected; however, he often struggled mightily, and rarely found a middle ground. Frustrations – by both the pitcher and the organization – grew as Astacio's inconsistencies baffled his managers. One scout called Astacio "probably the most inconsistent 60-grade pitcher in the game."[14]

Astacio had a scare in spring training in 1994, when team physicians detected a heart murmur. Although the diagnosis was ultimately determined to be insignificant, Astacio was sidelined for much of camp. Nonetheless he was ready to start the season and fanned 11 in his debut, a 6-0 loss to Atlanta on April 8. Astacio seemed to catch his stride during a six-start stretch beginning June 14, going 3-1 with a 1.88 ERA and holding batters to a .175 average, and leading sportswriter Tim Kawakami of the *Los Angeles Times* to declare, "There's no doubt Pedro has established himself as one of the top pitchers in the division."[15] Such a comment typified glowing perceptions of Astacio. In stark contrast were those voiced just weeks later when he failed to make it through the third inning in consecutive starts. Pitching coach Ron Perranoski said that Astacio's lack of English made it "difficult to make adjustments" during the game, suggesting that his struggles would continue because of a language barrier.[16] The Dodgers were in first place in the NL West when the players union began its strike on August 12, resulting in the cancellation of the rest of the regular season and postseason. Astacio finished with a 6-8 record and 4.29 ERA (highest among the club's starters) in 149 innings.

While baseball executives and union representatives haggled in the offseason over the future of baseball, Dodgers brass wondered what to do with the erratic, streaky Astacio, whose potential seemed as limitless as his flameout as a starter was likely. One report described Astacio as "teetering *this* close to mental disaster all the time" during the 1994 campaign, leading many to wonder if the high-strung flinger might be better suited as a reliever.[17] Calls for Astacio's banishment to the bullpen intensified when he went winless in his first five starts of the 1995 campaign before blanking the New York Mets on six hits on May 24, thereby recording his first victory since June 25 of the previous year. Losses in his next five consecutive starts resulted in his demotion. Beat reporter Bob Nightengale of the *Los Angeles Times* suggested that Astacio's "emotional fluctuations" and not his ability were the root cause of his "mystery struggles."[18] Used primarily in mop-up and low-leverage situations, Astacio fared better in the bullpen (3.40 ERA vs. 4.82 as a starter), or as team VP Fred Claire said, "had better focus."[19] The Dodgers captured their first division crown since they won the World Series in 1988. Astacio pitched in relief in each contest of the three-game sweep by the Cincinnati Reds, yielding just a hit in 3⅓ scoreless innings.

Astacio arrived at camp skeptical about the Dodgers' claim that he had a chance to regain a spot in the starting rotation. "They said it's my job to lose, but that doesn't mean anything," he said. "[L]ast year they told me I'd be back in the rotation."[20] After blowing up in his debut, Astacio produced his best and most consistent season in Dodgers blue. Though he didn't complete any of his 32 starts, he proved to be a dependable workhorse, logging 211⅔ innings with a sturdy 3.44 ERA (including a 2.95 clip over the last three months). Poor run support contributed to his misleading 9-8 record. According to the *Los Angeles Times*, three factors led to Astacio's success: He quickened his pace on the mound (he had been one of the NL's slowest workers), he relied much more on his fastball, and he seemed less demonstrative.[21] Astacio joined Hideo Nomo (16-11), Ismael Valdéz (15-7), and Ramón Martínez (15-6) to anchor the NL's best staff (a major-league-low 3.46 ERA) as the Dodgers finished in second place and captured a wild-card berth in Lasorda's final season in the dugout. The team was once again swept in the NLCS, this time by the Atlanta Braves. In his only appearance, Astacio hurled 1⅔ scoreless innings in Game Two.

The now 28-year-old Astacio arrived in camp in 1997 after yet another offseason filled with trade rumors, and also a new skipper, Bill Russell, who replaced the legendary Lasorda after 21 seasons. Astacio got off to a hot start, winning his first three decisions, while producing a 2.00 ERA a month into the season. In one of those victories, he tossed seven hitless innings against the Mets at Shea Stadium before yielding a leadoff double in the eighth. "He's one of the most underrated guys in this league," gushed pitching coach Dave Wallace.[22] Astacio then lost his next seven decisions, during which time he had an ugly altercation. Yanked after surrendering five runs in four dismal innings against the Cardinals in Los Angeles on national television, a visibly angered Astacio confronted Russell in the dugout and had to be restrained by third-base coach Joe Amalfitano after a shoving match.[23] (Three days earlier Valdez and Russell had a similar dugout confrontation.) Astacio immediately apologized in the press, but his fate was sealed. "When something like that happens in the dugout with the cameras there, you have to pay the consequences," said VP Claire, who fined Astacio an undisclosed amount.[24] Normally a quiet player in the clubhouse, Astacio was considered by some as too emotionally volatile to be consistently successful; on the other hand, some reporters sympathized with the pitcher, suggesting that the Dodgers never helped him settle into a rhythm as a starter and put too much pressure on him to conform to the "Dodger Way." On August 19, the Dodgers shipped Astacio to the Colorado Rockies for All-Star second baseman Eric Young. "[Astacio] has great ability, character and work ethic," said Claire about the transaction. "He pitched some outstanding games, (but never with consistency.)"[25]

Astacio wasted no time proving his worth to Rockies manager Don Baylor following the loss of the fan favorite Young. After fanning eight in a 6⅔-inning no-decision in his debut against the Houston Astros, in the Astrodome, Astacio won five consecutive decisions. Those victories included a career-high 12-strikeout performance in eight scoreless innings against Atlanta and an emotional six-inning outing with nine punchouts versus his former team in Los Angeles. After just six starts, pitching coach Frank Funk pronounced Astacio the best pitcher ever to wear a Rockies uniform.[26] The Rockies went 23-14 after acquiring Astacio to finish with a winning record (83-79; third place NL West) for the third consecutive season since they entered the league as an expansion team in 1993. "He came in and really took charge," said Funk of Astacio (5-1, 4.25 ERA in seven starts), and really fired up our ball club."[27]

A hot free-agent commodity in the offseason, Astacio signed a four-year deal worth more than $24 million with the Rockies. "He's one of our leaders," said Funk when spring training opened. "He has that aggressive, I-love-to-play attitude. He's got the work ethic of a high-school kid in his first major-league camp."[28] The Rockies, with the signing of free-agent pitcher Darryl Kile, were expected to challenge the San Francisco Giants and the Dodgers for the West crown in 1998. And then the season started. Astacio struggled mightily, yielding 27 earned runs in his first 20 innings (12.15 ERA). He's fighting with his control," said skipper Don Baylor. "He's up in the (strike) zone, and behind in the counts. You can't pitch like that."[29] While the Rockies limped to a 77-85 record, Astacio took a beating, producing the highest ERA in the majors among starters (6.23), tied for the major-league lead with 39 gopher balls, and led the NL by hitting 17 batters; still, he went 13-14, made 34 starts, set a new team record with 170 punchouts, and exceeded the 200-inning mark for the third straight season. Nonetheless, rumors swirled that Astacio's arm was injured – it wasn't. "[Astacio] bears no resemblance from the nasty right-hander" from 1997, wrote Denver sportswriter Ray McNulty.[30] Beat reporter Mike Klis noted that Astacio relied more on breaking balls instead of his heater.[31] Like all hurlers, Astacio had to adjust his pitching in Coors Field, with its thin air, where balls flew out of the park at a record pace in an era of home-run records. And that process wasn't easy, as the split in Astacio's home and away ERA indicated (7.39 to 4.90).

Astacio reached the heights and depths of his career in 1999, but for vastly different reasons. On the field he enjoyed his best season, consistently pitching deep into ballgames despite yielding a league-leading 38 home runs. His victory against the Milwaukee Brewers on June 6 might best capture Astacio's career at Coors Field. In 7⅔ innings, he surrendered four round-trippers and five runs while fanning 10 and emerged the victor when the Rockies exploded for eight runs (and also smashed four home runs) in the seventh. On July 6, he took revenge against the Dodgers, tossing a complete game with 10 punchouts and drove in the go-ahead run in a 5-2 victory at Coors Field. Not known as good hitter (.133 career average), Astacio had his most productive season at the plate, collecting 20 hits.

Just as Astacio seemed to realize the potential many had predicted for him, he was arrested on August 12 after a violent altercation with his estranged, pregnant wife, Ana, allegedly striking her in the face.[32] (It was his second marriage. His first, to Dorca Garcia Thomas, ended in divorce in 1995.)

Neither suspended nor fined by either the Rockies or the league, Astacio took the mound three days after the incident and tossed eight innings, fanning 11 in a 12-4 victory over the Montreal Expos in Denver, where the initial chorus of boos gradually turned to cheers for the pitcher. While the Rockies plunged to a last-place finish, Astacio completed a career year despite his legal distractions. He won 17 games (tying Kevin Ritz from 1996 for the franchise record), and set new club records in innings (232), complete games (7), and strikeouts (210, third best in the NL).

Astacio's charge of domestic abuse cast a dark shadow over his best season and raised questions about his future. On January 28, Astacio pleaded guilty to third-degree assault and received two years deferred judgment, thereby avoiding jail.[33] Soon thereafter the Department of Immigration and Naturalization Services (INS) informed Astacio that a felony or misdemeanor involving domestic violence was a deportable offense. (Astacio was a citizen of the Dominican Republic and had since reconciled with Ana.) Apparently unaware of the legal ramification of his plea, Astacio left the Rockies spring training in March and was granted permission to withdraw his guilty plea in an effort to remain in the United States with the formal trial set for early July. (The trial was subsequently deferred to November.) Despite his legal troubles, Astacio was the Rockies' Opening Day starter. After losing his first two starts, he won his next six decisions. Included was a four-start stretch with at least 10 strikeouts. He fanned 10 or more seven times during the season, and matched his career high of 12 punchouts in seven overpowering innings, yielding just two hits and one run in a 2-1 victory over the Chicago Cubs at Wrigley Feld on August 1. Seemingly headed to matching his totals from the previous season, Astacio injured his left oblique on September 1, making only three very brief starts thereafter before he was shelved the last two weeks of the season. He concluded the campaign with a 12-9 slate (5.27 ERA in 196⅓ innings) and racked up 193 strikeouts. Weeks after the season, he underwent arthroscopic surgery on his left knee to remove damaged cartilage that had bothered him for two years.

Astacio's legal woes were far from over. On November 13, he pleaded guilty to lesser charges, a single count of spousal harassment, and was sentenced to six months' probation; however, his residency status was still unclear.[34] INS eventually abandoned deportation procedures by the beginning of spring training. Astacio opened his 10th big-league season red-hot. On April 22, he tossed two-hit ball over eight innings to beat the Arizona Diamondbacks in Phoenix, 2-1, to improve his record to 3-1 and lower his ERA to 1.93 after four starts. And then the bottom dropped out. He won only three of his next 15 decisions with an ERA well north of 6.00, prompting trade rumors as the Rockies were headed to their second straight last-place finish in the NL West in three years. Despite Astacio's horrendous numbers, contenders still sought his services. In a cost-cutting move, the Rockies shipped Astacio, due to be a free agent at season's end, to the Houston Astros for pitcher Scott Elarton. Astacio had a renaissance of sorts (2-1, 3.14 ERA) before shoulder pain ended his season after just four starts.

Astacio was diagnosed with a torn labrum in the offseason, but decided to forgo possible season-ending surgery given his status as a free agent. The Mets took a chance a chance on the 33-year-old hurler, signing him to a two-year contract in January. Reunited with former Dodgers teammate Mike Piazza, Astacio emerged as one of the surprises of the season, winning his first three starts. On April 27, he threw 7⅓ hitless frames against the Brewers at Shea Stadium, ultimately tossing eight innings in a 2-1 victory. Mets beat writer Rafael Hermoso reported that the team was impressed with Astacio's "maturity" and "preparation" and how he mentored young hurlers on the club.[35] Teammates gave him the moniker Mule for his ability to carry them late into innings. On August 6, he tossed a complete-game three-hitter and fanned 10 (the 20th and final time he reached double digits in strikeouts) to beat the Brewers in Milwaukee, improving his record to 11-4 and lowering his ERA to 2.95 before the clock stuck midnight in his fairy-tale season. As the pain in his shoulder intensified, Astacio collapsed in his final nine starts, yielding 54 earned runs in 45 innings (10.80 ERA) while losing seven of eight decisions. Through it all, Astacio still took the mound every five days and never became a distraction for the last-place Mets. On the contrary, Hermoso described Astacio as "one of most jubilant members of the Mets' clubhouse, joking about almost everything and dismissing poor performances as if he had a bad hair day."[36]

Astacio spent four more seasons in the big leagues, battling an array of arm and shoulder injuries, chasing a dream. Occasionally he found lightning in a bottle. He made only seven appearances for the Mets in 2003, signed in the middle of the 2004 season with the Boston Red Sox, making five appearances in September during their historic run to the World Series (he was not on the postseason roster), and made 22 combined starts for the Texas Rangers and San Diego Padres in 2005. His 4-2 slate and 3.17 ERA for San Diego earned him his first and only postseason start. In Game Two of the NLCS he lasted only four innings yielding four runs (two earned) and was collared with the loss, 6-2, to the Cardinals in St. Louis. The 37-year-old Astacio finished his 15-year big-league career with the Washington Nationals in 2006, splitting 10 decisions in 17 starts, one of which was his second two-hitter for his 12th and final shutout, blanking the Braves, 5-0, on August 15 in the nation's capital.

The typically modest, media-shy Astacio was never an All-Star but he retired as one of the most productive pitchers from the Dominican Republic. At the time of his retirement following the 2006 season, his 129 victories (124 losses) ranked fourth behind Juan Marichal (243) and brothers Pedro Martínez (206)[37] and Ramón Martínez (135). (Astacio's total has since been passed by Bartolo Colon's 235 and Ervin Santana's 144, both as of 2017.) Astacio also became just the fourth Dominican hurler to log at least 2,000 innings, joining Marichal, Pedro Martínez, and Joaquín Andújar.

After his active playing days Astacio returned to his longtime residence and ranch in San Pedro Macoris, near where he grew up. In 2013, he donned a big-league uniform for the first time in seven years when he returned to the Rockies as a special assistant coach during spring training. As of 2017 Astacio still resided primarily in the Dominican Republic.

SOURCES

In addition to the sources cited in the Notes, the author also accessed Retrosheet.org, Baseball-Reference.com, the SABR Minor Leagues Database, accessed online at Baseball-Reference.com, SABR.org, and *The Sporting News* archive via Paper of Record.

NOTES

1 Owen Perkins, "In Camp With Rox as Coach, Astacio Thrilled to Help," MLB.com, February 28, 2013. m.mlb.com/news/article/42093506/in-camp-with-colorado-rockies-as-coach-pedro-astacio-thrilled-to-help/.

2   Quote by New York Mets GM Steve Phillips in Tyler Kepner, "Astacio's Health Is a Key Issue," *New York Times*, January 18, 2002: D2.
3   Perkins.
4   Randy Franz, "Performance Does the Talking," *Orange County Register* (Anaheim, California), March 26 1993: C1.
5   Pedro Astacio page, *WinterBall Data*, winterballdata.com/.
6   Ken Baxter, "Avila Led the Charge in MLB's Latin Revolution," ESPN, October 2, 2006. espn.com/espn/hispanichistory/news/story?id=2607258.
7   Allan Malamud, "(Notes) on a Scorecard," *Los Angeles Times*, July 6, 1992: C3.
8   Gordon Verrell, "LA Dodgers. Fly on the Wall," *The Sporting News*, July 13, 1992: 21.
9   Verrell.
10 "Scouting Report: Pedro Astacio," *The Sporting News*, August 13, 2001: 35.
11 Scouting Report, Pedro Astacio
12 Steve Dilbeck, "Astacio's Having Problems," *San Bernardino* (California) *Sun*, May 11, 1993: C2.
13 Associated Press, "Astacio, Dodgers blank Marlins," *San Bernardino* (California) *Sun*, September 13, 1993: C2.
14 "Scouting Report: Pedro Astacio."
15 Tim Kawakami, "Baseball Daily Report," *Los Angeles Times*, July 6, 1994: C9.
16 Maryann Hudson, "Baseball Daily Report," *Los Angeles Times*, July 24, 1994: C7.
17 "Caught on the Fly," *The Sporting News*, March 25, 1996: 5.
18 Bob Nightengale, "Dodgers Reconsidering Astacio's Starting Role," *Los Angeles Times*, June 16, 1995: C5.
19 Gordon Verrell, "Los Angeles Dodgers," *The Sporting News*, February 19 1996: 23.
20 Bob Nightengale, "(Baseball) Daily Report," *Los Angeles Times*, February 24, 1996: C6.
21 Bob Nightengale, "He Gets By With Help From Friends," *Los Angeles Times*, July 26, 1996: C1.
22 Bob Nightengale, "Los Angeles Dodgers," *The Sporting News*, April 28, 1997: 27.
23 Chris Baker, "Call It Dodger Blew – As in a Fuse," *Los Angeles Times*, June 9, 1997: C1.
24 Steve Springer, "Dodger Report," *Los Angeles Times*, June 10, 1997: C6.
25 Ross Newhan, "Baylor Looks for a Change From Astacio," *Los Angeles Times*, August 24, 1997: C9.
26 Mike Klis, "'Dodger Way' Isn't Working Well," *Gazette* (Colorado Springs, Colorado), September 21, 1997: SP 11.
27 Ray McNulty, "A Rockies' Attitude Adjustment," *Gazette* (Colorado Springs, Colorado), February 26, 1997: SP1.
28 Rob McNulty, "Preview," *Gazette* (Colorado Springs, Colorado), February 26, 1998: SP2.
29 Tony DeMarco, "Colorado Rockies," *The Sporting News*, April 27, 1999: 37.
30 Ray McNulty, "Rockies Better Batters in Beer-League Title," *Gazette* (Colorado Springs, Colorado), September 8, 1998: SP4.
31 Mike Klis, "Colorado," *The Sporting News*, May 22, 2000: 48.
32 "Rockies' Astacio Arrested," *CBS News*, August 12, 1999. cbsnews.com/news/rockies-astacio-arrested/.
33 "Rockies P Astacio Avoids Prison," CBS News, January 28, 2000. cbsnews.com/news/rockies-p-astacio-avoids-prison/.
34 Associated Press, "Astacio Sentenced to Supervised Probation," ESPN, November 13, 2000. a.espncdn.com/mlb/news/2000/1113/876164.html.
35 Rafael Hermoso, "It's Astacio's Turn to Take a Run at a No-Hitter," *New York Times*, April 28, 2002: G4.
36 Rafael Hermoso, "With Astacio Hurt, Mets Look to Cone," *New York Times*, March 21, 2003: S3.
37 Pedro Martinez was still active at time and had 206 victories; he finished with 219.

A RED SOX MEMORY

The 2004 Boston Red Sox club thrilled me. Having been born in 1945, I had suffered through the near-misses of the 1967, 1975, and 1986 Series and thus was so happy and relieved that the Sox had won a World Series in my lifetime. I was also happy for Broadway Charlie Wagner, who experienced a Series win at the age of 91 after devoting so much of his professional life to the Sox.

KIT CRISSEY

A RED SOX MEMORY

I remember distinctly a night in 2004. I drove from my New York apartment up to my postcard club in Yorktown Heights. As I came home via the Taconic Parkway, Game Seven of the ALCS was on the radio. I still remember my delight at each Red Sox home run against the haughty Yankees. Four wins after three losses!

That was the first and only time such a feat was accomplished in MLB history.

M (NEW YORK) FRANK

MARK BELLHORN

BY JASON SCHELLER

"We wouldn't have won the World Series without him."
– Kevin Millar[1]

Mark Bellhorn is quite possibly the most underrated player on the 2004 Red Sox team. While other players like David Ortiz, Curt Schilling, or Dave Roberts rightfully garner much praise for the success of the Red Sox' 2004 championship run, Bellhorn and his exploits receive relatively little attention. However, it can be successfully argued that without Bellhorn and his clutch play in the postseason, the Red Sox would not have won that World Series in 2004. Sportswriter Jackie MacMullan said of the switch-hitting second baseman, "You forget about Mark Bellhorn. He lulls you to sleep with those droopy eyes and that droopy hair and his insistence on examining every pitch as though it is a rare piece of art." MacMullan encapsulated fans' feelings about the switch-hitting Bellhorn, saying, "He'll drive you crazy this second baseman, who takes and takes pitches until he either walks or strikes out. Or hits incredible clutch home runs to win it."[2]

After a professional career that started in 1997 with the Oakland Athletics and led to short stints with the Chicago Cubs and Colorado Rockies, Bellhorn landed with the Red Sox. It was there that, in the 2004 season, he put up career numbers in walks (88), strikeouts (177), and on-base percentage (.373).

After helping the team win the World Series and ending the 86-year drought that had plagued the organization and its fans, Bellhorn was released on August 19, 2005, and picked up by the rival New York Yankees on August 30. His time there was short-lived. He appeared in just nine games, with just two base hits, and was released after the season. He signed with the San Diego Padres and spent the 2006 season with them before signing with the Cincinnati Reds in 2007. A free agent once again, he signed a minor-league contract with the Los Angeles Dodgers in 2008. Bellhorn finished his career as a second baseman for the Colorado Rockies' Triple-A affiliate at Colorado Springs in 2009.

Mark Christian Bellhorn was born on August 23, 1974, in South Weymouth, Massachusetts, to Theodore Bellhorn, a veterinarian who was a 1973 graduate of Auburn University, and Marilyn Bellhorn.[3] Shortly after Mark's birth, his family moved to Oviedo, a suburb of Orlando, Florida. Mark played basketball and baseball at Oviedo High School, graduating in 1992. Mark's mother had been a teacher but stayed home to take care of her child. Unsure of where his plate discipline developed, Bellhorn said, "Probably in high school. I think I was always that type of hitter. I always took pride in having a high on-base percentage. I always worked the count. I always liked to get into the at-bat and get a feel for what the pitcher was trying to do. I was trying to get hitter's counts (ex. 1-0, 2-0, 3-1) where I knew a fastball was coming."[4]

Bellhorn was drafted out of high school by the San Diego Padres in the 37th round of the June 1992 amateur draft but chose to play baseball at Auburn University. Bellhorn said he didn't feel ready for the professional baseball lifestyle and was more excited to play high-level college baseball. "I was picked in the 37th round and it didn't make sense from a financial perspective," he said. "I felt like I could do way better than 37th round, so maybe it gave me motivation." Bellhorn played for Auburn from 1993 to 1995 and helped lead the Tigers to the College World Series in 1994. He played in the World Baseball Cup for Team USA in 1994. For Auburn he hit .342 in 1995, with 12 home runs, 60 RBIs, and 11 stolen bases. He was named an All-American by the American Baseball Coaches Association. For his college career he batted .322 with 25 home runs, 43 doubles, and 138 RBIs.

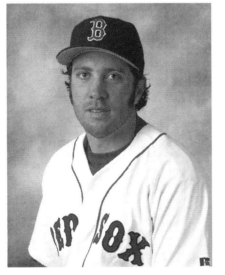

True to his expectations, Bellhorn was drafted in the second round in the 1995 draft, by the Oakland Athletics. With the Modesto Athletics of the advanced Class-A California League, he batted .258 with 6 home runs and 31 RBIs in 56 games.

For 1996 Bellhorn was moved up to the Huntsville Stars of the Double-A Southern League. In his first 23 games he batted .321 and Bellhorn was named the Player of the Month for May by the A's player development department.

Stars manager Dick Scott remarked, "He has a lot of poise. There are not many switch-hitters who have the power he has. … He's definitely a major-league prospect." Bellhorn ended the season as a utility infielder playing 55 games at second base, 57 at shortstop, and 12 at third base. He batted .250 with 10 home runs, 71 RBIs, 19 stolen bases, and 73 walks.

Bellhorn moved up to the Triple-A Edmonton Trappers of the Pacific Coast League in 1997, batting .328 in 70 games. In June he was called up to the Athletics to replace second baseman Scott Spiezio, on the 15-day disabled list because of tendinitis in his right hand.[5] He made his major-league debut on June 10, hitting an infield single off the Detroit Tigers' Willie Blair in his first at-bat. Bellhorn appeared in 68 games, playing third base, second base, and shortstop and batting .228. His first major-league home run came off Derek Lowe in Seattle on June 23, 1997.

Bellhorn spent most of the 1998 season with Edmonton, playing in 87 games at all four infield positions. He was called up twice by Oakland and played in 11 games between May 17 and June 21. He spent most of the 1999 season on the sidelines because of a torn tendon in his left wrist, but spent time with the Arizona Rookie League A's and the Midland Rockhounds of the Double-A Texas League.

Bellhorn played most of the 2000 season with the Sacramento River Cats, leading the PCL with 111 runs and 94 walks in 117 games. He finished second in the league with 24 home runs. Called up to Oakland in September, he was 2-for-13 in nine games.[6]

In 2001 Bellhorn played the outfield, a career first for him, in 18 games with Sacramento. He got into 38 games with the Athletics, as a utility infielder apart from one start in right field.[7] In the offseason Bellhorn was traded to the Chicago Cubs for minor leaguer Adam Morrissey. The 2002 season was among the best of Bellhorn's career. It was the first time in his career that he made the Opening Day roster, and he set a Cubs franchise record for home runs by a switch-hitter, hitting 27 round-trippers, a record that still stood in 2023. He played 77 games at second base but also spent time at the other three infield positions, and played one game (two innings) in left field.

On August 29, 2002, Bellhorn had the game of his career up to that point. Against the Brewers at Milwaukee's Miller Park, Bellhorn hit a home run from each side of the plate in the fourth inning. The first, from the right side with one man on base, was a towering 410-foot blast off Andrew Lorraine that landed in the center-field bleachers.

Later in the inning, with two Cubs on base, he homered off José Cabrera, a 380-foot shot that landed in the right-field bleachers. This made Bellhorn the only National Leaguer to homer from both sides of the plate in the same inning, and one of only three major leaguers to homer from both sides of the plate in the same game.[8] He finished the season with a .258 batting average, a career-high 27 home runs, and 56 RBIs in 146 games.

Bellhorn began the 2003 season as the Cubs' starting third baseman, but his patient approach at the plate coupled with new manager Dusty Baker's affinity for "aggressive" hitters saw Bellhorn traded in June to the Colorado Rockies. Of the trade, Bellhorn recalled in a 2005 interview, "I really don't know what happened that year. I kind of got off to a slow start with a new manager. I knew Dusty liked big guys who were more aggressive-type hitters. I don't know if he really liked my kind of approach."[9]

Bellhorn and minor-league pitcher Travis Henderson were traded to the Rockies for All-Star shortstop José Hernández. Rockies manager Clint Hurdle spoke optimistically of Bellhorn, saying, "Two years ago he hammered the ball pretty well. We feel pretty confident that he is a guy that we can bring in here, and hopefully get offensively charged again."[10] But Bellhorn's time in Colorado was marred by injury. He played in 48 games for the Rockies before being placed on the disabled list with tendinitis in his right shoulder, missing the first three weeks of August.

Bellhorn was at a pivotal moment in his career. He said, "I just felt that I had finally broken into the big leagues the year before and then the next year I couldn't do anything right. I lost playing time and felt very discouraged. I didn't think the Rockies were going to sign me again and thought I would be back in Triple A again. I went to winter ball in Mexico to try to find something."

Bellhorn was sent to the Red Sox in December; the team hoped he could fill the void at second base created by the departure of Todd Walker.[11] Bellhorn was "excited for the new start, and the chance to prove himself." While initially thought to be a utility infielder pickup for the Red Sox, he thought he had more to offer the team, and said, "I want to come in and compete for the second baseman's job. If I don't win it, then I can play a number of positions and help the team out."[12] The all-cash deal added depth to an infield that included Nomar Garciaparra, Pokey Reese, and Cesar Crespo.

Garciaparra struggled with injury throughout spring training and into July, barely able to field routine grounders, and was no longer an everyday starter at shortstop. On July 31 he was sent to the Cubs in a four-team deal that brought Montreal Expos shortstop Orlando Cabrera, Minnesota Twins first baseman Doug Mientkiewicz, and Los Angeles Dodgers outfielder Dave Roberts to the Red Sox.

Shoring up Boston's shaky defense led to a steadier role for Bellhorn in 2004. The extra playing time helped propel him to the best season of his career. Bellhorn started at second base, splitting time with the light-hitting Pokey Reese while Orlando Cabrera played consistently at shortstop.

The Red Sox started out hot, with a record of 15-6, but a losing streak in May saw the team play .500 baseball for the next three months. After the Garciaparra trade, the Red Sox offense caught fire. By the end of the season, Manny Ramírez and David Ortiz each had more than 40 home runs and, Johnny Damon hit .304 with 123 RBIs. Curt Schilling won 21 games while Pedro Martínez won 16, and the revamped defense was good enough to make Boston's pitching rotation one to be reckoned with.

Bellhorn played in 138 games, mostly at second base, with a .264 batting average, a .373 OBP, 17 home runs, and 82 RBIs. His 177 strikeouts were most in the American League but his 88 walks were third in the AL. Manager Terry Francona commented, "His concept of the strike zone has always been good. ... We knew coming in he could work the pitcher and run up the counts."[13] Perhaps the highest praise came from hitting coach Ron Jackson: "It's hard to explain his approach, but when you look around, if you go to sleep on him – BAM – he's going to bust you."[14]

In the American League Division Series, the Red Sox swept the Anaheim Angels, outscoring them 25-12. Bellhorn went 1-for-11 at the plate (.091), but drew five walks for a .375 OBP. He said, "I always struck out throughout my career. I know a lot of people think of that as a negative but that was part of my game. I always worked the count deep, so I wasn't a guy who swung at the first pitch. I don't think I struck out a lot in the clutch."[15]

In the American League Championship Series, Boston faced a New York Yankees team that had beaten them in 2003. The Red Sox dropped the first two games, at Yankee Stadium, then returned to Fenway Park only to be routed by the Yankees in Game Three, 19-8.

Both Bellhorn and Damon were having uncharacteristically difficult times at the plate during the ALCS. In four games Bellhorn had managed one hit and one RBI in 16 plate appearances. Teammate Dave Roberts said, "I tried to be a teammate, psychologist, and friend, pumping them up, telling them to be positive. They were getting booed, and I kept telling them to keep their heads high."[16] While Damon was not being screamed at by fans to take himself out of the lineup, Bellhorn was. He recalled, "What a great guy and teammate Dave Roberts was. I remember quite clearly how they were getting on both me and Johnny. I guess that's just part of the game, especially in places like Boston where the fans are so passionate about their sports and especially in the playoffs where everything is under a microscope." He went on to say, "As a player you just block it out as much as possible and focus on the job at hand. Lean on your teammates."

On the brink of extinction, the Red Sox won the legendary Game Four in 12 innings. Game Five went 14 innings, even longer than Game Four, and lasted 5 hours and 49 minutes, catapulting it to the top spot for the longest ALCS game. Red Sox relievers held the Yankees scoreless for the final eight innings. In the seventh inning, Bellhorn's double off Mike Mussina prompted Yankees manager Joe Torre to bring in Tanyon Sturtze. The Red Sox tied the score in the eighth. In the final at-bat of the marathon game, Ortiz blooped a single into center field, allowing Damon to score the game-winning run. Bellhorn said of the win, "It gave us a huge mental boost, the way we won. Especially the first night, and then to do it again. Going into New York, the last two games we felt like the pressure was on them."[17]

Game Six in Yankee Stadium, remembered as the "bloody sock game," saw Curt Schilling gut it out on a surgically repaired ankle, giving up only one run in seven innings. Bellhorn provided the run support, smashing a three-run homer off Jon Lieber in the fourth inning, putting the Red Sox on top 4-0. While the hit was initially ruled a ground-rule double, once the umpires conferred, they gave the home run to Bellhorn when it was discovered that the ball had bounced off a fan's hands in the left-field bleachers. "I thought it was probably going to be a double down the line and it ended up hitting off a fan's chest – home run."[18] Once Schilling exited the game, the bullpen held the Yankees in check and led the Red Sox to their third consecutive victory, 4-2, tying the Series at three games apiece.

In the winner-take-all Game Seven, the Red Sox came out swinging. Thanks to home runs by Damon, Ortiz, and Bellhorn, the Red Sox defeated the Yankees to advance to the World Series. Bellhorn's home run came in the top of the eighth inning with Boston up 8-3. On a 1-and-1 count, he hammered a Tom Gordon offering off the fencing attached to the right-field foul pole for his second home run in as many nights and the third of his career at Yankee Stadium. "That might have been the first hit I ever got off Gordon," Bellhorn said. "That was one of those swings where I swung and was like, 'Oh!' I was surprised how good I hit it. And it stayed fair and hit the pole."[19] The home run blunted any momentum the Yankees had built up for a comeback. Bellhorn said, "It was a huge momentum killer for the Yankees at the time. It pretty much silenced the crowd." In response to the home run, many diehard Yankee fans left the Stadium with a feeling reminiscent of Sox fans' hatred for Bucky Dent, cursing Bellhorn under their breath and, sometimes out loud. As diehard Red Sox fan Stuart O'Nan, who was in attendance that night, exclaimed, "From now until eternity Mark "F*cking" Bellhorn to Yankee fans."[20] As Bellhorn recalled, "Maybe I heard them do it a few times. ... Definitely a memorable home run for me."[21]

The Red Sox' victory catapulted them to the World Series where they faced off against the St. Louis Cardinals. In Game One Bellhorn continued his clutch hitting, leading to what he believed was the most memorable moment of his career. In the Boston eighth with the score tied, 9-9, after the Red Sox blew leads of 4-0, 7-2, and 9-7, Bellhorn sent a Julian Tavarez offering careening off the right-field foul pole to give the Red Sox an 11-9 lead and eventually the win. After the game Bellhorn said, "I just wanted to make a good swing at the pitch." *New York Post* columnist Mike Vaccaro put the home run in perspective, saying, "A good swing? What he made was a forever swing, a swing they will remember across New England for all time."[22]

In Game Two, Bellhorn was integral to the win for the Red Sox. In the fourth inning with two Red Sox on base, he doubled off the wall in center-field, scoring the two runners and extending the Red Sox lead to 4-1 as they won, 6-2. As Damon recalled, "Manny and David and myself, we weren't too big a factor tonight. But that's what's great about our team. It can be someone different every night. ... The offensive hero tonight: ... Bellhorn."[23] Bellhorn's heroics aside, it was also a game in which all the Red Sox runs were scored with two outs. Starter Curt Schilling became the first pitcher to win a World Series start with three different teams (Phillies, Diamondbacks, and Red Sox).[24] Bellhorn appeared on a *Sports Illustrated* cover on November 1, in a shot that captured him leaping over the Cardinals' Mike Matheny as Matheny slid into second base.

In Game Three, in St. Louis, Bellhorn again made a big impact. With men on second and third, Larry Walker came to the plate. Bellhorn, playing deeper than usual at second base, collected Walker's groundball and threw it to Ortiz at first base for the easy out. Ortiz spotted Jeff Suppan frozen midway between third and home and gunned the ball to Bill Mueller for the tag at third base to end the inning. With that lead, Pedro Martínez continued pitching masterfully in his last appearance with the Red Sox and closer Keith Foulke secured the win. In a postgame interview, when asked if the Red Sox had been lucky over the last few games because of the number of errors they committed, Bellhorn said, "That's the character of this team. Guys make mistakes and guys want to pick each other up."

The Red Sox won Game Four and swept the Cardinals, ending the 86-year "curse" that had plagued the Red Sox organization and its fans. Bellhorn was a key piece of that championship run and his clutch hitting put them in a position to win in the biggest games of the ALCS and World Series. Richard Johnson echoed Bellhorn's Game Three sentiments, saying, "It was a team where everybody contributed something. … This was a team where everybody found a way to pick it up and do something."[25] Bellhorn was precisely this type of player. He was not always consistent, but he was a clutch player when it mattered most.

In 2005 Bellhorn struggled offensively and his season was marred by injury. A sprained left thumb left him on the disabled list, making rehab starts at minor-league Pawtucket for 16 games. After his return he was released by Boston after refusing a minor-league assignment. He signed as a free agent with the Yankees on August 31. "It's unfortunate for me what happened this year in Boston, but there are no hard feelings," Bellhorn said.[26] However, once the Yankees expressed their interest in him, Bellhorn seemed optimistic, saying, "I wanted to go to a team where I was wanted."[27] Bellhorn made three starts for the Yankees, and had one pinch-running appearance in the Division Series.

After the postseason Bellhorn declined a minor-league assignment and chose to become a free agent.[28] He signed a one-year, $800,000 contract with the San Diego Padres, reuniting with former Red Sox teammates Alan Embree, Doug Mirabelli, Dave Roberts, and Scott Williamson.[29] Bellhorn played in 115 games for San Diego in 2006, batting .190 and hitting 8 home runs in 253 at-bats.[30]

Arguably his greatest game for the Padres came on May 28, 2006, against the Cardinals. He hit a towering home run that traveled 438 feet into the bleachers. At the time it was the second longest home run ever hit in Petco Park, then three years old. He also led the team in pinch-hit at-bats that season with 38.[31]

A free agent again after the 2006 season, Bellhorn signed a minor-league contract with the Cincinnati Reds with an invitation to attend spring training. He played in 99 games for the Reds' Louisville Triple-A affiliate, and in 13 August and September games for Cincinnati, going 1-for-14.

For 2008 Bellhorn was signed by the Los Angeles Dodgers to a minor-league contract ostensibly to play for the Triple-A Jacksonville Suns. However, Dodgers assistant GM DeJon Watson made clear that it was simply a minor-league signing with no intention of having Bellhorn fill a roster spot for Jacksonville or with the Dodgers. He was released on July 24.[32] Bellhorn was picked up by the Colorado Rockies on a minor-league contract in February of 2009, and played that year for the Triple-A Colorado Springs Sky Sox. After the season he retired as a player.

Since then Bellhorn has led a quiet life. He married Lindsey Bopp in May of 2013. As of 2023 they lived in Scottsdale, Arizona, with their two children. Since 2015 he has coached Arizona club league baseball at various age levels from 12 years old to high school. An avid golfer, he won the Arizona Stroke Play Championship in 2014. He displayed his trademark clutch "hitting" when he sank the first putt of the playoff round.[33] While many sources speculate that he owns multiple Dunkin Donuts franchises, he said, "No Dunkin Donuts franchises – I wish! Someone put that on my Wikipedia page 15 years ago and I have been asked about that multiple times."

Bellhorn's younger brother, Todd, born in 1976 in Lakeland, Florida, pitched at the University of Central Florida and was drafted in the ninth round by the New York Mets in 1998. He pitched for the Pittsfield Mets and the Capital City Bombers from 1998 to 2000.

Asked to summarize his career, Bellhorn said, "My career was an awesome experience. I feel extremely blessed to achieve my childhood dream of playing professional baseball. I had many ups and downs, but they only made me better. I went from thinking I wasn't going to have a job in 2003, while playing winter ball in Mexico, to being the starting second baseman of the World Series champion Boston Red Sox.

"I got to play for a lot of storied franchises, the Red Sox, Cubs, and Yankees. I wish I could've been a little more consistent in the big leagues, but I'm thankful for the opportunities that I got."

Of the 2004 Red Sox, Bellhorn said, "Being on that team and just experiencing the whole year with that group of guys – we had a lot of fun and we topped it off by winning the World Series. I especially loved those Red Sox vs. Yankees series It was like a college football rivalry game every time we played." Beyond the Red Sox, he said, "I enjoyed most all of the teams I played on (minors and majors). I just loved playing baseball and doing it for a job was icing on the cake for me."

"I'm sure most people will remember me for 2004 with the Red Sox, but I guess I just want to be remembered as someone who always hustled and played hard. Someone who always worked hard and was a great teammate."

SOURCES

In addition to the sources cited in the Notes, the author consulted Baseball-Reference, Retrosheet, Baseball Almanac, Stats Crew, and the Mark Bellhorn player file at the National Baseball Hall of Fame.

Thanks to Mark Bellhorn, the Boston Red Sox organization, Sarah Coffin of the Red Sox front office, and Rachel Wells and Roger Lansing at the National Baseball Hall of Fame, as well as Greg Fowler, Joe Johnston, and Holly Scheller for their support.

NOTES

1 MLB Network #WeKnowPostseason: Mark Bellhorn in 2004 interview with Kevin Millar. https://www.youtube.com/watch?v=44aWktxxTH0, accessed June 21, 2022.

2 Jackie MacMullan, "Bellwether," Boston Globe, *Believe It!!* (Chicago: Triumph, 2004), 16.

3 He began his career in small-animal practice in Lakeland, Florida. Dr. Bellhorn owned Seminole Veterinary Hospital in Sanford, Florida. In his later life he taught at the University of Tennessee, eventually moving on to become an associate clinical professor in the College of Veterinary Medicine at his alma mater, Auburn University.

4 Mark Bellhorn, email interview with author, June 16, 2023. Unless indicated, all otherwise unattributed quotations from Bellhorn come from this interview.

5 "Spiezio Expected Back in Lineup This Week," *Santa Cruz (California) Sentinel*, June 23, 1997: 16.

6 Bob Ryan, "Law of Averages Doesn't Apply Here," *Boston Globe*, April 28, 2004. http://archive.boston.com/sports/baseball/redsox/articles/2004/04/28/law_of_averages_doesnt_apply_here/, accessed July 12, 2022.

7 He hit just .135, and his OBP was but .210.

8 "Bellhorn Belts One from Both Sides: Becomes First NL Player to Do So in One Inning," *Santa Cruz Sentinel*, August 30, 2002: D-3. The Cubs scored 10 runs in the fourth inning and won the game 13-10.

9 Bruce Miles, "Mueller, Bellhorn Find Fame, Fortune with the Red Sox," *Chicago Daily Herald*, June 13, 2005.

10 Associated Press, "Rockies Swap Hernandez to Chicago," *Hays (Kansas) Daily News*, June 20, 2003.

11 He was acquired for $125,000. Though a number of reports mentioned a player to be named later, there was none. Email correspondence from Boston Red Sox, September 13, 2022.

12 Michael Silverman, "Who's on Second? Mark Bellhorn Says He's a Candidate," *Boston Herald*, December 16, 2023. https://www.milforddailynews.com/story/sports/2003/12/17/who-s-on-second-mark/41302268007/, accessed June 16, 2023.

13 Bob Ryan, "Law of Averages Doesn't Apply Here." http://archive.boston.com/sports/baseball/redsox/articles/2004/04/28/law_of_averages_doesnt_apply_here/, accessed July 12, 2022.

14 Allan Wood and Bill Nowlin, *Don't Let Us Win Tonight* (Chicago: Triumph Books, 2014), 59.

15 Wood and Nowlin, 59.

16 Saul Wisnia, *Miracle at Fenway: The Inside Story of the Boston Red Sox 2004 Championship Season* (New York: St. Martin's Press, 2014), 240.

17 Wood and Nowlin, 154.

18 Wood and Nowlin, 167.

19 Wood and Nowlin, 197.

20 Stewart O'Nan and Stephen King, *Faithful: Two Diehard Boston Red Sox Fans Chronicle the Historic 2004 Season* (New York: Scribner, 2004), 376.

21 Mark Bellhorn, email interview, June 16, 2023.

22 Mike Vaccaro, "Last Week's Goat Is Fenway's Darling," *New York Post*, October 24, 2004. https://nypost.com/2004/10/24/last-weeks-goat-is-fenways-darling/, accessed March 18, 2023.

23 Wood and Nowlin, 241.

24 Wood and Nowlin, 240-242.

25 Wisnia, 278.

26 Jim Cour, "Bellhorn Gets a Yankee Start: Infielder Switches Sides in New York-Boston Rivalry," *Albany (New York) Times Union*, August 31, 2005.

27 Cour.

28 "Transactions," *New York Times*, October 18, 2005.

29 "Baseball Notes: Dodgers Give Tomko $8.7 Mil," *Syracuse Post-Standard*, December 23, 2005.

30 "Reds Deal for Another Pitcher," *Cincinnati Post*, January 24, 2007.

31 "Bellhorn Hits Longest HR in Petco History in Win Over Cards," ESPN.com, https://www.espn.co.uk/story/2461613/pep-guardiola-bastian-schweinsteiger-must-decide-on-future, accessed March 18, 2023.

32 Tony Jackson, "Dodgers Sign Mark Bellhorn to Minor-League Deal," *Los Angeles Daily News*, May 16, 2008. http://www.insidesocal.com/dodgers/2008/05/16/dodgers-sign-ma/, accessed March 18, 2023.

33 "Arizona Stroke Play: Former MLB Star Bellhorn Wins It," amateurgolf.com, April 19, 2014. https://www.amateurgolf.com/12101-GolfNews-Ariz-Stroke-Play-Former-MLB-star-Bellhorn-wins-it, accessed June 16, 2023.

JAMIE BROWN

BY BOB LEMOINE

"I'll be part of that team for the rest of their life. Even though I wasn't a big part of the team, I'm still connected with it."
Jamie Brown, on his time with the 2004 Red Sox[1]

Jamie Brown pitched four games in the major leagues, all with the 2004 World Series champion Boston Red Sox. He was in his eighth professional season at that point as injuries had wreaked havoc on one season and the better part of two more. A steady control pitcher, Brown had an impressive 3.22 strikeout/walk ratio and 1.16 WHIP in eight minor-league seasons, but never had much opportunity at the major-league level. He finished his career overseas and found success in the Korean Baseball Organization.

Jamie Monroe Brown was born on March 31, 1977, in Meridian, Mississippi, to Charles Arnold Brown Jr., and Jenny (Thead) Brown. Charles worked as an electrician. Jenny worked as a hairdresser for a while until becoming a stay-at-home mother for her sons, Jamie and his brother, Aaron.[2]

Brown played high-school ball at West Lauderdale High School in Collinsville, Mississippi, and impressed his coach, local legend Jerry Boatner. "He threw strikes when he was in high school as a freshman," Boatner said. "I had one scout tell me that he was the best freshman he had ever seen."[3] As a freshman, Brown was the winning pitcher as West Lauderdale (33-5) won the state 3A championship, 8-1, over Ripley.[4] The team repeated as champion in 1993 by defeating Pontotoc. Sophomore Brown finished 13-0 that season.[5] He was undefeated (10-0, 0.94 ERA, 94 strikeouts in 52 innings pitched) and batted .367 his junior year and pitched the Knights (29-4) to a third straight title, 5-2, over Senatobia. "My arm felt good today, but my back was giving me troubles," Brown said after averaging 88-91 MPH on his pitches in the clinching game. "I was kind of nervous at the beginning."[6] Brown was selected as an all-state athlete and qualified for the National Amateur All-Star Tournament.[7]

Brown's senior year included an 18-strikeout game vs. Florence and a two-hit playoff victory against Forrest AHS. He finished the season 9-3 (1.90 ERA, 144 strikeouts), giving him a remarkable 43-5 high-school career record. In Game One of the playoffs, Brown threw a three-hitter while striking out 15 in a 4-2 victory over Simmons. The strikeout total propelled him to first place all-time in school history, surpassing Jay Powell, a native of Meridian who had an 11-year major-league career and won Game Seven of the 1997 World Series. "That was one of my goals when I started playing here," Brown said of the record. "I just came out with the fastball and then tried to keep them off balance." The Knights (30-5) later clinched their fourth straight state title.[8]

Brown was followed by Cleveland Indians scout Max Semler and selected in the 34th round of the June 1995 amateur draft by Cleveland, but he did not sign. He instead attended Okaloosa-Walton Community College in Niceville, Florida (later renamed Northwest Florida State College). He pitched masterfully for the Raiders, going 11-1 with a 1.90 ERA with 77 strikeouts in 77 innings. Brown was chosen as a third-team NJCAA All-American.[9] He transferred back home to Meridian Community College and was drafted by Cleveland again in the 21st round of the June 1996 draft. He continued his college career at Meridian CC and started 5-0 with a 2.32 ERA.[10] On May 15, 1997, he officially signed with Cleveland, and was assigned to Watertown of the short-season Class-A New York-Penn League.

Brown's professional debut came on June 19 when he allowed just two hits in five innings in a 15-0 thumping of Williamsport. "I was expecting to be nervous, first time out, first professional start," Brown said, "but I got out there and cleared my mind and everything." He threw 66 pitches, struck out two and walked none.[11] "He's got three quality pitches right now and he's got a plus arm," pitching coach Carl Willis said. "I think the ability is there, the arm's there, it's just a matter of, like everyone else, learning how to pitch. When to use the stuff you have.""[12] Brown finished the season 10-2 with a 3.08 ERA and a 1.11 WHIP.

Brown spent most of the 1998 season with Kinston of the Class-A Carolina League, where he went 11-9 in 27 starts with a 3.81 ERA and 1.19 WHIP in 172⅔ innings pitched. He finished the season with one start for Akron of the Double-A Eastern League. He arrived on such short notice that the seamstress didn't even have time to sew "Brown" on his uniform. The nameless pitcher allowed just two earned runs in seven innings. "I didn't even know my name was not on the shirt," he said. "I was more concerned with going out there and having a good game."[13]

Brown wouldn't be nameless in Akron for long, as he spent four seasons (1999-2002) in the Rubber City. He was added to the Cleveland Indians' 40-man roster in 1999 and threw 2⅓ scoreless innings in spring training. "I've learned how to pitch in front of a big crowd and against better hitters than what I was used to at Kinston," Brown said. "Coming into this season, I know what to expect at this level."[14] In 1999 he went 5-9 with a 4.57 ERA and 1.30 WHIP, winning his first three decisions but losing nine of his last 11, one being a wasted 10-strikeout performance against Portland on June 14.[15] Tendinitis in his right shoulder landed him on the disabled list most of July. Brown finished the season pitching one game for Triple-A Buffalo, winning with a five-inning relief effort.[16] He pitched over the winter and went 0-4 with a 5.55 ERA in eight starts with Maryvale of the Arizona Fall League.[17]

Brown added a sinker to his pitching repertoire in 2000. "Carl Willis worked with me on changing my delivery, which allows me to throw from a downhill plane and I'm getting more movement and sink on the ball," he said.[18] He started off hot in the chill of April, going 3-0 with a 2.16 ERA. "He's got a big-time sinker," said Willis.[19] Brown suffered soreness in his back and missed most of May but was still a strong 5-1 with a 2.63 ERA in early June. The same bad back forced him to miss August and September. No doubt the injury affected his final numbers: 7-6 with a 4.38 ERA and 1.25 WHIP.[20]

Brown was plagued with arm problems, which cost him most of the 2001 season. He was limited to four starts (5.03 ERA) and had Tommy John surgery in August. He was ready to pitch again by June of 2002.[21]

After returning, Brown went 9-5 with a 2.78 ERA in 103⅔ innings with a 1.10 WHIP. He won six straight starts in June and July with a 1.93 ERA over that span. From July 21 to August 5, he pitched at least seven innings in four straight starts. Brown allowed five hits in six shutout innings as Akron clinched the Eastern League Southern Division title on August 21. After a playoff victory, he became the winningest pitcher in Akron's history.[22]

In 2003 Brown began the year with Triple-A Buffalo (International League) and made his first start in late April after two relief appearances, throwing five scoreless innings. "This is my seventh year and I've always been a starter," he said. "I've never come out of the bullpen. It's a different feel. I'm still getting used to being a reliever. But I could do whatever, as long as I'm pitching."[23] He went 4-4 in 13 games with a 3.82 ERA and 1.01 WHIP for Buffalo before being traded to the Red Sox on June 22 for infielder Angel Santos. Brown moved from Buffalo to Pawtucket, the Red Sox' affiliate in the International League, where he was used in relief in 15 of 18 games with a 2.26 ERA and minuscule 0.87 WHIP. In 51⅔ innings, he struck out 39 while walking just five. "I try to throw strikes and hit my spots," Brown said. "My game is throwing strikes. I think I used to be a power pitcher before. After the surgery, now it's more location, location, location. I've always had pretty good control, but my velocity's down a little bit."[24]

Brown and a handful of other prospects were invited to Boston in January 2004 for a first-year winter development program. To avoid the shell shock rookies face of ordinary Boston realities such as traffic and directions, the Red Sox provided them an early look at the city. "The stadium's not the easiest to find and being here before for a couple of days and getting familiar with the area, it helped a lot," Brown said. "We were here for four days. We had a workout and some interview sessions and classroom work. And the main reason was to just learn the area of Boston."[25] It certainly helped, because Brown would soon return.

Brown began the 2004 season with Pawtucket and continued his effectiveness, going 3-1 with a 2.84 ERA in six starts, striking out 27, and walking only two in 38 innings while limiting opponents to a .199 batting average. Those numbers were more than enough to impress the Red Sox, who needed pitching help. Reliever Byung-Hyun Kim had been ineffective with a 6.23 ERA and was sent to Pawtucket and Brown was called up on May 12. "This is a dream come true," he said enthusiastically. "I was just waiting for the call. The last couple of years, I feel like I've had good numbers."[26] He had a good locker spot, between Pedro Martínez and Keith Foulke, and his first few hours in the clubhouse he spent playing cribbage with Scott Williamson. "We had an off day," Brown said of his interrupted Pawtucket schedule, "and I was just going to spend it with my family before I go off on a road trip."[27] Instead, Brown set off on a road trip with the Red Sox, visiting Toronto and Tampa Bay, where he made his major-league debut. After parts of eight seasons in the minors, the Mississippi native got his chance in the major leagues. The first-place Red Sox were 24-16, a half-game ahead of the New York Yankees in the AL East.

On May 20 the Red Sox trailed the Devil Rays, 8-6, in the bottom of the seventh. Brown came in for his major-league debut. He surrendered a ground-rule double to Geoff Blum and a single to Brook Fordyce as the Red Sox fell behind, 9-6. Brown pitched a scoreless eighth and Rocco Baldelli became his first strikeout. The Red Sox mustered no comeback and lost, 9-6. "I was just a little nervous and a little tense out there," Brown said. "I was anxious to get in there and get the first one out of the way."[28]

Brown had three more relief appearances in May. He threw a scoreless inning against Oakland on May 25 in a 12-2 Red Sox blowout. On May 27 he was knocked around for six hits and three runs in 2⅔ mop-up innings by the A's, who defeated Boston, 15-2. His final appearance was again in a mop-up role, finishing the last two innings of a 13-4 loss to Baltimore. Brown had no record in his four appearances with a 5.87 ERA and a 2.48 WHIP.

On June 9 left-hander Mark Malaska was activated from the disabled list and Brown was sent back to Pawtucket. He never returned to the major leagues. Malaska was not the left-hander the Red Sox wanted as they drove toward a postseason berth.

In early August they acquired lefty specialist Mike Myers from Seattle and to make room for him on the 40-man roster, Brown was designated for assignment.[29] He returned to Pawtucket and struggled, finishing the season 4-6 with a 4.82 ERA and 1.14 WHIP. The Red Sox won their first World Series in 86 years, and Brown received a World Series ring.[30] Although his time with the Red Sox was short, Brown enjoyed the experience and said Boston was a "one-of-a-kind place to play."[31]

Brown spent 2005-2008 overseas with the Hanshin Tigers of the Japan Central League and the Samsung Lions and LG Twins of the Korean Baseball Organization. His overall record in these four years was 28-23 with a 3.66 ERA and 1.26 WHIP, starting 71 of 76 games. His 11-9, 2.68 ERA, 1.050 WHIP (sixth best in the KBO) in 2006 helped Samsung win the Korean Series championship. Brown retired after the 2008 season.

Brown married Melissa Lang in 2000. He started his own investment firm, Munro Investments, LLC.[32] He also went back to his roots and became the pitching coach for his alma mater, West Lauderdale High School. As of 2022, their son Dylan was a star baseball athlete at West Lauderdale and signed with East Central Community College in Decatur, Mississippi. The Browns also have a younger son, Ridge.[33]

SOURCES

College statistics were taken from the baseballcube.com. Besides sources listed in the Notes, the author was aided by the following:

Baseball-reference.com

"Brown, Lang," *Franklin County Times*, February 25, 2001. Retrieved June 26, 2022. m.franklincountytimes.com/2001/02/25/feb-18-2001-5/

Familysearch.org

Findagrave.com

Retrosheet.org

NOTES

1. Jeff Edwards, "Diehard Red Sox Fan Fulfilling Dream … One Name at a Time," *Meridian* (Mississippi) *Star*, January 16, 2007. Retrieved June 13, 2022. meridianstar.com/sports/diehard-red-sox-fan-fulfilling-dream-one-name-at-a-time/article_b140cce-8abb-5196-b9b8-ddedffadb9a1.html.
2. Jamie Brown, interview with the author, July 10, 2022.
3. Austin Bishop, "Red Sox Call Up Jamie Brown," *Franklin County Times*, May 13, 2004. Retrieved June 14, 2022. Franklincountytimes.com/2004/05/13/red-sox-call-up-jamie-brown/.
4. "Mooreville Wins 2A Title," *Jackson* (Mississippi) *Clarion-Ledger*, May 29, 1992: 4C.
5. Robert Wilson, "West Lauderdale Rains Over Pontotoc in 3A," *Jackson Clarion-Ledger*, May 29, 1993: 1C, 4C.
6. Todd Kelly, "Warriors Can't Pierce Knights' Title Armor," *Jackson Clarion-Ledger*, May 20, 1994: 4C.
7. "Briefly," *Jackson Clarion-Ledger*, June 2, 1994: 2C; Bill Spencer, "Rolison Commands All-American Kudos," *Jackson Clarion-Ledger*, February 24, 1995: 4C.
8. Spencer, "Rolison Commands"; "Clinton Blanks Biloxi; Tupelo Nips Brandon," *Jackson Clarion-Ledger*, April 28, 1995: 4C; "No. 4 Prep Puts Heat on No. 3 Hillcrest Christian," *Jackson Clarion-Ledger*, May 3, 1995: 4C; Todd Kelly, "West Lauderdale Moves 1 Step Closer to Four-Peat," *Jackson Clarion-Ledger*, May 17, 1995: 4C; Derrick Mahone, "West Lauderdale Wins Crown 10-3," *Jackson Clarion-Ledger*, May 19, 1995: 4C; "Clarion-Ledger All-State Baseball," *Jackson Clarion-Ledger*, June 4, 1995: 6D;
9. "MCC Team Members Sign to Various Colleges," *Clarke County Tribune* (Quitman, Mississippi), November 27, 1996: 8A.
10. Steve Swogetinksy, "Talking Sports," *Clarke County Tribune*, March 26, 1997: 1B.
11. Rob Oatman, "Taylor Touches Off Tribe's 15-Run Tirade," *Watertown* (New York) *Daily News*, June 20, 1997: 15.
12. Rob Oatman, "Indians Losing Money," *Watertown Daily Times*, September 7, 1997: D5.
13. David Lee Morgan Jr., "Nameless, Not Winless," *Akron Beacon Journal*, September 6, 1998: D5.
14. David Lee Morgan Jr., "Brown Will Be the Man in Bowie," *Akron Beacon Journal*, April 8, 1999: B6.
15. David Lee Morgan Jr., "Morgan Still Fighting to Move Up," *Akron Beacon Journal*, June 15, 1999: D3.
16. David Lee Morgan Jr., "Many Are New to Young Team," *Akron Beacon Journal*, April 7, 2000: E13.
17. *2004 Boston Red Sox Media Guide*, 75.
18. David Lee Morgan Jr., "Cold nor Wait Keeps Brown from Shutout," *Akron Beacon Journal*, April 12, 2000: C5.
19. David Lee Morgan Jr., "Brown Undefeated as Aeros Win, 8-3," *Akron Beacon Journal*, April 27, 2000: D8.
20. *2004 Boston Red Sox Media Guide*, 75; David Lee Morgan Jr., "Aeros' 14-13 Victory a Long Time in Coming," *Akron Beacon Journal*, June 12, 2000: C3.
21. David Lee Morgan Jr., "Aeros Notes," *Akron Beacon Journal*, April 19, 2001: C3; David Lee Morgan Jr., "White, Bullpen, Lead Aeros to 6-3 Victory Over Ravens," *Akron Beacon Journal*, June 2, 2002: D9; Tom Reed, "Brown Records Bittersweet Record for Aeros," *Akron Beacon Journal*, September 2, 2002: C1.
22. *2004 Boston Red Sox Media Guide*, 75; David Lee Morgan Jr., "Aeros Clinch Southern Division," *Akron Beacon Journal*, August 22, 2002: C1, C5; "Brown Records Bittersweet Record."
23. "Brown Helps Herd Salvage Split with PawSox," *Buffalo News*, April 25, 2003: C7.
24. Matt Kalman, "Baseball – Brown Turns Right – Finds Way to Big Leagues," *Boston Herald*, May 13, 2004: 102.
25. Kalman.
26. Austin Bishop, "Red Sox Call Up Jamie Brown."
27. Gordon Edes, "He's All for Long Tossing," *Boston Globe*, May 13, 2004: 66.
28. Bob Hohler, "Hurling a Stinker," *Boston Globe*, May 21, 2004: D6.
29. Nick Cafardo, "Daubach Down, Malaska Called Up," *Boston Globe*, June 10, 2004: C6; Jeff Horrigan, "Baseball – Red Sox Notebook – Sox Add Myers to the Mix," *Boston Herald*, August 7, 2004: 41.

30 Jeff Horrigan, "Baseball – Red Sox Notebook – Sox Don't Blink an Eye – Series Rings to get Opening Showcase," *Boston Herald*, February 24, 2005: 108.
31 Brown interview with the author.
32 Brown interview with the author.
33 Drew Kerekes, "Jason Smith Credits Assistants, Players for West Lauderdale's Title," *Meridian Star*, June 11, 2021. Retrieved June 15, 2022. infoweb-newsbank-com.hpld.idm.oclc.org/apps/news/document-view?p=NewsBank&docref=news/18312A866888FFB8; Drew Kerekes, "West Lauderdale Sends 3 Baseball Players, 1 Soccer Player, to Next Level," *Meridian Star*, November 10, 2021. Retrieved June 19, 2022. infoweb-newsbank-com.hpld.idm.oclc.org/apps/news/document-view?p=NewsBank&docref=news/18634794F0C35A48; Brown interview with the author.

CHURCH BELLS RING IN MASSACHUSETTS HOMETOWN OF HALL OF FAME RED SOX SCRIBES

The first Red Sox World Series championship in 86 years was imminent. I left my living room and wide-screen television in the central Massachusetts town of Groton and jumped in the car with my 16-year-old son Samuel. We drove to the town center, listening to AM radio as Boston closed in on its clinching win over St. Louis.

The destination was the Union Congregational Church. It stood on Main Street a few hundred yards west of the First Parish Church. For 250 years the First Parish Church sanctuary had been a place of religious worship.

From the 1970s through the 1990s, the First Parish Church's downstairs vestry was the home to a once-a-year Hot Stove baseball worshippers' Sports Night starring Groton natives Peter Gammons and Dan Shaughnessy. It was the same room in which the two Groton native writers attended kindergarten nine years apart.[1]

Gammons and Shaughnessy were both born and raised in Groton, a quiet rural town in their youth and the same in 2004. Both wrote for the *Boston Globe* – Shaughnessy for his entire career and Gammons until he transitioned to national media. Both are in the Baseball Hall of Fame as recipients of the BBWAA Career Excellence Award, Gammons enshrined in 2004 and Shaughnessy in 2016.

The annual Sports Night was hosted by the Groton Men's Club, and featured roast beef stew for dinner. Three generations of Groton's men and boys filled the meeting hall. After dinner they peppered the esteemed scribes with sports questions. Most were about the Red Sox, their long championship drought and frustration, but there was always hope among the lifelong fans. Would this be the year?

By 2004 Sports Night was a fond memory, but Groton would forever be the hometown of Gammons and Shaughnessy. What better way to celebrate the Red Sox' first World Series win of our lives than by ringing Groton church bells?

Our car was parked on Main Street sidewalk outside the 180-year-old, white-steepled Union Congregational Church. My son and I listened to the final inning on the car radio. One out. Two outs. Three outs.

We raced to the church and opened the tall wood-paneled door to the foyer. A large rope hung from the ceiling, connected to the bells in the steeple. We took turns pulling the rope, and heard church bells ring, marking the end of an 86-year wait for a Red Sox World Series championship.

EVAN KATZ

1 Historical detail from Dan Shaughnessy, *At Fenway: Dispatches From Red Sox Nation* (New York: Three Rivers Press, 2010).

ELLIS BURKS

BY ROBERT BRUSTAD

Few players in the history of major-league baseball have displayed each of the prized "five tools," meaning the ability to hit for average and for power, to run, to field, and to throw. On that short list belongs the name of Ellis Burks, who began his major-league career as a 22-year-old rookie for the Boston Red Sox in 1987 and concluded it as a member of the 2004 Red Sox team that ended 86 years of frustration for the franchise with their World Series title. Burks had stops with four additional clubs, most notably with the Colorado Rockies, where he spent five seasons and where in 1996 he produced one of the greatest individual seasons in Rockies history.

Ellis Rena Burks was born in Vicksburg, Mississippi, on September 11, 1964. When he was 3 his family moved to the state capital, Jackson, where he completed elementary school and his father worked as an electrician. As a child in Jackson he had no real opportunities to play organized sports but he learned to love baseball by playing sandlot games with his cousins. He was not particularly skilled at the game as a child, however, and his cousins used to tease him because he batted cross-handed and they liked to inform him, "You don't know how to play, Ellis, you don't know how to play."[1]

At 10, the family moved to Fort Worth, Texas, and Ellis started to get serious about baseball, playing in a summer league after his freshman year at O.D. Wyatt High School. His varsity baseball coach, Bill Metcalf, would become an important influence upon him. As a sophomore, Burks was more than happy just to earn a varsity letter but Metcalf conveyed to the 15-year-old that he had uncommon instincts for the game and could become a special player.[2] As a senior, Burks transferred to nearby Everman High School, the local baseball powerhouse. He had an outstanding senior season at Everman, playing for coach Jim Dyer. It was at Everman that Burks adopted the batting stance of his favorite major leaguer, Jim Rice. "I tried to look exactly like that in high school," he once said. "I had his number, 14. I adopted his stance. My feet were pretty much placed the same as his in high school, junior college, and the minor leagues."[3]

Despite a torrid senior season at the plate, college scholarship offers were slow to materialize. On one occasion his grandmother, Velma Burks, asked him about his college plans and Ellis informed her that he would be going to Ranger Junior College, although the coaches at Ranger had not yet contacted him with an offer to play baseball.[4] He also entertained the thought that 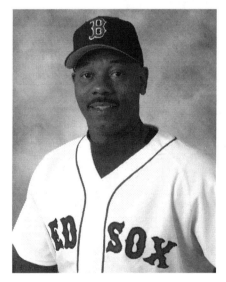 he might be selected in the major-league draft, but he escaped the notice of scouts despite the fact that he capped his impressive senior season by being the first high-school player to hit a ball out of Arlington Stadium.[5] (He did it in a high-school all-star game.) His grandmother died in March of his senior year but Ellis honored his promise to her and committed to Ranger even after other schools began to show interest.

At Ranger Junior College, Burks played for coach Jack Allen. Allen was a master of homespun homilies delivered to full effect with a Texas drawl and he had quite the influence on the 18-year-old Burks. On one occasion, Burks hit a routine groundball to shortstop and was running to first at slightly less than full speed. Allen surprised Burks by inquiring if he was, perhaps, nursing an injury of some sort. When Burks informed him that he was fully healthy, Allen lectured him in no uncertain terms and stated, "By golly, I don't care if you can throw a strawberry through a battleship or run a hole in the wind … on this team we play at full speed!"[6] It was a lesson Burks would never forget and his hustle became a trademark of his professional career. The Ranger team was a real powerhouse during Burks's freshman year and he led the parade by tearing the proverbial cover off of the ball throughout the fall season. He was excited because a number of scouts planned to attend a coming game, and he was shocked when game day arrived and Allen told him he wouldn't be in the lineup because the coach was afraid the scouts would see him and that Allen would lose Burks, his best player, in the coming January draft. Burks assured his coach that, even if drafted in January, he would not sign with a pro team until the end of the spring season and Allen relented and allowed Burks to play the game.

Indeed, the scouts had a very favorable opinion of Burks and on the advice of scout Danny Doyle, he was selected by the Red Sox with the 20th overall pick of the January 1983 draft. Five of Burks's teammates were also selected in that draft, including future major-league pitchers Mike Smith and Jim Morris. As Burks had promised Coach Allen, he did not sign with the Red Sox until the end of the spring college season.

Burks made his first stop in professional baseball with the Elmira (New York) Pioneers of the New York-Pennsylvania League as an 18-year-old playing short-season A ball in 1983.

At the plate he hit just .241 that season with two home runs but demonstrated his range of abilities as he stole nine bases and contributed five outfield assists. He was promoted to high-A ball at Winter Haven in the Florida State League the following season where he was a full three years younger than the league average but displayed a mature set of skills. In 112 games for Winter Haven, he stole 29 bases and contributed 12 outfield assists. Burks had the good fortune of meeting his idol, Jim Rice, then still with the Red Sox. "I met him in spring training. I was in 'A' ball, and I got called up for a split-squad game. He was in the clubhouse. I said, 'Excuse me, Mr. Rice, my name is Ellis Burks. It's a pleasure to meet you.' He said, 'Yeah, I know who you are, kid.'" Burks added, "I was like, whoa, how does he know who I am?" I happened to sit beside him on the bench that day. I was pretty much in awe. I was too scared to ask him any questions. The next year, I was on the roster, and he told the spring-training clubhouse attendant to put my locker next to his. It was unbelievable to grow up idolizing a guy, and now he wanted my locker next to his."[7]

Burks spent the 1985 and 1986 seasons at New Britain in the Double-A Eastern League and it was here that he really caught the attention of the big club. Red Sox coach Johnny Pesky became an admirer and declared that Burks "can run, hit, throw, and catch the ball. He may be ready for the big leagues sooner than people may think."[8] Burks's ascent through the Red Sox system was slowed slightly by two right-shoulder injuries but his power began to blossom with 24 home runs over the course of the two seasons. It was the 31 stolen bases that he collected during the 1986 season in New Britain, however, that really caught the attention of the Boston front office. The Red Sox system had many promising young hitters in addition to Burks, including Mike Greenwell, Brady Anderson, Todd Benzinger, and Sam Horn, but it was the baserunning abilities Burks displayed that made him stand out from the other quality hitting prospects as the big-league club was sorely deficient in basestealing. (The 1986 Red Sox finished a distant last in the major leagues in stolen bases with just 41, of which six were by 36-year-old first baseman Billy Buckner.)

Burks made a strong impression on the Red Sox with an outstanding spring training in 1987. He was the team's last cut, optioned to Triple-A Pawtucket.

The Red Sox did not have a strong sense of urgency to bring up their younger players to start the 1987 season; the team was coming off of a tremendously successful and memorable 1986 season in which they won their first American League pennant since 1975, and a heartbreaking seven-game loss to the New York Mets in the World Series. Lofty expectations for the 1987 Red Sox were misplaced as the team floundered to open the season. In late April, they had a 9-12 record and were in fourth place, 9½ games behind the high-flying Milwaukee Brewers. The Red Sox suddenly looked like a team that was past its prime and needed contributions from some of its talented prospects.

Burks had played a mere 11 games at the Triple-A level for Pawtucket when he was summoned to the big-league club. On the night of April 30, 1987, Boston manager John McNamara inserted 22-year-old Burks into the starting lineup as the Red Sox center fielder. Burks was batting ninth as the Red Sox faced pitcher Scott Bankhead and the Seattle Mariners in the Kingdome. Burks was hitless in three at-bats in a career that began with a weak groundball back to the mound, followed by a strikeout and a foul popup. He also dropped a line drive on which he had attempted to make a diving catch during the 11-2 Mariners victory. The game marked the first occasion that Burks had played on artificial turf,[9] a circumstance that contributed to a base hit skipping past him in the outfield. Burks reflected great dismay and determination. "I felt bad after that first game. Everything happened so fast and I was not happy at what happened. I just wanted to come right back in my next game and show it wasn't me," he told a sportswriter.[10] Skipper McNamara assured Burks that he would be in the starting lineup again the next game.[11] The next night in Anaheim brought out the "real" Burks as he collected his first major-league hit in the second inning, a double down the right-field line off Urbano Lugo that brought home two runs. He went 3-for-3 as he shook off the jitters. In that series against the Angels, he showed a dazzling display of speed by sprinting from shallow center field to haul in a drive hit by Gary Pettis. Burks apparently liked Angels pitching because he connected for his first major-league home run, against future Hall of Famer Don Sutton, in the third inning of a game back in Boston on May 10. He later hit five home runs during a single road trip and brought his home-run total to 10 by June 18. When he hit a go-ahead home run off the Yankees' Bob Tewksbury on June 21 it was the third time the rookie had provided the Red Sox with a game-winning blast.

Burks's success fueled the Boston youth movement. In short order, Todd Benzinger, Sam Horn, and Jody Reed were promoted to the big-league club to join Burks and Greenwell and the look of the team began to change. Burks split time in center with Dave Henderson and they became close friends rather than rivals. In fact, Henderson provided great help to Burks in outfield positioning and in reading hitters and Burks later identified Henderson as one of his greatest influences and closest friends in the game.[12] The front office liked what it saw from Burks so much in center field that it traded Henderson to Oakland on September 1. General manager Lou Gorman said, "Henderson's home run put us into the World Series. He did everything we asked of him, but Burks just came along and took his job."[13] Don Baylor, who had provided enormous offensive and leadership contributions during the previous season, was also traded, to Minnesota. The 1987 Red Sox finished 78-84 but the infusion of young talent brought great excitement to Beantown.

Burks's 1987 batting line exceeded all expectations with 20 home runs and 27 stolen bases to accompany 59 runs batted in and a .272 batting average. He became only the third Red Sox player to total 20 home runs and 20 stolen bases in the same season. He had 15 outfield assists, which as of 2017 remain the most in a season for a Red Sox center fielder. But Burks stood out for his entire game and his unusually refined skills, such as the ability to correctly read the flight of the ball off the bat. These defensive skills caught the attention of Lou Gorman who stated that Burks reminded him of a young Amos Otis.[14] Don Baylor was notably impressed by Burks' defensive prowess and paid him the highest of compliments by comparing him to Paul Blair.[15]

The young but talented Red Sox entered the 1988 season with high hopes. Burks set a personal goal of 40 stolen bases.[16] However, a bone chip in his ankle required offseason surgery and he was unable to open the season with the team. Upon returning, he compiled six multihit games in his first nine games. A jammed left wrist slowed him temporarily but he finished the 1988 campaign with a .294 average, 18 home runs, 92 runs batted in, and 25 stolen bases. On September 4, the Red Sox assumed a permanent hold on first place in the American League East on their way to an 89-73 record and the American League East title. Postseason play was less noteworthy as the Sox were swept in four games by the Oakland Athletics as former Red Sox pitcher Dennis Eckersley saved all four games and Dave Henderson threw some salt in Boston's wounds by going 6-for-16 with a home run. Burks was 4-for-17 in the series.

The 1989 season proved challenging for the team and for Burks. The team stumbled out of the blocks and was slow to recapture its form from the previous season. On April 30, the Red Sox faced the Texas Rangers in a game at Arlington as Nolan Ryan and Roger Clemens faced off on the mound. It was not much of a homecoming for Burks as a Ryan fastball in the first inning glanced off his shoulder and caught him behind the left ear. He was removed from the game and was not pleased with the situation. Burks said, "Why should I be when a guy who throws 100, throws one at my head?"[17] The same two pitchers were matched up in their next start, at Fenway Park on May 5. This time Burks exacted some revenge against Ryan and the Rangers by going 3-for-4 with a stolen base. In the seventh inning a Ryan fastball zipped under Burks's chin, causing Ellis to glare out at the mound and Ryan to take a step toward home plate. "I was making a statement," Burks commented.[18] In return, Ryan said, "Everyone was on edge because of what'd been said or written after the incident in Texas."[19] When order resumed, Burks fouled off a couple of pitches and then singled home Jody Reed to give the Red Sox the lead for good in a 7-6 victory.

New Red Sox manager Joe Morgan was very impressed with Burks and considered him to be highly capable in every aspect of the game. "He's way above average in everything," Morgan said. "Hitting, hitting with power, throwing, running, catching the ball. Everything. And he's a good fellow. The other day I yelled out to him, 'Burks, I hope you never change,' and he said, 'I won't change.'"[20] The biggest challenge Burks faced seemed to be staying healthy. While attempting to make a diving catch in a game against Detroit on June 14, he tore cartilage in his left shoulder. He underwent surgery and missed the next 41 games. The season came to an abrupt end for Burks during a September 6 game in Oakland in which Burks had gone 3-for-3 before he suffered a shoulder separation in a collision with Mike Greenwell in the outfield and surgery became necessary. Burks was limited to 97 games in the 1989 season, batting .303 with 21 stolen bases.

Burks completed a strong 1990 season that led to some overdue recognition as one of the top players in the game. He batted .296 and contributed 21 home runs and 89 runs batted in as the Red Sox compiled an 88-74 record and won the AL East Division title. His clutch hitting was particularly important as 23 of his first 43 runs batted in were delivered with two out. Against Cleveland on August 27, he became the 25th major leaguer to hit two home runs in one inning. The team's stay in the postseason was again brief; they fell once again in four straight games to the Oakland Athletics in the ALCS. Burks went 4-for-15 in the series. Burks received a Silver Slugger Award as a recognition of his excellence over the 1990 season. He was the only 20-home-run hitter that season for a Red Sox franchise traditionally known for its power. He also earned his first Gold Glove Award, joining fellow outfielders Ken Griffey Jr. and Gary Pettis. He was selected for his first All-Star team although he did not play in the game due to injury. Burks finished 13th in the American League MVP voting.

The subsequent two seasons in Boston brought a steady diet of frustration. The 1991 season was seriously compromised by tendinitis in both knees and continual back pain. The tendinitis disrupted Burks's timing and power at the plate and he had only two home runs in his first 29 games. The back pain increased over the course of the year and kept him out of the lineup for 11 games during a key late-September stretch run. The back problems proved to be a persistent foe over the coming years and Burks was later diagnosed with a bulging disk. His totals for the season reflected the extent to which he played hurt as he had only a .251 average with 14 home runs and 56 RBIs. A better reflection of the effects of the injuries was his uncharacteristically poor success rate on the bases with only 6 stolen bases in 17 attempts.

Trade talk percolated after the 1991 season but new Red Sox manager Butch Hobson was committed to Burks and batted him primarily in the leadoff spot in 1992. The knee problems compromised Burks's speed and these issues were compounded when he played on artificial turf. The back problem did not respond to rest and medication and his season was limited to 66 games and 235 at-bats, which yielded an uncustomary .255 batting average with 8 home runs and 30 runs batted in. The Red Sox did not tender Burks a contract for 1993 and he was left off the team's original 15-man protected list for the expansion draft, only to be pulled back when the Rockies selected Jody Reed.[21] Nonetheless, the Red Sox made no effort to sign him.

The Chicago White Sox emerged as the club with the greatest interest in Burks and he signed with the team in early January of 1993. The White Sox had assembled a talented and experienced team, and in spring training, GM Ron Schueler commented, " … Right now, Ellis looks as good as I've seen him look since I was scouting him years ago. If we can keep him going, he would give us a whole added dimension."[22] On April

16, and in his ninth game as a member of his new team, Burks made his return to Fenway Park. Facing Danny Darwin in his first at-bat of the game, Burks turned on a 3-and-2 pitch and launched a shot well over the left-field wall. As he rounded the bases, Burks received a standing ovation from the 26,536 fans. He commented, "It hasn't been an easy transition. … I gave it a lot of thought this winter how it would be in this game. In spring training it hit me – I was wearing different colored socks."[23] The 1993 season marked a strong return to form for Burks. He batted .275 with 17 home runs and 74 RBIs. More importantly, he was able to stay free of serious injury and played in 146 games. The White Sox realized expectations in winning 94 games against 68 defeats and claimed the American League West title. They met the Toronto Blue Jays in the American League Championship Series but fell, four games to two. Burks went 7-for-23 with a home run.

Burks became a free agent after the season and all indications were that he would re-sign with the White Sox, where he felt wanted and appreciated. "I'll take anything – three years, five years, ten years – whatever they want," he said. "It's been great here. One of the reasons I wanted to come here in the first place was a chance to win, and we're doing that."[24] But the White Sox offered only a two-year deal and wanted Burks to play right field[25] and so he was willing to consider other offers. The Colorado Rockies sorely needed a quality center fielder and offered Ellis a three-year, $9 million deal, which Burks accepted.

A new chapter in Burks's career began when he signed with the Rockies but the story had some familiar elements. In Colorado he was reunited with two teammates from his rookie year in Boston in manager Don Baylor and hitting coach Dwight Evans. Playing for the Rockies had an additional allure as the franchise had just set a major-league attendance record in their inaugural season by drawing nearly 4.5 million fans to Mile High Stadium. Playing there was a hitter's dream and a pitcher's nightmare as the altitude and reduced air resistance translated into additional carry on batted balls. Defense became a priority in this park, and particularly in the outfield, where outfielders needed speed and arm strength to handle the largest outfield in the majors. Playing 81 games a year in Denver also came with costs, including the physical demands of playing long games and chasing down a lot of batted balls yielded by a pitching staff that had the National League's highest ERA during the previous season.

The 1994 season was the second and final season for the Rockies at Mile High Stadium. They moved to Coors Field in 1995. Burks began the 1994 season just as he and the Rockies had hoped. He hit a home run off Curt Schilling of the Philadelphia Phillies in his first at-bat at Mile High Stadium and he was batting a lofty .354 with 12 home runs through his first 34 games. However, in a game against the Los Angeles Dodgers on May 17 he tore a ligament in his left wrist on a checked swing. He missed the next 70 games and when he returned to the club, every swing of the bat proved to be painful. He was limited to 42 games but still managed to hit .322 with 13 home runs. The 1994 season was shrouded by the specter of labor unrest and there was little movement in talks between owners and players as the season progressed. Indeed, the players union struck and the season concluded for the Rockies and all of the other major-league teams on August 11, and the 65,043 fans in attendance that night witnessed the last major-league baseball game to be played in Mile High Stadium, an otherwise forgettable 13-0 pasting of the home club by the Atlanta Braves. The Rockies finished 53-64 in their abbreviated season. Burks underwent surgery immediately after the season ended and his wrist remained in a cast for three full months following the surgery.

Resolution of the labor dispute was not reached until April 2, 1995, after a 232-day work stoppage that wiped out all 1994 postseason play. After an abbreviated spring training, the Rockies opened the 1995 season on April 26 in their brand-new ballpark, Coors Field. The 1995 lineup featured the "Blake Street Bombers," so named because Blake Street bordered the new ballpark on the east side and the lineup contained an assemblage of certifiable sluggers that included Burks, Andrés Galarraga, Dante Bichette, and Larry Walker. Vinny Castilla proved to be an unexpected but formidable additional power source and became the fifth member of the brigade. On April 26, the Rockies baptized their new park in unforgettable fashion as Bichette hit a three-run walk-off home run in the 14th inning off Mike Remlinger of the New York Mets to provide the 47,228 fans with an 11-9 victory. Burks was not able to join the fun until May 5 when he came off of the disabled list. The strong play of Mike Kingery in center field in his absence, and the presence of Bichette in left field and Walker in right field resulted in limited playing time for Burks for the rest of the season. His first home run of the season did not come until June 2 when he launched a walk-off pinch-hit three-run homer against Dan Miceli to beat the Pirates. Burks was able to play in only 103 games with 14 home runs and a .266 batting average to show for his injury-limited 1995 season. The team finished just one game behind the Los Angeles Dodgers in the National League West and they earned their first postseason berth courtesy of the wild-card spot. The Rockies lost three games to one in the first round of the postseason to the eventual champion Atlanta Braves as Burks went 2-for-6 in limited postseason playing time.

Burks arrived at spring training three days early in 1996 knowing that quality preparation and good health were going to be the keys to his success during the coming campaign. "For years I've just been trying to stay healthy and to get rid of that stereotype that I can't stay away from injuries," he said.[26] More than anything, he was determined to erase the memories of 1995 when he was relegated to a role as the Rockies' fourth outfielder. He was slotted to spend more time in left field during the season as manager Baylor wished to minimize the wear and tear on Burks and to see if center field might be a fit for the athletic Larry Walker. A full season of good health enabled Burks to have a remarkable turnaround in 1996 and he carried the Rockies offensively as injuries to Walker and Bichette severely affected the team's attack. Burks played in a career-high 156 games, and 129 of those games were spent in left field. His .344 batting average was second in the National League only to Tony Gwynn's .353 mark, and he led the league with 142 runs scored and also drove in 128 runs. Burks's 93 extra-base hits, 392 total bases, and .639 slugging average all led the league. Although some skeptics attributed his numbers to the "Coors Field Effect," his road statistics were more than sufficient to reject that notion. Away from home, Burks hit .291 with 17 home runs and had 49 runs batted in with a .903 OPS in 75 games. As Burks went, so went the Rockies in 1996. He batted .413 with 10 home runs when leading off an inning. He hit .362 with runners in scoring position and .369 with two outs and runners in scoring situations that year. Against the vaunted Atlanta Braves staff that featured three future Hall of Famers (Greg Maddux, Tom Glavine, and John Smoltz), Burks hit .380 (19-for-50). His 32 stolen bases were more than he had compiled in the previous five seasons combined. He joined Henry Aaron as the second player in history to record 40 home runs, 200 hits, and 30 stolen bases in a season. He finished third in the NL MVP voting behind Ken Caminiti and Mike Piazza and he received his second Silver Slugger Award. His WAR of 7.9 led the Rockies. Galarraga (47), Burks (40), and Castilla (40) became the first trio of teammates to reach 40 home runs in a season since Davey Johnson, Darrell Evans, and Henry Aaron accomplished the feat for the 1973 Atlanta Braves.

Burks became a free agent but was re-signed by the Rockies for the 1997 and 1998 seasons with an $8.8 million deal that included incentives. Burks had no regrets about re-signing and commented, "I signed early because I knew what I wanted. I'm sure I could have gotten a lot of money elsewhere. But money isn't the main issue with me."[27] Preseason expectations were high for the club in 1997 as Walker and Bichette were expected to make stronger contributions after their previous injury-plagued seasons. In fact, Walker contributed even more than expected with 49 home runs, 140 RBIs, and 33 stolen bases to accompany a .366 batting average that earned him the National League MVP Award. Burks began 1997 slowly but his first four hits were home runs. His biggest nemesis during the season was a groin injury that caused him to miss a full month and he reinjured the groin in his second game back. He also had wrist and ankle injuries that lingered throughout the season and limited him to 119 games. Nonetheless, he batted .290 with 32 home runs and 82 RBIs and had a .934 OPS. His season total of just seven stolen bases, however, was evidence of the physical limitations he encountered during the year.

As the 1998 season opened, Burks said he felt he could not continue to play center field beyond the current season due to the effects of the hamstring, back, and knee problems that continued to limit his mobility.[28] One of the major highlights of his season occurred on April 2, when he connected off the Diamondbacks' Brian Anderson for his 100th home run in a Rockies uniform. The Rockies fell from contention early in the season and they made a move to fill their need for a younger center fielder capable of patrolling spacious center field at Coors. At the July 31 trading deadline, they sent Burks to the San Francisco Giants for center fielder Darryl Hamilton and minor-league pitcher James Stoops. They later received another minor leaguer, Jason Brester, to complete the deal. Burks concluded his time with the Rockies with a .306 batting average and 115 home runs in 520 games, and his 1996 season will be remembered as one of the greatest individual seasons in Rockies history.

Burks was a solid contributor to the Giants, batting .306 with 5 home runs and 8 stolen bases as the team went 31-23 following his arrival to conclude the 1998 season in second place in the National League West. Manager Dusty Baker planned to play him in right field during the 1999 season and to provide Burks with scheduled rest days to reduce his injury risk. Two offseason knee surgeries resulted in pain and soreness that compromised his power as he began the season. As the season progressed, Burks began to drive the ball into the gaps. Despite playing just 120 games in 1999, he concluded the year with 31 home runs and 96 runs batted to go with a .282 batting average and a .964 OPS. He nearly became the first National League player to drive in 100 runs in fewer than 400 at-bats as he fell just four short of 100 in 390 at-bats. The Giants once again finished second in the NL West.

The 2000 season marked a strong return to excellence for Burks despite two additional knee surgeries in the offseason. He batted .344, which equaled his best mark, set in 1996 with the Rockies, and he complemented the high average with 24 home runs and 96 RBIs. Burks's contributions in San Francisco were duly noted as the team had the best record in the National League with a 97-65 mark and won the NL West title by 11 games over the Dodgers. They fell in four games to the New York Mets in the National League Division Series, in which Burks was 3-for-13 with a home run.

Burks became a free agent after the season and the American League seemed like the logical destination: He could serve as a team's designated hitter and limit his time in the field to accommodate the knee issues. In only 284 games in a Giants uniform, Burks had hit .312 with 60 home runs and 214 runs driven in. Remarkably, Burks had a better OPS with the Giants (.971) than he had in his previous five seasons in Colorado (.957).

The Cleveland Indians signed the 36-year-old Burks to a three-year, $20 million offer in 2001 with the hope that he could play 100 to 120 games a year. Burks broke his right thumb in mid-July but still hit 28 home runs and drove in 74 runs with a .290 batting average. The Indians won their division with a 91-71 record and headed to the ALCS, where they faced a Seattle Mariners team that had compiled an all-time major league record of 116 wins. Burks went 6-for-19 in the series with a home run but the Mariners prevailed in five games.

Burks assumed the designated-hitter role for the Indians during the 2002 season and showed what he could do when provided a full season with the bat. He played 138 games and had 32 home runs and 91 runs batted in to accompany a .301 average. He completed his fourth consecutive season with an OPS above .900 (.903) with each coming after the age of 34.

After the season, Burks required surgery on his left shoulder but he was in the Indians' starting lineup again on Opening Day in 2003. He began the season well and continued to drive the ball with authority through the early part of the year. However, right elbow pain hampered his swing and he was required to end his season on June 7 in order to undergo ulnar nerve reconstruction surgery. In his abbreviated third season with the Indians, Burks batted .263 with 6 home runs and 28 RBIs. The Indians released Burks after the season, but he was not yet ready to retire from the game.

Burks' career came full circle when he signed with the Red Sox as a free agent on February 6, 2004. At a press conference he said, "I can let you know that I will retire a Red Sox."[29] He was attracted to Boston by his wish to finish out his career where it had started and also felt that the team had a chance to reach the World Series. In turn, the Red Sox felt that Burks's leadership abilities provided an important contribution to a team hoping to finally end their World Series drought. Burks appeared in nine of the team's first 17 games but underwent additional knee surgery in late April. Although he was unable to resume playing for many months, Burks remained with the team and even accompanied the Red Sox on road trips as he recovered from his injury. His commitment to the team was duly noted and appreciated by his teammates and Burks later commented that he wanted to contribute in whatever way that he could to a team that he felt was destined to win the World Series.[30] After missing nearly five months with the injury, he returned to the lineup on September 23. In the season's next-to-last game, at Camden Yards in Baltimore on October 2, manager Terry Francona inserted Burks into the lineup for his 2,000th major-league game. Batting fifth and in the DH role, he singled in his first at-bat in the second inning of that game for his 2,107th and final career hit. In the bottom of the fourth inning he was replaced by rookie Kevin Youkilis. The Red Sox capped their dream season with their first World Series title since 1918 by sweeping the St. Louis Cardinals in the World Series although Burks was not on the roster for the playoffs.

The 2004 World Series title vanquished the bitter memories of previous seasons and will always be regarded as one of the greatest accomplishments in Boston sports history. A largely unknown part of the story involves the team's triumphant return home from St. Louis. As the plane approached Boston, Pedro Martínez asked for everyone's attention and delivered an impromptu speech in which he recognized the contributions of the players on the field in contributing to the historic accomplishment. As Martínez continued, he singled out "The Old Goat" in reference to Burks and provided special praise for the teammate who had remained with the club and who had contributed his knowledge and leadership over the five long months of his injury rehab. At the request of Martínez and his teammates, Burks led the team down the steps of the plane to the tarmac at Logan Airport carrying the World Series trophy overhead.[31]

Ellis Burks retired after the 2004 season with a .291 lifetime batting average to go with 352 home runs. He is one of just a few major league players to have hit 60 or more home runs with four separate teams. Injuries robbed Burks of the opportunity to put up even more impressive numbers and a possible berth in the Hall of Fame, but he looked back on his career with no regrets and said that he "loved every minute of it."[32] Burks received the respect of his peers for his professionalism and his willingness to play with pain. He remained in the game, working for the Cleveland Indians, Colorado Rockies, and San Francisco Giants.

The Ranger College baseball team now plays at Ellis Burks Field. As of 2017 Burks worked for the San Francisco Giants as an instructor, scout, and talent evaluator. He, his wife, Dori, and their daughters, Carissa, Elisha, and Breanna, resided in Chagrin Falls, Ohio. His son, Chris, began his own professional career in the Giants' minor-league system in the summer of 2017.

SOURCES

In addition to the sources noted in this biography, the author also consulted Baseball-Reference.com, Retrosheet.org, and the SABR Minor Leagues Database, accessed online at Baseball-Reference.com.

NOTES

1. Mel Antonen, "Red Sox Ellis Burks Steals Into the Spotlight: Fastest Player on the Team Learns by Survival," *USA Today*, April 8, 1991.
2. Author interview with Ellis Burks, November 20, 2017 (Hereafter cited as Burks interview).
3. Ellis Burks, as told to Matt Crossman. "My Idol," *The Sporting News*, July 6, 2009.
4. Burks interview.
5. Burks interview.
6. Burks interview.
7. Ellis Burks, as told to Matt Crossman.
8. "Minor Leagues," *The Sporting News*, May 20, 1985.
9. "Minor Leagues."
10. Joe Giuliotti, "Burks Brings Raw Speed to Red Sox," *The Sporting News*, May 18, 1987.
11. Burks interview.
12. Burks interview.
13. Joe Giuliotti, "In Boston, the Spotlight Shifts," *The Sporting News*, September 14, 1987.
14. Moss Klein, "AL Beat," *The Sporting News*, May 25, 1987.
15. Klein.
16. "AL East: Red Sox," *The Sporting News*, February 22, 1988.
17. "AL East," *The Sporting News*, May 15, 1989.
18. Phil Rogers, "Ryan-Roger Rematch Not So Hot," *The Sporting News*, May 15, 1989.
19. Rogers.
20. Jerome Holtzman, "Red Sox's Burks Really on His Way," *Chicago Tribune*, May 4, 1989.

21 Joe Giuliotti, "Boston Red Sox," *The Sporting News*, November 30, 1992.
22 Peter Pascarelli, "Bo or No, White Sox Look Like Contenders," *The Sporting News*, March 9, 1993.
23 Joe Goddard, "Burks Homers in Homecoming," *The Sporting News*, April 26, 1993.
24 Joe Goddard, "Burks Should Be Back in '94," *The Sporting News*, September 20, 1993.
25 Joe Goddard, "Chicago White Sox," *The Sporting News*, November 29, 1993.
26 Tom Verducci, "The Best Years of Their Lives," *Sports Illustrated*, July 29, 1996.
27 Tony DeMarco, "Colorado Rockies," *The Sporting News*, December 30, 1996.
28 Tony DeMarco, "Rockies," *The Sporting News*, March 23, 1998.
29 David Heuschkel, "Burks' Return: It's Been Ages," *Hartford Courant*, February 6, 2004.
30 Burks interview.
31 Burks interview.
32 Burks interview.

2004 WORLD SERIES (IN JAKARTA)

Our family of five lived in Asia for close to 20 years due to my job, but we were all from Boston, and baseball was just about the only sport we could continue to follow during that time (though the Super Bowl was always televised via satellite). Throughout the years, we were able to take advantage of the developing internet and increasing rollout of streaming audio from MLB. The *Boston Globe* online filled in the details. We were able to get to the occasional Sox game when we were visiting the US, but those games were never a part of a World Series run.

My father had emigrated to Boston from Lithuania in 1934 at the age of 18 not knowing anything about baseball. But he became a diehard Sox fan and took me to my first game in 1957 when I was barely 4 years old and we were living in Dorchester. Sadly, he died prematurely in 1966 at the age of 50 and I placed a Red Sox cap on his grave in 1967; he would have been smiling. My own three kids were born in Boston though we all left Massachusetts for good in 1982. But the kids already had caught Red Sox fever, so the Sox remain their home team. We were living in Connecticut, and I had popped open the champagne in 1986. (And yes, my premature popping of the cork was the reason we lost that year, not Bill Buckner.)

Barry posing while wearing a long-awaited t-shirt, along with long-time friend Suroto. Photo by Ellie Halpern.

In 2004, my wife, Ellie, and I were living in Jakarta, Indonesia. (The kids had moved back to the US to Boulder, Colorado.) It didn't seem to matter where we were living, once again it looked to be a disappointing season finish. Down 0-3 to the Yankees, we figured this was yet another one of those years. That year I was spending an enormous amount of money on phone calls to get inning-by-inning updates of the games. For that fourth playoff game against the Yanks, I was on a golf course in Bali, but on the phone with my son for the final few innings. I remember that when my son called out the end of the game's play-by-play to me on the phone, I was standing on the green and literally jumped and cheered as loud as I could. I then realized that I had disrupted at least a couple of other golfers on the course in mid-stroke.

For the fourth game of the World Series, I unfortunately had previously scheduled an important business meeting to attend. (Because of the massive time zone difference, night games in the US took place the next morning in Indonesia.) So I stressed over how I could get out of that meeting so that I could watch the game. By that time, the World Series games were televised live (via satellite at home).

After very carefully thinking about all of the pros and cons, I decided that you could always schedule a so-called "important meeting." So I stayed home – alone – and watched that fourth game. In the ninth inning, I arranged a telephone conference call with my kids and my mother (who was then 89 years old) so that we could all experience the thrill of the win and the end of the Curse.

So, even though I was 10,000 miles from Boston, I experienced the collective emotion of Red Sox Nation celebrating our amazing victory.

Once the Sox won the Series, I wanted the T-shirt, of course. I didn't know the fastest way for me to get one, so I ordered three, each shipped to a different address in the US, and had friends and family send them to me. I still have those three T-shirts, which I still proudly wear, and they're still in great shape!

BARRY HALPERN

ORLANDO CABRERA

BY TONY S. OLIVER

The Red Sox faithful's devotion to Nomar Garciaparra, cultivated through multiple All-Star seasons and batting titles, had seemingly reached its breaking point after a July 1, 2004, loss to the Yankees. While Garciaparra sat out the game due to his Achilles tendon injuries, his perennial rival Derek Jeter reached base twice and dove headfirst into the stands to snag pinch-hitter Trot Nixon's pop fly that allowed the Yankees to escape a 12th-inning jam without allowing any runs.

After the game, rumors that Garciaparra refused manager Terry Francona's request to pinch-hit in the late innings rubbed salt into the wound. Although a divorce seemed imminent, the July 31 trade to the Chicago Cubs shocked New England. Gone was the franchise shortstop and in his place was Orlando Cabrera, a less distinguished player who toiled in the relative obscurity of Montreal. Had this been a fantasy league swap, the commissioner might have fielded irate calls from players seeking to void such a lopsided transaction.[1] But baseball is not played on paper and the Boston front office was convinced that Cabrera was a better fit. They would have two scant months to prove their point.

Orlando Luis Cabrera was born on November 2, 1974, in Cartagena de Indias, a city on Colombia's Caribbean coast. His father, Jolbert Sr., was a former Florida Marlins scout who instilled a strong competitive streak in his sons, Jolbert Jr. and Orlando: "I learned my passion for winning from my father," Orlando once said. He hated to lose and so do I."[2] However, this was a dual baseball household, with his mother, Josefina, "a teacher for 44 years" who "would still find time to be at my baseball games and my brother Jolbert's. She really knew her baseball."[3] Josefina preferred that her sons be supervised on the diamond rather than unmonitored on the streets.

Although baseball is a distant second sport to soccer in the hearts of Colombians, the country boasts deep baseball roots. The game entered Colombia in the late nineteenth century, brought by Cubans and Panamanians to Cabrera's hometown. Baseball is king in Bolívar state, of which Cartagena is the capital; the country's first league was founded here in 1916.[4] The professional circuit (*Liga Profesional de Béisbol Colombiano,* or *LPB*), dates to 1948.[5] Although the nation has not produced many big leaguers (31 as of the beginning of the 2023 season), it boasts the first major leaguer born in Latin America, Lou Castro.[6]

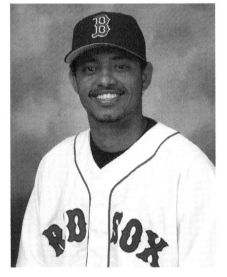

Cabrera began playing at 6 years old, often in the outfield. His slight build made teams wary of trusting him with a key defensive position, though Cabrera soon proved his mettle. When he moved into the infield, he modeled his game after Roberto Alomar and Barry Larkin, two future Hall of Famers against whom he would play in the big leagues. He soon moved from the sandlots to playing for an organized team, named Barakat after its mattress-making sponsor.[7] The brothers would often play together, and although Jolbert was seen as a better prospect – he signed with the Montreal Expos – Orlando worked hard to develop his skills: "I was 14 when my brother signed to play professional baseball. I thought if he could make it maybe I had a chance."[8] Although he would eventually reach 5-feet-9[9] and was listed at 195 pounds, his stature was still seen as an obstacle: "They signed my brother, but they didn't sign me. There were a lot of high expectations for me in Colombia, even from my family, but I figured it wasn't going to happen."[10]

Despite his father's connections, teams passed on Cabrera in no fewer than 15 tryouts, prompting him to enroll in college at his mother's urging. He continued to excel in athletics while studying maritime engineering, but both his father and scout William Marrugo remained in contact with various franchises. Another Colombian scout, Arturo DeFreites, a friend of Jolbert Sr.'s, enticed Montreal to sign Cabrera sight unseen. He bypassed the size concern by inflating the shortstop's height. Two months into the college semester, the Expos offered Cabrera a contract with a $7,000 signing bonus. He accepted it and was assigned to the Dominican Summer League.[11] The franchise almost backed out of the deal when Cabrera stepped off the plane, but he proved his ability on the field.

In 1994 Cabrera played 22 games in the rookie Gulf Coast League and batted a solid .315 (23-for-73) with 6 stolen bases. Unlike many Latin players on their first foreign experience, he was not alone, as brother Jolbert was also an Expos farmhand: "That was a big help. He helped me settle in and he taught me how to order food."[12] The GCL Expos also boasted two of the organization's top prospects: Vladimir Guerrero and Javier Vázquez, taking their first steps toward the big leagues.

Cabrera played with the Vermont Expos of the short-season Class-A New York-Pennsylvania League in 1995 and hit well (.282/.323/.407) in 65 games. He appeared in three other contests with the advanced Class A West Palm Beach Expos and went 1-for-5. He was promoted to the Class-A Delmarva Shorebirds of the South Atlantic League for the 1996 season and led the club with 134 games played, 580 plate appearances, 86 runs, 14 home runs, and 51 stolen bases, and made the league all-star team.[13]

Cabrera progressed through three minor-league levels in 1997. In 69 games for West Palm Bach, he hit .276/.340/.412 and was promoted to the Harrisburg Senators of the Double-A Eastern League. He improved his offense to .308/.378/.549 and thus prompted the Expos to move him up to the Ottawa Lynx of the Triple-A International League. Cabrera played 31 games for the Lynx and batted .262/.306/.385. He was now regarded mostly as a shortstop, and his defense steadily improved as he climbed the ladder. After committing 20 errors in 64 games in West Palm Beach, he had only 8 miscues in 66 contests with the Senators and the Lynx.

Once rosters expanded, Cabrera reached the major leagues in September but at first was used only as a pinch-runner, pinch-hitter, and late inning defensive replacement. On September 22 he made his first start and collected two hits in five at-bats against Greg Maddux. Cabrera had watched Maddux "pitch on the super-station [TBS] and I knew he always pitched outside so I was ready. I got two hits against a future Hall of Famer in my first game!"[14] For the Expos he hit .222/.263/.222 in 20 plate appearances and was praised by skipper Felipe Alou, who envisioned him as a leadoff hitter, saying: "He has good speed, is a pure base stealer, and hits the fastball."[15]

As the 1998 season began, rookies Brad Fullmer, José Vidró, and Cabrera were expected to join Grudzielanek in the infield. A 1-for-16 stretch in the Grapefruit League, punctuated by several defensive mistakes, led to a reprimand from skipper Alou.[16] Despite being ranked as the 92nd prospect in *Baseball America*'s preseason rankings, Cabrera began the season in Triple A and hit only .232/.298.294 in 66 games with Ottawa. Still, he was recalled on June 24. He hit his first major-league round-tripper on July 21, an inside-the-park home run against Mark Portugal of the Phillies. Since Cabrera was cheaper, a few years younger, and "already … a better defensive shortstop than Grudzielanek," the Expos traded the latter to the Dodgers.[17] Cabrera performed admirably in 79 games in both middle infield positions (.280/.325/.414).

Cabrera played winter league baseball in Venezuela with the Tigres of Aragua. Although official statistics are incomplete, he was credited with a .285 batting average and a .391 slugging percentage in 39 regular-season games and a .239 average in 16 postseason contests.[18]

Montreal named Cabrera as its starting shortstop for the 1999 season. He was dependable and played in 104 of the team's first 108 games before a severely sprained ankle in August forced him out of the lineup. After the season *The Sporting News* described him as "flashy and effective" though it added, "[O]ffensively, he had some good moments, but he neither hits for power nor average."[19] Like his teammates, he went 0-for-3 against David Cone on July 18; his third at-bat marked the final out of Cone's perfect game.[20]

During the offseason, Cabrera played in the winter league in Colombia to rehabilitate his injury. He reported to spring training with "pain only when … hitting and pivot(ing) on the ankle."[21] However, off-the-field tragedy struck as Jolbert Sr. died unexpectedly in 2000 and Cabrera suffered through a tough season: .237/.279/.393.

Cabrera focused on his physical conditioning and plate discipline during the offseason, as new teammate Tim Raines preached about working the count. Cabrera credited Raines with "making him more aware of the value of a walk" and showed "a better eye at the plate."[22] Often the cleanup hitter, Cabrera hit .267 in his first 43 games, made only two errors, and batted .324 with runners in scoring position.[23] He won a Gold Glove "despite playing 81 games on a surface that resembled a parking lot with holes."[24] He registered two 34-game streaks without an error, played in all 162 games, compiled a 2.1 Defensive WAR (fifth in the NL), and led the league's shortstops in fielding percentage.

Though Cabrera enjoyed playing with the Expos, the franchise's struggles in Montreal played a heavy role in his looming free agency. New Expos hitting coach Bill Robinson suggested that Cabrera work on hitting to the opposite field in the 2002 season.[25] Mixed results followed: Bothered by a bad back, Cabrera stole more bases and walked more, but his slugging percentage dropped by 48 points. He clashed with management early in the season, questioning their support when he was asked to bunt twice in a row in an extra-inning game. José Vidro, his double-play partner, had matured into a consistent .300 hitter, and Montreal boasted young prospect Brandon Phillips in the minor leagues, adding to the frustration. Perhaps the only highlight of the season was the June 21 game against Cleveland, which featured the Cabrera brothers as opponents for the first time in the major leagues.[26]

The Expos sought to sign Cabrera to a multiyear deal, but the parties could not agree to terms and the franchise started to explore trades. Cabrera's last full season in Montreal (2003) was his finest wearing the Expos uniform. He appeared in every game and hit .297/.347/.460 (105+ OPS) as the Expos finished in fourth place (83-79) in the competitive NL East.

Montreal struggled early in the 2004 season and Cabrera seemed lost at the plate (.246/.298/.336), but his fielding was spectacular (seven errors in 101 games). As the franchise played out the string before its move to Washington, it traded some of its assets to contending clubs. Cabrera was as shocked as anyone once he learned about his trade to the Red Sox from Expos manager Frank Robinson: "I thought, oh, my gosh, I'm in trouble" upon realizing he would replace Garciaparra.[27] He figured he would be dealt to a team without an established shortstop, not to one with an All-Star at the position.

Boston Globe columnist Dan Shaughnessy complained that "the club has some explaining to do because it didn't get enough for [Garciaparra] in the trade," bemoaning not necessarily

Garciaparra's departure, but rather what many Red Sox fans felt was an insufficient replacement.[28] Cabrera paid little attention to the newspapers thanks to counsel he received from former Expos teammate Pedro Martínez: "(He) gave me some good advice. He said, 'Do the interviews but don't ever read a paper here.'"[29] Cabrera acknowledged that "the first days were very hard with the media. Fans don't expect an idol to be replaced, but if he were, by someone from the same level … and I knew that I would not reach Nomar Garciaparra's level. … He was an offensive powerhouse, but he was not the same defensive player I was … so I had to play to my strengths and make the team more fundamentally sound."[30]

Despite the hostile press, Cabrera received the backing of the Red Sox pitching stars. Martínez noted, "I remember Cabrera as a young, good steady player at shortstop in Montreal, but he's gotten even better over the years. He's going to be a good player for us."[31] Curt Schilling agreed: "I know Cabrera from playing against him and he's one of the best shortstops in the game. He can hit and he can play good defense for us. He is a game-changer in the field for me."[32] Manager Terry Francona also provided a vote of confidence: "I saw him play when he was with Montreal and thought he was an excellent player. Everyone in Boston found out right away how good he is defensively. (Red Sox bench coach Brad Mills) was with him in Montreal last year. He thought (Cabrera) could again become the hitter he was last year and would thrive in this type of environment. He was right."[33]

Cabrera proved his worth from his very first at-bat. The Red Sox battled the Twins in Minnesota on August 1 and Cabrera, in Garciaparra's old third spot in the batting order, hit a home run against Johan Santana in the first inning. He made an error in the eighth inning that allowed the go-ahead run to score in a 4-3 Boston loss. However, Cabrera's value, as the front office anticipated, soon became apparent as the Red Sox defense improved. His sold hitting, though, was a bonus.

Ron Jackson, the team's hitting coach, helped Cabrera take advantage of his new surroundings: "I was hitting about .230 and (Jackson) said, 'Orlando, I want you to concentrate on pulling the ball. You've got that wall out here in left field, and if the ball is in the zone, I want you to pull it.' It was like a light went off from there on."[34]

Cabrera hit a robust .294 in the regular season for Boston, including a walk-off home run on September 22 against the Orioles. His ebullient personality fit in with the scrappy Red Sox but Cabrera knew when to be serious. After Manny Ramírez begged off playing a game because of a headache, Cabrera told he mercurial outfielder "There's no way you're coming out of the lineup. I've never been in the playoffs."[35] The statement convinced Ramírez, whose ill-timed requests were often the bane of management.

Perhaps nervous in his first postseason series, Cabrera hit .154 in the Division Series against the Angels but a blistering .379 versus the Yankees in the AL Championship Series. To Cabrera, the Red Sox "organization launched (my) career."[36] The ALCS "was amazing. It's something that will always live in my memory and my heart. It was one of the best-played series in my career, as a team to come back after that three-game deficit and win the next four, especially against the team that the Yankees had that year, it was special. After that, in the World Series, it was so much easier to win those four games, and it will always have a very big space in my mind."[37]

Often overlooked in Colombia, Cabrera now became the topic of incessant media attention. "I was doing interviews to every single news outlet in Colombia. It was crazy. Nonstop. … (T)here was so much excitement – I couldn't sleep. I was talking and talking and talking and thinking, 'Wow, this is incredible.'"[38] Cabrera hit .235 in the World Series, but the robust Red Sox offense did not need his bat. On the field, Cabrera's glovework was flawless as he played every Red Sox defensive inning in the postseason. Cabrera recalled "the friendship and the trust … the chemistry of the team" that galvanized the roster toward Boston's first World Series championship in 86 years.[39]

A first-time free agent, Cabrera was well-positioned to secure a lucrative contract. Boston chose to pursue Edgar Rentería instead of re-signing Cabrera. Though Rentería had been one of the few Cardinals whose bat was not silenced in the World Series, Cabrera had earned the pitching staff's trust. Years later, Cabrera would have a falling out with his business partner, Rentería's brother. The relationship between the two shortstops turned cold over a provocative *ESPN Magazine* article that planted the seeds of discord.

Cabrera was not the only playoff hero not to return in 2005. Mientkiewicz and Dave Roberts left for other teams, leaving the Red Sox without anything to show for the Garciaparra trade – except for the World Series trophy. A more nuanced look reveals other domino effects. The Red Sox received two draft picks from the Anaheim Angels as part of the compensatory draft; those extra slots yielded Jacoby Ellsbury and Jed Lowrie.[40]

The Angels signed Cabrera to a four-year deal worth $32 million, though Cabrera acknowledged that "it would have been nice to stay in Boston."[41] Indeed, the fans gave him a standing ovation when he returned as an opponent on June 3. "I will never forget that moment," he said in 2014.[42] Cabrera hit .257/.309/.365 in 141 games for the Angels in 2005 as they reached the ALCS but fell to the eventual World Series champion Chicago White Sox. Statistically he was arguably the AL's best shortstop, with a 19.6 UZR, 7 errors, and a .988 fielding percentage in 140 games.[43] However, Derek Jeter was the Gold Glove winner at shortstop.

Cabrera's 2006 statistics (.282/.335/.404) demonstrated marked improvement. Cabrera reached base in 63 consecutive games, the sixth-longest streak in major-league history, surpassed only by Ted Williams (three times) and Joe DiMaggio (twice). Despite baseball's sabermetric revolution, the accomplishment flew under the radar of many, including Cabrera himself: "It was a good run. With all the greatest players to have played the game, to even be on that list is crazy. It's just crazy, me doing that kind of stuff. I'm a free-swinging hitter. Reaching base every day? It was hard to believe I was doing it."[44]

Cabrera won his second Gold Glove in 2007 and finished 15th in the AL MVP voting with a career-high .301 batting average. His 11 sacrifice flies led the league for the second consecutive season. This was the last season Cabrera would enjoy with a permanent home. With one year remaining in his contract, the Angels traded him to the White Sox for pitcher Jon Garland.

Cabrera was durable for Chicago; he played 161 games and won the Defensive Player of the Year Award.[45] He overcame an awful start (.215 in his first 27 games and challenged scoring decisions that assigned him errors) to finish at .281/.334/.371 and a 14.9 UZR on the field. Though he butted heads with Ozzie Guillén over perceived lack of managerial support, the feisty former White Sox skipper lauded Cabrera's efforts: "He's a winner and always has been. … He had a great career."[46]

Cabrera became a free agent on November 1. He signed with the Oakland Athletics on March 6, 2009, and played in 101 games (.280/.318/.365) before the perennially cash-strapped club flipped him to Minnesota for Tyler Ladendorf. He helped the Twins in the stretch drive, providing veteran leadership and stability on the field while hitting .289, but hit only .154 in Minnesota's Division Series loss to the Yankees.

Cabrera returned to the National League in 2010 with the Cincinnati Reds and played in 123 games, his fewest since 1999. At age 35, his offense dipped to .263/.303/.354. A free agent again, he split the 2011 campaign with Cleveland (91 games, .244) and San Francisco (39 games, .222) after a July 30 deal for Thomas Neal.

After 15 years in "The Show," Cabrera retired before the 2012 season. "It was time," he said. "I love baseball too much to ever play at less than 100 percent."[47] His lifetime totals (1,985 games, 2,055 hits, 459 doubles, 985 runs scored, 123 home runs, 216 stolen bases, 21.33 WAR) are second among Colombian players, behind only Rentería. Though not a power hitter, his 459 career doubles surpass Hall of Famers Rod Carew, Jimmie Foxx, Roberto Clemente, Larkin, and Eddie Collins.

Cabrera hit .228 in 37 postseason contests, reaching the playoffs in six years (2004, 2005, 2007, 2008, 2009, 2010) with five different teams. Post-Boston, Cabrera played in 1,023 games and obtained 1,111 hits (.275 average). With his glove, Cabrera is credited with a .977 fielding average, above Hall of Famers Jeter, Larkin, and Luis Aparicio.

Cabrera was successful against Joe Saunders (14-for-27), Jae Weong (Seo) 2-for-22), Matt Morris (8-for-21), Brandon Duckworth (13-for-34), Liván Hernández (16-for-37), Félix Hernández (16-for-36), Maddux (16-for-47), and Schilling (15-for-44) but could not figure out Antonio Alfonseca (0-for-12), Octavio Dotel (0-for-20), Joe Nathan (1-for-17), Rick Porcello (2-for-18), Kris Benson (2-for-24), Barry Zito (3-for-32), and John Smoltz (4-for-27).[48]

During his playing days, Cabrera started the Prospect Sport Foundation, which has helped young baseball talent in Colombia, especially from ages 12 to 16. (Sixteen-year-olds can be signed to professional contracts in the United States.) He consults (as of 2023) with GenTrust Wealth Management in Miami to help young players handle the sudden influx of money that often accompanies a professional contract.

Cabrera paid $200,000 to repave streets surrounding his foundation's offices and a neighboring park, with plans for medical facilities. The foundation partnered with the US Embassy to conduct baseball clinics in 2019 taught by former major leaguers Yamid Haad, Sugar Ray Marimon, and Yhonathan Barrios.[49] Cabrera stressed the importance of the effort by noting that "Cartagena will always be the cradle of baseball in Colombia; I am convinced of our young talent, and we must support them."[50] He stressed the criticality of playing in the winter leagues and noted "some scouts and people who have not played (in the winter leagues) don't know the importance in the development of those youngsters. You find players who have competed in Triple-A, Double-A, the majors, the rookie leagues, and some who have not yet signed a contract."[51]

Nevertheless, a 2008 attempt to join the governing body for the league was unsuccessful due to disputes about sponsorship and funding. After that Cabrera focused his efforts on player development. He wishes it were more focused on development, noting that as the number of Colombians in the minor and major leagues has grown, the number of franchises in the Colombian league has dwindled. He commented, "Big leaguers don't play in Colombia because they weren't given the opportunity growing up, and now that they have reached the majors, they are being asked to play. They resent that."[52]

During the COVID-19 pandemic, he provided economic assistance to 77 coaches of the Bolívar State Baseball League.[53] Cabrera said he "wanted to support those coaches … to lend a helping hand, let them know we have not forgotten about them, and that the Prospect Sport Foundation depends on them."[54] The lockdown prompted the Cabrera brothers to collaborate on a podcast, *Colombianos MLB,* hosted by Diego Martínez that covered topics such as superstitions, how to learn English, the role of the agent, and how to overcome slumps.[55] The podcast is the top social media source for Colombian baseball.

Orlando joined Jolbert's coaching staff prior to the 2023 World Baseball Classic, Colombia's second appearance in the event. The entire Cabrera family cheered from the stands, led by their mother, Josefina. The team beat Mexico, 5-4, in its first game, but lost its next two contests, 7-5 to Great Britain and 5-0 to Canada. The team gave the United States a scare but lost 3-2 in a tight game that saw both nations struggle to hit. Six members of the roster were products of Cabrera's Foundation, adding an extra layer of pride to the occasion. Rentería was also a coach, thus reuniting the country's baseball triumvirate.

Orlando and his family live in New Hampshire. Being in New England keeps him close to the Red Sox faithful, who "are the way any fan base should be. If you show support for your team, you deserve to have a good team. The fan base in New England is always with you, you should always do your job, and if you do this, you will always be loved here."[56] Reflecting on his career during a TV interview, Cabrera noted that he "wasn't an All Star, but I had the privilege to walk among them. … My career, whatever I did, was always past my expectations."[57]

ACKNOWLEDGMENTS

Bill Nowlin for connecting the author to Katie Cabrera.

Katie Cabrera for connecting her husband, Orlando, to the author for an interview.

SOURCES

Unless otherwise specified, quotes stem from the author's telephone interview with Orlando Cabrera on June 27, 2023.

NOTES

1. The transaction, as complex as it was shocking, involved four franchises: Boston received Cabrera and Doug Mientkiewicz; the Twins obtained Justin Jones; the Expos received Francis Beltran, Álex González, Brendan Harris; and the Cubs obtained Garciaparra and Matt Murton.
2. Herb Crehan, "Orlando Cabrera Remembers the 2004 World Championship," *Boston Baseball History,* November 7, 2014. https://bostonbaseballhistory.com/new-orlando-cabrera-remembers-the-2004-world-championship/.
3. Crehan.
4. Gustavo Adolfo Acuña Romero, "El béisbol también se juega en municipios del Caribe," *El Espectador,* October 21, 2020. https://www.elespectador.com/deportes/mas-deportes/el-beisbol-tambien-se-juega-en-municipios-del-caribe-article/.
5. Mariano Panchano, "Colombia Making Its Mark in Baseball, One Step at a Time," MLB.com, March 4, 2023. https://www.mlb.com/news/featured/colombia-making-its-mark-in-baseball-one-step-at-a-time.
6. Castro was born in Medellín, Colombia, in 1876 and played 42 games for the Philadelphia Athletics of the American League in 1902. Esteban (Steven) Bellán, a Cuban, played with the Troy Haymakers (1871-72) and New York Mutuals (1873) of National Association (NA), but the NA is no longer considered a major league.
7. "Orlando Cabrera y el legado de una leyenda del béisbol colombiano," Infobae, November 3, 2022, https://www.infobae.com/america/colombia/2022/11/03/orlando-cabrera-y-el-legado-de-una-leyenda-del-beisbol-colombiano/.
8. Crehan.
9. Though often listed as 5-feeet-11, Cabrera is, by his own admission, 5-feet-9.
10. Art Davidson, "On Baseball: Cabrera Making It on His Own," *Milford* (Massachusetts) *Daily News,* October 3, 2004. https://www.milforddailynews.com/story/sports/2004/10/03/on-baseball-cabrera-making-it/41182959007/.
11. Baseball Cube, Orlando Cabrera page. https://www.thebaseballcube.com/content/player/993/prospects/.
12. Crehan.
13. Baseball Cube, Orlando Cabrera page. https://www.thebaseballcube.com/content/player/993/awards/.
14. Crehan.
15. Jeff Blair, "First Order Is to Find a Lead-Off Man," *The Sporting News,* September 8, 1997: 44.
16. Stephanie Myles "Baseball: Expos," *The Sporting News,* March 16, 1998: 22.
17. Stephanie Myles "Baseball: Expos," *The Sporting News,* July 13, 1998: 31.
18. Venezuelan League Statistics, Orlando Cabrera page. https://www.pelotabinaria.com.ve/beisbol/mostrar.php?ID=cabrorlo01.
19. Stephanie Myles "Baseball: Expos," *The Sporting News,* December 13, 1999: 68.
20. Expos at Yankees Box Score, July 18, 1999. https://www.baseball-reference.com/boxes/NYA/NYA199907180.shtml.
21. Stephanie Myles, "Baseball: Expos," *The Sporting News,* February 14, 2000: 60.
22. Stephanie Myles, "Baseball: Expos," *The Sporting News,* May 7, 2001: 27.
23. Stephanie Myles, "Baseball: Expos," *The Sporting News,* May 28, 2001: 47.
24. Stephanie Myles, "Baseball: Expos," *The Sporting News,* November 19, 2001: 50.
25. Stephanie Myles, "N.L. East," *The Sporting News,* December 24, 2001: 57.
26. Indians at Expos Box Score, June 21, 2022. https://www.retrosheet.org/boxesetc/2002/B06210MON2002.htm.
27. Crehan.
28. Dan Shaughnessy, "No Room for Neutrality," *Boston Globe,* August 4, 2004. https://www.boston.com/sports/baseball/redsox/articles/2004/08/04/no_room_for_neutrality/.
29. Crehan.
30. "Orlando Cabrera en 'el Magazine Deportivo': Entrevista con el ex-MLB exclusiva de Caribe Sports," originally streamed July 27, 2022, YouTube, https://www.youtube.com/watch?v=GlHZxQ7zp0Q.
31. Crehan.
32. Ben Shapiro, "Orlando Cabrera Retires: Looking Back on 3 Months That No Sox Fan Will Forget," *Bleacher Report,* January 19, 2012. https://bleacherreport.com/articles/1030622-orlando-cabrera-retires-looking-back-on-3-months-that-no-sox-fan-will-forget.
33. Davidson, "On Baseball: Cabrera Making It on His Own."
34. Crehan.
35. Jorge Arangue Jr., "Now It's Personal," ESPN, April 21, 2008. https://www.espn.com/espnmag/story?id=3356524.
36. Michael Smithers, "2004 World Champion Orlando Cabrera Visits Polar Park April 13 for 'Throwback Thursdays' Debut.," milb.com, April 18, 2023. https://www.milb.com/worcester/news/orlando-cabrera.
37. Smithers.
38. Ian Browne, *Idiots Revisited: Catching up with the Red Sox Who Won the 2004 World Series* (Thomaston, Maine: Tilbury House, 2014), 149.
39. Author's telephone interview with Orlando Cabrera, June 27, 2023.
40. Baseballism Blog. http://baseballism.blogspot.com/2011/02/why-do-teams-keep-passing-on-orlando.html.
41. Crehan.
42. Crehan.

43 For Ultimate Zone Rating, see https://www.fangraphs.com/players/orlando-cabrera/766/stats#fielding.

44 Bill Shaikin, "'A Good Run' for Cabrera," *Los Angeles Times*, July 9, 2005.

45 The DPOY award is now part of the Esurance MLB Awards and was voted by the fans. It is not connected to the Wilson Defensive Players of the Year Award (2012-present). For more information, consult Baseball Almanac, https://www.baseball-almanac.com/awards/defensive_player_of_the_year_award_plch.shtml.

46 Ozzie Guillén, "Rumbo a Chicago para una visita," Ozzie Habla, January 19, 2012. http://ozziees.mlblogs.com/tag/orlando-cabrera/.

47 Crehan.

48 "Selected Batter-Pitcher Matchups for Orlando Cabrera," Retrosheet. https://www.retrosheet.org/boxesetc/C/MUS0_cabro001.htm.

49 US Embassy in Bogotá, Colombia, August 30, 2019, @USEmbassyBogota. https://twitter.com/USEmbassyBogota/status/1167602979270250496.

50 "Ex beisbolistas de grandes ligas desarrollan en Cartagena las Clínicas de Béisbol," Noti Cartagena, date not published, https://noticartagena.com.co/ex-beisbolistas-clinicas-del-beisbol/.

51 "Orlando Cabrera en 'el Magazine Deportivo': Entrevista con el ex-MLB exclusiva de Caribe Sports."

52 "Orlando Cabrera en 'el Magazine Deportivo': Entrevista con el ex-MLB exclusiva de Caribe Sports."

53 Ernesto de la Hoz, "Cabrera entregó 77 mercados," *El Universal*, April 24, 2020. https://www.eluniversal.com.co/deportes/cabrera-entrego-77-mercados-DY2717948.

54 Juan Manual Ulloque, "'Hemos querido aportar un granito de arena en las necesidades de muchos afectados': Orlando Cabreda," *Primer Tiempo*, May 1, 2020. https://primertiempo.co/beisbol/hemos-querido-aportar-un-granito-de-arena-en-las-necesidades-de-muchos-afectados-orlando-cabrera/.

55 Orlando Cabrera and Diego Martínez, "El camino a las grandes ligas," Spotify Podcasts. https://podcasters.spotify.com/pod/show/elcaminohacialasgl/episodes/El-slump-en-el-bisbol-eepsl7.

56 Smithers, "2004 World Champion Orlando Cabrera Visits Polar Park April 13 for 'Throwback Thursdays' Debut," The016. https://the016.com/videos/25/29131/orlando-cabrera-interview-with-michael-smithers.

57 "Pillow Talk Show Episode 5: Orlando Cabrera," NESN, August 11, 2017. https://www.youtube.com/watch?v=I0valS3Vcbk.

FRANK CASTILLO

BY LUCA ROSSI

Frank Castillo was a right-handed pitcher who played 13 solid seasons in the major leagues, mostly as a starting pitcher, while recording over 1,100 strikeouts and 82 wins. In love with the game and his family, Frank had his best years with the Chicago Cubs in the early 1990s, close to making Cubs history in 1995 and eventually retiring with a World Series ring as a member of the memorable 2004 Red Sox team.

Frank Anthony Castillo was born on April 1, 1969, in El Paso, Texas, the son of John and Gloria Castillo. Frank grew up, along with his brother Joe and two sisters, Debi and Denise, in a family with a strong baseball tradition. His father, John "Joe" Castillo, was a professional baseball player himself from the same area (Jefferson High). Joe played in the Arizona-Texas League and signed a free agent contract with the Pirates organization,[1] but never made it to Pittsburgh.

Frank Castillo was drafted in the sixth round of the 1987 Amateur Draft (140th overall) by the Chicago Cubs out of Eastwood High School in El Paso, Texas. In that same draft Frank's teammate and fellow pitcher Butch Henry was drafted by the Cincinnati Reds in the 15th round.

It was with Castillo and Henry, leading the team as a great right-handed/left-handed starting pitcher combination, that the Eastwood Troopers won the 1987 Texas Region 1 Area Championship, eventually losing to Fort Worth Richland Hill in the State Championship Playoffs.[2]

In 2002 Castillo was inducted into the El Paso Athletics Hall of Fame.[3]

Castillo, who grew up watching Nolan Ryan on television, said he had dreamed of playing in Chicago's Wrigley Field. After being drafted by the Cubs, he said, "The thought of taking the mound at Wrigley is frightening. But it's a good feeling to know that I may get that chance."[4]

Castillo had signed a letter of intent with the University of Arizona but eventually signed a professional contract with the Cubs organization and began his pro career with the 1987 Wytheville Cubs (Rookie-Appalachian League) with an impressive 10-1 record and a 2.29 ERA, leading the league in wins and pitching five complete games. In that same debut season, Castillo also pitched and won one game for the New York-Penn League's Geneva Cubs (Class A).

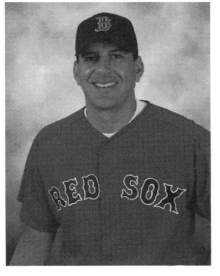

The following three seasons were marked by some serious injuries and excellent pitching performances while Castillo ascended through the Cubs' minor-league system.

He missed half of the 1988 season with a shin stress fracture and pitched only nine games with the Peoria Cubs of the Class-A Midwest League. In his limited work, he compiled a 6-1 record with a 0.71 ERA and 58 strikeouts in 51 innings.

In 1989 Castillo was 9-6/2.51 in 18 starts for Winston-Salem (Class-A Carolina League) and 3-4/3.84 in 10 starts after a call-up to the Charlotte Knights (Double-A Southern League), with almost 200 innings pitched overall.

Castillo missed the entire first half of the 1990 season with a stress fracture in his back, but in the second half of the season he was 6-6 with a 3.88 ERA for Charlotte, pitching 111⅓ innings with 112 strikeouts.

Castillo began the 1991 season in the Triple-A American Association with the Iowa Cubs and his first four starts (3-1, 2.52) earned him a call-up by the Cubs on June 27 and a spot in the starting rotation to replace Danny Jackson, who had been placed on the disabled list with a lower abdominal strain.

He made his major-league debut on the day he was officially called up, as the starter against the Pirates at Three Rivers Stadium in Pittsburgh. Castillo threw eight shutout innings and the Cubs led 3-0 going into the bottom of the ninth. After Castillo allowed back-to-back leadoff singles, Cubs manager Jim Essian called on his bullpen. Reliever Paul Assenmacher allowed the two inherited runners to score, and a third, tying the game. The Pirates won, 4-3, on a wild pitch from Heathcliff Slocumb, who had relieved Assenmacher.

On July 1 at Wrigley Field, Castillo faced the Pirates again, giving up five runs in seven innings. This time, it was the Cubs who came from behind, tied the game in the ninth and won in 13.

On July 5 Castillo earned his first major-league win, a 5-1 complete-game six-hitter against the St. Louis Cardinals at Busch Stadium. He won his next two decisions as well, both against Houston.

His best game of the year was a three-hitter against the Los Angeles Dodgers on August 27 at Wrigley Field. Castillo's record for his first season was 6-7 (4.35 ERA), with 73 strikeouts in 111⅔ innings.

In 1992 Castillo became a steady presence in the Cubs rotation and established himself as a major-league starter, pitching over 200 innings, compiling a 10-11 record (3.46 ERA) in 33 starts. He finished strong, with a 2.93 ERA over his last four starts of the year, including a win against the Montreal Expos on the last day of the season, working 8⅓ innings and striking out nine.

In 1993 Castillo made 25 starts and was 5-8 with an inflated 4.84 ERA. He also suffered from a lack of run support as the Cubs scored two or fewer runs in nine of his starts. After allowing 19 runs in 14 innings in August, he was moved to the bullpen and pitched in three games as a reliever to complete the season.

Castillo's 1994 season was marked by injuries; he pitched only 23 innings in four starts, going 2-1 with a 4.30 ERA. He began the season on the DL with a sprained finger on his pitching hand and didn't make his first appearance until May 15. After two starts, allowing 14 hits and 9 runs (8 earned) in 8⅔ innings Castillo was sent to Triple-A Iowa, where he was 4-2 with a 3.27 ERA before being called up in July after pitcher Anthony Young suffered a season-ending right elbow injury.

His return to the Cubs rotation, coming back from injury in late July, lasted only two games when the season was canceled after the players struck. His last 1994 start, on August 6, was his best performance of the year, a complete-game 7-1 victory over the San Diego Padres at Wrigley Field.

After baseball resumed in 1995, Castillo had his best season (11-10, 3.21), in 29 starts. He had two shutouts, the second of which, on September 25, was probably Castillo's best game as a Cub. In that game against St. Louis, Castillo, who had struck out 13 batters, was one strike out away from recording the first Cubs no-hitter since Milt Pappas hurled one in 1972. With two outs in the St. Louis ninth, Cardinals left fielder Bernard Gilkey, on a 2-and-2 count, tripled on a line drive that hit the ground in right-center field just inches from a diving Sammy Sosa.[5] Two pitches later, Castillo had the win on a fly ball to right field.

After the game, Castillo said, "I was too pumped up. I tried to throw it through a wall. I could really feel the energy of the fans. Sometimes you get caught up in that and try to do too much. It was one of those pitches that as soon as I threw it, I wanted it back. Sammy made a great effort. He almost made it."[6]

"When something like that does happen, you think you have a chance to accomplish," Castillo said. "It can be heartbreaking, but I'm looking at it as a positive."[7]

In 1996 Castillo started 33 games for a 76-86 Cubs team, striking out a career-high 139, but had a NL-leading 16 losses to go with only 7 wins (and a 5.28 ERA). The bright spot of the 1996 season was a shutout of the Dodgers in Los Angeles on April 28.

Castillo's 10-year stay with the Cubs organization ended on July 15, 1997. With a 6-9 record in 19 starts and a 5.42 ERA, he was traded to the Colorado Rockies in exchange for pitcher Matt Pool. The rest of Castillo's major-league career, which lasted until 2005, saw him pitch for several different organizations – Detroit, Pittsburgh, Toronto, Atlanta, Boston, Oakland, and Florida.

In Colorado, Castillo finished the 1997 season 6-3 for the Rockies before being granted free agency and signing a one-year deal with the Detroit Tigers. In 19 starts and 8 relief appearances, Castillo was 3-9 with the worst ERA (6.83) of his career in a very difficult year as Detroit lost 97 games.

Released by Detroit, he signed with the Pirates organization but spent the following season in Triple-A Nashville before signing with the Toronto Blue Jays as a free agent.

Castillo had a couple of very solid seasons in 2000 and 2001 with Toronto and Boston, winning 10 games each year as a member of the starting rotation. In 2000 he went 10-5 for the Blue Jays with a 3.59 ERA in 24 starts. A free agent after the season, he signed with the Red Sox. In 2001 he started 26 games for the Red Sox and was 10-9 with a 4.21 ERA. He defeated the Yankees twice in six days, on April 16 and 21.

Castillo started 23 games for the Red Sox in 2002. He was released at the end of a disappointing season (6-15, 5.07 ERA). He did, however, record his 1,000th career strikeout, becoming the sixth player to achieve that mark while pitching in a Red Sox uniform.[8]

In 2003 Castillo pitched in the minor-league systems of the Oakland Athletics and Atlanta Braves without being called up but did well enough to earn a contract for 2004 with the Red Sox. He started 25 games for the Triple-A Pawtucket Red Sox. Early in the season, Castillo was called up as a reliever and pitched in two games, securing the final out in the two losses, to the Orioles on April 15 and the Yankees on April 18, retiring Alex Rodríguez on a fly ball to center field. On the 19th he was returned to Pawtucket to make room for left-handed pitcher Lenny DiNardo, whom the Red Sox had acquired in the Rule 5 draft. From time to time, it appeared that Castillo might be recalled by the Red Sox, but he never was.

Despite appearing in only two games in April and facing a total of four batters, Castillo received a ring as a World Series champion.

A free agent after the season, Castillo signed with the Florida Marlins. He spent most of the season with Triple-A Albuquerque but made a final appearance in a major-league uniform on May 26, starting against the New York Mets in Miami and absorbing the 12-4 loss. His final play as a major leaguer was a walk allowed to Mets outfielder Cliff Floyd in the top of the fifth inning while his last career strikeout had come an inning earlier against Mets pitcher Kris Benson.

With that final game he ended his 13-year major-league career with a record of 82-104, a 4.56 ERA, 268 starts, 1,101 strikeouts, a near no-hitter, and a World Series ring.

Castillo briefly unretired and pitched in 26 games in 2007 and 2008 for the York Revolution of the independent Atlantic League. In 2011 Castillo became the pitching coach for the Mesa Cubs, a position he held until his tragic death in 2013.

On July 28, 2013, Castillo, 44 years old, drowned in Arizona's Bartlett Lake during a boat trip with friends while spending time with his family. Friends and family recalled him as a great teammate, a caring family man, and a player who had always loved and respected the game of baseball.[9] He was survived by his parents, his brother and sisters, his ex-wife Tracy, and two daughters. He is buried at Restlawn Memorial Park in his hometown of El Paso, Texas.

"Frank was a quiet guy, didn't say a whole lot. I hung out with him a lot, so I knew him at a different level than some others. A good dude and a good teammate." With those words Castillo's former Cubs teammate Brian McRae recalled his friend and teammate in an interview with the *Chicago Tribune*.[10]

SOURCES

All statistics, team, season, and game records are from Baseball-Reference.com.

NOTES

1. For Joe Castillo, see https://elpasobaseballhalloffame.org/inductee/joe-castillo/ and for Frank Castillo, see Rick Cantu, "1987: Eastwood Teammates Share Goal, Differ in Methods," *El Paso Times*, June 4, 1987. https://elpasotimes.typepad.com/morgue/2013/07/. Accessed December 27, 2022.
2. El Paso Athletic Hall of Fame, 2002 Induction Dinner Program. https://epahof.com/2002-dinner-program/.
3. El Paso Athletic Hall of Fame Inductees. https://elpasoathletichalloffame.com/inductees/.
4. "1987: Eastwood Teammates Share Goal, Differ in method." https://elpasotimes.typepad.com/morgue/2013/07/1987-eastwood-teammates-share-goal-differ-in-methods.html
5. Chicago Cubs vs. St. Louis Cardinals, September 25, 1995. No-hit bid final out and interview. https://www.youtube.com/watch?v=MLN9Ujo4HXk.
6. Paul Sullivan, "No Hitter, and Heart, Broken Up," *Chicago Tribune*, September 26, 1995. https://www.chicagotribune.com/news/ct-xpm-1995-09-26-9509260321-story.html. For his part, Gilkey said, "It seemed like everyone was against me. Everyone was yelling to me. I didn't want to see us on ESPN getting no-hit." Cubs first baseman Mark Grace went to the mound to return the ball to Castillo and said, "I saw his face on the mound. I almost started to cry. He came so close."
7. Sullivan.
8. The first 652 of his strikeouts were for Chicago.
9. Family obituary for ex MLB Pitcher Frank Castillo. https://kvia.com/news/2015/01/12/read-obituary-for-ex-mlb-pitcher-frank-castillo-rosary-is-tonight/.
10. "Former Cubs Pitcher Dies," *Chicago Tribune*, July 29, 2013. https://www.chicagotribune.com/sports/cubs/ct-xpm-2013-07-29-chi-former-cubs-pitcher-castillo-drowns-20130729-story.html.

RED SOX BASEBALL 2004 SEASON

Having Red Sox season tickets for 30 years put me in the middle of that enjoyable run in 2004. Over the years I witnessed many great games at face-value prices. Included, of course, were playoff games and none were crazier than those in October 2004 against New York. All of the series' early pent-up excitement was nearly doused completely by Game Three's 19-8 humiliation at Fenway. The 2003 meal of angst served by Tim Wakefield's last pitch in the Bronx had been regurgitated. I needed two brave souls for two of my four seats for Game Four and no one wanted to go and watch the Yanks celebrate on the infield with their next pennant trophy. After an extensive search and plea bargains, I finally filled the chairs 10 rows from the visiting dugout.

Remember this is the Twilight Zone-ish series that had me leave the house a mile away from Fenway on one day and never get home until the wee hours of the next morning. Three straight nights. This was only Game Four, yet "doom" was clearly in the crisp air.

It was a certified Yanks-Sox duel. The Evil Empire grabbed a lead on an Álex Rodríguez home run (an additional insult). The Sox then went up, but New York soon regained the lead. Suddenly it was the ninth inning and I sat there wondering how the Red Sox brass would explain not just losing again, but being swept, to a disgruntled Red Sox Nation after retooling after 2003's horrid finish.

By natural script, relief ace Mariano Rivera was out there, dealing his usual stuff. Somehow journeyman Kevin Millar didn't suck for an uncustomary high, inside pitch and walked.

Minutes later pinch-runner Dave Roberts stole second and many dusty history books cracked open.

With this prelude, Game Seven was the only way this whole episode could end after 86 years.

RICHARD DIXIE TOURANGEAU

CÉSAR CRESPO

BY TONY S. OLIVER

Dave Roberts stole *that base* in the ALCS. Doug Mientkiewicz caught the last out of the World Series. Trot Nixon was a perennial Red Sox fan favorite whose dirty uniform symbolized an unrestrained style of play. Nomar Garciaparra's sweet swing won consecutive batting titles (1999, 2000) and made the Fenway faithful swoon. Super-utility César Crespo, however, played in more games in 2004 than the better-known quartet. His appearances came in the first half of the season, and by the time he last wore the uniform, the franchise was two games out of the sole wild-card berth and once again trailed the New York Yankees in the AL East standings. As such, he was more of an extra than a minor character, not to be confused with the protagonists, and often forgotten without the aid of game recaps and box scores.

César Antonio Crespo Claudio was born on May 23, 1979, in Río Piedras, a neighborhood of San Juan, Puerto Rico, best known for the flagship campus of the University of Puerto Rico. He was raised in Caguas, a city on the outskirts of the San Juan metropolitan area. The city, named after the *Taíno* chieftain *Caguax*, who fought the Spanish *conquistadores*, has a rich baseball tradition. Its *Criollos* franchise has been a mainstay of the Puerto Rico Winter League, winning 20 titles and 5 Caribbean Series crowns. Native sons José "Cheo" Cruz, Victor Pellot (a/k/a Vic Power), and Juan "Tetelo" Vargas played alongside imports like Henry Aaron, Cal Ripken Jr., and Don Mattingly.

César's father, Felipe Crespo Sr., was a civil engineer and his mother, Carmen Claudio, was an occupational therapist, providing a comfortable middle-class upbringing for César and his three full siblings. In his youth, César played every position, but upon turning 15 he focused on shortstop and modeled his game after that of Roberto Alomar, though Mattingly and Rickey Henderson were his favorite players.

César attended the Catholic Notre Dame High School and was selected in the third round of the 1997 amateur draft, less than two weeks after his 18th birthday. Of the 30 prospects chosen in that round, nine made the major leagues. Crespo was picked ahead of Chone Figgins (fourth round), Eric Byrnes (fourth round), and Michael Young (fifth round). Almost seven years earlier, his brother Felipe Crespo had been chosen in the same round by the Blue Jays; the elder brother reached the big leagues with Toronto in 1996.

By now 5-feet-11 and 170 pounds, Crespo was assigned to the Capital City Bombers (Columbia, South Carolina) of the Class-A South Atlantic League. In 1998 the squad's 90-51 record topped the league and Crespo appeared in 116 games, most of them at second. However, shortly after the season ended, he and Brandon Villafuerte were traded to the Florida Marlins for Rob Stratton on September 12, 1998. Crespo's .252 batting average, 27 errors, and .948 fielding percentage did not concern the Marlins, who promoted him to the Brevard County Manatees of the Advanced Class-A Florida State League for 1999. Fortunes reversed as the club finished under .500 but Crespo hit .286 (.753 OPS), his zenith as a professional.

Crespo headed north to the Double-A Eastern League with the Portland (Maine) Sea Dogs in 2000. Under eventual big-league manager Rick Renteria, Crespo played all three outfield positions and the middle infield. He reached career highs in games, at-bats, plate appearances, runs, triples, RBIs, runs scored, walks, and strikeouts. During his time with the Marlins' affiliates, he met Euclides "Euky" Rojas, who would also join the Red Sox organization and coach in the Puerto Rico Winter League.

With a breakthrough campaign under his belt, the future looked bright for Crespo, but the trade winds blew in his direction. On March 28, 2001, he and Mark Kotsay went to San Diego in exchange for Matt Clement, Eric Owens, and Omar Ortiz. Crespo was assigned to the organization's top farm club; while the city's name was the same, this Portland was located thousands of miles away in the Pacific Coast League. The trade puzzled some, as "a week before the trade, Marlins manager John Boles likened the 21-year-old switch hitter to a young Tim Raines."[1] *Baseball America* had ranked Crespo as the 19th best prospect in the Florida organization.[2] Crespo was able to play with Henderson, one of his childhood idols, in both Triple A and the major leagues: he cherished the opportunity and said Henderson "was a great mentor and always treated me with respect."[3]

Crespo was called up and made his major-league debut on May 29, 2001. As the seventh hitter, he walked twice in four plate appearances against the Houston Astros. Moved to the leadoff spot the next day, he doubled off Wade Miller for his first major-league hit and enjoyed consistent playing time through the end of June before returning to the minors in July. For the season, he appeared in 133 combined games, and contributed a .209 average with the parent club, including a five-game hitting streak in mid-June.

Crespo's first home run was memorable. On June 7, 2001, the Crespos became the ninth pair of brothers to homer in the same game while playing for different teams. (As of the conclusion of the 2022 season, only Corey and Kyle Seager have repeated the feat.[4]) Felipe had two blasts, driving three runs, but César's shot in the seventh frame was the last run the Padres scored in their 10-8 victory.

Two days later, Crespo scored the go-ahead run on Kotsay's groundout against Seattle, snapping the Mariners' 15-game winning streak. At the end the month, though, he was back in Triple A, where he would "at [San Diego manager Bruce] Bochy's request … play shortstop" to further provide value off the bench.[5] After returning to the majors in September, he enjoyed his best game, clubbing two home runs, a double, and a single in the Padres' 15-11 loss to the Colorado Rockies on September 24.

Baseball Prospectus wrote that "he's never going to be a great hitter, but with his eye and speed he could have an above-average peak at second base or be a great utility player. He'd benefit from playing every day at Portland in 2022."[6] The Padres brass must have paid attention, as Crespo opened the season in Triple A.

The Padres regressed in 2002 and limped to a 66-96 record in the wake of icon Tony Gwynn's retirement. Fellow Puerto Rican Ramón Vázquez, acquired from the Mariners on December 11, played the lion's share of games at second base, so Crespo settled into a super-utility role. (Vázquez would join the Red Sox in 2018 as the team's bench coach.) Aside from a pair of games in April and a nine-contest stint in May, Crespo played most of the season with Portland. He featured as a defensive replacement during a late-season call-up. He started only two out of his 25 games for the year, though he defended all three outfield positions, third base, second base, and shortstop.

The Padres traded Crespo to the Red Sox on December 16, 2002, for fellow middle infielder Luis Cruz. He had a solid 2003 campaign with Triple-A Pawtucket, hitting .267 in 132 games, and alternated between right field and second base. Red Sox infielders Todd Walker and Garciaparra stayed healthy most of the year, and Crespo was not called up during the season.

Baseball Prospectus noted Crespo's potential value: "Crespo can play several positions, has above-average power for a middle infielder and a good eye at the plate. His youth and versatility will likely bring him back to the big leagues, probably in 2004. In the era of 12-man pitching staffs, versatility is everything."[7] The prediction came true, thanks to Crespo's torrid performance in the Grapefruit League. His two hits in a March 18 game against Cleveland brought his average to .462 (12-for-26).[8]

The Red Sox planned to bring glove man Pokey Reese as a backup infielder, but Crespo's hot bat gave the team pause. However, Garciaparra's nagging injuries landed the starting shortstop on the disabled list to begin the season, and freed another slot that Crespo earned thanks to his defensive flexibility.

Throughout April and May, Crespo appeared as a pinch-runner, pinch-hitter, defensive replacement, and occasional spot starter, spelling Reese, second baseman Mark Bellhorn, and the Red Sox outfielders. The dynamic was slated to change when Garciaparra returned from the DL, but Bill Mueller was sidelined through June, allowing Crespo to remain with the team. However, once the group was healthy, Crespo was the odd man out and he was designated for assignment on July 2.

Crespo fondly recalled his first taste of the Yankee-Red Sox rivalry. He appeared in all three games of an early season Red Sox series sweep, saying, "[T]he competition, after coming from San Diego, was intense. … [T]he goal was to win a championship." Among his teammates, he remembered "Manny Ramírez, Pedro Martínez, and David Ortiz making my life a whole lot easier in the big leagues. … [M]y hat's off to them. Since I got to the organization in 2003, they treated me with a lot of respect. Manny, David, and I would take early batting practice, and during the game I would talk to Pedro and he would teach me about the game itself."[9] Three days later, in a harbinger of things to come, Garciaparra returned to the lineup but was replaced by Crespo after a sixth-inning rain delay.

Crespo's last hit with the team, a single, came on June 6 in Kansas City against Chris George. The game, a 4-1 Boston victory, was marred by a freak play during his third plate appearance. With the bases loaded and one man out, Crespo weakly tapped a pitch toward first base. Pitcher Jason Grimsley ran to cover the bag, expecting a lob from first sacker Ken Harvey, but Harvey sought to throw Kevin Millar out at home. Grimsley was unable to duck, and the ball struck him in the face. Both Royals left the game after the harrowing collision.[10]

Crespo's final game with the Red Sox was a heartbreaker. Against the Yankees on July 1, Ramírez's solo homer off Tanyon Sturze broke a 3-3 tie in the top of the 13th inning, but the Yankees rallied against Curt Leskanic to win, 5-4.[11] Crespo entered the contest in the 11th as a pinch-runner for third baseman Kevin Youkilis. Crespo took second on a sacrifice and third on Johnny Damon's single but was left stranded after consecutive popouts by Bellhorn and Nixon. Crespo then took the field as the second baseman and Bellhorn moved to third. Crespo's last major-league plate appearance, in the 13th inning, doused a Boston rally as he grounded into a double play that also eliminated Dave McCarty from the basepaths. McCarty himself was a candidate for demotion.[12]

Crespo was stoic in the face of his demotion. After the Red Sox were swept by the Yankees in a crucial July series, he said, "[N]ot every day is a good day. They gave me an opportunity. I couldn't ask for more."[13] Although the Red Sox were in the thick of a pennant race, Crespo noted, "Offensively, I didn't do the job, so I can't ask for more. They gave me the opportunity, but I couldn't get my timing and I have to try to find my timing again, whether it's here in the organization or somewhere else."[14] Though barely 25, he was aware of the quagmire the minor leagues could offer: "I have to see what the organization is going to offer me if I go to Triple-A. I would love to stay in the infield, but last year I got stuck in right field the whole season. I didn't think that was productive for me."[15] Paradoxically, his defensive fluidity militated against a big-league return. An injury to Reese in late July opened a spot, but the team opted to sign veteran Ricky Gutiérrez instead.

Crespo performed admirably with Triple-A Pawtucket, hitting .272 in 55 games. A much-desired return to the majors did not materialize and Crespo watched his former teammates eradicate the Curse of Bambino from a distance. The franchise granted him free agency on October 4.

With the Red Sox, Crespo totaled 79 plate appearances in 52 games, 16 of them in the starting lineup. Among his 13 hits, three were for extra bases (two doubles, one triple) for a .165/.165/.215 slash line. He collected a pair of hits in a quartet of games (April 10, April 29, May 14, May 15). Even before the thrilling season became mythical, some reporters recalled that "Boston's road to the 2004 playoffs was not all walk-off home runs.… Remember César Crespo? He spent the entire first half of the season with the Red Sox … all over the place, too. He started games at shortstop, second base, center field and right field. Still, the Sox were 10-6 in games that Crespo started. They could have done worse for a utility guy."[16]

Crespo next suited up for the *Gigantes* of Carolina of the Puerto Rico Winter League, hoping to catch the eye of another major-league franchise. The Pittsburgh Pirates signed him on December 22, but he did not make the major-league roster. He spent 2005 with the Triple-A Indianapolis Indians and appeared in 111 games, contributing .265/.349/.409. He was not called up and was released on October 15.

The Atlanta Braves inked Crespo to a one-year deal on January 10, 2006, and assigned him to Triple-A Richmond. His offensive output regressed to .239/.326/.319 and Atlanta granted him free agency on October 15. Less than a month later, Baltimore offered Crespo a one-year deal and assigned him to Norfolk, his third International League team in as many years.

Before spring training, Crespo played for the Puerto Rican team in the 2007 Caribbean Series, going 3-for-10. He managed a .308 average in 15 plate appearances with Baltimore during spring training but was nevertheless sent to Triple A. His numbers with the 2007 Norfolk Tides (.244/.318/.318) did not merit a big-league call-up and the Orioles released him on October 29.

Crespo, however, was not done playing baseball. In 2008 he suited up for the *Mulos* (Mules) of Juncos in Puerto Rico's Amateur Baseball League, known as the Liga de Béisbol Doble-A de Puerto Rico. The league, founded in 1940, features blue-collar workers across the island playing on weekends, typically with their hometown teams. Crespo played six seasons with Juncos and was named the team's captain. He next signed with the *Toritos* (Bull Calves) of Cayey and retired after a subpar 2015 campaign. He averaged .345 across 136 contests from 2008 to 2015.

Though his .192 batting average (48 OPS+) in the major leagues was lower than his brother Felipe's .245 (85+) and César played in only half as many games as Felipe, he can nevertheless boast of playing for a team that won the ultimate baseball prize. He took part in the 10th-anniversary celebration of the championship of "the best team I ever played on."[17]

After hanging up his professional spikes, Crespo studied civil engineering at the Polytechnic University of Puerto Rico. Upon graduation, he joined one of his brothers and his father in the family business, C.A.C. Crespo Builders.[18] As of 2023, he and his wife lived in Caguas with their two young children.

ACKNOWLEDGMENTS

Alexis Figueroa for connecting the author with César Crespo.

NOTES

Unless otherwise noted, quotes stem from the author's interview with César Crespo on December 12, 2022.

1 Ken Rosenthal, "Inside Dish," *The Sporting News*, April 9, 2001: 54.

2 "Cesar Crespo Profile," *The Baseball Cube*, https://www.thebaseballcube.com/content/player/897/prospects/.

3 Author's telephone interview with César Crespo, December 12, 2022.

4 "Brothers Homering in the Same Game," *Retrosheet*, https://retrosheet.org/Research/VincentD/Brothers%20HR%20in%20Same%20Game.pdf.

5 "San Diego Padres," *The Sporting News*, July 30, 2001: 35.

6 *Baseball Prospectus 2002*, https://www.baseballprospectus.com/player/607/cesar-crespo/.

7 *Baseball Prospectus 2004*, https://www.baseballprospectus.com/player/607/cesar-crespo/.

8 David Borges, "Merloni Delivers for Cleveland," *Middletown* (Connecticut) *Press*, March 19, 2004. https://www.middletownpress.com/news/article/Merloni-delivers-for-Cleveland-11912453.php.

9 Crespo interview.

10 Box score, Boston Red Sox at Kansas City Royals, June 6, 2004, https://www.baseball-reference.com/boxes/KCA/KCA200406060.shtml. The collision can be seen on YouTube: https://www.youtube.com/watch?v=gyRW1idNr6k.

11 Box score, Boston Red Sox at New York Yankees, July 1, 2004, https://www.baseball-reference.com/boxes/NYA/NYA200407010.shtml.

12 Christina Karl, "Transaction Analysis: July 1-5," *Baseball Prospectus*, July 8, 2004. https://www.baseballprospectus.com/news/article/3049/transaction-analysis-july-1-5/#BOS. The writer's analysis: "[I]t's interesting to see that the Sox chose to keep a backup right-handed bat like Dave McCarty over a spare speedy utilityman like Crespo. … Crespo struggled pretty badly in a reserve role, so it isn't like he did much to help himself."

13 Phil O'Neill, "Sox Can Finally Field Full Lineup – Mueller Returns from Surgery," *Worcester* (Massachusetts) *Telegram & Gazette*, July 3, 2004: B4.

14 Bob Hohler, "Crespo Gets Short End of the Stick," *Boston Globe*, July 3, 2004: G5.

15 "Crespo Gets Short End of the Stick."

16 Bill Ballou, "Sadly, Many Red Sox Bit Players Kept Up with Jones," *Worcester Telegram & Gazette*, October 3, 2004: D8.

17 "Crespo Gets Short End of the Stick."

18 César Crespo Facebook Profile, https://www.facebook.com/cesar.c.claudio/about_work_and_education.

JOHNNY DAMON

BY MARK S. STERNMAN

A run-scoring-machine leadoff hitter with great speed (408 career steals) and good power (235 homers), Johnny Damon had "good range defensively but ... one of the worst outfield arms in the big leagues."[1] Offensively, Damon had his best years with Kansas City in 2000 and Boston in 2004, and won World Series titles with both the Red Sox in 2004 and the Yankees in 2009. Damon's legacy largely stems from his starring role in leading the Red Sox to the franchise's first championship in 86 years, notoriety that says as much about the outsized role of baseball in the Boston landscape and Damon's media-friendly personality as it does about Damon's considerable on-field accomplishments.

Johnny Damon owes his life to the Vietnam War. His parents, Jimmy and Yome, met in his mother's native Thailand, where his father served as a U.S. Army sergeant. Yome's father practiced holistic medicine, and his mother farmed. Yome gave birth to James Damon in Bangkok in 1971 and to Johnny in Kansas two years later. The family moved first to Illinois before settling in Florida, where Jimmy worked as a security guard and Yome as an office cleaner. "Johnny was like Yome, all nervous energy," an observer wrote. "Once, when he was 14, he took his mother's car to Daytona. ... Stopped by a police officer, Johnny said he'd forgotten his license. When asked his name, he gave the name of his big brother. The ruse worked ... when the officer didn't show up for the court date."[2]

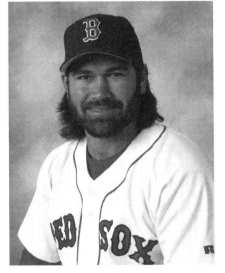

Leading up to the 1992 draft, *The Sporting News* called Damon, then a senior, "probably ... the best high school player available this year. 'He has great speed, is extremely strong, and his throwing has improved,' [Damon's] high school coach Danny Allie says. 'He's also got great power ... and 3.8-second speed to first base. A lot of guys have compared him to Ken Griffey Jr.'"[3]

Kansas City drafted Damon with the 35th pick in the first round of the 1992 draft. "A straight-A student in high school, he walked away from a baseball scholarship at the University of Florida to sign with the Royals for $300,000"[4] Aside from his future teammate Derek Jeter, Damon would have the best career of his fellow first-round draftees.

Displaying the same skills that he would show in the majors, Damon hit for average, stole scores of bases, and flashed occasional power in the minors. He won the J.G. Taylor Spink Award as the National Association Minor League Player of the Year for his performance in Wichita in 1995 even though he did not play a full season in Double A that year.

Called up from Wichita, Damon made his major-league debut against Seattle on August 12, 1995, leading off and playing center field. Facing Tim Belcher, Damon popped out to short in his first AL plate appearance. After flying out in his second at-bat, he tripled and scored in the fifth inning against Belcher, had an RBI single in the sixth off Salomón Torres, and singled against Torres again in the eighth as the Royals won, 7-2.

On August 31, Kansas City trailed Milwaukee 6-5 going into the bottom of the ninth. Damon hit his first homer in the majors to tie the game off Mike Fetters, and the Royals won in unusual walk-off fashion thanks to a bases-loaded throwing error on a pickoff attempt by Fetters. Damon's teammates had quickly taken to the talented rookie. "He's our sparkplug right now," first baseman Wally Joyner said.[5] "He's going to do just about everything you could want…," Royals manager Bob Boone said. "I'm pleased he's this good. But I'm not surprised."[6]

On August 10, 1996, Damon set a career high with seven RBIs in an 18-3 win over the Angels. But "he slumped near season's end ... as his confidence fell."[7]

After beginning 1997 as Kansas City's fourth outfielder, Damon rebounded somewhat although he had a career-worst 61.5 percent stolen-base rate, perhaps due to knee soreness that worsened in July and would necessitate offseason surgery.[8] Retrospectively, Damon credited Tony Muser, who replaced Boone for the second half of the season, with his resurgence. Damon recalled, "My first couple years, I didn't play every day. I would sit against left-handers sometimes. And then when Muser started managing ... he said, 'Guess what? You're going to be batting leadoff for me every day, and the only times you're not going to play is if you break something.'"[9]

Damon scored 100 runs for the first of 10 times in his career in 1998. In 1999, he hit over .300 for the first of five times for a Kansas City team that went 64-97 in spite of a strong outfield with Damon in left, Carlos Beltrán in center, and Jermaine Dye in right.

Damon's improved play ironically shortened his time with the Royals, as the small-market Kansas City franchise risked losing him for nothing as he approached free agency after the

2001 season. *The Sporting News* reported rumors of Damon going to the Yankees for Alfonso Soriano,[10] to the Mariners for Griffey Jr.,[11] or to the Dodgers for Eric Gagné.[12]

"There are clubs with higher payrolls in bigger markets that would give anything to have Johnny, because he's the one piece that a club thinks can cement the playoffs or World Series," said Royals general manager Hank Robinson.[13]

Because of or despite the rumors, Damon had his best year in a Kansas City uniform in 2000 with career highs in plate appearances (741), at-bats (655), runs (136), hits (214), doubles (42), steals (46), batting average (.327), on-base percentage (.382), slugging percentage (.495), OPS (.877), and total bases (324). He led the AL in both runs and steals.

In June, the Royals reportedly offered Damon a three-year contract for $15 million. "But Damon is adamant about a five-year deal," *The Sporting News* reported, adding, "He also labeled the average yearly salary Boston gave José Offerman, $6.5 million, as his 'starting point.'"[14]

Damon batted .436 in July 2000, .382 in August, and .322 in September. Kansas City had tapped Allard Baird as GM to replace Robinson. Baird, the scout who had signed Damon for the Royals, upped the KC contract offer to $32 million over five years, which agent Scott Boras rejected on Damon's behalf.[15]

Recognizing that Kansas City could not keep Damon, Baird shipped him to Oakland as part of a three-way deal that also involved Tampa Bay. "I was in Kansas City for five years," Damon said. "I had a home there. I had my family there. I had everything. It was great for me there, except for losing."[16]

Damon also liked hitting in Kansas City. "It plays fair. The waterfalls are cool. When I came up in the league, that was one of the toughest places to hit and to hit home runs. But as I developed, and as the years have gone by, it has become one of the easiest for me."[17]

Damon left the losing behind with the Royals. The A's had gone 91-70 in 2000 before falling to the Yankees in five games in the ALDS. Damon thought that he could help make Oakland take the next step. "Looking at this team on paper, I think we're the team to beat out there," Damon said. … "This is a great situation to be in."[18]

With Damon, Oakland improved to 102-60, but Seattle, which had also won 91 games in 2000, captured 116 in 2001. Damon did not enjoy his first trip as a visiting player to Kansas City, where "a radio station sponsored a 'Boo Johnny Damon Day' … including a sweepstakes for a free big-screen TV if he committed an error."[19]

The A's returned to the playoffs via the wild card but did so with only modest contributions from Damon, who failed to hit 10 homers for the only time from 1998 to 2009. Damon blamed it "partly (on) the A's strategy that calls for hitters to work the count to tire opposing pitchers. As a result, he said, he was less aggressive and found himself facing more two-strike counts."[20] Oakland would again face New York in the ALDS.

The series began in the Bronx. In his first career playoff game, Damon went 4-for-4 with a walk and two steals as the A's won 5-3. In Game Two, Damon doubled off Andy Pettitte and tripled off Mariano Rivera. Damon scored an insurance run after the triple as the A's triumphed 2-0 and needed just one win to advance to the ALCS. "It's hard to believe he was being called one of baseball's biggest disappointments at midseason and was being followed by rumors that he would be traded … because his contract was up at season's end. 'I know that he was very hard on himself for a time,' A's manager Art Howe said. 'Sometimes it just takes a person time to get adjusted to his surroundings.'"[21]

Neither Damon nor Oakland could keep up the good start. Damon went 3-for-13 as the Yankees won the last three games, eliminating the A's again and ending Damon's brief sojourn in Oakland as he signed with Boston as a free agent. "Damon wanted to play closer to his Florida home, where he and his wife, Angie, are raising twins who [turned] 3 in [2002]. 'Oakland did everything in their power to sign me,' Damon said. 'The biggest thing was the moving back to the Eastern time zone. It boiled down to my family.'"[22]

Boston won 82 games in 2001, but 93 games with Damon in 2002. "I had a feeling about this team when I signed in the offseason because of the attitude I bring," said Damon … "[W]ith guys like Rickey Henderson, Carlos Baerga, and Tony Clark … I feel we can do something special here."[23]

Damon brought both swagger and swat to Boston. "Damon has … been … the heart of the team," said [Sox teammate Pedro] Martínez. "He has done everything. He gets on base. He puts pressure on the other teams – on the catcher and the pitcher."[24] Damon led the American League with 11 triples, made his first All-Star team, and "benefited from the tutelage of hitting instructor Dwight Evans. Early in spring training, Evans noticed that Damon was releasing his top hand too soon, and he got Damon to keep both hands on the bat."[25]

In 2001, Damon started poorly but finished strongly. He did the reverse in 2002 when he "went through a difficult divorce from his high-school sweetheart, which may have affected him even more deeply than his active role in labor negotiations and the knee injury that slowed him but did not require postseason surgery."[26] Boston failed to make the playoffs in 2002, but reached the postseason in the remaining three years of Damon's Hub tenure.

Damon must have had flashbacks entering the 2003 ALDS. In his second playoffs, he faced Oakland, the team that had first taken him to the postseason. As in 2001, the A's won the first two games and needed just one more win to advance to the ALCS. Oakland lost the third game, 3-1, and the fourth game, 5-4, thanks in part to Damon hitting a two-run homer (the first of his 10 career playoff bombs) and throwing out José Guillén attempting to go first-to-third on a single.

Facing Barry Zito, Boston trailed 1-0 going into the top of the sixth of the deciding game. Jason Varitek homered to tie the game, and Damon followed with a walk. With two outs and two on, Manny Ramírez homered to give Boston a 4-1 edge. Behind Martinez, the Red Sox led 4-2 in the bottom of the seventh with two outs "when Jermaine Dye lifted a pop fly into shallow center. [Second baseman Damian] Jackson … sprinted into the outfield … while Damon came charging in, calling for the ball. The ball … landed in Jackson's … glove when … the right side of Jackson's head squarely struck Damon's head, also on the right side."[27]

Damon left the game in the next inning for a pinch-hitter, and the Red Sox held on to win in spite of Damon's departure due to a concussion. Later that week, Damon admitted, "I had no idea what was going on for the next four or five hours. … I was in really bad shape."[28]

Boston faced New York in an epic ALCS. Damon missed the first two games before returning to go 3-for-4 in Game Three, but he went just 1-for-16 in the final four games. Damon missed a key chance to blow the deciding contest wide open when Boston led 4-0 in the top of the fourth with runners on first and third and none out as Mike Mussina replaced Roger Clemens. Mussina fanned Varitek and induced a double play from Damon to keep the margin at four runs. The Yankees rallied to win the game and the pennant, 6-5, on Aaron Boone's 11th-inning walk-off homer.

Damon and Boston got their revenge in 2004. Damon set career highs with 94 RBIs and 76 walks. After not getting his hair cut in the offseason, Damon became "a cult figure virtually overnight."[29] As the longtime *Boston Globe* columnist Bob Ryan opined, "Johnny Damon is, and has always been, a good player, beard or no beard, hair down to his tushie or hair neatly cropped. He is a leadoff man whose job is to get on base and ignite an offense, and if you measure his value by looking at runs you'd have to say he's been pretty good."[30]

A master marketer, Damon rebranded the supposedly cursed Red Sox as carefree idiots, commenting, "Maybe it's not the greatest thing to say, but for the most part, we are. We just play the game. … We're not too bright of [*sic*] guys. In essence, we're idiots. We go out there and swing the bat as hard as we can. We make fun. … We've got the long hair, the ponytails."[31]

Boston swept Anaheim in the ALDS to set up an ALCS rematch against New York. The Red Sox dropped the first two games in the Bronx as Damon struggled. "It starts with me," said Damon, who fanned four times in four at-bats in the Game One loss, and followed with an 0-for-4, including one more strikeout, in Game Two. "I take full responsibility for these two games. … I'm very disappointed with myself."[32]

Boston returned to Fenway Park only to get shellacked 19-8. After the rout, Damon faced the media and confessed, "We're very upset. And we're definitely stunned. We thought we had the better team coming in and right now it doesn't look that way."[33]

The prospects of the Red Sox brightened after Boston won the next three games to force an elimination contest. Damon led off with a single and stole second, but a relay from Hideki Matsui to Jeter to Jorge Posada cut him down trying to score on a Ramirez single. The Red Sox led 2-0 in the second inning when Damon came up to bat against Javier Vázquez, who had just relieved Kevin Brown. On Vázquez's first pitch, Damon hit a grand slam that gave Boston an insurmountable lead. Damon later hit a two-run homer against Vázquez as well en route to a 10-3 win. "To do this against the Yankees in their ballpark is definitely a very special feeling," Damon said after the win that gave the Red Sox the AL pennant.[34]

Damon's postseason power continued as Boston sought to end its 86 years of baseball misery. He "ignited the Red Sox … with his left-field double in the first inning off Woody Williams that put the team on its way to an 11-9 win over the St. Louis Cardinals in Game 1 of the World Series. … 'This is the World Series, so you want to make an impact out there,' Damon said."[35]

Damon started the championship clincher with "a rope into the Cardinals' bullpen on the game's fourth pitch from Jason Marquis."[36] He later tripled as Boston swept St. Louis to win the 2004 World Series.

Helping bring the title back to a rabid baseball-championship-starved fan base transformed Damon from a baseball cult figure to a boldfaced name with broader celebrity appeal in Boston,[37] partially fulfilling a prediction Damon made at his post-signing press conference in Boston: "When we win a World Series," he said, "we're going to be put on a pedestal and be immortalized forever."[38] In Damon's case, the adulation lasted only a year, but the bitterness that began in 2006 lasted several seasons.[39]

In December 2004, he married for the second time, to Michelle Mangan, an event deemed worthy of a photo and extensive coverage on the society page of the *Boston Globe*.[40] But the Red Sox front office declined to engage with Damon as his contract approached its conclusion at the end of the 2005 season. "I'd like to finish my career here and get locked up for a long time," Damon said. "I know it's always been Red Sox policy to wait until after the season, but that can get hairy. … I'm in a good spot … but the Red Sox know that this is the best spot for me personally."[41]

For the second and last time in his career, Damon made the All-Star team in 2005, this time as a starter. He also had a 29-game hitting streak that ended in a loss to Tampa Bay. "I definitely felt like if I could have gotten past today, I could have taken it further," said Damon. "The funny thing is, the swing really hasn't felt great during this streak, and I'm amazed that it got up to 29."[42]

Boston's quick dismissal from the playoffs after an ALDS sweep by Chicago made Damon's regular-season accomplishments less meaningful. With the Red Sox trailing by a run in the sixth inning of the final game with two outs and the bases loaded, Damon worked the count full against Orlando Hernández. In his autobiography, published after the 2004 World Series, Damon had mockingly touched on the unique stylings of Hernández, writing, "He's one of those 50-year-old Cuban pitchers with all the funky motions and all the funny pitches and different speeds, but he knows what to do. … If he doesn't have his good stuff, he starts innovating."[43]

Hernández did indeed know what to do. "After a foul, El Duque fooled Damon with a wicked breaking ball that wound up in the dirt. Damon committed with his swing and was rung up to end the inning. 'The right pitch at the right time,' conceded Damon."[44] In his final plate appearance in a Boston uniform, Damon struck out swinging again for the second out of the ninth inning in a game the Red Sox lost, 5-3.

A month later, Boras began advocating for his free-agent client with a paper that "confidently predicts that Damon will join the 3,000 hit club in 2012, and … dares to place Damon in the company of Hall of Famers if he produces through 2015 the way he has [from 2002-2005]."[45]

The Red Sox offered Damon $42 million over four years,[46] but he signed with the Yankees for $52 million over four years instead. The *Boston Globe* editorialized on Damon's departure. In a particularly poor piece of Christmas Eve prognostication, Boston's paper of record wrote, "Marvelous as the beloved Idiot was in that championship season of '04, Red Sox fans needs to cast a cold eye on the future value of a weak-armed 32-year-old center fielder stationed in 2009 in the great expanse of Yankee Stadium."[47]

In 2006, Damon hit a career-high 24 homers in his first season in the Bronx, a figure he matched in 2009, when he brought great value to the Yankees outfield. In August 2006, a Boston writer conceded that Damon "has been worth every bit of the extra $12 million George Steinbrenner ponied up to take him away from the Red Sox. The Yankees got a very good player while taking one away from their biggest competition."[48]

While New York won the division with 97 wins in 2006, Damon could not deliver in the playoffs against Detroit, which knocked out New York in four ALDS games. Michelle gave birth to her first child and Johnny's third after the 2006 season. (They had a second child together after the 2008 season.) The Yanks slipped to 94 wins in 2007, which secured a wild card. In the ALDS, New York dropped the first two games at Cleveland and trailed 3-1 in Game Three going into the bottom of the fifth in the Bronx. Melky Cabrera hit an RBI single to cut the deficit to a single run, and Damon then hit a three-run homer as the Yanks rallied to an 8-4 win. But the Indians won the fourth game, meaning that Damon and New York had in consecutive years lost the ALDS in four games.

Under new manager Joe Girardi, the Yankees regressed and missed the playoffs in 2008. For the first time since 1999, Damon made most of his outfield starts in left rather than center field. His lighter defensive responsibilities may have led to his improved offensive performance. On June 7, Damon went 6-for-6 against Kansas City to tie a team record for hits in a game. His two-run single in the eighth tied the game at 10-10. After a David DeJesus homer in the ninth put the Royals back up 11-10, Posada tied the game with a homer in the bottom of the ninth before Damon hit a walk-off RBI single to give New York a wild 12-11 win.

In 2009, Damon relinquished his leadoff role to Jeter[49] and his center-field spot to Cabrera. The Yankees won 103 games for the first time since 2002 and got past the ALDS for the first time since 2004.

Damon made his most memorable contribution in pinstripes in Game Four of the World Series at Philadelphia. With the game tied, 4-4, two outs, and none on in the top of the ninth, Damon faced Brad Lidge and won a "nine-pitch battle … that sparked the winning rally. After going down, 0-2, he fouled off a number of pitches before lining a single into short left field. … Girardi called it 'an incredible at-bat.'"[50]

With Mark Teixeira up, the Phillies shifted to the right side of the infield with the switch-hitter batting lefty against the righty Lidge. Damon took off for second on the first pitch. After third baseman Pedro Feliz fielded the short-hop throw, Damon, after a brief hesitation, popped out of his slide and took off for the uncovered third base with Feliz in futile pursuit.[51] Damon received credit for two stolen bases on the play and, from one longtime Philadelphia baseball writer, credit for transforming the whole World Series.[52] "I'm just glad that when I started running, I still had some of my young legs behind me," Damon quipped.[53]

Lidge, possibly unnerved by his failure to cover third, then hit Teixeira. Álex Rodríguez doubled in Damon for a 5-4 lead, and Posada singled in two more runners to put New York up 7-4. Rivera preserved the win, putting New York up three games to one in the Series that the Yankees took in six games.

Seemingly picking a good time to go back into free agency, Damon and his agent Boras played a good hand weakly. The Yankees offered Damon a two-year contract for $14 million; Boras countered with $20 million over two years. New York turned down Boras, and Damon signed with Detroit for $8 million for the 2010 season.[54] Leaving the Tigers after a year, Damon joined Tampa Bay for 2011 and played in 150 games for the first time since 2004. The Rays made the playoffs, and Damon, batting fifth as the DH, got Tampa on the board with a two-run homer in Game One off C.J. Wilson in the only contest the Rays won as Texas took the ALDS.

Playing for his fourth team in four years, Damon signed with Cleveland after the 2012 season had already begun. Damon lasted less than four months with the Indians before the team released him. In November 2012, Damon joined Thailand as it attempted to qualify for the 2013 World Baseball Classic. "I'm enjoying the experience of playing for my mom's country," Damon wrote in a text to a reporter.[55]

In spite of his desire to keep playing, Damon's career ended with Thailand. As a famous former athlete, Damon appeared on reality TV shows such as *Celebrity Apprentice* in 2015 and *Dancing with the Stars* in 2018.

Baseball analyst Jay Jaffe aptly summed up Damon's career: "He was a very good and very popular player for a long time, but not quite enough for Cooperstown."[56] Underappreciated in the smaller media markets of Kansas City and Oakland, Damon thrived in a leadership role in Boston and continued to excel as a member of a strong supporting cast in the Bronx before becoming a baseball vagabond for the remainder of his impressive career as a professional hitter.

NOTES

1 Steve Rock, "Kansas City," *The Sporting News*, May 1, 2000: 36. Damon had a good glove to go along with his weak arm. His "major league-best streak of 249 games without an error ended … on August 31[, 2002] when he could not cleanly come up with a ground ball that turned out to be a game-winning hit. Damon had not committed an error in 592 chances dating back to August 27, 2000." Michael Silverman, "Boston Red Sox," *The Sporting News*, September 16, 2002: 63.

2 Gordon Edes, "Fortune of Soldier," *Boston Globe*, February 10, 2002.

3 Mike Eisenbath, "Martinez Follows in the Big Man's Footsteps," *The Sporting News*, May 11, 1992: 34.

4 Bob Hohler, "Johnny on the Spot," *Boston Globe*, March 29, 2002.

5 Dick Kaegel, "Kansas City Royals," *The Sporting News*, September 11, 1995: 28.

6 Alan Schwarz, "The Meaning of Johnny Damon," *Baseball America*, February 19-March 3, 1996: 12. This article and several others referenced below come from the National Baseball Hall of Fame and Museum's file on Damon. Thanks to Reference Librarian Cassidy Lent for scanning the Damon file.

7 La Velle E. Neal III, "Kansas City Royals," *The Sporting News*, November 25, 1996: 31.

8 Dick Kaegel, "Kansas City Royals," *The Sporting News*, September 1, 1997: 35.

9 "When It Clicked: Johnny Damon, Yankees," *Washington Post*, September 6, 2009.

10 Luciana Chavez, "Kansas City," *The Sporting News*, December 13, 1999: 65.

11 Jon Heyman, "Inside Dish," *The Sporting News*, January 10, 2000: 61.

12 Jason Reid, "Los Angeles," *The Sporting News*, July 17, 2000: 56.

13 Jeff Pearlman, "Force Three: The Hard-Hitting Young Kansas City Outfield Storms to the Top," *Sports Illustrated*, April 17, 2000.

14 Steve Rock, "Kansas City," *The Sporting News*, June 19, 2000: 29.

15 Gordon Edes, "He Can't Give Sox Royal Treatment," *Boston Globe*, November 12, 2000.

16 Chris Snow, "Damon Finds a Home Again," *Boston Globe*, June 8, 2002.

17 Steve DiMeglio, "Five Minutes with … Johnny Damon," *USA Today Sports Weekly*, May 19-25, 2004: 24.

18 Thomas Hill, "With A's, He's Johnny Dangerously," *New York Daily News*, February 28, 2001.

19 Bob Hohler, "Damon Loyal, but Not a Royal," *Boston Globe*, April 21, 2002.

20 Bob Hohler, "Leadoff Man Damon Sets a Positive Tone," *Boston Globe*, February 20, 2002.

21 Roger Rubin, "Damon Center of Revival," *New York Daily News*, October 13, 2001.

22 Bob Hohler and Gordon Edes, "Damon Touches Down," *Boston Globe*, December 21, 2001.

23 Gordon Edes, "No Waiting Damon," *Boston Globe*, April 23, 2002.

24 Michael Vega, "Starring Role for Damon," *Boston Globe*, June 27, 2002.

25 Nick Cafardo, "Damon Touches Bases," *Boston Globe*, May 1, 2002.

26 Gordon Edes, "Damon Not Buying A's Owner's Story," *Boston Globe*, March 17, 2003.

27 Gordon Edes, "Damon Hospitalized after Collision," *Boston Globe*, October 7, 2003. Damon and Jackson "couldn't hear one another in the loud playoff din, which is not uncommon." Roger Rubin, "Head Clear, Damon Takes Center Stage," *New York Daily News*, October 11, 2003.

28 Peter Botte, "Damon Likely Out Till Game 3," *New York Daily News*, October 9, 2003.

29 Jackie MacMullan, "Johnny on the Spot," *Boston Globe*, October 15, 2004.

30 Bob Ryan, "Damon Has Been Johnny on the Spot in This Heat Wave," *Boston Globe*, July 10, 2004.

31 Nick Cafardo, "Damon Is Having a Recurrence of Migraines," *Boston Globe*, October 8, 2004.

32 Kevin Paul Dupont, "A Low Point from the Top of the Order," *Boston Globe*, October 14, 2004. Damon credited Mussina for his sparkling performance in the opener. "He was pretty awesome. For him to make me look silly like that all day, that doesn't happen too often," said Damon, who was also fanned by Tom Gordon for the first out in the eighth. Peter Botte, "Damon Still in Swing," *New York Daily News*, October 14, 2004.

33 Roger Rubin, "Bosox Tipping Caps to Yanks but Damon Still Has Faith," *New York Daily News*, October 17, 2004.

34 Julian Garcia, "Damon's Suddenly Mane Man," *New York Daily News*, October 21, 2004.

35 Nick Cafardo, "Damon Takes the Lead," *Boston Globe*, October 24, 2004.

36 Jim McCabe, "Again, the Winners Were Happy Followers of Damon," *Boston Globe*, October 28, 2004.

37 "Damon was listed in the *Boston Herald* gossip column 64 times in 2004, or roughly once every five days." Tom Verducci, "The Yankee Clipper," *Sports Illustrated*, February 13, 2006: 64.

38 Bob Hohler, "Johnny Damon, Superstar," *Boston Globe*, July 11, 2005.

39 "I get booed. They absolutely despise me. I just have to say, 'You're welcome for '04. You're welcome for making it fun again over there.'" Peter Abraham, "Damon's Got Ear to Ground," *Boston Globe*, April 11, 2011.

40 Carol Beggy and Mark Shanahan, "Damon's Wedding Is a Rocking Hit for All," *Boston Globe*, December 31, 2004. Mangan also briefly became a minor media celebrity in Boston. A profile of her revealed that "Mangan and Damon both like Boston. 'It's a lot prettier than New York,' she says though there has been talk that he will head to the Yankees should the call come. 'I can't see him in a Yankees uniform,' Mangan says." Bella English, "Batting Around with Michelle Mangan," *Boston Globe*, October 1, 2005. Damon signed with the Yankees three months and two days after this article appeared.

41 Nick Cafardo, "Damon Enjoying Star Turn," *Boston Globe*, March 10, 2005.

42 Mike Petraglia, "Damon's Hit Streak Snapped at 29 games," MLB.com, July 19, 2005.

43 Johnny Damon with Peter Golenbock, *Idiot* (New York: Crown Publishers, 2005), 201. In a masterstroke of snarky brevity, columnist Dan Shaughnessy called the book "a work often compared with Tolstoy's 'Anna Karenina' and Dostoyevsky's 'Notes From the

44 Dan Shaughnessy, "Curses, Again," *Boston Globe*, October 8, 2005.

45 Gordon Edes, "What to Read into All This? Some Odd Chapters on Epstein, Damon," *Boston Globe*, November 23, 2005. In fact, Damon got his last hit, number 2,769, in 2012. He received a paltry 1.9 percent share of the 2018 Hall of Fame balloting. As Shaughnessy wrote, "I just got through checking out Scott Boras's dossier on Johnny, and until now I had no idea Johnny was better than both Willie Mays and Joe DiMaggio. What a crock." Dan Shaughnessy, "Is Johnny Damon Worth $10M a Year?" *Boston Globe*, November 27, 2005.

46 Gordon Edes and Chris Snow, "Damon Jumps to Yankees," *Boston Globe*, December 21, 2005.

47 "Steinbrenner's Folly," *Boston Globe*, December 24, 2005.

48 Nick Cafardo, "Damon Is Long Gone But Not Hard to Find," *Boston Globe*, August 19, 2006.

49 "When Girardi made the move, he stated a number of times that 'Johnny is really good at moving the runners over.' Clearly, the move was made to keep Jeter from hitting into so many double plays, as well…. Damon also pointed out that the move allowed him to really go for the long ball every once in a while." Kevin Kernan, *Girardi: Passion in Pinstripes* (Chicago: Triumph Books, 2012), 174.

50 Nick Cafardo, "Damon Smarter Than Most Idiots," *Boston Globe*, November 2, 2009.

51 youtube.com/watch?v=cCfmj6mnNoI (accessed May 21, 2018).

52 Jayson Stark, "Damon Steals the Show in Game 4," ESPN, November 1, 2009.

53 Nick Cafardo, "Damon, Yankees on the Verge," *Boston Globe*, November 2, 2009.

54 Bob Klapsich, "Johnny Damon, Scott Boras Really Blew This One," NorthJersey.com, February 23, 2010.

55 Benjamin Hoffman, "Unsigned for 2013, Damon Takes an International Step to a Possible Last Hurrah," *New York Times*, November 14, 2012.

56 Jay Jaffe, "One-and-Dones Pt. 3: Johnny Damon, Hideki Matsui Were Popular, but not Hall of Famers," *Sports Illustrated*, December 28, 2017.

A RED SOX MEMORY

The Red Sox were handed down to me paternally and pessimistically.

I remember telling my dad at 10 years old, down 3-0 in the '04 ALCS, "They could still come back." Was it pure ignorance for the probability of that happening or just untainted hope?

The 2004 season ignited my love for the Sox. For Neil Diamond, for the Dropkick Murphys, for batting helmets caked in pine tar, for giant illuminated Coke bottles, and for winning titles. I enjoyed it so much in 2004, I thought, "Why not do it three more times?"

ALEXANDER REARDON

MECHANICAL ENGINEERING CLASS OF 2017
VIRGINIA TECH

A RED SOX MEMORY

I was at Game Four of the ALCS at Fenway against the Yankees.

The Saturday night 19-8 loss in Game Three was vicious; it was almost like the Pinstripes were letting us know that we should realize we didn't belong on the same field.

I was at Game Four with my son. Tying it up in the ninth, winning in the 12th just felt so different, even though we were still down, three games to one. Day by day, game by game, it didn't matter how late we went to bed. There was so much electricity in the city. Winning the final two in New York topped it all. We knew the curse was going to be over. And we knew nothing would ever top this ALCS. Sweeping the Cards was great, but coming back with four straight wins over the Yankees provides the most vivid memories.

Loved the team, loved the chemistry.

VICTOR SON

CURRENT TOUR GUIDE AT FENWAY PARK.

BRIAN DAUBACH

BY KARL CICITTO

Brian Daubach was a first baseman-DH who was trapped in the minor leagues from 1990 to 1998. In 1999 he played for the Boston Red Sox and became a 27-year-old rookie sensation, earning the nickname "The Bellville Basher." From 1999 to 2002, Daubach hit 20 or more home runs for Boston in his first four seasons. After a year with the White Sox in 2003, he returned to the Hub and played 30 games for the 2004 Red Sox. His curse-busting teammates voted him a World Series winner's share and the team gave him a World Championship ring.

Daubach was known as a 4A hitter – too good for Triple A but not good enough for the major leagues. A minor adjustment to his batting approach in his sixth pro season transformed him.

Daubach overcame two major knee surgeries. Forged by a long, difficult path to the big leagues, he has coached and managed in the minor leagues for the Washington Nationals since 2011 with a humble, relatable style.

Brian Michael Daubach was born on February 11, 1972, in Belleville, Illinois, to Dale and Angie (Frisch) Daubach. His father was a letter carrier and his mother was a bookkeeper. He has two younger brothers, Brent and Brad. Brian grew up a Cardinals fan and attended the 1982 World Series with his family at Busch Stadium, 16 miles from Belleville.[1]

As of 2023 Brad was a special-education director at a high school, and Brent worked in stadium construction and was given a 2004 NLCS championship ring by the Cardinals, his employer at the time.[2]

Daubach played baseball for the Belleville American Legion, the St. Louis Flames youth team and Belleville Township High School West. As a senior at West, he was selected for the *St Louis Post-Dispatch's* All Metro first team,[3] batting .462 with 12 home runs.[4]

After graduating, Daubach was taken in the 17th round of the June 1990 amateur draft by the New York Mets. He was scouted by George Walden and signed on June 15, 1990, receiving a $30,000 bonus. He passed on a scholarship to attend St. Louis University.

Daubach debuted in professional baseball with the Gulf Coast Mets. He started poorly, batting below .200. Then a 30-game tear, a precursor of future streakiness, helped bring him to a respectable .270 final batting average. He returned home and started classes at Southern Illinois University; his backup plan to baseball was teaching or coaching.[5]

The Mets kept Daubach in rookie ball in 1991 with Kingsport in the Appalachian League. He improved defensively at first base, batted .243, and recognized that he was prone to striking out.[6]

In November of 1991, Daubach heard a crack in his knee while playing racquetball. He tore several ligaments, including the anterior cruciate, and underwent surgery. The injury cost him six weeks of spring training in 1992 before he joined the short-season Class-A Pittsfield Mets.[7] A year later, he had another knee surgery for a microfracture.

Daubach adjusted to playing first base with a knee brace in the cooler climes of Pittsfield, Massachusetts. He found it challenging to hit in Wahconah Park with its outsized dimensions – 440 feet in right center – for instance. His home runs dropped from seven to two. He was third on the team in strikeouts.

Over the next five seasons, Daubach worked his way through the Mets system. By 1995 he had improved marginally. In the midst of the player strike, he agreed to be a replacement player in spring of 1995 if the owners decided to start the season without Players Association members, but they did not.[8]

In 1996, Daubach's seventh professional season, he made a quantum leap, batting .296 with 22 home runs and 76 RBIs with Double-A Binghamton. The 24-year-old found his power stroke. But Daubach's path to the big leagues got more complicated. The Mets placed first baseman Roberto Petagine ahead of Daubach in Triple A.[9]

In October 1996 Daubach was informed by Mets general manager Steve Philips that he was being left off the 40-man roster and was a free agent.[10]

The Florida Marlins were the first to approach him. Daubach played winter ball for the Navegantes del Magallanes in Venezuela, where he batted .347 and, surprisingly, was among the league leaders in triples.[11] The Marlins watched him excel in the winter playoffs and signed him.

"The Marlins were an expansion team at the time," said Daubach, "but they were on their way and I was excited I was going to go to major-league spring training (with them) for the first time and they offered me $8,000 per month which was a whole lot of money to me back then because I'd never made more than $10,000 a year."[12]

He was assigned to the Triple-A Charlotte Knights for 1997. Charlotte manager Carlos Tosca expressed confidence in him from the start.[13]

Daubach delivered for the Knights. In 1997, he batted .278 with 21 home runs and 93 RBIs. In 1998 he had a monster year: He hit .316 with 35 home runs and 124 RBIs. He led the International League in round-trippers, RBIs, and doubles (45). He was in the top six for batting average and hits.[14] The word was that Daubach had learned to pull the ball effectively.[15]

Confirming that, Daubach explained "That is very true.... It was a minor adjustment I had to make in learning how to pull the ball. (I was) like a lot of the young players I work with now. Most of my HRs were opposite field (before I corrected) if I hit a ball to my pull side it would have topspin and be a double or the right fielder would catch it. I really believed I could do it the next year. I was happy to get a chance to come back to the Mets because one year I hit .240 or .250 with 10 home runs and as a first baseman, that doesn't bode well usually.... I was able to turn the corner the next year. ... Sometimes minor things go a long way when you talk about how really close hitting is ... then you feel better. It frees up your swing. That was really the only adjustment I needed and I was off and running."[16]

The humble Daubach deflected praise, adding: "Charlotte was a good place to hit. Small ballpark. I took advantage of it. And we had a great lineup around me, too."[17]

Daubach played in 10 games for the Marlins in 1998, making his major-league debut on September 10. His first major-league hit – a double – and first RBI came on September 26 against the Phillies' Curt Schilling.

Despite the outstanding season in Charlotte, Daubach was released by the Marlins on November 19, 1998. There were at least several possible explanations. He was going to be 27 years old in 1999. He was blocked from the Marlins roster at first base, where Derrek Lee was in place, and in the corner outfielder positions, where Mark Kotsay and Cliff Floyd were becoming settled in their roles. All three players were first-round draft picks.

"He was disillusioned when the Marlins released him. He was crushed. I think he was ready to go to Japan," said Jim Brueggeman, an old friend and a teacher from Belleville.[18]

On December 18, 1998, Daubach broke off talks with a Japanese team. He had received a call from Boston's general manager, Dan Duquette. The Red Sox signed Daubach to a minor-league contract and assigned him to Pawtucket for 1999. His contract called for $215,000. Since he had volunteered to be a replacement player, he did not receive the six-figure annual licensing pay that Players Association members get.[19]

Daubach's chances to make the club in spring training were iffy. Duquette brought in competition for the first-base job that opened when Mo Vaughn signed with the Angels. The field included former Rookie of the Year Bob Hamelin, 1998 holdover Midre Cummings, and veteran Mike Stanley. Reggie Jefferson was the incumbent at DH.

After Daubach hit a home run in spring training, Boston writer Gordon Edes referred to him in print as the Belleville Basher, a sobriquet that stuck.[20] (Tennis star Jimmy Connors was also from Daubach's hometown, and was nicknamed the Brash Basher of Belleville.)

Daubach played well that spring. On March 11 he came off the bench in the ninth inning and hit a two-out, two-run home run to walk off a 3-2 Boston win.[21] He tripled and notched two RBIs on March 13.[22] On March 19, he broke a 2-2 tie with a towering home run in the sixth inning of a 6-5 Boston win. At that time, Daubach was batting .357 and tied for the team lead in RBIs. Some observers assumed that he had made the team.[23]

Daubach finished spring training with a .313 average, 4 home runs, and 12 RBIs in 48 at-bats. He did well, though not as well as Stanley and Jefferson, who were slotted ahead of him. His performance was good enough, however, to make the Opening Day roster.[24]

The 27-year-old major-league rookie got into his first game of 1999 on April 9 and collected a double and a triple. But he was in just two more games before being sent to Pawtucket as Jefferson came off the injured list. The change seemed to make sense. The team had player options left on Daubach. Jefferson was under contract for $3,400,000, compared to Daubach at $215,000. Daubach returned to Boston, getting two hits on April 28. His playing time grew.

Through 14 games as of May 15, Daubach sported a .356 average and .431 OBP. He hit his first MLB home run, a dramatic one, on May 17. It was a two-out, three-run home run in the top of the ninth as Boston rallied for five runs in an 8-7 win in Toronto. (One sportswriter referred to Daubach in this game as Red Sox manager Jimy Williams's secret weapon, even somewhat secret to Williams himself.)[25]

On May 26 Daubach hit another ninth-inning home run to help the team save face in a 9-3 loss to the Yankees. On May 28 he hit a first-pitch homer in a 12-5 drubbing of Cleveland. He hit home runs in back-to-back games on May 31 and June 1; the latter was hit in the eighth inning and was decisive in a 5-4 win over Detroit. That blast was his second game-winning homer of the season. Daubach modestly told the press, "I don't know how I came through. I guess I'm just lucky in the clutch."[26]

On June 5 Daubach had three hits off the Braves' Greg Maddux and staked Boston to a 5-4 lead in the bottom of the eighth with an RBI single before the Red Sox bullpen blew it in the ninth. He was on an eight-game hitting streak with a .379 batting average.[27]

On June 7 Daubach hit his fifth home run in his last eight games.[28] On the 25th his two-run home run helped Boston to a 6-1 defeat of the White Sox.

On July 15 Daubach hit a home run to give the Red Sox a 6-3 lead in a win over the Phillies. He homered again on July 16 and again on July 24.

Daubach remained hot as a new month began. On August 1 he tied the Yankees in the fourth inning with a homer, doubled in the sixth, then scored to break the tie. Both teams continued to battle, and Boston hung on, 5-4.[29]

On August 4 Boston defeated Cleveland, 7-2, as Daubach reached base four times with two hits and two walks, part of scoring rallies in the first, fourth, and sixth innings.

Daubach then beat down the Angels in a three-game series in Anaheim. On August 6 his two-run homer made it 2-0, giving Boston all the runs needed to defeat the Angels, 5-1. The next night he got three hits including a double and a home run as the Red Sox bashed the Angels, 14-3. The following night, he doubled and homered again in a 9-3 victory.

Adding to this blissful run, Daubach homered and doubled in the same game for the third time in four games on August 10, this time in Kansas City. And he tripled in the in-between game on August 9, to boot.

Daubach did not cool down yet. On August 13 he had five RBIs on two doubles and a home run in an 11-6 victory over Seattle at Fenway Park.

Daubach's next game approached perfection. On August 14 he went 5-for-5 with six RBIs and his 19th home run of the season. That home run was his sixth in nine games; he batted .513 (20-for-39) with 20 RBIs in that span.

The lengthy streak was ending. As the season ground on, Daubach was tiring. He went 9-for-52 in September and October (.173).

Daubach finished his rookie season with a .294 average, 21 home runs, and 73 RBIs in 381 at-bats. He told this writer it had been a wild ride and that he was spent when September arrived. It was a lot to process for someone who had spent nine years in the minors and been released after an MVP-quality season in Triple A.

"You name it, (I felt) all the emotions that year. From making the team in spring training, to being sent down very early. I look back now, I was one of the last guys on the roster that had options and our pitching had gotten really thin, our starters had a couple of tough starts, our bullpen was thin. They had to send me down but Jimy Williams gave me his word that I'd be back in 10 days and I'd only have to stay down if someone else got hurt and sure enough, by May 15 I'm getting playing time (in Boston). It was quite the ride. I was very tired by the end of the year for sure. The emotions. I really struggled in September. I was having just a crazy year until September. It was a very emotional year for sure and something that made me stronger. Not only in baseball but through my life, and still does."[30]

The rookie was rewarded for his remarkable run when the Red Sox clinched the wild-card berth on September 29. They defeated Cleveland in the Division Series but lost to the Yankees in the Championship Series. He batted .212 in the postseason but hit a home run in each of those series.

Daubach was an important part of a joyous year. Fenway Park hosted the 1999 All-Star Game, when 80-year-old Ted Williams made a historic appearance. The team reached the postseason despite low expectations.[31]

Pedro Martínez struck out 313 batters and won his second Cy Young Award. Nomar Garciaparra batted .357 to lead the American League. The team advanced to the Championship Series for the first time since 1990.

Daubach contributed 31 multihit games. His 57 extra-base hits were fourth-best on the team despite his being a platoon player, getting 337 of his 381 at-bats against righties.

NESN, the TV network owned by the Red Sox, released a late-season promotional piece with a photo of Daubach that stated: "NESN delivers rookie sensation Brian Daubach and the Red Sox with 16 games in September!" In retrospect, Daubach thought that using him in this promotion was "crazy" given what Martínez and Garciaparra had done.[32]

The Belleville Basher finished fourth in the AL Rookie of Year voting and was one of only three players to receive a first-place vote. He was named to the Topps All Star Rookie team as its first baseman.[33]

Ironically, few in Boston had known who Daubach was before the season started. When asked if he had ever heard of him before the Red Sox signed him, manager Jimy Williams said, "To be very honest, no."[34]

In 2000 Daubach was back in Boston and the Red Sox were a contender. Pedro Martínez won his third Cy Young Award and Garciaparra batted .372 for his second crown. The team spent 25 days in first place before June was done. They finished in second place, 2½ games behind the Yankees.

Daubach hit 21 home runs and batted .248. He was an important cog, often batting third, fourth, or fifth. He missed a week after a nasty brawl on August 29 in which eight Devil Rays were ejected, suffering a hyperextended elbow. The fight was sparked when Pedro Martínez hit Gerald Williams with a pitch, and Williams charged the mound. Teammate Lou Merloni maintained that Daubach had only entered the fray to protect Martínez.

After returning to the lineup, Daubach endured a 9-for-57 stretch at the plate.[35] He had been on a streak before the altercation. There was some feeling that his injury broke his momentum and contributed to the team's losing the division to the Yankees. Boston was eliminated on September 29.[36]

The 2001 Red Sox added Manny Ramírez and David Cone to a talented roster that included Jason Varitek, Martínez, and Garciaparra. The team started strong. On July 31 they were in second place, 3½ games out of first with a 60-45 record. But injuries took a serious toll with Ramírez (hamstring), Garciaparra (wrist),[37] Varitek (elbow fracture),[38] and Martínez (shoulder)[39] the victims.

On August 16, after losing six of seven, the Red Sox fired manager Jimy Williams and replaced him with pitching coach Joe Kerrigan.[40] The change didn't help. Boston lost 15 of 21 games in September. They finished 13½ games behind New York.

Outfielder Trot Nixon spoke out about dysfunction within the team. "[P]eople not only disrespected the Red Sox uniform, they also disrespected themselves. ..."[41]

Daubach manned first base in most of his 122 games that year. He quietly had a decent season with 22 home runs and 71 RBIs. He was given the Jackie Jensen Award for spirit and determination by the Boston Baseball Writers. While there was talk about a major overhaul being needed for 2002, retaining Daubach seemed a sound option were they unable to land a big free agent like Jason Giambi. (They were not.)

A new factor made Daubach and his teammates uneasy in late 2001. The Red Sox were for sale. Prospective buyers of the team were visiting Fenway Park to inspect the facility before submitting their final purchase offers. It was presumed that once a new owner was announced, general manager Dan Duquette would be fired and his replacement would orchestrate an overhaul.[42]

Duquette, however, was busy in December preparing to sign arbitration-eligible players, including Daubach. Up to that point, the beefy first sacker-DH had been a Duquette blue-plate special, a big bang for a cheap buck.[43] He signed on January 22.[44] His salary rocketed from $400,000 to $2,352,000 for 2002. Finally, in his age 30 season, he made serious money.

The 2002 Red Sox had a new look. Grady Little was the new manager. Johnny Damon was in center field. Varitek, Garciaparra, and Martínez were healthier and ready to go full-time. Ramírez was healthy enough to play 64 games in left field and those who otherwise filled in for him included Rickey Henderson and Daubach.

Ownership had changed, too. The John Henry group said it would try to eliminate the corrosive clubhouse atmosphere of 2001. They fired Duquette on February 28 and replaced him with Mike Port as an interim.

Daubach played in 137 games in 2002 at first base and the outfield, making but five errors all year. He filled the designated hitter role at times, too.

He hit 20 home runs and in doing so tied a team record shared with Ted Williams, Tony Conigliaro, Jim Rice, and Nomar Garciaparra. Those are the only Red Sox players to start their career with four straight 20-home-run seasons.

Although Daubach delivered his fourth straight decent season, Boston did not offer him a contract for 2003. There is some thinking that the Red Sox showed restraint because salaries were falling.[45] It is also true that Daubach was entering his age 31 season. And he was going to be arbitration-eligible again if he stayed with the Red Sox.

Daubach signed with the White Sox for 2003 and took a pay cut, settling for $450,000. He played sporadically, stuck behind the well-established Frank Thomas (DH), Paul Konerko (first base), and Carlos Lee (outfield).[46] He played in 95 games with Chicago, batting .230 with 6 home runs in 183 at-bats, largely as a part-time first baseman and outfielder. He was released after the season.

In 2004 Daubach returned to the Red Sox as a backup first baseman, outfielder, and pinch-hitter and appeared in 30 games. He batted .227, playing his last game with the Red Sox on June 8. Daubach also played 93 games for Pawtucket, batting .271 with 21 home runs. His curse-busting 2004 Red Sox teammates voted Daubach a World Series share. The owners gave him a championship ring.

"Yeah, the guys were good to me," said Daubach. "And Mr. Henry and Larry (Lucchino) and Mr. (Tom) Werner appreciated the situation for what it was. A lot of players were on the Red Sox previously and part of the 86 years passed without winning. The Red Sox were gracious. To my knowledge they gave everybody a ring, no matter what role or job they had with the club."[47]

Daubach remembered how he was welcomed into the Boston clubhouse after they won the World Series in St. Louis:

"My dad was able to scrape up tickets and we went to the '82 World Series. The next time I was near the Busch Stadium field, I obviously wasn't on the 2004 Red Sox (postseason) roster, but I was with all the guys in the clubhouse with the trophy. It was weird because I never played in St. Louis, one of the few places I never got to play. The first time I was on the field was with the trophy. It was amazing."[48]

The Belleville Basher reached the end of his playing career in the minor leagues with the Mets in 2005 and the Cardinals in 2006. His last taste of major-league life was in 15 games in 2005 with the Mets, for whom he batted .120.

After taking extended time away from baseball at home in Belleville, Daubach launched his managerial and coaching career. In 2009 and 2010, he managed teams in the independent Can-Am League, the New Hampshire American Defenders and the Pittsfield Colonials, respectively. It was the 2007 Red Sox championship that pulled him out of Belleville and back into the baseball life in New England.

"You know, when you play baseball, especially straight out of high school, you're not really sure what you want to do. I did reboot and recharge (after retirement). And what got me back to Boston and Nashua was when I went to Opening Day at Fenway in 2008. The Sox had won in 2007 and wanted members of the 2004 team to be present with the Celtics' Bill Russell, Cedric Maxwell, the Bruins' Bobby Orr and Ken Hodge, and Teddy Bruschi and Wes Welker and a bunch of other guys from the Patriots. You know most of the '04 team was still playing. So I think it ended up being me, Curtis Leskanic, and David McCarty walking out on the field (on Opening Day). It felt great to be back in Fenway, so I just stayed there the rest of the year. I started working with WEEI and NESN. I started doing the radio show with Glen Ordway, *The Big Show*, two to three days of guest-hosting. Plus, I started doing pregame and postgames with NESN. It was pretty exciting so I stayed there the whole summer. The following year, 2009, I joined Nashua as a hitting coach, and the year after that as the manager. … I was ready to get back into baseball which was something I've done my whole life. I am really fortunate I got back in with an organization like the Nationals, where I am now."[49]

In 2011 Daubach began a long career in the Washington Nationals system as the manager of the Class-A Hagerstown Suns, where he was Bryce Harper's first professional manager.

In 2013 he managed Potomac of the Advanced-A Carolina League. In 2014 and 2015 he managed Harrisburg of the Double-A Eastern League. In 2016-18, he was the hitting coach with Triple-A Syracuse Chiefs of the International League.

In 2019 he was the hitting coach with the Fresno Grizzlies of the PCL, then was off in 2020 as COVID canceled the minor-league season.

On a personal note, Daubach married Kimberly Zimmerman in 2021. He has a son, Caden, from a previous marriage, who was born in 2004.[50]

In 2021 he became the hitting coach for the Rochester Red Wings of the Internal League, a post he still held in 2023.

Daubach's approach to leadership is nuanced. He said, "Managing in the minors is a little different from managing in the major leagues because obviously your prospects are going to play (a lot) … as far as on a daily basis, just be open with the guys, and teach as much as you can. I played 17 years and have coached another 14 or 15 years. I try to pass things along. But the big thing is I just try to be open. Some days it's being a good listener. Others it's being a good teacher. I think every guy is wired a little bit differently. It can change day-to-day. One day a guy needs an arm around him and another needs a kick in the butt. I think that's the beauty of any management role, but especially in baseball, where there is so much failure on the hitting side. … So you just try to bring the kids up, especially the ones who were high draft picks, they have a lot to live up to. It's a lot (of pressure). Especially with social media now. I try to be aware of everybody's situation. And to be available when they need you."[51]

Would he would like to manage again? Daubach had this to say:

"Yes. … I managed for five years, had some great players, at the time we were building up to (the Nationals') first World Series run. It was exciting to have a lot of young players drafted in the early 2010s. I had a chance to manage in Triple A. I just love the game. Love teaching, especially loved managing younger players because you see big strides can be made quickly, and when they later turn into World Series champions it's very rewarding. But Triple A is rewarding, too. Not only do you get to tell guys they're going to the major leagues, you have a 34-year-old bat that's trying to get back there. I've kind of been on both sides of that. I was a young guy coming up and trying to get there for the first time, and (I had to) go down to Triple A and fight my way back."

"(Helping others get there) is the best thing about coaching in the minor leagues."[52]

NOTES

1 Phone interview, Brian Daubach with Karl Cicitto, June 2, 2023 (hereafter Daubach-Cicitto interview).

2 Daubach-Cicitto interview

3 Mike Eisenbath, "The Mighty from '90," *St Louis Post-Dispatch*, June 21, 1990: 6D.

4 Norm Sanders, "West Hitter Signs Contract with Mets," *Belleville* (Illinois) *News-Democrat*, June 16, 1990: D1.

5 Norm Sanders, "Making the Grade," *Belleville News-Democrat*, September 11, 1990: D5.

6 Norm Sanders, "A Year in the Minors," *Belleville News-Democrat*, September 10, 1991: D5.

7 Norm Sanders, "Former Belleville West Slugger Works Way Back into Lineup," *Belleville News-Democrat*, July 6, 1992: D2.

8 Gordon Edes, "Base Tour," *Boston Globe*, June 11, 1999: E1.

9 Eisenbath, "In 7th Season, Daubach Still Optimistic," *St Louis Post-Dispatch*, July 13, 1996: 17.

10 Edes, "Base Tour."

11 "Batista Coquetea Con No-Hitter; Igor Debuta el Domingo con San Juan," *El Nuevo Herald* (Miami), December 4, 1996: 6B.

12 Daubach-Cicitto interview.

13 Earl Gault, "Marlins Spending Spree Could Make Tosca's Job Easy," *Rock Hill* (South Carolina) *Herald*, February 6, 1997: 1B.

14 Stats Crew, accessed May, 23, 2023: https://www.statscrew.com/minorbaseball/leaders/l-IL/y-1998.

15 Edes, "Base Tour."

16 Daubach-Cicitto interview.

17 Daubach-Cicitto interview.

18 Edes, "Base Tour."

19 Edes, "Daubach an Able Replacement," *Boston Globe*, May 27, 1999: C6.

20 Edes, "With a Deep Impact Garciaparra Is Back," *Boston Globe*, March 27, 1999: G6.

21 Larry Whiteside, "Saberhagen Strong in Mind, Body," *Boston Globe*, March 12, 1999: E2.

22 Whiteside, "Portugal Tuning Out the Negative," *Boston Globe*, March 14, 1999: E1.

23 Edes, "Gordon Shows No Signs of Strain in Hitting 92 MPH," *Boston Globe*, March 20, 1999: G3.

24 "How Red Sox Line Up for Opening Day," *Boston Globe*, April 5, 1999: D3.

25 Edes, "A Little Daubach Does It," *Boston Globe*, May 18, 1999: E1.

26 Edes, "Sox Go Long Way Around," *Boston Globe*, June 2, 1999: F1.

27 Rupen Fofaria, "No Minor Contribution," *Boston Globe*, June 6, 1999: D15.

28 Edes, "Rookie at Home Together," *Boston Globe*, June 8, 1999: E5.

29 Michael Smith, "Sox Rookies Rise to Occasion," *Boston Globe*, August 2, 1999: D5.

30 Daubach-Cicitto interview.

31 "1999 Season Predictions," *New York Times*, April 2, 1999. https://archive.nytimes.com/www.nytimes.com/library/sports/baseball/040499bbo-season-predictions.html.

32 Daubach-Cicitto interview.

33 Edes, "Gordon to Have Elbow Surgery," *Boston Globe*, October 28, 1999: E6.

34 Edes, A Little Daubach Does It," *Boston Globe*, May 18, 1999: G1.

35 Bob Hohler, "Brawl Set Off Some Bad Vibes," *Boston Globe*, September 29, 2000: F5.

36 Hohler, "Sox Slim Shot Slips Away," *Boston Globe*, September 30, 2000: F1.

37 Holhler, "These Parts Couldn't Drive the Red Sox Engine," *Boston Globe*, October 7, 2001: C14.

38 Hohler, "Curtain Cal: Team, Fans Send Ripken Off," *Boston Globe*, September 28, 2001: E3.

39 Hohler, "No Quick Return for Ace," *Boston Globe*, July 5, 2001: C6.

40 Hohler, "Duke Talks, Jimy Walks," *Boston Globe*, August 17, 2001: A1.

41 Hohler, "Nixon Has Few Regrets," *Boston Globe*, January 11, 2002: E4.

42 Hohler, "Duquette Wants Role Expanded," *Boston Globe*, October 9, 2001: F5.

43 Gordon Edes, "Base Tour," *Boston Globe*, June 11, 1999; E1.

44 "One-year Deal for Daubach," *Boston Globe*, January 23, 2002: F2.

45 Edes, "Less Dollars, More Sense in New Market," *Boston Globe*, December 22, 2002: C13.

46 Associated Press, "Daubach Returns to Red Sox," *Daily Hampshire Gazette* (Northampton, Massachusetts), March 17, 2004: D1.

47 Daubach-Cicitto interview.

48 Daubach-Cicitto interview.

49 Daubach-Cicitto interview.

50 Daubach-Cicitto interview.

51 Daubach-Cicitto interview.

52 Daubach-Cicitto interview.

REST IN PEACE, BABE

We always sat in the center-field bleachers in Fenway when we were kids. My dad claimed these were the seats with the best view of the field. We kids wanted to sit along the first-base line to have a better view of the pitcher's mound, where our father had pitched a championship game as a 14-year-old in 1937. Our dad's name was Babe.[1] Our mother was Ruth. We thought we had a unique connection to the greatest ballplayer of all time.

In 1964 our older cousin Steven's enthusiasm for Dick Stuart convinced us for a few months that the Sox could bring Babe Ruth's home-run record back to Boston. I was 13 and by August 25 I knew Stuart would never hit 61, but Steven could not be swayed. He believed.

Steven was 20 and had Down syndrome. His voice was loud and heavy, especially when he was excited, as he was that Tuesday evening. A couple of rows in front of us, I'd noticed a group of teenage boys turn and laugh each time Steven exclaimed, "Dick Stuart's gonna hit a home run tonight, right Uncle Babe?" My father must have noticed the boys, too. Without flinching, he answered, "Steven, if Stuart hits a home run this way, I'll catch the ball for you."

Stuart came to bat in the bottom of the fourth. He'd already made an error on a bunt by tossing the ball into left field and was greeted by a cacophony of boos from the 12,692 fans that

night.[2] As was his style, Stuart seemed unaffected when he stepped into the batter's box. Steven didn't seem to care either.

Over the din of jeers when the solid, crisp crack of the bat reached us in the bleachers, my father jumped up, balanced one foot on the seat in front of me and leapt into the aisle. He reached out his arm, the ball hit the concrete step and bounced straight into my father's bare hand. He climbed back to his seat and gave the ball to Steven, who stood up and showed it off proudly, vindicated, triumphant. Steven received an ovation from the raucous bleacher crowd, including the boys down front. I was awed. How'd my dad know Stuart was going to rap a line-drive home run into the center-field bleachers?

Baseball wasn't just a game in our family, it was a way to teach life lessons, so when spring arrived, we wanted to know if our dad thought the Sox could produce a miracle that season and win a World Series. His answer was always the same: "I hope they win during my lifetime." Babe passed away in 1996 but I like to think he was there that night of the final game of 2004 in Busch Stadium when a fan held up a placard that read, "Rest In Peace Babe." Watching in different cities, all four of Babe DeLuca's kids saw that sign that night. Maybe those words were meant for Babe Ruth, but for us, we believe it was a message for our dad.

KAREN DELUCA STEPHENS

1 Father's given name was Amedeo DeLuca and he was born in 1923, the year the Yankees won their first World Series championship.

2 Roger Birtwell, "Tigers Wallop Red Sox," *Boston Globe*, August 26, 1964: 39-40. Final score: Detroit 11, Boston 6.

LENNY DINARDO

BY SCOTT MELESKY

Lenny DiNardo's baseball career has been diverse, highlighted by a World Series ring, two no-hitters, setting collegiate strikeout records, and playing in the World Baseball Classic twice. DiNardo's time playing baseball spanned five years in the major leagues and 11 years including college, the minor leagues, the Dominican Republic Winter League, and in the Chinese Professional Baseball League. He has been a professional guitarist for over 20 years and has been an in-studio baseball analyst since 2017.

DiNardo, a left-handed pitcher born in Miami, Florida, was originally selected in the 10th round by the Boston Red Sox in the 1998 amateur draft but he did not sign. He attended Stetson University from 1999 to 2001 and was drafted by the New York Mets in the third round of the 2001 draft.[1]

DiNardo compiled a 10-18 record with a 5.36 ERA and 132 strikeouts in 94 games played for the Boston Red Sox, Oakland Athletics, and the Kansas City Royals. In his 10 years in the minor leagues, he had a 39-44 record with a 3.93 ERA and 655 strikeouts in 756 innings. Pitching for the Lamigo Monkeys in the Chinese Professional Baseball League in 2012, DiNardo had a 3-6 record with a 4.50 ERA. He also pitched for Italy in the 2006 and 2009 World Baseball Classics.

Leonard Edward DiNardo was born in Miami on September 19, 1979, the second of six children of Michael DiNardo Sr. and Elizabeth DiNardo. His father was a mail carrier, and his mother was a teacher's aide. In his high-school years he lived in Micanopy, in north central Florida, and attended Santa Fe High School in nearby Alachua. He dominated in his four years on the Santa Fe baseball team with a 33-8 record, including a no-hitter, and a 1.26 ERA. DiNardo was a four-year first-team All-Area and a first-team All-Stater in his junior and senior years. (He was a second-team All-Stater as a freshman and sophomore.) In his senior year, DiNardo was named a USA Today High School All-American and a member of the Florida State High School All-Star Game.[2]

Former Santa Fe High School baseball head coach Todd Gray saw DiNardo's major-league potential as he began his high-school career. His pitch speed and velocity were already significantly faster and harder than that of his teammates and opponents.

"Lenny was throwing 78-90 miles per hour as a sophomore," Gray said. "He had high velocity and could already throw a

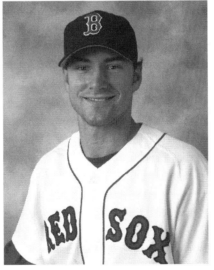

number of different pitches, which is rare in high school. Lenny always succeeded in anything that he put his mind to. He had a natural mindset for success."[3]

DiNardo was drafted in the 10th round by the Boston Red Sox, but chose to attend Stetson University and play under head coach Pete Dunn.[4]

Not signing with the Red Sox "was a tough call to make," DiNardo said. "I was a huge fan of Roger Clemens and had his poster on my wall. I felt that I had a lot of growing up to do and I wanted to work on strengthening up my pitching and I chose a three-year path that made me stronger as a pitcher and a baseball player. Pete was a great coach to play for. He told me when I signed with the school that he will give me a shot to learn to pitch which I very much appreciated. Stetson had a great coaching staff. I was also strongly influenced by coaches Larry Jones (Hall of Famer Chipper Jones's father) and Derek Johnson (in 2023, Cincinnati Reds Director of Pitching)."[5]

DiNardo added to the Stetson University baseball lineage with a historic season in his sophomore year, 2000. He won a school-record 16 games with one loss and a 1.90 ERA, and had a school-record 132 strikeouts in 132⅔ innings. In Stetson's 9-5 victory over Auburn in the opening round of the NCAA Atlanta Regional, DiNardo pitched eight innings and gave up four runs on 10 hits. Stetson defeated Auburn 13-10 in their second meeting in the regional before being eliminated by Georgia Tech 21-1 and 16-11 in the next round.[6]

"In every level of baseball, you face the crème de la crème of hitters," DiNardo said. "In college, I was now facing teams full of high-school All-Americans in every game. I really had to learn how to hit my spots as a pitcher. The season really rolled that year. Everything was clicking with my pitches; I am not a hard thrower, but I had to have my pitching command. When you stand on the mound and know that you will be able to get the hitters out, that goes a long way in winning ballgames. I really appreciated what Stetson did for me. They gave me a shot and made me into a good baseball player. They gave me every opportunity and put me in position to succeed as a baseball player."

In DiNardo's three seasons at Stetson, he finished with a school record of 35 wins with 10 losses. He was named a

Freshman All-American in 1999 and a Third Team All-American in 2001. DiNardo spent the summers of 1999 and 2000 with USA Baseball's Collegiate National Team and had an 8-1 record with a 2.29 ERA. He was inducted into the Stetson University Athletics Hall of Fame in 2007.[7]

"He was the perfect Stetson player," Dunn said. "We saw that he was a good player and fit the profile perfectly. Lenny was a tall left-hander with much velocity. He was outstanding and was a strike thrower. Lenny could strike out players with his eyes closed. He had a remarkable three-year career at Stetson. He was a role model and a team leader. The team looked up to him. He was everything a coach wanted on and off the field. Lenny was a great citizen, person, and player."[8]

In the 2001 draft, the New York Mets selected DiNardo in the third round. That summer he made his professional debut with the Brooklyn Cyclones of the short-season New York-Penn League. He pitched in nine games and was 1-2 with a 2.00 ERA with 40 strikeouts in 36 innings pitched. The Cyclones finished first in the league's Stedler Division with a 52-24 record. Because of the 9/11 terrorist attacks, the league championship series was canceled after Brooklyn won the first game. The Cyclones and the Williamsport Crosscutters were named co-champions.

"Brooklyn was a great city to play in," DiNardo said. "We were the first pro baseball team in that city since the Dodgers moved out in 1957. We were treated like celebrities and would play Pickle on our offdays with the local kids in the street. It was a lot of fun playing there."

DiNardo said Brooklyn coaches Howard Johnson and Bob Ojeda both had major impacts on his development as a professional baseball player.

"I learned so much from both of them about the game," DiNardo said. "Bob was 'old school' and hard-nosed and took me under his wing. He challenged us as rookies. Bobby wouldn't call us by our real names until we played in a game. He called me 'Jimmy New Guy' until I got my feet wet. Bobby told me that playing in the big leagues required a strong mental makeup in order to succeed."

In 2002 DiNardo was moved up to the Capital City Bombers (Columbia, South Carolina) of the Class-A South Atlantic League. He went 5-5 with a 4.35 ERA with 103 strikeouts in 101⅓ innings. DiNardo also got a major-league tutorial on diversifying his pitches when he took part in the Mets' spring training, a time that also foreshadowed his future music career.

"Al Leiter had a very strong influence on my learning how to throw a cut fastball," DiNardo said. "He was not a hard thrower but was a great pitcher. Al didn't really talk about it much, but I kept my eyes open on how he threw it. What also helped me develop my cutter was when I started playing guitar that season. The finger movement of playing chords on a guitar is very similar to throwing a baseball, which also helped me with my pitching development."

In 2003 DiNardo split time between the Port St. Lucie Mets of the High-A Florida State League and the Binghamton Mets of the Double-A Eastern League. He started the season with Binghamton, where he had a 1-3 record with a 3.60 ERA in 40 innings pitched. He was then sent down to Port St. Lucie, for whom he was 3-8 with a 2.01 ERA and 93 strikeouts in 85 innings.

After the 2003 season the Mets left DiNardo eligible for the Rule 5 draft, and the Red Sox drafted him. "My agent called me one morning and said I was a new member of the Boston Red Sox because of the Rule 5 Draft," DiNardo said. "He then tried to explain to me the rules on how to stay with the team. It was a lot to take in and I tried to just stay focused as a ballplayer and try to compete the best that I could."

DiNardo started the season on the disabled list with a left shoulder strain, but made his major-league debut on April 23, 2004, against the New York Yankees at Yankee Stadium. DiNardo pitched a shutout ninth inning in the Red Sox' 11-2 victory, striking out Hideki Matsui between groundouts by Gary Sheffield and Bernie Williams.

"My first game pitching at Yankee Stadium was an incredible experience," DiNardo recalled. "It was a very difficult and hostile environment to be a Red Sox player pitching against the Yankees in Yankee Stadium. The fans were brutal when I was in the bullpen, and I tuned them out when I was pitching. I told myself before I pitched that the field was the same dimensions that I pitched in high school and the only difference was that there were thousands of fans in the stadium. I trusted my game and pitched my best. I had to face Sheffield, Matsui, and Bernie Williams in the ninth inning. It all worked out for me as I was able to get them out and we won the ballgame."

On May 1 DiNardo worked three shutout innings of relief in a loss to Texas. He did not give up a run until his fifth appearance. In all, he made 22 relief appearances during the regular season with neither a win, loss, nor save.

"I really approached the season with my eyes wide open and my mouth shut," DiNardo said. "I wanted to soak it all in and learn from the best. This was an incredibly talented team that almost made the World Series a year before. The team had a great new manager under Terry Francona, and I learned so much from Pedro Martínez, Alan Embree, Mike Timlin, and Keith Foulke. Bronson Arroyo, Bill Mueller, and Gabe Kapler were also very supportive of me. Bronson told me that I belonged here and to just throw like I knew how and trust my pitches. It was an incredible feeling to be a Boston Red Sox player at the time when they finally won a World Series after 86 years. The fans were so loyal, loud, and passionate. Talk about being at the right place at the right time."

DiNardo's last appearance for the 2004 Red Sox came on July 4, 1⅔ scoreless innings in Atlanta. A blister on a finger of his pitching hand and a pulled back muscle required weeks on the disabled list and extensive rehab. Only at the end of the season was he able to return, with brief stints for Boston's minor-league affiliates in Sarasota, Portland, and Pawtucket, a total of five games and 11⅔ innings. With Pedro Astacio and Byun-Hyung Kim, he worked out in Fort Myers during the postseason, in case the Red Sox needed an emergency replacement.[9] He worked out with the team in Boston during the World Series but was not on the roster.

DiNardo split the 2005 season between Boston and Triple-A Pawtucket. He bounced back and forth between the teams five times during the season. For Pawtucket, DiNardo posted a 6-3 record with a 3.15 ERA with 93 strikeouts in 108⅔ innings. For Boston, he was 0-1 in eight games (one start) with a 1.84 ERA.

Before the 2006 season started, DiNardo competed in the 2006 World Baseball Classic as a member of Team Italy. (A great-grandfather was of Italian descent.) The team also had future Hall of Famer Mike Piazza. Italy finished with a 1-2 record in the tournament, with DiNardo taking both losses.

"It was a great experience to play for Team Italy in the World Baseball Classic," DiNardo said. "I loved the experience and appreciated what my great-grandfather did there. I got to play with Mike Piazza, Mike Gallo, and Jason Grilli on the team. Mike is a baseball Hall of a Famer and a consummate professional, but he is a very humble and a nice guy. He is very funny, and we would say lines from *The Godfather* to each other and crack each other up. The Italian kids loved us and would come into the dugout to see Piazza. Tommy Lasorda was Piazza's godfather and gave the team a great emotional and fiery pep talk which really fired the team before a game."

On May 7, 2006, DiNardo earned his first major-league win with a 10-3 victory over the Baltimore Orioles in Fenway Park. He pitched five innings and gave up one earned run on two hits. DiNardo walked five batters and struck out five.

"I felt like that I pitched a lot of games against the Baltimore Orioles," DiNardo said. "The first win was good, and it was a good feeling to get my first MLB win under my belt."

DiNardo was hampered by a bulging disk injury suffered when he was rear-ended in a car accident, one that lingered throughout the 2006 season. It limited him to 13 games and six starts for the Red Sox and a 1-2 record with a 7.85 ERA. DiNardo also spent time with Pawtucket, Portland, and the GCL Red Sox in the Gulf Coast League.

"It was a tough season," DiNardo said. On May 24, 2006, on the way to the ballpark, he was in an automobile accident. "I was in traffic and saw a car speeding up behind me. I braced for the impact, but I still ended up with a bulging desk. I had an epidural and the season was up and down for me as I dealt with the injury, but I was better in 2007."

In the offseason and as a Red Sox player, DiNardo became an active guitarist and backup singer and participated in the annual Hot Stove Music Concert in Boston for many years. He performed with Eddie Vedder of Pearl Jam, Evan Dando of The Lemonheads, Juliana Hatfield of Blake Babies, Kay Hanley and Stacy Jones of Letters to Cleo, Bill Janowitz of Buffalo Tom, and Joe Keefe and Sebastian Keefe of Family of the Year.[10]

In the studio, DiNardo sang backup vocals with Red Sox teammates Johnny Damon and Bronson Arroyo on the Dropkick Murphys' 2004 musical hit "Tessie." DiNardo also supplied backup vocals to Arroyo's debut music album, *Covering the Bases*, and played rhythm guitar on baseball journalist Peter Gammons' song "Model Citizen" on Gammons' debut album for Rounder Records, *Never Slow Down, Never Grow Old*.[11]

"I started playing guitar when I was in my early 20s, so it is surreal to have played in front of thousands of fans for good causes with all these legendary musicians," DiNardo said. "I was taught as a baseball player not to look into the crowd because it will distract you. I do the same as a musician. It is great to hear the cheering and the support from the fans, but I have to stay focused on hitting my chords. If I focus too much on the crowd, I will be distracted and miss my chords when I am playing."

Though he was an active musician, DiNardo continued playing baseball. At the end of the 2006 season, he appeared in 10 games for the Peoria Javelinas of the Arizona Fall League in order to prepare for the 2007 MLB season.

"I needed the work and faced a lot of great and elite hitters in the league," DiNardo said. "I was one of the older guys in the league, but the experience pitching there really helped me as a player."

On February 14, 2007, the Oakland Athletics selected DiNardo off waivers from the Red Sox. He had two productive seasons for Oakland. DiNardo compiled an 8-10 record with a 4.11 ERA in 35 games. He was versatile for the A's, with 20 starts and 15 relief appearances. June 10, 2007, was a historic day for DiNardo. In Oakland's 2-0 win over the San Francisco Giants, he got his only major-league base hit, a single off Matt Cain. DiNardo pitched six shutout innings in the game but got a no-decision.

In 2008 DiNardo split time with Oakland and Sacramento of the Triple-A Pacific Coast League. He started the season with Sacramento where he had a 6-5 record with a 6.69 ERA in 15 games. DiNardo finished the season with Oakland, where he compiled a 1-2 record with a 7.43 ERA in 11 games.

"I had 20 starts and 15 relief experiences with Oakland," DiNardo said. "It was a lot different than pitching in Boston. The Oakland-Alameda Coliseum is massive at 80,000 seats compared to Fenway Park; they draw 20,000 fans but it feels like 5,000. There weren't as many Oakland fans as Boston fans, but they were just as loud, passionate, and supportive. I got a lot of pitching experience and pitched in and was put in a lot of different game situations. I appreciated getting those different opportunities as a pitcher."

DiNardo signed a minor-league contract with the Kansas City Royals organization on December 20, 2008. Before he pitched for the Royals organization in 2009, DiNardo took part in his second World Baseball Classic for Team Italy. The team finished with a 1-2 record highlighted by a 6-2 upset win over Canada, but was eliminated by 7-0 and 10-1 losses to Venezuela. After playing in the WBC, DiNardo started the 2009 season with the Triple-A Omaha Royals. After going 10-5/ 3.32, DiNardo was called up to Kansas City and closed out his major-league career with an 0-3 record in five games.

"Kansas City was a nice place to play," DiNardo said. "I was pitching for a lot of different teams by the end of my career. I got to play in different countries around the world."

DiNardo tried to extend his major-league career when he signed a minor-league contract with Oakland on January 7, 2010. He began the 2010 season with Sacramento and posted a 2-5 record with a 3.40 ERA in 10 games. DiNardo also pitched in two games for the Athletics of the rookie Arizona League.

The 2011 season continued in the minor leagues for DiNardo. He was 3-5/6.49 for Sacramento and 1-2/3.51 for the Midland Rockhounds of the Double-A Texas League. Released by Oakland, he joined the Long Island Ducks of the independent Atlantic League of Professional Baseball, where he was 2-1 in three games. DiNardo ended the 2011 season with the Gigantes del Cibao of the Dominican Winter League. (3-5/2.22).

The year 2012 was an international season for DiNardo. He began the year in Taiwan, pitching for the Lamigo Monkeys in the Chinese Professional Baseball League, where he was 3-6 with a 4.50 ERA. Later DiNardo returned for another season with the Gigantes del Cibao. He was 0-0/ 38.57 in four games.

"I really enjoyed playing baseball in Taiwan," DiNardo said. "It was a great place to play baseball. There was lots of talent there. They did a lot of bunting in different types of situations in the game. I liked pitching there, but my lower back was giving me lots of problems."

After 12 years, DiNardo played his last professional baseball season in 2013. "I decided if I didn't get any MLB interest after the season, I would retire," DiNardo said. Again pitching in independent ball, he worked for the Atlantic League's Lancaster Barnstormers. He made franchise history on May 8, 2013, when he threw the team's first-ever no-hitter, a 9-0 win against the Long Island Ducks. DiNardo faced 28 batters, walked two, struck out eight, and recorded 15 outs on groundballs.[12]

"It was my second overall no-hitter in my baseball career. I threw one in high school. It felt really great throwing a no-hitter for Lancaster. Long Island was a very tough team made up of lots of former MLB and Triple-A players. I had a lot of support from my team on both the offense and the defense. They played very well. I was happy to throw the no-hitter in front of my wife [Julie] and oldest daughter. I thought that after I threw the no-hitter, I would hear from a MLB team but I did not hear from a single team and I knew my MLB career was over."

DiNardo finished the 2013 season and his professional career with a 5-9 record and a 5.25 ERA. He retired in August.

"I really enjoyed playing baseball," DiNardo said. "I felt that I got the most out of my pitching career and I worked hard and competed in every game that I played in."

DiNardo worked as a pitching instructor in Fort Myers and Naples, Florida, and in South Kingstown, Rhode Island, where he and his family live. In April 2017 he became an in-studio analyst for the Red Sox' flagship television station, the New England Sports Network (NESN).[13] Besides his TV duties, he has been a licensed realtor since 2017.[14]

SOURCES

In addition to the sources cited in the Notes, the author used the MLB.com, Baseball-Almanac.com, and StatsCrew.com websites for box score, player, team, and season pages, pitching and batting logs, and other material.

NOTES

1. Lenny DiNardo Hall of Fame. Stetson University Athletics. https://gohatters.com/honors/hall-of-fame/lenny-dinardo/44.
2. Email correspondence from Ricky Hazel, Stetson University associate director for athletics for communications, licensing and branding, Stetson University Athletics, May 16, 2022.
3. Author interview with Todd Gray, May 17, 2022.
4. In his 37-year coaching career, Dunn's teams won 1,312 games and made 17 NCAA Regional Tournament appearances. Sixty-two of his team members played professional baseball, and seven of them made it to the major leagues.
5. Author interview with Lenny DiNardo, May 17, 2023. Unless otherwise indicated, all direct quotations from Lenny DiNardo derive from this interview.
6. Hazel.
7. Hazel.
8. Author interview with Pete Dunn, May 24, 2022.
9. Bob Hohler, "Pesky Happy to be Back," *Boston Globe*, October 23, 2004: 61.
10. Lenny DiNardo Songs, allmusic.com. https://www.allmusic.com/artist/lenny-dinardo-mn0000385539.
11. Jim Sullivan, "Jocks and Rock – "Hot Stove Cool Music" Benefit Concert Comes back to Boston." WBUR News, April 25, 2017: 19. https://www.wbur.org/news/2017/04/25/hot-stove-cool-music-boston.
12. Burt Wilson, "Barnstormers' DiNardo Spins No-Hitter vs Long Island," LancasterOnline, May 9, 2013. https://lancasteronline.com/sports/barnstormers-dinardo-spins-no-hitter-vs-long-island/article_4cfbad11-991e-5ada-b2bb-e4f9ccc87dc7.html.
13. "NESN Announces Booth Talent for 2022 Red Sox Season," NESN.com, March 15, 2022. https://nesn.com/2022/03/nesn-announces-talent-roster-for-2022-red-sox-season/#:~:text=Jahmai%20Webster%20will%20serve%20as,to%20the%20roster%20Will%20Middlebrooks.
14. Peyton Doyle, "Lenny DiNardo: From Pitching Strikes to Pitching Homes," boston.com, March 23, 2023. https://www.boston.com/real-estate/real-estate/2023/03/31/lenny-dinardo-red-sox-pitcher-turned-realtor-broadcaster/.

ANDY DOMINIQUE

BY BOB LEMOINE

"It's an unbelievable feeling to be able to contribute to a team like this. I see how hard these guys work, and when I come up here from Triple A it's not a vacation."
Andy Dominique, after his first major-league hit with the 2004 Red Sox[1]

Andy Dominique played nine games in the major leagues, seven of them with the 2004 World Series champion Boston Red Sox. His first major-league hit was in the clutch and helped the Red Sox win a game in May. That career highlight for the hefty catcher-third baseman-first baseman came after eight seasons riding the buses in the minor leagues. "He is heavy around the middle and jowly, and doesn't have a hair on his head," wrote Steve Buckley in the *Boston Herald*. "His eyes suggest many late-night bus rides, truck-stop dinners and hotel mattresses that don't feel quite right."[2] It was a long journey to get there, but get there he did, and he has a World Series ring to show for it. Dominique's name is all over the baseball record books at his alma mater, the University of Nevada-Reno. Andy Dominique continued to inspire youth in Nevada, teaching the fundamentals of the game, while giving a firsthand account about patience, dedication, and overcoming extreme setbacks.

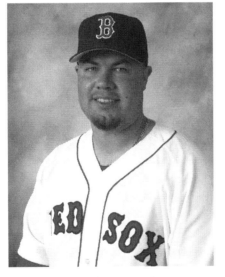

Andrew John Dominique was born on October 30, 1975, in Tarzana, California, to Jeff and Karole (Jones) Dominique. Andy had two siblings, Kris and Wendy. Jeff, a CPA, was the chief financial officer of multiple real estate companies. He also coached his sons, and was the local Little League president, high-school athletic booster president, and home football game announcer.[3]

Andy attended Bishop Alemany High School in Mission Hills. As a sophomore he batted .323 with 6 home runs and 23 RBIs. He also helped the Southern California Cardinals win the Mickey Mantle World Series youth championship over a team from Baltimore. Dominique batted .409 in the series at Waterbury, Connecticut.[4] As a junior, Dominique batted .393 with 2 home runs and 18 RBIs.[5]

Many, including Dominique, believed he would be drafted into the major leagues after he batted .493 in his senior year.[6] Others were doubtful, some attributing his body size (210 pounds and under 6-feet) as the reason. "I always hoped and thought I could play professional baseball," Dominique said. "I played with a lot of guys who knew for sure they were getting drafted out of high school. For me, it was a different story, because of my physical appearance. In baseball, it's a long season, and you've got to be in shape all the way to the end. There's always been a lot of question about a guy like myself, and it's something I'm trying to work on constantly."[7]

The next option was college, but Dominique struggled with dyslexia, which made SAT scores for college admission a major obstacle. He gave up his college dream, but his girlfriend encouraged him to seek tutoring and try again. His scores were good enough but all of his scholarships were rescinded, except one: Nevada-Reno. He enrolled, and Nevada became his home.[8]

Dominique set out to prove scouts were wrong by losing 19 pounds. "He's a real competitive kid," his coach at Nevada, Gary Powers, said. "He's quicker, a little more alert and has more stamina. We saw how he could swing the bat. It was a matter of setting himself in motion and getting him into condition to play. I think he's done a tremendous job."[9] In 56 games as a freshman, Dominique batted .317 with 8 home runs (.423 OBP, .896 OPS) as the starting third baseman. His batting numbers continued to impress as a sophomore when he batted .328 with 7 home runs (.387 OBP, .945 OPS). He played mostly third, but also first base and the outfield. He also played summer ball with the Kenosha Kroakers, champions of the new collegiate Northwoods League.[10]

Dominique's junior year power numbers were out of sight. He had a stretch of slugging 10 home runs in 11 games, batting .500 (17-for-34) over that stretch. "The ball's just popping off my bat," he said. "I'm not trying to hit home runs. And that's probably why I am doing so well. All I'm thinking about is driving the ball up the middle."[11] When he cracked home run number 15, he became the Wolf Pack's single-season home-run leader.[12] He finished the season batting .355 (.417 OBP, 1.138 OPS) with 17 home runs.

Dominique cemented his legacy at Nevada his senior year when he surpassed 35 career home runs, the Wolf Pack's all-time leader. He kept on going, becoming both Big West Player of the Year and second-team All-American. He batted .353 and crushed 30 home runs with 96 RBIs, still Nevada single-season records.[13] He left Nevada with several other school batting records that have since been surpassed, but his career home runs

(62), single-season home runs (30), and RBIs (96) still ranked all-time as of 2023.[14]

Dominique was discovered by Philadelphia Phillies scout Mitch Sokol.[15] The Phillies drafted Dominique in the 26th round of the June 1997 amateur draft. He was assigned to Batavia of the short-season Class-A New York-Penn League. He played first base and appeared in 72 games, batting .278 with 14 home runs, tied for the league lead. "I'm having fun," Dominique said. "But I'm not going to get too excited. The wheels could come off any time." He had a short commute, living with a family across the street from the club's Dwyer Stadium.[16] He was promoted to Piedmont of the Class-A South Atlantic League in 1998. He pounded 24 home runs and a team-record 102 RBIs, batting .282 with a .369 OBP.[17]

In 1999 Dominique was promoted to Clearwater of the advanced Class-A Florida State League. He batted .255 with 14 home runs and 92 RBIs and played the majority of his 130 games at catcher. His career-high 69 walks helped his .354 on-base percentage. In 2000 he was promoted to Reading of the Double-A Eastern League, where he batted .239 with 13 home runs.[18]

In 2001 Dominique batted .280 with 12 home runs and 49 RBIs in 76 games at Reading. He was promoted to Scranton/Wilkes-Barre of the Triple-A International League and batted a weak .170 in 40 games.[19] In March 2002 Dominique underwent knee surgery and in April was acquired by Boston. He played 103 games at Trenton of the Eastern League and batted .272 with 8 home runs.[20] Dominique dominated Double-A pitching in 2003, batting .361 (.454 OBP) in 32 games at Portland in the Eastern League. He was promoted to Triple-A Pawtucket and continued sizzling, hitting .305 with 13 home runs.

Dominique attended Fenway Park in January 2004 as a guest of Red Sox ownership. It was an orientation to help take away the shell-shocked response many rookies have when arriving in Boston. "It was something I'll never forget," he said. "So how will I react when I get that call? I have no idea. My emotions aren't there yet. But I know I'll be thinking about being a kid and dreaming of playing in the big leagues. That's where this all began."[21] His dream would soon be realized.

Dominique had spent eight long years in professional baseball. "When you've been playing minor league baseball for a long time," he said, "one of the questions you always get is, 'When are you going to quit?' And 'When are you going to stop playing and make some money?' I still play baseball, and I still love it. Keeping that in mind makes it a little easier to be in the minors."[22] His experience made him a leader in the Pawtucket clubhouse. "Everybody wants to be around Andy," fellow catcher Kelly Shoppach said. "He's funny. He makes you laugh. He's one of those guys you have respect for, not only because he's a good player, but because he leads you in the clubhouse. He's a class act."[23]

Dominique was batting .341 with 7 home runs and 38 RBIs at Pawtucket when he was called up to Boston on May 25 after Bill Mueller went on the disabled list. "It was a long road for me," said Dominique. "I was really happy for that day to come. I couldn't ask for anything better. I'm enjoying myself playing this game. It's a fun thing to come in to work and see the faces like you do and it makes you really appreciate what you do for a living."[24] He broke the exciting news to his parents on their 30th anniversary.[25]

Dominique made his major-league debut that night as an eighth-inning defensive replacement in left field for Manny Ramírez with Oakland blowing out the Red Sox, 12-2. As Dominique came to the plate in the bottom of the eighth, he received a lengthy standing ovation from the Fenway Park crowd, recognizing the 28-year-old's journey. "Whatever the reason was, it was an awesome feeling," Dominique said. "It's something I'll never forget."[26] In the bottom of the eighth, he struck out against Justin Duchscherer in his first at-bat.

Dominique chose an opportune moment for his first hit and RBI in the major leagues. The Red Sox hosted Seattle for a Sunday afternoon contest on Memorial Day weekend, May 30. The Red Sox were cruising with a 5-1 lead in the eighth when the Mariners erupted for six runs and led, 7-5. In the bottom of the eighth, Jason Varitek led off with a single that glanced off pitcher Shigetoshi Hasegawa. Dave McCarty doubled off the wall in left, sending Varitek to third. Johnny Damon, originally given the day off, pinch-hit for Gabe Kapler. Seattle manager Bob Melvin countered by summoning left-hander Eddie Guardado from the bullpen. Damon launched a deep fly to right, scoring Varitek to cut Seattle's lead to 7-6. Manager Terry Francona sent Dominique up to bat for Pokey Reese. Dominique singled to right to score McCarty with the tying run. He stayed in the game at first base and singled again in the 10th inning. McCarty hit a walk-off home run in the 12th inning and the Red Sox won, 9-7. "(Guardado) throws that good splitter out there and it was just a matter of me trying to get something up in the air. It just happened that I was able to stick it out there in right field," Dominique said.[27] The 31-19 Red Sox remained in first place by a half-game.

"I think every day there is something out there for us, and today it was out there for me to be able to get up there and get a base hit," said Dominique. "It's an unbelievable feeling to be able to contribute to a team like this. I see how hard these guys work, and when I come up here from Triple A it's not a vacation. I see how hard they work, day in and day out, and I want to work just as hard as them and hopefully not let them down. I want to prove that I am grateful for the opportunity to be here and to be a part of the team."[28]

Dominique's first major-league start, on June 9, was one to forget. In a scoreless game with San Diego, he failed to scoop Nomar Garciaparra's throw to first, which allowed a run to score, then overthrew Varitek at the plate, giving the Padres another run. Dominique went 0-for-4 and the Red Sox lost, 8-1. He was sent back to Pawtucket on June 11 when Scott Williamson was activated off the disabled list.[29]

Dominique was recalled in July when Trot Nixon went on the disabled list. He pinch-hit for Damon in a 12-5 Boston win over

Baltimore on July 26 and fouled out. When Orlando Cabrera was acquired, Dominique was again sent back to Pawtucket.[30] He was 2-for-11 in seven games. Boston went on to win the World Series and Dominique received a World Series ring.

Dominique was designated for assignment in September and signed to a minor-league deal by the New York Mets. After spring training, he was sold to the Toronto Blue Jays and sent to Syracuse of the Triple-A International League. He was batting .169 through 20 games in early May when Toronto needed an emergency catcher. Catcher Gregg Zaun was injured in a collision on the basepaths and went on the disabled list. Dominique was called up to replace him and he started on May 18 in Minnesota. Twins manager Ron Gardenhire tested the rusty catcher in the second inning and both Michael Cuddyer and Luis Rivas stole bases on poor throws to second. Dominique was pinch-hit for in the seventh and the Twins won, 3-2.[31]

Dominique's final major-league appearance was as a pinch-hitter for Vernon Wells on May 22 in a Toronto 9-2 loss to Washington. He flied out to right and was sent back to Syracuse. His season was cut short due to a foot injury in late June.[32] He signed a minor-league deal with Seattle in the offseason and was with them in spring training but sprained his knee. He was optioned to minor-league camp for rehab and played in exhibition games but was released in March. Dominique's major-league career had ended.[33]

Dominique returned to Nevada and in 2008 became a volunteer hitting coach for the women's softball team, which advanced to the NCAA Tournament. He became a full-time paid assistant in 2009 and continued with the club for several years.[34] In 2008, Dominique was inducted into the University of Nevada Athletics Hall of Fame.[35]

Dominique married Jennifer Huffman. They have a daughter, Cassidy. His father, Jeff, is the owner and writer of the *LA Dodger Chronicles* blog.[36]

In January 2017 Dominique suffered a devastating stroke that left him without speech or ability to write for six months. The stroke caused aphasia, making it difficult for him to communicate. "There was a blood vessel that just basically burst in his brain," his wife, Jen, disclosed. "That part of the brain basically fried, if you will, so he has to train a new part of the brain and the brain is such a unique, amazing organ, that it can be retrained."[37]

Andy recalled the long recovery process. "I couldn't say anything," he said. "I had to learn how to respond when people talked to me." He returned to the basics of the alphabet and simple word structure. He rarely went out in public. "His brain knows exactly what he wants to say, but it's disconnected from the mouth," Jen said.[38]

But recover he did and sure enough, Dominique went back to coaching. He became the coach of the baseball team at Wooster High School in Reno in 2019. "He slowly rebuilt his confidence," Jen said. "He's always had a heart and a desire to teach. When this opportunity came up, several people reached out and said, 'You should do it.' This is his next chapter of, post stroke, proving to himself that he can get out there."[39]

"Baseball is my life," Andy said. "I thought I was never going to do it again. That's why I want to (coach Wooster)." He is able to inspire players by his own example of overcoming obstacles. "Even in high school," Jen said, "He was told he would not amount to anything."[40]

"Nobody is going to tell him he can't do something," Jen said.[41]

SOURCES

College statistics were taken from the baseballcube.com

Besides the sources listed in the Notes, the author was aided by Baseball-reference.com, Familysearch.org, Findagrave.com, Retrosheet.org, and the following:

Dominique, Jeff. "A Father and a AAAA Player," in *LA dodger talk* blog, May 25, 2019. Retrieved June 28, 2022. ladodgertalk.com/2019/05/25/a-father-and-a-aaaa-player/.

"Meet Your Wolfpack," *Reno-Gazette Journal*, February 5, 1996: 2B.

NOTES

1. Rich Thompson, "Dominique Steps Up and Delivers," *Boston Herald*, May 31, 2004: 102.

2. Steve Buckley, "The Catchers in the Raw: PawSox Backstops Dominique, Shoppach Making Hay Down on the Farm," *Boston Herald*, May 9, 2004: B18.

3. Jeff Dominique, "What Drives a Free Agent," in the blog *LA dodger talk*. November 24, 2020. Retrieved June 28, 2022. ladodgertalk.com/2020/11/24/what-drives-a-free-agent/.

4. "Mission League," *Los Angeles Times*, March 6, 1992: C12; Tim Trepany, "Dominique Is Finally Rewarded With a Title," *Los Angeles Daily News*, August 15, 1991: S8.

5. Steve Elling, "Alemany's Dominique Chooses Nevada," *Los Angeles Times*, November 10, 1992: C7.

6. Eric Sondheimer, "Milligan Game Rosters Loaded with Prospects," *Los Angeles Daily News*, June 8, 1993: S1.

7. Reid Spencer, "No Matter What His Shape, Dominique Is a Heavy Hitter," *Charlotte Observer*, May 31, 1998: 18K.

8. Sondheimer, "Milligan Game Rosters"; Bill Ballou, "Man of Steel Isn't So Super – Damon Is Bigger and Slower," *Worcester Telegram & Gazette*, May 27, 2004: D4; Steve Henson, "Keeper of the Scores," *Los Angeles Times*, February 8, 1996: C9.

9. Eric Sondheimer, "Dominique Shedding His Old Image After Not Being Drafted/Ex-Alemany Star Loses 19 Pounds While at Nevada," *Los Angeles Daily News*, April 7, 1994: S9.

10. Andy Horschak, "Kroakers Win Title in Sweep," *Kenosha (Wisconsin) News*, August 14, 1995: 19.

11. Joe Santoro, "Dominique on Pace to Snap Home Run Record," *Reno Gazette-Journal*, March 19, 1996: 6C.

12. Joe Santoro, "Dominique Sets Packs HR Record," *Reno Gazette-Journal*, May 4, 1996: 4F.

13 Joe Santoro, "Dominique Caps Senior Season With MVP Award," *Reno Gazette-Journal*, May 16, 1997: 4E; "Dominique Named All-American," *Reno Gazette-Journal*, May 30, 1997: D1.

14 *2023 Nevada Baseball Record Book*, 49. Retrieved April 20, 2023. https://nevadawolfpack.com/documents/2023/3/13/Baseball_2023_RecordBook.pdf; Joe Santoro, "Dominique, a Pro at Last, Enjoying the Ride," *Reno Gazette-Journal*, August 24, 1997: 4D.

15 *2004 Red Sox Media Guide*, 101.

16 Dave Desmond, "Quick Beginning for Alemany's Dominique," *Los Angeles Daily News*, July 6, 1997: S11.

17 *2004 Red Sox Media Guide*, 102.

18 *2004 Red Sox Media Guide*, 102.

19 "Dominique Joins Red Barons," *Scranton Tribune*, July 17, 2001: B5.

20 John Nalbone, "Reeling Thunder Face Changes," *Trenton (New Jersey) Times*, April 27, 2002: E1; Van Rose, "Duckworth Baffles Columbus Hitters – Phillies' Projected No. 3 or 4 Starter Joins Triple-A Red Barons for the Day And Shuts Out Yanks' Farm Team Over 6 Innings," *Wilkes-Barre Times Leader*, March 17, 2002: 1C; *2004 Red Sox Media Guide*, 102.

21 Buckley.

22 Buckley.

23 Buckley.

24 John Connolly, "Dominique Gets Whiff of Success," *Boston Herald*, May 27, 2004: 112.

25 Jeff Dominique, "Welcome to Dodger Chronicles," in *LA Dodger Chronicles* blog. April 4, 2022. Retrieved June 28, 2022. ladodgerchronicles.com/welcome-to-dodger-chronicles/.

26 Ballou, "Man of Steel."

27 Thompson, "Dominique Steps Up."

28 Thompson, "Dominique Steps Up."

29 Mike Shalin, "Dominique Feels Heat," *Boston Herald*, June 11, 2004: 116; Jeff Horrigan, "Red Sox Notebook: Dominique Sent Back Down," *Boston Herald*, June 12, 2004: 44.

30 Phil O'Neill, "Injuries Keep Key Players Out," *Worcester Telegram & Gazette*, July 26, 2004: D2; Bill Ballou, "Cabrera Debut a Smash," *Worcester Telegram & Gazette*, August 2, 2004: D5.

31 John Lott, "Zaun Suffers 'Scary' Injury in Jays Loss," *Toronto National Post*, May 9, 2005: S6; "Bush Improves, but First Win Remains Elusive," *Toronto National Post*, May 19, 2005: S5.

32 Matt Michael, "Skychiefs Corner," *Syracuse Post-Standard*, July 22, 2005: C5.

33 Kirby Arnold, "Oldham Shines in Spring Start – Minor League Pitcher Thomas Oldham Subs for Felix Hernandez and Throws Three Scoreless Innings for the Mariners," *Everett* (Washington) *Daily Herald*, March 29, 2006.

34 "Dominique Goes Back to Nevada Softball Program," *Nevada Appeal*, August 19, 2009.

35 "Andy Dominique," Nevada Wolf Pack Hall of Fame. Retrieved June 27, 2022. nevadawolfpack.com/honors/hall-of-fame/andy-dominique/151.

36 "About Us," Dodger Chronicles. Retrieved June 27, 2022. ladodgerchronicles.com/about-us/.

37 Jim Krajewski, "After Suffering a Stroke, Dominique Named Baseball Coach at Wooster," *Reno Gazette Journal*, October 19, 2019: 2B.

38 Krajewski, 1B-2B.

39 Krajewski, 2B.

40 Krajewski, 1B-2B.

41 Krajewski, 2B.

A RED SOX MEMORY

In the ninth inning of Game Four of the 2004 World Series, with the Red Sox on the brink of victory, my wife and I debated whether to wake up our teenage daughter, Kelly, to watch on TV the expected history-making event to end the 86-year-old Curse. Kathie and I hesitated because 18 years earlier during Game Six of the 1986 World Series, we had awakened our then young son, Scott, to watch such a celebration, only for him to watch Mookie Wilson's groundball go through the legs of Bill Buckner to kibosh the victory ("You woke me up for this?"). Despite the bad jujus from that 1986 late-night episode, we did wake up Kelly, who watched in more amazement as I sat in stunned disbelief at the Red Sox victory while Kathie jumped for joy around the living room. Scott, now away at college, called to thank us for NOT notifying him this time and thus possibly jinxing the Sox. He then asked us to buy copies of the *Boston Globe* with its dramatic front-page headline for a keepsake.

CHARLIE BEVIS

ALAN EMBREE

BY BILL NOWLIN

Alan Embree was a left-handed reliever who pitched for 16 seasons of major-league ball and was a member of six teams that went to the postseason, going to the World Series twice – first with the 1995 Cleveland Indians and later with the triumphant 2004 Boston Red Sox.

Embree worked in 882 regular-season games, with a career earned-run average of 4.59. His won/lost record (not entirely meaningful for a specialist reliever) was 39-45. In the postseason, his ERA was a very impressive 1.66 in 31 games. Indicative of his specialist role was the fact that he worked fewer innings than games – he worked 21⅔ innings in those 31 postseason games, and 774 innings in his 882 regular-season games. His career WHIP (walks and hits per inning pitched) was 1.34.

Embree was born in The Dalles, Oregon, on January 23, 1970 and graduated from Prairie High School in Brush Prairie (Vancouver), Washington.[1] He lettered in basketball, baseball, football, and volleyball. He was All-Conference in baseball. At age 19, he was selected by the Cleveland Indians in the fifth round of the 1989 amateur draft. Credit for Embree's signing goes to scout Dave Roberts and scouting director Chet Montgomery. He wasn't an easy sign, but by September came to agreement.

He was a starting pitcher during his first years in the minors. In 1990 he was 4-4 (2.64 ERA) in 15 starts in rookie ball for the Appalachian League Burlington Indians. In 1991 he pitched in Single A, for the Columbus (Georgia) Indians of the South Atlantic League. He was 10-8 (3.59), with three complete games, one of them a shutout.

In 1992 Embree pitched for two teams and was called up to Cleveland in September. He started the season with Kinston (North Carolina) in the Class A+ Carolina League (10-5, 3.30) and then was advanced to Double A, pitching for Canton-Akron in the Eastern League (7-2, 2.28). Just a couple of days after Embree was called up, manager Mike Hargrove had him start on September 15 in Toronto against the Blue Jays. Embree's teammates staked him to a 3-0 lead in the top of the first. Taking the mound, he allowed one run on no hits in the bottom of the first. (A walk, a wild pitch, and a steal of third put Robbie Alomar in position to score on a sacrifice fly.)

Later in the game Embree gave up a two-run homer to Dave Winfield, and all told allowed five runs in 4⅔ innings of work. The final score was 5-4, Jays, and Embree bore the loss.[2] He started three more games that year, two of them wins (both coming after he'd left the game). His only other decision was also a loss, in his fourth start, on October 3 in Cleveland. Baltimore beat the Tribe, 7-1. Embree had given up four runs in four innings.

The years 1993 and 1994 were both with Canton-Akron, though Embree was plagued with arm problems in 1993 and appeared in only one game all season. He started the season on the DL with an MCL injury to his left elbow; giving it time to heal did not work and he had Tommy John elbow surgery in late June. He recovered and carried a full load in 1994, starting 27 games. He wasn't as effective as he had been, with a 5.50 ERA and a 9-16 record.

The Indians decided to convert Embree into a reliever and in 1995 he began the season in Triple A with the Buffalo Bisons.

On July 13 Cleveland sent Jason Grimsley down and called up Embree, who had already appeared in 30 games with an ERA of 0.89. He relieved in 23 games for Cleveland, though his ERA was 5.11. He was credited with three wins and bore two losses. It took him only a third of an inning (and five pitches) to pick up his first big-league win. He retired the only batter he faced at Jacobs Field, getting the last out in the sixth of a scoreless game against the visiting Oakland Athletics. He was thus the pitcher of record and when the Indians scored one in the bottom of the inning, he was in position to get the win in the 1-0 game. Two days later, he pitched the 11th and 12th innings and saw the Indians beat the Athletics again. He was sent back down, but quickly recalled, was sent back down, and called up again.

Embree pitched once in the ALCS, striking out the only Mariners batter he faced, and then pitched in four games of the six-game World Series, which Cleveland lost to the Atlanta Braves. He faced 14 batters over 3⅓ innings and was tagged for two hits and one run, but it was not a decisive one. His World Series ERA was 2.70.

In 1996 Embree opened the season with the team in Cleveland, but was optioned to Buffalo in mid-April for a while. He shuttled back and forth five times during the season, and he was kept busy in both places: For Buffalo he was 4-1 in 20 games (closing in 15 of the 20), and with Cleveland he worked in 24 games, 1-1, never working more than 2⅔ innings and seven times not even a full inning (in all, he pitched 31 innings in the 24 games). His ERA for the Indians was 6.39. Cleveland made it to the postseason, but was eliminated by Baltimore in the Division Series. Embree pitched in three of the four ALDS games, for a total of one inning. He gave up one run, hitting Rafael Palmeiro, who later scored on a grand slam hit off reliever Paul Shuey.

Dissatisfied with his '96 season, Embree said in February 1997, "One month I'd be good and the next month I'd be terrible. Then things would go like that from outing to outing. … I felt like I was a month behind all season." He kept active throwing throughout the winter months. "You can work out all you want," he said. "You can lift and run, but nothing takes the place of throwing to keep your arm strong."[3] He looked very good in spring training, said manager Mike Hargrove.

Near the end of spring training 1997, Embree was traded (with Kenny Lofton) to the Atlanta Braves for Marquis Grissom and David Justice. It was dubbed a "blockbuster" and "the biggest deal in club history" for the Braves.[4] It stunned both fan bases, and many of the players. "It was kind of like everybody's dog had been killed," said Tom Glavine.[5] Justice had hit the game-winning homer in Game Six of the 1995 World Series. Embree was described by some as a "throw-in" in the deal, to bring more balance to the deal. The deal was also one "motivated by baseball economics on both sides," according to Braves GM John Schuerholz.[6] Columnist Bob Nightengale was not kind, saying, "Embree, at best, is a mediocre pitcher. The man has a great arm, but Indians officials believe he lacks guts."[7] That Indians GM John Hart had disparaged Embree didn't sit well with him and even several years later it was reported that he had the words "No heart" and "Throw-in" written on the inside of his cap. In 2001, after Hart had announced it would be his last season with the Indians, Embree told *USA Today Baseball Weekly*, "I felt like calling him up wondering where he was going for his next job so I could stay away from him."[8]

Lofton had a very good year for the Braves, but Embree had arguably just as good a year at the tasks he was assigned. As the only left-hander in the Braves' bullpen, Embree appeared in 66 games, second only to Mark Wohler's 71, and his ERA of 2.54 was topped only by Greg Maddux (2.20) and right-handed reliever Mike Cather (2.39). He was 3-1. Getting the opportunity to work was key, in Embree's own view. "The more I'm out there, the more comfortable I feel," he said.[9]

The use of left-handed specialists had truly expanded by this time. Rangers GM Doug Melvin said, "You have to have them. You always need them. You don't necessarily need them as the closer. But you need them in the fifth and sixth or sixth and seventh for one or two batters because your starters don't go very far anymore. I think they're valuable to get one hitter out."[10] Right-handed relievers were more plentiful. Kevin Malone, Dodgers GM, said, "If you're left-handed, you've got a chance probably to pitch five years longer than one might expect."[11] Embree was what became known around this time as a LOOGY (Left-handed One Out Guy).

Embree signed a two-year deal with the Braves in January, but he traded uniforms in midseason again in 1998, traded straight up (on June 23) to the Arizona Diamondbacks for right-handed pitcher Russ Springer. It was pretty much a swap of "handedness" with the Braves needing a righty and the Diamondbacks needing a lefty (and the Braves having perhaps lost confidence in Embree). Both pitchers performed more or less the same throughout 1998, marginally better for their new club. Embree was, overall, in 55 games (35 with Arizona) with a combined 4.19 ERA. In November he was traded again, to the Giants for occasional outfielder Dante Powell. The D-Backs were looking for a center fielder.

Embree had a good 3.38 ERA in 1999 but (after signing a two-year deal in early February) slipped to 4.95 in 2000. He saw a little more postseason work in the National League Division Series with the Giants, pitching briefly in two games and retiring the five batters he faced.

In November he had minor surgery on his left elbow. After his career was over, Embree looked back on the help given him by his Tommy John surgery in 1993. "I was a power pitcher again," he said. "But I wasn't done. I took things from my rehab with me and created the maintenance program I followed throughout the rest of my career. The way I look at it is because of this maintenance program, it gave me seven to eight years onto my career."[12]

The next year, 2001, was not a good year at all. Embree appeared in 22 games for the Giants through June 26 but could never get on track. He had an 11.25 ERA for San Francisco, and it wasn't improving. Finally, they traded him, on June 29 (and had to put up some money, too), to get minor-league prospect Derek Hasselhoff from the Chicago White Sox. He pitched in 39 games for Chicago, and halved his ERA by working at a 5.03 pace. But that November, the White Sox granted him free agency. Two days after Christmas, Embree signed a one-year deal with the San Diego Padres.

It was like he'd been reborn. In 36 games for San Diego in 2002, Embree recorded an ERA of 1.26 and suddenly became a sought-after commodity. The Boston Red Sox worked a deal for him on June 23, sending the Padres two talented right-handed pitching prospects in Brad Baker and Dan Giese. He was energized, joining a team that was a possible pennant contender. He appeared in 32 games for the Red Sox with a 2.97 ERA. One outing may have exemplified his work as a lefty specialist. At Fenway Park on August 20, he was brought into a 2-1 game against the Texas Rangers in the top of the eighth. The Red Sox held the one-run lead, there were two outs, and there was a runner on third base. Embree was tasked with getting Rafael Palmeiro out. He threw one pitch. Palmeiro flied out to center. Embree's night was done. "He's throwing the ball now better than he has in his whole career," declared Red Sox manager Grady Little. "It makes you want to put him out there every single day."[13] Embree agreed he'd been going well: "This is as good as I've felt in a long time. I was scoped (elbow) the offseason before last, and that took care of the problem."[14]

In 2003 and 2004, after recovering from a shoulder injury in April 2003, Embree was a workhorse on two playoff-bound Red Sox teams, working in 65 games and then 71, with ERAs of 4.25 and 4.13. At the beginning of 2003, he was part of what the Boston media called "bullpen by committee." Red Sox GM Theo Epstein tried to be clear at the time: "That's not my choice of words." He called it "a deep, versatile, flexible bullpen with six quality options. … We believe the most critical outs in a game aren't necessarily in the ninth. They could, for instance, be in the seventh inning with the bases loaded, not in the ninth with a three-run lead."[15] Actually, Embree had not reported in top condition, which he admitted, going to Florida for a while in April to get his shoulder strength back. "I didn't prepare myself. … I failed myself," he told the *Boston Globe*'s Bob Hohler.[16] He'd come to love the intensity in Boston, though. "My mentality is better suited to this brand of baseball. I'm a guy that if it doesn't count, I [stink]. I've proved that. I like it when the game's on the line."[17]

Embree pitched in three games in the 2003 Division Series, and then in five of the seven games of the ALCS against the Yankees. In 4⅔ innings of ALCS work, he gave up three hits, but no runs. He was the winning pitcher in Game Six, securing the final two outs in the bottom of the sixth (including a one-out strikeout of Jason Giambi with men on second and third, followed by inducing a groundout), seeing the Sox score three runs to overtake the Yankees and go up 7-6 in the top of the seventh, and then not letting the ball get out of the infield in the bottom of the seventh. The score held up and he got the W.

In Game Seven, manager Grady Little left Pedro Martínez in too long and the Yankees scored three runs to tie the game, 5-5. Embree was the pitcher brought in after Pedro was taken out. He got the one batter he was asked to get. Mike Timlin closed out the inning. The Yankees' Aaron Boone homered off Tim Wakefield in the bottom of the 10th, sending the Yankees to the World Series and sending the Red Sox home.

The Red Sox got their revenge the next year, in storybook fashion. Once again they battled the Yankees in the ALCS, this time losing the first three games and getting clobbered 19-8 in Game Three. Embree gave up two runs in that game – half of the total of four he ever gave up in all his 31 postseason games. He was just one of six Red Sox pitchers to give up runs in the beatdown. Then Boston won two extra-inning games in a row, with David Ortiz knocking in the winning run both times. Embree pitched the 10th and part of the 11th in Game Four and got the last two outs in the top of the 10th in Game Five. The Red Sox took it to Game Seven, and built a very comfortable 10-3 lead over the Yankees. New York got two men on base and there were two outs. Manager Terry Francona asked Embree to relieve Mike Timlin and get the final out. That he did, getting Ruben Sierra to ground out, second to first.[18] Thus, a photograph well-known in New England which shows catcher Jason Varitek leaping into Embree's arms at the end of the game. The Red Sox were bound for their first World Series since 1986.

"It was the longest ground ball of my life," Embree said of the grounder. "It was a rollover, just as I planned it, and as it passed me toward Pokey (Reese) at second, it felt like it was taking an eternity. It felt like a moment frozen in time."[19]

The Red Sox swept the St. Louis Cardinals in the World Series. Embree pitched in three of the four games, earning a hold in Game Four.

The very next year, he experienced something unusual – Embree started the season with the Red Sox and ended it with the Yankees. With a world championship ring to his credit, he struggled over 43 appearances and held a 7.65 ERA. The Red Sox designated him for assignment, and then simply released him on July 19. Eleven days later, he signed as a free agent with the "pitching-starved" Yankees.[20] He had been in Sunriver, Oregon, fishing the Deschutes River for brown trout when he got the call. Commenting on going from the Red Sox to the Yankees, he said, "It's a beautiful ring. But that was last year. I'm trying to get one here right now."[21]

Embree worked in 24 games for New York, with a nearly identical 7.53 ERA. That November the Yanks released him, too.

He spent 2006 back with the Padres, and had a good year with a 3.27 ERA earned over 73 appearances. The Oakland A's worked out a two-year deal, signing Embree for 2007 and 2008. In 68 games in 2007, he worked a lot of them as the team's closer since Huston Street was injured for two months in the middle of the season. Embree filled the role well, and had a 3.97 ERA for the year.

At age 39, Embree pitched one last season in the majors, for the Colorado Rockies in 2009. He appeared in 36 games, but worked only a total of 24⅔ innings. His last decision was a win, on July 7 in a game against the Washington Nationals in Denver. The score was 4-4 after seven innings. With two outs, the Nationals got a man on first base and left-handed hitter Nyjer Morgan coming up to bat. Manager Jim Tracy called Embree in from the bullpen. Before he threw his first pitch to the batter, he picked baserunner Austin Kearns off first base, retiring the side. The Rockies scored one on a sacrifice fly in the bottom of the eighth and Tracy turned to Street, the closer, to secure the win. Embree had won the game without throwing even one pitch. Recalling the short outing after he game, he said, "I'm going, 'What just happened?' And then I came in and they went, 'You're done. Do you think you can go tomorrow?' I'm still in a daze."[22]

Three days later, Embree was hit in the leg by a line drive, fracturing his right tibia. He was out for the rest of the season.

Embree gave it one more shot in 2010 and signed a minor-league deal with the Red Sox. He appeared in eight games for the Triple-A Pawtucket Red Sox (3.68) and was called up to Boston, but wasn't used and was designated for assignment, and then released. Five days later, he signed with the White Sox again and they assigned him to play for their International League farm team, the Charlotte Knights. He was 0-1 in six games and was released on May 28. His career as a player was over.

Right near the end, the day he'd been released by the Red Sox, he expressed no anger: "I'm good with it. I've had a good career. I'm quite happy with where I am."[23]

Despite all the time he had spent in the National League, Embree's role was almost always as a lefty specialist, and so he rarely had the chance to bat. In his 882 big-league games he had only four plate appearances. He walked once, but was caught stealing. He struck out twice. His career batting average remains .000.

Embree's wife, Melanie, was a physical therapist he met during his rehab work after the Tommy John surgery. As of 2014, the Embrees lived in Bend, Oregon, where Melanie owned her own practice, Momentum Physical Therapy. Alan said, "I owe her a lot. She would probably say I didn't listen to her much, but I relied on her. I sought more advice from her than I did my trainers."[24] The Embrees have two children, Alan ("Ace") and Andie.

Embree worked as head baseball coach at Bend's Summit High School and also worked coaching the Bend Elks, an amateur team in the West Coast League, a wooden-bat collegiate baseball league in Oregon, Washington, and British Columbia.

SOURCES

In addition to the sources noted in this biography, the author also accessed Embree's player file from the National Baseball Hall of Fame, the *Encyclopedia of Minor League Baseball*, Retrosheet.org, Baseball-Reference.com, and the SABR Minor Leagues Database, accessed online at Baseball-Reference.com.

NOTES

1 Thanks to Kristin Wennerlind, librarian at Prairie High School, for explaining, "We are located in Vancouver, but many refer to the area (and location of our district) as Brush Prairie." Email to author, May 27, 2015.

2 Winfield said after the game, "The first time you face someone, you always like to leave an impression." Associated Press, "Winfield, Jays Stop Indians, 5-4," *Washington Post*, September 16, 1992: C6.

3 Sheldon Ocker, "Embree Employing Strong-Arm Tactics," *Chronicle-Telegram* (Elyria, Ohio), February 18, 1997

4 Bill Zack, "This One Really Is A BIG Deal," *Augusta* (Georgia) *Chronicle,* March 26, 1997: 6.

5 Zack.

6 Murray Chass, "Eyes on the Bottom Line: Braves and Indians Trade," *New York Times*, March 26, 1997: B13. The deal saved the Braves a reported $7.7 million. See Associated Press, "Justice, Lofton in Monster Trade," *Oneonta Star*, March 26, 1997.

7 Bob Nightengale, Braves' Bold Move Will Haunt Them," *The Sporting News*, April 7, 1997: 24.

8 Bob Nightengale, "Chatter," *USA Today Baseball Weekly*, April 18-24, 2001: 3.

9 Bill Zack, "Embree Emerges Early as Tight Closer," *The Sporting News*, April 21, 1997: 14.

10 Murray Chass, "Left-Handed Relievers Find Long Job Security," *New York Times*, February 21, 1999: SP2.

11 Chass.

12 Ben Montgomery, "Former Pitcher, Alan Embree, Credits Physical Therapy for Longevity," ptpubnight.com/2014/10/21/former-pitcher-alan-embree-credits-physical-therapy-longevity/

13 Bob Ryan," It's Good Work if You Can Get It," *Boston Globe,* August 2, 2002: E1.

14 Ryan.

15 Murray Chass, "Teams Are Playing Musical Chairs in Bullpens," *New York Times*, January 12, 2003: SP12.

16 Bob Hohler, "For Embree, Longer Stay Would Be Relief," *Boston Globe*, February 24, 2004.

17 Hohler.

18 Heading into the 2004 ALCS, Yankees Bernie Williams, John Olerud, and Sierra had a combined .133 batting average against Embree.

19 Ben Montgomery.

20 The phrase was used in an Associated Press article: "Embree Joins Yankees' Bullpen," *Albany Times Union*, July 1, 2005.

21 Tyler Kepner, "Boston to Oregon to Bronx, Embree Has New Uniform," *New York Times*, July 31, 2005: H5.

22 Thomas Harding, "Embree Earns 'W' Without Throwing Pitch," MLB.com, July 8, 2009.

23 Ian Browne, "Embree's Second Stint with Boston Ends," MLB.com, May 1, 2010.

24 Ben Montgomery.

KEITH FOULKE

BY KELEY RUSSO AND KAREN DELUCA STEPHENS

"I wish I had my own baseball card," Chris Singleton remembers Keith Foulke saying to him during a road trip in El Paso while they were playing together in the Giants' minor-league system. "He wasn't a guy who was highly touted, but I said, 'You're good, man. It's just a matter of time.' Now, here he is, however many years later, and he's one of the top closers in the game."[1]

Many kids in East Texas dream of becoming professional football players and Keith Foulke was no exception. In high school he played both football and baseball, but it was a baseball scholarship to Galveston Junior College that changed his aspirations and ultimately the trajectory of his professional sports career. Fate coupled with a competitive spirit and a desire to win found him on the mound on October 27, 2004. That cold October night would live on in the memories of Red Sox Nation, forever cementing Keith Foulke as one the game's heroes. The evening had an ethereal feeling with a total lunar eclipse, the first during a World Series. Because of cloud cover in St. Louis, the deep red moon was not visible, instead lending a copper hue to the sky over Busch Memorial Stadium.[2] But at the peak of the eclipse, while Red Sox fans "around the country watched with a red ball in the October sky[,]"[3] the Boston Red Sox won their first World Series in 86 years to end the Curse of the Bambino. Before the game Foulke said, "I hope we win tonight. I'm ready for this to be over."[4] All of Red Sox Nation would have agreed and to add to the historic significance – and the superstitions of that night – the game was played on the 18th anniversary of Game Seven of the Red Sox' loss to the Mets in 1986, a painful World Series memory for all Red Sox fans.

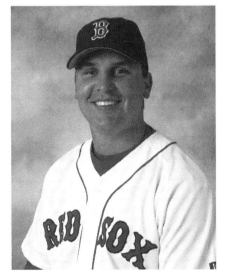

Even the way Game Four ended was unprecedented, with a final out at first base that every Red Sox fan, breaths held, watched as if time had stopped. Best described by Red Sox broadcaster Joe Castiglione, "A 1-and-0 pitch. Here it is. Swing and a groundball, stabbed by Foulke. He has it. He underhands it to first – and the Boston Red Sox are the world champions. For the first time in 86 years, the Red Sox have won baseball's world championship. Can you believe it?"[5] Foulke later recalled, "I was so excited when I saw the ball coming right back at me that I jumped higher than I needed to. That is a moment I will never, ever forget."[6] "But as soon as I had it and I tossed it towards first that's when everything was like 'holy cow, we actually did this.'"[7] All of this emotion is best captured by the image of catcher Jason Varitek leaping into Foulke's arms.

The 2004 Red Sox team, affectionately dubbed the Team of Idiots, was filled with large personalities and big talents, like Curt Schilling, Kevin Millar, Pedro Martínez, and David Ortiz. So, no surprise, Keith Foulke could go unseen. I was "never big on hyping myself as a closer, I was very quiet. Get the job done. Go celebrate with your boys."[8] A self-described "unextraordinary athlete," he made "the transition from little-known minor leaguer to All-Star reliever sound highly unlikely."[9] However, he closed out all four World Series games, with a win in the first game and a save in the fourth. In the 2004 postseason, Foulke pitched in 11 of the 14 Red Sox games, giving up only one earned run in 14 innings for an ERA of 0.64.

It was exactly this competitiveness and focus on constant improvement that came to define his baseball career.

The Red Sox' ability to close a game lacked cohesiveness and once again led to a frustrating loss against the Yankees in the 2003 Championship Series. By the end of 2004, the team bet on Foulke, who delivered exactly what was needed. From 2000 to 2004, Foulke was considered one of the best closers in baseball.[10] In a career spanning 11 years, he pitched in 619 games (786 innings) with 191 saves, 718 strikeouts to 194 walks, an ERA of 3.33, and a record of 41-37. In his All-Star season of 2003 with the Oakland Athletics, Foulke led the American League with 43 saves and ranked in the season's top 25 in 15 other major statistical categories.[11] For the 2004 season, the Red Sox were looking for a quality closer. Foulke's fastball was in the upper 80s and, as manager Terry Francona said, "Good teams have deep bullpens."[12] Although not as overpowering as Mariano Rivera, "from 1999-2004, Foulke was about as valuable as any reliever in the game, amassing a 2.43 ERA and 171 saves in 521⅔ innings. As a comparison during those same years, Rivera had a 2.20 ERA but threw 100 fewer innings."[13]

Keith Charles Foulke was born to US Air Force Sergeant Charles and Pauline (Hagen) Foulke at Ellsworth Air Force Base, South Dakota, on October 19, 1972. Chuck Foulke, a native of Youngstown, Ohio, had served in Vietnam. After he retired from the Air Force, the family, including 5-year-old Keith, moved to Texas, where Chuck became a deputy sheriff in Harris

County (Houston). Chuck, an avid baseball fan, encouraged his son's early love of sports and helped coach him, even working nights to make it possible. From an early age, Chuck said, Keith declared that he would be a professional baseball player. In Little League he learned proper throwing mechanics and the importance of control. By high school, his baseball skills were evident. Al Spangler, a 13-year major leaguer, was Foulke's coach at Hargrave High School in Huffman, Texas, and spotted his natural talent, describing him as "head and shoulders above everyone else.... He was by far the best athlete I ever had here."[14] In his senior year Foulke earned district MVP honors.[15]

In 1991, after graduating from high school, Foulke accepted his only scholarship offer and found himself at Galveston (Texas) Junior College. In the fall of his freshman year, the Galveston Whitecaps participated in the team's first fall baseball tournament. Head coach Dick Smith called Foulke "our outstanding individual of the tournament."[16] By his sophomore year, Foulke was chosen for the National Junior College All-Star team representing the US at an international tournament in Merida, Mexico. The US team finished third behind Cuba (first) and Mexico (second).[17] In May 1993 Foulke and the team went on to the Junior College Division 1 Baseball World Series in Colorado, losing in the sixth round. That summer Foulke pitched in the Alaska Summer League with the Anchorage Bucs and was the team's ace, helping to win their fifth straight championship with a 4-0 record and a 1.98 ERA. This drew the attention of the Detroit Tigers, who selected Foulke in the 14th round of the 1993 amateur draft, but Foulke did not sign.[18] Anchorage coach Ed Cheff was the baseball coach for Lewis-Clark State College, a powerhouse college baseball program in Lewiston, Idaho, and Foulke who was searching for a championship, enrolled there. Cheff taught Foulke the mental toughness he would eventually need for postseason play in the coming years. Soon he caught the eye of John Shafer, a scout for the San Francisco Giants, and was taken by the Giants in the ninth round of the 1994 draft.[19]

In 1993 Foulke met Mandy Nicole Whitted at Lewis-Clark State College. That Thanksgiving Mandy brought Keith home to Boise, Idaho, to meet her parents. Keith and Mandy married in July 1997. After the 2004 World Series, Mandy's mother, Pat Jones, recalled asking Keith during that first visit about his intentions with her daughter. Keith firmly stated he was going to become a major-league baseball player and make millions. Thinking it was youthful arrogance, Pat just smiled. "This table discussion has become part of our family lore," she said in 2004.[20]

When Foulke joined the Everett Giants of the Northwest League in 1994 he was coached by Keith Comstock, a left-handed pitcher who had sometimes relied on his screwball during his own career.[21] In the 1980s pitchers including Roger Clemens had regularly used the split-finger fastball, but by the time Foulke arrived with the Giants, the coaching staff discouraged the use of the splitter, believing that throwing it would reduce a pitcher's speed.[22] Foulke worried that this change in pitching philosophy might doom his career, even calling his father with his concern.[23] Comstock, however, showed Foulke how he threw a screwball, which Foulke adapted into his changeup, working on it for the next seven years until the late 1990s when he fully developed his "fastball up and in, and changeup down in the zone."[24] He learned early that control was his weapon and never sacrificed it for velocity, making him particularly effective against lefties.

Foulke moved through the Giants' minor-league system very quickly, being promoted to Shreveport of the Double-A Texas league in 1996. There he met Doug Mirabelli, his future Red Sox teammate, who said, "He was a very confident guy, he threw strikes and he had three good pitches."[25] On May 21, 1997, Foulke debuted with the Giants, and pitched in 11 games that season. But the Barry Bonds-led clubhouse of the Giants was a tough environment, with Foulke commenting, "I was pretty overwhelmed."[26] In July he was traded to the Chicago White Sox along with five other prospects, in what was called the "White Flag Trade," a controversial deal that many felt gutted the White Sox.[27] When he was moved from starter to the bullpen, his feelings were a bit mixed, "but I loved to pitch and moving to the bullpen was my ticket to a big-league career so I did it."[28] Foulke never pitched like a closer and didn't care to be called a closer. No matter where he was going to pitch in the game, he wanted to pitch the same way. But having been a starter, and one who liked to pitch multiple innings, ultimately helped him go further as a closer.

By 1998 Foulke was at home in the bullpen as the set-up man for closers Matt Karchner and Bill Simas. Late in the season he had arthroscopic surgery on his right shoulder to remove a bone spur.[29] After a painful season, the surgery increased his mobility and flexibility, and in 1999 results showed: a 2.22 ERA in 67 games and 105⅓ innings pitched, and a vote for the AL Cy Young Award. He was a workhorse on the mound, and in 2000 with Bob Howry struggling, Foulke was tapped as the White Sox' primary closer and was an integral part of their AL Central Division title with 34 saves.[30]

Foulke continued to thrive, recording 76 saves in 2000-2001. Strong performance, however, was not enough to keep Foulke in Chicago. Even though he ranked third on the White Sox saves list, he struggled, losing his closer spot in 2002 and going without a save from June 28 to September 16. After the season Foulke was traded to the Oakland A's for Billy Koch, one of the AL's top closers. The deal allowed Oakland some flexibility with payroll while still keeping a focus on performance. Chuck knew the move hurt his son, "[but] he won't make waves, he doesn't have an aggressive personality... and it was all the best for him, because the situation in Chicago was one of turmoil and confusion."[31] Reflecting on his years in Chicago, Foulke contrasted the experience with Boston where fan enthusiasm and media attention was far more intense. He said he valued his six seasons with the White Sox, playing with the same guys for five or six seasons and helping rebuild that team.[32]

Foulke's hard work paid off by the end of the season, becoming the A's closer. For Oakland GM Billy Beane, Foulke was "still one of the premier end-of-the-game guys in our league."[33] In 2003 he led the American League with 43 saves, was named to the All-Star team, and won the American League Rolaids Relief Man of the Year Award. *The Sporting News* named him 2003 AL Reliever of the Year. However, the 2003 season ended dramatically with the loss to the Red Sox in the Division Series. In one of baseball's fateful moments that later felt more like destiny, Foulke gave up the game-winning double to David Ortiz in Game Four. "Losing. I hated losing and that's all I really remember about that series," he said in 2014.[34]

After being granted free agency in October 2003, Foulke was wooed by Theo Epstein, who took him to a Celtics game at the TD Garden. There he saw up close the enthusiasm for Boston sports. At the time of the Boston offer, Foulke commented, "Just the excitement of playing for a team with this heritage and this history is something I want to do before I retire. I would love to be part of a championship."[35] It also didn't hurt that Foulke, a hockey fan, had a message on his answering machine from the Bruins hockey legend Bobby Orr, who told him, "You win in this town, you're forever idolized."[36] He signed with the Red Sox on January 7, 2004, with a deal structured to pay him up to $26.5 million if he was the regular closer for the team through 2007. About signing with the Red Sox rather than Oakland, Foulke said, "I want to be a winner before I go out."[37] At age 31 and after seven years in major-league baseball, he had secured the opportunity he had been looking for: He was part of a team built around winning a championship and was in a challenging major market. He described the 2004 Red Sox clubhouse as "very professional, many of the players had already done great things in baseball – MVPs, championship winners. There was hardware around the room."[38] He had played with Doug Mirabelli and Bill Mueller as well as Terry Francona, who had been Oakland's bench coach in 2003. Despite very different personalities, "when it came game time, everyone was there for the right reason. We didn't have egos in the clubhouse."[39]

The 2004 season started off strong for the Red Sox. They beat the Yankees in six of their first seven games in their April matchups. Foulke was a big part of the team's early strength, able to act as a neutralizer to the great Yankees reliever Mariano Rivera, something the Red Sox lacked in 2003. Mike Timlin, who had been crucial in the 2003 season welcomed Foulke as an addition to the bullpen. "Last year we didn't have the guy that could go out there and throw a scoreless [10th] and [11th]. The extra dimension we have – we have a three inning closer basically."[40] By the end of May, Foulke had converted 10 out of 11 saves and the team was essentially tied with the Yankees for first in the AL East.[41] Despite the strong start, July found the Red Sox lagging the Yankees by 7½ games. For Foulke the turning point started on July 24 with their three-game series against the Yankees. After a loss in the first game, the Red Sox won the next two games, which saw a memorable confrontation between Jason Varitek and Álex Rodríguez on the 24th, with Foulke nearly running down Johnny Pesky as he burst out of the bullpen to get to his teammates on the field. About that series, Foulke said that the Red Sox were "not cowering to the Yankees anymore. It was time to stand up for the team."[42] Foulke, earning a save in the third game, knew the significance of the wins. "That was an important series. We knew we had to get by the Yankees to win anything and that weekend showed we could handle them."[43] Foulke was right. The team's record improved to 45-20 and on September 27 they won the wild card over Tampa Bay exactly one month before their historic final game.

As the regular season wrapped up, Foulke's performance was phenomenal, with 32 saves and a 2.17 ERA.[44] Foulke found himself at the center of the Red Sox' sweep of the Angels in the Division Series, pitching in two of three games with a save in Game Two. In the ALCS against the Yankees, Foulke pitched in five games without allowing a run. With the Red Sox down 3-0 in the series, he threw 100 pitches over the next three days to help his team force Game Seven.[45] In Games Four and Five, he pitched for a total of four innings. Forgetting to bring his glove to New York, he had to borrow Curt Leskanic's glove to return to the mound to shut down the Yankees in the ninth inning of Game Six, popularly known as "the bloody sock game," and earn the save in the 4-2 Red Sox victory.[46]

Foulke's continued mental toughness and steady performance was critical as he pitched in all four games of the World Series against the Cardinals, finding himself on the mound in the bottom of the ninth inning of Game Four with the Red Sox leading 3-0. The first batter he faced, Albert Pujols, singled into center field when the ball went through Foulke's legs. Scott Rolen flied out to right field for the first out. Foulke then struck out Jim Edmonds, bringing Cardinals shortstop Edgar Rentería to bat. The first pitch was a ball and Pujols took second base. All season long, Red Sox Nation had been urged to believe: "Why not us?" With two outs and a runner on second, that belief once again was focused on Foulke, who had closed out a nailbiting ninth inning in Game Six of the ALCS on his 32nd birthday. On Foulke's 1-and-0 pitch, Rentería hit the ball back to Foulke, who took a slight hop when he caught it and in what seemed like an eternity to Red Sox fans, jogged toward first and tossed the ball to Doug Mientkiewicz for the out that gave the Red Sox their first World Series championship in 86 years. Foulke has said many times that the play was "one of the greatest moments of my life."[47] On a personal level for Foulke the moment was "a whole lifetime of joy and a huge release of satisfaction, that I'd reached my ultimate goal."[48] As "Why not us?" had become the rallying cry of the postseason, "Back to Foulke" has captured the euphoria and vindication all Red Sox fans felt with that final play.

Manny Ramírez was named the World Series MVP despite many sportswriters and fans believing the award belonged to Foulke, including Foulke himself. The New York Baseball Writers Association voted him the Babe Ruth Award, given to the player with the best performance in the World Series, essentially recognizing Foulke as their MVP. Speaking about the MVP award, Terry Francona said, "What Keith Foulke did was incredible. That's how you win – when people do special things."[49]

For Foulke, it did seem that the heroic effort was not without its downside. The 2005 season was the start of a challenging period for him, both personally and professionally. At the beginning of the season, he suffered with pain in both knees and his elbow. He had refused preseason surgery on his arm, which in 2012 he said he regretted, acknowledging that the decision to postpone "essentially ended my career as an effective pitcher."[50] He was not pitching well, was unhappy in his personal life, and his disappointment in his performance became a vicious cycle. "I wasn't helping the team. It was bad news."[51] His struggles seemed to continue when, on June 28, 2005, he lost a three-run lead and gave up a ninth-inning grand slam to Cleveland's Travis Hafner. He walked off the field to the fans booing and jeering him and later in the clubhouse in response to questions from reporters about his performance, Foulke said, "I'm more embarrassed to walk into this locker room and look at the faces of my teammates than I am to walk out and see Johnny from Burger King booing me. I'm worried about these guys, not everybody else."[52] The response struck some sportswriters as aloof and arrogant and generated a series of articles and commentaries on sports programs.[53] The fuss confused Foulke, who said he never intended his comment as a snub or criticism of the fans, but rather was meant to be taken as a joke, which further fueled the press. "The whole thought was (even if they don't believe), I still believe we're going to win the World Series whether I go out and blow a game against Cleveland in June or not."[54] Foulke felt his humor and sarcasm was taken out of context by the media, acknowledging that he didn't like the hero worship placed on athletes. "I spoke the truth to sportswriters," he said.[55] "I wasn't belittling anybody when I said that. I have better things to do than to try and put myself above everybody else."[56] He never saw himself any different than Johnny Burger King.

Foulke had surgery on one knee in July, then on the other before the 2006 season, but lost his closer position to Jonathan Papelbon. Without an offer extension from the Red Sox, Foulke signed with the Cleveland Indians in 2007 as a free agent, "but in my heart I knew I couldn't pitch at the big-league level."[57] He stepped down on February 16, 2007, before spring training. Cleveland's GM, Mark Shapiro, recalled what a professional and classy decision this was, with Foulke expressing that he didn't want to let his teammates down again.

On February 8, 2008, with his elbow surgery complete, Foulke left retirement and signed a one-year contract with the Athletics, where he was again a set-up man. Being on the West Coast let him be close to his family and he pitched in 31 games. In 2009, disappointed by no other forthcoming offers, he found himself pitching for the Newark Bears of the independent Atlantic League of Professional Baseball, turning down Triple-A offers he later regretted.

Independent teams are not farm clubs of major-league teams, so players strive to play well enough to sign with an affiliate. The Bears' strong reputation was a draw for many former major leaguers looking to get back to that level. Foulke wasn't alone. Two-time All-Star Carl Everett, former Yankee Shawn Chacon, former Oriole Jay Gibbons, and former All-Star closer Armando Benítez faced similar circumstances. The Bears decided to stockpile their roster with well-known players as a strategy for attracting fans and winning games. With a modest team record and minimal fan support, the strategy didn't work.[58] Foulke hoped going to Newark would get him noticed but receiving $948 every two weeks and missing his family in Phoenix, he acknowledged, "It's this or retire. I don't want to retire."[59] Like the others in the locker room, he had something to prove, after "going out on other people's terms."[60] His season started strong, with 12⅓ innings pitched and an 0.75 ERA,[61] but ultimately, there were no phone calls to the Bears, no major-league teams seeking help on the last day they could acquire players for their postseason rosters.[62]

Foulke retired from baseball in 2009. Matt Pouliot, sportswriter for NBC Sports, recognized Foulke as one of the best dozen players eligible but left off the Hall of Fame ballot in 2013, commenting that, "It seemed like he pretty much gave up his arm for the Red Sox's run in 2004, when he pitched 83 innings in the regular season and 14 more in the postseason (allowing just one run)."[63] Foulke's commitment to mentoring young ballplayers led to a role in player development for four seasons with the Red Sox, starting in 2016. As an adviser, helping young pitchers get into the big leagues, Foulke told the players he worked with to be "the best pitcher you can be on this pitch. Repeat, repeat, repeat."[64] He donated to the Huffman Little League and Huffman Athletic Booster, and sponsored the batting cages at the Hargrave High School baseball field, which have his name on them. "Many of the upgrades to our facilities are due to his generosity, time, and desire to help his alma mater," said Hargrave baseball coach Tom DeBerry.[65]

Foulke is the father of three boys. His oldest son from his first marriage, Kade, followed in his footsteps, enrolling in Galveston Junior College. He spent the summer of 2022 pitching for the Brockton (Massachusetts) Rox of the Futures Collegiate Baseball League with the sons of David Ortiz, Pedro Martínez, and Manny Ramírez. The league "ranks a few notches below the prestigious Cape Cod League" but provides players entering college and those playing at the Division level access to consistent playing time. ..."[66] As of 2023, after he and his second wife divorced, he resided in Arizona with his two younger sons, Kyler and Kasen. Foulke said he was watching as his sons developed as athletes if they chose and was leaving the coaching to others. "I've taken a step back and being 'just dad' to my sons," he said.[67]

For Foulke, coming to New England feels like a homecoming with each visit. "People still stop me on the street in Boston to thank me for what I did in 2004," he said. "I enjoy coming back to Boston every chance I get."[68] He's been seen raking the dirt on the Brockton Rox field, attending a UNH football game, or posing for photos with fans while attending a Rox game. For the 100th anniversary of Fenway Park in September 2012, Foulke threw the ceremonial first pitch to catcher Jason Varitek, with the two reenacting the famous World Series championship leap of Varitek into Foulke's arms. Winning the World Series "was the best moment of my life," he once said.[69] It was "the first time I've ever won anything. Not in Little League. Not in high school. Not in college."[70]

"At first, the victory was more of a personal thing," Foulke said in 2014. "My personal battle with baseball and the years of work and all the sacrifices. It wasn't until the parade that it soaked in. … There was a lot of emotion and that's when you learned that Red Sox blood runs through these people."[71] Red Sox fans would agree that "[we] were all a part of that groundball," he said in 2022.[72]

Adjusting to life after playing baseball in the big leagues has not always been easy, and as Foulke acknowledged, the shift to retirement happens abruptly from one day to the next.[73] But after a career that spanned 11 seasons, playing for four major-league teams, Foulke's heart ultimately belongs to Boston, he said. "I'm a Red Sox fan, and I live and breathe Red Sox baseball."[74]

SOURCES

In addition to the sources cited in the Notes, the authors consulted Baseball-Reference.com, Retrosheet.org, Baseball-Almanac.com, and Familysearch.org.

NOTES

1 Susan Slusser, "Closing a Chapter/Keith Foulke: A's Reliever Gets a Chance to Go Back to Chicago for All-Star Game and Show His Former Team They Made a Mistake," *San Francisco Chronicle*, July 12, 2003: C1. https://www.sfgate.com/sports/article/Closing-a-chapter-Keith-Foulke-A-s-reliever-2603717.php.

2 Joe Rao, "Lunar Eclipse Could Make Baseball History," NBC News, October 22, 2004. https://www.nbcnews.com/id/wbna6309920.

3 Dan Shaughnessy, *Reversing the Curse* (Boston: Houghton Mifflin, 2005), 226.

4 Pat Jones, "Pitcher's Mother-In-Law Shares in Red Sox Victory," *Centralia* (Washington) *Chronicle,* November 1, 2004. https://www.chronline.com/stories/pitchers-mother-in-law-shares-in-red-sox-victory,236430.

5 Howard Herman, "Keith Foulke, to the Joy of Red Sox Fans, Makes a visit to Wahconah Park," *Berkshire Eagle* (Pittsfield, Massachusetts), June 30, 2022. https://www.berkshireeagle.com/sports/local_sports/keith-foulke-to-the-joy-of-red-sox-fans-makes-a-visit-to-wahconah-park/article_c3e4f1e2-f620-11ec-a765-1f5e44dc35c5.html.

6 Tim Daniels, "Keith Foulke Talks 2004 Red Sox Title, Historic Comeback vs. Yankees in B/R AMA Session," BleacherReport.com, October 27, 2020. https://bleacherreport.com/articles/2915361-keith-foulke-talks-2004-red-sox-title-historic-comeback-vs-yankees-in-br-ama.

7 Herb Crehan, "Keith Foulke Remembers the 2004 World Championship," BostonBaseballHistory.com, September 23, 2014. https://bostonbaseballhistory.com/new-keith-foulke-remembers-the-2004-world-championship/.

8 Curse-Breaker ft. Keith Foulke, 2Seam, Episode 3, May 31, 2020, https://podcasters.spotify.com/pod/show/2seam/episodes/Curse-Breaker-ft—Keith-Foulke-eeqk9d.

9 Slusser.

10 "Fenway's Best Players: Pitchers." Fenway Park Diaries. https://fenwayparkdiaries.com/best%20players/keith%20foulke.htm.

11 Lewis-Clark State College, Warrior Athletic Hall of Fame, Baseball, 2015. https://lcwarriors.com/honors/warrior-athletics-hall-of-fame/keith-foulke/14.

12 Roch Kubatko, "Red Sox, Foulke Reach 3-Year Deal," *Baltimore Sun*, December 14, 2003. https://www.baltimoresun.com/news/bs-xpm-2003-12-14-0312140134-story.html.

13 Matthew Pouliot, "A Dozen Missed: The Best Players Left Off the Hall of Fame Ballot," NBC Sports, November 26, 2013. https://mlb.nbcsports.com/2013/11/26/a-dozen-dismissed-the-best-players-left-off-the-hall-of-fame-ballot/.

14 Slusser.

15 "Meet Your 1992 Galveston College Whitecaps," *Galveston Daily News*, February 2, 1992: 23.

16 Manuel Moreno Jr., "GC Makes the Grade after 1st Home Tourney," *Galveston Daily News*, October 16, 1991: 14.

17 Scott Archibald, "Whitecaps Well-Armed for Spring Campaign," *Galveston Daily News*, February 7, 1993: 19.

18 "Keith Foulke Trades & Transactions," Baseball-Almanac.com. https://www.baseball-almanac.com/players/trades.php?p=foulkke01.

19 Crehan.

20 "Pitcher's Mother-in-Law Shares in Red Sox Victory."

21 Bill Plaschke, "There Was No Quitting: Because Padres' Comstock Had to Keep Going/He Went Around the World," *Los Angeles Times,* July 10, 1987: 52. https://www.latimes.com/archives/la-xpm-1987-07-10-sp-1787-story.html.

22 "Split-Finger Fastball, Once Popular, Is Falling Away," *New York Times*, October 3, 2011: SP 6. https://www.nytimes.com/2011/10/02/sports/baseball/split-finger-fastball-use-of-a-popular-pitch-falls-off-the-table.html.

23 Keith Foulke, telephone interview with authors, August 7, 2023.

24 MLB Network Intentional Talk, "Keith Foulke Joins Intentional Talk," May 27, 2022. https://www.mlb.com/video/keith-foulke-joins-it.

25 "LCSC-to-San Fran Pipeline a Frequent Path to Pro Baseball," *Lewiston* (Idaho) *Tribune*, November 4, 2010. https://www.lmtribune.com/sports/lcsc-to-san-fran-pipeline-a-frequent-path-to-pro-baseball/article_710efa8d-b514-5bba-81b2-a73c73521dda.html.

26 Crehan.

27 Paul Sullivan, "Running Up the White Flag Can Work Out," *Chicago Tribune*, July 30, 2017: 3-5.

28 Crehan.

29 Scott Gregor, "Long, Difficult Season Taking Toll on Starter Sirotka's Mental Game," *Chicago Daily Herald,* September 10, 1998: 209.

30 Phil Watson, "White Sox: The Mount Rushmore of Sox closers: Keith Foulke," *Southside Showdown*, February 14, 2021.

30 https://southsideshowdown.com/2021/02/14/white-sox-mount-rushmore-closers.

31 Slusser.

32 Keith Foulke, telephone interview with authors, August 7, 2023.

33 ESPN Baseball, December 5, 2002. http://espn.com/mlb/news/2002/1203/1470567.html.

34 Crehan.

35 Allen Wood and Bill Nowlin, *Don't Let Us Win Tonight: An Oral History of the 2004 Boston Red Sox's Impossible Playoff Run* (Chicago: Triumph, 2014), 6.

36 Wood and Nowlin, 6.

37 "Foulke Signs Three-Year Deal with Red Sox," ESPN.com, December 13, 2003. https://www.espn.com/mlb/news/story?id=1685414.

38 Foulke interview.

39 2Seam, Curse-Breaker ft. Keith Foulke, Episode 3.

40 Tony Massarotti and John Harper, *A Tale of Two Cities* (Guilford, Connecticut: Lyons Press, 2005), 68.

41 https://bostonbaseballhistory.com/new-keith-foulke-remembers-the-2004-world-championship/.

42 Foulke interview.

43 Crehan.

44 Marc Normandin, "Red Sox Hire Keith Foulke as Player Development Consultant," SBNATION: Over the Monster, March 3, 2016. https://www.overthemonster.com/2016/3/3/11152438/red-sox-keith-foulke-2004-world-series-the-25.

45 Elliott Lapin, "Former Baseball Star Foulke Has Big Impact at Hargrave High Long After Playing Days," *Lake Houston Observer*, April 9, 2020. https://www.chron.com/neighborhood/lakehouston/sports/article/Former-baseball-star-Foulke-has-big-impact-at-15190821.php.

46 Crehan.

47 Gio Rivera, "16 Years Later: Interview with Keith Foulke on the 2004 Boston Red Sox," *Boston Sports Report*, May 22, 2020. https://bostonsportsreport445517378.wordpress.com/2020/05/22/16-years-later-interview-with-keith-foulke-on-the-2004-boston-red-sox/.

48 Wood and Nowlin, 265.

49 Wood and Nowlin, 269.

50 Gordon Edes, "Keith Foulke Catches Up," ESPN.com, September 27, 2012. https://www.espn.com/boston/mlb/story/_/id/8434045/keith-foulke-savor-boston-red-sox-2004-world-series-title.

51 Edes.

52 Nick Cafardo, "Closer Issue Open for Debate," *Boston Globe*, June 29, 2005: 46.

53 Michael Holley interview with Keith Foulke, "It's Johnny Cash vs. 'Johnny from Burger King,'" Boston Dirt Dogs, boston.com, July 1, 2005. https://bostondirtdogs.boston.com/Headline_Archives/2005/07/johnny_cash_vs_1.html.

54 Karen Guregian, "Just Humor Us: Foulke Won't Take Back 'Funny' Remark," *Milford* (Massachusetts) *Daily News*, July 2, 2005. https://www.milforddailynews.com/story/sports/2005/07/02/just-humor-us-foulke-won/41341142007/.

55 Keith Foulke, telephone interview with authors, August 7, 2023.

56 Guregian.

57 Edes.

58 Jack Curry, "In Newark, Playing for a Return to the Big Leagues," *New York Times*, September 9, 2009: B18. https://www.nytimes.com/2009/09/09/sports/baseball/09bears.html.

59 Steve Politi, "From World Series Hero to the Bush Leagues; the Fall Was Fast for Keith Foulke," *Newark Star Ledger*, June 11, 2009. https://www.nj.com/sports/ledger/politi/2009/06/former_boston_red_sox_closer_k.html.

60 Howie Kussoy, "Former Foulke Hero Toiling in Newark," *New York Post*, May 23, 2009. https://nypost.com/2009/05/23/former-foulke-hero-toiling-in-newark/.

61 Kussoy.

62 Curry.

63 Matthew Pouliot, "A dozen missed: the best players left off the Hall of Fame ballot," *NBC Sports*, November 26, 2013. https://mlb.nbcsports.com/2013/11/26/a-dozen-dismissed-the-best-players-left-off-the-hall-of-fame-ballot/

64 2Seam, Curse-Breaker ft. Keith Foulke, Episode 3.

65 Lapin.

66 Peter Abraham, "Sons Playing in Brockton for Love of the Game," *Boston Globe*, June 12, 2022: C9.

67 Keith Foulke, telephone interview with authors, August 7, 2023.

68 Crehan.

69 2Seam, Curse-Breaker ft. Keith Foulke, Episode 3.

70 Bob Ryan, "Worth the Wait," *Boston Globe*, October 29, 2004: 118.

71 Wood and Nowlin, 277.

72 Herman.

73 Foulke interview.

74 Joe McDonald, "For Polar Park Visitor Keith Foulke, Red Sox Championship Moment Still Rings True," *Worcester* (Massachusetts) *Telegram & Gazette*, August 19, 2021. https://www.telegram.com/story/sports/mlb/woosox/2021/08/19/keith-foulke-boston-red-sox-2004-world-championship-joe-castiglione/8204942002/.

NOMAR GARCIAPARRA

BY RALPH CAOLA

After seeing Nomar Garciaparra play, Red Sox great Ted Williams called Boston's general manager Dan Duquette and said, "That shortstop you brought up reminds me of a player, but I can't figure out who."[1]

Exuberant upon remembering, Williams called back. Without saying hello, he yelled, "DiMaggio! That's who he reminds me of, DiMaggio! The build, the face, the foot speed, the way he swings and the ease with which he plays the game."[2]

Born July 23, 1973 in Whittier, California, Anthony Nomar Garciaparra became a star in 1997, when he won the American League Rookie of the Year Award in a unanimous vote. In his first seven full seasons, he finished in the top 10 in voting for the Most Valuable Player Award five times and, in 2000, hit .372, the highest average by a right-handed batter since Joe DiMaggio hit .381 in 1939.

Garciaparra's early years were filled with positivity from fans, media, and management. He was the toast of Boston and, other than needing some occasional privacy, seemingly couldn't have been happier. But as his Red Sox career wore on, his mood darkened. By 2004, the last year of his contract, Garciaparra had become so dissatisfied, that, in a move once unthinkable, he was traded.

Thereafter, Garciaparra's career turned sharply downward. While he amassed 41.3 Wins Above Replacement[3] (WAR) in his first eight seasons, he totaled only three WAR in his last six.

A right-handed batter and thrower, Garciaparra spent 14 years in the major leagues, from 1996 through 2009. He played shortstop for the Boston Red Sox; later in his career, he split time at shortstop, third base, and first base with the Chicago Cubs, Los Angeles Dodgers, and Oakland A's.

Garciaparra has two sisters, Monique and Yvette, and a younger brother, Michael, a shortstop in the minor leagues from 2002 through 2010.[4] Nomar is married to former professional soccer star Mia Hamm, with whom he has three children.

His parents are Ramon and Sylvia. Garciaparra's middle name, Nomar, is "Ramon" spelled backwards. Nomar went by his middle name because it was unique. When someone yelled "Nomar," he could always be sure the person was calling him.

Ramon, born in Mexico, was a graphic artist and baseball aficionado who trained his son to be a contact hitter. When Nomar played T-ball, Ramon rewarded him with 25 cents each time he got a hit and fined him 50 cents each time he struck out.[5]

Ramon made sure Nomar knew how to play every position. "At supper [my dad] would draw diagrams of a diamond on a paper napkin and outline different game situations for me," Nomar said. "He'd say, 'Okay, one out, men on first and third, you're catching, runner goes, what are you going to do?'"[6]

Garciaparra attended St. John Bosco High School in Bellflower, California where he was an All-Star midfielder for the soccer team. He was also a placekicker and wide-receiver[7] on the football team and could kick a field goal from 60 yards.[8]

But Garciaparra's best sport was baseball. As a senior, he batted .492 and made California's All-Southern Section Baseball Team.[9] Major-league scouts noticed, and he was selected by the Milwaukee Brewers in the fifth round of the 1991 amateur draft.

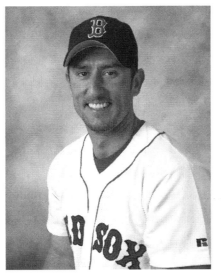

But rather than signing a contract, Nomar decided to go to college. He was recruited by several, including nearby UCLA, but chose to attend Georgia Institute of Technology (Georgia Tech).[10]

At Georgia Tech, Garciaparra became teammates with future major leaguers Jay Payton and Jason Varitek. From 1992 through 1994, the three combined to make Georgia Tech one of the best college teams in the country. Varitek and Garciaparra would later be teammates on the Boston Red Sox for parts of eight seasons.

As a freshman, Nomar was named Atlantic Coast Conference (ACC) Rookie of the Year. Georgia Tech finished 45-19 and was ranked as one of the top 25 teams in college baseball. Garciaparra was selected to the first team All-ACC and as a National College Baseball Writers Association first team All-American.[11]

That summer, Nomar made the 1992 US Olympic Baseball Team as a walk-on and became the starting shortstop. Manager Ron Fraser said, "He acts like he belongs."[12] Garciaparra was the only freshman and only walk-on to make the team.

Garciaparra suffered injuries as a sophomore in 1993 that contributed to a down year. Even so, the Yellow Jackets won the ACC Championship and were invited to the NCAA Division I Baseball Tournament.[13] After the season, Garciaparra played in the Cape Cod Baseball League, where he led the Orleans Firebirds to a championship. In 2002, Garciaparra was inducted into the Cape Cod Baseball League Hall of Fame.[14]

During Georgia Tech's 1994 season, new coach Danny Hall praised Garciaparra, saying, "Defensively, [Nomar is] as good as anybody I've ever coached and that includes [Hall-of-Famer] Barry (Larkin)."[15]

At the end of his junior season, Nomar was chosen to the All-ACC Team and named an All-American by Collegiate Baseball. He batted .437, second in the ACC between Payton and Varitek. With this powerful core, Georgia Tech led the nation in scoring with an average of 9.7 runs per game[16] and had an overall record of 47-16.

The record propelled the Yellow Jackets to the NCAA Division I Baseball Tournament. Georgia Tech scored 53 runs in five games on its way to winning the Midwest II regional. Garciaparra was named the regional's Most Outstanding Player.[17]

Consequently, Georgia Tech earned its first trip to the College World Series. In the semifinal game, with the score tied in the 12th inning, Garciaparra homered to give Georgia Tech the win and a spot in the finals.[18]

Nomar's father was at the game. "I always remember the smile on my Dad's face when I hit a home run to win a game in Little League," Garciaparra said. "He had the same smile on his face tonight."[19] But the Yellow Jackets' dreams of a national title ended after losing to Oklahoma in the finals. Nomar was named the All-Tournament Team shortstop.[20]

Garciaparra always wanted to be in the lineup—he was, as ballplayers say, a "gamer." During the College World Series, the first game of a doubleheader was played in 100-degree heat and a severely dehydrated Garciaparra had to be taken to the hospital and given intravenous fluids. After he was disconnected, he hurried back, but didn't arrive until the second game had just started. He begged to play, was inserted as a pinch-hitter and, on the first pitch he saw, hit a home run.[21]

Including the postseason, Garciaparra batted .427 and was one of only two college players to reach double figures in doubles, triples, and home runs.[22]

Growing up, Garciaparra had always been a good student and continued that excellence at Georgia Tech. He made the Dean's List every quarter and was an academic All-American in 1993 and 1994.[23]

In 2002, Garciaparra was named one of the ACC's 50 best players of all time.[24]

In June 1994, the Boston Red Sox chose Garciaparra 12th in the first round of the amateur draft. The Red Sox sent him to Sarasota of the Florida State League where he played 28 games and hit .295. In the Arizona Fall League, scouts couldn't remember a shortstop with so much range to his left.[25]

In 1995, the Red Sox promoted Nomar to the Trenton Thunder of the Double-A Eastern League. He played all 125 games and led the Thunder in stolen bases, triples, and runs. Although he committed 23 errors,[26] he led the league in assists.[27]

At an even 6-feet, Garciaparra weighed under 160 pounds in college, but by spring training of 1996, he was up to about 180. He had gained strength and a chiseled physique. Garciaparra said, "I knew I couldn't go out with the same body I had in college." Nick Cafardo of the Boston Globe wrote that since the previous year, "Garciaparra has become a 'big' shortstop."[28]

Garciaparra started the 1996 season with the Triple-A Pawtucket Red Sox, but injuries sidelined him until early July. After a short rehab assignment in the Gulf Coast League,[29] he returned to Pawtucket.[30] In just 43 games, Nomar batted .343, hit 16 home runs, drove in 46 runs[31] and was voted Pawtucket's Rookie of the Year.[32]

Thus Garciaparra was called up to the major leagues on August 31.[33] In his first start, he went 3-for-5 with a home run and two RBIs.[34] Former Red Sox player Johnny Pesky said, "I don't like to compare players, but this kid does remind me a lot of [Hall of Famer Luis] Aparicio."[35]

Garciaparra was so impressive in late 1996 and spring training of 1997 that he was the starting shortstop and leadoff hitter for Boston on Opening Day.

Garciaparra's first full season was auspicious. He hit safely in 30 straight games—an AL rookie record. He led the AL with 209 hits and 11 triples and led the majors in multi-hit games.[36] His 98 RBIs set a record for leadoff hitters and his 365 total bases were the fourth-most ever by a rookie and the most ever by a Red Sox rookie.[37] Garciaparra unanimously won the Rookie of the Year Award (fifth unanimous choice ever), finished eighth in MVP voting, and won a Silver Slugger Award. Even so, a humble Garciaparra said, "There's room for improvement in everything—offensively and defensively."[38]

But the Red Sox finished fourth in the AL East, 20 games out of first. Did Nomar think 1997 was successful? "It wasn't bad, personally. But we didn't win anything, so how can I say it was a success?"[39]

Nomar was wildly popular. Ted Williams said, "I'm looking at someone who is going to be as good as anyone who played the game. I say that, and, boy, I believe it, too. And, the best thing about it is, he's a terrific kid."[40]

In March of 1998, Garciaparra signed what became a seven-year contract for $44.93[41] million. Red Sox general manager Dan Duquette said, "Garciaparra has all the attributes our fans adore. He's got great work ethic, good leadership ability. He's everything you want a ballplayer to be."[42]

Nomar made a mockery of the sophomore jinx. He hit 35 home runs, scored 111 runs, and drove in 122. He had a 24-game hitting streak and finished second in MVP voting to Juan González, who had 45 home runs and 157 RBIs. The Red Sox finished 92-70, 22 games behind the New York Yankees, who won 114.

The 92 wins were enough to make the playoffs as the wild card. But the Red Sox lost the AL Division Series to the Indians, three games to one. With the Red Sox down to their final at-bat, Garciaparra exhorted Boston fans to cheer the Red Sox on. Afterward, he hugged his teammates and thanked the fans for their loyalty.[43] In the series, Nomar hit .333 with three homers and a double and drove in 11 runs.

In spring training of 1999, a member of the media suggested, with slugging first baseman Mo Vaughn gone, Garciaparra was now "The Man." He responded, "I don't know the definition of 'The Man.' There's no such thing as 'The Man.' Nobody's bigger than the game."[44]

Garciaparra continued to crush opposing pitchers, leading the American League with a .357 batting average. His On-Base-Plus-Slugging[45] (OPS) ranked third in the AL and was the highest of any shortstop in the majors.

In late September, Garciaparra was hit by a pitch on his right wrist.[46] Little did he, or anyone else, know the extent of the damage it caused or how much it would affect him in the future.

When asked about the baseball tradition in Boston and his relationship with the fans, Garciaparra said, "That's why I enjoy playing here so much. I can't think of a better place to win. [Winning here] would be one of the greatest days ever."[47]

The Red Sox won 94 games, enough to make the playoffs as the wild card. Boston beat Cleveland three games to two in the Division Series, but lost to the Yankees in the League Championship Series, four games to one. In the nine playoff games, Garciaparra hit .406, with four doubles, four home runs, eight runs scored, and nine RBIs.

Garciaparra followed his spectacular 1999 season with an even better one in 2000. Again he led the American League in batting average, improving to .372, the highest average by a shortstop in more than 60 years, and his OPS (1.022) was the third-highest by a shortstop since 1901. As if to punctuate the historic season, he finished with a 20-game hitting streak.

From 1997 through 2000, Garciaparra was arguably one of the three best players in baseball; only Álex Rodríguez (29.3) and Barry Bonds (27.8) accumulated more WAR than Garciaparra (27.7). In voting for AL MVP during that span, he finished eighth, second, seventh, and ninth.

In 2001, Rodriguez was making $22 million per year and Derek Jeter, $12 million. Garciaparra, relatively underpaid at $7.25 million, said he wasn't jealous, "I'm making enough to take care of myself and my family. I'm totally content."[48]

In its March issue, *Sports Illustrated* ran a story on Garciaparra's offseason training regimen. The cover featured a shirtless Garciaparra appearing puffed-up and looking nothing like the skinny kid he was in college.[49] The photo fueled suspicion Garciaparra had used steroids.[50]

Although Garciaparra felt discomfort in his right wrist in 2000, it hadn't bothered him enough to mention to the Red Sox medical staff. But on February 26, 2001, five days after he arrived at spring training, he awoke in significant pain. Two days later, an MRI showed a split tendon in the wrist.[51]

On April 2, Red Sox team doctor Bill Morgan performed surgery. The damage Morgan found was more extensive than he anticipated and, although he had to do significant repairs, said the surgery went well. Morgan estimated Garciaparra would be out eight to 12 weeks.[52]

The estimate turned out to be optimistic. Garciaparra didn't play for nearly 17 weeks and missed Boston's first 103 games.

He came back on July 29. When he stepped to the plate for his first at-bat, Boston fans gave him a 35-second standing ovation. His third time up, Garciaparra lined a homer that tied the game at 2-2 in bottom of sixth. The next inning, after the White Sox had taken a 3-2 lead, he smacked a two-run single, giving the Red Sox a 4-3 lead they never relinquished. The Boston press likened the hit to Carl Yastrzemski's clutch single on the final day of the 1967 season.[53] Garciaparra's triumphant return was front-page news.[54]

In his first seven games, Garciaparra hit .423, but the wrist was not fully healed. Shortly thereafter, he began missing games and his performance slid.[55] When he played his last game on August 26, the Red Sox were 71-58, in second place, only four games out of first. However, Boston proceeded to lose its next seven and 21 of its next 27. When the carnage ended, the Sox record had fallen to 77-79 and the team had been eliminated from playoff contention.

In the midst of the collapse, GM Duquette fired pitching coach John Cumberland in a ham-handed way. "That's why no one wants to (expletive) play here," said an angry Garciaparra.[56] It was a rare outburst of discontent. There would be more.

Teammate Scott Hatteberg said of Garciaparra, "Things have to change around here. I think he'll be very careful with his next contract." Hatteberg continued, "I can't imagine anything worse than what's gone on this year. It's been chaos the whole year."[57]

In 2002, the Red Sox sought to restore order. After John Henry took over as owner, he fired Dan Duquette as GM and Jimy Williams as manager. Initially, the changes seemed to help; at the end of May the Red Sox had a record of 36-15 and were in first place by two games. But, from June through August, Boston went 39-43 and fell 8½ games behind the division-leading Yankees. The Red Sox finished 93-69, in second place in the AL East, six games short of making the playoffs as the wild card.

Whatever lingering problems Garciaparra may have had with his wrist, they didn't keep him from playing; he missed only six games all season. He drove in 120 runs and tied for the league lead with 56 doubles—the most since 1936 and the second-most in Red Sox history. (Earl Webb, the all-time single-season doubles leader with 67, played for the Red Sox.)[58]

However, some negative signs appeared. Garciaparra's .310 batting average and .880 OPS were good, but down 27 and 83 points, respectively, from the averages he established from 1997 through 2000. A friend said, "He didn't completely trust the wrist."[59]

Late in the season, Garciaparra was particularly crabby. A notorious first-pitch swinger, he was upset about being criticized for not taking enough pitches. He complained about the way the press portrayed contract negotiations with the Players Association and groused about the lack privacy in the clubhouse.[60]

He started 2003 the same way he ended 2002: annoyed with the media. He said, "Somebody will write some (expletive) or whatever. Some (expletive) that I was unhappy. I'm damned if I do and damned if I don't … I'm in a no-win situation."[61] The working relationship became so strained Garciaparra had the clubhouse floor marked off with red tape, players on one side, media on the other.[62]

But, as ornery as he was with sportswriters, he remained kind to fans and civic groups. On an off-day in May, Garciaparra was the front man at a fundraiser for schoolchildren in Boston. Fans were thrilled to shake the hand of their hero. Garciaparra was able to get many Red Sox players to attend, a sign of the respect his teammates had for him. A generous Garciaparra thanked them, saying, "Days off are like gold to us and the fact that my teammates took time on their day off to come here, I can't tell you how big a deal that really is."[63]

Garciaparra followed an excellent May with an even better June, during which he hit .398 with an OPS of 1.090. On June 21, he went 6-for-6 and on June 24, went 5-for-5.

The two-month tear prompted Gordon Edes of the *Boston Globe* to write, "Garciaparra's current play, both offensively and defensively is equal to any comparable time before his wrist surgery in 2001."[64] Years later, Edes's colleague, Bob Ryan disagreed, writing, "I have always maintained [after the wrist injury, Garciaparra] never hit the ball as consistently hard again."[65]

At the end of August, Garciaparra was batting .323 with an OPS of .915, but September saw the shortstop swoon. In the season's final month, he batted only .170 with an OPS of .599.

The Red Sox again made the playoffs as the wild card. Boston beat the Oakland A's in the Division Series, but lost the League Championship Series to the Yankees, four games to three. The nail-biting series ended with Aaron Boone's 11th-inning home run in Game Seven.

In the first round, the Red Sox had just won a game to stave off elimination, coming from behind in the eighth inning. As the euphoric Red Sox were boarding the team bus, Garciaparra said, "Why is everyone so happy? As soon as we lose, everyone's just going to rip us."[66]

In the postseason, Garciaparra's batting average had been better than in September, but he got only two extra-base hits in 12 games. A scout said, "His bat looks slow, he looks like he's guessing, he looks lethargic. That's how it looks when you're struggling, but that's what I see, a slower bat."[67] The season-ending slump may have made the Red Sox wonder what version of Garciaparra lay in the future as free agency loomed at the end of the 2004 season.

In early December, the Red Sox tried to trade for Álex Rodríguez, a trade that would have made Garciaparra expendable. On his honeymoon, Nomar was shocked when he found out about the proposed deal in a newspaper. He said to interviewers, "How would you guys feel if *your employer* was trying to replace *you*?" Garciaparra's agent said, "[It] was a complete slap in the face."[68]

But perhaps not an unexpected one, since in spring training of 2003, Garciaparra had rejected the Red Sox contract-extension offer of $60 million over four years. Having originally asked for $68 million, Garciaparra offered to split the difference at $64 million. The Red Sox not only declined, but, citing a downward shift in the market, later reduced the offer to $48 million. These details were leaked by the Red Sox, which irked the intensely private Garciaparra.[69]

Even though the Rodríguez trade fell through, when spring training started, Garciaparra was more bitter than ever. He said, "When I heard about the [trade], I was thinking, well, the priorities are obviously not for me. They're obviously for someone else." He continued, "Am I still mad? … I was definitely hurt by a lot of it."[70]

Garciaparra did not play in the opening game of the 2004 season. He said his Achilles tendon had been injured March 5 when he was struck by a ball during batting practice, although no one witnessed the injury.[71] Team officials later speculated the injury had occurred in the offseason.[72]

Dr. Bill Morgan said, other than inflammation, there was nothing structurally wrong with the tendon. Morgan also said two weeks on the disabled list would be precautionary and, if the Red Sox were in a pennant race, Garciaparra would be playing.[73]

But, more than five weeks into the season, there was still no indication when he would rejoin the team. Red Sox manager Terry Francona said, "At the very beginning we thought it would be three or four days. I don't think anybody [thought his recovery] would be this long. I didn't, Nomar didn't, and the medical people didn't."[74]

In the *Boston Globe*, Dan Shaughnessy, ever-critical of Garciaparra, called the injury "mysterious" and the ball that hit Nomar in spring training "the magic bullet theory of sports injuries."[75] A reporter asked Garciaparra if, by delaying his return, he was "sticking it to the team."[76]

On June 9, after more than nine weeks, Garciaparra returned to the lineup. He started slowly, hitting only .235 in June, but recovered in July, posting a batting average of .386 and an OPS of 1.028.

On July 1, the Red Sox played a nationally-televised game against the archrival Yankees. Before the game, Garciaparra told Francona his Achilles was too sore to play. Only two Red Sox position players didn't participate in the dramatic, extra-inning game; one was Garciaparra. His decision to sit out stood in stark contrast to the effort of opposing shortstop Derek Jeter, who careened into the stands after making a game-saving catch. The Red Sox lost, 5-4.[77]

Garciaparra always publicly stated he wanted to stay with the Red Sox, but, after a mid-July meeting with Nomar, management emerged unconvinced. The combination of not getting the contract he wanted and the Red Sox trying to replace him with Rodriguez had thrown Garciaparra into a funk from which he was never able to recover. Team officials concluded Garciaparra was irreparably unhappy, would leave as a free agent, and the Red Sox would be left with nothing in return.[78]

Would Garciaparra have gone elsewhere? Probably so. Years later, Francona revealed, "He just got 'Bostoned-out.' Sometimes you just have to move on."[79]

So, on July 31, the trading deadline, the Red Sox sent Garciaparra and Matt Murton to the Chicago Cubs as part of a four-team deal in which the Red Sox got first baseman

Doug Mientkiewicz from the Minnesota Twins and shortstop Orlando Cabrera from the Montreal Expos.

After Garciaparra left, the personality of the team changed.[80] Without his brooding presence, the Red Sox were transformed into a carefree bunch of self-described idiots and cowboys. They also became more versatile, faster, and better defensively. About Garciaparra's replacement, Orlando Cabrera, Johnny Damon said, "[Now] we have someone who is dependable, someone who has won a Gold Glove, who is getting better."[81]

Indeed, the Red Sox got better. At the time of the trade Boston stood at 56-45. Thereafter, the Red Sox won 42 games, lost only 19, and finished with a record of 98-64, Boston's most wins in 26 years. In the playoffs, the Red Sox swept three games from the Angels, beat the Yankees in seven, and swept four from the St. Louis Cardinals to win the World Series. It was Boston's first World Series Championship since 1918, fulfilling the dreams of long-deprived Red Sox fans.

Garciaparra played the rest of 2004 and all of 2005 with the Cubs, then spent three seasons with the Los Angeles Dodgers before ending up with the Oakland Athletics in 2009. In the final five years of his career, Garciaparra was beset by injuries and played only 62, 122, 121, 55, and 65 games. His best season during this stretch was 2006, when he made the NL All-Star Team, won the National League Comeback Player of the Year award, and finished 13th in voting for the MVP Award.

Though his final seasons were mostly unproductive, Garciaparra had a terrific career, retiring with 1,747 hits, 229 home runs, 927 runs scored, and 936 RBIs. His father's training paid off; of expansion-era[82] players with slugging percentages above .500, Nomar had the fewest strikeouts per at-bat.

A six-time All-Star, Garciaparra hit more than .300 eight times and had a career batting average of .313, 11th-highest among players who started their careers after World War II. He got 190 or more hits six times, drove in more than 100 runs four times, and scored more than 100 runs six times.

From 1997 through 2003, Garciaparra ranked fourth in total WAR behind only Bonds, Rodríguez, and Andruw Jones. Not counting 2001, when he played only 21 games due to injury, he averaged nearly 7 WAR per season during this span. (Fangraphs rates a season of 6 or more WAR as MVP quality.[83])

Garciaparra's 41.2 WAR in his first eight seasons[84] are the fifth-most by a shortstop[85], ranking behind Cal Ripken (43.6) and ahead of Derek Jeter (36.9). Except Garciaparra and Álex Rodríguez, all of the retired players in the top 10 of this list ended up in the Hall of Fame, suggesting Garciaparra was on track for enshrinement before injuries derailed his career.

On March 10, 2010, Garciaparra signed a one-day contract with Boston so he could retire as a Red Sox.[86] He is currently (2019) an analyst for SportsNet LA, which carries the Los Angeles Dodgers.[87]

ACKNOWLEDGMENTS

This biography was reviewed by Bill Nowlin and Joel Barnhart and fact-checked by Mark Sternman.

NOTES

1. Tom Verducci, ".400 Reasons," *Sports Illustrated*, March 5, 2001: 34.
2. Verducci, 2001.
3. Steve Slowinski, "What Is WAR," https://library.fangraphs.com/misc/war/ Accessed July 13, 2019.
4. John Scher, http://www.espn.com/magazine/vol3no14test.html Accessed October 2, 2019.
5. Verducci, 2000.
6. John Scher, http://www.espn.com/magazine/vol3no14test.html Accessed October 2, 2019.
7. Jeffrey Denberg, "Word Gets Out On Garciaparra," *Atlanta Constitution*, April 14, 1994: E4.
8. Mark Stewart, *Nomar Garciaparra Non-Stop Shortstop* (Brookfield, Connecticut: The Millbrook Press, 2000), 7.
9. "High School Baseball," *Los Angeles Times*, June 21, 1991: C12.
10. Stewart, 7.
11. "For the Record," *St. Louis Post-Dispatch*, June 6, 1993: 8F.
12. Thomas Stinson, "Garciaparra Safe, Varitek Out as US Makes Final Cuts," *Atlanta Constitution*, July 11, 1992: D4.
13. Stewart, 11.
14. "Twelve Legends to be Inducted Into CCBL Hall of Fame," http://capecodbaseball.org/news/hofnews/?article_id=241.
15. Jeffrey Denberg, "Word Gets Out On Garciaparra," *Atlanta Constitution*, April 14, 1994: E4.
16. "Tech's Triple Threat," *Atlanta Constitution*, June 2, 1994: E1.
17. Mike De Giovanna, "'Unsung Hero' for Georgia Tech Belts Out the Titans Title Hopes," *Los Angeles Times*, June 9, 1994: C14.
18. De Giovanna.
19. De Giovanna.
20. Stewart, 17.
21. Stewart, 16.
22. Stewart, 16.
23. https://ramblinwreck.com/nine-tech-baseball-players-named-to-acc-anniversary-team/ Accessed June 28, 2019.
24. https://ramblinwreck.com/nine-tech-baseball-players-named-to-acc-anniversary-team/ Accessed June 28, 2019.
25. Stewart, 19.
26. Mike Shalin, *Nomar Garciaparra High 5* (New York: Sports Publishing Inc., 1999), 17.
27. Stewart, 16.
28. Nick Cafardo, "Garciaparra Powers Way Into Red Sox Plans," *Boston Globe*, March 4, 1996: 38.
29. Nick Cafardo, "Suppan's In Plans, But When," *Boston Globe*, July 7, 1996: 83.
30. Larry Whiteside, "Duquette Lays Groundwork But Will Wait to Deal," *Boston Globe*, July 12, 1996: 85.

31 Tony Massarotti, in the Boston Herald book *Nomar: Fenway's Favorite* (New York: Sports Publishing, LLC, 2002), 19.

32 Shalin, 19.

33 Michael Madden, "Trade Winds Blow As Deadline Looms," *Boston Globe,* September 1, 1996: 54.

34 Michael Madden, "Rookie Shows Why He's a Keeper," *Boston Globe,* September 2, 1996: 43.

35 Shalin, 25.

36 Shalin, 29.

37 Stewart, 29.

38 Shalin, 39.

39 Shalin, 41.

40 Shalin, 43.

41 https://www.baseball-reference.com/players/g/garcino01.shtml#all_br-salaries Accessed December 31, 2019.

42 Larry Whiteside, "Garciaparra Scoops a Record Contract," *Boston Globe,* March 11, 1998: D2.

43 Michael Silverman, in the Boston Herald book *Nomar: Fenway's Favorite* (New York: Sports Publishing, LLC, 2002), 49.

44 Steve Buckley, in the Boston Herald book *Nomar: Fenway's Favorite* (New York: Sports Publishing, LLC, 2002), 53.

45 http://m.mlb.com/glossary/standard-stats/on-base-plus-slugging Accessed August 23, 2019.

46 Gordon Edes, "Garciaparra Says Surgery Seems Likely," *Boston Globe,* March 28, 2001: E1.

47 Stewart, 47.

48 Bob Hohler, "He Doesn't Feel Shortchanged?," *Boston Globe,* January 12, 2001: E2.

49 Verducci, 2001.

50 Dan Shaughnessy, "Sour," *Boston Globe,* March 11, 2010: C1.

51 Gordon Edes, "Garciaparra Says Surgery Seems Likely."

52 Larry Tye, "Garciaparra Has Surgery on Wrist," *Boston Globe,* April 3, 2001: F1.

53 The Minnesota Twins and the Red Sox entered the game tied for first place. The Twins led 2-0 in the bottom of the sixth, when Yastrzemski banged a bases-loaded single to center that tied the game. The Sox went on to score five runs in the inning, beat the Twins 5-3, and won the AL pennant.

54 Gordon Edes, "Back With a Blast," *Boston Globe,* July 30, 2001: A1.

55 Gordon Edes, "Garciaparra is Sidelined," *Boston Globe,* August 29, 2001: F1.

56 Gordon Edes, "Garciaparra Comments Hang in Air," *Boston Globe,* September 5, 2001: D1.

57 Edes, "Garciaparra Comments Hang in Air,"

58 Peter May, "Garciaparra Battles on With Another 4-Hit Day," *Boston Globe,* September 17, 2002: F3.

59 Gordon Edes, "On Baseball," *Boston Globe,* December 6, 2002: D1.

60 Dan Shaughnessy, "Hot Garciaparra Cranks Out a Few," *Boston Globe,* September 1, 2002: C1.

61 Dan Shaughnessy, "Pique of His Career," *Boston Globe,* February 19, 2003: 79.

62 Peter Schworm, "One Last Short Stop," *Boston Globe,* March 11, 2010: A1.

63 Bob Hohler, "Garciaparra Proves to Be Kingpin With Mates," *Boston Globe,* May 23, 2003: E5.

64 Gordon Edes, "On Baseball," *Boston Globe,* June 25, 2003: F1.

65 Bob Ryan, "Sweet," *Boston Globe,* March 11, 2010: C1.

66 Dan Shaughnessy, "In Short, It Was Time for Him to Go," *Boston Globe,* August 1, 2004: C1.

67 Gordon Edes, "On Baseball," *Boston Globe,* October 15, 2003: F2.

68 Bob Hohler, "Fallback Plan in Place?," *Boston Globe,* December 19, 2003: D6.

69 Bob Hohler, "Fallback Plan in Place?"

70 Gordon Edes, "Shortstop Hasn't Forgotten, Forgiven," *Boston Globe,* February 25, 2004: F1.

71 Shaughnessy, "Sour."

72 Phil Rogers, "Nomar May Have Short Stop," *Chicago Tribune,* September 24, 2004: 4-1.

73 Bob Hohler, "Ruling May Be Out," *Boston Globe,* March 28, 2004: E1.

74 Bob Hohler, "Time Heals, but Very Slowly," *Boston Globe,* May 19, 2004: D6.

75 Dan Shaughnessy, "Looks Like a Short Stop Is Left for Fenway Fans," *Boston Globe,* June 10, 2004: C1.

76 Dan Shaughnessy, "Looks Like a Short Stop Is Left for Fenway Fans."

77 Dan Shaughnessy, "Having Found Another Way to Lose, Departure Right on Time," *Boston Globe,* July 2, 2004: E1.

78 Shaughnessy, "Sour."

79 Ryan, "Sweet."

80 Rogers, "Nomar May Have Short Stop."

81 Paul Sullivan, "Red Sox Fans Are Sad, but Glad," *Chicago Tribune,* October 10, 2004: 3-4.

82 1,000 or more games played since 1961.

83 Steve Slowinski, "What Is WAR," https://library.fangraphs.com/misc/war/ Accessed July 13, 2019.

84 In two of the seasons, he played fewer than 25 games.

85 To qualify, 800 games at shortstop were required.

86 Peter Abraham, "A Final Tug for Garciaparra," *Boston Globe,* March 11, 2010: C2.

87 https://dodgers.mlblogs.com/chase-utley-joining-sportsnet-la-broadcast-team-as-studio-analyst-a0f5b711748a Accessed August 17, 2019.

RICKY GUTIERREZ

BY MALCOLM ALLEN

Ricky Gutierrez played for six teams in 12 major-league seasons (1993-2004). Primarily a shortstop, he started all but one postseason game for three consecutive Houston Astros division winners. Two years after he suffered a serious neck injury, Gutierrez concluded his big-league career as a member of the 2004 World Series champion Boston Red Sox.

When Ricardo "Ricky" Gutierrez was born, on May 23, 1970, in Miami, his father was a catcher for the Leones de Yucatán in the Mexican League. Just 16 when he signed his first contract with the St. Louis Cardinals in 1956, Roberto Gutiérrez Herrera became known by his mother's surname in professional baseball, playing 20 seasons as Roberto Herrera. In the United States, he peaked in Triple A, from 1960 to 1962. His best statistical season came in Mexico with the 1969 Pericos de Puebla: .341 with 25 homers in 135 games.

Nicknamed "Musulungo," Roberto grew up as the son of a policeman in La Habana, Cuba.[1] He married Sonia Espalter in 1961, and their son, Roberto Jr., arrived the following year.[2] But professional baseball on the island was abolished after the Fidel Castro-led Cuban Revolution. In 1963 Musulungo departed the country for good. "Fidel gave us the approval," he explained. "He said that baseball players were not political."[3] Roberto Sr. did not see his wife or son again until 1966, when they, too, left Cuba on one of the Freedom Flights arranged by President Lyndon B. Johnson.

Ricky was introduced to baseball by his brother. "Since he was about 3, he has shown the ability to play ball," recalled Roberto Jr. "I gave him his first plastic bat when he was about that age and we used to play in the front yard. ... He caught on real fast."[4] Ricky grew up around the game. Roberto Jr., an outfielder, spent three seasons (1983-85) in the Baltimore Orioles' farm system. Their father – after retiring from playing following the 1975 campaign – became a longtime professional umpire. He officiated local minor-league and college contests, then headed off to winter ball. In the Venezuelan Winter League, for example, Musulungo remained an arbiter until 1998-99.[5]

Around the same time that he started grade school, Ricky attended Borrego Álvarez's baseball academy.[6] "You wouldn't see me without a bat in my hand, or outside throwing a ball," he said. "It was in me. I loved the game. I understood what I wanted to do from day one. It's all I dreamed of was just one day being in the big leagues."[7] He gained playing experience in the Hialeah Khoury League, Hialeah Community Baseball Association, and Hialeah Athletic Association, and he studied major leaguers.[8] "The guy I looked at was Ozzie Smith," he said. "Every game that was on TV, I always watched. I always charted it, I was just crazy about the game."[9]

In his junior year at American Senior High School, Gutierrez batted .602 (53-for-88) to lead Dade County Class 4A-3A players. He was named the MVP of the Apopka tournament.[10] "I thought I was good but I never thought I was great," he said. "I just got better and better." His speed and range at shortstop opened eyes. "The guy can get the ball in the hole and make the big play," said American coach José Ortega.[11] By the spring of his senior year, Gutierrez had signed a letter of intent to attend the University of Miami on a baseball scholarship.[12] The Hurricanes were headed for their ninth College World Series appearance in 11 years.

However, the Orioles had a "sandwich pick" between the first and second rounds of the June 1988 amateur draft. They used it to select Gutierrez 28th overall. "We didn't think he'd be there," said Baltimore's assistant GM, Doug Melvin.[13] Although the Orioles had future Hall of Famer Cal Ripken Jr. entrenched at shortstop at the major-league level, manager Frank Robinson noted that the organization lacked quality at that position in the minors.

"I want to play pro ball," Gutierrez told the *Miami Herald*. He signed with Baltimore through scout Jim Pamlayne for a $100,000 bonus.[14] That summer, Gutierrez debuted in the Rookie-level Appalachian League. In 62 appearances for the Bluefield (West Virginia) Orioles, he batted .245 and committed 34 errors. He made a good impression in the Florida Instructional League that fall, though, and Melvin said, "He has a chance to be a major-league prospect."[15]

In 1989 Gutierrez advanced to the full-season Class-A Carolina League, where he was the youngest player on the Frederick (Maryland) Keys' roster. Although he batted just .233 in 127 games, the Keys won the North Division, and his .943 fielding percentage led the circuit's shortstops.[16]

Gutierrez returned to Frederick in 1990 and showed substantial improvement: a .275 batting average in 112 games. He was named to the league's midseason and year-end all-star squads.[17] In his first taste of Double-A Eastern League action, he hit .234 in 20 games for the Hagerstown (Maryland) Suns at the end of the season.

Baseball America rated Gutierrez as the Orioles' top position-player prospect in 1991.[18] Back at Hagerstown to begin the season, he batted just .189 in his first 65 games. But his .408 (26-for-60) tear over his next 19 contests earned him a promotion to the Triple-A International League on July 17.[19] With the Rochester (New York) Red Wings, he hit .306 in 49 games. Although Gutierrez's .261 overall average between the two teams did not include much punch (11 doubles, 7 triples, and no homers in 449 at-bats), he drew 81 walks and stole 15 bases in 16 attempts.

Gutierrez returned to Rochester in 1992 and wound up playing more second base (82 appearances) than shortstop (53). The main reason was that he had been passed on the organization's depth chart by a younger, faster shortstop, Manny Alexander. Baltimore knew they would likely lose Gutierrez in the impending expansion draft for the new Florida Marlins and Colorado Rockies franchises, as he wouldn't make their 15-player protected list.[20] Four days after the contending Orioles dealt pitcher Erik Schullstrom and a player to be named later to the San Diego for southpaw Craig Lefferts on August 31, Gutierrez was sent to the Padres to complete the swap. He finished the season by playing in three games for the Las Vegas Stars, San Diego's Triple-A Pacific Coast League affiliate.

After a strong spring training in 1993, Gutierrez was one of the Padres' last cuts.[21] He spent only five games with Las Vegas, though. On April 13 he was called up to the majors when San Diego shortstop Kurt Stillwell went on the disabled list.[22] Gutierrez debuted that night at Jack Murphy Stadium, leading off the eighth inning as a pinch-hitter with the Padres trailing, 4-2. He struck out swinging against the Pirates' John Candelaria and spent the top of the ninth in right field, a position he had never played professionally.

The next night Gutierrez started at shortstop, batted leadoff, and went 1-for-6. His first major-league hit was a single against Pittsburgh's Randy Tomlin. By the end of April, Gutierrez had played five positions (adding second base, third, and left field) and raised his batting average to .364 with a 4-for-5 performance against the Mets. He wound up starting 108 of his 133 games and batting .251 with 5 homers. The Padres finished last in the NL West with a 61-101 record but he led the team with 76 runs scored.

Gutierrez was San Diego's Opening Day shortstop in 1994, but he didn't raise his batting average above .200 to stay until June 8. "Ricky is a good player, he just got off to a bad start," said Padres skipper Jim Riggleman. "Maybe he was pressing too much."[23] After the All-Star break, rookie Luis López played more frequently. Gutierrez batted .240 with one homer in 90 games (76 starts) before major leaguers went on strike in early August, ending the season prematurely. On December 28 he was traded to the Houston Astros as part of a 12-player deal that brought future NL MVP Ken Caminiti and center fielder Steve Finley to San Diego.[24]

Rookie Orlando Miller was the Astros' primary shortstop in 1995. As a reserve, Gutierrez went just 1-for-10 before May 12, when he was optioned to the Triple-A PCL. In 64 games with the Tucson Toros, he batted .301. On July 31 he returned to the majors to replace first baseman Jeff Bagwell, who had broken his hand. Then Miller injured his knee in a collision on August 15. Gutierrez capitalized on his chance to play every day and finished the season hitting .276 in 52 games. But Houston lost 11 consecutive contests with two regulars out and fell one game shy of a playoff berth.

Gutierrez batted .284 in 1996. Only 49 of his 89 games were starts, though, as he remained Miller's chief backup. The Astros coughed up the NL Central Division lead in September and missed the postseason again. In December Miller was dealt to the Detroit Tigers, but Houston had already signed free agent Pat Listach to replace him.

During spring training in 1997, Gutierrez broke his right thumb. He returned to the active roster on May 6 and became Houston's top shortstop because Listach was hitting so poorly. By the time Listach was released at the end of June, though, Gutierrez's bat had cooled off after a hot start, and the Astros had turned to slick-fielding Tim Bogar. As the season entered the second half, Gutierrez mostly started at third base, splitting time with sore-shouldered Sean Berry and lefty-hitting Bill Spiers.

Gutierrez scored a career-high four runs in Houston's 14-2 victory on September 4 in San Francisco, and Bogar suffered a season-ending broken forearm in the same contest. In the thick of the pennant race, Gutierrez returned to shortstop and helped the Astros secure the division title. He finished the regular season hitting .261 in 102 games (72 starts). Gutierrez was in the lineup for all three NLDS contests, but he went just 1-for-8 (.125) and Houston was swept by the Atlanta Braves.

In 1998 the Astros won a (then) franchise-record 102 games and repeated as NL Central champions.[25] Gutierrez was the regular shortstop and posted the NL's third-best range factor per nine innings (4.85) at that position. Two of his at-bats were particularly memorable. On May 6 at Wrigley Field, he grounded a third-inning leadoff single off the glove of Cubs third baseman Kevin Orie – the only hit allowed by Chicago rookie Kerry Wood in his 20-strikeout masterpiece. "Kerry was dumb enough to throw me a curveball there," Gutierrez joked 20 years later. "He should have just pounded me with fastballs and I would have had three strikeouts [that day] instead of two."[26]

When Gutierrez went down swinging against Bartolo Colón in Cleveland on June 26, it ended a 20-pitch battle, then the majors' longest at-bat since statisticians began tracking that data in 1988.[27] In 141 games, Gutierrez batted .261 for the second consecutive year. He achieved personal bests with 24 doubles and 13 steals. With Game Two of the NLDS tied entering the bottom of the ninth inning, he led off with a single against the Padres' Dan Miceli. Gutierrez took second base on a bunt, stole third, and scored the winning run on Spiers' single to even the series. The Astros' season ended after they lost the next two contests in San Diego, but Gutierrez batted .300 (3-for-10) in the playoffs.

In February 1999 Gutierrez and the Astros avoided a salary arbitration hearing by agreeing to a one-year, $2.2 million contract, nearly tripling his previous $800,000 base salary.[28] He hit .357 in Houston's first 19 games before a metacarpal bone in his left hand was fractured by a pitch thrown by the Diamondbacks' Armando Reynoso.[29] Shortly before the injury, Astros beat writer Carlton Thompson – noting Gutierrez's improved patience and ability to make contact – opined, "The most overlooked player in the starting lineup is SS Ricky Gutierrez. Pitchers seemingly view him as the one hitter in the lineup on which they can take a breather. That's a big mistake."[30]

Gutierrez returned after missing nearly six weeks, but played just over a month before a broken hamate in his left wrist forced him back to the disabled list.[31] The Astros and Cincinnati Reds were in a close fight for leadership of the NL Central Division when he came back on August 10. During Houston's 12-game winning streak from September 3 to 14, Gutierrez batted .459 (17-for-37), including two four-hit performances. For the third straight year, he hit exactly .261 and the Astros won their division, clinching on the season's final day. But Houston was eliminated in the Division Series for the third consecutive time, with Gutierrez going 0-for-10 in the three games he started against the Atlanta Braves.

That fall Gutierrez's tenure with the Astros ended when the club declined to offer him arbitration.[32] "I'm perfectly content to let Tim Bogar start the season at shortstop," remarked Houston GM Gerry Hunsicker before baseball's winter meetings.[33] On December 20 Gutierrez signed with the Chicago Cubs. He was guaranteed $2.5 million for 2000, with a club option for $3.4 million should they want him back for 2001. "Chicago was really the place I wanted to go," he said. "I've always liked playing there and in the ballpark, an old-time ballpark."[34]

When the Cubs opened the season with two games in Tokyo, Gutierrez was sidelined by a slight rib-cage strain.[35] Back in the US, he started all but one of the next 46 contests and batted .315 with 27 RBIs, including a career-high 5 on April 26 in Houston. He also went deep seven times, equaling his home-run total from the previous five seasons combined. Cubs beat writer Bruce Miles reported that Gutierrez had opened up his batting stance slightly at hitting instructor Jeff Pentland's suggestion, allowing hm to see the ball better and improve his plate coverage.[36] The same scribe later noted that Chicago's new shortstop was determined to prove himself as an everyday player, and observed, "Gutierrez is so smooth he almost looks nonchalant."[37]

On May 24, however, Gutierrez sustained two injuries on one play in Colorado. As one report described it, "Gutierrez was running to first when a twinge in his hamstring caused him to hobble. He fell to the ground and separated his throwing shoulder in the process."[38] He spent the next 24 games on the disabled list.

The Cubs lost 97 games and finished last in the NL Central Division, but Gutierrez batted .276 in 125 games, with career highs in homers (11), walks (66), and on-base percentage (.375). His 16 sacrifice hits tied for tops in the majors, and his .986 fielding percentage led NL shortstops.

In 2001 Gutierrez tied for the big-league lead in sacrifice hits (17) for the second straight year, and he established personal bests with 147 games, a .290 batting average, and 66 RBIs. "He's been one of our best clutch hitters," remarked Cubs coach Sandy Alomar Sr. late in the season. "If we have men on base, he's going to make contact. He's a patient hitter, a very dangerous hitter. But he's not flashy. He does what needs to be done."[39]

"He did the same in Houston – had a good year and nobody sees it," observed Marlins coach Tony Taylor, a friend of Gutierrez's father. "He plays every day and makes every day the same. He's very cool. He doesn't get too high or low."[40]

On July 12 Gutierrez hit his first big-league grand slam, in the bottom of the eighth inning of a deadlocked interleague contest against the crosstown White Sox. Both benches had been warned earlier after a pair of incidents at second base. After the Cubs' Eric Young knocked the ball loose from White Sox shortstop Royce Clayton's glove in the third inning, Gutierrez narrowly escaped a spiking by Chris Singleton in the following frame. "I'm lucky I didn't retaliate or I wouldn't have been in the game to do what I did," Gutierrez said.[41] His tiebreaking blast came right after the White Sox intentionally walked Young to load the bases.

The much-improved Cubs led their division as late as mid-August and finished 88-74. Chicago offered Gutierrez a two-year contract with a raise to return, but he wanted a four-year deal.[42] So the Cubs made him a free agent by not offering arbitration and traded for a younger shortstop with more power, Toronto's Alex Gonzalez.

Gutierrez and his wife hoped that he could reach a deal with his hometown Florida Marlins, but they already had a younger shortstop – also named Álex González – in place. On December 17 Gutierrez signed with the Cleveland Indians for three years and $11 million.[43] Although Cleveland was set at shortstop with perennial Gold Glover Omar Vizquel, they needed a second baseman after trading away future Hall of Famer Roberto Alomar the previous week. "Nobody can fill the shoes of Roberto Alomar," Gutierrez said. "I can just do the best I can and play like Ricky Gutierrez."[44]

Gutierrez had started only nine big-league games at second, none in the last five seasons. He worked out with former Gold Glover Harold Reynolds – the brother of his agent, Larry Reynolds – that offseason.[45] During spring training, Indians coach Robby Thompson – also a former Gold Glove second baseman – predicted, "If you're looking for spectacular plays and jump throws and this and that from him out at second base, you're not going to get that. He will be very steady. I think he'll turn the double play as well as anybody in the American League."[46]

In April, however, Gutierrez dove for a ball and injured his neck. He didn't tell anybody about it, and by the time he strained his groin on June 13, he was hitting .248 in 59 games, with 8 errors, and just 9 RBIs. He had grounded into more double plays (11) than any other AL player. After a trip to the disabled list, Gutierrez hit .323 (41-for-127) over a 35-game span, but the tingling sensation he had felt in his left arm since his April neck injury worsened.[47] When Gutierrez hurt his thumb during batting practice on August 15, he told a team doctor about his lingering symptoms. An MRI showed that a disc in his neck was pressing on his spine. "The doctor told me I could have been paralyzed," Gutierrez said. "Hearing that was a very scary thing."[48]

As described by the *South Florida Sun-Sentinel*, "[Dr. Kalman] Bloomberg removed the disc, replaced it with a bone graft and fused it with two screws and a plate. Gutierrez spent six weeks in a neck brace."[49]

Gutierrez began the 2003 season on the disabled list, but he returned to the Indians' lineup on June 24 after a 16-game rehabilitation assignment with the Triple-A Buffalo Bisons. He played in just 16 games as a third baseman-shortstop for Cleveland before he returned to the DL, though. "I think I rushed myself back, and we came to a conclusion that I still wasn't ready," he said that fall.[50]

About a week before Opening Day 2004, the Indians sent Gutierrez to the New York Mets for a player to be named later. New York's new shortstop, Kazuo Matsui, struggled in spring training after coming over from the Japan Pacific League, and former shortstop Jose Reyes' conversion to second base was slowed by a hamstring injury. Mets bench coach Don Baylor had managed Gutierrez with the Cubs and valued his experience. "He understands how to play and he plays to win," Baylor said.[51]

But Gutierrez batted just .175 in 24 games before he was released on May 24. "When I got released from the Mets, I sat home and debated about coming back or shutting it down for the rest of the year," he said. "But I talked to my family and my agent and we agreed the best thing was to get back to baseball, even if it was Triple-A."[52] He re-signed with the Cubs and wound up with their PCL affiliate in Des Moines with the understanding that he'd be allowed to pursue a major-league opportunity if one came along. That's exactly what happened on July 21, when the Boston Red Sox acquired him in a conditional deal.

Boston had just lost middle infielder Pokey Reese to a strained oblique and their Triple-A shortstop, Carlos Febles, was sidelined by a strained shoulder. "There were four or five guys we were looking at, and we didn't want to spend too much to get one," explained Red Sox GM Theo Epstein. "We were able to work out a deal to get Ricky without giving up anything. … If Ricky Gutierrez is healthy, he's a major league player."[53]

Gutierrez appeared in 21 games (eight starts) for Boston and batted .275. The Red Sox won 98 games and qualified for the postseason as the AL wild card. Although he wasn't on the active playoff roster, Gutierrez stayed with the team through their ALDS triumph over the Angels and their unprecedented comeback from a three-games-to-zero deficit against the Yankees in the ALCS. An Associated Press photo captured him – in uniform with his fist raised in triumph – charging out of the dugout after Boston won the pennant.[54]

After beginning spring training in an Indians uniform and bouncing through the Mets and Cubs organizations, the 34-year-old Gutierrez – though not on the postseason roster – found himself with a dugout seat for the World Series. "It's awesome. You dream about being here," he said. "The perfect ending would be winning the whole thing and being able to sit down, look at my hand, and see a big ring on my finger."[55] The Red Sox swept the St. Louis Cardinals to claim their first World Series championship in 86 years.

The Red Sox released Gutierrez after the season. In 2005 he went to spring training with the Seattle Mariners but he didn't make the team. He spent 35 games with the White Sox' Charlotte (North Carolina) Knights affiliate in the Triple-A International League, but batted just .183. In 2006, he returned to the PCL with the Padres' Portland (Oregon) Beavers farm club and hit .200 in 11 games. "When the writing's on the wall, your skills are not there anymore, it's time to probably come home and just be a father," he said. "I knew I wasn't that same player. I wasn't going to be able to help out a big league club anymore. So I made the decision to call it quits and retire."[56]

In 1,119 major-league games, Gutierrez finished with a .266 batting average, 38 homers, and 50 steals.

Back in Miami, Gutierrez focused on raising his four children – Aric, Brittney, Ricky Jr., and Kendrick – with Lisa (Jones), his spouse since 1994. "My proudest moment was marrying my wife," he said.[57] In addition to managing her four businesses, Lisa – a former basketball player for the University of Miami – coached Brittney's Flanagan High club in that sport.[58]

Gutierrez became the head coach of American Senior High's baseball squad. One of his players, outfielder Ricky Jr., was drafted in the 40th round by the Washington Nationals in 2012, but he opted to play football at the University of Connecticut. In 2014 Gutierrez led the Patriots to their first-ever Florida state title. The star of the team was future big leaguer Romy González.[59]

"At the end of my career I became a utility player," Gutierrez reflected. "So, in my mind, I had to always be ready and think like a manager, to know when I had to be ready for him. That helped me a great deal."[60]

Gutierrez returned to professional baseball in 2017 as the bench coach for the Reds' Daytona Tortugas affiliate in the Class-A Florida State League. He managed the same club to a 135-134 overall record over the next two years. In 2020 he advanced to the organization's Double-A Chattanooga (Tennessee) Lookouts farm club, but the season was canceled because of the coronavirus pandemic. Gutierrez skippered the Lookouts to a 58-54 finish in 2021.

In 2022, Gutierrez joined the Nationals' front office as the special assistant to the VP, international operations. He returned to the field in 2023 as Washington's "run prevention coordinator." Mark Zuckerman, a Nationals reporter for the Mid-Atlantic Sports Network (MASN), explained, "He's not an official member of the coaching staff, but he's in the dugout during games and works specifically with their middle infielders. Essentially an extra coach who specializes in infield defense."[61]

Gutierrez said, "My job is just to give them a bit of routine and make sure their game stays sharp," he explained. "Be there for them in any aspect, but mainly how to go about the game and to be ready for every day at a high level."[62]

SOURCES

In addition to sources cited in the Notes, the author consulted www.ancestry.com, www.baseball-reference.com, and https://sabr.org/bioproject.

NOTES

1. Regarding the nickname "Musulungo," SABR member Tony Oliver noted in an email to the author, "My grandfather (left Cuba in his early 30s) said he recalls the term being used for someone outlandish or out of the ordinary… Give the multiple "u" and the ending in -go, it may be a word from the Yoruba language."
2. Roberto Herrera, *The Sporting News* Player Contract Cards, https://digital.la84.org/digital/collection/p17103coll3/id/80117/rec/4 (last accessed January 31, 2023).
3. Francys Romero, "La Última Entrevista de Roberto 'Musulungo' Herrera," *On Cuba News*, February 4, 2019, https://oncubanews.com/deportes/beisbol/la-ultima-entrevista-de-roberto-musulungo-herrera/ (last accessed January 29, 2023).
4. Ken Plutnicki, "Father Catches Moment of Pride," *Miami Herald*, June 9, 1988: 85.
5. Falleció Roberto "Musulungo" Herrera," LVPB.com, December 27, 2018, https://www.lvbp.com/7267_fallecio-roberto-musulungo-herrera (last accessed January 30, 2023).
6. Plutnicki, "Father Catches Moment of Pride."
7. Anthony Uttariello, "Sunday Morning Chat: American Manager Ricky Gutierrez," *Miami-Dade High School Baseball*, March 17, 2013, https://miamidadehighschoolbaseball.com/2013/03/sunday-morning-chat-american-manager-ricky-Gutierrez/0106353 (last accessed January 31, 2023).
8. Plutnicki, "Father Catches Moment of Pride."
9. Uttariello, "Sunday Morning Chat: American Manager Ricky Gutierrez."
10. "Florida," *USA Today*, April 23, 1987: 14C.
11. Plutnicki, "Father Catches Moment of Pride."
12. "Florida," *USA Today*, April 19, 1988: 10C.
13. The Orioles had the additional first-round pick because their first-round selection in 1987, pitcher Brad DuVall, did not sign. Tim Kurkjian, "Stanicek Is Close but Not Ready to Return Just Yet," *Baltimore Sun*, June 4, 1988: 3B.
14. "No. 1 Pick Opts for College," *St. Louis Post-Dispatch*, June 12, 1988: F2.
15. Tim Kurkjian, "Redus' Agent Wants to Talk to Hemond," *Baltimore Sun*, November 1, 1988: 5B.
16. *Baltimore Orioles 1992 Media Guide*: 173.
17. *Baltimore Orioles 1992 Media Guide*: 174.
18. Gutierrez was Baltimore's number-three overall prospect, behind pitchers Arthur Rhodes and Mike Mussina. J.J. Cooper, "1983-2000 Top 10 Prospects Rankings Archive," *Baseball America*, January 22, 2019, https://www.baseballamerica.com/stories/1983-2000-top-10-prospects-rankings-archive/ (last accessed January 31, 2023).
19. *Baltimore Orioles 1992 Media Guide*: 173.
20. Jim Henneman, "Infielder Gutierrez Goes to Padres, Completing Trade for Lefferts," *Baltimore Sun*, September 5, 1992: 7C.
21. Buster Olney, "Gutierrez Is Nearly a Hero," *San Diego Times-Union*, April 15, 1993: D1.
22. Buster Olney, "Stillwell on the DL with Possible Break; Gutierrez Moves Up," *San Diego Times-Union*, April 13, 1993: D9.
23. Chris De Luca, "Wally's Worries," *The Sporting News*, June 13, 1994: 24.
24. In addition to Gutierrez, Houston received outfielders Derek Bell and Phil Plantier; pitchers Doug Brocail and pitcher Pedro Martínez; and infielder Craig Shipley. Heading to San Diego with Caminiti and Finley were shortstop Andújar Cedeño, pitcher Brian Williams, first baseman Roberto Petagine, and minor-leaguer Sean Fresh.
25. Houston's 102-60 record in 1998 surpassed the franchise's previous top mark, 96-66 in 1986. Twenty years later, however, the 2018 Astros went 103-59. As of 2023, Houston's 107-55 record in 2019 was the team's best.
26. Dan Wiederer, "Kerry Wood and 'the Greatest Game Ever Pitched,'" *Chicago Times*, May 6, 2018.
27. On April 22, 2018, the Giants' Brandon Belt had a 21-pitch at-bat against Angels pitcher Jaime Barria. "Belt Has 21-Pitch At-Bat, Later Homers," *South Florida Sun-Sentinel* (Fort Lauderdale), April 22, 2018: C4.
28. Carlton Thompson, "Astros, Gutierrez Agree to Deal, Avoid Arbitration," *Houston Chronicle*, February 10, 1999: 7.
29. Carlton Thompson, "Gutierrez Placed on DL," *Houston Chronicle*, April 29, 1999: 5.
30. Carlton Thompson, "Houston," *The Sporting News*, May 3, 1999: 31.
31. Carlton Thompson, "Fractured Hand Sends Gutierrez Back to DL," *Houston Chronicle*, July 11, 1999: 1.
32. Carlton Thompson, "Gutierrez Not Offered Arbitration," *Houston Chronicle*, December 8, 1999: 10.
33. Carlton Thompson, "Hunsicker on Lookout for Shortstop at Winter Meetings," *Houston Chronicle*, December 11, 1999: B7.
34. Gutierrez was to receive $2 million in 2001 but could choose to forfeit it and become a free agent. Or the Cubs could exercise their option and keep him in 2001 for a raise to $3.4 million. Paul Sullivan, "Gutierrez Fills Out Cubs' New Lineup Card," *Chicago Tribune*, December 21, 1999: 1.
35. Teddy Greenstein, "Baylor Already Competing," *Chicago Tribune*, March 29, 2000: 4-1.
36. Bruce Miles, "Young, Gutierrez Provide Boost at the Top of Lineup," *The Sporting News*, May 8, 2000: 27.
37. Bruce Miles, "Scouting Report," *The Sporting News*, April 30, 2001: 20.
38. "Cubs' Gutierrez Placed on DL," *National Post* (Toronto), May 27, 2000: A22.

39 Bonnie DeSimone, "Gutierrez Cool Under Pressure," *Chicago Tribune*, September 1, 2001: 3-1.
40 DeSimone, "Gutierrez Cool Under Pressure."
41 Tim Sassone, "Gutierrez to Sox: Spike This," *Arlington Heights (Illinois) Daily Herald*, July 13, 2001: 1.
42 Teddy Greenstein, "It's Down to Numbers; Gutierrez Wants to Stay, and Cubs Want to Keep Him," *Chicago Tribune*, December 6, 2001: 8.
43 George Diaz, "The Indians' Second Choice: Gutierrez Has a New Team and a New Position with the Indians," *Orlando Sentinel*, March 26, 2002: D5.
44 "Retooling Indians Sign Pair," *Memphis Commercial Appeal*, December 18, 2001: D3.
45 Steve Harrick, "Cleveland Indians," *The Sporting News*, December 31, 2001: 61.
46 Julius Whigham II, "Up to the Challenge," *Palm Beach Post*, March 15, 2002: 9B.
47 "Surgery Might Save Gutierrez' Neck," *Seattle Times*, August 21, 2002: D9.
48 "Gutierrez' Quick Recovery Amazes Indians," *South Florida Sun-Sentinel*, March 21, 2003: 10C.
49 "Gutierrez' Quick Recovery Amazes Indians."
50 Tim Dwyer, "Major League Advice," *South Florida Sun-Sentinel*, November 2, 2003: 14.
51 Charlie Nobles, "Mets Add Experience to Infield by Trading for Gutierrez," *New York Times*, March 29, 2004: 3.
52 Bryce Miller, "Gutierrez's Road Trip Ends with First Series," *Des Moines Register*, October 27, 2004: C5.
53 Adam Kilgore, "Gutierrez Relishes Latest Chance," *Boston Globe*, July 23, 2004: E6.
54 Associated Press, "Boston Is Boss," *Rochester Democrat and Chronicle*, October 21, 2004: D1.
55 Miller, "Gutierrez's Road Trip Ends with First Series."
56 Uttariello, "Sunday Morning Chat: American Manager Ricky Gutierrez."
57 Uttariello, "Sunday Morning Chat: American Manager Ricky Gutierrez."
58 Gary Curreri, "When Mom's the Coach, There'll Be No Sliding," *South Florida Sun-Sentinel*, January 6, 2009: C8.
59 Rick Duteau, "American Wins Its First State Title in School History," *Miami-Dade High School Baseball*, May 18, 2014, https://miamidadehighschoolbaseball.com/2014/05/american-wins-its-first-state-title-in-school-history/01014517 (last accessed February 5, 2023).
60 Uttariello, "Sunday Morning Chat: American Manager Ricky Gutierrez."
61 Mark Zuckerman, email to author, September 2, 2023.
62 Mark Zuckerman, "Nats Add Former Infielder Gutierrez to Coaching Staff," MASN Sports, March 19, 2023, https://www.masnsports.com/blog/nats-add-former-infielder-gutierrez-to-coaching-staff (last accessed August 29, 2023).

ADAM HYZDU

BY GEORGE "SKIP" TUETKEN

Adam Hyzdu was a multisport superstar at a high school known for superstar athletes including Buddy Bell, Barry Larkin, and Ken Griffey Jr. After being selected in the first round of the 1990 amateur draft, Hyzdu went on to have an interesting 18-year career in professional baseball. The slugging right-handed outfielder knocked out 273 minor-league home runs, and in parts of seven years in the major leagues he collected 19 more. Though he never got into as many as 60 major-league games in a season, he had some impressive highlights in the majors, including once being named the National League Player of the Week.

His parents, F. Michael Hyzdu (pronounced HIGHS-doo), a Missourian, and Shelley Dellaripa, from Virginia, met at Miami University in Oxford, Ohio.

Mike Hyzdu entered the business of selling stocks and bonds and giving financial advice. Soon after graduation, he accepted a job offer from Westinghouse Electric and the Hyzdu family of three moved to San Jose, California, where their second son, Adam Davis Hyzdu, was born on December 6, 1971. Shelley had a degree in counseling but primarily worked as a homemaker.

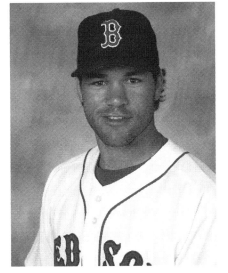

Working for a firm owned by H. Ross Perot, Mike was sent to Los Angeles for a six-month training course. He requested to be assigned to Ohio, and before Adam reached the age of 2, he became an Ohioan. In 1978 younger brother, James Marshall Hyzdu, was born.

From a very young age, Adam just seemed to love all sports. His father recalled that when Adam was about 4 years old, he kept bugging the big kids in the neighborhood to let him play with them, but he was just too young. Finally his brother Michael, 4½ years older than Adam, allowed him to take part by "being second base, not playing second base, but BEING second base."[1] That didn't satisfy him for long and he was soon joining in whenever he could. Once he was old enough to play T-ball, he clearly stood out.

By the time Adam entered Archbishop Moeller, an all-male Catholic high school in the northeastern suburbs of Cincinnati, he had played and excelled in plenty of sports, especially baseball and football. Through undefeated on Moeller's freshman wrestling team, he chose to concentrate on football and baseball. He was rapidly growing into his eventual professional playing frame of 6-feet-2 and over 200 pounds.[2]

Adam played quarterback and frequently kicked for Archbishop Moeller's football team and he helped lead the squad to the Ohio state championship game. Moeller lost, but Adam was named the game's Most Valuable Player. He set passing records that lasted for decades. Having thrown for 2,239 yards and 19 touchdowns in his senior year at Moeller, he was recruited to play football by many of the nation's top colleges, including Notre Dame, Duke, Kentucky, Miami, Stanford, and Tennessee. But baseball was his true love.

It wasn't only baseball that Adam fell in love with in high school. When a sophomore, he was introduced to Julie Theresa Berling and when they started talking they realized they both happened to have tickets to a coming Def Leppard concert, so they decided to go together. As Adam put it, "the rest is history" and they've been together ever since.[3]

Moeller High School has produced 31 players who have played professional baseball.[4] Hyzdu led the Moeller Crusaders in triples each of his seasons and his total of 14 triples broke the record of 12 that had been held by Hall of Famer Barry Larkin. His 22 home runs remain the school's career record.[5] Hyzdu is also the school's career leader in walks with 63, eight above the second-place total, which shows that he was patient and knew the strike zone and/or that pitchers were just afraid to throw him strikes. In his last two years Moeller won the league's championship and in his junior year they were also the state champs and ranked fifth in the nation.[6]

Adam also played a key role on some highly successful summer baseball teams, including two that won national championships. In 1988 his Midland Indians team became the Mickey Mantle 16U champs and the following summer his Midland Redskins won the Connie Mack 18U championship. Those stacked teams also included third baseman David Bell, who went on to play 12 years in the majors and catcher Mike Matheny, who played 13 years of major-league baseball and was a major-league manager for 10 years.

At least as many colleges tried to recruit Hyzdu for baseball as had tried to recruit him for football, and he eventually signed to play for coach Ron Polk and the Mississippi State Bulldogs. Adam's father said his son might have followed through had he been selected in any round of the baseball draft other than the first. In June of 1990, however, the San Francisco Giants selected him in the first round, and Adam signed a contract, with a $250,000 signing bonus with territory scout Herman Hannah, and became a professional baseball player.[7]

As an 18-year-old in 1990, Hyzdu played the outfield in 69 games for the Everett (Washington) Giants of the short-season Class-A Northwest League and collected 62 hits, including six home runs. He was promoted the next season to the Clinton (Iowa) Giants of the Class-A Midwest League, which put him about 2,000 miles closer to his Cincinnati hometown. He played in 124 games and helped Clinton end an 11-year playoff drought and win the Midwest League championship.

The next year Hyzdu was moved up once again, to the San Jose Giants in the Advanced-A California League. He hit .278 and led his team in base hits and total bases. On the troubling side, however, he also topped the team with 134 strikeouts, 58 more than any of his teammates, representing more than a quarter of his plate appearances.

In 1993 Hyzdu split his time between San Jose and the Shreveport Captains of the Double-A Texas League; for each team he struck out more than 25 percent of the time. Before the start of the 1994 season, he had gone to the Cincinnati Reds organization through the Rule 5 draft, was returned to the Giants, and was then traded back to the Reds for two minor-league pitchers. That year Hyzdu played for three teams in the Reds organization, the Winston-Salem Spirits (Class-A Carolina League), the Chattanooga Lookouts (Double-A Southern League), and the Indianapolis Indians (Triple-A American Association). He cut his strikeout rate considerably.

In August 1994, major-league players went on strike, ending the season and canceling the postseason, including the World Series. The following March, team owners planned to resume games by using replacement players. The very eccentric and twice-suspended racist owner of the Cincinnati Reds, Marge Schott, was fully onboard with her team's using replacement players. Hyzdu remembered it this way:

"Marge wanted to use me as the poster boy for the major league team in 1995 when they brought in replacement players. They brought 40 of us in and said we were competing for the 25 spots on the major-league roster. I proceeded to tell her I was not going to cross the line after her parading me around to the front office and telling everyone I would do the right thing. When I said thank you for the interest but I cannot play and I would not cross the union's wishes, she called me a weak little pussy and [said] that I would never amount to anything."[8]

When the strike ended, Hyzdu was sent back to Chattanooga, where he played well but was nevertheless released shortly before the start of the 1996 season. Late in April he signed with the Boston Red Sox and was sent to their Double-A team, the Trenton (New Jersey) Thunder. There he led the team in almost every batting category with 25 home runs, 80 RBIs, a .337 average, and a 1.042 OPS. The team was easily the best in the Eastern League with a record of 86-56. Hyzdu was promoted to the Pawtucket Red Sox in the Triple-A International League for the 1997 season and led his team with 23 homers and 84 RBIs, and helped the team improve to an 81-60 record. Showing an improved batting eye, he also led the team in walks with 72.

Hoping for a quicker path to the majors, Hyzdu opted for free agency after the season and signed with the Arizona Diamondbacks organization. He split the 1998 season playing for the Tucson Sidewinders in the Pacific Coast League and the Monterrey Sultanes in the Mexican League.???? Is there a story behind going to the Mexican League? He again became a free agent after the season and signed again with the Red Sox. Despite doing well in spring training, Hyzdu was sent back to Pawtucket, where in only a dozen games, he did not do well and was released.

While driving home to Cincinnati, Hyzdu received a phone call from Cam Bonifay, the general manager of the Pittsburgh Pirates. Bonifay asked Hyzdu if he would go to their brand-new Double-A Altoona Curve team specifically because some players there were "kind of headcases and running amok."[9] Altoona manager Marty Brown said he needed a high-character veteran who could take charge of the clubhouse and Hyzdu ended up doing that and a lot more. Brown told him, "Whatever you say goes."[10]

Playing in just 91 of Altoona's 140 games in 1999, Hyzdu nonetheless became its first star player, leading the team with 24 home runs, 78 RBIs, a .316 batting average, a slugging percentage of .612, and an OPS of 1.003. He also smashed five homers in 14 games for the Pirates' Triple-A team, the Nashville Sounds. Rather than a promotion the next season, he was sent back to Altoona, where he played in all 142 games and set team records of 31 homers, 106 RBIs, 94 walks, 285 total bases, and a .406 on-base percentage. He was named the team's Most Valuable Player for the second straight year and also was voted the MVP of the Eastern League.[11]

In 2018 Cory Giger, a longtime sportswriter for the *Altoona Mirror*, wrote of Hyzdu:

"To come through with clutch hit after clutch hit, ninth-inning home runs, pinch-hit homers to win games, the bottom line is he was a sensational player on the field. You don't become a legend anywhere unless you are first and foremost a great player. But because he was a great player who also accepted his role of being the leader, of being the older, mature guy on the team and of being the face of the franchise, that's what stood out to me. He accepted and appreciated what he could do for Altoona and the Curve.[12]

When Altoona's 2000 season ended, Hyzdu was called up to the Pittsburgh Pirates. Since Altoona was only about 100 miles from Pittsburgh, many Pirates fans were already well aware of his performance there and were rooting him on. He was almost 29 years old when he started as the left fielder in the second game of a doubleheader at Three Rivers Stadium on September 8, 2000, against the Cincinnati Reds. In his first major-league plate appearance, Hyzdu led off the bottom of the third inning with a single to right field off lefty Ron Villone. He didn't score, but the Pirates beat the Reds 3-1.[13]

Hyzdu collected his first major-league RBI on September 19 with a pinch-hit single that helped lead to a win in Philadelphia. The next night Hyzdu again was used as a pinch-hitter. His two-run homer in the 10th inning off righty Chris Brock drove in the final two Pirates runs in a 7-6 win.

Hyzdu's only other start for the 2000 Pirates came in the second game of a September 23 doubleheader. He had four at-bats in Milwaukee and got a single and his first two major-league doubles. In a dozen games with the Pirates, Hyzdu had batted .389 with an OPS of 1.056 and things were looking good for the coming spring.

But Hyzdu started the 2001 season back in Nashville and played in 69 games for the Sounds with a .291 batting average and 11 home runs. In early June he was called back to Pittsburgh, where he got into 51 games and hit five homers, but his batting average dropped to .208 so he started the 2002 season back in Nashville. This time he clubbed 10 homers with 50 RBIs before being recalled to Pittsburgh at the beginning of July. He started off well with a two-run home run in his first plate appearance, but it wasn't until his 10th game back that he caught fire.

On July 18 Hyzdu started in center field and knocked out two singles in three at-bats. The next day he collected three hits, including a home run, and four RBIs in a 12-9 win over St. Louis. On the next day he had the most productive game of his major-league career. He hit a three-run homer in the first inning, singled to center in the third, smashed another three-run homer in the fifth, and singled again in the ninth inning to drive in a seventh run in the Pirates' 15-6 thrashing of the Cardinals. Over the next four games Hyzdu got six more hits, including another home run. Those seven games gave him 15 hits, 4 homers, 7 runs scored, 12 runs batted in, a .556 batting average, a .586 on-base percentage, and a slugging percentage of 1.000. It also earned him a new watch as the prize for being named the National League Player of the Week.

On July 30, 2002, Hyzdu doubled in two of the Pirates' three runs in the eighth inning to beat the Colorado Rockies, 4-1. On August 18 he got a home run and two RBIs in a 3-2 victory over the Milwaukee Brewers. He followed that up on the 23rd with his first grand slam in a 6-3 win against the Brewers. On September 13 he doubled in a run and homered as the Pirates beat the Phillies 5-3.

Though Hyzdu started off the 2003 season driving in two runs and scoring another in a 6-3 win over the Mets and then smacking his second major-league grand slam on the last day of April to beat the San Diego Padres 8-5, things did not go well over the next three months. By the beginning of August his grand slam had been his only homer and his batting average was barely over .200. He performed much better in a starting role, as he mostly did in 2002, than he did when used as a pinch-hitter, a pinch-runner, or a late-inning defensive replacement, as was the case for him with the Pirates for most of 2003. Early in August he was sent back down to Nashville. In 40 games there he did pretty well with half a dozen homers, 18 RBIs, and an average of .282, but was nonetheless a free agent at the end of the season.

Hyzdu signed again with the Red Sox organization and returned to Pawtucket, where he had a terrific year. Of those who played more than a handful of games, he led the Pawsox with a .301 batting average, a .413 on-base percentage, and a slugging percentage of .568. He hit 29 home runs, scored 92 runs, and drove in 79, and his 84 walks were more than a dozen ahead of anyone else on the team. He was officially the Pawsox' Player of the Month of August.

It wasn't until Boston's Johnny Damon dislocated one of his pinky fingers diving back to first on a pickoff throw at the beginning of September, though, that Hyzdu was brought up to the Red Sox. Not wanting to put Damon on their injured list, the Red Sox instead designated pitcher Brandon Puffer for assignment to make room for Hyzdu.[14]

Hyzdu played in 17 games and the Red Sox went 12-5 in them. It wasn't until his sixth game of either being a late-inning defensive replacement for Manny Ramírez or as a pinch-runner that he got a plate appearance. It was on September 11 at Safeco Field in Seattle. The Red Sox were leading the Mariners 7-0 when Hyzdu replaced Ramírez to start the bottom of the seventh inning. After David McCarty singled and Pokey Reese walked with two outs in the ninth, he doubled in McCarty with the eighth run. Two more walks drove in the final run of the 9-0 Red Sox victory.

On the 15th at Fenway Park, Hyzdu ran for Doug Mirabelli in the sixth inning of a 6-6 game against the Tampa Bay Devil Rays and scored the go-ahead run on Manny Ramírez's sacrifice fly. The Red Sox eventually won 8-6. On September 29 at Tropicana Field in St. Petersburg, the Red Sox were losing 5-3 in the fifth inning when Hyzdu ran for Ramírez. He didn't score, but stayed in to play left and got to bat in the eighth and smashed a home run for the Red Sox' final run in a 9-4 loss. Finally, on October 2 at Baltimore's Camden Yards with Boston leading the Orioles 7-0 in the top of the sixth, Hyzdu batted for Johnny Damon and doubled to left, but was stranded. In the nightcap of that twin bill Kevin Millar was hit by a pitch in the seventh inning with the score tied at 5-5. With two on and one out, Hyzdu ran for Millar and scored the final run on Doug Mientkiewicz's triple in the second 7-5 Red Sox victory of the day.

Hyzdu's contributions to the soon-to-be World Series champion Red Sox embraced 11 plate appearances, three runs scored, a pair of RBIs, and an even .300 batting average. He had a .364 on-base percentage and an impressive .800 slugging percentage. His three hits were two doubles and a home run, which gave him an OPS of 1.164. In the outfield he played errorless baseball while collecting six putouts. Though not on the postseason roster, he and pitcher Lenny DiNardo continued to work out with the team throughout the postseason.[15]

As well as he had played in Pawtucket and Boston in 2004, the Red Sox clearly did not consider the 33-year-old Hyzdu to be a prospect any longer, so before the 2005 season started he was traded to the San Diego Padres for pitcher Blaine Neal. Neal pitched in eight games for Boston with no wins, one loss, and an earned-run average of 9.00. In 17 early-season games, Hyzdu played in 16 games in April for San Diego with only a couple of starts and was just 2-for-16. The Padres gave him one last start on May 2 before sending him to Triple-A Portland, Oregon. In that game Hyzdu came up with two outs and the bases loaded in the second inning. He drove in all three runners with a double to left, helping the Padres beat the Colorado Rockies 5-4.

For the Portland Beavers, Hyzdu's 11 home runs, .275 batting average, and .410 OBP were enough to convince the Red Sox that they might have had made a mistake in trading him away. So on July 19, 2005, they traded pitcher Scott Cassidy for him and Hyzdu joined the Red Sox organization for a fourth time. In five July games for Boston he was 0-for-6 before being sent to Pawtucket. He stayed there long enough to hit four home runs and collect 25 RBIs before returning to Boston for the September pennant drive.

Hyzdu played in seven of the Red Sox' final games and he got four hits and a pair of walks in 10 at-bats. His last game for Boston took place on October 2, the last game of the regular season. He went to center field, replacing Johnny Damon, to start the top of the seventh inning at Fenway Park. While there he made three putouts in center and led off the bottom of the seventh with a double to left. The next three batters struck out. Nevertheless, the Red Sox managed to hold on to a 10-1 win over the New York Yankees, moving into a first-place tie with them and becoming a wild-card entry in the playoffs for the third straight year. (The Yankees had one more head-to-head win over the Red Sox.)

A few days after the Red Sox were swept by the White Sox in the Division Series, Hyzdu was released. He signed for the 2006 season with the Texas Rangers, but played in only two games for them before being sent to the Oklahoma RedHawks in the Pacific Coast League. He spent the rest of the season there. It was his last season playing professional baseball in the United States. Though now 34, he nevertheless led the RedHawks in many categories, including runs scored, runs batted in, doubles, walks, and homers (19).

Hyzdu's Oklahoma numbers were impressive enough to get him recruited by the Fukuoka Softbank Hawks in the Japan Pacific League. One thing he recalled as being different from all his previous years was that when he signed to play baseball in Japan in 2007, it was the first time he knew exactly what team he would be playing for and exactly how much money he would be making. He ended up getting into only 47 games but hit 7 home runs and posted a batting average, on-base percentage, slugging percentage, and OPS that were each significantly above Fukuoka's team performances. It was his final year as a professional baseball player.

During parts of seven years, Hyzdu had been in 221 major-league games and collected 82 hits, of which more than 45 percent went for extra bases. His 19 major-league home runs in 407 plate appearances meant he hit a homer every 21.4 times he came up to bat. That frequency rate was better than those of Eddie Murray, Gary Sheffield, and Mel Ott, each of whom hit over 500 major-league home runs. It was, however, Hyzdu's minor-league statistics that were truly impressive. In 17 seasons in a variety of minor-league levels, he played in 1,703 games and had 1,642 hits. They included 355 doubles, 35 triples, and 273 home runs, meaning that over 40 percent of his hits went for extra bases. He scored 951 times and drove in over 1,000 runs. His 838 bases on balls gave him one walk every eight times he batted. His final minor-league statistics gave him a batting average of .276, an OBP of .366, a slugging percentage of .484, and an OPS of .850.

Though Hyzdu was always considered an outfielder, he played at least a little at every position except second base and shortstop in the minors; and in the majors he was an errorless first baseman in five games. In the 155 major-league games he played in the outfield, he was charged with only one error.

When Hyzdu returned from Japan in 2007, he was 35 years old, his baseball career was truly over, and he had to find something else to do. For about a year he worked for Children's Miracle Network Hospitals (CMNH), an organization that raises money for children's hospitals.

Meanwhile his father-in-law, Robert Berling, had been in the business of selling cars in Mesa, Arizona, until Adam and Julie gave him money in 2007 to start buying recreational vehicles. Adam said that "once Julie's dad sold his first RV, he was hooked. RVs are fun and happy and people love thinking about all the places they are going to go. Cars are cars, but RVs are an adventure."[16] After working for CMNH, he began working at Berling's dealership and, when Berling died of cancer in October of 2010, Adam took over running it. As of 2023 he was still running it. RVAZ Corral in Mesa is a place to visit, check out some recreational vehicles or tow-along campers, and even get an autograph from a former major-league baseball player.

Adam's parents Mike and Shelley had divorced, but have both remarried and were both still living in the Cincinnati area as were their two other sons. Adam's brother, Mike, is chaplain for the Columbus Clippers minor-league baseball team. Brother Marshall in 2023 was the president of Archbishop Moeller High School. The three Hyzdu brothers and their parents established a Hyzdu Family Scholarship, which is given annually for "a Moeller education to a student who participates in a co-curricular activity and displays Christian leadership among his classmates."[17]

Because of Adam's lengthy baseball career, he and Julie had lived in many different places before they settled in Arizona. Adam and Julie's first two children, Zac in March 1994 and Alexa in November 1996, were both born while Adam was still in the minor leagues. Having a family as a minor leaguer can be quite challenging and it certainly had been for the four members of the Hyzdu family. By the time Luke Hyzdu was born in December of 2000, however, Adam had finished his two outstanding seasons for the Altoona Curve and had even played a dozen games for the Pirates, so things were clearly looking up. His next six seasons were each split between Triple A and the majors, and though he still had to move around frequently, at least it was less of a financial struggle.

Despite the hardships of moving, however, at least the older children didn't have to worry about constantly changing schools. Until they reached high-school age, Julie Hyzdu home-schooled them in all but gym and math, which Adam handled. (Luke, the youngest, was home-schooled for only a year.) Like their father, both of the boys excelled in baseball during their high-school years. Zac was set to play baseball at Dallas Baptist University, but he suffered a broken back and was unable to do so.[18] After rehabbing, he made it on to the Grand Canyon University baseball team, but never quite recovered enough to play. After graduation he began working for his father and now handles financing at RVAZ Corral. Zac and his wife, Kendall, have also made proud grandparents out of Adam and Julie with two daughters. Since finishing college, Alexa has become a clinical counselor, first in California and then back in Arizona. Luke, meanwhile, played baseball at Scottsdale Community College after high school and then, after transferring, became a middle infielder for Texas A&M at Texarkana. In the spring of 2023, he played 44 games for the Eagles, mostly as their leadoff hitter, and batted a robust .344.[19]

John Wehner, a teammate of Adam Hyzdu with the Pirates and Altoona, who has since become a color commentator for the Pirates, told a sportswriter that Hyzdu had an amazing reputation with teammates and with fans. "He was also an engaging personality," Wehner said. "He had a smile on his face. He'd talk to anybody and everybody. He was one of those guys everyone liked." Wehner added that Adam "had a reputation like none that I've ever seen in the minor leagues."[20]

In mid-2023, when he wasn't watching one of his son Luke's college baseball games, or attending services at Sun Valley Church, where both he and Julie are active members, or going back to Cincinnati for a family reunion, or to Altoona to again be honored and remembered, Hyzdu could most likely be found working with his son Zac selling recreational vehicles at RVAZ Corral. If one went to their website and checked out their "Contact Us, About Us" information, one would find a picture of a Fleer 2001 Adam Hyzdu baseball card and the following sentence concerning his baseball career: "Adam played 18 years of professional baseball with the highlight being part of the 2004 World Champion Boston Red Sox!"[21]

SOURCES

Article researched by Andrew Tuetken.

In addition to the sources cited in the Notes, the author accessed a number of sources including Ancestry.com, baseballalmanac.com, Baseball-Reference.com, and retrosheet.org.

Thanks to both Adam Hyzdu and his father, Michael Hyzdu.

NOTES

1. Author interview with Mike Hyzdu on April 1, 2023.
2. Email from Adam Hyzdu on May 8, 2023.
3. Email from Adam Hyzdu on March 11, 2023.
4. https://www.baseball-reference.com/schools/index.cgi?key_school=fab6dbf6#site_menu_link.
5. Another member of the Hall of Fame, Ken Griffey Jr., had been second on that list with 17 homers.
6. Archbishop Moeller Crusaders Athletics, at https://letsgobigmoe.com/documents/2022/10/19/2022_Record_Book.pdf.
7. Email from Rod Nelson of SABR's Scouts and Scouting Research Committee on August 1, 2023.
8. Email from Adam Hyzdu on March 11.
9. Adam Berry, "This Altoona All-Star Remains a Pirates Cult Hero," MLB.com, November 14, 2019. https://www.mlb.com/news/adam-hyzdu-a-pirates-cult-hero.
10. Berry.
11. More than 20 years later, Hyzdu still held most of the Altoona Curve's franchise batting records for both a single season and a career. In 2000 the team announced that Hyzdu's uniform number 16 would be retired. Long after retiring from baseball, he returned in June 2018 to an Altoona Curve baseball game during which 1,000 Adam Hyzdu bobbleheads were given out. According to Mike Ryan, who played against Hyzdu in 2000 and who was the Altoona manager from 2017 through 2019, the Altoona fans still say "he's the greatest Curve player that's ever lived. … He was a man among boys at that time. I could see why this community and the organization was so excited by him." Berry.
12. Cory Giger, Altoona Curve, June 14, 2018, http://altoona.mlblogs.com/2018/06/14/all-time-curve-team-adam-hyzdu/.
13. Hyzdu's 1-for-3 outperformed fellow Archbishop Moeller grad Ken Griffey Jr.'s 0-for-4.
14. Puffer had been with Boston for one day and never got into a game.
15. They were both introduced with the team before the start of the World Series at Fenway Park and would have been available to be activated if someone who was on the roster had for injury or other reason been unable to continue playing. See the full broadcast of the game on YouTube, at https://www.youtube.com/watch?v=5rLWrD1ipio.
16. Email from Adam Hyzdu on June 6, 2023.
17. "Named scholarships," Archbishop Moeller High School, at https://www.moeller.org/support/named-scholarships.
18. Email from Adam Hyzdu on June 17, 2023.
19. https://thebaseballcube.com/content/stats/college~2023~22495/.
20. Berry.
21. https://www.rvaz.com/about-us.

BOBBY JONES

BY BUDD BAILEY

Bobby Jones certainly meets the qualities of a baseball lifer. He spent much of his time on the playing field and in dugouts for more than 40 years after playing in Little League, crossing the country frequently during that odyssey. Jones's dedication to the game eventually led to his appointment to the front office of an independent professional team in the fall of 2022.

Robert Mitchell Jones was born on April 11, 1972, in Orange, New Jersey. His family moved to Rutherford, a few miles north of Orange, in 1981. Bobby played Little League baseball for the Park Exxon team between 1982 and 1984. He became the fourth graduate of that Little League program to reach major-league baseball; he was preceded by Bill Hands, Brant Alyea, and Pat Pacillo.[1] Young Jones became a regular pitcher in 1983. As a 12-year-old in 1984, Bobby had a 4-5 record with an earned-run average of 2.82 and an opposing batting average of .216.[2]

At Rutherford High School, Jones was All-Bergen County in baseball, football, and basketball for three straight years.[3] He was inducted into the Rutherford High School Athletic Hall of Fame in 1990.

From high school Jones moved to Chipola College, a junior college in Marianna, Florida that has sent two dozen players to the major leagues. Its alumni include such players as Russell Martin, José Bautista, and Patrick Corbin; many others – including veteran manager Buck Showalter – were drafted but never reached the majors as players.[4]

On June 3, 1991, Jones was picked in the 44th round by the Milwaukee Brewers in major league baseball's free-agent draft. He didn't sign until May 13, 1992, and he was assigned to Helena (Montana) in the Pioneer League, the first of his 18 teams in pro baseball. He started 13 games there, compiling a record of 5-4 with a 4.36 ERA. In 1993 Jones moved up from rookie ball to Class A with Beloit (Wisconsin) of the Midwest League, for whom he went 10-10 with a 4.11 ERA. It was on to high Class A in 1994, as he joined Stockton in the California League. Jones slumped to 6-12 with a 4.21 earned-run average with the Ports. But he averaged a strikeout per inning that season (147 in 147⅔ innings).

Jones had been in the minor leagues for three seasons at that point and still hadn't moved past Class A. The Colorado Rockies took him in the Rule 5 draft on December 5, 1994. The Rockies had just finished their first year in the National League as an expansion team, and they took a chance that Jones could turn into a prospect.

Jones moved up to Double-A baseball in 1995 for the Rockies' organization, playing for New Haven (Connecticut) in the Eastern League. As a starter and closer for the Ravens, Jones was 5-2 with a 2.58 ERA and 70 strikeouts in 73⅓ innings. That was good for a midseason promotion to Colorado Springs in Triple A, but Jones struggled a bit at the higher level. He was used mostly as a starter, and finished 1-2 with a 7.30 ERA.

The lefty's role changed in 1996. Jones pitched in 57 games for Colorado Springs, none of them a start, and posted a 2-8 record with a 4.97 ERA. In 1997 the Rockies apparently changed their minds again about Jones; he had 21 starts for Colorado Springs, going 7-11 with a 5.14 ERA.

In 1997 Jones was called up to the major leagues for the first time. He debuted in a contest in Shea Stadium against the New York Mets, his favorite team as a child, on May 18. Jones did reasonably well.[5] He worked 5⅓ innings and gave up two runs on four hits with seven walks and three strikeouts. Jones left with the Rockies trailing 2-1. In his first major-league at-bat, Jones lined a single in the third inning off Dave Mlicki. Colorado took a 3-2 lead in the top of the seventh, but the bullpen allowed eight runs in the eighth. New York picked up a 10-4 victory.

Jones's next start was on May 23 at home against Houston. He wasn't quite as sharp, allowing six runs on 11 hits in 6⅔ innings. But the Rockies' offense provided some help. They had an 8-6 lead when Jones exited, and Colorado hung on for an 8-7 win, Jones's first major-league victory. On May 29 Jones started against the Florida Marlins. He had a no-decision in a 6-5 win in which he gave up four runs and seven hits in six innings. Jones's last appearance in a Rockies uniform for the year came on June 3 in St. Louis. After the Cardinals roughed him up for six runs on eight hits in 1⅓ innings, sending him to his first loss in the majors after a 15-4 St. Louis romp, and he was assigned to the minors.

Jones's brief stay in the majors in 1997 turned out to be a good warm-up for the following season. He made the Opening Day roster for the Rockies and stayed the entire season.

Jones started the season in the bullpen, and he struggled in the first half of April. But something clicked in the next couple of weeks, as the left-hander allowed four hits and one run in 9⅔ innings. "I didn't care what the situation was, I was going to keep plugging," Jones said of his struggles in his previous season. "I knew I could pitch at this level. I had days when I was outstanding, and I had days when I just played terrible. But I knew on those days when I was outstanding that I was better than a lot of guys in the minor leagues. That's why I felt like I could make it to the big leagues. It was just a matter of determination."[6]

Jones was moved to the starting rotation on May 24, and he threw seven innings of two-hit ball in beating Cincinnati. Jones's only complete game in the majors came on June 21, an 11-6 win over the Los Angeles Dodgers in Denver. He was something of a spot starter for most of the rest of the season, which was cut short by a knee injury suffered while fielding a bunt in a September 14 game against the Dodgers. The pitcher first hurt his knee while playing high-school football.[7]

Jones had 20 starts in 35 games, with a record of 7-8. He probably learned a lesson about pitching in the thin air of Coors Field, as he compiled a 5.22 ERA – average in that environment.

It was more of the same in 1999. Jones again started the season in the bullpen and threw in relief for the first month. He had his first start of the season on May 11 at Coors Field against the Mets, and his story took an unusual turn. The opposing pitcher was also named Bobby Jones. (For convenience, the "other" player will be called Bobby J. Jones here.) It was the first time in the twentieth century that two pitchers with the same first and last names started against each other. "There are not a lot of similarities outside of our name," Bobby M. Jones told the New York Times. "He's 6-4 and I'm 6-foot. He's white and I'm black. He's right-handed and I'm left-handed."[8]

The Rockies won, 8-5, and Bobby M. Jones earned the win, allowing two runs in five innings including a strikeout of the Mets' Jones. "I'll tell you the funniest thing that happened," Rockies coach Rich Donnelly said. "I was coaching third, and our Bobby Jones was hitting. We needed him to hit the ball hard somewhere to score a run. So I said, 'Come on, Bobby.' And the other Bobby Jones looked right at me. Then I heard the Mets in their dugout yelling, 'Come on, Bobby. Go get 'em.' And our Bobby Jones looked in their dugout. So their guy looked at me. Our guy looked at them. Perfect."[9]

Bobby M. Jones stayed in the Colorado rotation through the end of August, rarely going past six innings. He finished the year back in the bullpen, and his playing time was limited in September because he suffered from a pinkeye infection.[10] For the season he was 6-10 with a 6.33 ERA. Jones also had three starts back in Triple-A ball, going 2-1 for Colorado Springs.

Left-handed pitchers are often in demand from other teams, and the Mets may have noticed that Jones did well when pitching in New York. They completed a deal with the Rockies on January 14, 2000, acquiring Jones and pitcher Lariel González from the Rockies for pitcher Masato Yoshii.

That meant that two players with the same name were on the Mets' roster. The duo already had been receiving each other's mail quite a bit, and that problem would only get worse. The New York organization had gone through this once before in its history. The 1962 Mets had two right-handed pitchers named Bob Miller – a Bob Miller who went 1-12, and a Bob Miller who was 2-2. They were even roommates on the road.

Bobby M. Jones spent most of the 2000 season with Norfolk (Virginia), the Mets' Triple-A affiliate in the International League. He had a 10-8 record, starting 21 games with an ERA of 4.32. The Mets called him up to the majors a couple of times. In his first game in a New York uniform, he closed out a 7-1 win with a scoreless inning against Milwaukee on June 6. At one point, Bobby M. Jones was sent to the minors so the Mets could activate, yes, Bobby J. Jones. The left-handed Jones pitched in relief of the right-handed Jones three times during the season.[11]

Jones was recalled in early September and made eight appearances out of the bullpen the rest of the season. He finished 0-1 with a 4.15 ERA in 11 games. He ended the year with three straight scoreless appearances covering five innings. However, Jones had to watch the team win a couple of playoff series to reach the World Series, as he was not on the postseason roster. The New York Yankees defeated their crosstown rivals in five games to win the Series.

Arm troubles bothered Jones in 2001, starting with tendinitis during spring training. He spent most of the season on the disabled list, and saw very little action for three different teams in the minors one appearance with Norfolk, two with Double-A Binghamton, and four with Class-A St. Lucie.[12] He bounced back a bit a year later, appearing in 13 games (six starts) in Norfolk. Jones also pitched in 12 games for the Mets with no decisions and a 5.29 ERA.

Jones's time with New York came to a halt at the trading deadline on July 31, 2002, when he was shipped with Jason Bay and minor-league pitcher Josh Reynolds to the San Diego Padres for pitchers Jason Middlebrook and Steve Reed. The deal reunited baseball's two pitchers named Bobby Jones, as Bobby J. Jones had joined the Padres in the previous winter as a free agent. They started in back-to-back games, Bobby J. Jones on August 10 and Bobby M. Jones on the 11th.[13] Bobby M. Jones pitched in four games for the Padres, starting two, and had a 0-0 record with a 6.52 ERA. San Diego gave up on him after a month, releasing him on September 3.

On January 21, 2003, Jones signed as a free agent with the Atlanta Braves. He appeared in 37 games with Richmond of the Triple-A International League (1-3 record, 3.12 ERA) before the Braves released him on July 3. Six days later, the Kansas City Royals signed Jones and assigned him to Omaha, where he was 1-2 with a 3.65 ERA in 20 games. Jones was granted free agency on October 15, 2003.

Jones was 31 years old at that point, and may have been wondering if his major-league career was over. But the Boston Red Sox threw him a lifeline by signing him on November 12. Jones beat the odds in spring training and was on the team's roster at the start of the season. "This one takes the cake," he said about returning to the majors. "This one is way more special. After what happened the last one and a half years, this one is much sweeter."[14]

Jones's first action for the Red Sox came on April 7, when he threw two innings in a 10-3 win in Baltimore. A day later Jones wasn't as lucky, suffering a loss when he walked four batters in the bottom of the 13th inning in a 3-2 loss to the Orioles. The game ended when Jones missed the strike zone on a 3-and-2 pitch to Larry Bigbie. The evening became even worse for Jones and the Red Sox when mechanical problems grounded their plane for several hours; the sleepless group arrived in downtown Boston at 7:30 A.M. – less than eight hours before the home opener in Fenway Park.[15]

Finally on April 11, Jones gave up walks to the only two batters he faced – throwing only eight pitches in the process – in the 11th inning of a game against the Blue Jays. But Boston got out of the jam, and then won the game. It was no way to celebrate Jones's 32nd birthday, and those eight pitches were his final tosses in major-league baseball.

The Red Sox knew something was wrong at that point, and designated Jones for assignment on April 14. He decided to report to Triple-A Pawtucket. "When you walk that many guys in a row, it just gets disheartening," Boston manager Terry Francona said. "He needs to go back and get straightened out."[16]

Hampered by shoulder and elbow problems, Jones did not appear in any games for Pawtucket. Boston released him on October 8. Later that month, the Red Sox went on to win the World Series. Like all of the other players who were on the Boston roster that season, Jones received a championship ring from the team.

Jones wasn't quite done with baseball. He returned to New Jersey and pitched for the Newark Bears of the independent Atlantic League in 2005. Jones pitched 16 innings in five games for the Bears (0-0, 6.75 ERA), and that was enough to convince the Chicago White Sox to purchase his contract. He appeared in 16 games with Charlotte, Chicago's Triple-A affiliate, and he had an ERA of 8.39. He was released on October 15.

On February 17, 2006, the Detroit Tigers gave Jones one more chance by signing him. With Erie (Pennsylvania) in the Double-A Eastern League, Jones pitched in 28 games with 12 starts, going 3-4 with an ERA of 3.92. The veteran was selected for the roster of the Eastern League All-Star Game in July. That season was it for Jones's career, if one doesn't count a one-inning appearance with Rockland of the Canadian-American Association in 2013. Jones's major-league dossier: 99 games in six seasons, 14-21/5.77.

After retiring from playing, Jones turned to other ways to stay involved in baseball. He had a baseball academy in Montville, New Jersey, and later worked for Champions Way Sports Academy.[17] Jones also worked as a pitching coach at Don Bosco Prep and Montclair High School, and spent time as a pitching coach with the Rockland Boulders of the Can-Am League (now the New York Boulders of the Frontier League).

In 2016 Jones was named the manager of the Sussex County Miners in the Canadian-American Association. "I'm a baseball rat," he said when he was hired. "I'm very, very excited for spring training."[18] Jones guided a last-place team to a league championship in his third season on the job (2018). He and the Miners moved to the Frontier League in 2020, and Jones remained their manager through the 2022 season. For 2023 he was hired as the vice president and chief business officer of the New Jersey Jackals, a rival of the Miners in the Frontier League.

The timing of the new job worked out well for Jones, as the Jackals were moving their home games to Hinchliffe Stadium in Paterson, New Jersey. That ballpark hosted Negro League baseball in the 1930s and 1940s. "Moving to Hinchliffe Stadium is a new beginning for this team and I want to do everything I can to make it a winning team, and that will take people who want to win as much as I do," Jones said.[19]

The 2023 season marked the first time in decades that Jones wasn't sitting in a dugout during games. "I don't know if I'm going to miss it or not," he said before the season. "I might be too busy learning what I've got to learn and being involved in all the other aspects of running a team to miss it."[20]

Jones's son, Breyln, tried to follow in his father's footsteps. He also went to Rutherford High School, where he pitched. Breyln was selected in the 29th round of the amateur draft in 2019 by the Los Angeles Dodgers, and signed for a reported $125,000.[21] He pitched in seven games for the Dodgers' team in the Arizona Complex League in 2022, and was released. Bobby and his wife, Michelle, also had a daughter, Brianna.

SOURCES

In addition to the sources cited in the Notes, the author consulted Baseball-reference.com and Retrosheet.org.

NOTES

1 "The Bobby Jones File," https://www.charliesballparks.com/rll/jones.htm.

2 "Player Statistics: Bobby Jones," Rutherford Little League, https://www.charliesballparks.com/rll/roster/Jones-Bobby-1984.htm.

3 *New York Mets 2000 Media Guide.*

4 "Indians in Major League Baseball," Chipola Athletics, https://www.chipolaathletics.com/landing/index.

5 "The Bobby Jones File."

6 John Henderson, "Jones Battling Through," *Denver Post*, April 28, 1998, https://extras.denverpost.com/rock/grox0428c.htm.

7 Tracy Ringolsby, "Jones Out for the Season, but Won't Need Surgery," *Rocky Mountain News* (Denver), September 16, 1998.

8 Andrew Mearns, "There Was Once a Pitching Matchup Featuring Bobby Jones vs. Bobby Jones," MLB.com, May 11, 2017, https://www.mlb.com/cut4/on-this-day-in-1999-a-pitching-matchup-was-bobby-jones-vs-bobby-jones-c228115800.

9 Mearns.

10 *New York Mets 2001 Media Guide.*

11 *New York Mets 2001 Media Guide.*

12 "Camp Reports National League," *Chicago Tribune*, March 20, 2001: 3.

13 Mearns.

14 David Heuschkel, "Jones gets last spot in bullpen," *Hartford Courant*, April 4, 2004. https://www.courant.com/2004/04/04/jones-gets-last-spot-in-bullpen/.

15 Terry Francona and Dan Shaughnessy, *Francona: The Red Sox Years* (Boston: Houghton Mifflin Harcourt, 2013), 84.

16 David Borges, "Sox Set to Ship Jones Out," *Middletown* (Connecticut) *Press*, April 16, 2004, https://www.middletownpress.com/news/article/Sox-set-to-ship-Jones-out-11915512.php.

17 "2000 N.L. Champion Mets Pitcher …" http://www.centerfieldmaz.com/2020/04/2000-nl-champion-mets-pitcher-left.html.

18 Don Laible, "Bobby Jones 'Manager in Waiting,'" *Utica* (New York) *Observer-Dispatch*, April 10, 2016, https://www.uticaod.com/story/news/columns/2016/04/10/bobby-jones-manager-in-waiting/31993318007/.

19 Carl Barbati, "Bobby Jones Joins New Jersey as Vice President and Chief Business Officer," Frontierleague.com; November 1, 2022, https://www.frontierleague.com/sports/bsb/2021-22/releases/20221101nw5mc1.

20 "Bobby Jones Joins New Jersey as Vice President and Chief Business Officer."

21 Jennifer Ersalesi, "MLB Draft and RHS Graduate Breyln," *This is Rutherford.com*, June 25, 2019, https://www.thisisrutherford.com/post/mlb-draft-and-rhs-graduate-breyln-jones.

EMOTIONAL IMPACT OF 2004

After Aaron Boone's walk-off home run eliminated the Red Sox from a shot at the World Series in 2003, my wife went to bed, and I sat by myself staring at the television. I went into the kitchen and took out a butcher's knife. I wasn't going to do anything radical such as killing myself, but I gave serious thought to removing a part of a finger as a permanent reminder of just how painful this loss was. I talked myself out of it by deciding that from that moment on I would become a Cleveland Indians fan. They too had been waiting a long time for a championship (since 1948), but their fans didn't seem to take it so ridiculously seriously. That lasted for about six weeks, when I got a letter in the mail from the Red Sox asking if I would be interested in a partial season-ticket package. Of course, I forgot my pledge to the Indians and signed up for the tickets. One of the best decisions I ever made.

We both came from Long Island, but went to college in Massachusetts and made it our permanent home. I'd been a Yankees fan and enjoyed watching them win the World Series in 1961, 1962, 1977, and 1978. My father was a New York Giants fan but became a devout Yankees fan to encourage my interest in baseball. He gently called me out sometime during the 1980s and told me that if my kids were to develop an interest in baseball, they would likely be Sox fans, and that I should encourage them by being a Sox fan too. What kind of father would I be to root against the interests of my own sons? Besides, he said, how can you keep rooting for a team that is owned by George Steinbrenner? He made a lot of sense then, and over time my rooting interest in the Sox became more and more intense, as did my dislike of the Yankees. By the time 2003 came around, in my view the Red Sox-Yankees rivalry was good versus evil.

Come 2004, my wife and I feel as though we contributed to the breaking of the so-called "Curse of the Bambino." Game Seven of that year's ALCS was played on October 20, which is Mickey Mantle's birthday. I took my wife out to eat before the game but took a detour after dinner to a nearby town, Sudbury. We stopped in front of a large old house, which I pointed out had been owned by Babe Ruth when he played for the Red Sox. I told her that the two of us were there to persuade Ruth's spirit to renounce the curse. I also suggested that we talk with Mantle's spirit, because I believed that Mantle could convince Ruth that the 2004 Red Sox team was more in line with Mantle's and Ruth's personalities than the dull, drab 2004 Yankees. My wife stared at me in disbelief, and we sat there in silence for a good 15 minutes. We drove home, and as they say, the rest is history.

Those four World Series wins combined were nothing in comparison to watching the Sox win it all in 2004. Emotionally draining, but so satisfying.

JOHN TIERNEY

GABE KAPLER

BY DONNA L. HALPER

No matter where Gabe Kapler played during his 12 years in the major leagues, people who knew him made similar comments. Theo Epstein, general manager of the Boston Red Sox, said Kapler was "a real contributor on and off the field: an ideal teammate, a fan favorite, and the type of player who made the front office proud."[1] First baseman Rafael Palmeiro of the Texas Rangers said, "Kapler plays the game the right way – very hard at all times. And his passion for baseball really comes through."[2] And Milwaukee Brewers GM Doug Melvin said, "He has great work ethic. People love the way he plays the game."[3] While some sportswriters said he never fully lived up to expectations, Kapler still finished his playing career with a respectable .268 batting average, including 82 home runs and 386 runs batted in.

Gabriel Stefan Kapler was born on July 31, 1975, in Hollywood, California. His mother, Judy, was the director of a preschool, and his father, Michael, was a composer and pianist.[4] Growing up in Reseda, California, Kapler fell in love with baseball at an early age. He played T-ball at Reseda Park, and later played Little League ball in nearby Encino. At Taft High School in Woodland Hills, he played shortstop on the baseball team.

But when it came to his studies, things were not going well. Although Kapler enjoyed reading, academic subjects were a struggle. He was finally diagnosed with attention deficit disorder, and gradually learned to focus more, but schoolwork never came easy.[5] In his senior year at Taft, he began working out, as a way to cope with how awkward he felt. Bodybuilding helped him to gain more self-confidence, and he also got praise for doing it.[6]

After graduating from Taft in 1993, Kapler got a scholarship to attend Cal State-Fullerton, a top-tier baseball program. But instead of capitalizing on the opportunity, he spent much of his time partying. His immaturity cost him: after several months, he was asked to leave.[7] He came home and enrolled in Moorpark College, about 25 miles from Reseda. He recommitted himself to baseball, while continuing his bodybuilding regimen and eating a healthier diet. The result were noticeable: the young man who weighed 150 pounds in high school and was not a power hitter became a "sculpted 210-pounder" and a "crush-the-ball talent."[8]

Kapler demonstrated that talent for the Moorpark Raiders. In one of his best games as a freshman, he hit two three-run homers and had seven RBIs. He finished the year batting .352 with 4 home runs, 14 doubles, and 31 RBIs. In the June 1995 amateur draft, he was selected by the Detroit Tigers in the 57th round, and was sent to Jamestown (New York) of the short-season Class-A New York-Pennsylvania League, where he transitioned to playing the outfield. His low draft position concerned him; he hoped he would not be stereotyped as someone with little potential. Scout Dennis Lieberthal, who had recommended that the Tigers sign Kapler, assured him he would get ample opportunity to prove any detractors wrong.[9]

After batting .288 at rookie-level Jamestown, Kapler was moved up to low Class-A Fayetteville (North Carolina) of the Sally League, where he became one of the team's best hitters. He finished his season batting .300 with a league-leading 45 doubles plus 26 home runs and 99 RBIs. He hoped to move up to Double A in 1997, but the Tigers assigned him to Lakeland of the high Class-A Florida State League. At midseason he was batting .288 with 18 doubles and 40 RBIs; he finished with a .295 batting average, 19 homers, and 87 RBIs. In Detroit, the front office was so pleased with Kapler's progress that he was among a small group of Single-A and Double-A prospects invited to spend a six-game homestand with the major-league club in September.[10]

In 1998 Kapler was assigned to the Double-A Jacksonville Suns, and he picked up where he had left off. He was named the Southern League's player of the month for May: he hit .336 and drove in 36 runs in 27 games.[11] At the All-Star break, Kapler was batting .312 and leading the Southern League with 84 RBIs; he was named the MVP of the Southern League All-Star game. And just as Dennis Lieberthal had predicted, Tigers executives were taking notice. Said David Miller, director of minor-league operations, predicting a bright future for Kapler, "He's a sure-fire major leaguer."[12]

In late August, Kapler set a record for RBIs in a Southern League season when he got his 134th. He finished with a .322 batting average, 28 home runs, 47 doubles, and a record-setting 146 RBIs, earning the league's MVP award and being named 1998 Minor League Player of the Year by *USA Today Baseball Weekly*.[13] He also led Jacksonville to the playoffs.

After the Suns were eliminated, Kapler was called up by the Tigers in time for a series with the Minnesota Twins. He made his major-league debut on September 20, 1998, and got his first major-league hit (a single), as well as his first stolen base.

He went 1-for-4 as the Tigers lost 3-0, but it was exciting to be there, even on the last weekend of the season. He expressed his hope that he'd be in the majors in 1999. Larry Parrish, the Tigers' interim manager, could relate: After all, he had skipped Triple A and gone directly to the majors. He said the team would see how Kapler did during spring training and make a decision then.[14]

In January 1999 Kapler married his high-school sweetheart, Lisa Jansen;[15] the couple subsequently had two sons, Chase (born in October 1999) and Dane (born in November 2001). When Kapler reported to spring training, he attracted media attention right away. Few ballplayers were also bodybuilders, and by now Kapler was already on the cover of a fitness magazine.[16] But it wasn't just his physique that sportswriters noticed; it was the intensity with which he played the game. (One sportswriter described Kapler as "mentally tough, and physically buff.")[17] Kapler was determined to show that he was ready for the majors. After 55 spring training at-bats, he was hitting .418 with 4 homers and 15 RBIs. Even Tigers great Al Kaline praised Kapler's determination, saying, "He's going to will himself into being a big star."[18]

When the Tigers announced their 1999 Opening Day roster, Kapler's name was included. Although he was happy, he was realistic: he knew the Tigers had too many outfielders, and he might still end up in the minors. "Whether I stay two weeks or 15 years," he told reporters, "I'll do what I always do – go out and give it my best every day that I'm here."[19] But there weren't many opportunities. In the first three games, he got only six at-bats and one hit. By mid-April, the Tigers sent him to Triple-A Toledo, where he could play every day. Kapler soon began to hit the way he had the year before. After his average rose to .275, with 10 RBIs in 10 games, rumors began spreading that the Tigers planned to trade slumping outfielder Brian Hunter and bring Kapler back.[20] On April 28 the Tigers sent Hunter to Seattle for two prospects. Kapler was back in the big leagues again.

In his first game after being called up, Kapler hit his first major-league homer, with a man on board, in the eighth inning, as the Tigers beat Tampa Bay, 7-5. Later, Kapler was all smiles. "The first one is always going to be precious. I've got the ball in my pocket, and I'll probably send it to my dad tomorrow."[21] Kapler also proved he could hit for power: In mid-June, he hit two home runs (his first multi-homer game) and drove in four runs as the Tigers beat Seattle, 8-7; by the end of June, he was leading all American League rookies with 12 homers. That was the good news. The bad news was that his batting average was .224.[22] Kapler's inconsistency was a problem all season: he would get some hits, then go through a prolonged slump. He finished the year with 18 homers and 49 RBIs, but hit only .245. Some critics wondered if he should have been in Triple A after all.

Evidently, the Tigers organization decided Kapler wasn't a good fit; in early November, he was included in a nine-player trade that brought two-time American League MVP Juan González to Detroit and sent Kapler to the Texas Rangers. He admitted to being shocked and disappointed by the trade.

He hadn't expected that the Tigers would give up on him so soon, but acknowledged, "I was naïve to think I'd be in a Tiger uniform forever."[23]

Kapler showed up at spring training in February 2000 with something to prove. For someone who always played hard, he seemed even more determined to get results. On Opening Day, in a home game against the White Sox, he homered in his first two at-bats and then drove in a run with a single, much to the delight of the fans.[24] But then the entire team went into a slump, including Kapler, whose average dropped to .193 by the end of April. He continued to work with team batting coach Rudy Jaramillo and gradually his hitting improved.

The 2000 season was a disappointing one for the Rangers: after finishing first in the AL West in 1999, they finished last, at 71-91. Kapler, however, was one of the bright spots. He hit .302, with 134 hits and 32 doubles, all personal bests. He had 14 homers and 66 RBIs, and at one point in July and August, he had a 28-game hitting streak; when it ended on August 16, he had set a Rangers record.[25] But his season was interrupted by several stints on the disabled list. In May and June he missed 33 games with a strained hip flexor muscle. He also missed the last week of the season with a painful left shoulder injury. But despite playing in only 116 games, Kapler impressed the Rangers' management. He went home to Southern California to let his shoulder heal, feeling encouraged about his future.

In February 2001 Kapler signed a three-year, $5.6 million contract with the Rangers. But he continued to be injury-prone, missing the first several weeks of the season after tearing a muscle in his left leg during a spring-training game. Once he got back in the lineup, he hit his first career grand slam in a game against Cleveland in late April. After getting some timely hits in May, he found himself in a brutal slump in June. In late July, he was still slumping, and hadn't hit a home run since June 21. Most sportswriters, and Kapler himself, concluded he was having a subpar year; he finished it with a .267 average. Meanwhile, the Rangers had a management shakeup, which included hiring a new GM, John Hart; he was widely expected to make changes, since the team had a losing record once again.

By mid-2002, Kapler's playing time had been greatly reduced. He was hitting .260 with no homers and only 17 RBIs when he was sent to the Colorado Rockies at the July 31 trading deadline. Sportswriters described Kapler's career thus far as "disappointing,"[26] but Rangers manager Jerry Narron wished him well. "Gabe was having a difficult year.... I hope [the trade] revives his career. He's a pleasure to manage."[27] When Kapler got to the Rockies, the change of scenery was beneficial: in his first four weeks, he was batting over .350.[28] He finished the year with a combined .279 batting average, boosted by the .311 he hit during 40 games with Colorado. However, his power numbers were low: only two home runs.

By now a pattern had emerged. Each spring, baseball experts would predict that this year, Kapler would become a dominant player. Then, when it didn't happen, he would end up being traded. The 2003 season was no exception. Kapler hit only .224, with no home runs, in 67 at-bats, and the Rockies optioned him to Triple-A Colorado Springs. When he continued to struggle, the Rockies gave him his unconditional release on June 19. Five days later Kapler signed a minor-league contract with the Boston Red Sox; he understood that once he played himself back into shape, there was an excellent chance he'd be called up.[29]

Kapler's journey back to the big leagues began with Single-A Lowell, Massachusetts, where he got two hits. The next day, he was in Double-A Portland, Maine, where he played the first game of a doubleheader, going 1-for-3 (a double); and demonstrating his versatility in the field, he played first, center, and left.[30] Right after that game, Kapler was on his way to Boston, where he debuted against the Florida Marlins. He went 4-for-5 with two doubles, a triple, and three RBIs. The only downside was that the Red Sox lost the game, 10-9, but Kapler made many new friends. And proving his first game was no fluke, he went 3-for-4 with two home runs and four RBIs the next day – and this time, the Red Sox won, 11-7.

Kapler continued being a streaky hitter: after going an impressive 13-for-29 in his first 10 games, he went into an 0-for-18 slump in late July.[31] But manager Grady Little believed Kapler would turn things around. He did: By the end of August, his average stood at .296. In 68 games with Boston, Kapler finished with a batting average of .291; he hit only four homers, but he had 46 hits, including 11 doubles. He became an important role player, in a season when the Red Sox won the AL wild card, but then lost to the Yankees in the ALCS.

Kapler became a free agent in December, but he wanted to stay with Boston and even agreed to a pay cut, signing a one-year, $750,000 contract for 2004 (he had made $3.4 million the year before).[32] Why did he do it? "I had more fun [playing in Boston] last year than at any other time in my career," he explained. "The Red Sox fans have really been phenomenal. They've really embraced me."[33] They also embraced his unique "look": He not only had a bodybuilder's physique, but he also had multiple tattoos. Kapler, one of baseball's few Jewish ballplayers (along with teammate Kevin Youkilis), was not religious, but he was proud of his heritage: he had a Star of David tattooed on one leg and the phrase "Never Again" (referring to the Holocaust) on the other.[34] But while Jewish fans liked how he played, not everyone was comfortable with his body art, since the Jewish religion has historically opposed getting tattoos.[35]

By 2004, the Red Sox had a new manager, Terry Francona, and, having reached the ALCS the previous year, the players hoped that this year, the team would finally win it all. Kapler had a good spring training: At one point, he was 11-for-32, with 19 total bases; he also made some impressive fielding plays.[36] This was no surprise to Francona, who had been a bench coach with the Rangers when Kapler was there, and was already familiar with his intensity and versatility. The plan was for him to be a role player, filling in whenever an outfielder was injured or needed a day off.

Through early July, the Red Sox struggled, especially on the road, where they were 18-23.[37] They fell eight games behind the first-place Yankees before beginning to turn things around. By late August the Red Sox were within 4½ games of New York and continuing to win. And Kapler, who was hitting only .234 in early May, had boosted his average to .275, with 5 homers and 25 RBIs. Playing regularly helped: Because injuries sidelined right fielder Trot Nixon for much of the season, Kapler was in the lineup more. By season's end, he had appeared in 136 games, a record for him. And when he wasn't playing, he became known for his charitable work. He and his wife, who had been a victim of dating violence in a previous relationship, started a foundation that raised money for domestic abuse prevention programs.

Thanks to a strong second half, the Red Sox finished second to the Yankees and won the wild card. They swept the Anaheim Angels in the Division Series, setting up a rematch against the Yankees in the ALCS. Kapler did not play much in either series. He started Game One against the Angels and got a hit, but he did not start in Game Two, coming in as a pinch-runner and defensive replacement, and he was not in Game Three at all. Against the Yankees, he also saw limited playing time: He didn't play in the first four games, was a pinch-runner and defensive replacement in Game Five, a pinch-hitter and defensive replacement in Game Six, and didn't play in Game Seven. On the other hand, he participated in one of the most amazing comeback stories in playoff history, as the Red Sox, on the verge of elimination, won four games in a row, defeating the Yankees four games to three to go on to the World Series against the St. Louis Cardinals.

In the World Series, Kapler was once again a role player. He either pinch-hit or was a defensive replacement in the first three games. In Game Four he was a pinch-runner and late-inning defensive replacement; that meant he was on the field when the Red Sox recorded the final out, sweeping the Cardinals and winning the World Series for the first time in 86 years. As the players ran toward the mound to celebrate, Kapler (who wore number 19) was briefly standing next to Johnny Damon (number 18)[38] – of course, 1918 was the last time the Red Sox had won it all – until 2004.

After the season's triumphant conclusion, Kapler was one of Boston's 16 free agents. He decided to play in Japan, signing a $2 million contract with the Yomiuri Giants, who promised him the chance to play every day. Things in Japan did not go as Kapler hoped. He had difficulty adjusting, and in early July 2005, the Giants placed him on waivers. He was hitting .153 at the time, and no other Japanese teams claimed him. But the Red Sox were eager to have Kapler back, given how popular he was with the fans and in the clubhouse; by mid-July, the details were worked out. Kapler rejoined the Red Sox in early August. But he was only in 36 games before he suffered a ruptured Achilles tendon in a game against Toronto on September 14.

Kapler had surgery, spent months in physical therapy, and finally began rehabbing in early June 2006 at Double-A Portland. Sea Dogs fans, who recalled his brief appearance there in 2003, were eager to see him. After three consecutive rainouts, he finally got into the lineup, as the DH. He went hitless in three at-bats, but the next day, in a doubleheader against the Erie Seawolves, he went 2-for-4 and hit two doubles in the first game, and 2-for-3 with a triple and a double in the second game. (He also stayed late to sign autographs for fans who had waited.)[39] Then it was on to Triple-A Pawtucket; after getting three hits in the four games he played, he was back in Boston. He hit a double and a single in four at-bats, and he received a hero's welcome from the fans.[40]

Kapler hit .254 in 72 games. The Red Sox declined to offer him salary arbitration. He decided to retire at age 31 and accepted a position managing Boston's Single-A team, the Greenville (South Carolina) Drive. It was an opportunity to assist in the development of young players, and he was excited to begin.[41] Fans were excited, too: At the event to introduce him to season-ticket holders, he ended up signing autographs for over two hours.[42]

Kapler's Opening Day lineup included a familiar face: Red Sox starter Jon Lester, there on a rehab assignment after recovering from cancer. But the majority of the players had limited pro experience, including prospects Jason Place, an outfielder who was the Red Sox' 2006 first-round draft pick (and a Greenville high-school star); and pitcher Josh Papelbon, younger brother of Red Sox reliever Jonathan Papelbon. Kapler's first year had its ups and downs, as the Drive had a losing record, going 58-81. But some of the young players showed promise, and he enjoyed mentoring and motivating the team. Attendance was up, the players liked him, and while he made some mistakes, he said he learned a lot.[43]

Evidently, one thing Kapler learned was that he missed playing. He told reporters that managing had reawakened his competitive spirit; he felt physically healthy, and he believed he could still contribute to a major-league team.[44] In December, he signed a one-year contract with the Milwaukee Brewers, reuniting him with former Texas Rangers GM Doug Melvin. It turned out to be a good move. Filling in for Mike Cameron, who had been suspended for 25 games, Kapler hit .293 in April, with 4 homers and 13 RBIs. Even when he returned to being a role player, he continued getting timely hits and making key defensive plays. Then, in early September, he sustained a shoulder injury. At the time, he was batting .301 with 8 homers, 17 doubles, and 38 RBIs in 96 games. But he was unable to return for the remainder of the season.

Once again a free agent, Kapler signed with the Tampa Bay Rays, who liked his versatility, as well as his past success against left-handed pitching. Manager Joe Maddon used him in 99 games; he played all three outfield positions. Overall, he ended up hitting only .239, but that didn't tell the whole story. He had 8 home runs and 30 RBIs against lefties, and a .379 on-base percentage.[45] In late October the Rays re-signed him for the 2010 season.

But Kapler was unable to contribute much. He was hitting only .217 when he injured his hip in early June. He came back in July, but in mid-August, he was back on the DL with a sprained right ankle. He had not even been doing well against lefty pitching: His average was just .206. As a result, the Rays, who had numerous other outfielders available, were in no hurry to bring Kapler back, even when his ankle felt better.[46] He did not play again in 2010, and finished at .210 in just 59 games.

Kapler still believed he could play and tried to latch on with another team. He was invited to the Los Angeles Dodgers training camp, but while he got some hits and played hard, the Dodgers did not sign him. So he retired, after 12 years in the majors. He was a special-assignment scout for Tampa Bay for several years, and in June 2012, he joined two other Jewish former major leaguers, Shawn Green and Brad Ausmus, who were working with Team Israel in the qualifying round of the World Baseball Classic. Ausmus managed the team, and Kapler and Green agreed to be player-coaches. Kapler sustained a groin injury and couldn't play, but he was still able to coach. Team Israel won two games, but then lost and was eliminated.

In 2013 Kapler and his wife divorced. Kapler joined Fox Sports 1 as a baseball analyst, and then, in late 2014, he was hired by the Dodgers as director of player development. In late October 2017, he got the opportunity to manage again, this time at the major-league level, when the Philadelphia Phillies hired him. Major factors in the decision, according to GM Matt Klentak, were Kapler's "track record of leadership … progressive thinking, and working with young players." (By progressive thinking, Klentak was referring to Kapler's "fondness for analytics and sports science.")[47]

At first, many players responded favorably to Kapler's positive attitude, but as the 2018 season went on, some Phillies fans believed he was overly optimistic, especially when the team collapsed in the last 49 games, going 16-33 and ending up with a losing record, 80-82. Some also believed he relied too heavily on analytics, and wasn't responsive to how his players felt, which he later acknowledged was probably true.[48] He made some adjustments in 2019; in addition, the team acquired slugger Bryce Harper. But nothing worked. Kapler never won over the fans, and after the Phillies finished 81-81, he was fired. Looking back on the experience, he was philosophical about what happened. "I loved the city," he said, "But in the end, the fans were passionate about winning, and we didn't win enough games."[49]

He wasn't unemployed for long. San Francisco Giants President of Baseball Operations Farhan Zaidi hired him to take over for the retiring Bruce Bochy. Some fans were skeptical, given Kapler's record with the Phillies, but he proved that he could do the job. The 2020 season was shortened by the COVID-19 pandemic, and the Giants went 29-31, in a rebuilding year. One other noteworthy thing occurred in 2020: Kapler hired a female coach, Alyssa Nakken, who had previously worked in the Giants' front office.[50] This was no token hire, Kapler said. "She knows the game, [and] she knows what she is doing." He spoke about the importance of "representation"—that little girls will see her and possibly envision a role in major league baseball. "Alyssa is capable of doing anything she wants. I expect her to be a manager one day."[51] Meanwhile, Kapler and the players were getting along well, morale was high, and the fans couldn't wait for 2021.

It turned out to be a memorable season. Kapler guided the Giants to a league-leading 107 wins, the most in the franchise's history, resulting in a trip to the playoffs, after four consecutive years with losing records. The Giants lost to the Dodgers in the Division Series, but Kapler was proud of what his team achieved. And he noted that while he still utilized analytics, he had learned to listen more and micromanage less. "I've really started to respect, understand, and appreciate the feedback I'm getting from players," he said.[52] And the Baseball Writers Association recognized Kapler's leadership, naming him 2021 National League Manager of the Year.

If the Giants overachieved in 2021, they underachieved in 2022, going 81-81, but few sportswriters blamed Kapler; they respected his passion for baseball and acknowledged that his unconventional approach usually got good results.[53] He also established a reputation for speaking his mind, whether about baseball or current events. He credited his parents, especially his father, for teaching him to advocate for social justice. When his dad died in 2020, Kapler used his blog to publish a moving tribute to his influence,[54] and also got a new hand tattoo to honor him.

In 2023, the Giants continued to underachieve; they ultimately finished fourth, and failed to make the playoffs for the second year in a row. With only three games left in the season, Giants management unexpectedly fired Kapler. He ended his time in San Francisco with a record of 295-248. On social media, he thanked the fans, and told them he was "Looking forward to the next adventure." That next adventure turned out to be a job as Assistant General Manager with the Miami Marlins, focusing on player development.[55]

Through it all, Kapler has remained a proud nonconformist, aware that not everyone likes his politics (or his tattoos), but he believes in the importance of being true to himself. As he once told an ESPN reporter, "My message is, don't tone yourself down to make someone else comfortable."[56]

ACKNOWLEDGMENTS

The author would like to thank sports radio broadcaster and baseball historian Marty Lurie for helping to arrange the interview with Gabe Kapler.

SOURCES

Rob Neyer hosted a SABR podcast in 2020 during which Gabe Kapler discussed his views on social justice: https://sabr.org/sabrcast/episode/62.

The author consulted various newspaper databases, including Newspapers.com, NewspaperArchive.com, and GenealogyBank.com, as well as Baseball-Reference.com.

NOTES

1. Bob Hohler, "Kapler Says Sayonara and Heads Off to Japan," *Boston Globe*, November 23, 2004: F5.
2. Randy Galloway, "Rangers Will Be Fine Without Gonzalez," *Pittsburgh Post-Gazette*, March 18, 2000: D-8.
3. Vic Feuerherd, "Change of Plans: Kapler Back at It," *State Journal* (Madison, Wisconsin), March 20, 2008: F8.
4. Mark Herrmann, "Power to Surprise – Rangers' Kapler Not What You Would Expect," *Newsday* (Long Island, New York), April 12, 2000: A87.
5. Lynn Henning, "Kapler's Background Colorful, Exhaustive," *Detroit Free Press*, March 21, 1999: 1C, 10C.
6. T.R. Sullivan, "Gung-Ho Gabe Grows Up," *Fort Worth Star-Telegram*, March 5, 2000: 1C, 10C.
7. Alex Zola, "Detroit Outfielder Is Hailed as Next Hank Greenberg: Meet Gabriel Kapler, Jewish Tiger Who Shook Party-Boy Habits to Make It to the Majors," *The Forward* (New York), April 16, 1999: 26.
8. Rod Beaton, "Player of Year: Tigers' Kapler, Top Prospect, Was Drafted in 57th Round," *USA Today*, September 24, 1998: 3C.
9. John Klima, "Kapler Is Proving Low Draft Was Wrong," *Simi Valley* (California) *Star*, July 31, 1996: B4.
10. Steve Henson, "Fick's Stripes Astonish and Impress Tiger Brass," *Los Angeles Times*, September 7, 1997: C17.
11. "Gillespie Won't Play in All-Star Game," *Los Angeles Times*, June 13, 1998: C21.
12. Dave Desmond, "Minor League Baseball," *Los Angeles Times*, June 21, 1998: C18.
13. Gene Guidi, "Kapler Named Minors' Top Player," *Detroit Free Press*, September 10, 1998: 6D.
14. Gene Guidi, "Kapler's Debut in Rightfield: Single and Steal in Four At-Bats," *Detroit Free Press*, September 21, 1998: 3D.
15. Rod Beaton, "Player of Year: Tigers' Kapler, Top Prospect, Was Drafted in 57th Round," *USA Today*, September 24, 1998: 3C.
16. Eric Sondheimer, "Kapler's Career Has Received a Big Lift," *Los Angeles Times,* September 2, 1998: C9, C10.
17. John Lowe, "Babe in the City," *Detroit Free Press*, March 31, 1999: 1C.
18. Lowe.
19. Gene Guidi, "Tigers Fulfill Kapler's Prophecy," *Detroit Free Press*, April 2, 1999: 3C.
20. Gene Guidi, "Hunter Benching Fuels Trade Talks," *Detroit Free Press*, April 26, 1999: 5D.
21. "Weaver Finds Comfort Zone," *Ventura County Star*, May 1, 1999: C5.
22. John Klima, "Kapler Displays Power," *Ventura County Star* (Camarillo, California), June 29, 1999: C5.
23. "After Trade, Kapler Shakes Off Shock," *Port Huron* (Michigan) *Times Herald*, November 3, 1999: 6B.
24. T.R. Sullivan, "Eye Opener,*" Fort Worth Star-Telegram*, April 4, 2000: D1.
25. T.R. Sullivan, "Short Hops," *Fort Worth Star-Telegram*, August 17, 2000: 4D.
26. "Rangers Deal, but Rogers Remains," *Austin American-Statesman*, August 1, 2002: C1.

27 Alan Robinson, "Rangers Acquire Hollandsworth After Trading Kapler to Rockies," *Tyler* (Texas) *Morning Telegraph*, August 1, 2002: Section 4, 1.

28 "Rockies to Watch," *San Francisco Chronicle*, September 3, 2002: C7.

29 Bob Hohler, "Next Stop for Kapler," *Boston Globe,* June 25, 2003: F3.

30 Kevin Thomas, "Sea Dogs Notebook," *Portland* (Maine) *Press Herald*, June 29, 2003: 5D.

31 "Night of Pedro, Kim, and a Loss," *Portland Press Herald*, July 26, 2003: 5D, 8D.

32 "Red Sox Stand By Position," *Daily Hampshire Gazette* (Northampton, Massachusetts), December 23, 2003: D3.

33 Kevin Thomas, "Sox Fans' Support: Priceless," *Portland Press Herald*, February 9, 2004: C1.

34 Douglas Belkin, "Jews With Tattoos," *Boston Globe*, August 15, 2004: M7.

35 A thorough explanation of why Judaism has historically opposed tattooing can be found in "The Tattoo Taboo in Judaism." https://www.myjewishlearning.com/article/the-tattoo-taboo-in-judaism/.

36 Howard Ullman (Associated Press), "Kapler Set to Step In for Nixon," *North Adams* (Massachusetts) *Transcript*, March 20, 2004: B4.

37 Charles Odum (Associated Press), "Nine-Run Rally Lowe Point of Terrible Trip," *Quincy* (Massachusetts) *Patriot Ledger*, July 5, 2004: 19.

38 Ben Walker (Associated Press), "Red Sox Say Goodbye to Ghosts and Curses," *Lynn* (Massachusetts) *Daily Item*, October 29, 2004: C1.

39 Kevin Thomas, "Quite the Finish," *Portland Press Herald*, June 12, 2006: C1, C7.

40 Mike Fine, "Kapler Has 2 Hits in First Game Since Sept. 7," *Quincy Patriot Ledger*, June 20, 2006: 24.

41 Nick Cafardo, "New Manager Kapler Has an Extensive To-Do List," *Boston Globe*, January 28, 2007: C10.

42 Willie T. Smith III, "Fans Get to Know Kapler," *Greenville* (South Carolina) *News*, February 4, 2007: 5C.

43 Willie T. Smith III, "Drive End Record Year with Victory," *Greenville News*, September 4, 2007: 2C.

44 "Former Sox OF Kapler Looking to Resume His Playing Career," *Biddeford* (Maine) *Journal Tribune*, September 21, 2007: B3.

45 Tony Fabrizio, "Rays Re-Sign Kapler," *Tampa Tribune*, October 28, 2009: S4.

46 Tony Fabrizio, "Team Won't Rush Kapler's Return," *Tampa Tribune*, September 4, 2010: S4.

47 Rob Maadi (Associated Press), "Phillies Hire Gabe Kapler as Manager," *Cincinnati Enquirer*, October 31, 2017: 4C.

48 Scott Lauber, "Kapler Begins New Job Defending Himself," *Philadelphia Daily News*, November 14, 2019: A41.

49 Gabe Kapler, telephone call with the author, August 4, 2023.

50 Nakken, a former college softball player, was hired as an assistant coach, working with the players on baserunning and outfield defense. On April 12, 2022, she made history when she was called into the Giants-Padres game to coach first base, making her the first woman to coach on the field in a regular season major-league game.

51 Gabe Kapler, telephone call with the author, August 4, 2023.

52 Noah Trister (Associated Press), "Cash, Kapler Win Manager of the Year Awards," *Merced* (California) *Sun-Star*, November 18, 2021: 1B.

53 Chris Biderman, "Her Moment, Her Job," *Sacramento Bee*, April 20, 2022: 3A.

54 Gabe Kapler, "Saying Goodbye," *Kaplifestyle*, December 31, 2020: https://kaplifestyle.com/2020/12/31/saying-goodbye/.

55 Steve Adams, "Marlins to Hire Gabe Kapler as Assistant General Manager," *MLB Trade Rumors*, December 1, 2023, https://www.mlbtraderumors.com/2023/12/marlins-hire-gabe-kapler-assistant-general-manager.html

56 Tim Keown, "Being Gabe Kapler: Inside the Mind of the San Francisco Giants' Nonconformist Manager," ESPN.com, May 13, 2022: https://www.espn.com/mlb/story/_/id/33904139/mind-san-francisco-giants-nonconformist-manager.

BYUNG-HYUN KIM

BY ROBERT P. NASH

Byung-Hyun Kim, or BK, as he was known to his teammates, was one of the first and most successful major-league players from South Korea. Although he is most remembered for devastating back-to-back blown saves in Game Four and Game Five of the 2001 World Series, those failures obscure the fact that for several years he was one of the top closers in the major leagues. With a quirky submarine-style delivery, he threw pitches with unexpected velocity and movement that at times made him almost unhittable, especially by right-handed batters. His finest years were as a closer, but he never embraced that role, strongly preferring to be a starter. When he finally did become a starting pitcher in the later years of his career, he was unable to perform at the same high level. In addition to overcoming the challenge of language barriers and cultural differences, he was hampered by various injuries over the course of his career.

Born in Gwangju,[1] South Korea, on January 19, 1979, Kim was a 1997 graduate of Gwangju Jeil High School, a school noted for producing baseball talent.[2] His prodigious pitching ability was evident at an early age. After being chosen for the Junior National Team in 1996, he was a member of the South Korean National Team in 1997 and 1998.[3] He shined in various international competitions, including a dominating June 1998 performance against Team USA in Tucson, Arizona, in which he struck out 15 batters.[4] After graduating from high school, he attended Sungkyunkwan University in Seoul, but his higher education was cut short when the Arizona Diamondbacks signed him as an amateur free agent in February 1999.

After arriving in the United States in late March, Kim was sent to the El Paso Diablos, Arizona's Double-A affiliate in the Texas League. Working out of the bullpen, he made 10 appearances, picking up two wins with a 2.11 ERA and 32 strikeouts in 21⅓ innings before being promoted in mid-May to Triple-A Tucson. He started only three games for the Sidewinders when he was called up to the Diamondbacks on May 28. On arriving in New York for a series against the Mets, Kim revealed that his dream was to strike out Mark McGwire, Mike Piazza, Sammy Sosa, and Mo Vaughn.[5] He didn't wait long to cross one of those names off his list. On the very next day he made his major-league debut. At 20 years old, he became the youngest player in the major leagues, and only the third Korean-born player after Chan Ho Park (1994) and Jin Ho Cho (1998).

With the Diamondbacks holding a slim 8-7 lead, Kim was sent out in the bottom of the ninth inning to close out the game. Mets manager Bobby Valentine tried unsuccessfully to rattle the young rookie by questioning the size of his glove.[6] Kim retired the Mets' Edgardo Alfonzo, John Olerud, and Mike Piazza in order, to record his first major-league save. In striking out Piazza to end the game, the Diamondbacks catcher, Damian Miller, reported that Kim had thrown "a couple of Nintendo sliders … the ones you see in the video games with the huge bend on them."[7]

While Kim did not have any more saves during the season, he became a bullpen regular, appearing in 25 games, primarily as a set-up man. His rookie season was shortened by an injury in late July that landed him on the disabled list, followed by a rehab stint in Tucson. After missing nearly two months, he returned to the Diamondbacks in late September, making three relief appearances to end the season, including picking up his first major-league win on October 2. In only their second season of existence, the surprising Diamondbacks won the NL West with a 100-62 record. Kim, however, was not included on the postseason roster, as Arizona lost in the NLDS to the New York Mets.

When injury-plagued Diamondbacks closer Matt Mantei began the 2000 season with two stints on the disabled list, Kim took over as the primary closer. Over the first half of the season, he was impressive in that role, making 34 appearances, and converting 14 of 16 save opportunities with a 1.94 ERA. After recording his last save of the season on July 5, however, he slumped badly, blowing three straight save opportunities. At the end of July, he was sent down to Tucson to work on his pitching issues. He was only there long enough to make two starts before being recalled, but by then a healthy Mantei had reclaimed the closer role. For the remainder of the season, Kim was used mainly as a set-up man, and was unable to recapture his earlier success. In his final 27 appearances of the season, he gave up 26 earned runs in only 29 innings of work (an 8.07 ERA). After winning the NL West in 1999, the Diamondbacks fell back to third, with an 85-77 record, 12 games behind the San Francisco Giants.

After only eight appearances in April 2001, Mantei went down at the end of the month with a season-ending elbow injury that ultimately required Tommy John surgery. Kim was again inserted into the team's closer role. He appeared in a career-high 78 games with a 2.94 ERA, saving a team-leading 19 games as the Diamondbacks won the NL West. His 98 innings pitched were one of the heaviest workloads among relievers.

Kim initially continued his regular-season dominance in the postseason as the Diamondbacks defeated the St. Louis Cardinals in the NLDS and the Atlanta Braves in the NLCS to win their first National League pennant. Over the two series, Kim appeared in four games pitching 6⅓ scoreless innings, allowing only one hit, and collecting three saves, including a two-inning save in the pennant-clinching game, a tight 3-2 victory over the Atlanta Braves.

Kim's luck ran out in the World Series against the New York Yankees. He did not appear until Game Four in Yankee Stadium with the Diamondbacks holding a 2-1 Series lead. On Halloween night he was sent to the mound in the bottom of the eighth inning with the Yankees losing 3-1. Kim, who had not pitched in 10 days, struck out the side and remained in the game for the ninth inning to face the top of the Yankees order. Derek Jeter grounded out and Paul O'Neill singled, before Bernie Williams struck out swinging. With two outs, Tino Martinez then hit a two-run home run to tie the game. Kim put on two more men with a walk and a single before getting the final out of the inning with a strikeout. Surprisingly, Kim was left in the game to pitch the 10th inning. After retiring the first two batters, he surrendered the game-winning home run to Jeter.[8]

Despite Kim's throwing a season-high 61 pitches in Game Four, Arizona manager Bob Brenly inexplicably went to him again on the very next night with the Diamondbacks leading 2-0 in the ninth inning. After a leadoff double by Jorge Posada, Kim got two outs before giving up yet another gruesome game-tying two-run home run, this time to Scott Brosius. Kim was mercifully replaced by Mike Morgan, who got the final out of the inning, but the Yankees went on to win 3-2 in the 12th inning to take a 3 games to 2 lead.[9] After Kim's two monumental blown saves, it was noticed that only once before in the entire history of the World Series had a team come from behind with two outs in the bottom of the ninth inning to tie the game with a two-run home run.[10]

Kim did not pitch again in the Series, but fortunately for him and his teammates, the Diamondbacks came back to win the final two games, dethroning the three-time defending champion Yankees in seven games. In only their fourth year of existence, the Diamondbacks became the youngest franchise to win the World Series, and Kim became the first Asian-born player on a World Series-winning team.

Despite his nightmare 2001 World Series performance, Kim returned as the Diamondbacks' closer in 2002. With Matt Mantei recovering from Tommy John surgery, for the first time Kim was the team's closer for the entire season. He responded with the best year of his career. Early in the season his manager, Bob Brenly, wryly commented, "If he has any lingering effects from what happened last year, he's hiding them well."[11]

On May 11, Kim joined an exclusive pitching fraternity. In the bottom of the eighth inning, with the Diamondbacks clinging to a 5-4 lead over the Philadelphia Phillies, he threw an "immaculate inning," striking out Scott Rolen, Mike Lieberthal, and Pat Burrell in succession on nine straight pitches.

In the following month, he gained a measure of redemption when the Diamondbacks traveled to New York for an interleague series with the Yankees. On June 12, in his first mound appearance in Yankee Stadium since his disastrous 2001 World Series performance, he entered the game with a 7-5 lead in the bottom of the eighth inning. He struck out the side and got out of a ninth-inning jam for his 17th save of the season. Afterward he joyously hurled the game ball from the pitcher's mound over the left-field wall. Teammate Mark Grace joked, "I think that was his best fastball of the year."[12]

In July Kim was selected as an All-Star, becoming only the second Korean-born player to make an All-Star team.[13] He had a role in the most controversial All-Star Game in its history. Kim entered in the top of the seventh inning with two outs, a man on base, and the National League holding a 5-3 lead. He promptly gave up three straight hits before getting the final out, giving the American League a 6-5 lead. The game lasted until the 11th inning, ending in an infamous 7-7 tie.[14] Kim, however, immediately bounced back from his weak All-Star Game performance to get saves on three straight days, earning him recognition as NL Player of the Week.

Kim ended the regular season with a team-low 2.04 ERA in 72 games. His 36 saves set a new Arizona season record, breaking Gregg Olson's record of 30 set during the Diamondbacks' first season, 1998.[15] The Diamondbacks won the NL West for the third time in four seasons but were swept by the St. Louis Cardinals in the NLDS. Kim's only appearance was in the deciding third game, when he was brought on in the eighth inning to keep the score close with the Diamondbacks behind 4-3. Instead, he gave up two runs on two hits and three walks as the St. Louis Cardinals eliminated the Diamondbacks, 6-3.

Although Kim had proved himself as an elite closer, he regularly made it clear that he preferred to be a starting pitcher. Manager Brenly went so far as to say that Kim "despised" being a closer.[16] With a healthy Mantei returning from Tommy John surgery, Kim finally got his chance to join the starting rotation for the 2003 season. Brenly commented, "If he has done as well as he has the last few years in a role that he did not like, I'm anxious to see what he is going to do in a role that he wants."[17] Kim made six starts in April before going on the disabled list at the end of the month with an ankle injury. After three rehab appearances in Tucson, he returned to the Diamondbacks, making a quality start in a no-decision on May 27.

Despite a 1-5 record over his seven starts, Kim had pitched well, with a 3.56 ERA. Two days after his last start for the Diamondbacks, the Boston Red Sox, needing to bolster their pitching staff, traded their All-Star third baseman, Shea Hillenbrand, for Kim. Interestingly, with his acquisition the Red Sox had fielded four of the first five Koreans to play in the major leagues.[18] Five of Kim's first seven appearances for the Red Sox were as a starter (2-1, 3.10 ERA). When the team's closer-by-committee approach wasn't working out, however, he was pressed into service as the closer at the beginning of July.[19] He performed impressively in that role, converting 16 of 19 save opportunities with a 2.28 ERA over the final three months of the season.

In 12 September appearances, Kim did not give up a single earned run. He recorded three wins and five saves in those games as Boston edged out the Seattle Mariners by two games for the league's wild-card playoff spot. On September 22 he picked up his 16th and final save of the season, which surprisingly would turn out to be the last save of his major-league career.

Kim's only appearance in the postseason came in Game One of the ALDS in Oakland against the Athletics. He entered the game in the bottom of the ninth inning with the Red Sox nursing a 4-3 lead. In the process of getting two outs, he also put two men on base with a walk and hit batter. Manager Grady Little then pulled his closer for Alan Embree, who gave up a game-tying single in a game that Boston ultimately lost in the 12th inning.

When the Red Sox returned home for Game Three down two games to none, Kim was ungraciously booed during pregame introductions. The young pitcher who had played such a vital role in the Red Sox getting to the postseason responded with a slight smile on his face and a raised middle finger. An official apology for his ill-advised gesture was issued afterward on his behalf by the Red Sox. Years later he candidly explained, "In the heat of the moment, I was just being honest with my emotions. When the fans booed me, I felt really misunderstood, and all of that frustration came out."[20] With his status questionable due to reported stiffness in his right arm, Kim did not pitch again in the divisional playoff as Boston swept the next three games to defeat Oakland. He was also left off the roster for Boston's heart-breaking ALCS loss to the Yankees, in which they certainly could have used a healthy Kim in their bullpen.

During the offseason, the Red Sox signaled that Kim would not be returning as the team's closer in 2004 by signing free agent All-Star closer Keith Foulke. Foulke was coming off a 2003 season in which he led the American League with 43 saves for the Oakland Athletics. At the same time, Boston's management demonstrated their desire to retain Kim's services by signing him to a two-year, $10 million contract.

Under new manager Terry Francona, Kim was projected to be the team's fifth starter, joining Derek Lowe, Pedro Martínez, Tim Wakefield, and the newly acquired Curt Schilling. Kim began the season on the disabled list with a right shoulder strain. After a rehab start in Sarasota and two more in Pawtucket, he finally made his Fenway Park debut on April 29 in the first game of a doubleheader against the Tampa Bay Devil Rays. In his first appearance on the mound since his obscene gesture to jeering fans during the 2003 divisional playoffs, he pitched five scoreless innings, allowing only one hit to pick up the victory. He was cheered by the large hometown crowd, leading him to joke afterward, "Maybe the fans who don't like me didn't show up."[21]

Sadly, that was the high point of Kim's 2004 season. Poor outings in his next two starts put him back in Pawtucket on May 11. He made only a couple of starts there before landing on the disabled list again with back issues and lingering shoulder problems. At the end of May, he traveled to South Korea for medical treatment, and did not return until late June. Most of the remaining season was spent in Pawtucket, but he never recovered his effectiveness, going 2-6 for the PawSox with a 5.34 ERA in 22 games, including 19 starts. Bronson Arroyo was the beneficiary of Kim's lost season, filling in capably as the team's fifth starter.

Kim was finally recalled by Boston in late September, making four appearances out of the bullpen and retiring the final 10 batters he faced. He appeared in only seven games (three starts) in his two brief stints with Boston, going 2-1 with a 6.23 ERA. It was the worst ERA of his major-league career. He was ineligible for the postseason as the wild-card Red Sox staged a dramatic playoff run that culminated in their first World Series title since 1918.

Given Kim's 2004 struggles, it was no great surprise when just before the opening of the 2005 season, he was traded to the Colorado Rockies for veteran catcher Charles Johnson, minor-league pitcher Chris Narveson, and cash. Neither acquisition ever played a game for the Red Sox.[22] Rockies general manager Dan O'Dowd acknowledged the gamble they were taking on Kim, saying he "is someone we want to take a flier on. You never get a guy like this when he is going good. But he's not that far removed from being an All-Star and a dominant young closer."[23]

Other than a couple of spot starts, for the first two months of the season Kim worked out of the Rockies bullpen. In early June, however, due to injuries and trades, he landed a spot in the starting rotation for the rest of the season. Although he was only 5-9 as a starter, his 4.37 ERA as a starter was among the best on a team that finished last in the NL West with a 67-95 record.

On August 5, the Rockies acquired Sun-Woo Kim (no relation) off waivers from the Washington Nationals. He became the only Korean teammate Kim had during his major-league career. "Sunny" Kim made his first appearance for Colorado on August 8 in the first game of a doubleheader, and "BK" Kim pitched the second game. It was the first time that pitchers with the same last name had started both ends of a doubleheader since June 22, 1974, when brothers Jim Perry and Gaylord Perry accomplished the feat for the Cleveland Indians.[24]

After re-signing as a free agent with Colorado for the 2006 season, Kim was a member of the South Korean team that finished third in the inaugural World Baseball Classic played in March. Belatedly joining the Rockies for spring training, he strained the hamstring in his right leg and started the season on the disabled list. After three rehab starts with the Colorado Springs Sky Sox, the Rockies Triple-A affiliate, he made his season debut with the Rockies on April 30. He went 6⅔ innings, giving up only one run to pick up the victory. For the first and only time in his major-league career, Kim spent the entire season in the starting rotation. His 27 games started, 155 innings pitched, and 129 strikeouts were all career highs.

On May 22, in his fifth start of the season, Kim pitched against fellow South Korean and former high-school teammate Jae Weong Seo of the Los Angeles Dodgers. It was the first time in major-league history that two Korean-born pitchers had faced off against each other as starters.[25] Although Kim gave up only one earned run in six innings, he was charged with the loss in the Dodgers' 6-1 victory.

In his next start, on May 28, against the San Francisco Giants, Kim earned an unwelcome place in the record books. In the bottom of the fourth inning, he delivered the pitch that Barry Bonds hit for his 715th home run, moving him ahead of Babe Ruth on the all-time list, second only to Henry Aaron.[26] Kim got the last laugh, however, picking up the win in a 6-3 Rockies victory.

Kim ended the season with an 8-12 record and a 5.57 ERA as the Rockies finished in a tie for last place in the NL West with a 76-86 record.

After two appearances in relief and one start to begin the 2007 season, Kim went on the disabled list with a bruised thumb. He made five rehab starts with Colorado Springs, but on May 13, a day after his last start for the Sky Sox, he was traded to the Florida Marlins for right-handed reliever Jorge Julio. Five days later he was plugged into the Marlins' starting rotation. Over the next 2½ months, he made 13 starts before being released at the beginning of August. The Arizona Diamondbacks claimed him off waivers, but after two bad outings he was released again. Several days later he rejoined the Marlins, where he finished out the season. As it turned out, all three of Kim's former teams made it to the 2007 postseason. Colorado defeated Arizona in the NLCS before losing to Boston in the World Series.

On September 28 at Shea Stadium, the site of his 1999 debut, Kim got the start in what turned out to be the last game of his major-league career. He picked up the victory for his 10th win of the season (a career high), finishing with a respectable combined record of 10-8, but a not-so-respectable 6.08 ERA. In a nine-year career with four teams, Kim compiled a 54-60 record with 86 saves in 394 games (87 games started) and a 4.42 ERA.

Still only 28 years old after the 2007 season, Kim attempted to extend his major-league career by agreeing to minor-league contracts with the Pittsburgh Pirates in 2008 and the San Francisco Giants in 2010. He was unable to make it out of spring training for either club. After a 2010 season with the Orange County (Fullerton, California) Flyers of the independent Golden Baseball League, he played for the Tohoku Rakuten Golden Eagles in the Japan Eastern League in 2011. For the next four years he played for the Korean Baseball Organization's Nexen (Seoul) Heroes (2012-2013) and his hometown Kia (Gwangju) Tigers (2014-2015). It was clear, however, that he was not the pitcher he had once been.

At age 39 Kim staged one last comeback, with the Melbourne Aces of the Australian Baseball League. Although he appeared in only nine games during their brief 2018-2019 season, he struck out nine batters in 9⅔ innings with a 0.93 ERA. That performance allowed him to retire on a high note, with him saying, "I was happy with myself in that moment, and that's when I decided to walk away."[27] In reflecting on all the highs and lows of his career, he commented, "I'm fine with how it happened. Now, it's all a good memory."[28]

In his post-baseball retirement, Kim became an owner of multiple restaurants, including one in San Diego, California, as well as being active as a television personality in his native South Korea.

SOURCES

Unless otherwise indicated, statistics and team records were derived from baseball-reference.com and retrosheet.org.

NOTES

1. Also transliterated as "Kwangju." "Birthplace of Byung-Hyun Kim Identified," SABR Biographical Research Committee Monthly Report, November/December 1999: 1, http://sabr.org/research/biographical-research-committee-newsletters.

2. Andrew Keh, "Where School Spirit Is Metaphysical," *New York Times*, October 3, 2015: D2. Two of Kim's high-school teammates, Jae Weong Seo and Hee-seop Choi, also made it to the major leagues.

3. *2004 Boston Red Sox Media Guide*, 154.

4. Phil Villarreal, "Korean pitcher Fans 15 in Rout of Team USA," *Arizona Daily Star* (Tucson), July 1, 1998: D6.

5. "Young Gun … Byung Gun," *Sports Illustrated*, June 7, 1999: 31. Kim would eventually strike out Piazza, Sosa, and Vaughn on multiple occasions. McGwire faced Kim only twice in his career during the regular season, drawing two bases on balls, one of them intentional.

6. Jason Diamos, "Mets Fall 2 Runs and a Few Tricks Short," *New York Times*, May 30, 1999: 8-2.

7. "Young Gun … Byung Gun."

8. Stew Thornley, "October 31, 2001: Jeter becomes Mr. November," SABR Baseball Games Project, https://sabr.org/gamesproj/game/october-31-2001-jeter-becomes-mr-november/.

9. Stew Thornley, "November 1, 2001: Scott Brosius deja vu in the Bronx," SABR Baseball Games Project, https://sabr.org/gamesproj/game/november-1-2001-scott-brosius-deja-vu-in-the-bronx/.

10. Tom Verducci, "Desert Classic," *Sports Illustrated*, November 12, 2001: 41-42. In Game Five of the 1964 World Series in Yankee Stadium, Tom Tresh of the New York Yankees hit a two-run homer in the ninth inning off future Hall of Fame pitcher Bob Gibson to tie the game, 2-2. The St. Louis Cardinals, however, won in the 10th inning with Gibson going the distance.

11. Stephen Cannella, "Saved!" *Sports Illustrated*, May 13, 2002: 48.

12. Jack Curry, "Same Kim, Same Site, but a Different Result, *New York Times*, June 13, 2002: D4.

13. Chan Ho Park of the Los Angeles Dodgers made his only All-Star Game appearance the year before, in 2001.

14 See Stew Thornley, "July 9, 2002: All-Star Game ends in a historic tie," SABR Baseball Games Project, https://sabr.org/gamesproj/game/july-9-2002-all-star-game-ends-in-a-historic-tie/, accessed April 7, 2023; Jack Curry, "No Winner, Loser or M.V.P., but Plenty of Boos," *New York Times*, July 10, 2002: D1, D3. The second All-Star Game of the 1961 season, played on July 31, also ended in a tie.

15 Kim's record stood until 2007 when it was broken by José Valverde, who finished the year with 47 saves.

16 Ken Rosenthal, "D-backs Playing a Game of Risk," *The Sporting News*, March 10, 2003: 50.

17 Daniel G. Habib, "Starting with Closers," *Sports Illustrated*, March 17, 2003: 46.

18 The three Koreans to play previously for the Red Sox, all pitchers, were Jin Ho Cho (1998-1999), Sang-Hoon Lee (2000), and Sun-Woo Kim (2001-2002).

19 Daniel G. Habib, "Boston's Bullpen Gamble," *Sports Illustrated*, March 17, 2003: 42-46.

20 Tim Rohan, "After a Career of Being Misunderstood, Byung-Hyun Kim Is at Peace," *Sports Illustrated*, July 3, 2019, https://www.si.com/mlb/2019/07/03/byung-hyun-kim-diamondbacks-yankees-world-series, accessed May 14, 2023.

21 Marvin Pane, "For Starters, Kim Gets Warm Fenway Reception," *Boston Globe*, April 30, 2004: E5.

22 Johnson was released on the day of the trade, and Narveson was sent to Pawtucket, before being released in August.

23 Troy E. Renck, "Rockies to Roll the Dice with Kim," *Denver Post*, March 31, 2005: D1.

24 Troy E. Renck, "Rockies 4-5, Marlins 3-3, (First, 11 innings) – Mohr's Homer Blasts Him into Lead," *Denver Post*, August 9, 2005: D1.

25 Bill Shaikin, "Dodgers Foil Rockies with Dogged Defense," *Los Angeles Times*, May 23, 2006: D1.

26 Coincidentally, Kim's countryman, Chan Ho Park, gave up Barry Bonds' 71st home run during the 2001 season, which moved Bonds past Mark McGwire for the single-season record. See Alexander Harriman, "October 5, 2001: Barry Bonds hits 71st home run to set new single-season record," *SABR Baseball Games Project*, https://sabr.org/gamesproj/game/october-5-2001-barry-bonds-hits-71st-home-run-to-set-new-single-season-record/.

27 Rohan.

28 Rohan.

A RED SOX MEMORY

The third game of the ALCS. Red Sox and Yankees. The Sox had lost the first two games and it looked as though they were headed for a third defeat, with a likely cataclysmic postseason, typically bleak, a tumble into the abyss. I came to the game with a few other people. We sat in Section Two with a panoramic view of the impending disaster with a cadre of out-of-town reporters taking up the rows at the top end of the section. As each nail was driven into the Sox' postseason coffin, we could hear them announce traumatic statements such as, "That was Jeter's four millionth RBI – setting another MLB record," or even worse, "A-Rod's home run drove in three runs and also miraculously cured seven pediatric patients over at Children's Hospital, all with the same swing of the bat!"

The citizens of Section Two started throwing crumpled papers, and an occasional hot-dog roll up at them, but it did no good at stemming the verbal inhumanity. In the eighth inning the so-called fans began drifting out, few remaining to witness the end. My friends were eager to leave, but if the Red Sox are still out there facing disaster, then we must stay, too! They threatened to leave me behind. I said, "Fine, it's a nice night for a walk home, even if it'd be 26 miles all the way back to Mudville, where there also was no joy," and with time enough to contemplate the significance of being a diehard Red Sox fan.

JOANNE HULBERT

CURTIS LESKANIC

BY JESSE ASBURY

In a 2004 column written for ESPN previewing the American League Championship Series between the New York Yankees and the Boston Red Sox, Bill Simmons broke down the bullpen matchup as follows: "In extra-inning games, I'd take (Derek) Lowe and Leskanic over any of the … Yankee guys. And you *know* there's going to be one game that goes past midnight. It's Yanks-Sox, for God's sake."[1] Just one week later, Curtis Leskanic would enter Red Sox lore as a key figure in an extra-inning game that ended well past midnight and helped change a franchise's destiny.

Curtis John Leskanic was born on April 2, 1968, in Homestead, Pennsylvania. This small borough in Allegheny County, just a few miles southeast of Pittsburgh, also produced Negro League pioneer and Baseball Hall of Famer Cumberland Posey. Curtis's mother, Helen Eckbreth Leskanic, worked as a hairdresser and as a cook at a local restaurant. His father, Lawrence Leskanic, played semipro baseball in his 20s before pursuing a career in the steel industry in Pittsburgh.[2] Curtis has another well-known family member: Cousin Katrina Leskanich was the lead singer of the band Katrina and the Waves, famous for their 1983 hit "Walkin' on Sunshine."[3] In his youth, Leskanic said, "everyone had a glove, and everyone had a ball" in his hometown, so he spent a great deal of time playing baseball with his friends in the local parks.[4] Leskanic attended Steel Valley High School in nearby Munhall, where he lettered in baseball and football. His college years began at the Community College of Allegheny County in West Mifflin, Pennsylvania. After spending one year there, he spent one year at Gulf Coast State College in Panama City, Florida, where he played on the baseball team. But after just one year of junior-college ball, Leskanic found that it "wasn't all it was cracked up to be"[5] and soon sought a transfer to a major college.

It was at Louisiana State University, under the tutelage of legendary manager Skip Bertman, that Leskanic truly began his road to the majors. In 1988, his first year in Baton Rouge, he appeared in only two games, throwing a total of 1⅓ innings.[6] But 1989 was his breakout season. Working as both a starter and a reliever, he pitched in 29 games, starting 15. In 115⅔ innings, he compiled an impressive 120 strikeouts and posted a team-leading ERA of 3.19.[7] He also recorded a conference-leading 15 wins, which was good enough to break LSU's single-season record. Leskanic was named second team All-SEC.[8] The loaded Tigers, whose roster featured six future major-league pitchers,[9] clinched a spot in the 1989 College World Series. The sixth-seeded Tigers opened with a loss to Miami followed by wins against Long Beach State and a rematch against Miami.[10] A loss to Texas eventually ended LSU's run in Omaha, but Leskanic's baseball career was only beginning.

Despite only having one full year of major college baseball under his belt, Leskanic impressed Indians scouting director Chet Montgomery enough that Cleveland selected him in the eighth round of the June 1989 amateur draft. He began his professional career in 1990 in High-A ball with the Kinston (North Carolina) Indians of the Carolina League. He worked exclusively as a starting pitcher in 1990, compiling a 6-5 record with a 3.68 ERA in 14 starts. He stayed with Kinston for the 1991 season, again working only as a starter. His record improved to 15-8, and he shaved almost a full run off his ERA from the year before.

On March 28, 1992, Leskanic and pitcher Oscar Munoz were traded to the Minnesota Twins for first baseman Paul Sorrento. Leskanic did not appear in the majors for his new team, instead spending the 1992 season pitching with the Double-A Orlando Sun Rays and the Triple-A Portland Beavers. He started 26 of the 31 games in which he appeared, ending the season with 168 innings pitched and a combined 10-13 record.

The Twins left Leskanic unprotected for the 1992 expansion draft to help fill the rosters of the two new teams added to the National League for the 1993 season, the Florida Marlins and the Colorado Rockies. In a draft where 72 players were selected, Leskanic was drafted with the 66th pick by the Rockies. Reflecting on the draft five years later, Rockies general manager Bob Gebhard considered Leskanic one of his "pleasant surprises," along with third baseman Charlie Hayes and Vinny Castilla.[11] Indeed, Leskanic spent the rest of the decade occupying a crucial role on Colorado's roster.

Leskanic began the 1993 season once again in the minors, pitching with the Triple-A Colorado Springs Sky Sox. He also appeared in seven games for the Double-A Wichita Wranglers. He posted a combined 7-5 record and an ERA of 3.96 before he was called up to the majors. Leskanic made his major-league debut on June 27, 1993, getting the start against the San Francisco

Giants at Candlestick Park. Pitching seven innings, he gave up five runs on seven hits, including a two-run home run by utility infielder Mike Benjamin in Leskanic's seventh and final inning pitched.

In a battle of expansion teams on July 8, 1993, Leskanic recorded his first major-league win, against the Florida Marlins. Pitching 6⅔ innings, Leskanic shut out the visiting Marlins, striking out five and walking two. Surprisingly, the only hit he allowed was to Marlins starting pitcher Pat Rapp. A trio of Colorado relievers helped secure the 3-2 win for Leskanic and the Rockies.

Leskanic's – and the Rockies' – growing pains continued throughout the inaugural 1993 season. Appearing in 18 games (eight as a starter), Leskanic posted a subpar 5.37 ERA with only 30 strikeouts in 57 innings pitched. The Rockies as a team ended their first season with 67 wins and 95 losses, 37 games behind the division-winning Atlanta Braves. Leskanic also encountered his first off-field setback that August when he was arrested for drunk driving after crashing his car in a Denver suburb.[12] He escaped the crash uninjured, but it was not his last brush with danger behind the wheel.

Leskanic began the 1994 season back in the minors with the Sky Sox. Working only as a starter, he recorded a 3.31 ERA in 130⅓ innings. When he returned to the majors late in the season, he appeared in eight games, getting the starting nod in three of them. His final start in the strike-shortened season came on August 5 against the Los Angeles Dodgers in Denver's Mile High Stadium. Pitching opposite Ramón Martínez, Leskanic took the loss, allowing five Dodgers runs in 5⅔ innings. This game ended up being the final start of his major-league career. Leskanic appeared only in relief roles for his final nine seasons.

The next season, 1995, was Leskanic's first full season in the majors. It was also Coors Field's first season as the Rockies' home ballpark. On April 26 the Rockies hosted the Mets for the first regular-season game played there. The home fans got their money's worth as the game went to extra innings with the score tied, 7-7. Leskanic came on in the 11th, eventually pitching three innings and allowing one run on a single by José Vizcaíno in the 13th. Dante Bichette's walk-off home run in the 14th inning ended the 11-9 slugfest and gave the Rockies their first win in their new home.

As for Leskanic, he went on to lead the National League in games pitched in 1995, appearing in 76. He led all National League relievers with 107 strikeouts.[13] Despite mainly working as a set-up man for closer Darren Holmes, Leskanic did get the occasional opportunity to close out a game. In a Sunday afternoon game on June 4, Leskanic earned his first career save, against the visiting Pittsburgh Pirates. He locked down the ninth inning, allowing no baserunners and striking out one to secure a 4-1 Rockies win. It was the first of 10 saves for Leskanic in 1995, second only to Holmes's 14 for the team lead. By season's end, Leskanic had compiled a 6-3 record with a 3.40 ERA in 98 innings pitched.

In only their third year of existence, the Rockies made their first postseason appearance, winning the wild card by one game over the Houston Astros. Their reward was a Division Series matchup against the soon-to-be World Series champion Atlanta Braves. The Braves eliminated the Rockies three games to one. Leskanic took the loss in Game One, giving up a ninth-inning solo home run to Chipper Jones that broke a 4-4 tie. He recorded a hold in Game Three, facing two batters in the seventh inning and one in the eighth before being removed for Bruce Ruffin.

Leskanic followed up his strong 1995 season with a subpar 1996. While he still managed over one strikeout per inning as he had the year prior, and while he recorded six saves and a 7-5 record over 70 games pitched, his ERA nearly doubled, to 6.23. But 1996 proved to be rough year for the entire Rockies pitching staff, who posted a collective 5.59 ERA. Conversely, five Rockies position players hit over .300, and three hit at least 40 home runs. Coors Field, in only its second season as the Rockies' home ballpark, was already earning its reputation as a hitter's dream and pitcher's nightmare.

Leskanic's role as a reliable set-up man for the Rockies continued throughout the remainder of the 1990s. From 1997 to 1999, he appeared in a total of 184 games, pitching 219 innings and striking out 185. He recorded four more saves in limited closing opportunities behind the recently acquired Jerry DiPoto and Dave Veres. While his ERA during this time was hovering around 5.00, his park-adjusted ERA+ was actually just above league average. On June 9, 1999, Leskanic recorded the last "first" of his career when he hit his only major-league home run, against the visiting Seattle Mariners. Facing Mariners reliever Rafael Carmona in the bottom of the seventh with two men on, Leskanic went deep down the left-field line to drive home the Rockies' final three runs in a 16-11 win.

Exactly seven years from the day Leskanic was drafted by the expansion Rockies, he was traded to the Milwaukee Brewers on November 17, 1999, for fellow reliever – and future Red Sox teammate – Mike Myers. After a midseason trade sent incumbent Brewers closer Bob Wickman to Cleveland, Leskanic took over the role for the remainder of the 2000 season and finished the year with 12 saves. In addition to these saves, he compiled a 9-3 record, struck out 75 batters and recorded what was then a career-best 2.56 ERA in 73 appearances.

Unbeknownst to Brewers coaches and staff, Leskanic spent much of the 2001 season pitching through the pain of a torn rotator cuff and a torn labrum in his throwing shoulder.[14] Despite the pain, he pitched in 70 games and recorded 17 saves working as the team's primary closer. At the end of the season, he underwent surgery to repair both tears and endured months of rehabilitation, often working six days a week in the hopes of expediting his return.[15] He was only able to resume pitching at the end of the 2002 season, appearing in just eight games with a pair of Milwaukee's farm clubs. When asked during spring training in 2003 about his decision to pitch through the pain during the 2001 season, Leskanic said, "I might [have been] sore, but I'm not going to say a word. ... I'm a football player in a baseball body."[16]

Leskanic returned to the Brewers to start the 2003 season. He did not finish it there. Despite putting together a sparkling 4-0 record with a 2.70 ERA in the first half of the season, he was traded to the Kansas City Royals for outfielder Alejandro Machado and pitcher Wes Obermueller on July 10. His second half with the Royals was even more impressive –a 1.73 ERA and a pair of saves in 27 appearances. The Royals re-signed him for the 2004 season on December 1, 2003, only to release him on June 18 of the next year. In 19 games with the 2004 Royals, his ERA ballooned to 8.04, and his won-lost record was an equally disappointing 0-3.

After his release, two teams showed interest in the free-agent reliever: the Boston Red Sox and the New York Yankees. Leskanic's former Rockies teammate Jerry DiPoto, now working as a scout for the Red Sox, reached out to Leskanic and told him he would fit in perfectly in Boston. Leskanic agreed, saying that "I'd never make it as a Yankee. In a Boston uniform, I could just be me."[17] So just four days after being released by Kansas City, the veteran reliever signed with the Red Sox. Johnny Damon later recalled vouching for Leskanic's talent in a conversation with general manager Theo Epstein before the signing: "This guy has a good arm. Please at least take a look."[18] His first chance to pitch for his new team came on June 25, when he threw one inning in relief of Pedro Martínez in a rain-shortened eight-inning 12-1 blowout win over the visiting Philadelphia Phillies. Leskanic struck out one and did not allow a baserunner in his Fenway Park debut. On July 8 against the Oakland Athletics, Leskanic pitched a perfect 10th inning in relief of closer Keith Foulke to record his first win as a member of the Red Sox. As DiPoto predicted, Leskanic fit right in with the collective "Idiot" personality of the 2004 Red Sox. He certainly looked the part as well with his five-o'clock shadow and his long hair flying out of the back of his hat with every pitch.[19]

Despite on occasion being referred to as "Let's Panic" by fans and media members frustrated by some of his past relief outings, Leskanic put together a streak of 10 consecutive scoreless appearances for the Red Sox from August 20 through September 14, a crucial stretch in the season during which Boston was able to distance itself from the Oakland Athletics in the race for the wild card.[20] On September 27 the Red Sox clinched the wild card with a win over the Tampa Bay Devil Rays. Leskanic came on in the seventh with two runners on and retired the next two batters, ending the inning and the Devil Rays' threat.

In the Division Series, the Red Sox made quick work of the West Division champion Anaheim Angels, sweeping them in three games by a combined score of 25-12. Leskanic did not appear in the series. The American League Championship Series was a rematch from the year prior, with the Red Sox facing off against the rival New York Yankees. Leskanic was called into action early in Game One, appearing in the fourth inning to relieve a struggling Curt Schilling. With the Red Sox already down 6-0, Leskanic walked the first two men he faced before getting Álex Rodríguez to ground into a double play and striking out Gary Sheffield to end the inning. In Game Three, Leskanic came on in the fourth with the game tied, 6-6, and gave up a three-run home run to Sheffield and a double to Hideki Matsui before being pulled for Tim Wakefield.

Leskanic's next – and last – appearance in the ALCS came in a must-win Game Four at Fenway Park on October 17. In a game perhaps best remembered for Dave Roberts' steal of second base in the bottom of the ninth, Leskanic's late-game heroics may have been just as important. After nine hard-fought innings, the game went to extra innings with the score tied, 4-4. Leskanic entered in the top of the 11th in relief of Myers, the man for whom he was once traded, with the bases loaded and two outs. He got Bernie Williams to fly out to center to end the inning and the Yankee threat. With the game still tied, he came out again to pitch the 12th. He gave up a hit to Jorge Posada to open the inning and then took a hard grounder off his leg from the bat of Rubén Sierra. Undeterred, Leskanic fielded the ball and threw Sierra out at first. He retired the next two batters he faced, ending the frame by striking out Miguel Cairo. David Ortiz's two-run home run in the bottom of the 12th sent Red Sox fans home happy and gave Leskanic the win in one of the wildest games in postseason history.

That clutch performance in Game Four was the last game Leskanic ever pitched in the majors. By this point in his career, Leskanic himself admitted he was pitching on fumes: "It was all adrenaline; my arm was pretty much done."[21] Theo Epstein concurred, stating, "He had no right pitching in the big leagues with the way his shoulder was at that point ... and he's making huge pitches, getting huge outs for us."[22] The Red Sox proceeded to win their next seven games, taking the pennant in seven over the Yankees and earning the franchise's first World Series victory in 86 years after a sweep of the St. Louis Cardinals. After the 2004 season, Leskanic announced his retirement. When reflecting on his final season, which started by being released by the Royals and ended with a World Series victory, Leskanic said it was "like falling out of a dump truck and ending up on a cloud."[23]

In the 2007 World Series, the Red Sox faced the Rockies. Leskanic, who had postseason experience with both teams, had difficulty picking a team to root for, saying that he "just wanted to see a good series."[24] The Red Sox swept the overmatched Rockies in four games. At the 2008 Red Sox home opener, Leskanic and his 2004 teammate Dave McCarty appeared in the pregame festivities, carrying their team's World Series trophy. Leskanic and McCarty's role in this celebration served as a reminder to Red Sox Nation that their once-moribund franchise had now won *two* championships in the last four seasons.[25] Leskanic also spent the 2008 season working as a scout for the Red Sox from his home in Florida.[26]

Despite these opportunities to still be involved in the game he loved, Leskanic admitted that he had difficulty adjusting to life after his playing career ended: "When I retired, I was a bitter, miserable, and self-endowed jerk."[27] In 2011 Leskanic was arrested near his home in Altamonte Springs, Florida, and charged with driving under the influence. His daughter was with him in the car, where he was found by police hunched over the steering wheel. His blood/alcohol level was over four times the legal limit, and, as a result, he had to be sent to the hospital as a precaution before being sent to jail.[28]

After this second drunk-driving incident, Leskanic found strength in his faith to help him overcome his demons, saying that "God humbled me."[29] He began volunteering his time at local jails, telling his story to warn others of the dangers of driving under the influence.[30] As of 2023, he was the owner and manager of Tres Jolie Medical Spa in Longwood, Florida. His wife, Susan, also works for the spa.[31] Leskanic still finds time to go back to Boston periodically to watch Red Sox games, work with local charities, and visit with teammates and friends.[32] In 2023 he said that people still recognized him and thanked him for his role in helping the Red Sox beat the Yankees in 2004 and end the Curse of the Bambino.[33] When asked in 2021 about his time with the 2004 Red Sox and his extra-inning Game Four win, Leskanic said it was like a dream come true: "Of course, when you're a kid, that's all you think about. … To be in that situation … was surreal."[34]

SOURCES

In addition to the sources cited in the Notes, the author consulted Baseball-Reference.com and Retrosheet.org.

NOTES

1. Bill Simmons, *Now I Can Die in Peace* (New York: Random House, 2009), 281.
2. Author interview with Curtis Leskanic, April 29, 2023.
3. John Paschal, "Relatively Important: When Performers Run in the Family," fangraphs.com, May 28, 2019. https://tht.fangraphs.com/relatively-important-when-performers-run-in-the-family/.
4. April 29, 2023, interview.
5. April 29, 2023, interview.
6. *2020 LSU Baseball Yearbook: Baseball at the Box*. https://issuu.com/lsuathletics/docs/2020_lsu_baseball_yearbook
7. *2020 LSU Baseball Yearbook*.
8. *2020 LSU Baseball Yearbook*.
9. The six future major-league pitchers on the 1989 LSU roster were Leskanic, Paul Byrd, Ben McDonald, Chad Ogea, John O'Donoghue, and Russ Springer
10. *2020 LSU Baseball Yearbook*.
11. Irv Moss, "Rockies and Marlins Took 72 Players," *Denver Post*, November 18, 1997. https://extras.denverpost.com/rock/rock1127.htm.
12. "Notes," *San Bernardino County* (California) *Sun*, August 20, 1993: C3.
13. "Sports Briefs," *Indiana* (Pennsylvania) *Gazette*, January 30, 1996: 15.
14. Arnie Stapleton (Associated Press), "Injured Brewers Closer Leskanic Back," *Midland* (Texas) *Daily News*, February 23, 2002. https://www.ourmidland.com/news/article/Injured-Brewers-Closer-Leskanic-Back-7056329.php.
15. Stapleton.
16. Stapleton.
17. Interview with Leskanic, April 29, 2023.
18. Ian Browne, *Idiots Revisited* (Thomaston, Maine: Tilbury House, 2014), 112.
19. Browne, 112.
20. "2004 World Champion Boston Red Sox. Curtis John Leskanic." http://www.redsoxdiehard.com/worldseries/ players/leskanic.html.
21. Allan Wood and Bill Nowlin, *Don't Let Us Win Tonight* (Chicago: Triumph Books, 2014), 134.
22. *Don't Let Us Win Tonight*, 135.
23. *Don't Let Us Win Tonight*, 266.
24. Jeff Birnbaum, "Where Are They Now? Curtis Leskanic," MLB.com. https://web.archive.org/web/ 20140826015229/http://newyork.yankees.mlb.com/news/article.jsp?ymd=20080926&content_id=3553486&vkey=news_col&fext=.jsp&c_id=col.
25. Dan Shaughnessy, "Red Sox' Home Opener a Success All Around," *Boston Globe*, April 8, 2008. http://archive.boston.com/sports/baseball/redsox/articles/2008/04/08/red_sox_home_opener_a_success_all_around/?page=1.
26. *Baseball America Directory 2008: Your Definitive Guide to the Game* (New York: Simon & Schuster, 2008), 27.
27. facebook.com/curtis.leskanic/about_details.
28. Gary Taylor, "Curtis Leskanic: Former Pro Baseball Pitcher Arrested on DUI Charge," *Orlando Sentinel*, September 14, 2011. https://www.orlandosentinel.com/sports/os-xpm-2011-09-15-os-former-baseball-player-dui-20110914-story.html.
29. facebook.com/curtis.leskanic/about_details.
30. linkedin.com/in/curtis-leskanic-791bab88?trk=people-guest_people_search-card.
31. linkedin.com/in/curtis-leskanic-791bab88?trk=people-guest_people_search-card.
32. Interview with Curtis Leskanic, April 29, 2023.
33. April 29, 2023, interview.
34. Jessica Eley, "Fox 35 Speaks to Former Red Sox Pitcher Who Won 2004 World Series," Fox 35 Orlando, November 2, 2021. https://www.fox35orlando.com/news/fox-35-speaks-to-former-red-sox-pitcher-who-won-2004-world-series.

DEREK LOWE

BY BILL NOWLIN

In 2004, as the Boston Red Sox won their first world championship in 86 years, right-handed sinkerball pitcher Derek Lowe earned the rare distinction of winning the clinching game in the Division Series, the League Championship Series, and the World Series itself.

He won 176 regular-season games pitching for seven different major-league teams, but his most notable tenure was with Boston, where he also threw a no-hitter in 2002, was a two-time All-Star, and was 70-55 with a 3.72 earned-run average.

He began his career with the Seattle Mariners, but came to Boston midway through his first season in one of the most lopsided trades in baseball history.

Lowe was born and raised in the Detroit suburb of Dearborn, Michigan, on June 1, 1973, the son of Don and Dianne Lowe. Dianne worked as a nurse and Don as a repairman. Derek grew up in an athletic family and told writer Herb Crehan, "Everyone in the family was involved in sports: uncles, aunts, cousins, everyone. I wouldn't change a thing about the way I grew up. I played whatever sport was in season: golf, soccer, basketball, and baseball. Playing and adapting to the different sports made me a better athlete."[1]

He graduated from Dearborn's Edsel Ford High School, where he lettered in four sports: basketball, golf, and soccer, as well as baseball. And he was an All-League honoree in four sports. He was expected to attend Eastern Michigan University on a basketball scholarship (Lowe was 6-feet-6 and is listed in baseball-reference at 230 pounds.) His all-league selection in baseball had been as a shortstop, though, not a pitcher, but he was drafted as a pitcher – despite winning only a pair of games in high school. "I was pitching my sophomore year against the number one team in the state in the playoffs, and the other team had kids that were getting looked at for the draft, so pro scouts were at the game. I lost the game but Seattle Mariners scout Ken Medeja noticed and started following my high school career. Seattle was drafting tall pitchers at that time hoping they would fill out in time and I fit that build. Long story short, I was drafted in the eighth round even though only winning two high school games."[2]

Unsurprisingly, Lowe was a Tigers fan growing up. "Chet Lemon. He was my man," he said in 2003. "But then I started playing shortstop, and I wanted to be Alan Trammell."[3]

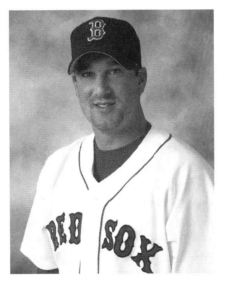

"He was a typical high school kid," said Pat Wyka, athletic director at Edsel Ford for 25 years. "He wasn't 100 percent focused. ... He did not have a good senior pitching season." But he was good enough to catch the eye of the Mariners' scouts.[4]

In the June 1991 player draft, it was the Seattle Mariners who drafted Lowe, in the eighth round, the 214th pick overall. Starting out with 213 prospects having been rated higher in the draft, Lowe wasted no time in signing, on June 7. Medeja is credited with the signing. The 18-year-old Lowe was sent to rookie league in Arizona, started 12 games, and built a 5-3 record with a 2.41 ERA, striking out 60 and walking 21.

He was advanced slowly through the system, working for Bellingham, Washington, in 1992, where he was 7-3 with a 2.42 ERA, nearly identical to that from rookie league. Lowe struggled at higher levels of play and was 21-25 over the next three seasons while giving up more than five runs per nine innings. He split 1996 between the Port City Roosters in Double A (in North Carolina) and the Mariners' Triple-A Tacoma Rainiers of the Pacific Coast League.

Lowe began the 1997 season with Tacoma but a very early-season injury sent Seattle left-hander Tim Davis to the 15-day disabled list and resulted in Lowe's being called up to join the major-league Mariners on April 24. His debut came two days later in Toronto. The score was tied, 3-3, when he was brought on in relief to pitch the bottom of the sixth. He got through his first three innings and got the first out in the bottom of the ninth. Otis Nixon reached on a single to third base and then stole second. Another infield single, to shortstop, put two men on; Nixon had to hold at second base. Manager Lou Piniella called on Norm Charlton to relieve. Charlton got a fly out but then yielded a single, which resulted in the loss of the game being charged to Lowe.

After another relief stint, Lowe was optioned back to Tacoma, but then recalled again and got his first start on May 27 against the Twins. He worked five innings and gave up four runs, but had a no-decision. Lowe's first win came – in Detroit – on June 6, thanks to a pair of two-run homers by José Cruz Jr. Lowe appeared in six June games and three in July. He held a 2-4 record with a 6.96 ERA in 53 innings, when he was optioned back to Tacoma in July

That's when the Mariners dealt Lowe to Boston in a July 31 trading-deadline deal. The Mariners really need to bolster their bullpen and acquired Heathcliff Slocumb from the Red Sox for Lowe and minor-league catcher Jason Varitek. Years later, Varitek said that he and Lowe were pretty raw: "He was a one-pitch pitcher, and I couldn't catch, hit, or throw."[5]

With Boston's Triple-A Pawtucket Red Sox, Lowe was 4-0 in 1997 with a 2.37 ERA (the last time he worked in the minor leagues) and in September he was called up to the big-league club, where he was 0-2 in 16 innings but with a solid 3.38 ERA.

Lowe's first two games in 1998 were starts, and losses. He relieved in 13 games, then got a few starts again, losing all five decisions in his next eight starts. He was 0-7 by the end of June, with an ERA of 4.23. He finished the year 3-9, with the three wins all coming in relief. His 4.02 earned-run average was, however, slightly better than the team's 4.18. The Red Sox made it to the postseason, losing the Division Series to Cleveland, three games to one. Lowe worked 4⅓ innings in the ALDS, giving up one run on three hits, the eighth run of nine in a 9-5 Game Two loss.

The Red Sox noted that Lowe had pitched much better in relief than when starting, and in 1999 they had him work exclusively out of the bullpen, pitching in 74 games, closing 32 of them and earning 15 saves (he was 6-3). His ERA for the year was 2.63. Come the postseason, one earned run in four innings cost him a loss in Game One of the Division Series, again against the Indians. Lowe won Game Three thanks to a big six-run bottom of the seventh at Fenway Park. The Red Sox advanced to the ALCS, facing the Yankees.

Lowe had a superb 2000 season, closing 64 games (most in the league) and earning a league-leading 42 saves (tied with Todd Jones of the Tigers). His ERA was an enviable 2.56 and he was honored in midseason by being named to the American League All-Star team. Won-lost records tend not to mean much for relievers; he was 4-4.

One could see 2001 as a transition year. By July 29 Lowe was 4-8, with 21 saves and a 4.15 earned-run average. There was a mixed bag of closers – by year's end, Lowe had closed 50 games, but Rod Beck had closed 28, Ugueth Urbina (acquired from the Expos on July 31) had 13, and Rolando Arrojo 11. The team also changed managers in midseason, with pitching coach Joe Kerrigan replacing Jimy Williams as manager. Lowe finished 5-10 with a 3.53 ERA; the team's ERA was 4.15.

Grady Little became Red Sox skipper for 2002; the team itself was under new ownership. Tony Cloninger became the pitching coach. Lowe returned to starting games and in his fifth start (April 27) he threw a no-hitter against the Tampa Bay Devil Rays, with only one third-inning base on balls. Lowe had an interesting take on the battle of wits between batter and pitcher when it comes to a no-hitter: "You need some luck, or good fortune, and you need to remember the pressure is on the batter because you are pitching well and they aren't having any success."[6]

It was the first time a pitcher had both had a 40-save season and thrown a no-hitter. Lowe won a career-high 21 games in 2002, against only eight losses, with a season ERA of 2.58 and a WHIP of 0.974. He was again named to the All-Star team. After the season, Lowe placed third in the Cy Young Award voting.

In 2003, when the Red Sox came to within a few innings of making it to the World Series, Lowe worked to a 17-7 record, though with an ERA of almost two runs per game higher – 4.47. The number of walks he'd allowed had jumped from 48 in 2002 to 72 in 2003. Walks haunted him in the 2003 postseason, too. In Game One of the ALDS, he came into a 4-4 tie game in Oakland to pitch the bottom of the 11th, and then again the 12th. In the bottom of the 12th, he walked two batters, sandwiched around a couple of groundouts, and then issued an intentional walk to load the bases – before giving up the one hit he'd allowed, an unexpected bunt single by catcher Ramon Hernandez.

In ALDS Game Three, Lowe started and gave the Red Sox seven innings of one-run ball. They won the game on Trot Nixon's two-run homer in the bottom of the 11th. In the deciding Game Five, back in Oakland, Boston was ahead 4-3 heading into the bottom of the ninth. Scott Williamson walked the first two batters he faced. Grady Little called on Lowe, who retired the side with two strikeouts after a sacrifice. In the ALCS, Lowe lost both Game Two (6-2) and Game Five (4-2), ending up with an 0-3 record for the 2003 postseason. After the Sox lost to the Yankees in extra innings in Game Seven, Lowe said, "That was the quietest clubhouse I have ever been in. Nobody said a word. Of course there wasn't anything to say."[7]

That was reversed in 2004, as noted above. Lowe had a mediocre regular season, again slipping a full run in ERA from 4.47 to 5.42. His record was 14-12. In the postseason, new manager Terry Francona, well aware of how Lowe had slipped, said he was asking him to work out of the bullpen. Lowe thought about going home, but Francona asked him to sleep on it. He accepted the assignment. And he won the clinching game in all three rounds of the postseason – getting the win in relief in the deciding Division Series game, winning Game Seven of the ALCS (allowing just one run in six innings) and winning Game Four of the World Series with seven shutout innings. He had also started Game Four of the ALCS, allowing three runs in 5⅓ innings. Afterward, he admitted Francona had been right: "I probably would have left me off the roster I had pitched so poorly. But it was tough to go back to the bullpen."[8] All's well that ends well; he had a world championship ring.

Lowe was a free agent and in January 2005 signed a four-year deal with the Los Angeles Dodgers. There were rumors that the Red Sox had concerns about his drinking, and did not put on a push to re-sign him. Lowe started 35 games for the Dodgers in 2005, tied for the lead in the National League. He cut down his walks, struck out more batters, and brought his ERA down nearly two runs (a one-hitter – a single by the first batter in the game – on August 31 helped) to 3.61, but his record was just 12-15 (the Dodgers were 71-91). He won 16 games in 2006, enough to tie for the league lead with five others. Lowe's four years with Los Angeles were remarkably consistent, year to year, and he never missed a turn in the rotation, leading the league once more in starts in 2008 (and once more tied with several others). In that year's postseason he won the first game of the Division Series, but lost the first game of the NLCS, 3-2.

And then it was on to Atlanta for three seasons, Lowe again cashing in as a free agent and again twice leading the league in games started (in 2009 and in 2011, tied with five others in 2009 and two others in 2011). But he also led the National League in losses in 2011 (9-17, after winning 31 games in the two prior years). His ERA had crept back up over 5 (to 5.05). He'd started 2009 well enough, but the second half of the season was subpar by his standards. And 2010 was, as well, even a little more so; but suddenly in September Lowe got a second wind and reeled off five consecutive wins, becoming Pitcher of the Month and helping the Braves secure the wild card as he himself finished with an even 4.00 ERA on the season. He pitched very well in the Division Series against the San Francisco Giants, but ended up with an 0-2 record, saddled with losses of 1-0 and 3-2.

Like most pitchers, Lowe didn't hit that well (.149, with a .201 on-base percentage, in 534 plate appearances). His one home run was one of the bright spots of his 2011 season. On August 31 he homered at Turner Field, leading off the third inning against Washington Nationals pitcher John Lannan. Lowe worked a 3-and-2 count, with a couple of fouls mixed in, homering to deep left field on the eighth pitch to give Atlanta a 2-0 lead in a game Lowe won, 3-1.

Lowe was pretty good fielding his position, with a career .975 percentage, five times tied for being best among pitchers.

After the 2011 season, the Braves didn't see enough of a future in Lowe, given those 17 losses and his declining effectiveness, so they settled for some degree of salary relief and swapped him on the last day of October to the Cleveland Indians for 23-year-old lefty minor leaguer Chris Jones, with the Braves paying a reported two-thirds of Lowe's hefty salary for the final year of their four-year deal.

The Indians saw him as a fourth or fifth starter, but as a veteran with experience who might provide some help. Indeed, hoping for a comeback season, Lowe got off to an excellent start with the 2012 Indians and was 6-1 by May 15, but seemed to run out of steam and was 2-7 over June and July, while watching his ERA climb from 2.15 on May 20 to 5.52. The team released him on August 10.

The Red Sox and Orioles both showed some interest, and Lowe himself said he just needed a "tune-up." But three days later the team he had caught on with was the New York Yankees. He was asked to work back in the bullpen. On the 13th, he had what was only his second relief appearance (excluding the postseason) since 2001. He threw four innings of two-hit scoreless relief in his first game and was credited with a save. Over the remainder of the season, Lowe won one and lost one, with a 3.04 earned-run average in 17 relief appearances, and pitched in the postseason for the last time, throwing two innings of relief in three games, giving up three runs in three Yankees losses though never involved in any of the decisions.

Lowe ended his career with a win. A free agent again, he wanted to continue as a starting pitcher but the versatility he offered had appeal and he signed a minor-league deal with the Texas Rangers in the spring of 2013. Expected to make the big-league team, he did just that. The Rangers used him in relief nine times. When starter Nick Tepesch was struck by a line drive in the top of the second inning of the April 20 home game against visiting Seattle, Lowe was brought in for long relief and worked four full innings of no-hit relief, credited in the ultimate 5-0 win. But after he was tagged for eight runs over his final three appearances, in 2⅓ innings, the Rangers designated him for assignment on May 20. There was no interest from other teams and in mid-July Lowe announced his retirement.

Lowe said he'd go back to rooting for the Tigers. "I'm not going to go to the Hall of Fame, so I don't feel like I need to have a retirement speech," he said. "But I was able to play 17 years on some pretty cool teams and win a World Series. So, everyone's got to stop playing at some point, and this is my time."[9]

Lowe has been married twice. He had two children with his first wife, Trinka, and adopted the son she had from a prior relationship. Lowe later became involved with Fox Sports Net broadcaster Carolyn Hughes during the first of his Dodgers years while she was covering the team. His first wife, Trinka, had apparently had an affair with married German soccer star Stefan Effenberg.[10] Following divorces from their respective spouses, Lowe and Hughes married in December 2008.

In his years since baseball, Derek Lowe has been able to enjoy being retired from the game. In June 2016 he said, "I am just splitting time between Florida and my home state of Michigan, spending a lot of time with family, and golfing quite a bit."[11]

Lowe is a survivor of squamous cell carcinoma and has donated time to a number of causes that fight cancer, including the Melanoma Foundation of New England and the National Council on Skin Cancer Prevention.

SOURCES

In addition to the sources noted in this biography, the author also accessed Lowe's player file from the National Baseball Hall of Fame, the *Encyclopedia of Minor League Baseball*, Retrosheet.org, Baseball-Reference.com, Rod Nelson of SABR's Scouts Committee, and the SABR Minor Leagues Database, accessed online at Baseball-Reference.com.

NOTES

1. Herb Crehan, "Derek Lowe Remembers the 2004 World Championship," BostonBaseballHistory.com, June 30, 2014.
2. Email to author, June 15, 2016.
3. Associated Press, "Baseball the Right Choice for Lowe," ESPN.go, March 11, 2003, at sports.espn.go.com/mlb/news/story?id=1392434.
4. "Baseball the Right Choice for Lowe,"
5. Tony Massarotti, "'Tek Support," *Boston Herald*, April 28, 2002: B24.

6   Crehan.
7   Crehan.
8   Crehan.
9   Tom Pelissero, "Derek Lowe 'Officially' Threw His Last MLB Pitch," *USA Today*, July 17, 2013.
10 "Inside Track," *Boston Herald*, September 8, 2008.
11 Email to author, June 15, 2016.

BLANKETED BY RED SOX MEMORIES

I was fortunate to accompany my father, Bill Enos, when he was invited by the Red Sox to attend Games One and Two of the 2004 World Series in Boston. Dad had retired in 1992 after 19 years as a Red Sox New England amateur area scout. He then became a scouting consultant until 2002, even after a 2000 move to Arizona. He was honored to have worked for the best organization in baseball.

Upon his retirement, Dad watched every Sox game on NESN or the MLB Network, and kept up with the box scores, MLB drafts, and New England players in pro ball as he continued his dedication to his beloved hometown team. At age 84, with over 64 years' service in professional baseball, Bill had attended many World Series and Championship Series games, but in 2004 there was no way he would miss the opportunity to watch the Red Sox play the Cardinals, the team that first signed him as a 16-year-old from Cohasset, Massachusetts.

As a World War II Navy seaman and on inactive status with the St. Louis Browns, Bill was stationed on Tinian in the Northern Marianas during the 1944 World Series between the Browns and the Cardinals. Unfortunately, a typhoon hit in the ninth inning of Game Six, knocking the radio off the shelf, so the sailors waited for a day to learn the outcome.

Upon returning home from the Pacific in 1946, Bill played in the minors for the Asheville Tourists and the Miami Sun Sox and was thrilled to obtain '46 World Series tickets to see the Red Sox play against the Cardinals at Fenway Park. He planned to take his father, Abraham, but that was not to be, as Abe suffered a fatal heart attack on September 24. Bill wrote to his Miami manager, future Hall of Famer Paul Waner, and invited him to stay at the family home in Cohasset during the Series. Waner sent his regrets since he had to remain in Sarasota. Consequently, he asked his cousin to the games, knowing that Abe would have insisted they attend this historic event. Thus, the Sox-Cardinals matchup in 2004 would bring back bittersweet memories of the father he lost 58 years prior.

Bill Enos and Bill Lajoie. Photo by Anne Enos.

The whirlwind weekend began for us on October 22, 2004, with a last-minute plane trip from Arizona and attendance at the World Series Gala at the JFK Museum that night, followed by the two exciting games on October 23 and 24.

The World Series affords baseball folks the chance to renew old friendships and Dad reunited with Bill Lajoie, a player he signed in 1955 for the Baltimore Orioles immediately after the College World Series in Omaha. In 2004 Lajoie was employed by the Red Sox as a special assistant to GM Theo Epstein in scouting. Bill Lajoie had a long career in baseball including leading the 1984 Detroit Tigers to a World Series championship as general manager.

The weather was cold and windy, especially as our blood had thinned from Southwest desert living, so I purchased a heavy Red Sox fleece blanket to keep us warm during the game. To avoid the rush of the crowds, we didn't get to our seats for the opening ceremonies, so Dad sat in a folding chair next to the entrance of the Green Monster seats and "raved" with an employee while I watched from "backstage" as the Dropkick Murphys entered the park.

For both games, we huddled under the blanket, seated in the front row of the center-field bleachers along with Red Sox current and retired baseball scouts including Frank Malzone, Joe McDonald, Buzz Bowers, Dick Berardino, and Ray Crone Jr. I vividly remember seeing Jim Edmonds' amazing over-the-shoulder catch right in front of us in Game Two. I'll never forget the excitement of winning both games against the Cardinals with outstanding pitching performances for both clubs. And of course, the crowd was abuzz about the status of Curt Schilling's ALCS ankle injury.

The Red Sox logo blanket became a familiar source of comfort as Dad aged and his body, but not his mind, deteriorated. In his later years, he cuddled up under it as he continued to watch Red Sox telecasts. When he entered hospice care for the last two weeks of his life in December 2014, the blanket continued to provide solace and warmth, even as he took his last breath. And as most diehard Red Sox fans would say, he was at peace, under a Red Sox blanket of love.

ANNE ENOS

MARK MALASKA

BY JOHN VORPERIAN

Mark Malaska served as a major-league baseball relief pitcher during two seasons. In 2003, the 6-foot-3, 191-pound left-hander broke into "The Show" with the Tampa Bay Devil Rays. He then joined the 2004 Boston Red Sox in their fabled World Series championship run. During his major-league career, Malaska appeared in 41 games and posted a 3-2 won-lost record, with 36 innings pitched, 29 strikeouts, 24 walks, allowing 2 home runs for a 3.75 ERA. He earned a championship ring with the Red Sox.

Dennis Mark Malaska was born on January 17, 1978, in Youngstown, Ohio, to Dennis and Darlene Malaska. Dennis was a teacher at the city's Chaney High School. On September 12, 1980, the couple had their second child, a son, David.

Located in the northeast section of Ohio in Mahoning County, Youngstown once had a vibrant steel industry. But in the 1970s that economic sector was in decline. The municipality's population totaled under 140,000. The Malaska family resided on the city's south side.

From 1992 to 1996, Malaska attended Cardinal Mooney High School in Youngstown. Established in 1956, the private Roman Catholic school boasts such notable alumni as San Francisco 49ers owner Denise DeBartolo York, former boxer Ray "Boom Boom" Mancini, past Oklahoma football head coach Bob Stoops, and former US Representative James Traficant. A gifted athlete, Malaska earned a total of six varsity letters in baseball and basketball. During his interscholastic sports years for the Cardinals, his outstanding performance on the diamond and the hardwood secured the teenager All-Steel Valley honors in both sports.

When it came to Cardinals basketball, Malaska was positioned either at guard or forward. In addition to interscholastic competition, he also participated in community cage leagues.

But in baseball, the left-handed hitter and thrower was a standout outfielder with a strong arm and quick bat. In his senior season at Cardinal Mooney, he hit .462. Also, he was the top hitter in the 1996 Connie Mack state tournament with a .536 batting average.[1]

Looking toward college, Malaska received athletic scholarships in both sports as well as academic scholarships. Purdue, Ball State, Duke, Georgia Tech, Bowling Green, Toledo, Clemson, Ohio University, and Florida State all made bids for this student-athlete. As to the athletic scholarships, the better deals were baseball offerings. Thus, he decided to pursue a single athletic endeavor – baseball. From among the various proposals, Malaska eventually selected an institution of higher learning less than 60 miles from his hometown – the University of Akron. He made the choice in large part due to a tragic incident and to keep close to his family.

On July 21, 1997, there was a life-changing experience that nearly upended Malaska's dream and desire for baseball. That day Mark was playing in a local league game. From the stands his father and brother saw him make four hits, including three home runs, and notch eight RBIs. However, a stellar day on the ball field turned by night into a horrific nightmare for Mark. That evening, his brother David lost his life in a fatal traffic accident. Some contemporary reports chronicle that Malaska began to think of turning away from baseball. Yet, with the support of his parents he nonetheless went onward with his athletic career.

In 2003, upon reflection of that fateful date, Malaska commented, "Along with the loss, along with my mourning and grief, something else happened on that Sunday, I began to see a larger picture in life and I have never been under any pressure doing things since then."[2]

Mark attended the University of Akron from 1996 to 2000 and majored in exercise physiology. His freshman year, he was redshirted in baseball. In subsequent seasons, Malaska hit .296, .318, and .326 and built a college career total 100 RBIs and 13 home runs. He handled the positions of outfield – primarily center field – and relief pitcher.

Malaska's athletic feats made entries into the Akron record books. He set single-game records for runs scored (5), doubles (3), and RBIs (10). In the NCAA offseason, he further developed his baseball skills by playing for the Danbury Westerners (Danbury, Connecticut) in the New England Collegiate Baseball League.

Founded in 1993, the NECBL was created to be an amateur wooden-bat summer circuit with the avowed goal of permitting student athletes to improve their chances of showcasing their talents for pro scouts. Its inaugural season commenced in 1994. The league's season runs from early June to early August. Its motto: "Keep Your Eye on the Dream."[3]

Danbury was managed by Moe Morhardt, a former backup first baseman for the Chicago Cubs who played in parts of the 1961 and 1962 seasons. Malaska said of Morhardt, in a 2023 interview: "Best coach I've ever had. Simplified the game mentally and it clicked for me and my career took off due to him."[4]

In his initial NECBL season, Malaska made the loop a personal playground with his ballplaying exploits. He ranked third for the league's batting title. Mark led the league with 40 runs, 113 total bases, 7 triples, 58 hits, and 26 extra-base hits. In 41 games, he had 163 at-bats, for a .356 average, with 40 RBIs and 11 home runs.[5]

Malaska was named as an outfielder to the 1998 All-League Team. He was crowned as the league's 1998 NECBL Outstanding Pro Prospect.

Morhardt's 1998 team complied a 25-17 record, which earned the Westerners a bid to the first round of the NECBL playoffs. They were defeated by the Middletown Giants, three games to one.

In the NECBL 1999 season, Mark repeated as the league's Outstanding Pro Prospect. Named to the All-League Team, Malaska topped the NECBL with 41 RBIs, ranked second in extra-base hits with 19, and batted .317. He was named MVP of the NECBL All-Star game.[6]

Danbury finished with a 23-19 record. The Westerners entered the playoffs and got to the championship series. Middletown again took the NECBL crown, three games to one.

During the fall of 1999, Akron held its annual Scout Day. Mark threw some batting practice. "When some of his pitches reached 90 MPH on the radar guns, major-league scouts began to notice."[7]

In his final season at Akron, the Zips lacked a closer. Malaska was offered the chance to fill the team's need. He recalled, "The coaches talked me into pitching." The left-hander said, "I wanted to play every day. I love to hit. Scouts told my coach I could make it to the next level as a pitcher."[8] In 24 innings Mark put up a 3-1 record with four saves and a 1.12 ERA. His dual-position performance during the 2000 NCAA season earned him being named to the All Mid-American Conference First Team.

In a 2023 interview, Malaska recalled that at Akron's Scout Day, as an outfielder he was projected to go as a 15th- to 20th-round pick. But the talent evaluators at some 2000 pre-draft workouts in Chicago, Cleveland, Pittsburgh, and Milwaukee were telling him that as a pitcher he could go in the top 10 rounds.[9]

In 1998 the Tampa Bay Devil Rays and the Arizona Diamondbacks joined major-league baseball as expansion ballclubs. On June 5, 2000, Tampa Bay selected Malaska in the eighth round (226th overall) of the major-league amateur draft. Tampa Bay scout Matt Kinzer, a former pitcher with the St. Louis Cardinals and Detroit Tigers, signed the 22-year-old on June 19, 2000. According to *Baseball America*, Malaska received a $35,000 signing bonus.[10]

Kinzer, having also been an NFL replacement player for the Detroit Lions, may not have been shocked by Malaska's side job – bouncer. The offseason occupation came about because, as Malaska recalled, "I frequented that bar, had a reputation as a fighter and knew pretty much everyone in town so they figured I'd be good to stop or defuse any problems. I was also dating a popular bartender there at the time."[11]

Malaska was assigned to Tampa Bay's low Class-A club, the Charleston RiverDogs (South Atlantic League). He was there for only a month. After two innings and two runs given up, he was assigned to the short-season Hudson Valley Renegades (New York-Penn League) of Wappingers Falls, New York.

Concerning the move to a lower level of ball, Tampa Bay minor-league director Tom Foley said, "We wanted to give him more opportunities to pitch."[12]

On July 25, 2000, Hudson Valley's number 5 starter, Nate Comer, was slated to pitch, but was injured. Malaska was tagged to start in an away game against the Queens Kings, a New York Mets affiliate. He pitched four innings, without a decision.

His second start was on August 18. With a 0-1 record and a 7.07 ERA, he entered a home game at Dutchess Stadium against the Boston Red Sox affiliate Lowell Spinners. Although the Renegades lost 1-0, the 22-year-old threw five shutout innings. About his outing, Malaska said, "Every time that I go out there, I'm improving, I'm learning the little things, the normal things that experienced pitchers already know."[13]

With the Renegades, Malaska was in 10 games, five of them as starter, with a record of 0-2 in 40⅓ innings pitched, 36 strikeouts, and a 4.91 ERA.

In 2001 Malaska found himself back with the Charleston RiverDogs. As a starter in 25 games, he posted a 7-12 record, 157 innings pitched, 152 strikeouts, and a 2.92 ERA with one complete game. Malaska ranked eighth among South Atlantic League starters in strikeouts and his ERA placed him in the 12th slot.

His 2001 season included a stint with Devil Rays' Advanced Class-A club, the Bakersfield Blaze (California League). During that tenure, with 17⅔ innings pitched, he had a 2-1 record, with 13 strikeouts and a 4.08 ERA. That year overall, Malaska tied the Tampa Bay organizational lead in strikeouts.

In 2002 Mark was cited by *Baseball America* as the 29th rated prospect in the Devil Rays organization. At Bakersfield, he had a 7-4 record with two complete games. The California League All-Star tossed 91⅓ innings with 94 strikeouts and only 12 walks, with a 2.96 ERA. He placed second in the California League in shutouts with two.[14]

That same season, Malaska got playing time for the Rays of Florida – the Double-A Orlando Rays (Southern League). At this higher level of baseball, Malaska appeared in 12 games, 11 of which he started. In 70⅔ innings pitched he went 4-5, with one save, one complete game, 49 strikeouts, and a 3.69 ERA.

Malaska and right-hander Brandon Backe led the six Tampa Bay minor-league clubs in complete games with three games each for 2002.

The next year, Malaska played on two Devil Rays farm clubs – Orlando and then Tampa's Triple-A affiliate, the Durham Bulls (International League). At Orlando, in 19 relief appearances he went 1-1 with one save and a 2.16 ERA. Promoted to the Bulls, he made 15 relief outings and had a 1-1 record with a 4.30 ERA.

Tampa Bay needed a left-handed arm in the bullpen, and Malaska was called up.

On July 17, 2003, his first day with the Devil Rays, the 25-year-old made his major-league debut. In a home night game at Tropicana Field against the Texas Rangers, manager Lou Piniella called Malaska in from the bullpen in the top of the ninth inning. The Rangers were leading 11-3.

Malaska replaced Brandon Backe, who had just walked Rangers third baseman Donnie Sadler. (Coincidentally, Backe was also originally a position player converted to a pitcher.) With a man on first, Malaska faced Bo Díaz. He walked the Texas catcher. The Rangers' leadoff hitter, Michael Young, hit into a fielder's choice that forced Diaz but now put runners at the corners. Center fielder Doug Glanville singled to left field, allowing Sadler to score and Young to advance to second. Texas shortstop Álex Rodríguez – later named the 2003 AL MVP – came to the plate. Malaska got Rodriguez to hit into a double play, ending the frame. Malaska said by getting "ARod .... to ground into a double play it was def my 'welcome to the big leagues' moment."[15]

Nine days later, with one scoreless inning of relief in between, Malaska got his first major-league win, against the Chicago White Sox on July 26 at US Cellular Field. In a tie game, he faced Carl Everett in the bottom of the fifth and retired him to close out the inning. Tampa Bay scored four runs in the top of the sixth and ultimately prevailed, 10-6. As the pitcher of record at the end of five, Malaska was awarded the win.

For the 2003 season, the Devil Rays rookie appeared as a reliever in 22 games with 16 innings pitched, 17 strikeouts, a 2-1 record and a 2.81 ERA.

Nonetheless, after the season ended Tampa placed him on waivers.

On December 8, 2003, Red Sox general manager Theo Epstein announced that Boston had claimed Malaska off the waiver wire. On March 30, at the end of spring training, he was optioned to the Triple-A Pawtucket Red Sox.

During the 2004 season, Malaska was shuffled between the Triple-A PawSox and the parent club. Perhaps two ardent Red Sox fans best described his pitching efforts during Boston's legendary run to make the fall classic. In their book *Faithful*, which chronicled the renowned season, novelists Stewart O'Nan and Stephen King have an entry for the April 9, 2004, home game against the Toronto Blue Jays. To try to safeguard a 5-4 lead after six innings, manager Terry Francona called upon "Mystery Malaska who didn't make the club … brought up from Pawtucket because we went through the entire pen last night."[16] The writers noted that the left-hander was to face tough Toronto batsmen Frank Catalanotto, Vernon Wells, and 2003 AL RBIs leader Carlos Delgado. "And he does, one-two-three, Mystery Malaska!"[17]

On April 11, in an extra-inning day game against the visiting Blue Jays, "Mystery" Malaska logged his first victory as a Boston Red Sox pitcher. With the score knotted, 4-4, he was brought in the 11th inning and replaced another left-hander, Bobby Jones. Malaska faced three batters, struck out one, and got the other two out. He returned in the 12th inning and retired the side in order. In the bottom of the 12th, Boston's Bill Mueller walked and David Ortiz homered to win the game, 6-4.

On May 14 Boston recalled Kevin Youkilis from Pawtucket and optioned Malaska to the Rhode Island farm club. On June 9 he was promoted back to Boston as Red Sox right-hander Jamie Brown was returned to the PawSox. On June 22 the Red Sox signed right-hander Curtis Leskanic and relegated Malaska to Pawtucket. On July 21 Boston recalled both Malaska and Kevin Youkilis from the PawSox. With second baseman Pokey Reese on the 15-day disabled list and reliever Scott Williamson recovering from injury, the Red Sox were making moves to bolster their infield and pitching positions.[18]

Malaska's final game as a member of the Boston Red Sox occurred on July 24, 2004, at Fenway Park against their archrivals the New York Yankees. After a six-run rally by the Yankees in the sixth inning that eliminated a one-run Red Sox lead, New York led 9-4. With two outs, Malaska was brought in from the bullpen. Hideki Matsui was at the plate. Earlier in the inning the Yankee outfielder had doubled to start the scoring spree. Malaska got the New Yorker out on a called third strike, gave up a leadoff homer in the seventh to Rubén Sierra and then saw the next two Yankees reach on errors. He was replaced by Alan Embree. The contest finished with a come-from-behind ninth-inning 11-10 Red Sox victory.

On August 6, 2004, Malaska was returned to Pawtucket. With the International League club, his 2004 season numbers were a 1-1 record, one save, 36⅓ innings pitched, 31 strikeouts, and a 4.21 ERA. With Boston, he had also been 1-1, with 20 innings pitched and a 4.50 ERA.

He received a World Series ring as part of the 2004 Boston Red Sox championship team.

Throughout the 2005 season, the 27-year-old remained with Pawtucket. He had a 5-3 record, one save, 87 innings pitched, 86 strikeouts, and a 4.14 ERA. After the season he was released by the Boston organization.

On January 11, 2006, Malaska returned to the Devil Rays and signed as a free agent. But during spring training he abruptly left camp. Contemporary news articles had statements made only by his father as to Mark's departure. Those reports note Malaska felt he could pitch in "The Show" but there was a lack of desire to continue as a pro ballplayer. On March 15, 2006, he retired from baseball.

However, there was much more going on with Malaska, the man. In a 2023 interview he capsulized his career as that of a fringe big leaguer. The back-and-forth from the minors to the majors had taken a mental toll on him. In fact, he believed he deserved to be called up by Boston in the late 2005 season.

"I was tired. Mentally. I was engulfed in the party life off the field and was battling alcohol addiction."[19] His brother's death was ever-present. "I was carrying a lot of that baggage too. I sat at my locker after the game and just decided that was it. I couldn't do it anymore. Wanted a 'normal' life. I told some people at home I was injured but I was fine physically. So I just left without saying a word and drove 21 hours home and never looked back. Didn't return any of my agent's calls or media outlet calls."[20]

Malaska returned to his Providence, Rhode Island, residence. He got married, but his battles with alcohol dependency took a toll on the union. Less than two years later, he found himself divorced.

In 2011 Malaska discovered his soulmate, Shelby, and married her. Having moved back to Ohio, he sought and got help to deal with his personal demons. He conquered his addiction problems.[21]

His off-the-field employment path took him into the world of finance and sales.

Even so in his post-baseball career, there were accolades. Malaska was inducted into the NECBL Hall of Fame in 2010. In 2012 Cardinal Mooney High School inducted him into its athletic Hall of Fame. And two years later, the Danbury Westerners retired their first number, Malaska's 15.

How did the southpaw feel about pitching in Fenway Park with the looming Green Monster? "The Green Monster didn't bother me. I was just thrilled to play in such a historic ballpark."[22]

Looking back at the Red Sox' 2004 legendary breaking-the-curse campaign, his fondest memory is that April 11 game. "Pitching a few scoreless innings on Easter Sunday and getting the win on a Big Papi walk-off home run with my parents in town."[23]

As of 2023, Malaska plied his financial expertise as the business manager for a Youngstown automotive dealership, #1 Cochran Cars. He resided in Canfield, Ohio, with his wife, Shelby; son, Benjamin; and daughter, Alexandra.

NOTES

1. "Baseball's Mooney Malaska Hoping for a Bright Future in Boston," December 23, 2003, *Vindicator* (Warren, Ohio), https://vindyarchives.com/news/2003/dec/29/baseball-mooneys-malaska-hoping-for-bright-future/.
2. He added, "My dad was always very active with me and he always encouraged me, but he was hands off, never pressuring me to play." "Baseball's Mooney Malaska Hoping for a Bright Future in Boston."
3. http://www.necbl.com/view/necbl/.
4. Author interview with Mark Malaska, September 20, 2023.
5. http://www.necbl.com/files/uploaded_documents/2083/1998_NECBL_Season_Stats006_2.pdf.
6. http://www.necbl.com/files/uploaded_documents/2083/1999_NECBL_Season_Stats_2.pdf.
7. Sal Interdonato, "Ex-Outfielder Gets More Time on Mound for Renegades," *Middletown* (New York) *Times Herald-Record,* August 19, 2000.. https://www.recordonline.com/story/news/2000/08/19/ex-outfielder-gets-more-time/51195800007/. Accessed October 14, 2023.
8. Interdonato.
9. Malaska interview, September 20, 2023.
10. https://www.baseballamerica.com/stories/2000-draft-signing-bonuses/.
11. Malaska interview, November 20, 2023.
12. Interdonato.
13. Interdonato.
14. https://www.statscrew.com/minorbaseball/l-CALL/y-2002.
15. Malaska interview, October 29, 2023.
16. Stewart O'Nan and Stephen King, *Faithful: Two Diehard Boston Red Sox Fans Chronicle the Historic 2004 Season* (New York: Simon & Schuster, 2005), 44.
17. O'Nan and King, 44.
18. https://fenwayparkdiaries.com/2004%20red%20sox/sox%2007-21-2004.htm.
19. Malaska interview, November 20, 2023.
20. Malaska interview, November 20, 2023.
21. Malaska interview, November 4, 2023.
22. Malaska interview, September 20, 2023.
23. Malaska interview, September 20, 2023.

ANASTACIO MARTÍNEZ

BY ERIC CONRAD AND MARK MOROWCZYNSKI

Anastacio Euclides Martínez was a right-handed pitcher who spent 13 years playing professional baseball, mostly in the Red Sox organization. He spent most of his career as a starter before being converted to a reliever in 2003. He played one season in the majors, appearing in 11 games for the World Series champion 2004 Red Sox, appearing in 11 games (10⅔ innings) with a 2-1 record, five strikeouts, and an 8.44 ERA.

Martínez was born on November 3, 1978, in Villa Mella, Distrito Nacional, Dominican Republic. He attended high school at Liceo Santa Cruz de Villa Mella. Recalling his childhood, he said, "My mom and dad were always very close. We spent lots of time together and always looked out for each other: I have happy memories with my family." His parents, Pedro Martínez and Susana Martínez Gonzalez, had a family farm – a working ranch – and Pedro sold meat as a butcher, while his mother took care of the family and the ranch. "My parents were attentive and always supported everything I did," Anastacio said. "I practiced baseball here in Villa Mella before being signed. My life was just studying and playing baseball at that moment."[1]

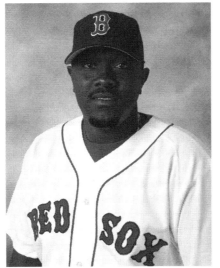

Martínez was signed by the Red Sox as a nondrafted free agent on January 6, 1998. He pitched two games for the Dominican Summer League Red Sox that year before being promoted to the rookie-level Gulf Coast League Red Sox in Fort Myers, Florida. He appeared in 12 games (starting 10), compiling a 2-3 record with a 3.18 ERA and 50 strikeouts in 51 innings.

Martínez began the 1999 season with the Augusta GreenJackets of the Class-A South Atlantic League, starting 10 games with a 2-4 record and a 6.30 ERA. He finished the year with the short-season Class-A Lowell Spinners, going 0-3 in 11 starts with a 3.68 ERA.

Martínez played for two teams in 2000, appearing in two games for the GCL Red Sox (going 0-1 with a 9.45 ERA) before returning to the GreenJackets. On August 20, 2000, he took a no-hitter into the ninth inning against the Asheville Tourists two days after teammate Eric Glaser pitched a no-hitter against the Hagerstown Suns.[2]

He gave up a one-out single to Jim Rinne on his 130th pitch of the game. Martínez recorded 14 strikeouts. It was the first time he pitched past the seventh inning and the first time he threw over 100 pitches that season.[3] In a postgame interview, Martínez said, "I was upset that it didn't happen, but I feel very proud of what I did today. I wish I could have pitched a no-hitter, but I think this is a pretty good day for me."[4] Augusta catcher Kelly Ramos said, "He has very good stuff, and that is the best stuff he's had this season. It is too bad that he didn't get his no-hitter, but he should be happy with what he did today. The last two or three starts he is pitching the best he has pitched all year."[5]

Martínez had 23 starts for Augusta that season, with a 9-6 record, a 4.64 ERA, and 107 strikeouts in 120 innings pitched. The GreenJackets went 83-58 that year, winning the division title.

As the 2001 season began Martínez was promoted to the Sarasota Red Sox of the High-A Florida State League. He began to pitcher deeper into games, going six innings or more in 17 of his 24 starts, and improved as the season went on. His April ERA was 5.79 after five outings. In his next 20 starts, his ERA was 2.77.[6] Martínez led the team with 145 innings pitched, 24 games started, and 123 strikeouts. He ended the season with a 9-12 record and a 3.35 ERA. He pitched a career-high 145 innings.

Martínez played the entire 2002 season with the Trenton Thunder of the Double-A Eastern League, compiling a record of 5-12 and 139 innings pitched. He struck out 127, the second most of any Red Sox minor-league pitcher and was third in strikeouts in the Eastern League. His record doesn't fully reflect his performance. When allowing three runs or fewer, Martínez received a loss or a no-decision in 12 of those starts. He allowed two runs or fewer in 11 starts.[7]

2003 saw Martínez's role change from starter to relief pitcher. He started in Triple A with the Pawtucket Red Sox but was moved down to the Double-A Portland Sea Dogs.[8] On July 22, 2003, Martínez and Brandon Lyon were traded to the Pittsburgh Pirates for Scott Sauerbeck and Mike González.

Martínez was assigned to the Altoona Curve of the Double-A Eastern League, for whom he pitched in only three games. Ten days later the same trade essentially occurred again, in reverse. The Pirates sent Martínez, Brandon Lyon, and Jeff Suppan back to Boston for Mike González and Freddy Sanchez. This was due to elbow concerns with Lyon's elbow.[9] Martínez finished the season with Portland, leading the team in saves with 14 through 40 innings pitched. He did not allow an earned run in 25 of his 34 outings and allowed more than one earned run just once.[10] He was called up back to Triple-A Pawtucket on

August 1, and finished the season with a record of 2-1, with 15 strikeouts in 14 innings pitched.

With the Pawtucket Red Sox in 2004, Martínez pitched in 38 games, with a 3-3 record, 57 strikeouts in 58⅔ innings, and a 3.74 ERA over the course of the year. He was called up to the Red Sox in May, and won his first appearance in relief of fellow Dominican Pedro Martínez (no relation) against the Toronto Blue Jays on May 22, 2004. He relieved Pedro in the seventh inning with the game tied 2-2. He pitched a perfect seventh, beginning by striking out Simon Pond. Orlando Hudson then grounded out and Frank Menechino flied out to center. Mark Bellhorn gave the Red Sox a 3-2 lead with a bases-loaded single in the bottom of the inning. Martínez gave up a bunt single to Reed Johnson to open the eighth and was relieved by Alan Embree. Keith Foulke closed the game in the ninth. All three relievers pitched scoreless ball.

After the game Pedro Martínez said, "I'm happy to see Anastacio get a win in his first try. I'm very happy for him. This game was televised live in the Dominican Republic so his family got to see him. It's his first win. I know how big that is."[11] Pedro then acted as an English interpreter for Anastacio for a postgame interview; Anastacio said he "had butterflies before the first pitch, but I was comfortable after that."[12]

Anastacio later recalled that game. "It was an unforgettable experience: My family was super happy at home, enjoying and celebrating the triumph. It was an honor to have stood in for a person so important in my country like Pedro Martínez. No matter how many times I talk about it, I always feel proud to have relieved a gentleman like him. I had a good relationship with him; we supported each other and kept an eye out for each other. He's a tremendous human being and a tremendous person."[13]

Anastacio continued to work out of the bullpen with the Red Sox, frequently entering the game in the seventh. He picked up his second win on May 30 against the Seattle Mariners, entering in the 11th against the heart of the order to face Raul Ibanez, Bret Boone, and John Olerud. Martínez stranded one runner in the 11th and in the 12th allowed no runners to reach base, including Ichiro Suzuki. In the bottom of the 12th, right fielder Dave McCarty hit a two-run walk-off home run off J.J. Putz for a 9-7 win for Boston.

Martínez's next notable outing was on June 9 against the San Diego Padres. He entered in the seventh with the Red Sox down 4-0. Mark Loretta led off the inning with a double and Phil Nevin homered, leaving the Red Sox down 6-0 when he completed the inning. Boston lost the game 8-1.

Three days later, on June 12, Martínez relieved Tim Wakefield in the fifth inning against the Los Angeles Dodgers with the Red Sox down 5-2 and the bases loaded. It was the worst outing of his season; he allowed all three inherited runners to score, hitting a batter and giving up a single and two walks to leave the game down 9-2 with three on. Mark Malaska allowed two of those runners to score, leaving Martínez charged with four earned runs.

Martínez's final appearance in the majors, and with the Red Sox, came on July 2 against the Atlanta Braves. He entered the game in the bottom of the 11th and allowed a single to Adam LaRoche. The 12th didn't go as smoothly. A single by Mark DeRosa and a double by Rafael Furcal set up a walk-off three-run home run by Nick Green to end the game 6-3. He was optioned back to Triple-A Pawtucket, where he finished the season.

Martínez's cousin, catcher Angel "Sandy" Martínez, also played (later in the season) for the 2004 Red Sox. They are the only relatives to play for a Red Sox World Series champion team.

In March 2005 the Red Sox released Martínez but re-signed him two weeks later. He spent the entire season once again in Pawtucket. He appeared in 35 games (6 starts). His record was 3-4 with one save over 58⅔ innings with 46 strikeouts. Martínez was released on October 15, 2005.

The Washington Nationals signed Martínez on February 6, 2006, and assigned him to the Double-A Harrisburg Senators. He started two games, going 2-0 with a 3.65 ERA and 11 strikeouts through 12⅓ innings pitched before being promoted to the Triple-A New Orleans Zephyrs. Martínez continued to work as a starter in 24 games. He led the team with 115 strikeouts in 128⅔ innings. He allowed the second most earned runs on the team, ending his season with a 4.48 ERA and a 5-11 record. At the plate, he recorded five hits and two RBIs, the sum total of all his minor- and major-league career.

After the season, Martínez joined the Estrellas de Oriente of the Dominican Winter League. He started three games, going 0-1 with a 2.45 ERA.

On January 18, 2007, the Nationals optioned Martínez to the Double-A Harrisburg Senators. He was used as a starter, going 0-2 with a 4.88 ERA through 24 innings pitched before being moved back up to Triple A with the International League's Columbus Clippers, where he split his time starting and in relief. (2-3, 4.73 ERA).

On June 20, 2007, the Nationals sold Martínez's contract to the Detroit Tigers,[14] who optioned him to Triple-A Toledo. He was once again used as a starter and reliever, finishing 4-4, 4.24. Again he played in the Dominican Winter League for the Estrellas de Oriente

The 2008 season was Martínez's last in Organized Baseball. He started the season with Toledo, but was sent down to the Double-A Erie SeaWolves after going 2-7 with a 5.29 ERA. For the SeaWolves he made only three appearances in relief, and was released on September 5, 2008. Martínez once again pitched in the Dominican Winter League with the Estrellas de Oriente.

For the 2009 season, Martínez signed with the Sinon Bulls in Taichung, Taiwan, of the Chinese Professional Baseball League. Once again he worked in the dual role of starter and reliever.

Martínez recalled his playing time in Taiwan, including difficulties he faced. "It was very difficult to play in Taiwan, especially with the language, but we survived," he said. "If you like to play baseball, you have to get used to surviving however you can. At first it was difficult, but I got used to it in the end.

But it was hard being in a place so different from my home. One time we practiced at a university where they had never seen or met anyone with my skin color – everyone was surprised and staring. But it was a good experience, and I was with one of my friends as well, Wilton Veras."[15]

Martínez returned to North America for the 2010 season with the Calgary Vipers of the independent Golden Baseball League as a starter. He made nine starts in his 10 appearances and finished with a 2-4 record, 43 innings pitched, and a 7.74 ERA. As a batter he was 4-for-15.

As of 2023 Martínez worked with José Offerman at his baseball academy in the Dominican Republic.[16] He and his wife, Nieves, have a daughter, Susan. In his 2023 interview, he said, "I have my wife and my daughter. She's 10 years old. Our life here is quiet and relaxed." Looking back on his career, he recalled, "There is nothing better than being beside so many superstars like Pedro Martínez, David Ortiz, and Manny Ramírez. I don't think there is a better experience than that. It was unforgettable and so special."[17]

SOURCES

Sources used include a telephone interview conducted with Anastacio Martínez on September 23, 2023, and multiple articles from the *Augusta Chronicle* and the *Boston Globe*. Thanks as well to Sandy Martínez.

Statistics were taken from the *Red Sox Media Guide*, Baseball-Reference.com, and Baseball Almanac.

NOTES

1. Anastacio Martínez, telephone interview, September 23, 2023. Interview conducted and translated from Spanish by Emma Conrad.
2. Rob Mueller, "Single in Ninth Inning – Spoils Second No-Hitter," *Augusta* (Georgia) *Chronicle*, August 21, 2000: C01.
3. *2004 Boston Red Sox Media Guide*, https://archive.org/details/bostonredsoxmedi2004bost/.
4. Mueller.
5. Mueller.
6. *2004 Boston Red Sox Media Guide*.
7. *2004 Boston Red Sox Media Guide*.
8. Rich Thompson, "PawSox' Trek Tough Without Stars," *Boston Herald*, May 23, 2003.
9. Bill Ballou, "Back to Boston for Suppan, Lyon," *Worcester* (Massachusetts) *Telegram & Gazette*, August 1, 2003.
10. Mueller.
11. Alan Wood, "Going Deep for the Win," *Nashua* (New Hampshire) *Telegraph*, May 23, 2004: C-1.
12. Wood.
13. Martínez interview.
14. https://www.baseball-almanac.com/players/trades.php?p=martian01.
15. Martínez interview.
16. https://www.instagram.com/jobaseballacademy/?hl=en.
17. Martínez interview.

A RED SOX MEMORY

On October 17, 2004, the morning after the Yankees trounced the Red Sox to take a three-games-to-none lead in the ALCS, my friend Brett called my Maryland home to commiserate.

"I know this isn't much consolation," he said. "But if the Red Sox somehow make the World Series, we've got tickets to Games One and Two at Fenway." Brett worked for a travel agency that sold sports-themed packages. He'd run into future Sox President Sam Kennedy the night before, and Sam promised to hook us up with Series tickets.

Of course, trailing 3-0, we'd likely never get to use them. Brett and I had been attending Red Sox games together since meeting at Quinnipiac College in Connecticut in 1976.

We'd been to numerous home openers, Yaz's final game in 1983, and spring training games in Winter Haven, but never a Series game.

I pretty much forgot about the tickets as the Sox rallied to win Games Four and Five. Finally, about halfway through ALCS Game Six, I took a leap of faith and reserved a flight and hotel room in Boston.

As we parted on the T following Game Two, I told Brett, "Our lives could be changing forever." He nodded. I only wish the rest of his life was as happy as those two chilly nights in Boston. Brett passed away six years later.

WALT CHERNIAK

PEDRO MARTÍNEZ

BY NORM KING

Fred Claire wasn't a politician. However, like many politicians, the erstwhile executive vice president of the Los Angeles Dodgers said one thing when he was talking about Pedro Martínez in 1992, ended up doing the opposite, and regretted his action.

"I won't trade Pedro Martínez, I don't care who they offer," said Claire.[1]

Well, he did trade Martínez, and lost the services of one of the best pitchers of the last 50 years, a three-time Cy Young Award-winning pitcher with a career 219-100 record and a lifetime 2.93 ERA. More on the trade later.

Pedro Jaime Martínez was born October 25, 1971, in Manoguayabo, Distrito Nacional, Dominican Republic, the fifth of six children born to Paolino and Leopoldina Martínez. Manoguayabo was a poverty-ridden town nine miles from the country's capital of Santo Domingo, and the family lived in a tin-roofed hovel with dirt floors. Paolino supported the family by working as a janitor and performing odd jobs, while Leopoldina took in laundry. The Martínez children grew up poor, but they were well dressed for school and they took their education seriously.

They also took baseball seriously…very seriously. Pedro, along with his older brother Ramón, had pitching in their genes thanks to Paolino, who was a top-flight pitcher during the 1950s (he played with future big leaguers Felipe and Matty Alou, both of whom said he was good enough to play in the majors) with a mean sinkerball.

"I was too poor to leave the country," Paolino said. "When the Giants invited me for a tryout, I didn't have cleats. So I couldn't go to the tryout."[2]

Nonetheless, the young Martínez boys grew up playing baseball, using tree branches or other sticks they could find to fashion bats. For balls they would re-enact the French Revolution with their sisters' dolls. "When my sisters came home from school, they'd find [the dolls] with no head and they would go, 'Mommy! Mommy!'" he said.[3]

In addition to having his father as a pitching role model, Pedro looked up to his brother Ramón both on and off the field. Almost four years older than Pedro, Ramón became de facto head of the household when Paolino and Leopoldina divorced when he was 13, showing a maturity and leadership that influences Pedro to this day.

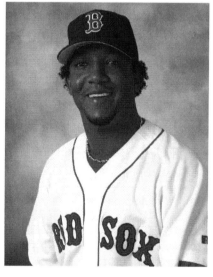

"What I know of baseball, and life off the field, I owe to Ramón," said Martínez. "Everything I am I learned from Ramón."[4]

Ramón pitched for the Dominican Republic team during the 1984 Olympics in Los Angeles at age 17, and was signed as a free agent by Los Angeles Dodgers scout Raphael "Ralph" Avila on September 1 of that year. The Dodgers sent him to their baseball academy back in the Dominican Republic to begin his professional career.

In the grand tradition of annoying little brothers everywhere, 13-year-old Pedro tagged along when Ramón went to the academy. Avila eventually noticed him tossing a ball around and decided to put the radar gun to his fastball – it clocked in at 80 miles per hour. Wisely, Avila told Pedro to keep on pitching. Pedro did just that, and in 1988, Avila signed Pedro, now 16, to get him into the Dodger fold before he could turn professional. Pedro continued pitching locally in 1988-89 with the Dodgers' Dominican Summer League affiliate, going a combined 12-3 over the two seasons.

Finally, in 1990 at age 18, he began his climb through the Dodgers' minor-league system with Great Falls of the rookie-level Pioneer League. His season was a harbinger of things to come, as he went 8-3 with a 3.62 ERA. His victory total was the highest on the team, as was his walk total of 40 in 77 innings.

His performance earned him a trip through the southwest United States in 1991. He started off in Bakersfield of the Class-A California League, where he won all eight of his decisions with a 2.05 ERA. Since it was clear that he was too good for that level, he then moved to San Antonio of the Double-A Texas League, and while his record there was only 7-5, he had a sparkling 1.76 ERA, prompting the parent club to move him yet again, this time to the Albuquerque Dukes of the Triple-A Pacific Coast League. Martínez struggled at this level, only going 3-3 with a 3.66 ERA.

Overall, Martínez went 18-8 with a 2.28 ERA and 192 strikeouts and 66 walks in 177 1/3 innings pitched, becoming the first player to go through three levels in the Dodgers' system in one season, since brother Ramón did it three years earlier. *The Sporting News* named him its minor league player of the year.

"Although Pedro stands just 5-9 and weighs about 160 pounds, his fastball has been clocked at 90 mph," wrote Mike

Eisenbath. "He also has a wicked changeup that seems to be a family gift."[5]

It was in spring training 1992 that Claire uttered his fateful words. Martínez was doing well at Dodgertown, the team's spring training facility in Florida at the time, and his reputation was growing to the extent that other teams asked about him. At the time, he wasn't going anywhere except Albuquerque, because the Dodgers felt that another year of seasoning at Triple A was in order for the 20-year-old.

In 1992, Martínez went 7-6 with a 3.81 ERA, but with 124 strikeouts in 125 1/3 innings pitched and only 57 walks. His overall season earned him a September call-up and his first major-league start, a 3-1 complete game loss at Cincinnati.

Pedro had a good spring training in 1993 but was sent down again to Albuquerque just before the season began, but after pitching only three innings in one game with the Dukes, he returned to the Dodgers on April 9 after reliever Todd Worrell was placed on the 15-day disabled list.

He got into his first Dodger game that year, coming on for brother Ramón, who had only given up one run in six innings to the Atlanta Braves, but was down 1-0. Pedro gave up two more runs in 1 2/3 innings. The final score was 3-0. Pedro and Ramón became the first brothers to pitch in the same game for the same team since Rick and Mickey Mahler did it in 1979 for, as it happens, the Braves.

His next appearance, and first loss of the season, came the following night in the Dodgers' opener home against St. Louis. Gerald Perry of the Cardinals arrived at the ballpark less than hour before game time because he thought it was a night game. Martínez wished he had stayed away because Perry hit a three-run homer off him in the seventh inning to erase a 7-5 Dodgers lead. The final score was 9-7 St. Louis.

Although the season didn't start the way he would have wanted, Pedro righted his pitching ship and went on to have a very good rookie year. He appeared in 65 games, all but two of them in relief, and finished with a 10-5 record and a fine 2.61 ERA. Perhaps his most impressive statistic was his 119 strikeouts in 107 innings pitched.

Good rookie season notwithstanding, Claire did indeed hear a trade offer that he couldn't refuse, and in November sent Martínez to the Montreal Expos in exchange for speedy second baseman Delino DeShields. For the Expos it was a cost-cutting move, as DeShields made $1,537,500 in 1993 and was eligible for arbitration. Martínez, on the other hand, had made $114,000 the previous season and couldn't go for arbitration for another two years.

The Dodgers had used Martínez almost exclusively in relief because they didn't think he had the size and strength to pitch deep into ballgames. The Expos saw him as a starting pitcher despite weighing less than 160 pounds, and put him into the starting rotation with Ken Hill, Jeff Fassero, Butch Henry, and Kirk Rueter.

It is well known among baseball aficionados that the 1994 Montreal Expos had the best record in baseball at 74-40 when their season and a possible World Series appearance were derailed by a players' strike. The pitching staff had the lowest ERA in the National League (3.56), and Martínez was a major contributor to the team's success. He went 11-5 with a 3.42 ERA and 142 strikeouts in 144 2/3 innings.

He also became known as a headhunter for his tendency to pitch high and inside, and acquired the nickname "Senor Plunk" from the Montreal media. He led the league in hit batsmen with 11, got thrown out of 12 games and got into three fights. That first fight occurred on April 13, when Reggie Sanders charged the mound after being hit on the elbow by a Martínez pitch with one out in the eighth inning. Even Sanders' teammates thought it highly unlikely that Martínez tried to deliberately to hit him at that point because Martínez was pitching a perfect game at the time.

"That's the way you've got to pitch," said Reds catcher Brian Dorsett, who broke up the no-hitter in the ninth by hitting a single with nobody out in the top of the ninth. "You've got to bust them in and keep them honest."[6]

"He's not trying to hit anyone," said Expos pitching coach Joe Kerrigan. "He isn't a malicious kid."[7]

An Expos fire sale saw the Expos lose Hill, Larry Walker, Marquis Grissom, and John Wetteland prior to the 1995 season. What had been a powerhouse the year before was an also-ran team that finished last in the National League East Division with a 66-78 record. Nonetheless, Martínez continued improving, going 14-10 with a 3.51 ERA and 174 K's in 194 2/3 innings. He hit 11 batters again, but that represented an improvement because he pitched 30 more innings than he had the previous year, and left him in third place among league leaders behind Mark Leiter of the Giants with 17 and Darryl Kile of Houston with 12.

The highlight of Martínez' 1995 season, and perhaps of his career, came on June 3 against the Padres in San Diego. That night Martínez became only the second pitcher in history to take a perfect game into extra innings. Harvey Haddix went 12 perfect innings for the Pirates against the Braves in 1959 before losing his no-hitter and the game in the 13th. Pedro was perfect through nine, but the score was still 0-0. The Expos scored once in the top of the 10th, but Martínez gave up a double in the bottom of the 10th to leadoff hitter Bip Roberts. Closer Mel Rojas relieved him and got the next three hitters to preserve the win.

The Expos bounced back in 1996 with an 88-74 record, missing out on the National League wild card by two games. On the surface, it looks as if Martínez' season wasn't quite as good as the year before; he went 13-10, with the highest ERA of his career to date, 3.70. His won-loss record was hampered by the fact that the Expos only scored 22 runs in the 10 losses. Nonetheless, he got his first All-Star nod and gave up two hits in one inning of work as the National League shut out the American League, 6-0, in Philadelphia.

Any questions about Martínez' abilities were answered in 1997. In the same season that DeShields left the Dodgers after three unspectacular seasons (.241 batting average and .326

on-base percentage from 1994-96), Martínez went 17-8, led the league with a 1.90 ERA, 305 strikeouts, and 13 complete games. He also struck out two American League hitters in one inning of work at the All-Star Game. He became the first and only Cy Young Award winner in Expos history, receiving 25 of 28 first-place votes (Greg Maddux got the other three). For Martínez, the award was more than a mere personal accolade, as he became the first Dominican pitcher to win it. Not only was he proud of that, he felt that fellow Dominican Juan Marichal should have won it at least once during his great career. He even gave his award to Marichal at a banquet after the season ended. Marichal, though deeply touched by the gesture, returned it back to Martínez.

From an Expos standpoint, the first Cy Young Award in the team's history was worth celebrating only because it increased Martínez' trade value. Pedro was one year away from free agency and Expos management wanted to trade him while they could still get something for him. Eventually they sent him to the Boston Red Sox for Carl Pavano and Tony Armas. After the trade, Martínez signed a six-year contract with the Red Sox worth $75 million, making him the highest-paid pitcher in baseball at the time.

The 1997 Red Sox under Jimy Williams finished fourth in the American League East Division with a 78-84 record. With Martínez in the rotation in 1998, Williams suddenly became a much better manager, piloting the Red Sox to a 92-70 record, good enough for second place in the division and the wild card playoff spot. Pedro had another magnificent season, going 19-7 with a 2.89 ERA and 251 strikeouts. He was an All-Star for the third straight season — for the American League this time — but didn't appear in the game. He finished second in the Cy Young voting behind Roger Clemens of the Toronto Blue Jays.

Martínez also got his first taste of postseason action, as he took the mound in Game One of the American League Division Series against the Cleveland Indians. Pedro pitched seven strong innings, giving up three runs, striking out eight and not giving up any walks as the Red Sox won easily, 11-3. It was his only appearance of the series, as the Indians went on to win the next three and move on to the American League Championship Series.

Martínez had a season for the ages in 1999. He won the pitcher's triple crown, leading the league in wins (23 against four losses), ERA (2.07), and strikeouts (313). He not only started and won the All-Star Game for the American League at Fenway Park, but he did it in style, striking out five of the six batters he faced in two innings' work. He was also chosen the game's MVP.

The Red Sox again made the playoffs as the wild card in a rematch from 1998 against the Indians. Martínez started Game One and pitched four scoreless innings before leaving with a strained back muscle. Cleveland scored in the bottom of the ninth to win it, 3-2. Boston won two of the next three to knot the series at two going into Game Five. Meanwhile, the knot in Martínez' back disappeared.

Bret Saberhagen started the decider for Boston and was replaced by Derek Lowe in the second inning. After three innings, the score was 8-7 Cleveland. The Red Sox tied it in the top of the fourth; then on came Martínez in the bottom of the inning. What happened next became part of Red Sox lore.

For the next five innings, Martínez completely silenced the Indian bats. He threw 97 pitches, allowed no runs and no hits, walked three and struck out eight. In the meantime, the Sox scored four more runs to take a 12-8 lead. Martínez showed a sense of style by striking out Omar Vizquel to end the game and the series.

Martínez was the only bright spot in the ALCS against the Yankees, which the Bombers won in five games. Roger Clemens was now with the Yankees, and what was hyped as a big showdown between Pedro and Clemens in Game Three at Fenway ended up as games that are hyped as big showdowns often do. The Sox hammered Clemens for five runs in two innings and won going away, 13-1. Martínez pitched seven scoreless innings for the win.

While the Y2K scare was nothing more than hype in the hi-tech industry, Martínez' year 2000 deserved all the publicity it got. He won his second consecutive Cy Young Award by unanimous vote with an 18-6 record, and he led the American League in ERA (1.74), shutouts (4), and strikeouts (284). His season was especially impressive because it came at the height of the steroid era, when the overall American League ERA that year was 4.91. He held opponents to the lowest on-base percentage against (.213) in 100 years.[8] The Red Sox finished second yet again in their division, but did not make the playoffs.

The 2001 season was an odyssey of frustration and disappointment for Martínez as he contended with major injury for the first time in his career. He missed two months after with a minor rotator cuff tear, and did not pitch the rest of the season after a September 7 3-2 loss to the Yankees. He also got into a dispute with general manager Dan Duquette, who said in early September that Martínez was healthy enough to pitch. "I think Dan knows as much about medicine as I do, maybe less," said Martínez. "That's why I'm surprised he said I'm healthy."[9]

For the year, Martínez was 7-3 in 18 starts with a respectable 2.69 ERA in 116 2/3 innings pitched.

Pedro bounced back in 2002 with a vengeance. He reached the 20-win plateau for the second time (20-4), won the ERA and strikeout titles (2.26 ERA, 239 K's) and was voted to the All-Star team, although he didn't play in the game (the infamous 7-7 tie in Milwaukee). He also finished second in the Cy Young Award voting to Oakland's Barry Zito.

Pedro's 2003 season will be remembered for two controversial incidents he was involved in during that year's ALCS against the Yankees.

Martínez had a 14-4 record that season and won the ERA title again with a 2.22 average. Red Sox manager Grady Little started limiting the number of innings Martínez worked and gave him an extra day's rest whenever he could. The Red Sox finished 95-67 and earned them their first playoff berth since

1999. After defeating the A's in the ALDS, the Sox hooked up in a memorable series that was a slugfest in more ways than one.

Martínez got his first start in Game Three with the ALCS tied at one game apiece. The Yankees had just gone ahead, 3-2, in the fourth when Martínez hit right fielder Karim Garcia with a pitch. No fight erupted, but it charged up an already electric atmosphere, and the benches emptied in the bottom of the inning when Clemens threw at Manny Ramírez.

Baseball brawls generally involve players from both teams running on the field and shouting "Oh yeah?" at each other. For some reason, the Yankees' 72-year-old bench coach Don Zimmer decided to take a run at Martínez, who wasn't in a very good mood himself after blowing a lead in the top of the inning. Martínez threw Zimmer to the ground, and while no one was injured, the game did suffer a black eye. Zimmer later admitted the encounter was his fault.

Although Martínez lost that game, the Red Sox hung in and forced a Game Seven. Little went with his ace, which was a good idea, at least for most of the game. Going into the eighth, the Red Sox led 5-2. With one out and a run in, and Hideki Matsui coming up, Little went to the mound and asked Martínez if he had anything left. Martínez said he did, but it turned out he was wrong.

"Little went to the mound, spoke to Martínez and patted him with encouragement, but then turned and stepped back to the dugout, not knowing that he was about to join Bill Buckner in Red Sox lore," wrote Buster Olney.[10]

Matsui hit a ground-rule double, which left runners at second and third. Yankee catcher Jorge Posada then got a bloop hit that drove in two runs and tied the game. Aaron Boone hit the series-winning homer off reliever Tim Wakefield in the 11th.

Since it's easier to replace managers than star pitchers, Little was fired after the 2003 season and Martínez stayed in the rotation. He wasn't quite as dominant in 2004, for even though he had a 16-9 record, his ERA was an un-Pedro-like 3.90. The Red Sox made the playoffs again in what proved to be an historic season for the team.

The Yankees and Red Sox met again in the ALCS. Martínez lost Game Two, going six innings in a 3-1 defeat. The Yankees wore out home plate with all the times they crossed the plate in a Game Three 19-8 battering, giving them a 3-0 series lead. But then the Yankees forgot they had to win four games.

The Sox stayed alive by winning Game Four, 6-4, in 12 innings. Pedro pitched Game Five and allowed four runs, leaving after six innings down 4-2. The Sox tied it in the eighth and won it in the 14th to make the series 3-2. After Curt Schilling's courageous outing in Game Six, the Sox completed the comeback in Game Seven. Martínez pitched the seventh inning and allowed two runs on three hits, but the Red Sox won the game easily 10-3.

After such an inspired comeback by the Sox, the World Series was anti-climactic, as they easily disposed of the St. Louis Cardinals in four straight games. After a mediocre ALCS, Martínez was excellent in his only World Series start, pitching seven shutout innings in Game Three and getting the win in a 3-1 Red Sox victory.

In the joyous victors' clubhouse at Busch Stadium, Martínez took a moment to remind fans of the departing Montreal Expos how important the city was to him by sharing the Red Sox victory with them.

"I'm glad I got it [the World Series win] and I would like to share it with the people of Montreal that are not going to have a team anymore," he said in an interview. "My heart and my ring is [sic] with them, too."[11]

Winning isn't everything in sports, nor is it the only thing. Professional sports is a business and like any businessman, Martínez took the opportunity to shop his wares to the highest bidder once he became a free agent after the 2004 season. That bidder turned out to be the New York Mets, who signed Martínez to a four-year, $53 million deal in December 2004 that included a $3 million signing bonus. The Red Sox worried how long his shoulder might hold up and had offered $40.5 million over three years. In addition to the salary, Martínez' contract included incentive clauses for winning the Cy Young Award and being named to the All-Star team as well as a luxury suite at Shea Stadium.

Martínez proved to be worth the price to the Mets, at least for the first year. He was 15-8 in 2005 and made the All-Star team. On a personal level, Pedro married his sweetheart Carolina Cruz that year, whom he met through his Pedro Martínez and Brothers Foundation in 1998 when she was a sophomore at Boston College. She was able to attend the university on a scholarship provided through the foundation.

In 2006 he made the All-Star team again, but only went 9-8 with an astronomical 4.48 ERA as injuries to his hip, calf, and toe limited him to 23 starts. He underwent major surgery for a torn rotator cuff that October, and missed the Mets' postseason, which saw them come within one game of going to the World Series. While the operation may have relieved pain, it cost him velocity on his fastball. It took 11 months for Martínez to recover, and he didn't make his first start of the 2007 season until September 3 against the Reds in Cincinnati. That was a milestone game for Martínez, as he became only the 15th pitcher to record 3,000 strikeouts when he got Aaron Harang on an 87 mile-per-hour fastball. For the season, Martínez went 3-1 in five starts with a 2.57 ERA.

The decline continued in an injury-filled 2008, as Martínez had the worst season of his career, a 5-6 won-lost record with a 5.61 ERA for a team that went 89-73. The Mets missed the playoffs by one game and there's no doubt having Pedro pitching at top capacity would have vaulted them over the Brewers and into the wild card.

The *annus horribilis* that was 2008 also included great personal sadness for Martínez, as his father died of brain cancer in July at the age of 78.

When the 2009 season began, Martínez could relate to the proverbial teenage girl waiting for the phone to ring on a Saturday night. Martínez was a free agent, but the 37-year-old's age and mediocre statistics did not attract teams. Finally, the Philadelphia Phillies, who were hoping to repeat as World Series champions, signed Pedro to a one-year $1 million contract on July 15. They hoped he could provide them with some quality starts and help them overcome injuries to their pitching staff. After three starts in the minors, he returned to the majors on August 12 at Wrigley Field and was the winner in a 12-5 Phils victory over the Cubs. He went five innings, gave up three earned runs, and struck out five.

Martínez contributed to the Phillies winning the National League East Division by compiling a 5-1 record with a 3.63 ERA in nine starts. He didn't play in the NLDS against the Colorado Rockies, which the Phillies won in four games. He pitched magnificently in Game Two of the NLCS against the Dodgers, going seven scoreless innings and leaving with a 1-0 lead. The bullpen couldn't hold on and the Phillies lost, 3-1. It was the team's only loss in the series, which they won in five games.

Then came the World Series against his old rival from the Red Sox days, the hated Yankees. Pedro started Game Two and gave up three runs in six-plus innings. Yankee starter A.J. Burnett was almost unhittable that night and the Yankees won, 3-1.

In what turned out to be the last game of his career, Martínez started Game Six with the Phillies down three games to two. He just didn't have it that night, giving up four runs in four innings as the Bombers won the game, 7-3, and the Series.

Overall, Martínez had a decent season, but something was missing and he knew that the time had come to hang up the spikes.

"You find yourself alone, ironing your clothes again and you find yourself moving your car and parking and driving by yourself home late at night after being on the road," said Martínez in an interview. "After achieving what I achieved in baseball, I felt like if I was going to go through all of that just to achieve a little bit more, I would rather not."[12]

Retirement has been good for Martínez, who is both a deeply religious man and a proud Dominican who has not forgotten his roots despite the millions he earned playing baseball. He and Carolina run the foundation, which is headquartered in Santo Domingo. His foundation has built a three-story school, and a facility that offers kids the chance to learn computers, English, and music as well as how to battle domestic violence and teenage pregnancy.

He received a unique honor in 2011, when the Smithsonian Institution's National Portrait Gallery unveiled a painting of him done by Susan Miller-Havens.

He has also re-established ties with the Red Sox by becoming a special assistant to general manager Ben Cherington in January 2013. He celebrated another World Series win with the team that same season.

Martínez received a player's ultimate accolade on January 6, 2015 when he was elected to the National Baseball Hall of Fame in his first year of eligibility. His name appeared on 91.1 percent of the ballots from the Baseball Writers Association of America. On his plaque he is depicted wearing a Red Sox cap.[13]

After his induction that July, the Red Sox retired his number 45. An autobiography, *Pedro*, co-authored by Michael Silverman, was published by Mariner Books in 2015, and is available both in English and Spanish language editions.

He also began work that year as a studio analyst for the MLB Network. He has continued to work on television as an analyst.

In 2018, Martínez was inducted into the Canadian Baseball Hall of Fame.[14]

Not bad for a kid who had to tear off dolls' heads to play the game he loved.

SOURCES

In addition to the sources cited in the Notes, the author also consulted:

http://www.mlbtraderumors.com

http://www.jockbio.com

http://www.baseball-reference.com/

http://www.nytimes.com/

http://dev.baseballlibrary.com/ballplayers

http://www.boston.com/sports/baseball/redsox/articles/2003/10/08/thrills_were_in_season/

http://www.hardballtimes.com

http://ftw.usatoday.com

http://www.nydailynews.com/

http://mlb.com

http://www.playerwives.com/mlb/boston-red-sox/pedro-Martínezs-wife-carolina-cruz-de-Martínez/

NOTES

1. "Pedro Martínez turning some heads in Dodgers' camp," *Ocala (Florida) Star Banner*, March 2, 1992.
2. Peter Gammons, Clemson Smith Muniz, "Pedro Martínez could throw Boston its best party in a long, long time," *ESPN Mobile Web Archive*, July 10, 2012 (note that this date refers to when the archived article was put on the ESPN website. It was probably written soon after Martínez was traded to the Red Sox in late 1997.)
3. Mike Shalin, *Pedro Martínez: Throwing Strikes* (Sports Publishing LLC, 1999), 21.
4. Shalin, 23.
5. Mike Eisenbath, "Minor League Player of the Year," *The Sporting News*, October 28, 1991.
6. Tim Kurkjian, "An Inside Job," *Sports Illustrated*, April 25, 1994.
7. Tim Kurjkjian, "Baseball," *Sports Illustrated*, May 16, 1994.
8. Statistics provided by the book *Red Sox Threads*, by Bill Nowlin published by Rounder Books.
9. Howard Ulman, "Martínez Criticizes Duquette," *Pittsburgh Post-Gazette*, September 5, 2001.
10. Buster Olney, "Boone's Blast, Rivera's Arm Lift Yankees," *ESPN the Magazine*, October 2003.

11   Television interview, *Reseau des sports* October 27, 2004. http://www.youtube.com/watch?v=RUXq7ZVXgvU
12   Sean Deveney, "Happily retired Pedro Martínez reflects on time with Red Sox," *sportingnews.com*, April 20, 2012.
13   He said, "I cannot be any prouder to take Red Sox Nation to the Hall of Fame with the logo on my plaque. I am extremely proud to represent Boston and all of New England with my Hall of Fame career. I'm grateful to all of the teams for which I played, and especially fans, for making this amazing honor come true." ESPN.com News Services, "Pedro Martinez opts for Red Sox logo," January 22, 2015. https://www.espn.com/mlb/story/_/id/12211099/pedro-martinez-rep-boston-red-sox-hall-fame-plaque
14   His page is available at: https://baseballhalloffame.ca/hall-of-famer/pedro-martinez/. Regarding his induction, see Joseph Zucker, "Pedro Martinez on Canadian Baseball Hall of Fame Induction: 'Extremely Honored'," bleacherreport.com, June 18, 2022. https://bleacherreport.com/articles/10039131-pedro-martinez-on-canadian-baseball-hall-of-fame-induction-extremely-honored

A RED SOX MEMORY

The magical year of 2004 has so many memories for me, but one story stands out during the Yankee series. That year I worked for Michael Rutstein selling his *Boston Baseball* magazine outside Fenway. On the night of Game Four against the Yanks, trailing three games to none, Mike came to us and suggested that perhaps they should just drop this game and start fresh next year. We all thought he had lost his mind. Well, we went out and had a good night, and so did the Sox. We spent the rest of the playoffs teasing him and not letting him forget it throughout the whole next season. The atmosphere outside Fenway was unbelievable. Lots of eager fans, lots of media, and lots of fun. A time I'll never forget.

DAVID SOUTHWICK

ANGEL "SANDY" MARTÍNEZ

BY ERIC CONRAD AND MARK MOROWCZYNSKI

Angel "Sandy" Martínez was a catcher for eight years in the major leagues, from 1995 to 2004. He played in 218 games for six major-league teams, finishing with a career slash line of .230/.284/.333 with 6 home runs, 51 RBIs, and a 33 percent caught-stealing percentage. He caught Kerry Wood's historic 20-strikeout game for the Chicago Cubs in 1998.

Martínez was born on October 8, 1970, in Villa Mella, Distrito Nacional, Dominican Republic. He grew up on the family farm with six brothers and three sisters and was raised by his mother. He said she had a strong work ethic, got up every day, never complained, and made sure there was food on the table. She inspired him to work hard with the hopes of being able to take care of her through baseball. Baseball was a constant in his life; he played the game with his cousins all the time growing up. He lived close to Jesús Figueroa, a former player and longtime batting-practice pitcher and bullpen coach for the Toronto Blue Jays,[1] who was instrumental in his development throughout his entire career.[2]

Right fielder José Herrera was from Villa Mella as well, and both broke into the big leagues the same year, Herrera with Oakland. As an 8-year-old, Martínez was struck in the face in the on-deck circle when his teammate accidentally let go of the bat swinging at a pitch. This left a visible scar and a lump above his nose near his right eye that he would carry for the rest of his life.[3]

Martínez as a catcher threw right-handed but batted from the left side. He stood 6-feet-2 and was listed at 200 pounds. He played for six major-league teams over the course of his eight-year major-league career, the Toronto Blue Jays, Chicago Cubs, Florida Marlins, Montréal Expos, Cleveland Indians, and the Red Sox.

Martínez honed his skills in Santo Domingo at a large sports complex complete with several basketball courts and baseball fields where, he said, a game was always being played. The complex also had the facilities of the New York Mets and Pittsburgh Pirates, and he was able to train with their players and continue his skills growth.[4]

Signed by the Blue Jays in 1990, Martínez played 44 games for their Dominican Summer League team that year. Sandy initially only spoke Spanish and learned English while playing. He split the 1991 season between the rookie-level Medicine Hat Blue Jays and the advanced Class-A Dunedin Blue Jays in the Florida State League. This was the first time Martínez really left his home and it was an eye-opening experience playing in Idaho and Montana as part of the Pioneer League North Division. One of the unfortunate learning experiences he encountered (along with his teammates) was racism. He said that some people shunned them due to their color of their skin when they went out for pregame or postgame meals. Looking back 33 years later, Martínez said, "People didn't want to be around us. You got to go through it."[5]

In 1991, his first season, Martínez exemplified the attributes he'd have as a big-league catcher: defense-first as a catcher and struggling at the plate (.177 batting average). In 1992 with the Medicine Hat Blue Jays and Dunedin Blue Jays, his hitting improved to .249 in 239 plate appearances, with 6 home runs and 43 RBIs.[6]

Photo courtesy of the Pittsburgh Pirates.

With Hagerstown of the Class-A Sally League in 1993, season, Martínez again improved at the plate, batting .263 with 9 home runs and 46 RBIs. He returned to High-A Dunedin for the 1994 season, playing 122 games and batting .260.

Martínez opened the 1995 season in the Double-A Southern League, playing for the Knoxville Smokies. In 41 games, he hit for a .229 average. He was ranked as the 77th best prospect by *Baseball America,* eight spots ahead of future Montréal Expos teammate and Hall of Famer Vladimir Guerrero.[7]

After injuries to Randy Knorr, Carlos Delgado, and Lance Parrish,[8] the Blue Jays brought Martínez up to the majors in June 1995. He made his major-league debut on June 24 against the New York Yankees at Yankee Stadium, catching right-hander Juan Guzmán. The Yankees won the game, 10-2, with Martínez catching the entire game. He went 1-for-4, with a single to center off fellow Dominican Josías Manzanillo as his first major-league hit. He hit his first major-league home run in his next game, a three-run homer off Roger Clemens against the Red Sox at Fenway Park in Boston on June 27.

Martínez stuck with the Jays the rest of the season, appearing in 62 games for manager Cito Gaston, batting .241 driving in 25 runs. He was projected as part of the rebuilding Blue Jays' youth movement with, among others, Shawn Green, Alex Gonzalez, Tomás Pérez, and Carlos Delgado.[9]

In his rookie season Martínez went by his true first name, Angel. In an interview in 1996, his second season, Blue Jays broadcaster Jerry Howarth noted that "Sandy" was written on his catcher's mitt and asked about it. Martínez answered, "Ever since I was a baby, my mother has called me Sandy. Angel is my first name, but no one in my family or my friends ever calls me that. Only here. I just haven't mentioned it to anyone." Howarth said, "Sandy, thank you for sharing that with me. No longer are you Angel Martínez. From now on you are Sandy Martínez. Are you okay if I tell everyone what you just shared with me right here for our interview?" In a book published in 2019, Howarth related, "He said that would be fine. Tom threw it down to me in the dugout and I opened up that postgame interview with the new Sandy Martínez story. I am proud to say that from that point on in his eight-year major league career, he was called Sandy."[10]

In 1996 Martínez settled into his role as the Blue Jays' primary backup catcher behind Charlie O'Brien. He started 68 games and came in as either a pinch-hitter or a replacement catcher in eight more. The 76 games were the most Martínez played in a major-league season. On May 11 he produced the game-winning hit in the bottom of the 11th off Red Sox pitcher Heathcliff Slocumb, scoring Juan Samuel from second base.

Martínez finished the season with a .227 batting average, 3 home runs, and 3 triples (tied with five others for second-most in the majors for a catcher in 1996. He made three errors with a 35 percent caught-stealing rate. After the Blue Jays signed catcher Benito Santiago in December 1996, Charlie O'Brien became the primary backup. Martínez was sent back down to Triple A so he could catch every day.[11]

Martínez began the 1997 season with Syracuse of the Triple-A International League and was the primary catcher for 92 of the team's 142 games. In early September he was recalled to the Blue Jays after Santiago was hit on the hand with a pitch.[12] In a starting assignment on September 10 vs. the Oakland A's, he got his only at-bats of the season. He went 0-for-2 with a walk, a run scored, and one caught stealing.

The Blue Jays traded Martínez to the Chicago Cubs on December 11, 1997, for a player to be named later, who turned out to be Trevor Schaffer.[13]

Martínez caught Kerry Wood's 20-strikeout game for the Cubs on May 6, 1998, at Wrigley Field. It was the first time Martínez had caught Wood. The game began with Wood hitting home-plate umpire Jerry Meals directly in his mask with a fastball. Meals said, "First pitch. I'll never forget it. How could I? As an umpire you hardly ever get drilled right in the mask with the first pitch of the game."[14] Wood recalled, "I remember Biggio trying to get a look at me. He just sort of half-squared around like he was going to bunt – just to get a look at the pitch and time it. And I think maybe his barrel got in front of Sandy Martínez's mask and Sandy lost sight of it and never got his glove back up to it."[15]

Martínez said of Wood's pitching, "… [I]t was unbelievable. … Everything I called, he already had the grip for it. He only shook me off three or four times that game. … That day it seemed like we were communicating mentally. It was just a game you can't really describe. I feel very lucky for catching it."[16] He told another sportswriter, "I didn't know until the seventh inning that he had that many K's. In the seventh inning, for some reason, I looked to left field and the bleachers, and saw all the K's and said, 'Damn, we got so many.' I didn't realize he had that many K's. The only thing I had in my mind was to try to win the game."[17] Martínez is tied with four other catchers for most putouts in a nine-inning game (20).[18]

Martínez made his only postseason appearance against the Atlanta Braves in Game Three of the 1998 NLDS. He singled and scored a run off Greg Maddux in the bottom of the eighth inning in his only at-bat. The Braves won the game, 6-2, to sweep the series. Martínez finished the 1998 season with 45 appearances for the Cubs, and career-high stats for batting average (.264), slugging percentage (.391), and OPS (.754).

Martínez appeared in 17 games for the Cubs during the 1999 season, where his offensive numbers declined. He batted .167 with one home run and one RBI. The Cubs released him at the end of the season and the Florida Marlins signed him on December 6, 1999.

Martínez started the 2000 season with the Marlins, getting into seven games before being optioned to Triple-A Calgary. He was recalled in September for three more games before entering free agency in October. This was a recurring pattern for his remaining time as a player in professional baseball: spending most of his time with the Triple-A affiliate and a few games with the major-league club.

Martínez was signed by the Montréal Expos as a backup catcher in 2001 and appeared in one game, on Opening Day against the Chicago Cubs at Wrigley Field on April 2, 2001. Starting catcher Michael Barrett was ejected in the eighth inning for arguing with plate umpire Rick Reed. Martínez grounded into a double play in his only at-bat, in the ninth inning.[19] Vladimir Guerrero knocked in the Expos' go-ahead run in the top of the 10th. Martínez left the game after injuring his elbow.[20] Martínez later had Tommy John surgery, ending his season.

Martinez spent most of the 2002 season with the Expos' Triple-A affiliate, the Ottawa Lynx, batting .226 before entering free agency again. He was signed and released by the Tampa Bay Devil Rays, and the Kansas City Royals, playing 24 games for the Royals' Triple-A affiliate in Omaha Royals before being released on June 8, 2003. He then played in 34 games for the Piratas de Campeche of the Mexican League.

For 2004 Martinez signed with the Pittsburgh Pirates but was traded at the start of the season to the Cleveland Indians, who sent him to Triple-A Buffalo. (He batted .274 with 17 home runs for Buffalo and played in one game for the Indians.) On August 31, in time for postseason eligibility, he was sold to the Red Sox.[21]

Martinez appeared in three games and went hitless in four at-bats. His cousin, right-handed pitcher Anastacio Martínez, also played (earlier in the season) for the 2004 Red Sox, earning a victory in relief of Pedro Martínez (no relation). Anastacio's entire major-league career consisted of 11 games with the Red Sox that year. Sandy and Anastacio Martínez are the only relatives to play for a Red Sox World Series champion.[22]

Martinez returned to the minors for three more seasons, ending his playing career with three games for the Albuquerque Isotopes of the Pacific Coast League in 2007. He never played against his cousin Anastacio in a regular-season game but hit a two-run home run off him in a spring training game for the New York Mets in 2006.[23] "I told him not to throwing anything close to me. He threw a fastball inside, then another fastball up and in, then a curveball and I hit a home run. I was laughing around the bases and I said, 'Don't throw anything close!' but we laugh about it now," said Sandy.[24]

In 2007 Martinez signed with the Dodgers but was released by the end of spring training. He spent time in the Marlins farm system. In 2008 he tried to focus most of the year on recovering from a meniscus injury but by the end of the year the pain was still there and he finally retired from playing.

Martínez began managing the Washington Nationals' Dominican Summer League team in Boca Chica, Dominican Republic, in 2011. As of 2023 he was also the on-field instructor for the Nationals' year-round baseball academy based at the same location. The academy moved to a new upgraded facility in 2014, and Martínez said, "Compared to where we were before, things have gotten better, the kids have gotten better and we're showing it."[25]

He is the father of two sons, former Arizona Diamondbacks minor-leaguer Sandy Martínez (catcher) and Angel Martínez, as of 2023 an infielder in the Cleveland Guardians farm system. His wife, Indhira, is an accountant and lawyer.[26]

SOURCES

Sources used include a telephone interview conducted with Sandy Martínez on June 14, 2023. Details from his early career are mostly based on *Toronto Star* articles. Multiple articles on Kerry Wood's 20-strikeout game include articles from the *Chicago Tribune*, *Sarasota Herald-Tribune*, and MLB.com. Statistics were taken from Baseball Reference, Baseball Almanac, and ESPN.

NOTES

1 Figueroa is the longest-serving member of the Toronto Blue Jays. He joined as a batting-practice pitcher in 1989. CBC News: https://www.cbc.ca/news/canada/toronto/jays-batting-practice-pitcher-1.3762860.

2 Sandy Martínez, telephone interview, June 14, 2023.

3 Marty Ormsby, "Martinez Accepts Role as Jays' Backup Catcher," *Toronto Star*, May 2, 1996.

4 Martínez interview.

5 Martínez interview.

6 Ormsby.

7 1995 Baseball America MLB Prospect Rankings https://www.thebaseballcube.com/content/prospects_mlb/1995~BA/.

8 Richard Griffin, "Fancy Prose Can't Conceal Jays' Lineup Woes," *Toronto Star*, February 15, 1996.

9 Jim Byers, "Blue Jays: Give Us Time and We'll Rebuild," *Toronto Star* October 3, 1995

10 Jerry Howarth, *Hello, Friends! Stories from My Life and Blue Jays Baseball* (Toronto: ECW Press, 2019), accessed via Google Books, June 2023.

11 "Ball Notes," *Toronto Star*, March 13, 1997.

12 Allan Ryan, "Banged-Up Jays Throw One Away," *Toronto Star*, September 4, 1997.

13 1997 Major League Transactions, Baseball Reference. https://www.baseball-reference.com/leagues/majors/1997-transactions.shtml.

14 Dan Wiederer, "Kerry Wood and 'the Greatest Game Ever Pitched': The Oral History of May 6, 1998, at Wrigley Field," *Chicago Tribune*, May 6, 2018. https://www.chicagotribune.com/sports/cubs/ct-spt-kerry-wood-20-strikeout-anniversary-20180501-htmlstory.html.

15 Wiederer.

16 Chris Anderson, "Part of Baseball History," *Sarasota Herald-Tribune*, February 24, 2003. https://www.heraldtribune.com/story/news/2003/02/24/part-of-baseball-history/28741218007/.

17 Alyson Footer, "Remembering the Most Dominant Start Ever," MLB.com, May 6, 2023, https://www.mlb.com/news/kerry-wood-astros-recall-20-strikeout-game-c274851112.

18 The other catchers are Rich Gedman (catching Roger Clemens' first 20-strikeout game), Dan Wilson (catching Randy Johnson's second 20-strikeout game), and Wilson Ramos (catching Max Scherzer), each of whom caught 20-K games. Jerry Grote caught 19 strikeouts by Tom Seaver and caught a pop foul for a 20th out.

19 *Baseball Reference*, https://www.baseball-reference.com/boxes/CHN/CHN200104020.shtml.

20 ESPN Baseball, "Cubs Unable to Mount Rally in 10th," https://www.espn.com/mlb/2001/20010402/recap/monchc.html.

21 Gordon Edes, "Red Sox Notebook," *Boston Globe*, September 1, 2004: C7.

22 Bill Nowlin, *Boston Red Sox Firsts: The Players, Moments, and Records That Were First in Team History* (Essex, Connecticut: Lyons Press, 2023), 130.

23 MLB game recap, ESPN, March 15, 2006. https://www.espn.com/mlb/recap/_/gameId/260315120.

24 Martínez interview.

25 James Wagner, "In Dominican Republic, Nationals Want Prospects to Be Comfortable, but Not Too Comfortable," *Washington Post*, January 7, 2015. https://www.washingtonpost.com/sports/nationals/in-dominican-republic-nationals-want-prospects-to-be-comfortable-but-not-too-comfortable/2015/01/07/d75f3cd2-8b70-11e4-a085-34e9b9f09a58_story.html.

26 Martínez interview.

DAVE MCCARTY

BY JEFF ENGLISH

On September 27, 2004, the Boston Red Sox trailed the Tampa Bay Devil Rays 2-0 when Red Sox first baseman Dave McCarty led off the top of the fifth inning with a line-drive single to left-center field. He took second base on a walk and scored on a three-run home run by center fielder Johnny Damon. Boston tacked on two more runs to finish the top half of the fifth inning with a lead of 5-2. The Red Sox added two more runs in the eighth inning on solo home runs by McCarty and catcher Jason Varitek and went on to win the game 7-3, clinching a berth in the postseason for a second straight year.

McCarty arrived in Boston off waivers from the Oakland Athletics in August 2003. The Red Sox were his seventh major-league club since he debuted with the Minnesota Twins a decade earlier. McCarty had earned a reputation as a highly regarded defensive asset at first base and in the outfield and one of the more dependable right-handed pinch-hitters in the American League. He had enjoyed his best season three years before in Kansas City, when he batted .278 with 12 home runs in 270 at-bats. Shortly after his arrival in Boston, McCarty recognized that he had joined a club with a much loftier set of expectations than his previous teams.

"There were a lot of teams I had played on earlier in my career that were kind of rebuilding and you did not have that same mindset of hey, we are working towards a championship. Nobody cared what their individual numbers were but rather, did we win the game? Guys were really pulling for each other. Then in 2004 with the few changes they made, it was the best group of guys I ever played with."[1]

The best three years of McCarty's career were his last three, with the 2003-05 Red Sox, for whom he hit at a .286 pace. When he retired, he went out on top.

David Andrew McCarty was born to Dennis William and Joan Gush McCarty on November 23, 1969, in Harris County, Texas, which includes the city of Houston. Dennis worked as an electrical engineer and though Joan worked several different jobs over the years, she was mainly a stay-at-home mom looking after David and his younger sister.

As a boy, David played multiple sports, including football, but upon reaching Sharpstown High School in 1984, he chose to focus on baseball and basketball. On the diamond he pitched and played first base and the outfield. He batted right-handed and threw left-handed. He grew to become 6-feet-5 and was listed at 210 pounds, finishing his career at 243.[2]

Asked about his time on the mound at Sharpstown, McCarty recalled, "Like a lot of younger left-handed pitchers, I was kind of wild and did not really have the kind of arm strength I had when I grew into my body when I got older."[3] Wild or not, colleges around the country took notice, some viewing McCarty as a potential dual threat at the plate and on the mound. As he told ESPN in 2004, "Some colleges were recruiting me more to pitch than hit."[4] Under the guidance of longtime coach Dick Janse, Sharpstown was widely regarded as an annual high-school baseball powerhouse in Texas, having captured a state title in 1982 while boasting two future big-league hurlers in Rusty Richards and Greg Swindell.[5] Like Richards and Swindell before him, McCarty always imagined he would wind up playing baseball at the University of Texas. But other schools sought him out. "When Stanford jumped in, I (went) out for a visit," he said.[6] Stanford had won back-to-back College World Series during his junior and senior years in high school, which McCarty said made an impression. "And then I got out to the Bay Area and saw the weather and the quality of education. Nobody else could match that, so it really forced me to change my mind."[7] His four years at Sharpstown yielded three first-team all-district and All-Houston selections, two district Player of the Year awards, and a spot on two all-state teams. He graduated from Sharpstown High School in 1988, and in May was named the Outstanding Male Scholar-Athlete at the 12th Annual Greater Houston High School Spring Sports Dinner.[8]

McCarty excelled at Stanford, starting 166 games at first base from 1989 through 1991, including a streak of 133 straight. During the summer of 1989, he played in Massachusetts with Cotuit of the Cape Cod Baseball League.[9] As a sophomore in 1990, he batted .336 with 12 home runs and 69 RBIs and was selected to compete for the United States in the Goodwill Games and the World Championships, where he batted an astounding .445 across both tournaments.[10] In 1991 McCarty enjoyed one of the finest seasons in Stanford University history. In 62 games he batted .420 with 24 home runs and 66 RBIs, and nearly half of his 100 hits went for extra bases.[11] Across one 26-game stretch he hit .490 with 10 home runs and 32

RBIs. His .420 season batting mark was the second highest in school history. McCarty was rewarded for his effort by being chosen First Team All-American, First Team All-Pac-10, and Pac-10 Southern Division Player of the Year. *Baseball America* named him Player of the Year and he was viewed as a likely early first-round draft pick.

McCarty graduated from Stanford with an economics degree in 1992 and was inducted into the Stanford University Athletics Hall of Fame in 2008.[12]

On June 3, 1991, the Minnesota Twins selected McCarty with the third pick in the first round of the amateur draft, making him the second-highest pick in school history. He signed his first professional contract 12 days later and received a reported $390,000 signing bonus.[13] McCarty was sent to the Visalia Oaks in the high Class-A California League, where he responded by batting .380 in 15 games with 3 home runs and 8 RBIs. His performance was rewarded with a promotion to the Orlando Sun Rays in the Double-A Southern League. In 28 games in the outfield, he recorded four assists while batting .261 with extra-base power and a knack for getting on base.

McCarty began the 1992 season rated by *Baseball America* as the number-22 prospect in the game. He opened the season once again in Orlando, and in 129 games he split time between the outfield and first base. He registered a strong offensive showing that included 18 home runs and 79 RBIs, and earned a late-season promotion to Portland in the Triple-A Pacific Coast League. In just seven-regular season games at Portland, he batted .500 with a home run, 8 RBIs, and a 1.286 OPS. In the first three games of the first round of the PCL playoffs against the Vancouver Canadians, he erupted for four home runs and a near .500 batting average.[14] Vancouver won the matchup three games to two, but the Twins front office was taking notice of McCarty's performance.

McCarty entered spring training in 1993 as *Baseball America*'s 16th rated prospect in the game. As the spring got underway, McCarty swung the bat in a way that suggested the rating might be far too low. On March 19 he had a three-hit day and scored three runs in a 10-6 victory over the Texas Rangers that pushed his preseason average to .345 with a team-best 3 home runs and 11 RBIs.[15] In March *The Sporting News* reported that despite his torrid spring, he held out little expectation of making the big-league roster to begin the season. The Twins had signed future Hall of Famer Dave Winfield the previous December and McCarty acknowledged that. "It hurt (my chances) a lot, but a team can't pass on a player like Winfield. It would sound ridiculous if I said, 'Poor me. I'm playing behind Dave Winfield. Yes. Of course, I am.'"[16] At the end of spring training, McCarty was sent to Minnesota's minor-league camp for reassignment. He found his way back to Triple-A Portland, where began the season by recording a .398 average and a .637 slugging percentage in 31 games.[17]

In mid-May Minnesota outfielder Shane Mack went on the disabled list with soreness from a separated shoulder. The Twins purchased outfielder-first baseman McCarty's contract from Portland and the 23-year-old found himself in the starting lineup on May 17 in Minnesota against the New York Yankees. He wasted little time securing his first big-league hit with a sixth-inning single off starter Jimmy Key; indeed, he hit safely in 18 of his first 20 games.

McCarty hit his first big-league home run on June 2 in Minnesota off Texas Rangers starter Roger Pavlik. But he began to struggle and his average fell to .256 by the end of July. With just 52 games under his belt, he was optioned back to Portland. Recalled August 14, he remained with the Twins for the rest of the season. With few exceptions, including a four-hit, two-double day in a 9-5 win over Texas in early September, McCarty's difficulties at the plate persisted. Despite a home run in the final game of the season, against the Seattle Mariners, his batting average sat at .214 with just two home runs in 350 at-bats. Noting that there was pressure to produce with power at the plate, McCarty in an interview with the author cited changes to his swing as one of the primary culprits for his struggles. As he recalled, "We started making changes to my swing and it really got kind of screwed up. It got longer, slower, and so it just did not work out at all."[18] Ultimately it contributed to McCarty's placing additional pressure on himself.

"But then when things did not work out well that first year, I struggled after having been messed around with my swing, it really kind of affected my confidence. And that I think caused me to struggle some. And then in 1994 I just could never seem to get enough at-bats to really get going."[19]

Although he was expected to start the 1994 season in Triple A, McCarty broke spring training with the Twins. He started at first base against the California Angels on April 7 and was 2-for-3 with a walk and a stolen base. But as the season progressed, concern grew over McCarty's lack of production, as well as uncharacteristic miscues in the field. *The Sporting News* observed that although McCarty "was supposed to be a power threat, (he) had one RBI in his first 37 at-bats this season and 22 RBI in 387 big-league at-bats."[20] After playing in just 44 games through the end of June and batting .260, McCarty was sent to the Salt Lake City Buzz in the Pacific Coast League. His hitting did not improve even at the lower level.[21] Reflecting on a difficult 1994 season, McCarty commented to the author, "What comes first, the chicken or the egg? If you are not hitting well enough you are not going to get the at-bats. But if you do not get the at-bats, you are not going to hit well enough. From then on in my career, I had a tough time getting at-bats in the big leagues."[22]

McCarty began the 1995 season in Minnesota, at first base, where the recently retired Kent Hrbek's departure left a big hole to fill.[23] As the season got underway, McCarty never seemed to find his groove, and after 25 games at first base and in the outfield, his average sat at .218 with no home runs and only 4 RBIs in 55 at-bats. On June 8 he was traded to the Cincinnati Reds for John Courtright, a pitcher notable for a big-league career that spanned a single inning.

The Reds sent McCarty to Triple-A Indianapolis (American Association). He drove in 32 runs in just 37 games, batting .336 and once again found his slugging power. He was traded again, to the San Francisco Giants as part of an eight-player deal on July 21.

The Giants optioned McCarty to the Phoenix Firebirds in the PCL, and he picked up where he had left off in Indianapolis. In 37 games for the Firebirds, he batted .351 with nearly half of his 53 hits going for extra bases. His performance brought him a call-up to the Giants in September and he delivered a ninth-inning game-winning single against the Montreal Expos in his second game (and first start) as a Giant. In limited playing time in 12 games, McCarty batted .250 with 2 RBIs.

In 1996 McCarty made the Giants out of spring training.[24] His first hit came on April 22 in his seventh at-bat of the young season, a three-run home run as a late-inning replacement for Barry Bonds in an 11-8 loss to the Houston Astros. In early June McCarty found his way to the 15-day disabled list after he sprained his right ankle by tripping on his shoes on the way to the bathroom.[25] The 1996 season saw McCarty receive more opportunities to pinch-hit than in any other season. And he responded with two home runs and nine RBIs in the role. McCarty recalled, "At that point in my career, I really did not know how to do it. It is one thing to go up there and pinch-hit if you have been rotting on the bench versus getting regular at-bats and on days you are not starting you are the go-to pinch-hitter. It is just a whole different animal."[26] The 1996 Giants finished in fourth place in the National League West Division. McCarty hit 6 home runs in 175 at-bats to go with a .217 batting average.

Despite a strong showing at Giants camp in the spring of 1997, McCarty was reassigned to the minor-league camp. Before the move, he had hit safely in eight of 10 games, going 9-for-16 with 3 doubles, 6 RBIs, and 5 runs scored. He spent all of the 1997 season back at Phoenix, where he put up some of the best offensive totals of his career. McCarty batted .353 and slugged 22 home runs. His 92 RBIs were the eighth-highest in the PCL and his OPS of 1.009 ranked him fifth.

The Seattle Mariners traded for McCarty in late January of 1998. He saw limited action in the majors – four games in late May and four in early June – but spent most of the season with the Tacoma Rainiers, his fourth Coast League team. In 108 games, he batted .317 and got on base at a clip of .411.

After the season McCarty opted for free agency rather than accept a return to Tacoma.[27] He signed a minor-league contract with the Detroit Tigers on December 18 that included an invitation to spring training.[28] But he spent all of the 1999 season at Toledo in the Triple-A International League. His 31 home runs were a career high and second-best in the league.[29] He spent all of 2000 and 2001 in the majors. After the 1999 season, he had signed as a free agent with Oakland. He swung the bat exceptionally well the A's 2000 spring training, The Sporting News noting that McCarty "has made superb plays in the field, has a strong throwing arm, and bashed two homers in one inning of a game."[30] But near the end of spring training, Oakland sold his contract to the Kansas City Royals.[31]

McCarty found a good match in Kansas City and played in 103 games for the Royals in 2000. He batted .278 with 12 home runs in 270 at-bats. He had four hits in a 13-11 win over Boston on June 1, and his sixth-inning grand slam off Cleveland starter Chuck Finley contributed to a 10-5 win for the Royals on July 19. On August 16, he snapped a 15-at-bat hitless streak by driving in three runs on three hits in a 9-3 win over Minnesota and followed that up with a two-run double and a run the following day. Of his arrival in Kansas City, McCarty said, "Oh yeah. I got a chance to play and then, all the sudden, I put up good numbers. I led the American League in pinch-hitting and just really blossomed, I thought. Once I got to Kansas City, I really knew what I needed to do, and I was also getting the at-bats I needed to stay fresh."[32] In 23 pinch-hit at-bats in 2000, McCarty had nine hits for a .391 average with a home run and 9 RBIs.

In 2001 McCarty played in 98 games, 68 of them at first base. He got two hits on Opening Day against the New York Yankees. But his average hovered in the low .200s for much of the season, resulting in fewer and fewer at-bats. He recovered slightly in August and September to finish at .250 for the season with 7 home runs.

McCarty was in the starting lineup on April 3, 2002, and doubled in three at-bats in a 1-0 Royals loss to the Minnesota Twins. But he managed only two more hits in his next 29 at-bats, and with a batting average sitting at .094, he was released by Kansas City on May 15. Six days later he signed as a free agent with the Tampa Bay Devil Rays. He split the remainder of the season at Triple-A Durham, where he batted .325 in 29 games, and with the Devil Rays, batting just .176 in 12 games. After suffering a knee injury, he had surgery and spent the rest of the year rehabbing it at home.[33] On August 7, 2002, he was released by Tampa Bay and on November 27 he again signed with the Athletics.

Despite a strong spring camp. McCarty spent most of the 2003 season with Triple-A Sacramento. In 91 games he batted .270 with 15 home and 72 RBIs. He was called up on July 7 to fill a roster spot created when Jermaine Dye went on the disabled list.[34] Splitting time between the outfield and first base, he batted .269 in eight games.

On August 4, 2003, the Red Sox selected McCarty off waivers from Oakland. Boston needed a right-handed bat off the bench, but as *The Sporting News* noted, "What the team likes about him most is his glove at first base."[35] He played in 18 games between August 5 and September 28, going 11-for-27. The Red Sox were in a pennant race that went down to Game Seven of the American League Championship Series. McCarty played in only 16 games, but his .407 batting average made a sufficiently good impression that he was kept on the postseason roster. He got into just two games and struck out in his one plate appearance, against the Yankees in the ALCS. And the Red Sox signed him again for 2004.[36]

Expectations were exceptionally high for the Red Sox in 2004. They had acquired starting pitcher Curt Schilling in a trade with the Arizona Diamondbacks in November, and signed free agent closer Keith Foulke in January. On December 4, former Philadelphia manager Terry Francona was hired to replace Grady Little as Boston's manager. Players arrived for spring training in high spirits, ready for another run at the Yankees.

McCarty had a strong spring at the plate in 2004. He homered and drove in two runs against Baltimore on March 21 in Fort Lauderdale, and hit a three-run home run against the Yankees in Tampa three days later.[37]

First baseman-outfielder Dave McCarty – who played 11 seasons in the major leagues – pitched in three games, all during the 2004 season. He pitched in the home opener at Fenway Park and the final game of the regular season, as well as an inning on June 12. They were the only three pitching appearances of his big-league career, but he acquitted himself well and can look back on a 2.45 career earned-run average.[38]

McCarty connected for his first hit of the 2004 season on April 19, an eighth-inning double that put him in position to score the go-ahead run in a 5-4 win over the Yankees.

The 2004 team was full of team players. McCarty played in 89 games, 10th on the team in games played. He played first base: 67 games (20 of them complete games), left field in 10, and right field, in 7, and was the designated hitter in 3. McCarty was a very solid first baseman: His career fielding percentage in 368 major-league games stands at .990.

McCarty was a reserve as the postseason began but didn't get into any games. The team went with Bill Mueller and Kevin Youkilis at first base.

In January 2005, the Red Sox re-signed McCarty as a free agent. He opened the season with Boston and appeared in 13 games as a late-inning defensive replacement, mostly at first base, but Kevin Millar had a hold on the starting slot there and – with a .500 batting average (two singles in four at-bats, with two RBIs) – he was released on May 2, "granted free agency" in baseball parlance.

At this point, the 35-year-old McCarty chose to retire. He told an interviewer in 2013 that the Red Sox had actually had a deal in place to trade him to the Baltimore Orioles, but the Orioles had averaged more than 30 games out of first place for the four preceding years and the prospect didn't appeal to him. He said to himself, "I've been on enough bad teams, I can't go back to that. I'd rather go out on top, I'm done. Boston was a special place to play. And it was a special group of guys, too. … That's why I retired when I did."[39]

McCarty worked as a part-time baseball analyst on the New England Sports Network (NESN) from 2006 to 2008. He became a principal with Lee & Associates of Oakland, buying, leasing, and selling office, industrial, and investment properties in the East Bay. McCarty and his wife, Monica, lived in Piedmont, California, with their two children. Monica was very successful in her own career, described by her husband as "a successful Scottish historical romance novelist [who has] hit both the *New York Times* and *USA Today* best-seller lists."[40]

Dave and Monica later moved to Oakland, "having downsized after our now adult kids flew the coop."[41]

"My main hobbies," he said, "my wife and I like to travel, we golf quite a bit, we like hiking and swimming, just trying to live a healthy lifestyle. Trying to evade the inevitable decline."[42]

McCarty said he kept in touch with some of his 2004 teammates and values the chemistry that team had. When they held a 10-year reunion in 2014, "There were some of those guys I literally had not seen in 10 years. Because they went off to a different team after 2004 or whatever, and then here we are seeing each other 10 years later, and the whole group, it is like, it could have been two days. We did not skip a beat. We still had that connection together."[43]

He added, "My wife always says, and it is true, really winning that World Series made all the kind of journeyman, up and down and getting traded and released all over the place, it made the whole baseball experience really worth it."[44]

NOTES

1   Interview with the author September 29. 2023. Hereafter, "McCarty interview."

2   Email from David McCarty, December 5, 2023.

3   McCarty interview.

4   https://www.espn.com/mlb/spring2004/columns/story?columnist=stark_jayson&id=1754705.

5   https://www.uiltexas.org/baseball/all-tournament-team/1981-1982-5a-baseball-state-results; https://www.chron.com/sports/highschool/article/Dick-Janse-former-Sharpstown-coach-passes-at-81-12230848.php.

6   McCarty interview.

7   McCarty interview.

8   https://www.chron.com/sports/article/Local-players-among-list-of-top-scholar-athletes-1653847.php.

9   Jack Thomas, "A 'Touching' look at Cape League," *Boston Globe*, July 19, 2004: B1.

10 United Press International, "Stanford's McCarty Named Top Baseball Player," *Cape Girardeau* (Missouri) *Southwest Missourian,* May 3,1990: 3B. https://books.google.com/books?id=osQfAAAAIBAJ&pg=PA7&dq=McCarty+Stanford+baseball+1990&article_id=5271,3990483&hl=en&sa=X&ved=2ahUKEwi69JvfyvSCAxURD1kFHU2sAWcQ6AF6BAgFEAI#v=onepage&q=McCarty%20Stanford%20baseball%201990&f=false.

11 https://www.thebaseballcube.com/content/player/727/.

12 McCarty left an indelible mark on the Stanford University record books. His 24 home runs in 1991 remain the second-highest single season total while his career average of .359 is still the second highest in program history. He ended his career sixth all-time in doubles (44) and seventh with 155 RBIs. https://gostanford.com/honors/stanford-athletics-hall-of-fame/david-mccarty/38.

13 https://www.baseball-almanac.com/players/trades.php?p=mccarda01. Kevin Murphy was the scout credited with his signing. In a 2023 email, McCarty said the bonus was just a bit higher, $395,000.

14 Jeff Lenihan, "Minnesota Twins," *The Sporting News*, September 21, 1993: 34.

15 Associated Press, "McCarty Has Big Game for Twins," *Salina* (Kansas) *Journal*, March 20, 1993: 20.

16 Jeff Lenihan, "Trombley Wonders Why He Isn't Starting," *The Sporting News*, April 5, 1993: S-30.

17 Associated Press, "Major Step Forward for McCarthy [sic]," *Galveston* (Texas) *Daily News*, June 12, 1993: 19.

18 McCarty interview.

19 McCarty interview.

20 Twins manager Tom Kelly suggested McCarty's inconsistency on defense was somehow related to his lack of production at the plate. But McCarty disagreed, telling *The Sporting News*, "I don't think one was related to the other, but the fielding surprised me. I've always taken that for granted. I don't know what happened." Jim Souhan, "Minnesota Twins," *The Sporting News*, July 11, 1994: 36.

21 In 55 games for the Buzz, he hit .253 with 3 home runs in 228 plate appearances.

22 McCarty interview.

23 McCarty told the Associated Press that Hrbek was "such a mainstay in the clubhouse," and credited him for his ability to "keep the mood very light and make it a lot of fun for everybody else." Associated Press, 'Twins Trying to Replace First Baseman Hrbek," *Greenwood* (South Carolina) *Index-Journal*, April 17, 1995: 7.

24 "McGwire Sure Isn't Hurting for Power," *San Francisco Examiner*, printed in the *Santa Cruz* (California) *Sentinel*, March 31, 1996: 19.

25 Sacramento Bee, "Giants Rained Out; Suffer Injury," *Santa Cruz Sentinel*, June 7, 1996: 13.

26 McCarty interview.

27 Jim Street, "Seattle," *The Sporting News*, October 12, 1998: 76.

28 "Transactions," *Indiana* (Pennsylvania) *Gazette*, December 19, 1998: 17.

29 It was increasingly clear that the now 29-year-old McCarty could more than handle the pitching in the highest of minor leagues. He also found other ways to contribute at Toledo, including two innings in two games on the mound. He spent significant time during the season at first base and at all three outfield positions.

30 Susan Slusser, "Oakland," *The Sporting News*, May 13, 2000: 54.

31 The Royals needed a viable defensive upgrade at first base over Matt Sweeney, who had struggled to make even the routine plays in camp. Steve Rock, "Kansas City," *The Sporting News*, April 3, 2000: 39. Sweeney came through in the regular season, playing in 159 games and driving in 144 runs, with a .991 fielding percentage.

32 McCarty interview.

33 McCarty interview.

34 "Transactions," *Salina Journal*, July 9, 2003: 26.

35 "Boston Red Sox," *The Sporting News*, August 18, 2003: 36.

36 McCarty's lone opportunity in the Series was as a pinch-hitter in the eighth inning of Game One, but in response to a pitching change he was removed for a different hitter before making an actual plate appearance. Boston advanced to the American League Championship Series against the New York Yankees, losing in seven games. McCarty had one at-bat, striking out in a pinch-hit appearance in the eighth inning of a 6-2 loss in Game Two.

37 "Linescores," *Greenwood Index-Journal*, March 22, 2004: 12; Associated Press, "A-Rod Hurt Against Boston," *Ukiah* (California) *Daily Journal*, March 25, 2004: 7.

38 For an article detailing McCarty's pitching, see Bill Nowlin, "First Baseman Dave Mccarty Pitches Three Times During the Magical 2004 Red Sox Season," SABR Games Project. https://sabr.org/gamesproj/game/october-3-2004-first-baseman-dave-mccarty-pitches-for-third-time-during-magical-red-sox-season/. In his September 2023 interview, McCarty said he had "kind of messed around with [pitching] for years" and had thrown a bullpen for the Red Sox coaching staff in 2003 and was invited to work out with pitchers and catchers in 2004 spring training. In early 2004, there had been word that "the Red Sox have backed off McCarty's pitching experiment but [his agent, and former ballplayer Joe Sambito was] "hoping the team would continue to allow McCarty to pitch." Nick Cafardo, Exercising Caution on Nixon," *Boston Globe*, March 18, 2004: C2. After McCarty's Opening Day outing, catcher Kevin Cash said, "He had some good stuff, first-pitch slider and a couple of sinkers. He knows what he's doing up there." Joe Burris, "Blue Jays Come Out Swinging," *Boston Globe*, April 10, 2004: F5. Cafardo said that Sambito was said to have been McCarty's boyhood hero, now his agent. He devoted a full column to McCarty's mound debut. "McCarty Isn't King of the Hill," *Boston Globe*, April 10, 2004: F8.

39 Regarding the Red Sox teams he'd been on, he said, "There wasn't any of that selfishness that you see on every team, where some guys are just worried about their stats, and putting up their numbers. It was completely different. Guys were, from 1 to 25, everybody was pulling to win. It didn't matter if I was 0 for 4, but we won. Everybody was happy. Nobody was skulking around." Interview with Allan Wood on April 29, 2013.

40 Todd Civin, "Through the Eyes of ... David McCarty, World Champion Human Being," *Bleacher Report*, March 31, 2009. https://bleacherreport.com/articles/147987-through-the-eyes-ofdavid-mccarty-world-champion-human-being. Monica McCarty has a website available at https://www.monicamccarty.com/index.php.

41 McCarty email, December 5, 2021.

42 He added: "One thing they never tell you about playing professional sports is that the bill comes due. You beat the crap put of your body for all those years. From the time I was 50, I could not run because my left knee was so shot. I finally got a partial replacement when I was 51 and I wish I had done it sooner. That is pretty young to be having that done. And even now, my back hurts, my neck hurts, my right hip is starting to hurt. My right knee is OK, but eventually that will go. That is the bill."

43 McCarty interview.

44 McCarty interview.

RAMIRO MENDOZA

BY NICK MALIAN

Ramiro Mendoza was signed as a free-agent starting pitcher in 1991 by the New York Yankees, but as his career progressed, he became a bullpen staple and occasional spot starter to support the pitching needs of both the Yankees and Boston Red Sox. The transition from starter to reliever suited Mendoza, who went 23-19 with a 5.09 ERA in 62 games as a starter and 36-21 with a 3.68 ERA in 280 games as a reliever during his 10-year major-league career. He earned the nickname El Brujo, Spanish for the Wizard, for his ability to fool batters with his four-seam fastball, slider, sinker, and changeup.[1] He was also one of three players to win a World Series for both the Yankees and the Red Sox.[2]

Ramiro Mendoza was born on June 15, 1972, in the town of La Enea, in the small southern province of Los Santos, Panama.[3] He is one of several prominent major leaguers from Panama, including Hall of Famers Rod Carew and Mariano Rivera. Growing up poor in Panama with aspirations of playing baseball meant sacrificing as a family. They farmed and sold tomatoes to make ends meet and when they earned enough, Mendoza could afford bus fare to travel to the ballpark.[4] If not, he would spend the night at the ballpark to avoid paying extra fare. The scout who signed Mendoza in 1991, Herb Raybourn, said of him, "Of all the kids I've ever signed, he had the hardest time because he had trouble just getting to play."[5]

Mendoza debuted in the Yankees' minor-league system with the Greensboro Hornets and the GCL Yankees in 1993 and then bounced around between Rookie and Triple-A ball until 1996, when he debuted in the majors to support an injury-laden pitching staff on May 25 against the Seattle Mariners. In front of a sold-out Kingdome, Mendoza pitched six innings and gave up seven hits and three earned runs and struck out six Mariners including Ken Griffey Jr. and Edgar Martinez, both looking, to earn his first major-league win.[6] His six strikeouts in his first game were a record for Panamanian pitchers, which was later tied by Humberto Mejía in 2020.[7]

Mendoza appeared in 12 games in 1996 and started in 11. His second career start was in sharp contrast to his debut. Against the California Angels, he pitched only 3⅔ innings and gave up six hits. The Yankees' offense was stifled, and the Angels won, 4-0. His next three starts were also unimpressive. In that stretch, he pitched 13⅔ innings and allowed 26 hits and 14 earned runs (9.22 ERA) and went 0-2, with one no-decision.

Mendoza earned wins in his next two starts, against the Cleveland Indians and Minnesota Twins, that brought his season record to 3-3. In his final five appearances, he made four starts and pitched in relief once, in his final game of the season. He went 1-2 with a 7.78 ERA and finished the season with a 4-5 record and a 6.79 ERA. The Yankees finished first in the AL East. Due to pitching injuries suffered by the Yankees, there was talk that Mendoza would make the playoff roster; however, that did not occur.

Mendoza's transition to the Yankees in 1996 from their minor-league system was aided by teammates Ruben Rivera and Mariano Rivera.[8] Mendoza and Rivera developed a special bond that transcended the typical teammate friendship. In 1997 while having a catch with Rivera, Mendoza witnessed "a gift from God" as Rivera put it. One of the most famous pitches in baseball was born, Rivera's devastating cutter. "The ball was moving, and (Mendoza) thought I was making the ball move," Rivera said, claiming "I have no control over this. The ball is moving, and I have no control." Rivera become one of the greatest closers of all time and led a modern baseball dynasty because of that pitch.[9] And although Mendoza's career was markedly different than Rivera's, he too played an instrumental role in his team's success.

Mendoza began the 1997 season with Triple-A Columbus (International League). The Yankees had signed David Wells in the offseason, and it was unclear whether Mendoza would crack the starting rotation. However, a hernia injury landed Dwight Gooden on the disabled list in early April and Kenny Rogers was moved to the bullpen to boost his confidence, and that opened the door for Mendoza to heavily contribute in 1997.[10]

Mendoza made 39 appearances (15 starts) and had an 8-6 record. As a starter, he was 5-5 with a 4.93 ERA; in relief he was 3-1, 2.93. He pitched 133⅔ innings, the most he would pitch in his major-league career. Despite logging the fifth-most innings of all Yankees pitchers during the regular season, Mendoza pitched only 3⅔ innings in two postseason games.

Mendoza was brilliant in his postseason debut. He pitched in relief in Game One of the Division Series against the Cleveland

Indians. Replacing David Cone in the top of the fourth inning after Cone gave up six earned runs, Mendoza gave up one hit, struck out two, and did not give up a run.[11] The Yankees were unfazed by the 6-1 deficit when Mendoza entered the game: They scored eight runs over three innings to win, 8-6. The Yankees manager Joe Torre said of Mendoza's performance, "I thought, obviously he was the difference. He put the tourniquet on it."[12]

Game Four of the ALDS was a different story for Mendoza. He replaced Mariano Rivera to start the ninth inning of a 2-2 game. Cleveland's Marquis Grissom led off the inning with a single to right field. Bip Roberts sacrificed Grissom to second. Then Omar Vizquel slapped a single up the middle that hit off Mendoza's glove and bounced past Derek Jeter, scoring Grissom for a walk-off victory. The Yankees lost the next night and were ousted from the postseason.

The 1998 Yankees capped off a historic 114-win regular season by sweeping the San Diego Padres to claim their first of three consecutive World Series titles. The 1998 season was also a career year for Mendoza. In 41 pitching appearances, 14 as a starter, he finished with a career-high 10 wins and a 3.25 ERA, a career low. Mendoza started 11 of his first 13 appearances and posted a 4-1 record. However, the debut of the Cuban phenom Orlando Hernández on June 3 shifted Mendoza's role from starter to reliever. In his remaining 28 appearances during the regular season, 25 in relief and 3 as a starter, Mendoza finished with a record of 6-1, one save, and five holds.

Mendoza pitched only 5⅓ innings in the postseason. In the ALCS against Cleveland, he replaced Andy Pettitte with two outs in the bottom of the fifth inning with the Yankees trailing 6-1. He held Cleveland in check, giving up three hits and no runs before being replaced by Mike Stanton in the seventh. The Yankees lost the game 6-1.

In Game Six of the ALCS, Mendoza held Cleveland to one hit and no runs over three innings. He replaced David Cone in the top of the sixth with a 6-5 lead. The Yankees scored three more runs in the bottom of the inning and won the game and the ALCS, 9-5. Mendoza earned his first postseason hold and his first trip to the World Series.

Mendoza pitched in relief in Game Three of the World Series against the San Diego Padres. He replaced Graeme Lloyd in the bottom of the seventh inning with one out and the Padres leading 3-2. Mendoza struck on the first batter he faced, Carlos Hernández. He then gave up a soft hit to left field by Chris Gomez, who was thrown out by Shane Spencer trying to stretch it into a double. The Yankees added three runs in the eighth to take a 5-3 lead. In the bottom of the inning, Mendoza gave up a one-out double to Quilvio Veras. Rivera replaced Mendoza and the Padres scored a run, but Rivera closed out the ninth inning and gave Mendoza his first postseason win.

In 1999 Mendoza had a 9-9 record in 53 appearances, predominantly as a reliever. In 12 postseason games, he was limited to three pitching appearances, two in the ALCS against the Boston Red Sox and one in the World Series against the Atlanta Braves.

In Game Two of the ALCS against the Boston Red Sox, Mendoza replaced Allen Watson in the top of the eighth inning; he struck out Butch Huskey and got José Offerman to fly out, ending the inning. The Yankees won, 3-2. Mendoza entered Game Five in the bottom of eighth with one out and got five consecutive outs to earn his first postseason save and clinch the ALCS for the Yankees.

Mendoza's 2000 season was highlighted by a near-perfect outing in his first start of the season, on April 15 against the Cleveland Indians. He brought the perfect game to the top of the seventh inning with one out at Yankee Stadium, when Carlos Febles lined a single off third baseman Clay Bellinger's glove that broke up the perfect game. "I was on pace to do something special. … I just hope that in the future I get the chance to go out there and try to do something special," Mendoza said.[13] Manager Joe Torre's plan for Mendoza in this game was to limit him to 80 pitches. He entered the seventh inning having thrown 74. Mendoza had also developed a blister on his right middle finger which gave him problems gripping the ball. After Mendoza gave up an RBI double to Jermaine Dye, Torre took him out. Through 6⅔ innings, Mendoza gave up two hits and one run and earned his second win of the season.

Mendoza's season was cut short on August 6 when he was placed on the 15-day disabled list for weakness in the back of his shoulder that also kept him out of the postseason. He pitched only 65⅔ innings in 14 games and finished with a 7-4 record.

With Jeff Nelson having left for the Seattle Mariners, the Yankees' expectation for 2001 was for Mendoza to become the set-up man. However, as he recovered from shoulder surgery in 2000, the Yankees expected to be patient with Mendoza.[14] By season's end, however, he had appeared in 56 games, pitching 100⅔ innings, the most by anyone the bullpen, and was 8-4, 3.75.

The Yankees relied heavily on Mendoza in the postseason. He pitched in eight games, three in the Division Series, three in the Championship Series, and two in the World Series, which the Yankees lost to the Arizona Diamondbacks. Against Arizona he struck out 10 batters in 12⅓ innings and had a 0.73 ERA.

In the 2002 regular season, Mendoza pitched in 62 games, the most of his career. His ERA over 91⅔ innings was 3.44 The 2002 season was the first in which he did not make a start. In the postseason, the Yankees lost to the eventual World Series champion Anaheim Angels in the Division Series. Mendoza pitched twice in relief, giving up two runs in 1⅔ innings (13.50 ERA).

In Game Four, Mendoza replaced David Wells in the bottom of the fifth inning with the Yankees trailing 6-2 and two Angels on base. Mendoza faced two batters and gave up a single and double that accounted for three runs. This was Mendoza's final postseason appearance for the Yankees.

The Yankees cut Mendoza loose after the 2002 season. "It hurt me to see that the Yankees didn't sign me saying they had no money," he said.[15] Mendoza then signed a two-year, $6.5 million contract with their archrivals, the Red Sox. Red Sox general manager Theo Epstein said, "We're very happy to have him in our bullpen. It is up to (manager) Grady (Little), but we've discussed how he fits in perfectly with how we want to use our bullpen this year. He's a versatile guy and could pitch some of our most critical innings."[16]

The 2003 season with the Red Sox was Mendoza's worst as a professional. His record in 37 games was 3-5 with a 6.75 ERA and a 1.77 WHIP in 66⅔ innings. On July 5 Mendoza made his first start since June 2001, facing the Yankees, and pitched five shutout innings to help blow out Roger Clemens and the Yankees, 10-2. He earned his second win of the season.

Mendoza finished the 2003 season on a high note. In front of a sellout crowd at Fenway Park against the Baltimore Orioles on September 25, he struck out Brian Roberts to close out a 14-3 victory that clinched the AL wild card.[17] Mendoza did not pitch in the postseason, in which the Red Sox were eliminated by the Yankees in the ALCS.

The historic 2004 season for the Boston Red Sox did not start well for Mendoza. After he pitched one inning in the third game of the season, Mendoza was placed on the 15-day disabled list with a sore shoulder. He was reactivated on July 15 and finished the season 2-1 with three holds in 30⅔ innings, with a 3.52 ERA, better than the team ERA of 4.18.

In the Red Sox postseason run, Mendoza pitched twice, both in the ALCS against the Yankees. In Game One he pitched one inning, gave up a hit and hit one batter. In Game Three, Mendoza replaced Bronson Arroyo in the top of the third inning with the score tied 4-4 and gave up two runs; one on a single by Bernie Williams and one on a balk. Mendoza hit Miguel Cairo to lead off the fourth inning and was replaced by Curt Leskanic, who gave up a home run to Gary Sheffield two batters later. Cairo's run broke the 6-6 tie and gave Mendoza the loss. He did not pitch again in the ALCS or World Series.

Mendoza was not re-signed by the Red Sox in the offseason. He signed a minor-league contract with the Yankees' Triple-A team, the Columbus Clippers. In eight games he went 1-0 with one save and 0.75 ERA. He also pitched in two games for the Rookie Gulf Coast Yankees. On September 1, the major leagues' roster expansion day, his contract was purchased by the Yankees.

Mendoza pitched for the Yankees the same day against the Seattle Mariners. He relieved Alan Embree in the bottom of the eighth inning with Seattle ahead 2-1. Mendoza gave up two runs and two hits and the Yankees lost 5-1. At age 33, this was Mendoza's last major-league game appearance.

In his 10 seasons in the majors (1996-2005), Mendoza pitched in 342 games (797 innings) and finished with a 59-40 won-lost record and 16 saves. His career ERA was 4.30.

But his baseball career was not over: From 2006 to 2012, Mendoza pitched in the minor leagues, in Venezuela, and for Panama in two World Baseball Classics.

In 2006 Mendoza re-signed with the Columbus Clippers and pitched in 24 games (2-5, 6.96). In 2008-09 he pitched in Venezuela and went 4-0 with a 1.62 ERA in 21 games. He returned to the United States in 2009 and pitched in 17 games for the Newark Bears of the independent Atlantic League and earned a 4-4 record. Pitching for Panama in the 2009 WBC, Mendoza made one appearance, in an elimination game against the Dominican Republic. He pitched four innings, allowed five runs, and took the 9-0 loss.[18]

In 2012, as a 40-year-old, Mendoza rejoined the Panama team in the World Baseball Classic qualifying tournament. "It is a wonderful experience," he said. "I [am coming] to do my part to help the boys, but I know they have a lot to offer for Panama."[19] Mendoza pitched in two games in the qualifying tournament. In the first game against Brazil, Mendoza entered the fifth inning with the score 2-2 with men on second and third. He gave up an RBI single that gave Brazil a 3-2 lead and eventual victory. In the second game he pitched, Mendoza was ejected in the seventh inning for hitting Colombia's Steve Brown. Despite that, he earned the win for Panama and advanced to the final against Brazil. Brazil beat Panama 1-0 to advance to the tournament. Mendoza did not pitch. Of the four qualifying tournaments that year, Mendoza pitched 8⅔ innings, the most of any pitcher.

Advancing to the major leagues from a challenging and humble life in Panama, Mendoza pitched in every role imaginable, including several high-leverage situations in the regular season and playoffs. As of 2020, he resided in Florida with his wife, Cinthia, and three children. His last venture in baseball was working for a sports agency providing financial guidance to young ballplayers.[20]

SOURCES

In addition to the sources cited in the Notes, the author consulted Baseball-reference.com.

NOTES

1   TV Max, "Ten Facts About Ramiro Mendoza, 'El Brujo' from Santeno Who Triumphed in the Major Leagues," TVN Panama, June 25, 2020, accessed June 6, 2022. https://www.tvn-2.com/tvmax/beisbol/ramiro-mendoza-brujo-grandes-ligas_1_1170557.html.

2   Johnny Damon and Eric Hinske are the other two players. Mike Rosenstein, "Ex-Yankees World Series champ: Fenway Park gives Red Sox a huge advantage in AL Wild Card game, nj.com, October 5, 2021, accessed June 28, 2022, https://www.nj.com/yankees/2021/10/ex-yankees-world-series-champ-fenway-park-gives-red-sox-a-huge-advantage-in-al-wild-card-game.html.

3   TV Max, "Ten Facts About Ramiro Mendoza, "El Brujo" from Santeno Who Triumphed in the Major Leagues."

4   Jack Curry, "On Baseball; Mendoza Speaks Pitch by Pitch," *New York Times*, October 20, 1999: D4.

5   "On Baseball; Mendoza Speaks Pitch by Pitch."

6   Associated Press, "Griffey Not as Clutch This Time," *Santa Cruz (California) Sentinel*, May 26, 1996: 16.

7   Justin Lane, "The Panamanian Humberto Mejia Will Pitch Again in the Major Leagues," Midiario.com, August 17, 2020, accessed September 9, 2022. https://www-midiario-com.translate.goog/deportivas/el-panameno-humberto-mejia-volvera-a-lanzar-

en-grandes-ligas/?_x_tr_sl=es&_x_tr_tl=en&_x_tr_hl=en&_x_tr_pto=sc.

8 Aurelio Ortiz G, "'El Brujo' Mendoza Recalled His First Spell with the Yankees 24 Years Ago," Midario.com, August 17, 2020, accessed June 6, 2022. https://www-midiario-com.translate.goog/deportivas/el-brujo-mendoza-recordo-su-primer-hechizo-con-los-yankees-hace-24-anos/?_x_tr_sl=es&_x_tr_tl=en&_x_tr_hl=en&_x_tr_pto=sc

9 Scott Miller, "Mariano Rivera: Birth of the Cutter Was 'Gift from God,'" Cbssports.com, July 14, 2013, accessed June 9, 2022, https://www.cbssports.com/mlb/news/mariano-rivera-birth-of-the-cutter-was-gift-from-god-part-4-of-5/.

10 "Rogers Is Sent to the Bullpen and Quickly Brought Back," *New York Times*, June 15, 1997: Sports, 8.

11 Associated Press, "Yanks Send Message with Game 1 Rally," *Capital*, Annapolis (Maryland) October 1, 1997: 17.

12 "Yanks Send Message with Game 1 Rally."

13 Jack Curry, "A Brush with Perfection in Mendoza's First Start," *New York Times*, April 16, 2000: 4

14 Buster Olney, "Baseball Yankees Notebook; After Having Surgery, Mendoza Won't Be Rushed Back," nytimes.com, February 20, 2001, accessed September 7, 2022. https://www.nytimes.com/2001/02/20/sports/baseball-yankees-notebook-after-having-surgery-mendoza-won-t-be-rushed.html.

15 Aurelio Ortiz G, "'El Brujo' Mendoza Recalled His First Spell with the Yankees 24 Years Ago," Midario.com May 25, 2020, accessed February 6, 2023.

16 Mark Pratt, "Red Sox OK $6.5M, Two-Year Mendoza Deal," *Midland* (Michigan) *Daily News*, December 29, 2002, accessed September 9, 2022. https://www.ourmidland.com/news/article/Red-Sox-OK-6-5M-Two-Year-Mendoza-Deal-7140117.php.

17 Associated Press, "Red Sox Have Wild Ride to Playoffs," *Hays* (Kansas) *Daily News*, September 26, 2003: 12.

18 Omar Marrero, "Dominican Republic Bounces Back in WBC," *San Diego Union-Tribune*, March 8, 2009, accessed September 10, 2022. https://www.sandiegouniontribune.com/sdut-bbi-wbc-panama-dominican-republic-rdp-030809-2009mar08-story.html.

19 Jose Pineda, "Mendoza Wants to Don No. 55 for Panama," mlb.com, accessed December 2, 2022. https://www.mlb.com/news/ramiro-mendoza-wants-to-help-panama-reach-world-baseball-classic/c-39951966.

20 "'El Brujo' Mendoza Recalled His First Spell with the Yankees 24 Years Ago."

A RED SOX MEMORY

The 2004 baseball season felt like a nor'easter of emotions as the Sox ebbed and flowed season-long behind the despised Yankees, culminating in the "Greatest Comeback [Collapse] in Baseball History" and a sweep of the Cards in the Series. You couldn't have asked for a better Hollywood-type script of a movie.

I attended no games that season but I grokked many a minute of the Sox' trip on TV. Fave memories and moments include Ortiz's October smashes, Bellhorn's batting feats, Mueller's single up the middle, the Bloody sock, Varitek and A-Rod, Pedro's pitching, Dave Roberts' enthusiasm, Theo's midseason moves, Damon's grand slam, Terry's pitcher handling, Millar's quips, Castiglione's "Can you believe it?" I could go on and on but to summarize: "What a ride!!"

SEAMUS KEARNEY

DOUG MIENTKIEWICZ

BY RYAN PALENCER AND BILL NOWLIN

There are only five players in baseball history to have earned both an Olympic Gold Medal and a World Series ring. One of these men also has a Gold Glove on his mantle…that man is Doug Mientkiewicz.

Mientkiewicz, a 12-year major-league baseball veteran finished with a .271 career batting average. He played for seven different team and points to his longevity in the game as one of the things that he was most proud of.

"(I most valued) staying in the big leagues," Mientkiewicz said. "It is hard. I played around a lot of good people, good teammates, great cities. There were a lot of good friendships and a lot of really good memories."[1]

Douglas Andrew Mientkiewicz was born on June 19, 1974, in Toledo, Ohio, to Leonard and Janet Mientkiewicz. "My mom worked at the University of Miami for like 25 years. She was like an administrative assistant. My dad was an electrical contractor who had his own small business."[2]

Doug attended the private Westminster Christian School in Florida and was a high school teammate of Álex Rodríguez, a year ahead of him. Mientkiewicz was selected as an All-State player in both football and baseball. Mientkiewicz was a 12th round pick by the Toronto Blue Jays in 1992, but opted to go to college at Florida State instead. The decision paid off, as Mientkiewicz hit .371 with 19 home runs and 80 RBIs in his third season with the Florida State Seminoles. He was named to the All-Tournament team in the 1995 College World Series. Riding that momentum, he was selected again by the Minnesota Twins in the fifth round in 1995. He signed in late July and appeared in 33 games for the high-A Fort Myers Miracle.

His first full year was 1996; he played in 133 games for Fort Myers and drove in 79 runs with a .291 batting average.

In 1997 he was advanced to the Eastern League's New Britain (Connecticut) Rock Cats. He hit .255 the first year but in 1978 – his age 24 season – blossomed with a .323 batting average in 138 games, with 16 homers and 88 runs batted in. He was named to the league All-Star team as a designated hitter. This earned him a look with the Twins and he had his major-league debut on September 18 against the Detroit Tigers. Though he went 0-for-3 in the contest, it did not take Mientkiewicz long to pick up his first hit the following day. In 25 big-league at-bats in 1998, Mientkiewicz hit .200 with a double and two RBIs.

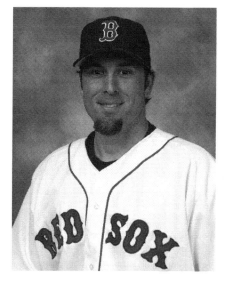

Though Mientkiewicz saw some success on the field, the Twins were in a huge drought as a group. They finished the season 70-92. Their most recent winning season had been 1992 and they strung together four straight 90-loss seasons from 1997 to 2000. With low expectations, the Twins then put it all together and finished second in the American League Central in 2001. The following three seasons, with Mientkiewicz manning first base, Minnesota claimed three straight A.L. Central crowns.

"We were in a rebuilding phase there," Mientkiewicz said. "We brought respectability back to that town that deserved it. That city really got us, because we were not high profile, big name guys at the time. We were kind of the blue-collar type and that town really fed off us and we fed off them."

While he played with seven different teams, by far his longest stop was with the Twins. He played in parts of seven different seasons with the team, and he said that it will always feel like his baseball home.

"I was professionally born as a Twin," Mientkiewicz said. "I was fortunately to come up with mostly the same group from A-Ball all the way to the big leagues. I am still in contact with a lot of those guys. People didn't think we were very good at the time and we made the playoffs. Looking back at those teams, there were some pretty good guys on that team."

Mientkiewicz stood 6-foot-2 and is listed at 195 pounds. He batted left-handed and threw right-handed. He was, however, was far from a typical, power-hitting first baseball in the early turn of the century. Most corner infielders were expected to hit homers in the bunches and drive in runs by the hundreds. This was not Mientkiewicz's game. He was a finesse hitter, but a solid on-base guy. Where he made his biggest difference was with the glove.

Mientkiewicz knew that he was never going to fit the mold, but he knew that he was good enough at his niche to last and fit what the Twins wanted him to do. This belief in his defensive abilities paid off when he was awarded the 2001 Gold Glove at first base.

"The Gold Glove, for me, was about the only thing I could win, as a first baseman," Mientkiewicz said. "I had to do things that other guys didn't do…That was pretty much catch everything that comes this way and turn hits into outs. That is the way that [manager] Tom Kelly wanted it and that is how I got my chance. Defensive players have longer chances to bail themselves out of offensive slumps. I think that my glove earned me a lot of at bats and jobs that maybe that outside world didn't understand. I was hoping to win a lot more than one [Gold Glove]. With just the one, I am in a pretty high-profile fraternity and that means a lot to me."

However, Mientkiewicz's time in Minnesota was not always peaches and cream. After his cup of coffee in 1998, he had some high expectations coming into the 1999 campaign. Unfortunately, those were not realized. Mientkiewicz hit just .229 in 327 at-bats. The 2000 campaign was not that much better, as he spent most of the season with the Salt Lake City Buzz in Triple-A, only playing in three Twins games – the team's final three games of the year. He had made the league's All-Star team but, nonetheless, Mientkiewicz found his confidence at an all-time low. However, the timing was actually on his side, as he was selected to represent Team USA in the Sydney Olympic Games in baseball. A grand slam in one game was a game-winner, and he hit a walk-off home run in the bottom of the ninth inning to send Team USA to the final Gold Medal round. "Just being on the gold medal stand and hearing the national anthem is something I'll never forget."[3]

This is something that Mientkiewicz credits with saving his baseball career ultimately. "It instilled confidence in what I did. It put me back on the map with the Twins."[4]

Years later, he added, "The Gold Medal, without it, I don't think that I would have even played ever again," Mientkiewicz said. "I was just in a bad spot. I just had come down from the big leagues and had really gotten beat up. I started having some success in Triple-A…It put me in a place where, if I don't play back in the big leagues, I have done something that not many people can say they have done. It gave me confidence and had me believing in myself again"

For the tournament, Mientkiewicz went 12-for-29 with two home runs in nine total games. As for the success, Mientkiewicz credits the work he put in growing up with his father.

"I always felt like I was better built for a two-week tournament than I was for a six-month season," Mientkiewicz said. "I have always had a knack…I think it came from my dad preaching that it was always bottom of the ninth and two outs when we took batting practice, down by a run. What are you going to do? That situational thinking really prepared me for tournaments and playoffs. I had a knack for slowing it down because my dad emphasized those situations. I went out there and had a solid two weeks."

In 2001, he was back with the big-league Twins for the full season, playing in 151 games and leading the team in batting with a .306 average. He homered 15 times and his 74 RBIs placed him third on the Twins. The team finished in second place, six games behind the Division-leading Cleveland Indians. This was the year he won his Gold Glove. He was also named the Twins' MVP for 2001. How did he become a Gold Glove first baseman? "Countless hours with my old man hitting me ground balls on the concrete for years."[5] He said he wanted to be known as a "gamer…a blue-collar, lunch-pail kid."[6]

With a 94-67 season, the Twins won the Central Division in 2002, though Mientkiewicz had something of an off-year, his average dropping 40 points to .261 and his RBIs dropping by 10. While his career playoff numbers don't showcase this fully, Mientkiewicz has displayed that he is a clutch player. In his first playoff series, Mientkiewicz smacked two home runs in the 2002 American League Division Series in over the Oakland A's, a solo home run in Game One and a two-run homer in the Game Four. This was the Twins' first playoff series win in over a decade, and Mientkiewicz was a catalyst. In the ALCS against the Angels, Mientkiewicz hit .278 with a double, but the Twins were defeated, four games to one.

Mientkiewicz rebounded in 2003, batting an even .300 and achieving a career-high on-base percentage of .393. He only committed four errors all season long, a .997 fielding percentage. The Twins lost the Division Series to the New York Yankees, winning the first game but then dropping three in a row. Mientkiewicz was 2-for-15, both singles.

Before he got the opportunity for his third straight playoff performance with the Twins, he was traded by the team that developed him. In 78 games with the Twins, he'd hit .246. When he was in a slump, things really ate at him to a degree that seems surprising. Both he and his wife talked about it in a late June interview that presents an interesting story of a hitter haunted by slumping.[7] He remembered slumps for along time to come. In May 2001, he told Bob Nightengale about his 1999 season. "I wake up every morning and remember what it was like, It's still very fresh in my memory. And to be honest, I don't want to ever forget that feeling. That year was an embarrassment. It was hard for me to even look at myself…I didn't deserve to be here…There wasn't a player even close to being as bad as I was."[8] Hard on himself, for sure.

On July 31, 2004, Mientkiewicz was traded as part of a four-team trade by the Minnesota Twins to the Boston Red Sox.[9] This was pretty fitting, because Mientkiewicz remembers seeing what happened to the Red Sox just the season before, when they lost to the Yankees in the ALCS in seven games.

"I remember sitting there, watching that ALCS the year before," Mientkiewicz said. "I lived in Miami at the time and was already making plans to go see David [Ortiz] and the guys in South Florida. At the time, I wasn't a really big Yankee fan."

His Twins teammates were said to see him go. Torii Hunter says, "This is hard, man. I've never see anyone play defense like this cart. And Dougie is chemistry."[10]

The trade happened while the Red Sox were in Minneapolis visiting the Metrodome. He literally walked from the home clubhouse to the visitors clubhouse.

Down the stretch, Mientkiewicz did not put up tremendous numbers; he only hit .215 in 107 at-bats for the Red Sox, but he was ready when October hit, for a cursed team who had not won a World Series in 86 years. Red Sox manager Terry Francona used him as a late-inning defensive replacement in each of the three ALSG games, in the final four ALCS games, and in all four World Series games. Mientkiewicz didn't get to bat much, but went 2-for-4 and played a strong defensive first base, taking over for Kevin Millar near the end of each game. Indeed, in 178 career postseason chances, Mientkiewicz never committed even one error.

The Red Sox swept the Angels and earned that rematch with the Yankees.

However, things started to look grim again for Boston, as they fell down three games to none, smacked 19-8 in Game Three. However, Mientkiewicz knew that if any team was built to come back from that, it was that 2004 Red Sox squad.

"It was really a special group because they made us feel welcome for the guys who came over later," Mientkiewicz said. "You know they got their hearts ripped out the year before, and turn around and stay strong enough that they can come back and do it again and finish it. That group may not have been the most talented, but they were the most battle tested. The care for one another was through the roof and I think it gets lost in the shuffle, but I think because we cared so much about one another, won us more games than we might care to admit even in the playoff run."

The following two games were won by the Red Sox in the 12th and 14th innings. They also took Games Six and Seven to earn the World Series appearance against the Cardinals. Riding the momentum against the Yankees, the Red Sox steamrolled the Cardinals, outscoring them 24-12 in the four-game sweep. While he got only one at-bat, Mientkiewicz was in a great spot, providing a defensive replacement at first base in all four games. With two outs in the ninth of game four, Edgar Rentería grounded softly back to Keith Foulke, who flipped on to Mientkiewicz at first for the final out, earning him a spot forever in Red Sox lore.

Red Sox broadcaster Joe Castiglione uttered the words that will live in the memory of a generation of Red Sox fans: "Swing and a ground ball stabbed by Foulke. He has it. He underhands to first and the Boston Red Sox are the World Champions. For the first time in 86 years the Red Sox have won Baseball's World Championship. Can you believe it!"

"We always joked that we hadn't won one in 86 years, if you think we are going to do it the conventional way, you're crazy," Mientkiewicz said. "Getting down 3-0 was not exactly the best of situations, but looking back to win that one the way we did, I think that team will be remembered and grandkids will tell their grandkids. It will keep moving on and be a folklore. I was lucky to be in the right place at the right time a lot of times."

Doug Mientkiewicz kept the ball. He'd not even realized he had it until 20 minutes later when his wife Jodi asked where it was. He looked in his glove, saw it still there, pulled it out and put it in her purse. Unfortunately, he also remarked to a reporter, "That's my retirement fund."[11] That didn't set too well with many in Red Sox Nation. There were even death threats.[12]

Who was the rightful owner of arguably the most valuable ball in Red Sox history, the one that when caught ended an 86-year-long championship drought? How much was the ball worth? The Boston Globe's Dan Shaughnessy called the bell the "Hope Diamond of New England sports." He noted that the ball which had eluded Bill Buckner was auctioned off for $93,500 (purchased by action Charlie Sheen), that the Carlton Fisk hit off the left-field foul pole to win Game Six of the 1975 World Series had gone for $113,273, that Barry Bonds' 73rd home run ball sold for $450,000, and that Mark McGwire's 70th home run ball had sold for $3 million. He quoted Boston area sports memorabilia dealer Phil Castinettti as saying, "It might be worth a million dollars."[13]

A minor controversy developed and one of the authors of this article was asked to debate the issue with noted Harvard Law School professor Alan Dershowitz, the discussion printed in the Boston Globe Magazine.[14]

The Red Sox and Mientkiewicz agreed to loan the ball to the Hall of Fame for a year, but in November the Red Sox filed suit against the first baseman and in December 2005 the two parties agreed to submit to arbitration.[15] In the end, the ball was donated to the National Baseball Hall of Fame. "Me, my family, went through hell and back. I'm glad it's over," said Mientkiewicz after the matter was finally resolved.[16]

Following that win, Mientkiewicz played five more major-league seasons with the Mets, Royals, Yankees, Pirates, and Dodgers before retiring in 2010 as a minor-league player for the Marlins.

In January 2005, the Red Sox had traded him to the New York Mets for minor-leaguer Ian Bladergroen. He played first base in 87 games for the Mets, six more games than fellow first baseman Chris Woodward. He hit for a .240 average, with 29 RBIs. The Mets added Carlos Delgado in 2006; Mientkiewicz was granted free agency in November 2005.

In mid-December, he signed with the Kansas City Royals and a pattern developed where each October or November he was granted free agency and then signed with a brand-new team for the following season.

With the Royals in 2006, he played in 91 games, batting .283 and driving in 43 – through July 25. A back problem was discovered and in late August he underwent season-ending back surgery for a herniated disc.[17] Next up was a year with the New York Yankees in 2007. In 72 games (more than any other Yankee first baseman that year), he hit .277 and drove in 24. A midseason broken wrist cost him three months of playing time, from June 3 through September 3. The 2008 season saw him hit for the very same average (.277) for the Pittsburgh Pirates, and drove in 30. He had initially signed a minor-league deal with an invitation to spring training, and had made the team. He appeared in 125 big-league games, many as a pinch-hitter and some for late-inning work behind Adam LaRoche.

Mientkiewicz started the 2009 season with the Los Angeles Dodgers, but after a two-run pinch-hit double in the April 16 game separated his right shoulder when diving into second base, requiring surgery that kept him out almost the full season. He rehabbed with the Triple-A (Pacific Coast League) Albuquerque Isotopes.[18]

That August his wife Jodi had heart surgery. He was brought back up to the big leagues in September and played in 13 games for the Dodgers, almost exclusively as a pinch-hitter. For the year as a whole, he was 6-for-18 with Los Angeles. He had hoped to return in 2010 and signed to a minor-league contract with the Dodgers in December, but was released by the Dodgers on April 3, 2010. On May 6, he signed with the Florida Marlins, appeared in four games for their Triple-A affiliate New Orleans Zephyrs. Eight days after signing, he was granted free agency. He announced his retirement as a player.

In the majors, he had appeared in 1,087 games, with a career .271 batting average (and .360 on-base percentage). He homered 66 times and drove in 405 runs. His lifetime fielding percentage of .9963 fielding percentage is said to rank fifth among major-league first basemen.

He took a position as a hitting coach working in rookie ball for the Dodgers.[19]

In 2012, he worked as hitting coach for the rookie-league Ogden (Utah) Raptors of the Pioneer League. For 2013, he was made manager of the Class-A Fort Myers team in the Florida State League. The Miracle won the South Division title, but lost out in the playoff semifinals.

In 2014, repeating as manager, Mientkiewicz and the Miracle went all the way, beating Daytona three games to one in the finals. After the season, he was one of three finalists for Ron Gardenhire's replacement as manager for the Twins. Instead the Twins selected Paul Molitor. He admitted to being "Crushed. I thought I was ready."[20] He was named to manage the Chattanooga Lookouts, the Twins' Double-A team in the Southern League. He led that team to a league championship, his second in as many years.

It was the Lookouts again in 2016, then the Miracle for 2017 and then – in the Detroit Tigers system, the International League's Toledo Mud Hens in 2018. In both years, his teams made the playoffs but were eliminated in the first round of the playoffs. In 2019, the Mud Hens finished third in the West Division and Mientkiewicz was relieved of his position.

He was hired by ESPN to work as a college baseball analyst on its ACC Network, beginning with the 2020 season but the season was placed on hold due to the COVID-19 pandemic and at the time of the March 28 interview, all concerned were waiting for baseball to resume.

SOURCES

In addition to the sources cited in the Notes, the authors also relied on Baseball-Reference.com, Retrosheet.org, and the Doug Mientkiewicz player file from the National Baseball Hall of Fame.

NOTES

1. Ryan Palencer interview with Doug Mientkiewicz on August 27, 2019. Unless otherwise indicated, all direct quotations come from this interview.
2. Bill Nowlin interview with Doug Mientkiewicz on March 28, 2020.
3. Seth Livingstone, "Mientkiewicz Had Had A Pronounced Impact," *USA Today Baseball Weekly*, April 3-9, 2002: 37.
4. Adam Kilgore, "Mientkiewicz Has Golden Memories," *Boston Globe*, August 15, 2004,
5. Steve Serby, "Serby's Dunday Q&A with…Doug Mientkiewicz," *New York Post*, February 27, 2005: 46.
6. Serby.
7. Jim Souhan, "Twins: Hitting Slump Consumes Doug Mientkiewicz," *Star-Tribune*, June 27, 2004.
8. Bob Nightengale, "Unpronounceable but Unstoppable," *USA Today Baseball Weekly*, May 9-15, 2001: 5.
9. The Boston Red Sox sent Nomar Garciaparra and Matt Murton to the Chicago Cubs. The Montreal Expos sent Orlando Cabrera to the Boston Red Sox. The Chicago Cubs sent Francis Beltran, Alex Gonzalez, and Brendan Harris to the Montreal Expos. The Chicago Cubs sent Justin Jones to the Minnesota Twins.
10. La Velle E. Neal III, "Gone by Game Time: Four-team Swap Sends Gold Glover to Red Sox," *Star-Tribune*, August 2, 2004:
11. Dan Shaughnessy, "For Now, He's Having A Ball," *Boston Globe*, January 7, 2005.
12. Wayne Drehs, "The Lesson of Doug Mientkiewicz," *ESPN.com*, April 30, 2011.
13. Dan Shaughnessy.
14. Clare Leschin-Hoar, "Field of Schemes," *Boston Globe Magazine*, February 13, 2005: 320. Bill Nowlin took the position that tradition would dictate the ball remained Mientkiewicz's. Prof. Dershowitz essentially argued that Red Sox fans should decide. Both agreed that perhaps a charity should benefit.
15. Chase Davis, "Sox Drop Suit over Series Ball," *Boston Globe*, December 17, 2005.
16. Associated Press, "Mientkiewicz Says Last-Out Ball from 2004 Series Headed to Hall," *Oneonta Star*, April 26, 2006.
17. Associated Press, "Mets Cut Ledee to Make Room for Green," *Utica Observer-Dispatch*, August 25, 2006.
18. Kevin Baxter, "Dodgers' Doug Mientkiewicz Toughs Out A Comeback," *Los Angeles Times*, August 2, 2009.
19. Jon Heyman, "Mientkiewicz Makes Bold Boast; Did He Help or Hurt Managerial Chance?", *CBS Sports*. October 22, 2014.
20. Chip Scoggins, "Mientkiewicz Manages Through his Frustration," *Star-Tribune*, March 30, 2015.

KEVIN MILLAR

BY KAREN DELUCA STEPHENS AND KELEY RUSSO

Kevin Millar has a phrase he keeps close. "Against All Odds," tattooed on his upper left arm, captures the unlikeliness of a 12-year career in major-league baseball that began with the Florida Marlins in 1998 and led to a position on the Boston Red Sox team that broke an 86-year world championship drought to win the 2004 World Series. During a 2001 interview while playing for the Florida Marlins, Millar, who was batting an impressive .326 at the time, said, "I'm not supposed to be here. "I'm the outcast. I'm that guy."[1]

How did he get there against all odds? At 21 he was undrafted and, he admits, did not have a natural toolbox of size or speed to be a professional baseball player. Yet, he didn't let a series of initial disappointments and setbacks douse his dreams because what he did have was passion for the game: an insatiable desire to play ball, a dedicated work ethic developed as a young boy, and an infectious team spirit. "I'm a baseball player. … I love this game. I love this game. I love this game. This is all I know."[2]

Kevin Charles Millar was born on September 24, 1971, in Monterey County, California, to Charles "Chuck" Millar and Judy (Heary) Millar while his father was in the military. His early love for baseball certainly seems to have been in his DNA. Less than two months before her son was born, Judy was on the field playing fast-pitch softball and Chuck had played park league baseball before serving in the US Army during the Vietnam War. The young family settled in Valencia in Los Angeles County's Santa Clarita Valley, where Chuck worked as a lab technician and Judy as a dental hygienist. The story his parents tell is that at age 2 Kevin picked up a bat and, standing in front of a mirror, practiced his swing and batting stance and, according to his father, he slept with his bat.[3] It was around this time, too, that his parents divorced but during his childhood his parents lived about 10 minutes from each other. Trying to find an outlet for her young son's zeal for the game led Judy to tell a white lie and enroll her son in T-ball when he was six months shy of his fifth birthday. For his part, Chuck installed mercury vapor lights in his backyard and bought a pitching machine so his son could hit Wiffle balls as long as he wanted. According to Kevin, "We'd go buy a hundred Wiffle balls and play all day, all night."[4]

At this time youth baseball in Santa Clarita had grown in popularity with the success of the William S. Hart Boys Baseball program, and Kevin took the opportunity to play for two different league teams. "I was playing a 40-game schedule when everyone else was playing 20 games," he said.[5] In 1984 Millar's Hart team was 44-0 and won the Bronco Division World Championship in the Pony League World Series, played that year in St. Joseph, Missouri.[6] When he was 14 his mother moved to Los Angeles, but Millar remained in Valencia to attend Hart High School, which had a successful baseball program. He lived with his father, and for a while with his aunt, Carrie Millar, and her husband, Wayne Nordhagen, who played eight seasons in major-league baseball, and encouraged his young nephew to work hard toward his dreams. "He was my guy, I wanted to be like him," Millar said of Nordhagen.[7] In his early high-school years Millar described himself as a "third-string second baseman and a late-bloomer, but my dad always inspired me and never said 'no' to my playing. In the baseball toolbox, I think there should be a sixth tool, a kid's heart."[8]

His early years of persistence paid off. When he retired from the majors his slugging average was a solid .452 while his OPS was .810, an average that places him in the upper ranks of major-league statistics for power hitting combined with getting on base, a skill that did not go unnoticed by the Red Sox franchise in 2003. Nevertheless, the road to a World Series championship was for Millar, like his Red Sox team, one of several tough breaks and disappointments. Yet, he never doubted he would play in the majors, confessing, "I got frustrated, even angry about my playing time. But I never gave up on my dream."[9]

Los Angeles baseball in the 1980s drew a lot of attention. The Dodgers posted multiple division titles throughout the late '70s and '80s and won two World Series championships. In nearby Anaheim Nolan Ryan was breaking records for the Angels, bringing them a division championship in 1979. In his junior year Millar moved to Los Angeles to live with his mother and enrolled in University High School just at the time Frank Cruz and Hal Kurtzman began their legendary high-school coaching careers there. That first year at University, Millar played on the school's team that went to the final rounds of the citywide championships in Dodger Stadium.[10]

After his senior year Millar did not receive a single offer to play at the collegiate level. Undeterred, he attended Los Angeles City College, where he was coached by Dan Cowgill, who remembered Millar calling him at 7:00 A.M. saying, "Let's go to the park and hit."[11]

After two years at Los Angeles City College, Millar was again undrafted but was offered his one and only recruiting opportunity to play college ball at a Division I school, the result of a fortuitous coincidence. Jim Gilligan, the coach at Lamar University in Beaumont, Texas, spotted Millar remaining on the field after practice to field groundballs. Impressed with his work ethic, Gilligan offered him a scholarship. Millar jumped at the chance and enrolled at Lamar, a decision that was life-changing.

The early 1990s were a period of turmoil in Los Angeles with gang violence and police riots. Both Millar's parents had remarried and with his mother moving to Los Angeles, Millar's life had often been full of change. Arriving at Beaumont as a punk kid from LA, he immediately liked the slower-paced, close-knit community. In 1992 Gilligan's determination turned the Lamar team around and it was recognized by the NCAA for achieving the biggest improvement over a previous season.

Millar's contribution was evident. He led the Cardinals in runs, hits, home runs, and RBIs and was awarded All-Sun Belt Conference honors and the Al Vincent Award, given to Lamar's top hitter. Then he played collegiate summer baseball with the Harwich Mariners of the Cape Cod League where he is posted as the team's starting left-fielder.[12] Returning to Lamar for the 1993 season, he was instrumental in bringing the team (44-18) the Sun Belt Conference regular-season, that led to a a berth in the NCAA Central Regional Championships although the team did not advance beyond the regional tournament.[13] After his senior year at Lamar, when he batted .324 with 54 RBIs, 54 RBIs, Millar was overlooked again although he had been told he had a good chance of being selected somewhere near the middle of the draft.[14]

Millar, a self-proclaimed "fake drinker.[15] He bought a 12-pack and checked into a motel. "I sat there by myself, thinking baseball was over for me," he said. "I got smashed, and I cried and cried. It was the first time this game brought me to tears."[16]

He did not give up. Another break came his way, part coincidence, part good fortune, and part the result of Millar's unflinching goal of playing in the majors. Sam Hughes, who played for Louisiana Tech and whose father, Gary Hughes, was the Florida Marlins' director of scouting, told his father about Millar. According to Hughes, Sam said, "Dad, this guy can play. He loves the bat more than anything."[17] Jim Gilligan, his coach at Lamar, encouraged him to fly to St. Paul for tryouts in the newly formed Northern League. Millar signed his first professional contract with the scout, Dan Lunetta, with the St. Paul Saints on June 8, 1993.[18] Millar played alongside Leon Durham, a two-time Cubs All-Star first baseman and outfielder. The two became roommates and, in interviews, Millar credited Durham's experience and encouragement as crucial to building his own confidence that he had what it took to play in the big leagues. Millar hit .260 with 5 home runs and 30 RBIs in 63 games. His contract and those of two others were sold to the newest major-league team, the Florida Marlins. Millar's contract sold for $5,000.and on September 20, 1993, Millar signed with the Marlins.[19] Millar said he ended up with about $900 as a signing bonus and, feeling flush, returned to Beaumont and invited his friends to an Outback Steakhouse to celebrate.[20] A few days shy of 22, defying the odds with no agent and having been overlooked in the draft on multiple occasions, Millar finally had a big-league contract.

Millar's next hurdle was to succeed in the minor leagues, where he spent the next four years with the Kane County Cougars, Brevard County Manatees, Portland Sea Dogs, and the Triple-A Charlotte Knights. In 1994 with Kane County of the Class-A Midwest League, Millar was named an all-star. In 1995, because the players' strike was ongoing, the Marlins ordered Millar and several other nonroster players to report to spring training for possible use as replacement players. The offer was $5,000 for spring training and an additional $5,000 if they made the Opening Day roster. The players were told that if they didn't show up, they would be expected to turn in their uniforms.[21] Millar complied with the demand for the sake of staying in baseball. He was not a member of the players union and at the time the consequences for showing up for spring training were unclear.

"I was not a replacement player," he said. "I never reaped the benefits from the union then crossed the line. I was a guy from the Northern League who had bad timing, who was told by the Marlins farm director, John Boles, I had no choice."[22] He only had a few at-bats and decided to quit the replacement team before regular season began.[23] Nevertheless, Millar was regarded as a replacement player when he eventually reached the major leagues. When the strike resolved one day before Opening Day, the replacement players did not take the field but there were repercussions. After the strike the union agreed to give players like Millar all the benefits of regular union members, but not membership in the union or union representation in negotiations. "No one knew at the time. No big-league players came down and talked to the minor league," Millar said.[24] However, he's never been ostracized. He's been a union supporter all his life. "Guys understand I came through a weird way to get to the big leagues as a nobody. ... I've never had problems with my teammates," Millar said.[25] However, financial consequences continue. Replacement players were allowed to play on the postseason teams, but not allowed to benefit from any commemorative merchandise, or be featured by name on video games or other types of games, such as the American Professional Baseball Association simulation board game where replacement players are assigned an APBA fake name. Millar is known as Mike Butcher.[26]

As a nonprospect, a guy who wasn't drafted, who didn't have a team with an investment in his future, Millar had to work for his playing time in the minors. His breakthrough came in 1997, his last full year with the Portland Sea Dogs of the Double-A Eastern League, when he hit .343 with 32 home runs and 131 RBIs and was named Eastern League Player of the Year.[27] While playing for the Sea Dogs, Millar set a minor-league record of reaching base in 71 straight games.[28] His record was tied by Kevin Youkilis (2003) and Mookie Betts (2013-2014), and was broken by Andrew Velazquez of the Arizona Diamondbacks in 2014.

Millar also put in time in the winter leagues in the Dominican Republic and in the Mexican Pacific League for three seasons beginning in 1995 along with future Red Sox teammate Keith Foulke. In 1995 Millar met his future wife, Jeana, at a friend's wedding in Beaumont. They were married in October 1999 and lived in Beaumont for the next 20 years.

Millar made the Marlins in 1998 as a third baseman. "That moment is something you live for," he said.[29] He made his major-league debut on April 11 and drew a pinch-hit walk in his first at-bat. Injured in his second game, he was sent back to Triple-A Charlotte Knights for the rest of the season. He spent the first month of the 1999 season with Triple-A Calgary Cannons, and was called up on May 21. He remained with the Marlins through 2002. In the four full seasons Millar played for the Marlins, he batted .296; his best year was 2001, when he batted .314 with 20 home runs and 85 RBIs. On the field he alternated between first and third bases as well as the outfield.

Baseball is filled with celebrities and superstars, but the heart of the game lives in those ballplayers who have toughed it out without much fanfare or spotlight. Upbeat, energetic, and never giving in are qualities that propelled Millar throughout his career. As Marlins catcher Mike Redmond once said, "There are guys who fall through the cracks, and they have to do every little thing they can to get noticed. Kevin's stuck around for one reason – he's a gamer."[30] And then there is the fact that Millar's personality, his enthusiasm for playing a game he loves, can be infectious and add some levity when needed, like when he sprayed doe urine on his bat for good luck in the Opening Day game with the Marlins in 2002, or growing out his beard during his 25-game hitting streak that season.[31] About his ribbing and joking around the clubhouse, Millar was clear: "it's because I don't like cliques. ... Guys on a team need to like one another, top to bottom."[32] The South Florida Chapter of the Baseball Writers Association of America voted him their "Most Improved Player" in 2001 and in 2002 they gave him their "Good Guy" Award.[33]

When Theo Epstein and the Red Sox organization began building their team for the 2003 season, Millar was on their radar. For the 2003 season the Red Sox brought on several nontendered players, including David Ortiz and Bill Mueller. Millar could hit and get on base. By the end of the 2002 season, his career batting average with runners in scoring position was .318, and with the bases loaded it was an impressive .421. Not only could he hit under pressure, he could also bring a spirit of levity and camaraderie to the team, overcoming a defeatist mentality that often arose at crucial moments, and could help break an 86-year old curse to ultimately bring home the biggest prize of all, a World Series championship trophy to Boston. Epstein knew Millar could be a leader in the clubhouse.[34]

In true Kevin Millar fashion, getting to Boston was not without a few bumps in the road. In January 2003 the Marlins signed Todd Hollandsworth of the Texas Rangers to a one-year, $1.5 million contract. All of Millar's career had been spent with the Marlins and although he was well-liked within the organization and by Marlins fans, his position in the outfield made him vulnerable when the left-handed Hollandsworth was signed.[35] The Marlins sold Millar's contract to the Chunichi Dragons of the Japanese Central League. On January 9, 2003, Millar signed a two-year contract worth $6.2 million plus a signing bonus of $500,000 with additional bonuses for the next two years and a $3 million player option for 2005. For the contract to go through, Millar had to clear waivers. For Millar, 31, who had begun his career nearly a decade earlier making $320 every two weeks, the Chunichi offer was an opportunity he could not let slip pass.[36] Millar and his wife planned to depart for Japan on January 29 with Millar as their starting left fielder.

Two things changed Millar's career and the outcome of the 2004 Red Sox season. First, Epstein placed a waiver claim on Millar. Millar rejected it, and became a free agent. He then signed with the Dragons. Epstein continued to press his waiver claim, stating he would consider various "resolutions that could help him land Millar."[37] Millar made it clear that he would honor his contract with Chunichi,[38] but said he would prefer to stay in the US majors had he been given the right offer.[39]

The second event was the impending US military invasion of Iraq in early 2003. Both Jeana Millar and Millar's father, Chuck, who had served as a medic in Vietnam, said they did not want the family residing outside the United States with the nation at war. In early February Millar, Jeana, Chuck, and Millar's agents, Sam and Seth Levinson, met in New York with Mitsuo Kodama, director of baseball operations for the Dragons. Kodama refused to release Millar from his contract.[40] The only way Millar would be free to walk away from his contract and sign with the Red Sox was if his agents could prove that his contract with Chunichi was invalid.[41]

While further discussions were taking place, representatives from Nippon Professional Baseball went to Millar's home in Beaumont to try to convince him to adhere to his contract. Millar insisted that he would not report to Japan as planned on February 10. The Chunichi club said it was prepared to sue Millar for breach of contract.[42] Meanwhile Millar indicated that the Red Sox would have to match the contract the Dragons offered him, which would be multi-year and could come close to $6 million.[43] However, Nippon Commissioner Junnosuke Nishikawa reiterated that the league would obligate Millar to uphold his contract. With the February 10 deadline approaching, the Nippon league said that coming to Japan was Millar's only option.[44]

Of concern to Major League Baseball was the effect the situation might have on its future relationship with the Japanese league. It became evident that a way for Japan to exit the dispute while maintaining dignity was at stake.[45] After six weeks of negotiations with the help of Commissioner Bud Selig, a deal to release Millar was brokered. Chunichi released Millar from his contract and was paid between $1.2 million and $1.5 million by the Marlins. The Marlins then sold Millar's contract to the Red Sox for $1.5 million: $1.2 million was payment for Millar and $300,000 was a donation to the Marlins Community Foundation, part of which was donated by Millar. The deal was official on February 14. A few hours later Jeana and Kevin loaded up their car and drove straight for 16 hours to Fort Myers, where Millar and Epstein met for the first time.[46]

About joining the Red Sox, Millar said, "The most exciting thing in looking at this roster at the guys Theo brought in...You're going to have a lot of guys pulling from the same rope instead of three or four pulling from different ropes."[47] For Epstein, Millar was an ideal addition to his 2003 lineup, calling him one of the better unknown hitters in baseball.[48] "You've got to watch this guy play to appreciate him," Epstein said. "He's an outstanding teammate. He really fits in with a lot of the guys we have here. He's going to get dirty and get on base."[49] The Marlins' deal with the Red Sox gave them more flexibility in their salary negotiations that season, and they went on to win the World Series.

Joining the Red Sox with a starting position at first base and with a career batting average of .321 with runners in scoring position and .421 with the bases loaded, Millar was ready to put the contract ordeal behind him. Lighthearted by nature, he arrived in Fort Myers ready to show he was a fierce competitor on the field.[50] Millar's rallying cry "Cowboy Up" captured the camaraderie of the 2003 team.[51] Fans thought of Millar as the "Cowboy" and often greeted him with the cheer when he came to bat. Millar was part of the lineup that set a team record for slugging at .491. When the heartbreaking 2003 Red Sox season ended in a playoff loss to the Yankees, Millar had a batting average of .276, a .472 slugging average, and 25 home runs, a season high for him.

"Cowboy Up" whenever Millar and the Red Sox struggled carried over into the 2004 season, with a new manager, two new pitchers added to the bullpen, and a new starter, Curt Schilling. In midseason Millar hit a slump at the plate, and was faced with rumors of a possible trade, coupled with some rough treatment by the hometown fans. He hit three home runs against the Yankees in a Fenway Park game on July 23, and although the Red Sox lost the game, he believed it was a turning point for him. He said that the pain of the tough loss to the Yankees the previous season lent to the grit and determination of the 2004 team.[52]

No better example of Millar's belief in the power of attitude for a winning team was his response to Dan Shaughnessy before Game Four of the 2004 ALCS.[53] In an article written after Game Three, Shaughnessy had called the team "a bunch of frauds."[54] The phrase ignited a fire in Millar. In a pregame interview that was caught on video, Millar, punching his hand into his glove, challenged Shaughnessy with the phrase "Don't Let Us Win Tonight" that became a prediction and a rallying cry for the remainder of the ALCS and the World Series. About Game Four Millar said, "We had the chance to shock the world."[55] That night in Fenway Park in the ninth inning of Game Four, Millar's legendary walk against Yankees relief pitcher Mariano Rivera sparked the greatest comeback in major-league history. Approaching the plate, Millar's goal was a home run, like his ninth-inning home run off Rivera in 2003, but after one fastball that he fouled off, Millar waited for Rivera to make a mistake with his inside cutter, which he did. Once on first and replaced by Dave Roberts, the grit the Red Sox had displayed that whole season was magnified. "The 2004 Red Sox were a talented ballclub, but we were also scrappy. And we were relentless," he said. "We were a bunch of guys who cared. And we showed that you could win a championship being who you are."[56]

Millar hit .282 in his three seasons with the Red Sox with 52 home runs and 220 RBIs. In 2005 his power hitting dipped with only 9 home runs. In January 2006 he signed a $2.1 million, one-year contract with the Orioles, with the hopes that he would bring both his batting power and charisma to a team that had suffered a rocky 2005 season.[57] He spent three seasons with Baltimore and although an Oriole, Millar was invited back to Boston for Game Seven of the 2007 ALCS to throw out the first pitch.

In 2009 Millar signed a one-year minor-league contract with the Toronto Blue Jays. The following year he signed a minor-league contract with the Chicago Cubs but was released in spring training. He retired as a player on April 10, 2010, and joined MLB as a studio analyst. In May he joined the New England Sports Network (NESN) as a Red Sox analyst.[58]

To no one's surprise, in early May 2010, Millar signed to play with the St. Paul Saints, with whom he began his career 17 years earlier. His contract with MLB Network allowed him to play while continuing with his broadcasting obligations.[59] He played six games for the Saints. Millar explained that his return to the team had not only been to have another shot at playing baseball but was also to show support and encouragement for young players in the independent league. Millar was invited back to the Twin Cities in 2017 to celebrate the Saints' 25th anniversary; he was back on the field with a one-game contract and hit a two-run home run. "Without the Saints, I would never have been a big leaguer. I was just a regular guy – but if you believe in something, go for it," he said.[60] In August 2022 the Saints retired Millar's number 15 in recognition of his contribution to the team and independent baseball.[61]

In 2011 Millar joined Chris Rose to co-host the MLB Network talk show *Intentional Talk*.

During his 12-year major-league career, Millar played 1,427 games and batted .274 with 170 home runs and 699 RBIs. Millar continues to co-host the MLB show, which has become the network's longest-running talk show. In April 2012 he was back at Fenway Park with Pedro Martinez to lead the toast to celebrate the 100th anniversary of the ballpark. Millar has also been involved with the Good Hands in the Stands Charitable Foundation at the NCAA College World Series.

As of 2023, the Millars lived in Austin, Texas with their four children. Two of their sons were playing high-school baseball. Millar tells his children as well as any young person with hopes of playing in the major leagues that more than talent, baseball requires mental maturity. "I'm you. I'm the guy who thinks he's not going to make it. Dream and learn how to fail. The game is a failure sport, but inspiration is the kid who has a dream. When you have to grind you appreciate it more because of the grind."[62]

Millar returned to Fenway Park in 2022 to join the NESN broadcasters and continued in 2023. He has joined the ranks of Boston sports' most colorful figures.[63]

In return, Millar has said of coming to Boston in 2003, "It was the greatest thing that ever happened in my life."[64]

SOURCES

In addition to the sources cited in the Notes, the authors consulted Baseball-Reference.com; BaseballAlmanac.com; FamilySearch.com; Ancestry.com; BaseballAmerica.com; and

Tony Massarotti and John Harper, *A Tale of Two Cities* (Guilford, Connecticut: The Lyons Press, 2005).

NOTES

1. Dave Joseph, "Kevin's Heaven," *South Florida Sun-Sentinel* (Fort Lauderdale), July 1, 2001: 41.
2. "Kevin's Heaven."
3. Tyler Kepner, "Kevin Millar's Unconventional Path to the Pros," *New York Times*, March 10, 2010. https://archive.nytimes.com/bats.blogs.nytimes.com/2010/03/10/kevin-millars-unconventional-path-to-the-pros/.
4. "Kevin's Heaven."
5. Herb Crehan, "Kevin Millar Remembers the 2004 World Championship," BostonBaseballHistory.com. https://bostonbaseballhistory.com/new-kevin-millar-remembers-the-2004-world-championship/.
6. Kevin Millar, telephone interview with authors, October 23, 2023.
7. Millar interview.
8. Millar interview.
9. Crehan, "Kevin Millar Remembers the 2004 World Championship."
10. Ray Riotan, "University Does More with Less," *Los Angeles Times*, June 9, 1988: 15.
11. Dave Joseph, "Kevin's Heaven.'
12. https://www.reddit.com/r/baseball/comments/gcps67/all_time_team_for_every_team_in_the_cape_cod/
13. https://lamarcardinals.com/honors/cardinal-hall-of-honor/kevin-millar/99.
14. "Kevin's Heaven."
15. https://sportsspectrum.com/table-forty/2022/04/05/podcast-former-mlb-player-kevin-millar-wife-jeana/.
16. Jeff Pearlman, "A Character Guy," *Sports Illustrated Vault*, August 26, 2002. https://vault.si.com/vault/2002/08/26/a-character-guy-strike-talk-have-you-down-then-watch-the-marlins-wacky-kevin-millar-who-keeps-everybody-laughing/.
17. "Kevin's Heaven."
18. Howe Sports Data International, San Mateo, California, February 7, 1994.
19. Pearlman, "A Character Guy."
20. Crehan, "Kevin Millar Remembers the 2004 World Championship."
21. Juan Rodriguez, "Though Not a member, Millar Supports Union," *South Florida Sun-Sentinel*, August 24, 2002, 45.
22. Joe Capozzi, "Millar warns: Don't cross union," *Palm Beach Post*, August 24, 2002:52.
23. "Millar supports union."
24. Rodriguez, "Though not a member, Millar supports Union."
25. Rodriguez, "Though Not a Member, Millar Supports Union."
26. https://www.baseball-almanac.com/legendary/replacement_players.shtml.
27. Jeff Pearlman, "A Character Guy." https://vault.si.com/vault/2002/08/26/a-character-guy-strike-talk-have-you-down-then-watch-the-marlins-wacky-kevin-millar-who-keeps-everybody-laughing/
28. David, "Millar Time–The Long and Winding Road," BaseballRoundTable.com, June 26, 2017. https://baseballroundtable.com/millar-time-the-long-and-winding-road/
29. Jeff Pearlman, "A Character Guy," *Sports Illustrated Vault*, August 26, 2002.
30. "A Character Guy."
31. David Heuschkel, "Millar's on His Way," *Hartford Courant*, February 16, 2003: 37. https://www.courant.com/2003/02/16/millars-on-his-way/.
32. David O'Brien, "No teammate is safe from Millar's barbs," *South Florida Sun Sentinel*, March 3, 2002: 50.
33. Crehan, "Kevin Millar Remembers the 2004 World Championship."
34. Millar interview.
35. "Marlins Get Hollandsworth."
36. Ben Walker, "Millar Financial Victim," *Stuart* (Florida) *News*, January 11, 2003: 39.
37. Juan Rodriguez, "Red Sox Make Claim for Millar," *South Florida Sun-Sentinel,* January 15, 2003: 45.
38. Bob Hohler, "A Changeup from the Sox," *Boston Globe*, January 14, 2003: 74.
39. Murray Chass, "Millar Makes Case to Stay in Majors," *New York Times*, February 4, 2003: D7. https://www.nytimes.com/2003/02/04/sports/plus-baseball-millar-makes-case-to-stay-in-majors.html.
40. Jayson Stark, "Millar Wants Out of $6.2M agreement with Dragons," ESPN.com, February 13, 2003. https://www.espn.com/mlb/news/2003/0203/1503537.html.
41. Gordon Edes, "MLB: Sox Can't Make Deal for Millar," *Boston Globe,* January 20, 2003: 67.

42 https://www.bostondirtdogs.com/2004/Chasing_Steinbrenner_excerpt.html.

43 Bob Hohler "Not Getting Off Cheap with Millar," *Boston Globe*, January 17, 2003: 92.

44 Gordon Edes, "MLB Will Stay Out," *Boston Globe*, February 1, 2003: 79.

45 Gordon Edes and Nick Cafardo, "Millar Resolution in the Works," *Boston Globe*, February 7, 2003: 72.

46 Gordon Edes, "Sox Put Finishing Touches on Millar," *Boston Globe*, February 15, 2003: 50.

47 Jeff Horrigan, "At long last, Millar arrives at Red Sox camp," *Milford Daily News*, February 16, 2003. https://www.milforddailynews.com/story/sports/2003/02/17/at-long-last-millar-arrives/41241027007/

48 Gordon Edes, "MLB's Clout Helped Break Millar Logjam," *Boston Globe*, February 16, 2003: 85.

49 David Heuschkel, "Millar's on His Way," *Hartford Courant*, February 16, 2003: 37. https://www.courant.com/2003/02/16/millars-on-his-way/.

50 Bob Hohler, "Hoping His Time Has Arrived," *Boston Globe*, February 17, 2003: 56.

51 https://www.baseball-reference.com/bullpen/2003_Boston_Red_Sox.

52 Brian Jones, "Former Red Sox Star Kevin Millar Reflects on 'Painful Times' Before Winning 2002 World Series (Exclusive)," popculture.com, May 5, 2022. https://popculture.com/sports/news/former-red-sox-star-kevin-millar-reflects-painful-times-before-winning-2004-world-series-exclusive/.

53 "Kevin Millar Recalls Confronting Dan Shaughnessy During 2004 ALCS," cbsnews.com, October 5, 2017. https://www.cbsnews.com/boston/news/kevin-millar-dan-shaughnessy-2004-alcs-toucher-rich/.

54 Dan Shaughnessy, "Time to Show Some Guts or Go Belly-Up," *Boston Globe*, October 15. 2004: 79.

55 Millar interview.

56 Bill Nowlin and Allen Wood, *Don't Let Us Win Tonight: An Oral History of the 2004 Boston Red Sox's Impossible Playoff Run* (Chicago: Triumph Books, 2014), Kindle edition, Foreword.

57 "Orioles Sign Millar to 1-Year Deal," espn.com, January 12, 2006. https://www.espn.com/mlb/news/story?id=2289745.

58 "Kevin Millar Joins MLB Network as Studio Analyst," nesn.com, April 22, 2010. https://nesn.com/2010/04/kevin-millar-joins-mlb-network-as-studio-analyst/.

59 Tim Dierkes, "Kevin Millar Signs With St. Paul Saints," mlbtraderumors.com, May 5, 2010. https://www.mlbtraderumors.com/2010/05/kevin-millar-signs-with-st-paul-saints.html.

60 David Karpinski, "Millar Time – The Long and Winding Road," BaseballRoundTable.com, June 26, 2017. https://baseballroundtable.com/millar-time-the-long-and-winding-road/.

61 Dean Spiros, "Saints Retire No. 15 of Kevin Millar, Who Gave the Team 'Someone To Cheer For,'" TwinCities.com Pioneer Press, August 13, 2002. https://www.twincities.com/2022/08/13/saints-retire-no-15-of-kevin-millar-who-gave-the-team-someone-to-cheer-for/.

62 Millar interview.

63 "Kevin Millar Part of Boston Tradition of Appreciating Colorful Characters," nesn.com, May 27, 2010. https://nesn.com/2010/05/kevin-millar-the-latest-in-longstanding-boston-tradition-of-appreciating-colorful-characters/.

64 Hayden Bird, "Kevin Millar Discussed the Legacy of the 2004 Red Sox, and Why He Thinks Trevor Story's 'Going to Be Fine,'" boston.com, May 6, 2022. https://www.boston.com/sports/boston-red-sox/2022/05/06/kevin-millar-red-sox-2004/.

A RED SOX MEMORY

I've lived in the Boston area, and a Red Sox fan since 1977. The playoff series with the Yankees (especially Game Four) made those 27+ years *almost* worthwhile.

I was disappointed that the World Series started just two days later. I would have preferred attending a celebratory parade the day the Red Sox beat New York – even if it meant conceding Game One to St. Louis).

NORM GINSBERG

DOUG MIRABELLI

BY MATT PERRY

Between the minor and major leagues, there are thousands of baseball players trying to make a name for themselves. Some can hit home runs; others are great at striking out batters. One, Doug Mirabelli, was able to stand out and become a two-time World Series champion because he could do what most catchers can't always do: catch a knuckleball.

Drafted by the San Francisco Giants as a fifth-round pick in 1992, Mirabelli played for the Giants, Texas Rangers, and San Diego Padres, but is best known for his stints with the Boston Red Sox as the preferred batterymate of knuckleballer Tim Wakefield. The Red Sox even went as far as securing a police escort from the airport after reacquiring him from the Padres to make sure that Mirabelli arrived to Fenway Park in time to catch Wakefield.

Douglas Anthony Mirabelli was born on October 18, 1970, in Kingman, Arizona, to parents Frank and Karen Mirabelli. His family moved to Las Vegas, Nevada, where his father worked as a blackjack dealer in the casinos. His mother worked in human resources for the Nevada Power Company. After Frank Mirabelli retired from the casinos, he bought a neighborhood bar and restaurant. Doug attended Valley High School, the same high school as major leaguers Greg Maddux, Mike Morgan, and Tyler Houston attended, and became a standout for the Vikings baseball team. He helped lead the team to two state championships.

After his senior year in 1989, Mirabelli was selected by the Detroit Tigers in the sixth round of the June 1989 draft. Instead he played baseball at Wichita State University. From 1990 to 1992, the Shockers were the Missouri Valley Conference champions, and they were the runners-up in the 1991 College World Series, losing to LSU.

Mirabelli was a 1990 *Baseball America* freshman second-team All-American, a 1991 *Baseball America* third team All-American, a 1992 American Baseball Coaches Association second-team All-American and Collegiate Baseball third-team All-American, the Wichita State MVP in 1992.[1] Over three seasons, Mirabelli hit .341 and threw out 46 percent of baserunners attempting to steal. In 2002 he was inducted into the school's Athletics Hall of Fame.[2]

Mirabelli was selected by the San Francisco Giants in the fifth round of the 1992 draft. His career began in the California League with the San Jose Giants for the 1992 and 1993 seasons. He was promoted to Shreveport of the Double-A Texas League for 1994. In 1995 and '96 he played mostly at Shreveport with some time at Triple-A Phoenix and a brief call-up to the Giants at roster expansion time in 1996.

In a 2002 interview Mirabelli discussed his 1996 call-up to the majors. "Because I was in Double-A, I thought they were calling me up to Triple-A for the playoffs," Mirabelli said. "When they said the big leagues, I went numb."[3] He played in nine games for San Francisco Giants that year, making his major-league debut in a game against the Philadelphia Phillies on August 27, catching in the top of the ninth inning and flying out in the bottom of the inning. He got his first major-league hit on September 1 against the New York Mets, a double against pitcher Bobby Jones in the seventh inning.

For the next three seasons, Mirabelli moved between the majors and minors, appearing in six games for the Giants in 1997, 10 in 1998, and 33 in 1999. He spent all of 2000 in the majors, appearing in 82 games and batting .230 with 6 home runs and 28 RBIs. He was 0-for-2 in the NL Division Series against the New York Mets.

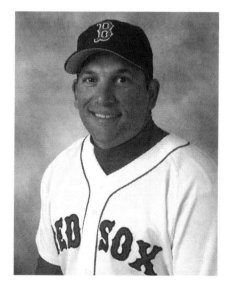

After the 2000 season, the Giants, flush with catchers, sold Mirabelli's contract to the Texas Rangers. Mirabelli had spent 10 years in the Giants system, and manager Dusty Baker said, "It's never easy to tell somebody goodbye, especially someone who's been in the organization so long."[4]

Mirabelli didn't spend too much time in Arlington, where he was a backup to future Hall of Famer Pudge Rodriguez. On June 12 he was traded to the Red Sox for pitcher Justin Duchscherer.[5]

By his second season with the Red Sox, Mirabelli had accepted his role with the team, telling the *Southeast View*, "For a long time, I had a hard time with backing up. I always wanted to play every day, but then you realize you're a backup catcher and you just deal with it," adding, "I'm not saying I don't want to play every day, but I'm comfortable with my role on this team, very much so."[6]

In 2002 Mirabelli began catching knuckleballer Tim Wakefield. He told the *Southeast View*, "It's like catching a fly ball. It's like reaching into a bucket and trying to catch a minnow. They're flying everywhere and you have to catch one of them. … It's hard to do, but I use a bigger glove and it seems to help."[7]

He told the paper how much he enjoyed playing in Boston, saying, "When I came over here, I fell in love with the place. I felt at home and I feel Fenway (Park) is great for my swing, and the fans and the atmosphere there are great."[8]

Mirabelli began playing more regularly as Wakefield got a spot in the rotation during the 2003 season. Before the season, the *Boston Globe* reported that manager Grady Little "expects to use [Jason] Varitek as he did last year, having him catch every starter except Tim Wakefield, who will work with Doug Mirabelli."[9]

Mirabelli appeared in 55 games that season, starting in 43 of them. He improved offensively, batting .258 and posting a .755 OPS. He caught all but two of the 202⅓ innings thrown by the 11-7 Wakefield during the season.[10]

At the end of the season, Mirabelli's contract was up. The Red Sox re-signed him to a one-year deal worth a reported $825,000 which avoided arbitration, and also had the Red Sox "retaining one of the game's top backup catchers."[11]

Expectations were high for the 2004 Red Sox after their devastating loss to the New York Yankees in Game Seven of the 2003 American League Championship Series on walk-off home run. In that series he caught Games One and Four, both wins, and replaced Varitek in the ninth inning of the Game Seven loss.

Mirabelli responded in 2004 by having his best offensive season in the majors, batting .281 with an .893 OPS and 32 RBIs. He played in 59 games with 41 starts as catcher, still mainly working with Wakefield.

Mirabelli didn't play at all during the 2004 divisional round against the Angels, and played only in Game Three of the ALCS, a 19-8 massacre that put the Red Sox down three games to none and set the stage for their historic comeback. Mirabelli praised Tim Wakefield, a starting pitcher who volunteered to enter the game in relief and help keep the bullpen intact. Wakefield pitched for 3⅓ innings, allowing other arms in the bullpen to be saved for the four must-win games that the team had ahead of them.

"At the end of the day, you don't want your bullpen to get blown out because we've still got four games we need to play," Mirabelli told authors Alan Wood and Bill Nowlin for their book *Don't Let Us Win Tonight*. "Hopefully. For him to be able to go out there and suck up some innings for us, that was a huge help. He loses his start the next night, but Derek Lowe is not a bad fall-back plan."[12] (Lowe started Game Four, a Red Sox victory, instead of Wakefield.)

The team had confidence that if they could take the series to seven games, they could win it. "We realized it wasn't a perfect situation for us, but there was a lot of hope and positive feelings that with our pitching we could see ourselves right back in this thing again," Mirabelli said. "I think we always had a feeling that if it got to Game Seven, the pressure would be so high on the Yankees that we would win. We just had to get to Game Seven."[13] Mirabelli and the team felt that they hadn't played their best baseball through the first three games. "There was always a sense of what we knew we were capable of doing. We knew this wasn't an accurate showing of what our offense was all about. All we needed was one positive feeling that we could get something done."[14]

These feelings were correct, and the Red Sox were able to accomplish the "impossible," becoming the first team in major-league history to erase a 3-0 series deficit, winning their first American League pennant since 1986.

The Red Sox were set to face the National League champion St. Louis Cardinals, a rematch of the 1946 and 1967 World Series. As expected, the team was feeling good after defeating the Yankees. Mirabelli said, "Our confidence was skyrocketing. It wouldn't have mattered at that point who we were playing, because when you get a team that's hot, you don't want to play that team."[15]

Wakefield got the start in Game One, meaning that Mirabelli would be starting. Varitek, the usual starting catcher, said before the game, "Doug and I have built a tremendous bond over the years. We help each other offensively, defensively, with the pitchers. We both want to accomplish the same thing. We want to win a championship. There's no question we go with Doug tonight."[16]

In the third inning, Mirabelli singled to left field off Cardinals starter Woody Williams. He said, "I had one at-bat in Game Three of the ALCS, popped up to second base. That's the only at-bat I had in a long time, so I had some nerves going, for sure. … I hit that ball really well. It was one of those hits that you can't even get to second base on because it bounces right back to the left fielder."[17] He scored on Orlando Cabrera's single three batters later. Even after starter Wakefield was replaced by Bronson Arroyo in the fourth inning, Mirabelli continued to catch until Varitek pinch-hit for him in the sixth.[18]

Mirabelli did not play again during the World Series, as the Red Sox won the next three games, sweeping the Cardinals and winning the World Series for the first time in 86 years.

After the World Series, Mirabelli re-signed with the Red Sox for two years and $3 million, making him "the highest-paid backup catcher in the majors." Varitek was also a free agent after the season, and Mirabelli stressed the importance of their tandem: "We said we were a package deal, and I still want to it to be that way. … You can't lose Varitek, regardless of what the situation is. The guy was the leader on our team. If you don't have Varitek, you don't have that team."[19]

Varitek eventually re-signed and the arrangement between the two catchers continued for the 2005 season. Mirabelli started in 33 games as the catcher and four as DH. His offensive numbers slipped slightly, at .228 with a .721 OPS. The Red Sox again made the playoffs as a wild card but were swept in the divisional round by the eventual World Series champion Chicago White Sox. Mirabelli started in the final game of that series.

During the 2005 winter meetings, the Red Sox traded Mirabelli to the San Diego Padres for second baseman Mark Loretta. Wakefield wondered, "What the heck is our team going to look like next year?" The *Globe* noted that Wakefield was 16-8 with a 3.66 ERA with Mirabelli catching him and 0-4 with an 8.86 ERA pitching to Varitek.[20]

Mirabelli's replacement, Josh Bard, struggled to catch Wakefield. During an April 26 game in Cleveland, Bard had four passed balls, one less than the team record. The *Globe* reported that "Bard, if he continues to catch Wakefield all year, stands to make a run at the Sox' season record of 26, set by Mike Macfarlane in 1995, Wakefield's inaugural year with the Sox."[21]

"Where have you gone, Doug Mirabelli?" wailed the *Globe*. "With Josh Bard struggling mightily with Tim Wakefield's knuckleball (10 passed balls in five starts), some Sox fans have expressed nostalgia for Wakefield's former battery-mate."[22]

On day after that article appeared, the Red Sox brought Mirabelli back to Boston to resume his role as Wakefield's backstop. The trade may have been surprising, but what became the story was Mirabelli's return trip to Fenway Park.

There was speculation that Red Sox GM Theo Epstein had some regrets over the trade, saying, "The game against the Indians motivated him to move on perhaps the most famous trade for a backup catcher in the history of baseball – a trade he now considers the worst he's ever made."[23]

"Instead of being patient and coming up with a creative situation, we got caught up in some of the panic that was enveloping our clubhouse," Epstein said. "I got too close to the situation and made a really reactionary move."[24]

The Red Sox sent catcher Bard and prospect Cla Meredith to San Diego in exchange for Mirabelli. The day the trade was made, the Red Sox were to play the Yankees on national television and Tim Wakefield was to start. It was Johnny Damon's first game back at Fenway Park since he left the Red Sox for the Yankees. Mirabelli, overjoyed, left San Diego on a private jet at 10:15 A.M. Pacific time. "To say I was excited would be an understatement," he said.[25]

He said the plane was cleared to go over airspace in Cleveland and New York, a move that was not routine for planes. "I guess with airplanes they typically don't go over other airspace, they have to go around it. But for this occasion, they cleared us straight over Cleveland," Mirabelli said, adding, "The pilot said to me after we got cleared over New York, 'I don't even know who you are, but I've carried hearts and lungs and never had this much clearance over airspace.'"[26]

Mirabelli landed at Boston's Logan Airport at 6:48 P.M. and hopped into an SUV that was being driven by a Massachusetts state police officer. Epstein said, "We regularly use police escorts to get the team in and out of Logan, so the traveling secretary [Jack McCormick] had an idea. He set it up."[27]

Mirabelli changed into his uniform in the back of the car as the driver, Sgt. Dave O'Leary, took Storrow Drive, a busy road that was full of traffic. To get through the traffic, Sgt. O'Leary used his lights and sirens.

"People were pulled over on the side of the road," said Mirabelli. "They saw the police car. It was bumper to bumper, and they were pulling over letting us through."[28]

As all this was going on, Wakefield was being warmed up by Jason Varitek, who was prepared to catch if Mirabelli did not make it to the park on time. He did make it on time, pulling up to the stadium at 7:02 and borrowing Wily Mo Pena's shoes.

Wakefield recalled seeing his friend and teammate again for the first time, saying, "I walk into the dugout, and I walk into the tunnel right before the national anthem, and who do I see? Mirabelli – full uniform, full gear, full everything, just walking at me. I gave him a big hug and welcome back."[29]

The game started eight minutes late at 7:13, and after a few warmup pitches, Mirabelli was back playing for the Red Sox. He was so rushed that he played the entire first inning without a cup, a piece of equipment that is essential for catchers. "I forgot my cup. It was in the police car. I didn't see it, and it was floating around in the back of a police car. I went through the first inning without a cup, and [before the] second inning I ran in and put one on."[30]

Wakefield was grateful to have Mirabelli back on the team. "Dougie was a great catcher. To be able to do what he did, to catch me – he had the best hands I've ever thrown to. Unbelievable."[31]

Although everything worked out for the Red Sox that night, the Massachusetts State Police have said that if the same situation ever occurred, they would handle things differently.

"We wouldn't do something like that again, certainly not with lights and siren. As a public safety agency, that was not an appropriate use of our assets," a spokesman said.[32]

Back on the team, Mirabelli and Wakefield found the same success they had before he left for San Diego. He had a total of 12 passed balls during the season, two more than Bard had in his first six starts.

When Varitek had to undergo surgery on his knee in August, Mirabelli stepped into the starting role and played in 57 games for the Red Sox. Plagued by injuries, the Red Sox finished 86-76 and missed the playoffs.

Learning from the previous offseason, the Red Sox kept Mirabelli, signing him to a one-year contract worth $750,000.[33]

The Red Sox turned it around for the 2007 season and Mirabelli's offense improved slightly over the previous season. With Varitek back, he reverted to his standard role as Wakefield's personal catcher and started in 33 games for Boston. The Red Sox finished 96-66, first in the American League East, and swept the Anaheim Angels in the Division Series.

Mirabelli made his only playoff appearance in Game Four of the Championship Series against the Cleveland Indians. The Red Sox lost that game, 7-3, but they went on to win the Series and sweep the Colorado Rockies in the World Series. For the second time in four seasons, Mirabelli and the Boston Red Sox were World Series champions.

At the end of the season, the 37-year-old Mirabelli filed for free agency. The Red Sox re-signed him for a $550,000 base salary with incentives that could bring his salary to $1 million.[34] But the catcher's skills had eroded and he was released during spring training.[35]

Wakefield said he was "shocked," adding, "I'm saddened by the whole situation, but it's a business decision on their part. I feel like [Kevin] Cash can do a good job, but I'm really going to miss Doug, especially with the way he's handled me and the comfort level. I'll miss his friendship. We've been together for eight years. We went through a lot of stuff together. It's unfortunate it happened that way, but we have to get past that and understand that I'm still an employee here."[36]

After being released. Mirabelli retired as a player. He has occasionally returned to Fenway Park, including in 2012 to honor Wakefield's retirement, catching the ceremonial first pitch from the knuckleballer.[37]

In 2009 Mirabelli was named head coach of the St. Francis High School baseball team in Traverse City, Michigan.[38] In 2013-14, Mirabelli worked for his old boss Theo Epstein as a scout for the Cubs. In 2015 Mirabelli joined the Florida Gators softball team staff as a volunteer assistant coach.[39]

As of 2023 Mirabelli lived in Traverse City with his wife, Kristin. They have three children, Emma, Molly, and Joey.

NOTES

1. "Doug Mirabelli (Baseball, 1990-92)," Wichita State Athletics, https://goshockers.com/news/2015/6/23/BSB_0623153518.aspx.
2. Todd Dewey, "Former Valley Standout: Catcher Finds Niche," *Southeast View* (Las Vegas), August 14, 2002.
3. Dewey.
4. Henry Schulman, "Mirabelli to Texas; $75,000 to Giants," *SFGate*, March 28, 2001, https://www.sfgate.com/sports/article/Mirabelli-To-Texas-75-000-To-Giants-2937299.php.
5. "Rangers-Red Sox Trade Could Mean Pitcher for Oklahoma or Tulsa," "News on 6," June 13, 2001, https://www.newson6.com/story/5e3681b42f69d76f62096129/rangersred-sox-trade-could-mean-pitcher-for-oklahoma-or-tulsa.
6. Dewey.
7. Dewey.
8. Dewey.
9. Bob Hohler, "Varitek's in a Position of Strength/Offseason Work Should Help Play," *Boston Globe*, February 15, 2003: D3.
10. Bob Hohler, "Mirabelli a Good Catch, so Sox Hold On to Him," *Boston Globe*, December 21, 2003: C10.
11. Hohler.
12. Allan Wood and Bill Nowlin, *Don't Let Us Win Tonight* (Chicago: Triumph Books, 2014), 95-96.
13. Wood and Nowlin, 100.
14. Wood and Nowlin, 85.
15. Wood and Nowlin, 213.
16. Wood and Nowlin, 221.
17. Wood and Nowlin, 223.
18. https://www.baseball-reference.com/boxes/BOS/BOS200410230.shtml.
19. Bob Hohler, "Mirabelli Signs for Two Years," *Boston Globe*, November 30, 2004: E1.
20. Chris Snow and Gordon Edes, "Red Sox Work on Renteria Deal," *Boston Globe*, December 8, 2005: C1.
21. Snow, "Can't Catch a Break; Passed Balls by Bard Let Indians Run Off with Win," *Boston Globe*, April 27, 2006: C1.
22. Gordon Edes, "They Must Produce Answer/Hitting in Clutch Has Lagged so Far," *Boston Globe*, April 30, 2006: C8.
23. Tim Healey, "The Doug Mirabelli Trade: An Oral History," *FanGraphs*, April 29, 2016.
24. Healey.
25. Healey.
26. Healey.
27. Healey.
28. Healey.
29. Healey.
30. Healey.
31. Healey.
32. Healey.
33. Bob Duffy, "Lugo Hopes to Hit It Big; He Finds Fenway a Welcome Sight," *Boston Globe*, December 14, 2006: E6.
34. Amalie Benjamin, "Red Sox to Re-Sign Mirabelli: Catcher Will Take Pay Cut for 2008." *Boston Globe*, January 11, 2008: F2.
35. Nick Cafardo, "Mirabelli Release Is Cash-Conscious," *Boston Globe*, March 14, 2008: E1. Cafardo wrote, "According to team sources, the 37-year-old Mirabelli's bat had slowed since last season, when he appeared in 48 games and hit just .202 with 5 home runs and 16 RBIs. His defense, particularly his throwing arm, has declined. In the end, the Red Sox decided Kevin Cash, as solid as there is defensively, was the better option."
36. Nick Cafardo, "A Heap of Good News on the Mound," *Boston Globe*, March 16, 2008: C7.
37. Jon Couture, "Waves of Emotion for Tim Wakefield on His Big Day in Boston," *Springfield Republican*, May 16, 2012: C7.
38. Mark Urban, "Gladiators hire Mirabelli," *Traverse City* (Michigan) *Record-Eagle*, January 5, 2009.
39. "Doug Mirabelli Joins Gator Softball Staff," *FloridaGators.com*, September 9, 2015, https://floridagators.com/news/2015/9/9/31183.aspx.

BILL MUELLER

BY KEVIN BLEY

Every young boy imagines coming up to bat when defeat seems certain and delivering the big hit. However, William Richard Mueller, in his St. Louis suburban yard, could not have imagined a scenario or set of circumstances quite as improbable.

Bill Mueller was born the only child of William Romeo and Barbara Ann (Poleweski) Mueller on March 17, 1971, in Maryland Heights, Missouri, a suburb in northwest St. Louis County. He enjoyed playing multiple sports but was particularly drawn to baseball. His father would frequently come home from his job as a purchasing agent for McDonnell Douglas to practice with Bill after school. While practicing in their long driveway, Bill, who threw and batted right-handed, attempted some left-handed swings. The switch-hitting seed was planted, and it grew into a regular practice; he was fully a switch-hitter by high school.

As a child, Mueller participated in Ballwin Athletic Association baseball leagues. Summers during high school were spent playing for Maryland Heights American Legion Post 213. He tried to emulate certain skills from the players he watched: the soft fielding hands of Ozzie Smith; the strike-zone discipline of Ryne Sandberg; the hand and eye coordination of Willie McGee; the basestealing of Vince Coleman.

Mueller played football, basketball, and baseball at De Smet Jesuit High School in Creve Coeur, Missouri. He made limited varsity appearances through his sophomore year but became a force in his junior and senior years. "Bill got where he was because he was an over-achiever," recounted De Smet's varsity baseball coach, Greg Vitello. "He was relentless. We'd do a drill of 100 groundballs and he wouldn't quit until he completed them all in a row perfectly."[1] The determination resulted in a scholarship to Southwest Missouri State University (now Missouri State) in Springfield, Missouri.

"The first time I saw (Mueller), he was playing right field for the Maryland Heights Legion team. He ran harder on and off the field than any other player ran the bases that day," Southwest Missouri State head baseball coach Keith Guttin recalled. "He could beat you in more ways than any other player in my 38 years of coaching."[2]

Mueller started for the Bears all four years and became the single-season record holder for runs, hits, singles, and walks, as well as career marks for runs (234), hits (289), total bases (398), walks (154), and stolen bases (65). His .376 batting average still stood as of 2020 as the Missouri State record for a four-year career.[3] He has been inducted into the Missouri State Athletics and Missouri Valley Conference Halls of Fame. Perhaps Mueller's slightly below-average player size (5-feet-11, 175 pounds) resulted in his later-round drafting by the San Francisco Giants; he was selected in the 15th round of the 1993 June amateur draft.

During college summers, Mueller played in three collegiate leagues: St. Louis Metro League (1990 Yankees), Jayhawk League (1991 Wichita Broncos), and Cape Cod League (1992 Bourne Braves).

The Giants assigned Mueller to Everett, Washington, of the short-season Class-A Northwest League. Playing mostly third base, he finished second on the team in batting average (.300). In 1994 with San Jose of the High-A California League, Mueller again displayed solid offensive numbers, finishing among the top hitters (.302). He progressed in 1995 to the Shreveport Captains of the Double-A Texas League, where the hits kept coming. After 88 games, Mueller (.309) was promoted to the Triple-A Phoenix Firebirds and finished well (.297 BA). By now, he was sniffing at his major-league shot.

Mueller went to 1996 spring training with a legitimate chance to make the big-league squad or at least earn consideration during the season. He started the season in Phoenix, but the call to join the Giants came quickly after a minor injury to Shawon Dunston. Mueller flew to Chicago to join the club against the Cubs on April 18. He started on the bench but pinch-hit for Shawn Barton in the top of the seventh inning. The result was a fly out to left in the Giants' loss. The next day unfolded similarly with Mueller starting on the bench. He entered the game at third base in the eighth inning and batted in the ninth. The outcome this time was a single to left field – Mueller's first major-league hit. The reward? A flight back to Phoenix to continue developing at Triple A. However, there was a high probability of returning later in the season if he performed as he had in past seasons. He did.

In five minor-league stops from 1993 to 1996, Mueller batted between .297 and .309 – the picture of consistent and successful hitting. He returned to the Giants at the end of July 1996 and quickly saw starts as fellow third baseman Matt Williams was lost for the season with a shoulder injury.[4] Mueller finished the season with an impressive .330 batting average. He had earned his major-league status, but the team stumbled to last place.

In the offseason, Brian Sabean replaced Bob Quinn as the Giants' general manager and soon traded the popular Williams to the Cleveland Indians for José Vizcaíno, Julián Tavárez, Joe Roa, and Jeff Kent. To many, the trade looked foolish; Williams had been key to the Giants' offense and defense. Sabean stuck to his reasoning and proved his case. "I know if we had stayed on the same path we would have Rich Aurilia playing shortstop and Bill Mueller at second," Sabean said. "I think we upgraded both those positions."[5]

After the trade Mueller was the starting third baseman for the 1997 Giants but split some time with Mark Lewis. He nonetheless appeared in 128 games. He hammered his first major-league home run on the road, against the Florida Marlins on June 3 facing rookie pitcher Rob Stanifer. On July 23 in San Francisco, Mueller went 4-for-4 at the plate with a home run and five RBIs in a rout of the Philadelphia Phillies. The Giants finished the season on top of the American League West with Mueller holding the team's highest batting average (.292). The eventual World Series champion Florida Marlins swept the Giants in the Division Series but Mueller hit a home run in Game One.

The 1998 season included more playing time for Mueller and higher marks in most offensive categories. Personal highlights included a two-home-run game against the Arizona Diamondbacks on April 5. Both came off starter Andy Benes and were the only Giants runs in the 3-2 road loss. Mueller belted his first career grand slam on September 19 against the visiting Los Angeles Dodgers' Ismael Valdéz. Four-hit games on May 21 against the Milwaukee Brewers and September 16 at Arizona helped keep his average high (.294) for the season. The Giants completed the season in second place, 9½ games behind the San Diego Padres.

The first inning of Opening Day is full of anticipation and butterflies. Brett Tomko was the starting pitcher for the Cincinnati Reds when the Giants visited on April 5, 1999, and was perhaps not in midseason form. A low pitch struck Mueller in his first at-bat, breaking his left big toe.[6] After healing, he entered a three-game rehabilitation stint with Triple-A Fresno which included five hits and six RBIs. He rejoined the Giants on May 17. Seven games later, on May 25, Mueller and the Giants visited his hometown of St. Louis and Mueller hit his second career grand slam, over the left-field wall off Kent Mercker during a 17-1 rout. In keeping with the previous season, Mueller finished with a .290 batting mark and the Giants finished in second place.

To gain additional power and strengthen the bench, the Giants signed free-agent third baseman Russ Davis in the offseason. Trade rumors swirled about Mueller, but Brian Sabean moderated them and explained the third-base job: "Billy Mueller obviously is a guy that we know. It's up to Russ to come in here and press the issue for the team. I feel confident it will work out for everyone, and everyone will get enough at-bats."[7] Mueller was the starting third baseman, but Davis had 33 starts throughout the year. The Giants began the 2000 home schedule at their new Pacific Bell Park (later named Oracle Park). In the first inning, Mueller got a single, the first hit by a Giant in the ballpark. The Giants won 97 games and took the National League West. However, it was a less impressive year by Mueller's standards. His average dropped to .268 and competition for third base was forming in Davis, Ramón Martínez, and prospect Pedro Feliz. As in 1997, the Giants fell in the Division Series, this time to the New York Mets three games to one.

The trade buzz from the previous offseason didn't have long to resurface. Mueller was dealt to the Chicago Cubs on November 18 for pitcher Tim Worrell. "As things went forward, we decided we were not going to give Billy a multiyear deal, with Pedro Feliz coming in from Triple A and having Russ Davis also, who has produced at that position in the past," Sabean said.[8] Giants manager Dusty Baker added his thoughts on Mueller: "Certainly we were not in a hurry to get rid of Billy, because he was one of our favorites and a gutsy ballplayer, but the Cubs wanted Billy real badly. You hate to lose him big-time. We raised him. But I think this will be a good situation for him."[9] Mueller observed, "There have been a lot of guys in major-league baseball who've been traded more than once. It's just a new experience for me and that's why I'm excited about meeting new people and a new staff and learning a new philosophy and seeing the game in a new light. You never know what can help you."[10] The optimism made an impression on both teams.

Mueller opened the 2001 season on an offensive tear. As the Cubs wrapped up a visit to St. Louis on May 13, he was batting .312 and playing brilliant defense. Starting the game at third, he hit an RBI triple in the first and scored. Then came bad news for the Cubs. While tracking a foul popup, Mueller ran into a wall and broke his patella – an injury that sidelined him until August 13. The Cardinals won the game, 13-4, sweeping the Cubs, and took over first place. "He's irreplaceable at third base," said teammate Kerry Wood. "He's a Gold Glove third baseman, in my opinion, and [losing him] is the worst thing about the whole road trip. It will be tough to come back from that."[11] After returning to the Cubs, Mueller endured an 0-for-14 stretch before regaining his early-season production; he finished the season batting .295. Wood's prophecy was accurate. The Cubs finished third in the National League Central.

The knee injury lingered and Mueller had surgery on March 11, 2002, to clean up the affected area before the start of the season.[12] He began the season on the disabled list, returning on May 6. Mueller yielded average numbers offensively for the Cubs through the beginning of September, but his last month was much improved. The Cubs were out of contention early and decided to deal Mueller back to the Giants for cash and pitching prospect Jeff Verplancke on September 4. "It's an opportunity to be back in San Francisco where it's familiar to me," Mueller said. "I just want to do whatever comes my way to help these guys."[13] Mueller was to fulfill a bench role and help the Giants try to catch the first-place Diamondbacks down the stretch. Since the trade occurred after September 1, Mueller was not eligible to join the Giants' postseason roster. "It's unfortunate that I can't stay with them if and when they make the playoffs, but I'm going to do whatever I can to help," he said.[14] The Giants wound up in second place in the division, but won the wild-card spot and defeated the Cardinals in the NLCS to capture the National League pennant. They lost to the Anaheim Angels in the World Series. After the season Mueller became a free agent.

On January 4, 2003, Mueller signed with the Boston Red Sox. Good times were ahead for both Mueller and Boston in the 2003 season. Hits came early for Mueller – by the end of May, he was batting .379. They kept coming all season. By the All-Star break, Mueller had hit 30 doubles. He had three four-hit games: June 27 (Marlins), July 10 (Blue Jays), and September 8 (Orioles). On the road against the Texas Rangers on July 29, he had a game for the record books. In the top of the third, Mueller led off with a home run off R.A. Dickey. Batting from the right side against Aaron Fultz in the seventh, Mueller placed his second home run in the left-field seats – this time a grand slam. Again, in the eighth with the bases loaded, now batting left-handed, he connected for another grand slam (his third home run of the game) against Jay Powell. Through the 2021 season, Mueller is the only major leaguer to hit a grand slam while batting right-handed and left-handed in a game. "You never come to the ballpark thinking you're going to do anything like this," Mueller reflected after the game. "I'm just trying to have some good at-bats, and I guess some of my good at-bats went over the wall tonight."[15]

The season ended for Mueller with career highs in hits, doubles, triples, home runs, and RBIs. He was awarded the Silver Slugger Award at third base. It was his top season in batting average (.326) and the best in the American League, just edging teammate Manny Ramírez by .001. "I'm not a stats guy," Mueller said as he downplayed the batting title. "I don't show up at the park to do things like that. I show up to help the team."[16] Help the team he did – the Red Sox won the American League wild-card position and faced the Oakland Athletics in the Division Series. They skirted by the A's after losing the first two games, but later lost to their traditional rivals, the New York Yankees, in seven games in the Championship Series. It was a slow postseason for Mueller (8 hits in 12 games) after a tremendous regular season.

The 2004 season began well for the Red Sox despite early injuries sidelining Trot Nixon and Nomar Garciaparra. However, Mueller was battling pain in his knee again. "This is an issue I've been dealing with for quite some time," he confessed.[17] In May Mueller and the team decided surgery was necessary to prevent inflammation caused by degeneration. He was shelved from May 20 through a rehab assignment in late June, finally rejoining the Red Sox on July 2. Mueller's bat started to heat up and he ended the season batting .283, which was 21 points higher than his pre-surgery average. On July 24 Mueller popped a walk-off home run against the Yankees in a wild game at Fenway Park that included a brawl and a three-run bottom of the ninth. Red Sox manager Terry Francona wishfully observed, "I hope we look back a while from now and we're saying that this brought us together. … I hope a long time from now we look back and say this did it."[18]

The Red Sox went on to again win the wild card. They swept the Anaheim Angels in the Division Series to face the Yankees in a Championship Series rematch. The Yankees took the first two games of the best-of-seven series at home and the third, an embarrassing 19-8 loss, at Fenway Park. To make things worse, they trailed 4-3 in the bottom of the ninth of Game Four facing the pitcher known as the Sandman, future Hall of Fame closer Mariano Rivera. Defeat was in the air. Kevin Millar led off with a walk and was lifted for a pinch-runner, Dave Roberts. Roberts stole second to get into scoring position. Up stepped Mueller … and hope.

Up the middle. Roberts will come to the plate. The throw by Williams. Bill Mueller has tied it.

Joe Buck calling Mueller's game-tying single off Rivera in the ninth inning of Game Four of the 2004 American League Championship Series.[19]

Mueller had singled to center field and scored Roberts to tie the game. The Red Sox went on to win the game in the 12th inning on a walk-off home run by David Ortiz. The next night, Ortiz repeated with another game-winning RBI – this time, a single in the 14th inning. The Red Sox prevailed in the next two games in New York and won the American League pennant. No team had ever come back from an 0-3 deficit to win a playoff series.

The World Series was against the team for which Mueller grew up cheering. The Cardinals had won 105 games in the regular season, but the Red Sox were riding an emotional high after their astounding come-from-behind victory. The Red Sox made quick work of the Cardinals, sweeping the Series and earning their first World Series championship in 86 years. Mueller had a nice Series at the plate: .429 batting average with two RBIs. He reflected on his experience with two outs in the bottom of the ninth of the final game: "I remember standing at third base and looking up in the stands and saying, 'I can't believe it, we're going to be World Series champions.' Just seeing the Boston Red Sox fans standing up in Busch Stadium, I'm like, 'Man, what an unbelievable thing. I never want to forget this feeling. I never want to forget how I'm feeling right now at this moment.' That was a dream come true."[20]

Mueller responded in 2005 with a characteristic performance: .295 batting average, 10 home runs, 62 RBIs. The Red Sox took the wild card for the third consecutive year and tried to repeat in the postseason but were swept by the Chicago White Sox in the Division Series.

Although never one to break out with noteworthy power, Mueller was difficult to strike out during his career and gave consistent quality at-bats. Similarly, he never won the coveted Gold Glove Award, but fielded commendably (.958 career fielding percentage). During his first (and last) Hall of Fame eligibility year, 2012, Mueller received only four votes and was dropped off future baseball writers' ballots. But Mueller's career earned him respect among teammates and fans who affectionately dubbed him "Billy Ballgame."[21]

Free agency, which Mueller entered at the end of the season, did not last long. He and the Los Angeles Dodgers made a two-year agreement official on December 15, 2005. Ned Colletti and Grady Little, the Dodgers' new general manager and manager respectively, both had experience with Mueller, Colletti as the Giants' assistant general manager and Little as the Red Sox manager in 2003. "Every successful team has true baseball players with the makeup, drive and desire of Bill Mueller," said Colletti. "His ability to hit from both sides of the plate will give Grady additional maneuverability."[22]

As usual, Mueller got out of the gate in 2006 with solid hitting. Through April he was batting .299, but there was trouble with his right knee again. The next seven games showed that the knee was too troublesome. Mueller underwent his third surgery. Recovery was more difficult than before, and the "degenerative, arthritic changes" ultimately led to the choice in November to retire from playing.[23]

Mueller was far from finished with baseball. The Dodgers kept him on as a special assistant to the general manager. In June 2007 Eddie Murray was fired from his job as hitting coach and Mueller "agreed to help us bridge the gap," Colletti told reporters.[24] After about a month, Mueller was officially assigned the role and finished the season before reverting back to special assistant. He remained in this position through the 2012 season and then moved into scouting for the Dodgers for an additional season.

In 2014 Mueller returned to the Cubs as their hitting coach. It was short-lived as he resigned after just one season. The decision was tied to the termination of assistant hitting coach Mike Brumley. The Central Division rival Cardinals quickly contracted with Mueller to assist hitting coach John Mabry in 2015. Mueller spoke about the importance of coach relationships: "Having known [Mabry] for as long as I have, I know who he is and he knows who I am. There were other [organizations] … that I could have been a part of. … [A]gain I search for the right relationships."[25]

Mueller shifted to first-base coach for the 2016 season when José Oquendo had to temporarily vacate his third-base coaching role due to surgery. He returned to the assistant hitting coach role in 2017 with an extended personal leave of absence in June. In 2018 the Cardinals' front office was unsatisfied with results by July 14 and decided to shake up much of the coaching staff. Mueller was fired along with Mabry and manager Mike Matheny.

While playing or coaching with the Red Sox, Dodgers, and Cardinals, Mueller tried to choose uniform numbers to reflect the birthdates of his children. With his wife, Amy, Mueller has three children: daughter Alexis and two sons, Tucker and Dawson.

In 2022, Mueller joined the coaching staff of the Washington Nationals as a quality control coordinator assisting prospective players in development.

ACKNOWLEDGMENTS

This biography was reviewed by Bill Nowlin and Len Levin and fact-checked by David Kritzler.

SOURCES

Statistics have been taken from Baseball-Reference.com and Retrosheet.org.

Content includes the author's interviews with Greg Vitello, Keith Guttin, and Bill Mueller in 2020.

NOTES

1. Author interviews with Greg Vitello in April and May 2020.
2. Author interview with Keith Guttin in April 2020.
3. missouristatebears.com.
4. Tony Blengino, "Once Upon a Fractured Season: Matt Williams and the 1994 Home Run Chase," *Forbes*, March 19, 2020.
5. David Bush, "GM Defends Williams Deal / Sabean: 'I Am Not an Idiot,'" SFGATE, November 16, 1996. sfgate.com/sports/article/GM-Defends-Williams-Deal-Sabean-I-am-not-an-2959131.php.
6. Associated Press, "McGwire's First Isn't Enough for St. Louis," *Los Angeles Times*, April 6, 1999.
7. Henry Schulman, "Giants Sign Third Baseman Davis," SFGATE, January 25, 2000. sfgate.com/sports/article/Giants-Sign-Third-Baseman-Davis-2781142.php.
8. Henry Schulman, "Giants Give Up Mueller to Cubs / Reliever Worrell coming to S.F.; 3B Davis re-signs," SFGATE, November 20, 2000. sfgate.com/sports/article/Giants-Give-Up-Mueller-To-Cubs-Reliever-Worrell-2727354.php.
9. Schulman, "Giants Give Up Mueller to Cubs."
10. Schulman, "Giants Give Up Mueller to Cubs."
11. Teddy Greenstein, "Mueller, Cubs Hit Wall," *Chicago Tribune*, May 14, 2001.
12. "Cardinals' Ankiel Put on DL," *Washington Post*, March 29, 2002.
13. Associated Press, "Giants Trade Minor League Pitcher for Mueller," ESPN, September 4, 2002. espn.com/mlb/news/2002/0903/1426924.html.
14. Associated Press, "Giants Trade Minor League Pitcher for Mueller."
15. Associated Press, "Mueller Has Grand Time in rout of Rangers," ESPN, July 30, 2003. espn.co.uk/mlb/recap?gameId=230729113.
16. Ron Kroichick, "Hitting 8th: Bill Mueller, the AL's Batting Champion," SFGATE, October 1, 2003. sfgate.com/sports/kroichick/article/Hitting-8th-Bill-Mueller-the-AL-s-batting-2584869.php.
17. Ken Davis, "Mueller to Have Knee Surgery," *Hartford Courant*, May 26, 2004.

18. Dan Shaughnessy, "Red Sox Win Slugfest with Yankees / Mueller Slams Dramatic Homer, 11-10," *Boston Globe*, July 25, 2004.
19. youtube.com/watch?v=IBPe0gRI2IE.
20. Ian Browne, *Idiots Revisited: Catching Up with the Red Sox Who Won the 2004 World Series* (Thomaston, Maine: Tilbury House, 2014).
21. See, for instance, https://browniepoints.mlblogs.com/billy-ballgame-calls-it-a-career-9b05191716dc and https://thesportsdaily.com/news/so-long-billy-ballgame/
22. "Report: Dodgers Sign 3B Mueller," ESPN, December 14, 2005. espn.com/espn/wire/_/section/mlb/id/2258856.
23. Steve Henson, "Mueller's Knee Injury Might Threaten Career," *Los Angeles Times*, June 23, 2006.
24. Tony Jackson, "Eddie Murray Fired by Dodgers," *Los Angeles Daily News*, June 14, 2007.
25. Brendan Marks, "Cardinals' New Assistant Hitting Coach Bill Mueller on The Press Box," InsideStl.com, November 19, 2014. insidestl.com/cardinals-new-assistant-hitting-coach-bill-mueller-on-the-press-box-2/1937156.

A RED SOX MEMORY

In a three-month period in 2004, I donated a kidney to a stranger, watched my longtime boss (US Sen. John Kerry) lose the presidential election, and finished my first season as a partial season-ticket holder for the Red Sox. At the time and ever since, I felt overjoyed to have the chance to donate an organ, bittersweet about having worked for the Democratic Party nominee, and responsible as a regular paying customer for my least favorite baseball team winning a World Series.

MARK STERNMAN

A RED SOX MEMORY

I sat dejectedly at Fenway Park, having witnessed the 19-8 loss against the Yankees. My wife predicted we would come back; we did not believe her and yet there I was in front of the TV during Game Four of the World Series. (My wife was watching from Cape Cod.) Without realizing it, I had crossed my legs early on in the game and decided that it would not be possible for us to win if I uncrossed my legs. After the win, both my legs had gone to sleep, and I had no feeling in either one. I promptly fell to the floor as I cheered the Sox on. It would take a long while before I could put any weight on my legs again.

From my wife, Judy Ramírez: On October 19, as I was driving to our friends' home – the Cormiers – to watch the game, listening to Sox commentators talking about the game. One of them mentioned that the date was October 19 and it occurred to me that yesterday was the 18th and so, since we won on the 18th, we would win on the 19th (18/19), thereby reversing the curse of 1918!! It was in that moment that I knew with certainty that this was the year!! The ALCS that year was THE SERIES!!! The World Series was just the frosting on the cake. Shortly after, my friend Larry and I both got tattoos to commemorate the win.

Joey Ramírez with Billy Arrington. Courtesy of José Ramírez.

From son José Ramírez Jr. (Joey): The victory cigar I smoked after beating the Cardinals was the last from the box I had bought in Cuba in 1994. Old, stale, and the best cigar I've ever had. [In the photo, Joey has the Sox jacket on, next to his friend Billy.]

From son Jason Ramírez: My favorite memory taught me a valuable lesson in celebrating. I was in attendance at the ALCS Game Four. In the bottom of the ninth, the closest Yankee fan lit his celebratory cigar. He lit that cigar before the first pitch of the inning.

From my friend Larry Cormier: After the Red Sox loss in 2003 to the Yankees, I was absolutely convinced that, like my father, I would never see a Red Sox championship in my lifetime. My kids were not and bet me that I was wrong. So, I said, "If the Sox win the World Series before I die, I will get a tattoo." If you know me, you would also know that this was equivalent to "Hell freezing over."

On October 27, 2004, the Sox did it and my kids quickly reminded me of our bet. Weeks later and with a big smile on my face, I was in the last place on earth anyone would expect me to be ... a tattoo parlor in New Hampshire. Along with my best friend's wife (Judy Ramírez, who thought it was a great idea to have a lasting memento), we both got tattoos and we both have worn them proudly ever since.

JOSÉ RAMÍREZ

MIKE MYERS

BY ROBERT EMERSON

Unique in every respect, left-handed submarine pitcher Michael Stanley Myers brought a presence to the mound that exhibited the definition of left-handed specialist. In a 13-year career with nine major-league teams, Myers made his presence known as a one-trick pony with a few more tricks up his sleeve. Myers, the premier LOOGY of the late 1990s and early 2000s, was part of an analytical overhaul of how a bullpen can be utilized.

Born on June 26, 1969, in Arlington Heights, Illinois, to Warren Myers, a high-school math teacher, and Carol Myers. Michael was their second oldest child, his siblings being older brother Gary and younger brother Don.[1] Growing up a Cubs fan, he excelled in pitching at Crystal Lake High School, graduating from there in 1987 and pitching at Iowa State University soon thereafter. In 1988, his freshman year, he appeared in 18 games and recorded 46 strikeouts.

In 1989 Myers worked as a starter for the Iowa State Cyclones and was named to the All-Big Eight second team, with 6 wins and a team-high 62 strikeouts. That summer he was named a Cape Cod Baseball League all-star for the Brewster Whitecaps. In 1990 Myers was named to the Big 8 All-Tournament team. In the fourth round of the June amateur draft, Myers was selected by the San Francisco Giants, and soon made his pro debut for the Everett Giants of the short-season low Class-A Northwest League.

Finishing 1990 with a 4-5 record in 14 starts with a 3.90 ERA, Myers moved up to the Class-A Clinton Giants (Midwest League) in 1991, where he accumulated a 5-3 record in 11 games started. In 1992 he split his time Clinton (1.19 ERA in 7 starts) and the High-A California League San Jose Giants (2.30 ERA in 8 starts) before getting a different chance come the winter.

On December 7, 1992, the Florida Marlins took Myers in the Rule 5 draft, and a strong spring training threw him into the Marlins' projected starting rotation for 1993. The acquisition of pitchers Chris Hammond and Luis Aquino in the last week of spring training hurt Myers' chances of making the big-league roster, and two days before the season started he was sent down to the Triple-A Edmonton Trappers (Pacific Coast League), starting 27 games with a 7-14 record and a 5.18 ERA. He earned an invite to 1994 spring training.[2]

Myers spent all of 1994 in the minors, struggling in his time in Edmonton with a 1-5 record and a 5.55 ERA in 12 games. Demoted to Class-A Brevard County (Florida State League),

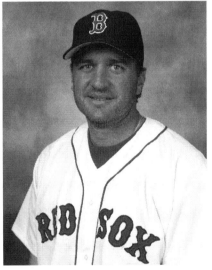

he fared better in three games with a 0.79 ERA. In 1995 it took a while for him to prove himself in spring training again, but took longer after the players strike in the majors prematurely ended the 1994 season and the beginning of the 1995 season.

Nevertheless, Myers made his major-league debut on Opening Day, April 25, 1995, pitching one inning of scoreless relief in an 8-7 loss to the Los Angeles Dodgers. His only other appearance for Florida, another scoreless inning, came in a loss to Atlanta on May 2. He was optioned to the Triple-A Charlotte Knights on May 7. In Triple A that year, he had a 5.65 ERA with an 0-5 record in 37 games as a reliever.

When the Marlins traded for Buddy Groom from the Detroit Tigers on August 7, it was for a player to be named later. Two days later, Myers was named as the player. Optioned to the Triple-A Toledo Mud Hens, Myers appeared in six games before being called up to Detroit on August 30, making his Tigers debut against the Chicago White Sox. Myers finished the year as a left-handed specialist for the 60-84 Detroit Tigers, Sparky Anderson's last year managing in the majors.

Myers improved his pitching after a tip from Tigers broadcaster Al Kaline. After a rough outing against the Minnesota Twins on September 6, Myers' three Detroit appearances resulted in two-thirds of an inning of work, with 11 batters faced and a 67.50 ERA. Hall of Famer Kaline suggested Myers drop his pitches down and work from a submarine release.[3] In a situation where it couldn't hurt to try, Myers' remaining eight Detroit appearances resulted in a more respectable 3.18 ERA.

All told, Myers had a 9.11 ERA in 11 appearances with a won-lost record of 1-0. His one decision came in a game against the Baltimore Orioles at Tiger Stadium on September 19. He was the pitcher of record as he worked a scoreless top of the fifth inning in a game the Tigers won 7-4.

Myers' submarine delivery and situational pitching against lefties gave him great durability throughout his career. Beginning in 1996 and through 2007, he appeared in at least 64 games in each season. In 1996 Myers led both leagues in games pitched with 83, despite pitching only 64⅔ innings. His high number of appearances and 5.01 ERA represented only part of the struggles of the 1996 Tigers, who lost a league-high 109 games.

The 1997 Tigers improved to a more respectable 79-83 record, with Myers leading the American League in games pitched with 88. In 49 of his appearances, he came in with runners on base. Because most of his work was facing lefties, he accrued only 53⅔ innings pitched with a 5.70 ERA. He was 0-4.

On November 20, the Tigers traded Myers, Rick Greene and Santiago Pérez to the Milwaukee Brewers for right-handed reliever Bryce Florie. The Brewers knew that Myers had struggled in his time in Detroit but hoped that NL hitters would not be used to the submarine motion he employed.

Their hopes were upheld. In 70 games in his first year for the Brewers, Myers dramatically improved his earned run average to 2.70 in 50 innings of work. He was 2-2. Perhaps NL batters adapted to his submarine delivery in 1999; his ERA climbed to 5.23 in 71 appearances and 41⅓ innings.

On November 17, 1999, the Brewers shipped Myers to the Colorado Rockies for right-handed reliever Curtis Leskanic, and Myers entered the new millennium with his second expansion team. The 2000 season saw an improvement on Myers' part despite the notoriously hitter-friendly home ballpark, Coors Field.

In 78 games pitched in 2000 (third most in the NL), Myers' 1.99 ERA in 45⅓ innings was the best to come out of the Rockies bullpen, and his 2.6 bWAR was fifth best on the team, tied with starting pitcher Pedro Astacio and closer José Jiménez. His park-adjusted ERA+ of 294 led the Rockies staff. Myers' opponent batting average of .160 was a franchise record that was held for 18 years until it was broken by Adam Ottavino with .158 in 2018.[4]

Myers continued his durable streak in the league in 2001, pitching in 73 games and posting a 3.60 ERA in 40 innings pitched. On January 7, 2002 the Rockies traded Myers to the Arizona Diamondbacks for catcher JD Closser and outfielder Jack Cust.[5]

With Arizona Myers saw his appearances go down and ERA go up. Pitching in 69 and 64 games in 2002 and 2003, he had ERAs of 4.38 in '02, and 5.70 in '03. Myers made his postseason debut in the 2002 National League Division Series against the St. Louis Cardinals, facing two batters in Game Two and four in Game Three, not allowing a run in either game. After the 2003 season Myers became a free agent.

On January 19, 2004, Myers signed a minor-league contract with the Seattle Mariners worth $550,000. He made the major-league roster out of spring training and appeared in 50 games for the Mariners, racking up a 4.88 ERA. On August 6, after the Mariners had placed Myers on waivers, he was claimed by the Boston Red Sox. He appeared in 25 games for the Red Sox with a 4.20 ERA, and finishing the season with a 75 games pitched.[7]

Myers' time with Boston in 2004 saw him make a return to postseason pitching. He earned a hold in the Red Sox' Game Two victory over the Los Angeles Angels in the ALDS; he faced one batter and struck him out on four pitches. In Game Three he walked the only batter he faced, José Molina, who scored when Vladimir Guerrero hit a grand slam off Mike Timlin. This was largely forgotten by the time David Ortiz hit a two-run homer in the bottom of the 10th and the Red Sox headed to the AL Championship Series against the New York Yankees.

Myers made three appearances against the Yankees, with varying success. His worst game, in a 19-8 blowout, was the last Red Sox loss in the 2004 postseason, with Myers pitching the last two innings, allowing 2 earned runs in a 19-8 shellacking. The Red Sox famously overcame the three-games-to-none deficit. Myers pitched in Games Four and Five– in the 11th inning of both games – facing one batter in each, granting an uneventful four-pitch walk to Hideki Matsui in Game Four and striking out Matsui when the Yankees batter led off the 11th.

Though he warmed up in the bullpen several times during Game One of the World Series, he was not called upon to pitch during the Series, but Myers had arrived in Boston in time to be a part of the historic Red Sox playoff run and he earned a World Series ring for his efforts after the Red Sox swept the St. Louis Cardinals in four games. Asked if he regretted not getting into one of those games, he said, "Absolutely not. ... No, because if I did, the scores could have been completely different."[6] Better that Boston won the games than him having to be called upon to help.

Oddly, Myers joined the Cardinals soon after the World Series, signing as a free agent on December 22, 2004, but he was back with Boston when the Red Sox acquired him in a March 29 trade for minor leaguers Carlos De La Cruz and Kevin Ool. Myers had one of his better years in 2005, with a 3.13 ERA in 65 games, with 37⅓ innings pitched, cementing his place as one of the best LOOGYs in the majors. His 749 games pitched up to this point with only 456⅔ innings pitched showed his one-out efficiency.

There was one more playoff appearance. Myers faced one batter in Game Three of the 2005 ALDS against the Chicago White Sox, and walked him. The Red Sox were swept by Chicago, the White Sox ultimately winning the 2005 World Series.

Myers was a free agent once more. On December 16 he decided he would continue his career with the New York Yankees, signing a two-year deal worth $2.4 million.

In 2006 Myers pitched in 62 games for the Yankees, working 30⅔ innings. A 3.23 ERA was a modest success for Myers' career, and he made sure to make himself worth every dollar. He continued to showcase his durability in the 2007 season, appearing in 55 games (40⅔ innings) as of August 7. Despite a 2.66 ERA, he was designated for assignment on that date, and he signed a deal with the Chicago White Sox on August 20 to finish out the season (17 games, 13⅔ innings pitched, 11.20 ERA). The White Sox released him on October 30.

Myers signed a minor-league deal with the Los Angeles Dodgers on February 3, 2008, and was invited to spring training, but was released on April 24. He retired as a player shortly thereafter.

Myers had pitched in 883 games, accumulating 541⅔ innings pitched. He fared much better against left-handers, with righties hitting a much better .301 against him compared with the lefties' .219 average in 157 more at-bats than right-handers. The epitome of a specialist, he holds the major-league records of 227 appearances with five pitches or fewer, and 503 appearances with 10 pitches or fewer.[7]

On March 17, 2009, Myers was named a special assistant to Donald Fehr, executive director of the Major League Players Association, and continued in the role under Fehr's successors, Michael Weiner and Tony Clark.[8] As a liaison between the union and its members, Myers was still active in the role as of 2023.

Since 2005, Myers, his wife, Robyn, and their children Christian, Daryl, and Laryssa, have resided in Castle Pines, Colorado, near Denver. All three children have followed in their father's footsteps, with Christian and Daryl both playing high-school and collegiate baseball and Laryssa playing high-school volleyball.[9]

SOURCES

In addition to the sources cited in the Notes, the author consulted Baseball-Reference.com.

NOTES

1. Obituary of Michael Myers' father, Warren Myers, *Arlington Heights* (Illinois) *Daily Herald*, September 3, 2021. https://www.legacy.com/us/obituaries/dailyherald/name/warren-myers-obituary?id=23837729.
2. Gordon Edes, "Florida Marlins; Fly on the Wall." *The Sporting News*, March 29, 1993: 18. Gordon Edes, "Florida Marlins; Shallow Pitching," *The Sporting News*, January 10, 1994: 39.
3. Jeff Horrigan, "Red Sox Notebook: Myers Owes Tiger Legend," *Milford* (Massachusetts) *Daily News*, August 8, 2004. https://www.milforddailynews.com/story/sports/2004/08/08/red-sox-notebook-myers-owes/41376611007/.
4. *2023 Colorado Rockies Media Guide*, 51.
5. Bob Baum, "Diamondbacks Acquire Reliever Myers," *Midland* (Michigan) *Daily News*, January 6, 2002. https://www.ourmidland.com/news/article/Diamondbacks-Acquire-Reliever-Myers-7074840.php.
6. Marvin Pave, "Glad This Sidearmer on Their Side," *Boston Globe*, June 6, 2005: 44.
7. Sean Forman, "Keeping Score: Many Games, Few Innings," *New York Times*, April 30, 2010, archive.nytimes.com/bats.blogs.nytimes.com/2010/04/29/many-games-few-innings/.
8. Richard Sandomir, "Ex-Pitcher Helling Is Named Assistant to Fehr," *New York Times*, March 18, 2009, www.nytimes.com/2009/03/18/sports/baseball/18helling.html.
9. Lynn Zahorik, "America's Favorite Pastime Is a Family Affair," *Castle Pines* (Colorado) *Connection*, May 1, 2016, www.castlepinesconnection.com/americas-favorite-pastime-is-a-family-affair/.

A RED SOX MEMORY

Game Four of the 2004 World Series. I was there and still have all the memorabilia from that night. Unfortunately, I didn't take up one of the offers of the many Red Sox fans outside Busch Stadium seeking to purchase tickets. I remember walking up the street from my office going to the game by myself and this one Bostonian comes up to me with 12 hundred-dollar bills fanned out saying he has to be at the game. I guess Cardinal red ran too strong in my blood and I turned him down. My team had not been in the World Series since 1987. This was not what would become a regular thing in St. Louis in the next few years. It was something I didn't want to give up, and you also thought maybe the Redbirds could come back.

Drew Barrymore and Jimmy Fallon. I was sitting next to my brother at the end of the game pointing out who are those two nuts (a blonde girl and a kid in jeans) running around the field as the Sox were jumping all over each other after the last out. Just wasn't sure what was going on. Didn't even think about it until the next morning when at work one of my employees who had seats right next to the Red Sox dugout told me she had been in the restroom earlier in the game when Drew Barrymore walked in and she recognized her and then watched her as they went back to their seats nearby and then saw her run out onto the field after the final out.

ED WHEATLEY

JOE NELSON

BY BOB WEBSTER

Joe Nelson was drafted by the Atlanta Braves in the fourth round of the June 1996 major-league amateur draft. The day after he was drafted, his scout, Mack "Shooty" Babitt, came over to Nelson's house to discuss a signing bonus with Nelson and his parents. Shooty asked Nelson what he wanted. Nelson had already done some research and came up with a number. It was $105,000, plus $38,500 for school. He wrote the number on a piece of paper and showed it to Shooty. Shooty asked if he could use his phone.

After a couple of minutes, Shooty handed the phone to Nelson. It was the Atlanta Braves GM John Schuerholz, who said, "Welcome to the Atlanta Braves, we'll give you exactly what you asked for."[1]

The Braves signed their fourth-round pick the year before for $435,000 and Nelson knew that, but the scenario was different and Nelson knew what he wanted.

Joe Nelson's family held a party to celebrate the signing and Nelson asked Shooty if he left anything on the table. Shooty said, "You didn't leave anything on the table, you got exactly what you wanted." A few years later, Shooty said, "Man, you left a ton of money on the table!"

When Nelson reported to Eugene, Oregon, a few days later and met other players, Mark DeRosa informed him that players drafted after Nelson were upset with him because the Braves refused to sign them for more than Nelson got.

"I don't regret it, but the guys behind me regretted it," said Nelson.[2]

Joseph George "Joe" Nelson was born in Alameda, California, on October 25, 1974, to George and Paula Nelson. George was then and in 2023 still was in the car sales business. George and Paula split up when Joe was 6 years old and George was out of the picture as Joe grew up, but the two developed a strong relationship as adults.[3]

Joe joined sisters Joeli Yaguda, who is six years older than Joe, and Shannon Nelson, three years older.

Joe's mother, Paula, was a stay-at-home mom and a radio DJ for a few years. In 2023, she was living in Arizona with Joe's stepfather, Larry Rodriguez. Paula drove Joe to every practice and game growing up. "My mom was the person who always made sports possible; she would drive me and was always taking me to camps or playing catch in the back yard," Nelson said. He added, "Larry was instrumental in my development as a player starting at age 15. He was at every game I ever played in from 15-18 and really taught me about mental toughness and playing with a chip on my shoulder."[4]

Joe was a huge Oakland A's and Raiders fan and despised the Giants and 49ers. He was born on October 25 and his mother took him to a Raiders-49ers game two days later. His grandfather had season tickets and took Joe and his mother to every game.

Two early highlights of Nelson's sports career were at age 6, when he turned an unassisted triple play in T-ball, and at age 12, when he played on the California Pee Wee state football championship team.[5]

Nelson attended St. Joseph's Notre Dame High School in Alameda, where he was a standout in baseball and basketball. In his junior year, he was a member of the Division I California State Championship basketball team. His backcourt mate was senior Jason Kidd, who went on to a successful NBA career. On the baseball diamond, Nelson played shortstop and pitched, and Kidd was leadoff man and center fielder. "Joe was Mr. Baseball," Kidd said. "He pitched a little, but he played more shortstop. And he could really handle the bat. He loved to play baseball. He was a gifted athlete."[6]

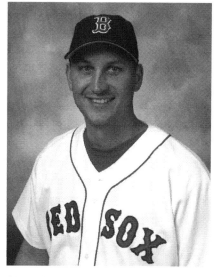

As a senior in 1993, Nelson had a 5-0 record as a pitcher and batted .489. He was named the East Shore Athletic League's Player of the Year.[7]

After high school, Nelson played baseball at Seminole (Oklahoma) State College in 1994 and 1995, where he batted .380 with 150 RBIs over the two seasons.

Lloyd Simmons, his coach at Seminole, saw some potential as a pitcher, but told Nelson that he needed to come up with a split-finger pitch. The traditional split-finger grip between the index and middle finger was too uncomfortable for Nelson, so he tried it with the ball between the middle and ring fingers and it worked, so when he moved on to the University of San Francisco, he used the pitch regularly. The pitch was called the Vulcan changeup, named after a lookalike hand gesture on *Star Trek*. He never pitched at Seminole, but Simmons said to Nelson when he left for USF, "You'll pitch in the big leagues someday."[8]

Nelson pitched in 14 games with the University of San Francisco in 1996 and was 4-1 with a 2.33 ERA. In 54 innings, he gave up 45 hits and struck out 52.

At Eugene of the short-season Class-A Northwest League, Nelson compiled a 5-3 record with a 4.37 ERA. In 70 innings he allowed 69 hits and struck out 67 batters.

Nelson moved up to the Durham Bulls of the High-A Carolina League for 1997. In 25 games, 24 as a starter, he threw 124⅔ innings and had a 10-6 record with an ERA of 4.76. His progression through the minors stayed on track, he pitched for the Greenville Braves of the Double-A Southern League in 1998 and put together a 6-9 record.

Nelson split the 1999 season between Greenville and the Triple-A Richmond Braves. Used primarily as a reliever, he posted a 2.37 ERA with eight saves at Greenville. Promoted to Richmond, he was 2-3 with a 4.54 ERA before going down with an elbow injury in August, requiring Tommy John surgery.[9]

Nelson said he asked his orthopedic surgeon if there were any cute nurses at the hospital where he was scheduled for an MRI and was told yes. At the hospital he was introduced to a woman who he thought was a nurse. She was actually a physician, a radiologist resident doing the MRI. Nelson asked her why she wasn't married because he didn't see a ring. She said she was always at the hospital and never dated doctors. He told her that lucky for her he wasn't a doctor. He got her to go to the game that night and they went out afterward, and the night after that, and the next night. Nelson and the doctor, Teresa Cortinas, eventually married.[10]

After limited action in 2000 recovering from the injury, Nelson pitched for Richmond in 2001, posting a 1.13 ERA in 29 games with eight saves. He was named International League Pitcher of the Month in May.[11] His work earned him a promotion to Atlanta in June after John Smoltz went on the disabled list. Nelson made his major-league debut on June 13, 2001, against the Toronto Blue Jays in the SkyDome in Toronto. Nelson entered the game in the bottom of the seventh, replacing Matt Whiteside. The Jays led 8-3. In one inning of work, Nelson gave up four runs on three hits, a walk, and a hit batter.

On June 19 Nelson pitched an inning against the Florida Marlins and surrendered five runs on four hits, including a grand slam by Cliff Floyd. What had happened? He was lights out in Richmond just a month earlier. It turned out that he had a torn labrum in his right shoulder. "I tried to fight through it at obviously the biggest time in my career," said Nelson, "But you can't pick when they call you up the first time. If I could, I would have said, 'Come get me' four weeks ago. Getting up here was one thing, staying up here is another. ... But I will be back healthy."[12]

He didn't get the chance with the Braves. On August 2 he was released. A week later he signed with the Boston Red Sox and was assigned to the Trenton Thunder of the Double-A Eastern League. In four games he pitched 4⅓ innings, giving up eight runs on nine hits when he blew out his shoulder again. Thanks to a call from Nelson to John Schuerholz of the Braves, the Braves took care of the labrum surgery and rehab.[13]

Nelson was released by the Red Sox and missed the rest of 2002 and all of 2003 in rehab.

On March 30, 2004, Nelson signed with the Red Sox again and was assigned to the Portland Sea Dogs of the Double-A Eastern League. In 30⅓ innings he gave up only 16 hits and struck out 49 with an ERA of 2.37 and 13 saves. This earned him a promotion to the Pawtucket Red Sox of the Triple-A International League. In 21⅓ innings with Pawtucket, Nelson gave up 27 hits and struck out 31. He had a 4.64 ERA.

An injury to Lenny DiNardo created an opportunity and the Red Sox promoted Nelson on July 10. He pitched in three July games for the Red Sox, giving up five runs on four hits. On July 21, with a 16.88 ERA, the Red Sox sent him back to Pawtucket.

Before his call-up to the Red Sox, on a Pawtucket day off, Nelson and three teammates drove to Boston to watch the Red Sox play. They were down on the field prior to the game and Red Sox manager Terry Francona asked if any of the four wanted to see the clubhouse. Three said yes, but Nelson told Francona that he didn't want to go into the clubhouse until he was on the team. A month later, Nelson was on the Red Sox and Francona remembered what Nelson said.[14]

Nelson was not on the Red Sox postseason roster and was released on October 5, 2004. He signed as a free agent with the New York Mets on January 11, 2005, but was released on April 1.

On April 19 Nelson signed with the Tampa Bay Devil Rays and was assigned to the Durham Bulls of the International League. In 46 innings, Nelson struck out 62 while surrendering 41 hits. He was released on July 25 and signed with the St. Louis Cardinals six days later. The Cardinals assigned Nelson to the Springfield Cardinals of the Double-A Texas League, where he struck out 22 batters in 13⅓ innings.

Nelson became a free agent after the season and signed with the Kansas City Royals. He started the 2006 season with the Triple-A Omaha Royals. On April 21 the Royals' David DeJesus was placed on the disabled list and Nelson was summoned from Omaha.[15] He spent the rest of the season with Kansas City, pitching in 43 games and posting 9 saves. He won his first major-league game, against the Red Sox, on September 9 at Fenway Park when the Royals exploded for six unanswered runs in the top of the 12th inning. His record was 1-1.

At the Royals' spring training in February 2007, Nelson was diagnosed with shoulder soreness. A month later he underwent labrum surgery for the third time and missed the entire 2007 season.

Released by the Royals after the season, Nelson signed with the Florida Marlins. He began the 2008 season with the Triple-A Albuquerque Isotopes, where in 19 games he racked up 11 saves. The Marlins called him up on May 26. "That's what spring training was for me – proving I was healthy again, proving to myself I was healthy and proving to the Marlins I was healthy," Nelson said.[16] With the Marlins, he enjoyed his best season by far, 3-1 with an ERA of 2.00 in 59 games and 60 strikeouts in 54 innings. On September 28 he picked up the win in the final game of the season and the last major-league game at Shea Stadium. Nelson entered the game in the bottom of the seventh with the score tied 2-2 and pitched a one-two-three inning. In the top of the eighth, Wes Helms and Dan Uggla hit back-to-back home runs and the Marlins took a 4-2 lead which they held to preserve the win for Nelson.

Earlier in the season, on July 18, Nelson's wife, Teresa, was in labor with their third child. Alexander was born at 3:30 P.M. and the Marlins had a game that night. Marlins manager Fredi González asked Nelson if he was going to make it to the game that evening. Since the mother and baby were both doing well and Teresa saw that Joe was champing at the bit, she said that he could go to the game as long as he made it on *SportsCenter* that evening. He went to the ballpark and told the pitching coach what she had said.

With the visiting Philadelphia Phillies up by a score of 4-2, Nelson came in to pitch the ninth inning. After he struck out Pedro Feliz, Carlos Ruiz singled to third. Nelson then struck out Greg Dobbs and Jimmy Rollins to end the inning by striking out the side. His teammates gave him a framed lineup card that was signed by members of the team.[17]

After the 2008 season, Nelson was once again a free agent. He signed with the Tampa Bay Rays on December 30 and started the 2009 season on the big-league roster. In 42 games, Nelson was 3-0 as a middle reliever.

This was a fun time for Nelson to be a member of the Rays. On May 16 he introduced the Rays' lineup on the Fox broadcast in the voice of Bill Murray's character in *Caddyshack*, groundskeeper Carl Spackler.[18]

That was just a day after ESPN did a spot on Nelson's "Vulcan changeup grip," where Nelson offered to be a "hand stunt double" in the next movie since the new Mr. Spock, Zachary Quinto, reportedly had to have his fingers glued to do the "live long and prosper" gesture that Nelson used as a pitching grip.[19]

His last game for the Rays was on July 31. Jeff Bennett was released by the Braves and signed by the Rays, and to make room for him, Nelson was sent to the Durham Bulls, where he remained for the rest of the season.

Released by the Rays after the season, Nelson signed again with the Red Sox and was assigned to Pawtucket. On May 19, 2010, he was called up after Josh Beckett was placed on the 15-day disabled list. He pitched in eight games for the Red Sox, giving up 14 hits in 8⅓ innings.

Red Sox pitching coach John Farrell said of Nelson, "He's shown lots of perseverance, both from a physical standpoint and what he's come back from and never being a guy who was guaranteed anything."[20]

The Red Sox released Nelson on June 21 and he was picked up by the Seattle Mariners three days later; they sent him to their Triple-A affiliate in Tacoma. With the Rainiers, Nelson pitched in eight games before being released on July 26.

"My career came to an end from self-sabotage in a way," Nelson wrote in an email to the author. "I have always been goal oriented, and from the time I started playing professionally I wanted to make an Opening Day roster and make a million dollars a year. I achieved both in 2009 and I made the fatal flaw of not setting new goals. It took me so long to get to the mountain top, I just didn't have it in me anymore. I had lost the desire to do all the work. I have no regrets in baseball at all, I played a kids' game my entire life and made a living at it. I truly had a blessed life, and thank GOD every day for the life I get to live.

"I told Theo Epstein that I needed a job and I had no idea what path to take; scouting, coaching, or player development. He sent me to meet Allard Baird (my GM in Kansas City). We scouted a game in Portland, Maine, and it turns out I was a scout my entire career. I see things other people didn't on a baseball field. I was never the best player, so I had to use video and look for flaws in hitters' approaches, and scouting was similar. I had to write a lot of reports for various teams and worked with some great people; Theo Epstein, Ben Cherington, Allard Baird, Jared Porter, Tom Allison, to name a few. There are so many people in this great game who took the time to share with me their knowledge and experience and made me the best scout and baseball guy I could be. When the Cubs let me go during COVID, I was gutted."[21]

Nelson scouted for the Red Sox in 2011, the Mariners from 2012 to 2016, and the Cubs from 2016 to 2020.[22]

Nelson's wife's career is going strong and he is now the homemaker; makes lunches for school, drives their children to school and back, makes breakfast and dinner, and coaches a couple of local teams in flag football.[23]

Nelson received a World Series ring for his part in the Red Sox 2004 World Series championship team.

Nelson played 13 seasons in professional baseball but did not make an Opening Day roster until his 12th season at age 34. He persevered through four major surgeries and lots of rehab to survive in the game as long as he did. He put up some really good numbers when his arm was healthy and it would be interesting to see how his career would have panned out if he was healthy all of those years.

Joe and his wife, Dr. Teresa Cortinas, live in Jupiter, Florida, and are the parents of three children, Sofia, Olivia, and Alexander.

SOURCES

In addition to the sources cited in the Notes, the author used Retrosheet.org and Baseball-Reference.com for stats and game information. Thanks to Joe Nelson for telephone interviews and email correspondence.

NOTES

1. Telephone interview with Joe Nelson, October 12, 2023
2. Nelson telephone interview.
3. Email correspondence with Joe Nelson, September 29, 2023.
4. Nelson email.
5. Nelson email.
6. Mark Hale, "Reliever Was Kidd's Backcourt Mate," *New York Post*, February 16, 2005, retrieved from: www.nypost.com/2005/02/16/reliever-was-kidds-backcourt-mate/.

7   "Nelson Voted ESAL's Player of the Year," *Oakland Tribune*, May 26, 1993: 47.

8   Dick Kaegel, "Nelson Takes Spot in Kansas City 'Pen,'" www.milb.com/news/gcs-71373, May 15, 2006; Rob Cox, "Second Thoughts," *Arkansas Democrat Gazette* (Little Rock), May 4, 2009. https://www.arkansasonline.com/news/2009/may/04/second-thoughts-20090504/.

9   "Reliever Joe Nelson Still Going Strong After Four Surgeries," NESN.com, March 8, 2021. www.nesn.com/2010/03/reliever-joe-nelson-still-going-strong-after-four-surgeries/.

10 Nelson email.

11 Carroll Rogers, "Calls Costly After Nelson Call-Up," *Atlanta Journal*, June 13, 2001: 63.

12 Carroll Rogers, "Nelson on DL After Two Outings," *Atlanta Journal*, June 21, 2001: 91.

13 Telephone interview with Joe Nelson, October 4, 2023.

14 Telephone interview October 4, 2023.

15 Bob Dutton, "Baird Unfazed by Comments," *Kansas City Star*, April 22, 2006: 76.

16 Marlins Daily Report, "Nelson Called Up to Bolster Bullpen," *Miami Herald*, May 27, 2008: 73.

17 Telephone interview, October 4, 2023.

18 Rays Report, "Impersonation of the Day," *Tampa Bay Times*, May 17, 2009: 28.

19 James Borchuck, "Star Trekking," *Tampa Bay Times*, May 17, 2009: 12.

20 NESN Staff, "Reliever Joe Nelson Still Going Strong…"

21 Nelson email.

22 Telephone interview October 12, 2023.

23 Nelson email.

TROT NIXON

BY TIM PEELER

No one was going to give Trot Nixon a speeding ticket.

Not for the inspirational leader of the Boston Red Sox, the left-handed outfielder with the dirty uniform and the grinder spirit who became a fan favorite for wanting to win just a little bit more than most. His country was under attack, his wife was in the hospital, and he was eager to meet their first child.

Nixon woke up that morning – September 11, 2001 – after barely an hour of sleep, thanks to a plane trip from New York to Tampa and an all-night card game with teammate Morgan Burkhart.[1]

When the phone rang at 5 A.M., he knew immediately his wife was likely in labor and that his son was on the way into the world. He knew it was going to be a long day to get back to Boston from the Gulf Coast of Florida.[2]

He also knew it would be well worth the travel ahead.

Surely it was, but Nixon's 19-hour trek to meet his firstborn was more difficult and traumatic than he could have ever imagined.[3]

For Nixon, hardly a patient man working in the most impatient baseball town in the American League, the journey back to Boston wasn't even the hardest part. The world looks different when seen through the smoke of the Pentagon on fire while driving on Interstate 95 and through the dust caused by the collapse of the Twin Towers at the World Trade Center.

It almost made what happened two years later, when Nixon's improbable return to the lineup to help the Red Sox win their first World Series championship in 86 years, seem small by comparison.

So, Nixon did what worked for him throughout his professional baseball career: simplify and focus.

Born for Baseball?

Christopher Trotman Nixon was born in Durham, North Carolina, into a family with tobacco-farming and baseball roots. His father, Dr. William P. Nixon, a former high-school teammate of Jim "Catfish" Hunter, became a physician in Wilmington, North Carolina, moving his family to the coast before his son could walk, much less Trot.

The young athlete grew up at a Wilmington quarterback factory, terrorizing high-school opponents in both football and baseball unlike few who had ever competed in a state known for good athletes.

Throughout his prep career, the hallways of New Hanover High School echoed with the memories of highly decorated NFL signal-callers Roman Gabriel and Sonny Jurgensen. They traveled through stops at North Carolina State and Duke, respectively, to realize their NFL dreams.

Neither, however, pulled off the dual-sport feat that Nixon did as a senior when he was named the state's most valuable football and baseball player and the *USA Today* North Carolina Athlete of the Year.

In the fall of 1992, Nixon led New Hanover's undefeated football team to the second round of the state's 4A playoffs.[4] N.C. State, the state's most successful Division I football program at the time, signed him to a scholarship to be part of a quarterback lineage that includes NFL passers Gabriel, Erik Kramer, Philip Rivers, and Russell Wilson.

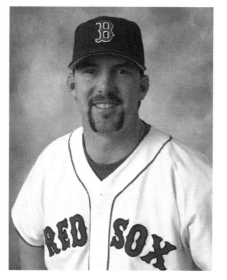

In baseball, Nixon was even better, taking New Hanover's 1993 team to the school's first state championship since 1959,[5] when it was still called Wilmington High. Surely, he could excel in both sports at N.C. State, as Gabriel did from 1959 to 1961.

New Hanover's title run, after years of disappointment in the state playoffs, mirrored what happened during Nixon's major-league career, particularly after he and future New York Mets draftee Fletcher Bates called their teammates together following a season-opening loss to Garner High and gave them whatfor. They announced in that meeting their intention to carry the team over the hump that had blocked the program for more than three decades.

"Our team had a get-down-and-dirty attitude," said head coach Dave Brewster in a 10th-anniversary profile in the *Wilmington Star-News*. "They were gritty."[6]

Nixon was practically unstoppable, hitting 12 homers, driving in a state-record 56 runs and posting a 12-0 record with a 0.40 earned-run average on the pitcher's mound. He was successful in 20 of his 21 stolen-base attempts and struck out only twice all season.

The team didn't lose another game.

The Red Sox, at the suggestion of longtime scout Jeff Zona, made Nixon the seventh pick of the 1993 draft – the second high-school player taken after number 1 overall selection Álex

Rodríguez and 14 spots ahead of future Red Sox captain and teammate Jason Varitek.[7]

Before Nixon could embark on the professional baseball career he knew would follow, he had to get football out of his system.

Choosing a Sport

In late July 1993, Nixon and his dad made the 2½-hour drive to Raleigh into a maelstrom of confusion that was the Wolfpack football program. Just before the start of camp, the coach who recruited Nixon, Dick Sheridan, announced his retirement, citing health issues. He was replaced by quarterbacks coach Mike O'Cain.

The prospective freshman showed up every morning at 7:30 to prepare for two-a-day workouts, knowing he had three weeks before the start of classes to decide his baseball future, while his father and family adviser Ron Shapiro of Shapiro, Robinson and Associates negotiated with the Red Sox.

Just as Nixon looked as though he might be the third Red Sox first-round pick to not sign with the team, joining Jimmie Hacker in 1970 and Greg McMurtry in 1986, he took an accidental hit on his throwing elbow, a scare that hastened his decision to play baseball.

On August 25, 1993, he and the Red Sox agreed to terms, with a then-club-record signing bonus of $890,000 and a promise for a spot on the 40-man roster in 1994 and 1995.[8]

"I really did want to play college football and baseball and experience the full college atmosphere," Nixon said 30 years later. "I wanted to do it at N.C. State, and I was dead serious about it.

"But I was also dead serious about my dream to play professional baseball."[9]

Making Hard Decisions

Nixon spent five years in the minors, honing his offensive and defensive skills.

"It becomes a job real quick," Nixon said. "You've got to fine-tune things and get better if you want to be successful. To me, getting drafted was not successful. My dream was to get to the big leagues and win."

That didn't happen in the first half of Nixon's first Triple-A season. Specifically, things weren't going well on May 11, 1997, when he was playing for the Pawtucket Red Sox and the parent team came to McCoy Stadium for its annual exhibition game. Nixon was hitting under .150 and thought it was the right time for a pregame break.

"We don't have time to take days off," hitting coach and Red Sox legend Rico Petrocelli told the 23-year-old first-round pick with exactly four major-league at-bats.

"He got on me hard," Nixon said. "I needed it."[10]

By the end of the season, Nixon had raised his batting average to .244 and finished with 20 homers and 61 RBIs, good numbers on a good team in the International League.

The next season also started slowly for a prospect who was showing some age.

"I was sitting on the back steps of the outdoor batting cages in Louisville at a real low point in my career," Nixon said. "It was like I was hanging on a cliff, about to fall off. I told myself, 'God gave you the ability to play the game, and right now you aren't using that ability. You can't get out of your own way.'"[11]

What Nixon needed was a little joy from the game, a kid-like perspective of putting passion into his play.

"Sometimes you lose that pure love of the game," he said. "So sitting on the steps of that batting cage, I made the decision to get back to that point, to play hard, to play with joy."

He also made some technical adjustments, moving his front foot up in his stance and switching to a heavier 35-ounce, 36-inch bat. He finished the year with 23 homers, 74 RBIs, and 26 stolen bases.

Sticking in the Big Leagues

It's hard for any major-league player not to forget his first hit. For Nixon, it was a dream scenario.

He was briefly called up to the Red Sox in September 1996, fulfilling a contractual obligation to be part of a late-season roster expansion. Mostly, he was there to observe, with no anticipation of making a meaningful contribution.

The night before the next-to-last game of the season, left fielder Mike Greenwell told Nixon he would be in the starting lineup the next day against the eventual World Series champion New York Yankees. Nervously getting ready for his first at-bat, Nixon took a practice swing and accidentally dropped his bat on Yankees catcher Joe Girardi's head.

On the first pitch he saw from Ricky Bones, however, Nixon pulled a single to right field and eventually found himself standing on third base.

"Was that your first hit?" Wade Boggs asked him. "I hope you get a ton more."

Nixon got another hit later in the game and saw 13 more games as a late-season call-up in 1998.

He played well enough in his second stint that manager Jimy Williams put him on the postseason roster. He started in right field in Game Three of the American League Division Series against the Cleveland Indians and went 1-for-3.

Cleveland won the series three games to one, but the message was clear for Nixon: Be ready to play – with passion, with joy, and with dirt on his uniform – in 1999.

A Platoon Stalwart

Nixon played the majority of his first two full seasons in right field as half of a platoon with either Damon Buford or Darren Lewis.

He started slowly in 1999, just 4-for-38 in the first 12 games, and he was hearing whispers that general manager Dan Duquette was ready to ship Nixon out of Boston, by either trade or demotion. One afternoon he was called into the manager's office.[12]

"Tough going right now," Williams said.

Nixon braced for the worst.

"We're going to change some things up," Williams told him. "You're going to keep playing, don't worry, but we're going to change up your stance. We're going to simplify things.

"You're going to be good, kid."[13]

Nixon had better than a .320 batting average for the month of May, hit ..393 in July, and cemented an enduring love for the manager who put unwavering faith in his abilities. Still playing in a platoon, Nixon was comfortable batting in the bottom two slots in the lineup, hitting all 15 of his home runs and driving in 49 of his 51 runs from the eighth and ninth positions.[14]

The next year, Williams was ready to make even bigger moves with Nixon, first putting him in the leadoff spot, then moving him down to either second or third. He played 102 games in the top third of the lineup, with all 12 homers and 58 of his 60 RBIs from those slots.[15]

"Next to God giving me my abilities, my parents and my coaches growing up who taught me the game, I owe my career to Jimy Williams," Nixon said. "That's probably a bold statement, I know, but everyone on the team knew that if they had something bad to say against Jimy, they better not say it around me."

In the Air on 9/11

When Nixon's plane left Tampa International Airport at 6:30 A.M. on September 11, 2001, he dozed off almost immediately. He slept deeply, with the satisfaction of a player finally riding a breakout season.[16]

He was awakened by an announcement from the pilot about a detour to Norfolk, Virginia, but a commotion in the cabin and the panic-stricken face of a flight attendant suggested anything but a routine mechanical problem. The next pilot announcement came with a wings-vertical bank to the left: "The President of the United States has ordered all aircraft in American airspace to the ground."[17]

Nixon learned just how traumatic the morning had been in US airspace when he landed in Norfolk, Virginia. He called his parents in Wilmington. He called his wife in Boston, now in full labor. And he called a cousin in Hertford, North Carolina, to make arrangements to be picked up as quickly as possible.

Finally, he talked to his wife's doctor and said for the first time what he knew hours earlier: "I'm not going to be there in time for the delivery."[18]

Neither his wife nor her doctors knew what was going on in New York, Washington, or rural Pennsylvania, the sites of terrorist attacks that day. Nixon finally had to give her the details on the phone.

Nixon's cousin took him to their grandparents' home in Hertford, where his father, mother, and younger sister picked him up to begin the race to Boston to be with his wife. They sped through Washington, around New York City, and into Massachusetts. Late in the evening, Nixon loaded on three Mountain Dews, took over the driving from his father, and he stepped on the accelerator.[19]

He knew his wife, Kathryn, was in good hands, as Bitsy Hatteberg, wife of teammate Scott Hatteberg, spent the entire day in the delivery and recovery room with her. He kept driving through the night as the rest of his family slept.

Sometime around 3:30 A.M., Nixon made it to the Boston hospital where his new family waited for him and held his son, Chase, in his hands.[20]

World Series Champion

In addition to the birth of his son, Nixon had plenty to be proud of in 2001. He hit 27 home runs and drove in 88 runs. It was the first of three consecutive seasons in which he had at least two dozen homers and 75 RBIs. He was not only solidly in the Red Sox lineup, he hit third in the batting order for much of the year.[21]

Nixon overcame the Red Sox decision to fire Williams in August of 2001[22] and endeared himself to successors Joe Kerrigan, Grady Little, and Terry Francona over the next three years for his hard play in the field. He became the emotional leader of the Dirt Dogs, the name pitcher Paul Quantrill gave Nixon and several other Red Sox players.[23] It's a nickname still used by Boston.com on the top of its Red Sox fan page.

Nixon was the perfect embodiment of that dusty spirit. His locker-room nameplate read "Volcano" because, said first baseman Brian Daubach, "he could erupt at any time."[24]

He did just that from 2001 to 2003, the three most productive seasons of his career. Fully healthy, he averaged 26 home runs, 90 RBIs, and 5 stolen bases, while hitting .273 in the top half of the lineup. He had career highs with 28 home runs and a .306 batting over 134 games in 2003, earning him a three-year, $19.5 million contract extension.[25]

It took a while for Nixon's lava to flow during the 2004 season. On a 12-hour drive from Wilmington to Fort Myers, Florida, for spring training, Nixon exacerbated a bulging herniated disk problem in his lower back. It cost him the first 63 games of the season.

Not long after he returned, he pulled the quadriceps in his left leg, an injury that team physicians thought might sideline him through the end of the season. Off and on, Gabe Kapler, Dave Roberts, and Kevin Millar filled in for Nixon in right field but combined (11 home runs, 61 RBIs, and 5 stolen bases), they could not match Nixon's averages in those categories for the previous three years.

Privately, Nixon knew he could be ready for postseason play. Silently, Red Sox owner John Henry helped make that happen by sending Nixon to work with a physical therapist who was more connected to Boston University and the NHL's Boston Bruins than he was to the Red Sox medical staff of trainer Jim Rowe, assistant Chang Lee, and physical therapist Chris Correnti.

Under the close direction of Brookline, Massachusetts-based physical therapist Scott Waugh, Nixon did off-ice hockey workouts for six weeks, gaining a deeper understanding of how onerous and odorous their training for short bursts on the ice truly was.

"Hockey locker rooms are tough," Nixon said. "They smell like the world's biggest dirty sock."[26]

Waugh helped Nixon's impatience with the process.

"We won't worry about what's going to happen at the end of the year," Waugh told him. "I'm going to train you like a hockey player. Early on, it's going to suck, but I think it will pay off.

"Let's simplify and get to work."

By the end of August, Nixon was ready for his first trip to the minors in six years.

He played one game for the Sarasota Red Sox and three for Pawtucket. He ripped 9 hits in 24 at-bats. He felt game-ready, but when he returned to Boston's active roster on September 7, he was in danger of disrupting a red-hot lineup that had won 19 of 22 games.

Sporting an unsightly Mohawk haircut, Nixon pinch-hit in five of his first six games, including a two-run homer in a loss to Tampa Bay. In his lone start, he had two hits, including a double, in four trips to the plate.

"It was the best I had ever felt in my life," Nixon said.[27]

Because of his extended absence, there were whispers that general manager Theo Epstein might not include him on the postseason roster, but that wouldn't have set well with the established star, even though he had contributed only 6 home runs and 23 RBIs in 48 regular-season games.

"Theo, I'm not missing this ride," Nixon said.[28]

What happened over the next three weeks was too good to believe, even for a Dirt Dog with big dreams. Nixon played in 13 of the 14 postseason games and, just as he had the year before, he produced at the most critical times.

He had just two hits in two games against the Anaheim Angels, but both drove in critical runs.

He felt completely healthy to face the Yankees, in a rematch of the previous year's American League Championship Series.

After the Red Sox lost the first three games and faced elimination, Nixon wasn't sure what would happen.

"It was kind of an impossible situation," he said.

Nixon credited Varitek, the veteran catcher and team captain, for producing a winning strategy for the famous "Four Days in October."

"Varitek rarely ever spoke, but when he did, we all listened," Nixon said. "All he said was that we all knew what we needed to do. He told us to focus on each half-inning. If they score one in the top, we score two in the bottom. Just win each half-inning. And that's what we did – everyone was just totally locked in."

"It was all such a fairytale ending just to get to the World Series."[29]

The Cardinals never really had a chance in the 4-0 sweep. In the final game of the season, in the game that ended the Red Sox' 86-year championship drought and was played on the 18th anniversary of the Game Seven loss to the New York Mets in the 1986 World Series, the oft-sidelined Nixon had three doubles and drove in two of his team's three runs to send New England into pandemonium.

"It really was the most magical season in Red Sox history," Nixon said. "I owe everything I was able to do that year to the Man Upstairs and John Henry.

"He took a chance to go a little different route on my rehab, and it paid off for me."[30]

Breaking the famed Boston curse was the headline of the season, of course, but Nixon's contributions earned him a spot in Red Sox lore as well. He was the first of Boston's 78 first-round picks in franchise history to help the Red Sox win a World Series title.[31]

The club's homegrown talent – including first-round picks Jacoby Ellsbury, Clay Buchholz, Blake Swihart, Jackie Bradley Jr., and Andrew Benintendi – helped win three subsequent titles in 2007, 2013, and 2018.

Breaking Away

Nixon had two more injury-laden seasons with the Red Sox, in which his power numbers and productivity dwindled to his pre-2001 numbers. Including the championship season, Nixon had just 27 homers over three seasons, as his Dirt Dog style continued to take its toll on his body.

In 2004, he had managed to come back with great force after the herniated disk and quad injury but that didn't happen in the following years.

In 2005 he had both an oblique strain and arthroscopic surgery at the end of the season.[32]

In 2006 he had an early season groin strain and missed a month with a biceps strain.[33]

The club did not offer salary arbitration and pulled back on a two-year extension, choosing instead to offer a five-year, $70 million contract to J.D. Drew to take over right field.[34]

Nixon and agent Michael Moss began looking for new places to play and chose to sign a $3 million, one-year deal with the up-and-coming Cleveland Indians,[35] who needed the experience of an outfielder with five different trips to the postseason.

Nixon was again saddled with injuries and eventually gave up his position in right field to prospect Franklin Gutierrez, as the Indians jumped out to a fast start. He went weeks without playing but made a deal with Indians manager Eric Wedge to lead the team's clubhouse after the team lost three consecutive series following the All-Star break.

"I told Eric I would take over the clubhouse, and he could run the team," Nixon said. "It was a good young team. We made it fun. I was happy because I was making an impact on the young players."[36]

The Indians won the American League Central Division, finished tied with the Red Sox for the most wins (96) in the American League and clobbered the wild card Yankees in four games in the Division Series.

Cleveland went up three games to one against the Red Sox but lost the last three games for a chance to go to the World Series. As Nixon walked out of Fenway Park for the last time as a major-league player, a group of fans gave him an appreciative ovation for all that he meant to the club, from the days he chose to sign a contract instead of playing college football to breaking the most famous curse in professional sports history.

"I don't think the people who were there know what that meant to me," Nixon said. "I wasn't a great player. Without the injuries, I could have been a lot better. But I cared about the game. I cared about my teammates. I cared about the city of Boston.

"All I ever wanted to do was win, and I was a part of a team that won it all."[37]

After Baseball

Nixon signed with the Arizona Diamondbacks in January 2008 and was assigned to three different minor-league teams in the first half of the season. In June he was traded to the New York Mets and was called up for his first-ever action in the National League on June 12.[38]

He played just 11 games for the Mets, then signed a contract with the Milwaukee Brewers in the offseason.[39] He was released before the season started.

Nixon thought about pursuing a career in coaching, broadcasting, or front-office work, but the pull of raising his sons, Chase and Luke, was too strong and he retired to Wilmington.

"I talked with Grady Little about it," Nixon said, "and he told me, 'The one regret of my career was that I was never there to see my boys growing up. If you can afford it, stay there in Wilmington and watch your boys play.'"

"I had some opportunities to stay in baseball, but I just wanted to be with my wife and kids."[40]

Both boys had outstanding high-school careers and both chose to play college baseball at N.C. State, the school where their dad once entertained the idea of being a football and baseball star.

Nixon watched them play every game, and he never missed a birthday.[41]

In December 2023, Trot Nixon was voted into the Boston Red Sox Hall of Fame as a member of the Class of 2024.

NOTES

1. Christopher Trotman Nixon, personal interview with Timothy Michael Peeler, September 1, 2022, Doak Field at Dail Park, North Carolina State University, Raleigh, North Carolina. Hereafter, Nixon interview.
2. "Athletes Share Their 9-11 Memories," *ESPN: The Magazine*, September 19, 2011. https://www.espn.com/espn/story/_/id/6942890/athletes-kevin-durant-dale-earnhardt-jr-abby-wambach-more-share-their-9-11-memories-espn-magazine.
3. Nixon interview.
4. North Carolina High School Athletic Association, 1992 football playoff bracket, 1992 Football State Championship Bracket – NCHSAA.
5. North Carolina High School Athletic Association, 1993 baseball playoff bracket, https://www.nchsaa.org/bracket/1993-baseball-state-championship-brackets/.
6. Chuck Carree, "10 Years Ago, New Hanover Baseball Ruled the State," *Wilmington Star-News*, May 11, 2003. https://www.starnewsonline.com/story/news/2003/05/11/10-years-ago-new-hanover-baseball-ruled-the-state/30516185007/.
7. Baseball Reference, 1993 Baseball Draft, https://www.baseball-reference.com/bullpen/1993_Amateur_Draft.
8. Nick Cafardo, "Hobson Planning Four-Man Rotation," *Boston Globe*, August 27, 1993: 51.
9. Nixon interview.
10. Nixon interview.
11. Nixon interview.
12. Bob Ryan, "Williams Made the Right Move by Trusting Nixon," *Boston Globe,* September 16, 1999: C5.
13. Nixon interview.
14. Baseball Reference, 1999 season splits, https://www.baseball-reference.com/players/split.fcgi?id=nixontr01&year=1999&t=b.
15. Baseball Reference, 2000 season splits, https://www.baseball-reference.com/players/split.fcgi?id=nixontr01&year=1999&t=b.
16. Nixon interview.
17. Nixon interview.
18. Nixon interview.
19. Nixon interview.
20. Nixon interview.
21. Baseball Reference, Trot Nixon season stats, https://www.baseball-reference.com/players/n/nixontr01.shtml.
22. Nixon interview.
23. Bob Hohler, "It Centers on Nixon," *Boston Globe*, July 19, 2001: C1, C5
24. John Powers, "Starry Bursts by Nixon," *Boston Globe*, June 13, 2001: 87.
25. Associated Press, ESPN.com, February 6, 2004.
26. Nixon interview.
27. Nixon interview.
28. Nixon interview.
29. Nixon interview.
30. Nixon interview.
31. Boston Red Sox MLB First Round Draft History, ESPN.com, https://www.espn.com/mlb/draft/history/_/team/bos.
32. "Trot Nixon Goes to the DL," UPI.com, July 27, 2005, https://www.upi.com/Sports_News/2005/07/27/Trot-Nixon-goes-to-the-DL/44481122505527/.
33. Associated Press, "Red Sox Place Nixon on DL, Activate Wells," ESPN.com, July 26, 2006.
34. Gordon Edes, "Exciting Signs," *Boston Globe*, December 6, 2006: C1 33.
35. Associated Press, ESPN.com, January 19, 2007.
36. Nixon interview.
37. Nixon interview.
38. Associated Prress, "Nixon Traded to Mets to Help Injury-Riddled Outfield," ESPN.com, June 14, 2007.
39. Associated Press, "Brewers Add Outfielder Nixon," ESPN.com, December 18, 2008. https://www.espn.com/mlb/news/story?id=3779852.
40. Nixon interview.
41. Nixon interview.

DAVID ORTIZ

BY BILL NOWLIN

"He's a superhero without a cape. That's the way we see him."
– Alex Cora[1]

Several of the biggest base hits in Boston baseball history came off the bat of "Big Papi," David Ortiz. He sports three world championship rings and then wrapped up his career with one of the best final seasons any player has ever enjoyed. Within months of leaving the game, he was honored by the Red Sox, who retired his jersey number 34. He had already become an instant icon in Red Sox Nation.

Had he done no more than lead the 2004 team to triumph over the Yankees and then the Cardinals, he would still go down in team history for his key role in helping them win their first World Series in 86 years. But he came up big again in 2007 and was overpowering in 2013.

Ortiz hit 541 home runs in the course of his major-league career, and 632 doubles. The only two batters before him to hit 500 homers and 600 doubles were Hank Aaron and Barry Bonds.

And Ortiz was, as a *New York Times* subhead once said, "a maestro in the statistics-defying art of clutch hitting."[2]

The toast of the town in Boston, David Americo Ortiz Arias came from the humblest of backgrounds. He was born in Santo Domingo, Dominican Republic, on November 18, 1975, but from around the age of 14 grew up in the community of Haina, on the southern coast just west of the capital. The city of around 84,000 people has been dubbed the Dominican Chernobyl and is considered to be one of the most polluted cities in the world. "According to the United Nations, the population of Haina is considered to have the highest level of lead contamination in the world, and its entire population carries indications of lead poisoning."[3] The problem almost certainly emanated from the Baterías Meteoro battery plant, a now-closed automobile battery recycling smelter. David Ortiz himself said, "Piles of batteries, some as high as three-story buildings, could be found in the city. That alone put our lives in danger. ... [B]attery acid and lead would seep into the soil."[4]

As if that weren't enough, the city was plagued with "Shootings. Stabbings. Drugs. Gangs. ...We were poor and our neighborhood was teeming with violence and crime." One day on his way to the bodega, young David saw a man murdered right in front of him.[5] Had it not been for the values instilled in him by his parents, Enrique and Angela, he might have grown up to a different life entirely – or lost his own life at an early age. Enrique worked at automotive repair, "from parts to repairs to sales," though he rarely had more than a moped himself. Angela originally worked as a secretary for the Department of Agriculture in Santo Domingo, but she "was always taking on jobs to pick up extra money. She would sometimes travel to other parts of the Caribbean, as far away as Curaçao and St. Thomas, to buy clothes and sell them to tourists at local hotels."[6] They worked hard, sacrificing to help provide for David and his younger sister, Albania.

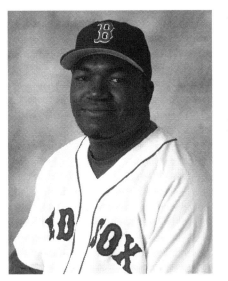

David had talent at sports, basketball as well as baseball, with his father pushing hard for him to pursue baseball. David spent a lot of time at the Florida Marlins facility but elbow inflammation cropped up and they let it be known he wasn't being seen as a prospect. A *buscón*[7] named Hector "Machepa" Alvarez took David under his wing and a week and a half after David turned 17, he signed with the Seattle Mariners for $7,500 to $10,000.[8] He was sent to play rookie ball in Peoria, Arizona, in the summer of 1994. His salary was $59 per week.[9] He was far from home, in an alien environment, and he struggled. Had it not been for his sense of obligation to his parents and a competitive fire within himself, he might not have persevered. That first summer he played in 53 games and batted .246. In the summer of 1995, however, he bumped his average up to .332.

Ortiz was left-handed and grew to stand 6-feet-3 to 6-feet-4, listed at 230 pounds.

In his third year, Ortiz was assigned to the Class-A (Midwest League) Wisconsin Timber Rattlers in Appleton, Wisconsin. There he had five roommates, all Dominican, living in a two-bedroom home. (Until he made the majors, David always played professionally as David Arias, not David Ortiz.) That summer of 1996 saw him begin to hit for power as well as average, with 18 homers and 93 RBIs (both leading the team by a considerable margin), and a .322 batting average. Primarily a first baseman, he was now making $400 a week. He was voted the best defensive first baseman in the league.[10]

He also met a young woman from Kaukauna, Wisconsin, named Tiffany Brick. She was a photography student in Madison, and a fast-pitch softball player who had been voted "Most Athletic Girl" in her high school. They hit it off immediately and within two weeks, he says, the word "marriage" first came up.[11]

The Timber Rattlers made the 1996 league playoffs, but lost out in the final round.

On September 13 that year, Ortiz became the player to be named later in a trade with the Minnesota Twins, completing a deal made on August 29, when the Mariners acquired Dave Hollins in what may well have been a cost-cutting move for the Twins.

Ortiz played for four teams in 1997. First he was sent to Fort Myers to play in the Twins Class-A Florida State League team there. He hit .331 in 61 games, earning him a promotion to Double-A ball (with the Eastern League's New Britain Rock Cats in New Britain, Connecticut). There he hit 14 homers (.322 BA) in 69 games. He was promoted to Salt Lake City of the Triple-A Pacific Coast League and appeared in 10 games there, then became a September call-up to the Twins.

Ortiz's first two major-league at-bats came as a pinch-hitter during interleague play at Chicago's Wrigley Field. On September 2 he hit a fly ball out to deep left-center field. On September 3 he doubled to deep right-center for his first major-league base hit. He was 2-for-5 with his first run batted in on September 8 and, by season's end, had made a bit of a mark with just one home run, but with 16 hits in 49 at-bats (.327).

As a youngster, the first player who had made an impression on him, watching the 1991 World Series on a simple TV in the Dominican Republic, was Kirby Puckett. As soon as he was able, Ortiz took the number 34 in tribute to Puckett. But the Twins were no longer the team that had inspired him back in 1991. Not since 1992 had they won as many as half their games; they played in the uninspiring Metrodome, and they were near the bottom of the league in terms of attendance. Ortiz also had a difficult relationship with manager Tom Kelly.[12]

Through the first games of the 1998 season, Ortiz was hitting over .300 with 20 RBIs, and second on the Twins in slugging, but a broken right wrist saw him unable to play from May 9 to July 9, and hampered his power numbers for the year. (Interestingly, he'd stayed in the game after breaking his wrist, and even homered later in the game.)[13] He hit .360 in 18 September games, finishing with a .277 batting average. For the year, he drove in 46 runs despite missing two months; no one else on the Twins drove in more than 77.

In 1999, although the Twins were clearly in need of a big bat, Ortiz was one of the first players cut in spring training and he spent most of the year back in Salt Lake City. He put up some big numbers there, batting .315 with 30 homers and 110 RBIs. When called up in September, however, he was playing with a torn ACL and proved a very disappointing 0-for-20 at the plate, with 12 strikeouts.

There followed something of a journeyman season in the year 2000. Ortiz appeared in 130 big-league games, mostly as a DH, batting .282, and driving in 63 runs. His RBI total placed him fifth on the Twins; he ranked third in slugging percentage.

In 2001 he appeared in only 89 games, almost all as the DH. Another wrist fracture sidelined him for 2½ months. Though he hit 18 homers in the end (from August 9 through August 12, he homered in four consecutive games), he hit for only a .234 average, driving in 48 runs. He'd started off really hot, with 15 RBIs in his first 16 games, and was hitting .311 at the time of the injury. He clearly never fully recovered that season. He had shown plate discipline; in both the 2000 and 2001 seasons, he drew enough walks to add another 82 points to his on-base percentage. The Twins payroll in 2001 was the lowest in the majors when the season began.[14]

On New Year's Day 2002, tragedy struck; Ortiz's mother, Angela Rosa Arias, was killed in an automobile accident. Those who have watched David Ortiz hit home runs over the years will recall that, ever after, when he crossed the plate he would point heavenward to share the moment with his beloved mother.

The year 2002 was Ortiz's first exclusively in the major leagues, and he appeared in 125 games. (A mid-April surgery to remove bone chips in his knee cost him almost a month on the DL.) Ortiz hit .272, with 20 homers and 75 RBIs, totals that would have both been higher had he not missed so many games. Even then, he ranked third on the Twins in the latter two statistics. He appeared in 15 games at first base, but was typically the DH. The Twins made the postseason and Ortiz's ninth-inning double drove in the game-winner in the final Division Series game against the Athletics. The Twins lost the ALCS in five games to Anaheim; Ortiz hit .313 but drove in only a pair of runs.

Still skimping on payroll, the Twins weren't prepared to pony up the money needed to sign Ortiz to a new contract and they didn't want to go to arbitration with him, which might have forced them to pay him double the $900,000 or $950,000 he was being paid.[15] They tried to trade him, but every team in baseball passed, and so they simply released him on December 16, 2002.[16] Hard as it may be to believe today, the man who soon became perhaps the best DH in history and one of the most fearsome clutch hitters in postseason play was simply released. He was a man without a team. Notably, though, Tiffany Ortiz's response was, "Good. Now we can apply for a job in Boston."[17]

And Red Sox pitching ace Pedro Martínez (who was dining in the same restaurant in Santo Domingo the evening Ortiz got the word that he had been released) got to work, peppering the Red Sox front office with phone calls and telling them they simply had to sign David Ortiz. They did, with new Boston GM Theo Epstein offering a one-year deal for $1.25 million. It wasn't a big commitment at the time, and the pursuit of Ortiz barely made the Boston papers. The team had Shea Hillenbrand, and was engaged in negotiations to sign Kevin Millar and Jeremy Giambi. But Ortiz put on something of a show in Dominican Winter League ball, batting .351 with 23 RBIs in 20 games.[18]

The Dominican team won the Caribbean Series, and Ortiz was named MVP.[19]

The signing itself was famously dubbed an example of the Red Sox "shopping at Wal-Mart."[20]

Indeed, Epstein had proven a thrifty shopper, spending $5.3 million and landing David Ortiz, Kevin Millar, and Bill Mueller.[21] Millar fired up the ballclub with his "Cowboy Up!" movement in 2003 and his "Don't Let Us Win Tonight!" mantra in 2004. Mueller hit .326, good enough to win the American League batting title in 2003. And Ortiz, well, within three years he was being compared to Babe Ruth and described as "one of the all-time baseball bargains."[22]

Ortiz was expected to contend for the first-base slot. Epstein sent scout Dave Jauss to look him over and said, "He showed good hands and feet around the bag. Jauss gave a really good report. We're comfortable with him defensively, and more than comfortable with him offensively."[23]

It wasn't that Epstein needed Pedro Martinez and Manny Ramírez to speak up for Ortiz; he had already been tracking him back when Epstein was working for the Padres.[24]

Ortiz was given the locker next to Manny Ramírez. In both his autobiographies, Ortiz talked about the wholly different approach to the game (and the different atmosphere) he felt he encountered in the Red Sox organization and clubhouse. "I felt like I just got out of jail, bro," he wrote. I felt like I could hit the way I wanted to hit."[25]

Ortiz got off to a slow start with the 2003 Red Sox, hitting only one homer in April and batting just .200 as of May 1. He homered only once in May, but brought his batting average up to .272. Ortiz was still being passed over for others, until Pedro Martínez took the unusual step of telling Red Sox manager Grady Little that he wanted Ortiz in the lineup whenever he was pitching. Hillenbrand had been traded, and Giambi suffered numerous injuries and, ultimately, shoulder surgery. The job fell to Ortiz by default.

It was during this first season with the Red Sox that Ortiz acquired the nickname "Big Papi," bestowed on him by Red Sox broadcaster Jerry Remy.[26]

He homered only twice in June. But he added eight in July as he started to get on a roll. He hit two home runs in a July 4 game at Yankee Stadium and then two more in the next day's game as well, the first visiting player to ever do so.[27]

His first game-winning hit for the Red Sox was a pinch-hit single in the bottom of the ninth on July 26 against the Yankees. That one at-bat was described at length and in context by Jackie MacMullan of the *Boston Globe*.[28] From July 27 through August 7, 12 consecutive base hits were all extra-base hits (five doubles, two triples, and five homers). There were several games in which he seemed to make all the difference, such as a 5-4 win in 10 innings in Chicago, when Ortiz drove in four of the runs, including the game-winner.

By the end of the season, one which saw the Sox reach the playoffs, Ortiz had 31 homers and 101 RBIs. His .592 slugging percentage was tops on the team. He ranked fifth in league MVP voting.

Boston dropped the first two games of the 2003 ALDS to Oakland, but then took the next two. Ortiz hadn't had a base hit until the bottom of the eighth in Game Four, but he doubled and drove in two runs, winning the game for the Red Sox, 5-4, and sending the Series to Game Five, where the Red Sox prevailed. In the American League Championship Series against the archrival Yankees, Ortiz hit a two-run homer to kick off Game One. The next runs he drove in were in Game Six, his two-run single in the third making the score 4-1, his three RBIs in the game proving the margin in Boston's 9-6 win.

Ortiz's solo homer in the top of the eighth in Game Seven extended the Red Sox lead to 5-2 and it looked like a trip to the World Series was in the cards … until Grady Little asked Pedro Martínez, to return to the mound and pitch another inning – only to see Pedro cough up three runs, see the game become tied, and watch the Red Sox lose it in the 11th. Any trip to the World Series would have to wait until 2004.

Ortiz said the 2003-04 offseason was full of sleepless nights for him. "The Game 7 loss to the Yankees had torn me up, knowing that we were just five outs away from going to the World Series. Anytime I got close to contentment, I'd feel the sting of that loss."[29]

He worked hard and came back better than ever. In 2004, now secure as a starter (34 games at first base, 115 as DH), he put up bigger numbers than ever: 41 homers (second in the league only to teammate Manny Ramírez's 43), 139 RBIs, a .301 batting average. Ortiz and Ramírez were a potent combination in Boston's batting order. Six times that season, they went back-to-back; on August 22 in the eighth inning of a game at Comiskey Park, they homered on consecutive pitches –first Manny off Freddy Garcia, and then Ortiz off reliever Dámaso Marté. Two teammates both hitting 40 homers, driving in 100 runs, and hitting for at least a .300 average had been done only eight other times since Babe Ruth and Lou Gehrig did it in 1931.

Ortiz was rewarded by being named to the American League All-Star squad for the first of 10 times. He homered in the All-Star Game. In May he had been signed to a new two-year contract with a team option for 2006.

The Red Sox finished second to the Yankees in the AL East. As the wild-card team, they took the first two games from Anaheim in the ALDS. In the bottom of the 10th in Game Three, after the Angels had overcome a 6-1 deficit to tie the game, Ortiz came up with two outs and homered to the opposite field off Jarrod Washburn to advance the Sox to the ALCS – where they faced the Yankees again. In the ALDS, Ortiz was 6-for-11 with four RBIs and five walks.

He drove in two runs in Game One against the Yankees, but the Red Sox lost the first three games, Game Three an embarrassing 19-8 beatdown in Boston. The story of Game Four and all that followed has been told at great length elsewhere.[30] The game went into the bottom of the ninth with the Yankees leading, 4-3. Two of the three Red Sox runs had been knocked in by Ortiz in the fifth. With Mariano Rivera on the mound, Kevin Millar walked, pinch-runner Dave Roberts stole second, and Bill Mueller drove Roberts in to tie the game. With the bases loaded, Ortiz popped up to second and the game went into extra innings. But Rivera wasn't going to be around if Ortiz got up again and, he said, "I liked my percentages against anyone who wasn't him."[31]

In the bottom of the 12th inning, with the score still tied, Ortiz got another opportunity. Paul Quantrill was pitching and Manny Ramirez singled to left field. Ortiz, as a DH not needing to play the field, studied Quantrill on video, and he was ready. He homered into the right-field stands, winning the game 6-4 and sparing the Red Sox the ignominy of being swept. And "David Ortiz became the only player in baseball history to hit two walk-off home runs in the same postseason" while the Red Sox became the first team since the 1910 Chicago Cubs to be the only team down three games to none and win Game Four in extra innings.[32]

No team had ever come back after losing the first three and won it all, but simply the reprieve of taking Game Four offered some salve to Red Sox fans.

Next up was Game Five. The fourth game had ended after midnight, in the early hours of October 18. The fourth game started that evening. Ortiz drove in the first run of the game, in the first inning. The Yankees took a 4-2 lead into the eighth, and Ortiz homered to make it 4-3, then watched a Jason Varitek sacrifice fly off Rivera tie the game. Ortiz led off the bottom of the 10th and struck out. Facing reliever Esteban Loaiza in the 12th, he walked but was caught stealing.[33] The game went into the 14th inning, Loaiza still on the mound. He alternated strikeout, walk, strikeout, walk, then faced Ortiz again. It was a 10-pitch at-bat. On that final pitch, Ortiz singled to center, driving in Johnny Damon, and for the second time on the same calendar date, he'd given the Red Sox a sudden-death, extra-inning walk-off win.

Suddenly this was a different Series entirely. Both teams went back to Yankee Stadium for Game Six. With four runs in the fourth, three on Mark Bellhorn's three-run homer, the Red Sox took that one, setting up another Game Seven.

One could well say the Red Sox were giddy with success with the Yankees uptight and maybe panicked. Ortiz hit a two-run homer in the top of the first. Damon drove in six runs. The Red Sox won it easily, 10-3. Ortiz had driven in 11 runs in the ALCS and was named MVP. In back-to-back ALCS against New York in 2003 and 2004, he had homered five times and driven in 17 runs.

After winning four in a row to overtake the Yankees, the Red Sox won the next four games, too, sweeping the St. Louis Cardinals in the 2004 World Series. For the first time in 86 years, the Red Sox were world champions.

Ortiz had driven in four runs, all in Game One, the first three coming on a three-run homer in the first inning.

And everyone knew he had come through in the clutch when the Red Sox were in the depths.

In the summer of 2005, Mariano Rivera stated what had become evident. Ortiz had developed as a hitter. "He used to have holes on the inside. You'd go outside. Holes? Now they're not there anymore."[34] Ortiz's work with video became legendary, it being written, "David Ortiz of the Red Sox does not look like a computer nerd, but he is. Ortiz is a slave to the laptop, hunkering over it several times a day, especially during games, to analyze at-bats. He wants to see how pitchers approached him, how he reacted and whether they had a counter-response."[35]

With Ortiz as a designated hitter, the Red Sox were always faced with a choice when playing in a National League ballpark, for interleague play or in the World Series: Do they play him at first base and thus keep him in the lineup, or do they opt for a perhaps improved defense by using their regular first baseman, whoever he may be at the time? The decision was easier because Ortiz was a very good fielder, with decent range. Over the course of his 20 seasons in the big leagues, he handled 2,169 chances with only 22 errors – a .990 fielding percentage. He also recorded 164 assists, a particular one a highlight indicating good situational awareness. It came in Game Three of the 2004 World Series, the first game in St. Louis. It was only the second game Ortiz had started at first base since July 22, and it had rained earlier in the day so he had been unable to take infield practice. But when the moment came, he was ready. In the bottom of the third inning, with the score 1-0 in Boston's favor, Cardinals starting pitcher Jeff Suppan led off and singled. After Edgar Rentería doubled to right field, the Cardinals had runners on second and third with nobody out. Larry Walker grounded to second base, and Mark Bellhorn threw to first base to get Walker. Ortiz recorded the out, but alertly had his eye on Suppan, who had indecisively headed toward home but then decided to retreat to third, only to be caught when Ortiz took a couple of steps toward third and fired the ball across the infield for a double play. The Cardinals failed to score in the inning.

Although the team enjoyed no postseason success in 2005, David Ortiz had a very good regular season. He led the majors in runs batted in, with 148. He upped his home run total to 47 but again finished second. He hit an even .300 and walked 102 times, just barely edging his OPS over a magic mark – to 1.001. His best single day was probably an August 12 game against the White Sox; he was 4-for-5 with two homers and drove in six runs. The Red Sox won, 9-8. After a game on September 6, when a solo Ortiz home run beat the Angels in the bottom of the ninth, 3-2, Red Sox ownership presented him with a plaque they had prepared and held for the right moment, proclaiming him the "Greatest Clutch Hitter in the History of the Boston Red Sox."[36] They couldn't have known how much history was yet to be written.

The Red Sox did make the postseason, but it was the White Sox' turn to break an even lengthier curse than the Red Sox had suffered. They swept Boston in three games in the Division Series; Ortiz hit .333 with one homer. The White Sox beat Houston and won their first World Series since 1917.

Early in 2006, Ortiz played for the Dominican Republic team in the World Baseball Classic. He hit three home runs (and walked once with the bases loaded) but Japan won the tournament and four players either matched or exceeded Ortiz's three homers.[37] In April he agreed to a four-year extension of his contract with the Red Sox, for an amount thought to be $52 million.[38]

In 2006 Ortiz had 31 home runs before the All-Star break. He set a franchise record with 54 home runs, this time leading the league. (Jimmie Foxx had held the Red Sox record, with 50 homers in 1938.) Ortiz's 137 RBIs also led the American League, as did his 355 total bases. It was a year that Boston finished third, however, and out of the postseason.

And speaking of clutch performances, in just the four-year stretch from 2003 through 2006, Ortiz had 15 "walk-offs" – two in 2003, five in 2004, three in 2005, and five in 2006.

The Red Sox had finished in second place eight years in a row, 1998 through 2005, and then third in 2006. In 2007 they were in first place from April 18 on and never once relinquished the spot.

The team won another world championship in 2007, again by a sweep (this time over the Colorado Rockies). Ortiz hit a career-high .332 batting average, and his .445 on-base percentage led the league. He homered 35 times and drove in 117 runs. His 1.066 OPS was the highest of his career; this was the third year in a row he topped 1.000.

After homering and driving in two runs to help beat the Angels 4-0 in Game One of the Division Series, the Angels walked him four times in Game Two. He homered again in Game Three, and Boston swept that series with Ortiz batting .714. It took the full seven games to beat Cleveland in the ALCS. Ortiz contributed three RBIs and seven runs scored; he hit .292. In the World Series, he drove in four runs and scored four. He was 5-for-15 with three doubles.

An amusing story surfaced in April 2008. It turns out that Gino Castignoli, a member of the construction crew building the new Yankee Stadium, had buried a Red Sox jersey bearing Ortiz's number 34 in concrete. When the story emerged, the team ordered jackhammers to work to remove the offending jersey.[39] (The jersey was later placed on auction on eBay to raise money for the Jimmy Fund, and fetched $175,110.)[40]

The next two times the Red Sox reached the postseason, Ortiz was unable to match his high standards of production. In 2008 he had a difficult year; playing in only 109 games, he hit .264 with 23 homers and 89 RBIs. He became an American citizen in June, but a serious left wrist injury on Memorial Day weekend made an already difficult season (due to a slow start) even more so. The team beat the Angels in four Division Series games with just one RBI from Ortiz, an insurance run on a single in Game One. They were down one game to three to Tampa Bay in the Championship Series with Ortiz even driving in one run, and with manager Joe Maddon employing a fairly dramatic defensive shift when Ortiz came to bat. Game Five was at Fenway Park, and when the Red Sox came up to bat in the bottom of the seventh, they were losing 7-0 and on the brink of elimination. After Dustin Pedroia drove in one run, Ortiz hit a three-run homer and put them back in the game. They scored three more runs in the eighth to tie it, and J.D. Drew won the game with a two-out RBI single in the bottom of the ninth. Ortiz knocked in the fourth run of a 4-2 win in Game Six, but the Rays prevailed in Game Seven. Ortiz had hit just .154 in the ALCS.

Shifting against Ortiz was often effective, though he had a significant number of opposite-field hits and was even known to lay down a successful bunt toward third base on occasion.

In the midst of the 2009 season, a story in the *New York Times* reported that both Ortiz and Manny Ramírez had turned up in 2003 on a list of players who had tested positive for steroids. That year was the first year of testing for steroids, and all tests were meant to be anonymous.[41] Ortiz vehemently denied ever knowingly taking any substances that might have resulted in a positive test, and said he believed that all players should be tested. If anyone was found guilty, he suggested a penalty greater than any ever employed: "Ban them for the whole year."[42]

Ortiz has reportedly never been informed as to the substance for which he reportedly tested positive, and thus remains in the dark. Given that it was the first year of testing, the tests may also have been faulty. The same article said that Barry Bonds had not tested positive, but a later retest did show the presence of steroids. Years later, Commissioner Rob Manfred announced on October 2, 2016, that there were "legitimate scientific questions about whether or not those were truly positives," acknowledging that the tests were flawed, and that it was "entirely possible" that, in reality, Ortiz had not truly tested positive.[43] In the 13 seasons after 2003, and the 7½ seasons after the *Times* article, Ortiz was tested numerous times and no positive test ever occurred.

The Angels swept the Division Series in 2009. Ortiz was 1-for-12 (.083) with a single. During the regular season, he'd suffered a very slow start and at one point did not homer for 149 at-bats. He came to feel he might have been over-thinking his approach to batting and decided to "act like I was in Little League" – just to play to have fun, and unclutter his mind.[44] In the end, he hit for a .238 average but he had found his stroke and done damage: he drove in 99 runs. He homered 28 times.

The Red Sox didn't see the postseason again until 2013.

Ortiz's batting average picked up in 2010 and 2011 (.270 and .309). He'd had a very slow start in 2010 (.143 at the end of April, with one homer, and not passing .200 until May 14) and some became alarmed, thinking age had caught up with him. By the end of the season, though, he had 32 homers and had driven in 102 runs – numbers most players would give anything to attain. The team finished in third place.

In 2011 the Sox finished third again. Ortiz hit steadily throughout the season, falling four RBIs short of the 100 mark, homering 29 times.

In 2012, signed to just a one-year deal, he had a very strong first half, but a severely strained right Achilles tendon saw him only appear in one game after July 16. He played in only 90 games, though he drove in 60 runs, homered 23 more times, and hit .318. Under manager Bobby Valentine, the Red Sox finished in last place. Though not something we want to dwell on here, Ortiz absolutely shredded Valentine in his book *Papi: My Story*.

The year 2013 was a magical year, though it started with the horrible tragedy of the Boston Marathon bombing. It was April 15 – Patriots Day – and the Red Sox, per local tradition, started the game at 11:05 A.M., timed to end around the time the first runners of the Boston Marathon crossed the finish line, just two subway stops from Fenway Park. Ortiz was not in the game, but he was at the ballpark. He was still rehabbing from the Achilles problem, and didn't play his first game until April 20. The Patriots Day game ended at 2:08, and the team dressed to head for the charter going to Cleveland for the next day's game. At 2:40, two bombs exploded 12 seconds apart and three young people were killed, including 8-year-old Martin Richard. Dozens were injured and the city was under a "shelter in place" situation later in the week after the bombers killed an M.I.T. police officer and drove off without being caught. Ortiz was in Greater Boston all the time, and lived through what area residents experienced.

The team seemed to draw on the sense of togetherness, embodied in the "Boston Strong" movement, and in a powerful speech before the next Fenway game, an unfiltered Ortiz said, "This is our fucking city. And nobody is going to dictate our freedom. Stay strong."

Ortiz opened his season with a 2-for-4 game, kicking off a 15-game hitting streak. After the first nine games, at the end of April, he had 15 RBIs and was batting .500. He rarely missed a game after he got started, appearing in 137 games and batting .309, with 103 RBIs and 30 homers. The Red Sox rocketed from worst to first, from a 69-93 record in 2012 to 97-65. They beat Tampa Bay and then Detroit, and played the St. Louis Cardinals in the World Series. One of the most celebrated home runs of his career came in Game Two of the ALCS. The Tigers had won the first game, 1-0, and were leading 5-1 heading into the bottom of the eighth inning in Game Two.

Three and a half months earlier, on June 23, Joaquin Benoit had struck out Ortiz in the ninth inning of a game in Detroit. Ortiz filed the pitch away in his mind and was waiting for another chance to attack it. With Boston baserunners loading the bases, manager Jim Leyland called on Benoit to pitch to Ortiz. Big Papi was waiting.[45] Swinging at Benoit's first pitch, Ortiz hit a grand slam into the Red Sox bullpen to tie it. The Sox won it in the ninth. Clutch? No fan would say otherwise.[46]

There was no certainty the Red Sox would win the World Series. The Cardinals were up two games to one, and the score was 1-1 at the midpoint of Game Four. "We were playing like zombies," Ortiz said later. "Quiet, no emotion, a little stiff."[47] So he called a quick meeting right then and there in the dugout and basically gave them a pep talk, telling them how rare it was to get to the World Series, that they were better than St. Louis, and it was time to get going. A Jonny Gomes three-run homer in the top of the sixth followed, and the team never looked back.

Ortiz hit a spectacular .688 in the World Series (11-for-16), with eight bases on balls giving him a .760 on-base percentage. It was the highest batting average in World Series history. He drove in six runs and scored seven (two on his own home runs). The Red Sox won it in six games, and Ortiz collected his third world championship ring in 10 years (2004, 2007, and 2013). He was named Series MVP.

And after the Series, owner John W. Henry called on Ortiz, offering him a contract that in effect offered him a player option for as long as he wanted – a contract for the life of his playing career.[48]

In each of his next three seasons – his last three as a ballplayer – Ortiz drove in more than 100 runs, each season knocking in more runs than the season before. In 2014 he had 35 homers and drove in 104 runs. In 2015 he had 37 homers and drove in 108 runs. And in his final season – 2016, having announced his retirement before the season began – he had perhaps the best year any player has ever had in his final season. Playing in 151 games, he hit for a .315 batting average, led the major leagues with 48 home runs, led the American League with 127 RBIs (tied with Edwin Encarnación), and led all of baseball in slugging (.620) and OPS (1.021).

It would have been nice to say Ortiz went out with another ring, but the Cleveland Indians swept the Red Sox in the ALDS. Ortiz was 1-for-9, the one hit a double. After the season, Ortiz was recognized for the second time with baseball's Hank Aaron Award (the first time had been in 2005). He won his seventh Silver Slugger Award.

Retirement awaited, though Ortiz was often seen around Boston during 2017. David and Tiffany Ortiz continued to maintain their principal residence in Massachusetts, with their three children, Jessica, Alexandra, and D'Angelo. There had been a time early in 2013 when the couple had separated, but in time they reconciled. Tiffany later told him, "As clutch as you were on the field, you did that and more to win me back and put our family back together again."[49]

For David, his number 34 was retired during the summer. He had a street named after him, as was the bridge that spans the Mass Pike as people leave Kenmore Square to go to Fenway Park. And he became Dr. David Ortiz when Boston University bestowed an honorary degree on him in May 2017.

Ortiz was active in charitable endeavors, and also saw his second autobiography published. Following a very moving visit to a Dominican hospital in February 2005 where he encountered children recovering from heart surgery, he established the David Ortiz Children's Fund in 2007 and partnered with Massachusetts General Hospital and CEDIMAT, the first Diagnostics and Advanced Medicine center in the Dominican Republic. The Fund sponsors an annual golf tournament in La Romana, DR, and has raised more than $2 million. It reckons to have "saved over 500 lives in the Dominican Republic" and helped others in New England.[50]

For his career as a whole, Ortiz hit better against right-handed pitchers, batting .294 for his career against them as opposed to .268 against lefties. He faced more right-handers, of course, but hit 421 homers off them as opposed to 120 off left-handers. Against Blue Jays pitching, he homered 62 times; against the Orioles, 55 times, and against both the Rays and the Yankees, 53. As the season progressed, he seemed to hit more home runs. In May: 79. In June, he hit 86. In July: 95. In August: 105. And in September/October, he hit 102. More of his home runs were hit on the road (300) than at home (241). Conversely, he drove in more runs at home (953) than away (815).

On September 13, 2017, the Red Sox announced a mutual long-term commitment between the ballclub and Ortiz: "In his new role, Ortiz will act as a mentor for current players, participate in recruitment efforts, make a variety of special appearances for the club, and work in a business development capacity for Fenway Sports Management and its partners."[51]

David Ortiz was shot in the back on June 9, 2019, while seated outdoors at the Dial Bar and Lounge in Santo Domingo. Within the first 10 days after the shooting, 11 suspects were arrested with several more still at large, but on June 19, prosecutors announced that Ortiz had not been the intended target of a contract killing, but that the gunman had been after another man who was seated near Ortiz. Many Dominicans were skeptical.[52] In the meantime, reportedly suffering injuries to both intestines, his gall bladder, and liver, he had been brought to Boston for medical treatment, where he underwent multiple surgeries over a period of more than a month at Massachusetts General Hospital. He was released from the hospital on July 26.

On September 9, before the Monday evening game against the Yankees, David Ortiz bounded up the steps of the Red Sox dugout and out onto the field to throw out the game's ceremonial first pitch. He spoke a few words, thanking the fans in Boston for their support and thanking a couple of the Yankees for making the time to come visit him. He had his big smile, was full of energy, and sat in seats next to the dugout for most of the game – at one point giving the jersey he had worn to a youngster seated several rows behind him. Big Papi was back.[53]

A postscript on walk-offs

Following up on walk-offs, the number any player can have is limited by the fact that you can have only one in a home game. David Ortiz had 20 in regular-season play. Two players had more – Frank Robinson (26) and Dusty Baker (21). No player in history had ever had more than two walk-offs in the postseason – but David Ortiz hit three of them in 2004.

David Ortiz walk-off hits
For the Twins:
April 4, 2000 – tie-breaking single in the ninth
July 31, 2002 – single in 10th
September 25, 2002 – home run in the 12th
For the Red Sox:
July 26, 2003 – single off the Wall in the ninth, against the Yankees
September 23, 2003 – HR in the 10th
April 11, 2004 – HR in the 12th
June 11, 2004 – single in the ninth
October 8, 2004 – HR in bottom of the 10th to clinch a win in the ALCS against the Angels
October 17, 2004 – home run in the 12th to win Game Four of the ALCS against the Yankees
October 18, 2004 – single in the 14th to win Game Five of the ALCS against the Yankees
June 2, 2005 – Three-run HR in the ninth to come from behind and beat the O's
September 6, 2005 – HR in the ninth
September 29, 2005 – single in the ninth
June 11, 2006 – Three-run HR in the ninth to overcome a 4-2 deficit
June 24, 2006 – two-run homer in the 10th
June 26, 2006 – single in the 12th
July 29, 2006 – single in the ninth
July 31, 2006 – three-run homer in ninth to overcome two-run deficit
September 12, 2007 – two-run homer in the ninth to overcome one-run deficit
August 26, 2009 – tie-breaking solo homer in the ninth
July 31, 2010 – three-run double in the ninth to overcome two-run deficit
June 6, 2013 – three-run tie-breaking homer in ninth
May 14, 2016 – double in the 11th

SOURCES

In addition to the sources noted in this biography, the author also accessed the *Encyclopedia of Minor League Baseball*, Retrosheet.org, and Baseball-Reference.com.

NOTES

1 Peter Abraham, "Ortiz Was All That Mattered at Fenway," *Boston Globe*, June 10, 2019: C4.

2 Jack Curry, "An Island of Calm in a Sea of Doubt: Ortiz's Clutch Hitting Keeps Red Sox Moored Despite Struggles," *New York Times*, September 17, 2005: D1.

3 worstpolluted.org/projects_reports/display/50.

4 David Ortiz, with Michael Holley, *Papi: My Story* (Boston: Houghton Mifflin Harcourt, 2017), 2.

5 *Papi: My Story*, 2-3.

6 *Papi: My Story*, 9, 125. David's father's name was Americo Enrique Ortiz and he had wanted to be a ballplayer himself. That aspiration was one of the reasons he worked closely with David, and encouraged him every step of the way. See David Ortiz, with Tony Massarotti, *Big Papi: My Story of Big Dreams and Big Hits* (New York: St. Martin's, 2007), 20-23.

7 A buscón in the Dominican Republic is a free-lance scout and agent. The word is Spanish for searcher.

8 In *Big Papi*, he said it was $7,500. In *Papi: My Story*, he said it was $10,000.

9 *Papi: My Story*, 13.

10   David Ortiz, with Tony Massarotti, *Big Papi*, 69.

11   *Papi: My Story*, 18.

12   In both of his autobiographies, Ortiz expresses his dissatisfaction with Kelly.

13   Gordon Edes, "Sox Officially Bring in Ortiz," *Boston Globe*, January 23, 2003: E3. Also see *Big Papi*, 95-96.

14   Murray Chass, "Surprising Twins Give Foes a Run for Their Money," *New York Times*, April 24, 2001: D1.

15   Bob Hohler, "Epstein Negotiating for Millar," *Boston Globe*, January 18, 2003: F3.

16   See, in particular, *Big Papi*, 191-192. The Associated Press said Ortiz was "released … before the draft to make room for shortstop Jose Morban." See, for instance, AP, "Anderson Released by Pirates," *Augusta* (Georgia) *Chronicle*, December 17, 2002: C4.

17   *Papi: My Story*, 38. David and Tiffany had sealed their longstanding relationship with marriage on November 16.

18   Bob Hohler, "Epstein Negotiating for Millar."

19   Joe Burris, "Opportunity Knocks for Sox' Ortiz," *Boston Globe*, June 12, 2003: C8.

20   Gordon Edes, "Sox Officially Bring in Ortiz."

21   Tyler Kepner, "Red Sox Trying to Picture the Parade," *New York Times*, February 8, 2004: SP1.

22   Harvey Araton, "New Babe in Boston Has Torre Looking for the Right Move," *New York Times*, October 1, 2005: D1.

23   Araton.

24   Gordon Edes, "Smashing Success," *Boston Globe*, September 12, 2003: E1.

25   *Big Papi*, 128.

26   Ricky Doyle, "Where Did David Ortiz's 'Big Papi' Nickname With Red Sox Come From?' NESN.com, October 3, 2016. See nesn.com/2016/10/where-did-david-ortizs-big-papi-nickname-with-red-sox-come-from/.

27   The last Yankee to do so was Roger Maris in 1961, hitting two homers in each game of the July 25, 1961 doubleheader. Gloria Rodriguez, "After a Boom, the Red Sox Go Bust," *New York Times*, July 7, 2003: D3.

28   Jackie MacMullan, "Ortiz's Bat Does Talking in the Ninth," *Boston Globe*, July 27, 2003: D1.

29   *Papi: My Story*, 62.

30   The author's admittedly biased preference is the oral history of the season as told by 59 players, coaches, support staff, and others in Allan Wood & Bill Nowlin, *Don't Let Us Win Tonight: An Oral History of the 2004 Boston Red Sox's Impossible Playoff Run* (Chicago: Triumph Books, 2014).

31   *Papi: My Story*, 80.

32   *Don't Let Us Win Tonight*, 137.

33   Ortiz did steal 17 bases in his regular-season career. He was caught nine times.

34   Jack Curry, "Big Guy, Big Numbers, Big Smile," *New York Times*, July 14, 2005: D1.

35   One of the better articles on Ortiz's work with video is Jack Curry, "A Scientific Hitter in the Computer Age," *New York Times*, October 12, 2007: D1.

36   Chris Snow, "A Blast, Like the Past," *Boston Globe*, September 7, 2005: F1.

37   Seung-Yeop Lee, KOR – 5; Adrian Beltre, DOM – 4; Derrek Lee, USA – 3; Hitoshi Tamura, JPN – 3; and David Ortiz, DOM – 3.

38   Associated Press, "Ortiz Agrees to Four-Year Extension," *Register-Star* (Rockford, Illinois), April 11, 2006: 27.

39   Karen Matthews, Associated Press, "Sox Shirt Found in Yanks' New Stadium," *Daily Northwestern* (Evanston, Illinois), April 14, 2008: 15.

40   Joshua Robinson, "Ortiz Jersey Cemented at the New Yankee Stadium Brings $175,110," *New York Times*, April 5, 2008: D3.

41   Michael S. Schmidt, "Stars of Red Sox Title Years Are Linked to Doping," *New York Times*, July 30, 2009: A1.

42   Schmidt.

43   Alex Speier, "Commissioner: 'Entirely Possible' Ortiz Did Not Test Positive in 2003," *Boston Globe*, October 2, 2016.

44   Jack Curry, "To Enjoy the Game Again, Ortiz Tries Playing It as if He Were a Boy," *New York Times*, September 26, 2009: D5.

45   See Ortiz's description in *Papi: My Story*, 195, 200.

46   Benjamin Hoffman of the *New York Times*, however, wrote an article entitled "Ortiz's Consistency Comes Across as Clutch." See the newspaper on October 15, 2013: B12. The eighth-inning homer saw Tigers right fielder Torii Hunter make a valiant effort to catch the ball before it landed in Boston's bullpen. He fell into the pen, both legs upraised behind him, forming something of a "V" while City of Boston policeman Steve Horgan, stationed in the bullpen, raised both of his arms in a celebratory "V" – creating an iconic image captured by *Boston Globe* photographer Stan Grossfeld. See, for instance, sports.yahoo.com/blogs/mlb-big-league-stew/boston-cop-fenway-bullpen-celebrates-david-ortiz-grand-132350182—mlb.html.

47   *Papi: My Story*, 204.

48   *Papi: My Story*, 207. Henry told Ortiz it was "a contract that allows you to play as long as you want to."

49   *Papi: My Story*, 205.

50   davidortizchildrensfund.org/.

51   Media release, Boston Red Sox, September 13, 2017. The actual description of his duties was vague in the extreme, so much so that Craig Calcaterra ran a piece headlined, "David Ortiz Will Be Doing … Um, Stuff and Things for the Red Sox." See nbcsports.com/2017/09/13/david-ortiz-will-be-doing-um-stuff-and-things-for-the-red-sox/. Chances were thought to be his work would be in a "player development consultant" role, along the lines of Carl Yastrzemski and Dwight Evans, but with Ortiz perhaps more active.

52   Danny McDonald, David Abel, and Aimee Ortiz, "David Ortiz Was Not Intended Target in Shooting, Officials Say," *Boston Globe*, June 20, 2019: A1. See also David Abel, "Many Are Skeptical of Mistaken-Identity Explanation," *Boston Globe*, June 20, 2019: A8. A detailed summary of the story, informed by a visit to the Dominican Republic, is Danny Gold, "David and the D.R.," *Sports Illustrated*, July 29–August 5, 2019.

53   In his first comments to an English language publication, he talked about the experience to the *Boston Globe*. See Bob Hohler, "Near Death, Ortiz Pushed Through Despair," *Boston Globe*, September 15, 2019: 1, C9.

BRANDON PUFFER

BY BILL NOWLIN

Right-hander Brandon Puffer pitched in 85 major-league games, but is perhaps better known in some circles for the World Series Championship ring he earned in 2004 as a member (however briefly) of that year's legendary Boston Red Sox – despite the only pitches he threw at Fenway Park being *against* the Red Sox, rather than for them.

"I think I could have been a great idiot," he said the following year.[1]

The 2004 Red Sox were self-described as "The Idiots," a moniker popularized by center fielder Johnny Damon.[2] That year's team won the Red Sox' first World Series in 86 years (since 1918) and had done so only after coming back from being down three games to none in the best-of-seven American League Championship Series against the archrival New York Yankees.

One could look up Puffer's name to see how he contributed to the team and not find his name listed in any of the statistics for the 2004 Red Sox. He was on the team for one day, sitting in the Red Sox bullpen at Fenway Park on September 2 and ready to work if called upon. The pen needed an extra arm available since it had worked 6⅓ innings in a 12-7 win over the Angels on September 1.[3]

In the Thursday evening game, starting pitcher Derek Lowe worked 7⅓ innings and manager Terry Francona called in relievers Mike Myers and Keith Foulke to wrap things up, which they did, facing five batters.

Johnny Damon hurt his right pinky finger diving back in to the first-base bag during the game, dislocating his finger. He went for X-rays right after the game, and the Red Sox felt they needed to make a move so they called up outfielder Adam Hyzdu – Pawtucket's player of the month in August – and Puffer was designated for assignment.[4] He never did appear in a game for the Red Sox.

Puffer had pitched at Fenway Park once earlier in the 2004 season – but against them, not for them. It happened on June 10, and he came to Boston as a member of the San Diego Padres. Curt Schilling started for the Red Sox and worked seven innings, giving up two runs. Ismael Valdéz was San Diego's starter. He left after four-plus innings, having surrendered four runs. Padres manager Bruce Bochy had Puffer relieve Valdéz.[5] Puffer had been with the big-league club for four weeks. He was 0-1 with an ERA of 4.15. This was his 12th appearance of the season. With two inherited runners on base and nobody out, the first batter he faced was David Ortiz, whom he struck out. He was instructed to intentionally walk Manny Ramírez, loading the bases. Nomar Garciaparra doubled off the left-field wall, driving in two runs, both charged to Valdéz. Puffer struck out Jason Varitek but then Kevin Millar doubled, driving in two more.

Puffer retired the side in order in the sixth. In the seventh he loaded the bases with nobody out but worked out of the jam. In all, he had worked long relief – three full innings – allowing two runs on four hits and a walk, striking out four. The game was a 9-3 loss for the Padres, the loss assigned to Valdez.

When Puffer reappeared at Fenway in September, he said, "Even just coming here as a visitor, just the buzz around here was unbelievable. Being able to put this uniform on and play here is even a lot sweeter."[6]

Puffer put the Red Sox uniform on – wearing number 52 – but the next day he was gone again. On the morning of September 2, he got a call. He hadn't left Pawtucket yet, though the season had just ended. "I had to get up there pretty quickly. So I did. As you can imagine, it was a whirlwind. I got a uniform, went out and played catch during batting practice. I'm still just kind of floating around at Fenway. I sat in the bullpen." After the Damon injury and with Lowe having given the bullpen a break, the Red Sox called up Hyzdu. "They needed a roster spot, so they sent me out. I was there one full day. After batting practice the second day is when Francona and Theo Epstein and them called me in and told me the bad news. Terry was very gracious. He said, 'Man, we don't ever do this. I don't understand this. I don't know why they did this to you.' I said, 'I got a day here and I enjoyed every bit of it.'"

Photo by Louriann Mardo-Zayat.

He'd spent one night in a Boston hotel. The Red Sox flew him back to Mission Viejo, leaving rather promptly. "I was supposed to fly out a day later, but my 10-year high-school reunion was the next day. I asked the traveling secretary if they could fly me out immediately so I could make my reunion. I was able to do that. They were great, all the way through. It was awesome. If you gave me the choice I'd rather have been at Fenway again, but …"[7]

On October 15 Puffer once more became a free agent. It was the fifth of 10 times he entered free agency. He never did pitch for the Red Sox but he did get a World Series ring. Principal owner John W. Henry wanted everyone who was on the team to get a ring – and Brandon Puffer had been there, in the bullpen, on the team, ready to work, albeit just for one day. The team reached out to him the following spring asking for his ring size. It was an "18-carat white gold ring … encrusted with diamonds and adorned with a ruby 'B.'"[8]

Brandon Puffer had a remarkable career. He had fallen in love with sports as a child and – though basketball was his favorite sport earlier on, it was in baseball that others saw him having greater potential.

Brandon Duane Puffer was born on October 5, 1975, in Downey, California, about a dozen miles southeast of Los Angeles. His parents were Gary and Liz Puffer, and Brandon had a younger brother, Todd. Gary Puffer worked for Oakley Sunglasses, starting when it was a much smaller company. "Most of the time, he worked in Health and Safety, making sure that the warehouse and stuff was up to code," said Brandon. "He bounced around a little bit, managed different departments, but for the most part worked in Health and Safety."[9]

Since January 1994, Liz Puffer has worked in pastoral care at Saddleback Church in Lake Forest, California, the so-called "megachurch" founded by Pastor Rick Warren. It's the largest church in the state of California, and one of the largest churches in the country.[10] "My mom just started volunteering at the church after Pastor Rick started it. It was smaller. We'd meet in the local high school auditorium. As the church grew, our family continued to go. They continued to elevate her role. I think she's been with them over 30 years now. She's Pastor Liz." She works in pastoral care. In 2021 Liz Puffer and two others became the first women ordained as pastors, an act that engendered serious negativity within the Southern Baptist Convention.[11]

The family had moved from Downey to Mission Viejo a couple of years after Brandon was born, and shortly after Todd, who is a year and a half younger than Brandon, was born. At that point, he explained, "my grandma bought a little house in Mission Viejo, Orange County. She felt it would be a better place for us to grow up, so my parents rented from her, and then eventually bought the home. They're still in the same home that we grew up in. It was a blessing to grow up there, for sure."

Asked about his brother, Brandon said, "Todd – he's pretty much my best friend. He played some football in junior college. He's in the corporate world and has his own company now, in the finance space. [Source Tax Incentives, in Franklin, Tennessee.] He has an awesome family. He's doing great."[12]

Gary Puffer was a Dodgers fan and Brandon himself was a fan of pitchers like Fernando Valenzuela and Orel Hershiser – though he also became a big fan of Dave Winfield when Winfield threw a ball to him one day at Anaheim Stadium. He called himself a "tunnel-vision type of kid" who always wanted to be a professional ballplayer when he grew up.[13]

Come high-school time, Brandon attended Capistrano Valley High School in Mission Viejo.

At age 18, he was selected by the Minnesota Twins in the 27th round of the June 1994 amateur draft. He learned of his selection over the high-school intercom system: "Attention Capistrano Valley High School; your fellow Cougar, Brandon Puffer, has officially been selected in the Major League Baseball draft by the Minnesota Twins!"[14] His signing scout was Scott Groot.[15]

It was nearly eight years before Puffer made it to the majors. Indeed, it wasn't until that same year that he even rose as high as Triple A. He definitely paid his dues in the minors.

His first assignment was to Rookie-level ball in Lee County, Florida (at Fort Myers), with the Twins team in the Gulf Coast League. In the summer of 1994, he worked solely in relief, throwing 35⅓ innings in 18 games, 2-2 with a 3.06 ERA.[16]

After he returned to California, he learned to his surprise that his former high-school girlfriend (they had broken up before he got drafted) was seven months pregnant. It was a secret she had kept from her own father. She herself "sadly had to remove herself from the parenting scenario." She and Brandon were still together throughout that first rookie ball season and only broke up after her mother said that was the only way they would sign over all custodial rights. Brandon's parents filled the breach. Liz and Gary Puffer took Darrin in. The family had full custody since his very first day. "Saints," he called his parents, "they are the ones who took primary responsibility for raising my son, Darrin."[17] Darrin was born on December 21, 1994. Brandon was a father at age 18. He has written that Darrin "never truly knew his birth mother."[18]

Darrin grew up with a father absent both while playing baseball and while in prison, but with the loving care of his grandparents. "He is an adventurer now," Brandon said in March 2023. "I just got off the phone with him. He's in Missoula, Montana, snowboarding. He's heading to Alaska next week to do commercial fishing – the *Deadliest Catch*-type stuff. Make some money, and then he'll go surf for a couple of months. He's just living the dream."

Brandon Puffer returned to Fort Myers the following summer, getting into 14 games (five of them starts) and was 0-3 with a 2.88 ERA. Now he was earning money – such as there was at rookie-level ball – to support himself but also to be able to contribute something toward raising Darrin. He did what he could to make money during the offseasons, and sometimes during the season. He variously worked as a food deliveryman, at a local golf club, local fitness center, working on warranties at Oakley, and as a "wine consultant" at Costco.

It wasn't as though he was playing in front of large crowds. "You had more people at your high-school games," he said.[19]

In May 1996 the Twins released Puffer and he signed as a free agent with the California Angels, spending most of the time with the Boise Hawks of the Short Season-A Northwest League. There was one game for the Angels' Rookie-level team (a loss) but 16 with the Hawks, for whom he was 2-0 despite a 4.45 ERA. In 1997 he pitched in six games for Boise and then in 10 games for the Class-A Midwest League Cedar Rapids Kernels. He had neither a win nor a loss all season. The Angels released him in December, by which time they had renamed themselves the Anaheim Angels.[20]

The next month, in January 1988, Puffer signed with his third big-league organization, the Cincinnati Reds. He was 2-7 (6.93) for the Class-A Charleston (West Virginia) AlleyCats, but did markedly better for the Double-A Chattanooga Lookouts, with a 3.12 ERA (no decisions) in seven appearances.

The Reds placed him in Iowa in 1999 with the Class-A Clinton LumberKings. He worked in 59 games, as a closer in 55 of them, and he recorded an excellent 1.99 ERA. The Reds released him, though, after the season. The Colorado Rockies signed him next, but by May 18, 2000, they had released him. He'd given up 13 earned runs in 14⅓ innings of work for Asheville.

It was in the year 2000 that Puffer married for the first time – to Jennifer, whom he had met in Charleston while he was with the AlleyCats. The couple had two daughters together – Morgan and Ashlynn. The life of a ballplayer wasn't easy, of course, moving from team to team and city to city, and at one point, they separated but then got back together again, after a couple of years. Though he had been sober for five years, in spring training 2004 "some of those old habits crept back." They ended up getting divorced, but "[w]e remained close, for our girls. They're in West Virginia with their mom. One's in nursing school and the other's a freshman in high school. Next week, we'll have a grandson. I'll be out there in two weeks to hang out with them and see my new grandson."[21]

There was, later, a second marriage as well, to a woman who had been a single mom for a number of years. He was able to help her raise her two daughters and see them through middle school and high school.

Puffer had a brief stint in independent baseball – the Atlantic League – where he pitched for the Somerset Patriots (Bridgewater, New Jersey) for two months before being signed by the Houston Astros. Houston is where he first got a shot in the majors, but it still took another couple of years to get there.

His first assignment was with the Kissimmee Cobras in the Florida State League, an Advanced A league. He closed 18 games with a 1.27 ERA. He was placed with Double-A Round Rock in 2001. Working relief in 56 games (closing 33 times), he was 6-1 with an ERA of 2.07. He began the 2002 season in Triple A, with the New Orleans Zephyrs, where he had a 1.80 ERA in 11 appearances at the highest level he had yet pitched. It was there during a game where he learned he had been called up to the big leagues by an announcement over the ballpark's loudspeaker: "Brandon Puffer! You have been selected to join the Houston Astros!"[22]

Puffer's major-league debut came in April. He joined the team in Cincinnati and manager Jimy Williams put him into his first game on April 17, to throw the bottom of the ninth in a game Houston was leading, 7-2. He struck out the first batter he faced, Todd Walker. He hit Jason LaRue in the back, walked Wilton Guerrero, but then got Barry Larkin to ground into a force play at second base, and then struck out Juan Encarnación.

Puffer didn't give up a base hit until his third outing, but then he gave up four of them and was tagged for three runs. His first decision was a loss, in his fourth game, on April 23. His next decision was a win, but that didn't come until his 22nd outing, on June 29 against the Texas Rangers. He had worked four innings of one-hit ball and seen the Astros come from a 5-0 deficit to an 8-5 win. Typically, though, he worked in short relief – he appeared in 55 games and threw 69 innings. His year-end record was 3-3 (4.43).

In 2003 Puffer spent most of the season in New Orleans again. He was called up to the Astros, first appearing on April 25 in Montreal and stuck with the team through the end of May, appearing in 11 games, without a decision, and with a 4.95 ERA. He got one other call and worked to six batters in two games over the July 4 weekend in Pittsburgh, but that was it – his end-of-season ERA was 5.14. With New Orleans, he did work in 44 games, 7-3 with a 2.91 ERA. The Astros released him in November.

San Diego was next; Puffer signed with the Padres in January 2004. After 22 appearances with the Triple-A Portland Beavers, he was called up to the major-league team, appearing in 14 Padres games from May 13 through July 1, 0-1 with an ERA of exactly 5.00. On July 2 he was traded to Boston, reporting to the Triple-A Pawtucket Red Sox. The Red Sox had planned to use him in the bullpen, but on that very same day they had acquired Jimmy Anderson in trade from the Chicago Cubs. They decided to go with Anderson and so optioned Puffer to the PawSox.[23] There he worked in 24 games with a 3.26 ERA (3-2). As noted above, he was a member of the Boston Red Sox for just the one day – September 2 – assigned a uniform and a locker, worked out before the game, but sat out the game in the bullpen.

It may seem difficult to believe, but having already been signed by seven major-league organizations, Puffer still had five more with which he signed before he retired.

In December 2004 he signed with the San Francisco Giants. They placed him with the 2005 Triple-A Pacific Coast League Fresno Grizzlies. He was called up in mid-June for a little more than a week, appearing in games on June 18, 23, and 26. He was hit for runs each time, and for five of them in 1⅓ innings on June 26 in Oakland, his last game in the major leagues. Working in 54 games for Fresno, his ERA for the year was a disappointing 5.52.

One sees in retrospect that Puffer's time in the majors was over. His career record was 3-4 (5.09). As a batter in the National League, he seemed to be adept at striking out. He had eight plate appearances in 2002 without a hit and with five strikeouts. He did contribute with a sacrifice bunt in the August 20 game hosting the Cubs. Both baserunners advanced, and then both scored on José Vizcaíno's single. The two runs gave Houston a 7-4 lead, but was a game the Cubs ultimately won, 14-12. Puffer was charged with six of those runs, and the loss. By the end of his career, he had nine at-bats and had struck out seven times.

Fielding in the big leagues, Puffer committed only one error in 39 chances, with the Padres in 2004, ruining what would otherwise have been a career 1.000 fielding percentage to balance his .000 batting average. A run scored on the throwing error fielding a bunt, but it was the fifth run in a 7-1 loss to the Rockies.

The Astros gave Puffer another look in 2006, and it was back to Round Rock but he didn't have nearly the success he had enjoyed the first time round. With a 4.47 ERA in 37 games, he was released on July 25 – signing three days later with the Oakland Athletics. He spent the rest of the season with their PCL club in Sacramento, but was released after the season.

Puffer played winter ball in Venezuela for Leones del Caracas, only recording 10 innings of work but four decisions. He is shown as 2-2 with a 1.80 ERA.[24]

In February 2007 Puffer signed with the Pittsburgh Pirates, but before the end of spring training he was released on March 20 – signing three days later with the Texas Rangers. He was 31 years old. He spent 2007 in Double A with the Frisco RoughRiders in Frisco, Texas, working in 51 games – all in relief – and finished 3-3 (3.20). A brief visit to Venezuela that winter saw him work all of two scoreless innings for LaGuaira. It was around this time that he began to think that his future might lie in coaching – as a bullpen coach.

In 2008 Puffer turned 32 years old and he was hired by Frisco as a player-coach. He knew that part of his role with that team had been to serve as a sort of mentor to the younger players, someone they could look up to. It might well have led to a next step in baseball, transitioning to becoming a coach. He led chapel for the team. He pitched again and this time put up a dramatic won-lost record of 8-0 in 39 appearances, despite a 3.90 ERA.

Frisco made it to the league finals that year, but on September 12 was eliminated in the final game, 10-3, by the Arkansas Travelers. Hours later, Brandon Puffer began his journey from the bullpen to the state pen – the Texas State Penitentiary at Huntsville.

He had held himself apart from the others on the team, almost all significantly younger players, but the guys kept at him, urging him to come out and party. At the end of their season, he gave in. He'd taken Adderall before the game, and mixing it with alcohol was, in a sense, playing with fire. He says he's always been an "all-in" type of guy. Just taking a drink or two in a social setting was not the way he was. He doesn't remember all the details, but he did end up on trial on the charge of "burglary of a habitation with the intent to commit sexual assault."

Even after the others had turned in, he was still going. There was an apartment in the complex where they were staying that had been the scene of a number of parties, and he decided to visit. The woman who lived there hadn't locked the door and he let himself in uninvited (the "burglary" part of the charge) and "I tried to take my clothes off and get in bed with her."[25] "I'll never forget the scream," he wrote later.[26] The next day he was in an orange jumpsuit.

The felony charge could have seen him receive up to 99 years in prison. He was fortunate to have impressed a number of people he had encountered along his journey in life and even had Nolan Ryan appear as a character witness during his trial. Puffer was convicted on July 2, 2009, and sentenced to five years in prison.

Prison was a learning experience, which he details at length in his book. The sound of his prison door clanking shut after he had entered his cell changed his life. There was indeed no way out, no technicality that might spare him from conviction. His first cellmate was a man serving three life sentences, having killed three people.

There came a moment of remarkable clarity; one might call it an epiphany. Essentially, that first day in the small, hot cell was the first day of the rest of his life. He has since developed the moniker of "Coach Puff Positive" and (even just to talk on the telephone or see him on a podcast) one instantly perceives the positive outlook he takes toward life. He says it began that very first day in prison. "I committed myself to being the best inmate I could be and initiating positive interactions with those I came in contact with."[27] He became known for his cheerful, positive demeanor in prison, maybe something of an anomaly – someone who just started smiling and adapted to prison life. It came from an acceptance of a situation that was literally inescapable, but also in that "surrender" – putting himself in the hands of God – he found peace and meaning.

Nonetheless, he was cut off from his two daughters and had almost no communication at all during his time in the penitentiary.

He served 3½ years of his sentence. He was released on September 21, 2012. Looking back on his time in prison, Puffer takes as positive an attitude as one can imagine. He says he was glad he went through the experience because of what he learned. He just wishes that there had not been a victim involved and that the families that were hurt had not been. He has reached out through the Victims Assistance Program to ask for forgiveness and to tell her how truly sorry he is, but understands that she may well prefer not to bring up any bad memories.

Puffer's relationship with Round Rock Express owner Reid Ryan and family helped him land a position with the club after his discharge, working at its ballpark, Dell Diamond, doing maintenance work – pressure washing the facility, painting, and the like.[28] He began to offer a few private lessons. In time he became an outreach coordinator for the club. "And then I branched off and started a youth and high school program."[29]

With a friend, Brian Gordon, Puffer founded a new enterprise named GPS Texas Baseball. The two were teammates at Round Rock in 2006. Gordon had been a seventh-round draft pick of the Arizona Diamondbacks in June 1997 and he put in his time in minor-league ball as well – in all, playing 18 seasons of professional baseball.

Puffer talked about Gordon: "We met in the Round Rock/Austin area. We trained together in every offseason. We were both working at the Dell Diamond, the Triple-A team here. I would give pitching lessons. He would give hitting lessons. There were two cages. And we just became very close friends."

"We created GPS to help advocate for youngsters to go and play in college. Our whole thing is to try to use our experience as baseball players – he played 10 years as an outfielder and eight as a pitcher. He played for the Yankees. Pitched for the

Rangers. We try to use that experience to make them better baseball players, but more importantly just better young men. I always draw from my struggles and what I went through, to try to help them."

"That my passion now. We just absolutely love it. We're just trying to help these kids be better on and off the field."[30]

Four players from the GPS program have been drafted by major-league teams: Matthew McMillan (Angels, 2018), Mason Montgomery (Rays, 2018). Jimmy Lewis (Dodgers, 2019), and Justin Lange (Padres, 2020). "It's really neat to walk them through that process – what to expect, and all that good stuff."[31]

In February 2023, a new chapter in life began as Brandon and Yvette Puffer married. Yvette founded and is the owner/operator of Sedro Trail Assisted Living & Memory Care, which serves elderly folks with Alzheimer's needs at the end of life.[32]

SOURCES

In addition to the sources cited in the Notes, the author consulted Baseball-Reference.com and retrosheet.org. Thanks to Brandon Puffer for the March 2023 interview.

NOTES

1. Henry Schulman, "Giants Notebook: Puffer's Reward Has Nice Ring to It," SFGate.com, March 29, 2005. https://www.sfgate.com/sports/article/GIANTS-NOTEBOOK-Puffer-s-reward-has-nice-ring-2719621.php/. Accessed February 19, 2023.

2. For background to the moniker, see Ian Browne, "Genius Moniker: Origin of '04 Sox 'Idiots,'" MLB.com, February 5, 2021. https://www.mlb.com/news/2004-red-sox-idiots-nickname-explained. Accessed February 19, 2023. Damon's autobiography is entitled *Idiot: Beating "The Curse" and Enjoying the Game of Life*, written with Peter Golenbock (New York: Crown, 2005).

3. Puffer had been acquired from the San Diego Padres on July 2 for a player to be named later and had been placed with the Triple-A Pawtucket Red Sox. Puffer had worked in 24 games, closing 21 of them, with a 3.25 ERA and a record of 3-2. The player named later was infielder-outfielder Peter Ciofrone, who spent eight seasons in the minor leagues but never made the majors. Thanks to Sarah Coffin and the Red Sox Baseball Operations Department for the information identifying Peter Ciofrone.

4. Damon missed four games, returning on September 7. Hyzdu stuck with the team the rest of the season, playing in 17 games, usually as a late-inning defensive replacement. He hit .300 in 10 at-bats.

5. "We did get our butts kicked, so I feel like I contributed a little bit to the Red Sox that season." Brandon Puffer, on Granger Smith Podcast, episode 80. https://www.youtube.com/watch?v=IrDWf7WXD1w.

6. Bob Hohler, "Sore Shoulder Sidelines Ortiz," *Boston Globe*, September 3, 2004: F6.

7. Puffer interview.

8. Peter Abraham, "A Red Sox 2004 World Series Ring Up for Grabs," boston.com, August 15, 2013. There is a story behind the ring being "up for grabs." At a low point, in trying to provide for his family, Puffer sold the ring. http://archive.boston.com/sports/baseball/redsox/extras/extra_bases/2013/08/a_red_sox_2004_series_ring_up_for_grabs.html. The night of Abraham's column, the ring was going to be offered to the highest bidder on the television show *Pawn Stars*. The ring was apparently withdrawn from sale because one of the cast members objected, perhaps due to Puffer's felony conviction. Puffer's story leads one to think of another Red Sox player – Brayan Villareal – who got a ring as a member of the 2013 World Series champion Red Sox. He pitched in a total of one game (August 20 in San Francisco), facing one batter (Marco Scutaro). The bases were loaded in the bottom of the ninth, the score tied 2-2. Villareal thew four pitches, walking Scutaro, which forced in the winning run for the Giants.

9. Interview with Brandon Puffer on March 3, 2023. "When he started, it was extremely small. In fact, I took an offseason job there with him and there was three or four of us doing warranty. It was pretty cool to watch it grow when he was there. Afterwards, he was a driver for a couple of companies. He's been medically disabled for quite a while now. He's OK, but he went through some different things with brain surgery, a heart attack, and stuff."

10. https://saddleback.com/.

11. Ruth Aguantia, "Rick Warren's Saddleback Church Ordains Its First Female Pastors, Gets Mixed Reactions," *Christianity Daily*, May 10, 2021. https://www.christianitydaily.com/articles/11796/20210510/rick-warren-s-saddleback-church-ordains-its-first-female-pastors-gets-mixed-reactions.htm, accessed February 22, 2023. Rick Warren retired in 2022. The "mixed reactions" culminated in the church being expelled from the Southern Baptist Convention in February 2023. See Peter Smith (Associated Press), "Southern Baptists Oust Popular Saddleback Church Over Woman Pastor," wrdw.com, February 23, 2023. https://www.nbcnews.com/news/us-news/southern-baptists-boot-saddleback-church-woman-pastor-rcna71714. See also Deepa Bharath and Peter Smith (Associated Press), "Saddleback Church Doubles Down on Support for Female Pastors," *Atlanta Journal-Constitution*, March 1, 2023. https://www.ajc.com/news/nation-world/saddleback-church-doubles-down-on-support-for-female-pastors/V5VSHPKYXFAN3ARSA7R5HJI3UM/. Accessed March 5, 2023.

12. Puffer interview.

13. Granger Smith podcast.

14. Brandon Puffer, *From the Bullpen to the State Pen* (North Haven, Connecticut: Streamline Books, 2022), 11.

15. "I got to know some of the other scouts a little better. They seemed to be around a little more frequently. The Twins kind of came out of nowhere. I don't really remember him out there all that much, but we became closer after signing. We became pretty good friends." Puffer interview.

16. Minor-league life could be a struggle. "Meals and hotel rooms were sometimes taken out of our salaries. And we rarely got to choose our meals … just kind of the same thing mostly every day. The buses we traveled in were pretty brutal as well. There's just a lot about minor league baseball that isn't ideal." *From the Bullpen to the State Pen*, 20.

17. *From the Bullpen to the State Pen*, 31.

18. *From the Bullpen to the State Pen*, 25. Respecting her and her family, Puffer preferred not to name Darrin's mother, who had managed to keep the pregnancy secret from her father, even for some period of time after Darrin was born.

19. Granger Smith podcast. In the March 2023 interview, he was asked about Fort Myers – spring training, extended spring training, and then rookie ball for the second summer in a row. "It was a long

stretch there, in the same hotel room. As you know, the minor leagues don't get paid very well. For me, I had to pay for medical insurance for Darrin and all those things. At the end of every two weeks, the max I would receive was like $200."

20 The team name was changed on November 19. Bonnie Hayes, "On Deck: New Image; Stadium, Logo, Name are fresh … Now About the Team …," *Los Angeles Times*, Orange County Edition, November 20, 1996: 1.

21 Puffer interview. During the two years they were separated, Puffer had another son, Brenton, born in 2005. "He's a junior in high school. He lives in Southern California. He's a left-handed pitcher." For the first 14 years of Brenton's life, his father says, it was "totally the opposite of what I did for Darrin by stepping up. It's embarrassing to admit but I really just cowarded. One of my major prayers – along with making redemption with the young lady that was the victim – was that I would one day be able to make amends with Brenton. And I have. We message each other all the time. I've met him several times when I go out there to visit my parents. But for the first 14 years of his life, I had nothing to do with them. His mom graciously kind of slowly let me back in there. They're still very guarded, which I understand. But he's pursuing baseball. That's his dream and passion."

22 *From the Bullpen to the State Pen*, 36, 42.

23 Anderson himself was gone after July 14, having worked a total of six innings in five games with an ERA of 6.00. He joined Pawtucket, where he worked to seven batters in just one game, and no more.

24 I went to winter ball five or six years, to Puerto Rico and Venezuela. If my memory serves me, a lot of times they will call in imports just for the playoffs. You don't go for the whole season. You just go for the holidays, for a round robin. I think that's what it was. I was just down there for the playoff series." Puffer interview.

25 Granger Smith podcast.

26 *From the Bullpen to the State Pen*, xv.

27 *From the Bullpen to the State Pen*, 100. In the March 2023 interview, he added, "Everybody has to choose how they're going to do their time. I made the choice I was going to take a positive attitude. I was going to be a light in a pretty dark place. I saw a lot of things that you wouldn't want to see. For the most part, I was just kind of able to keep my head down and stay positive." There have been some fellow inmates with whom he has at least occasional contact. I'm heading up to Dallas right now for a baseball tournament I'm coaching and I connected with one of the guys I was doing time with, who lives up there. I had some people reach out to me and say, 'Hey, you really encouraged me.' It's been pretty neat to be able to know that even in an environment like that you can have a positive impact."

28 "Their family was so supportive of me throughout the year – including the time I was in prison – and Reid specifically told me to reach out after I had gotten out, because he'd have some work for me." *From the Bullpen to the State Pen*, 125.

29 Granger Smith podcast.

30 Puffer interview. Brian Gordon appeared in five major-league games, three for the 2008 Texas Rangers and two for the 2011 New York Yankees. One of the other coaches, Ryan Langerhans, also has major-league experience, playing from 2002 through 2013 with six different big-league teams. For more on GPS Texas Baseball, see https://www.gpstexasbaseball.com/.

31 Puffer interview.

32 https://www.sedrotrailassistedliving.com/.

A RED SOX MEMORY

My memories of the 2004 Red Sox are clutch performances by David "Big Papi" Ortiz and Curt Schilling pitching through a torn tendon sheath in the postseason. Their resilience to overcome the odds impacted me to this day. I still get tears of happiness when Keith Foulke tosses the ball to Doug Mientkiewicz for the third out to win the 2004 World Series. Euphoria is the emotion I get when I think back to 2004.

SCOTT MELESKY

A RED SOX MEMORY

I remember Game Four of the World Series as if it were yesterday. I was in Amherst, Massachusetts, that night, staying at the Campus Hotel. A bunch of us were watching the game on a TV in the lobby. And when the Red Sox finally won their first World Series in 86 years, we screamed and cheered and hugged each other as if we'd all been friends for years. An amazing and magical moment in an amazing and magical season.

DONNA HALPER

MANNY RAMÍREZ

BY BILL NOWLIN

"Manny being Manny" – the simple phrase seemed to instinctively capture the essence of his baseball persona. He was one of the greatest right-handed hitters of the past 50 years. As of 2015, he ranked ninth all-time in career slugging percentage (.5854), has 555 major-league home runs (placing him number 14 – and he's got another 29 postseason home runs – more than any other player), and is number 32 in career on-base percentage (.4106). He won the American League batting crown in 2002 and was World Series MVP for the Boston Red Sox in 2004. He's a 12-time All-Star, with nine Silver Slugger awards, and he's third all-time in grand slams.

And yet his judgment was questionable. He was suspended for 50 games for testing positive for banned substances in 2009, and when he tested positive again in 2011, he retired rather than take the prescribed 100-game suspension.[1]

He's been called a hitting savant. And with his "fielding miscues, baggy uniforms, flowing dreadlocks, big hits, and tired anecdotes, the public is left with caricatures of Manny as a carefree goofball and spoiled superstar."[2] He earned over $200 million as a major leaguer. Yet biographers Rhodes and Boburg also write that, however inscrutable he may be, he "defines himself by what he is least known as – a dedicated athlete, a well-regarded teammate, and a beloved father, husband, and son."[3]

Ramírez was also beloved by fans entranced by his hitting and his charisma at the three main stops on his career route – Cleveland, Boston, and Los Angeles. Each time, he burned bridges behind him, leaving fans disappointed, or worse, though one wouldn't know that from the statistical record alone.

Named after his father (and a statesman of ancient Athens) as Manuel Aristides Ramírez, he was born on May 30, 1972, in Santo Domingo. His high school, though, was George Washington High School in New York City. An outfielder throughout his career, he was a first-round pick of the Cleveland Indians (the 13th pick overall) in the 1991 draft.

Manny moved to New York when he was 13. His mother, Onelcida, had worked a desk job at a dermatological institute in the Dominican Republic but in New York had to take a job as a seamstress in a sewing factory. Father Aristides had worked as an ambulance driver and then, after marriage, driving tank trucks. In New York he was a factory worker and sometimes in and out of work. Manny was the only son in what seemed a matriarchal family, with his mother and his grandmother Pura; he had three older sisters. They moved into an apartment building in a Washington Heights neighborhood that was heavy with drug dealers and murders.[4] But Manny himself had started playing baseball at age 5, playing with the proverbial stick and bottlecap in the DR – and even announcing at 7 his ambition to play professionally. In New York he found Highbridge Park near the apartment and signed up for Little League under coach Carlos "Macaco" Ferreira. Bizarrely, Manny kept baseball separate from family and not even his sisters or mother knew he was ultimately named New York City Public High School Player of the Year, his sister Evelyn admitting, "When we found out that Manny was drafted, we had no idea. I mean, nobody knew about it. Somebody called us and told us to turn on the television … the six o'clock news. We knew he loved to play baseball, but we had no idea."[5]

Manny was active in Brooklyn's Youth Service League ball from the age of 14, and played here and there in the various boroughs, not always letting school get in the way of baseball. He was often the first on the field and the last to leave. It is likely that school attendance being a prerequisite for sticking on the high-school team helped get him through school. He may also have been cut a little slack; "maybe that was when he began to realize that for a gifted athlete like him, the rules did not apply."[6]

Manny's lack of English-language skills left him unsure of himself in situations where conversation was called for, but his work ethic showed from an early age in punishing workouts, waking as early at 5 A.M. on a regular basis to get in his running – and quite often running up hills in the city, tugging a 20-pound tire behind him secured by a rope around his waist. Even years later, teammates on, say, the Boston Red Sox, mentioned that no one worked harder in the weight room and with training than Manny Ramírez. Under the baggy uniforms was a sculpted body that might have been featured in a fitness magazine; as a major leaguer, he was listed as an even 6 feet tall and 225 pounds.

Once on the Washington High team under coach Steve Mandl, Manny truly excelled. As early as age 17, he made the first of two trips to New Mexico with the Youth Service League to play in the Connie Mack World Series.[7] He hit for a .630 batting average in his junior year and was named to the All-City team. In his senior year, he surpassed that, batting .650. He was named New York City Player of the Year.

Needless to say, scouts began to pay attention – even if it meant making the trip into neighborhoods one could understatedly deem dodgy. Cleveland Indians scout Joe DeLucca followed Ramírez carefully, but also at a bit of a distance so the other scouts wouldn't see how interested he was. He wanted to make Manny a first-round pick, but there were 12 other teams picking first. Indians scout George Lauzerique told DeLucca, "No Latin-American immigrant kid has even been drafted in the first round," but that didn't faze DeLucca, who stuck to his guns.[8] The Indians selected Ramírez in the June 1991 draft, and signed him with a $250,000 bonus.

The Indians had Ramírez attend a two-week minicamp and then go to Burlington, North Carolina, for rookie ball in the Appalachian League. He did well – hitting .326 with 19 homers and more than one RBI a game – 63 RBIs in 59 games.

Ramírez's 1992 season was a tougher one. The Indians asked him to play winter ball in the Dominican Republic, but he quit after 15 days and returned to New York. Playing for the Kinston Indians, in the high Class-A Carolina League, he got off to a very slow start, but he started to hit in June and the beginning of July – when he broke the hamate bone in his left hand, costing him the rest of the season. He hit just .278 in 81 games.

In 1993 Ramírez was assigned to the Canton-Akron Indians (Double-A Eastern League), got into 89 games (.340, 17 HR, 79 RBIs) and got himself called up to Triple-A, to the Charlotte Knights (International League). He played in another 40 games and drove in 36 runs, with a .317 average – and also got himself called up to the major leagues, to Cleveland. He was later named *Baseball America*'s Minor League Player of the Year.

When he got the call, Ramírez asked Charlotte manager Charlie Manuel, "Can you come with me?"[9] The sentiment was emblematic of his attachment to certain mentors along the way. Needless to say, Manuel couldn't drop everything – he had the Knights on the way to the league pennant. Ramírez joined the Indians in Minneapolis on September 2 and was 0-for-4, though three of the balls were well-hit fly balls. The very next day, they played at Yankee Stadium, with lots of Manny's family and friends at the game. He hit a ground-rule double to left field his first time up, flied out in the fourth, hit a two-run homer to left in the sixth off Mélido Pérez, and then hit another one – also to left – off Paul Gibson. Two homers, three RBIs, and a 7-3 Cleveland victory.

It was quite a splash but Ramírez struggled from that point on, getting only six more hits in 45 at-bats, with two more runs batted in and no more extra-base hits of any kind. With one exception, he DH'd, and pinch-hit in four games – and, perhaps a little oddly, pinch-ran in five. He ended the season, after appearing in 22 games, batting .170.

The Indians, once again, asked Ramírez to play winter ball. It was another fiasco; he even took one of the team buses and drove off, AWOL for the day. He wasn't welcomed back.[10]

The 1994 season ended with a players' strike. The Indians played 113 games, and Ramírez appeared in 91 of them. It was his official rookie year, and he came in second in Rookie of the Year voting, though compared to the rest of his stats, it was one of his least productive years. He did drive in 60 runs.

The Indians opened the 1995 season in Texas. The team went on to Detroit, and after they left, there was a typical Manny moment – he'd left his paycheck in a boot underneath his locker. It had to be shipped onward to him. Ramírez himself hit 11 homers in just the month of May. (He was named AL Player of the Month.) He made the All-Star team for the first time, drove in 107 runs (helped by 31 homers), and helped the Indians reach the World Series. He hit only .222 in the Series itself (with a .364 on-base percentage), with one homer, but there was only one Indian who hit higher – Albert Belle with .235. The Cleveland offense was clearly lacking – 19 runs in six games, losing to the Atlanta Braves.

Ramírez's early career was replete with a number of fielding and baserunning lapses. He was cut slack, of course, given his hitting – in 1996 he drove in 112 runs, with 33 homers. He hit for a higher average in 1997 (.328) but his RBIs declined to 88. Matt Williams, Jim Thome, and David Justice each drove in just over 100. The Indians made the postseason again, and went all the way to the World Series once more, playing the Florida Marlins. At one point or another, the Indians held a lead in each of the seven games, but in the end they lost four. Ramírez contributed some key hits in the first couple of rounds, but was 4-for-26 (.154) in the World Series. Average alone was deceptive; he drove in six runs in the seven games.

Occasional lapses aside, Ramírez had a strong and accurate arm. Twice he led the AL in assists from his position: 1996 as a right-fielder, with 19, and in 2005 as a left-fielder, with 17.

There was a time when Manny paid an unannounced visit to his old high school, and wandered into the gym where coach Steve Mandl was talking to the baseball team. Asked if he wanted to say anything to the team about hitting, Manny said, as simply as possible, "See the ball. Hit the ball."[11]

With 45 homers and 145 RBIs in 1998, Ramírez had an exceptionally productive season, despite a batting average six points under .300. At one point in September, he homered in four at-bats in a row and eight times in a five-game stretch. It was the second year he made the All-Star team, and the first year in what became a string of 11 consecutive annual All-Star selections. The Indians beat Boston in the ALDS but lost to the Yankees in the ALCS. Ramírez hit two homers in each round, batting .357 and .333 respectively.

There were thoughts, though, that Ramírez's fielding may have cost the Indians the chance to get to another World Series. It was Game Six, at Yankee Stadium, and the Indians had just scored five runs in the top of the fifth to pull to within a run of New York. (Thome hit a grand slam, but Ramírez had struck out with the bases loaded.) In the bottom of the sixth, Derek Jeter tripled to right field to drive in two big insurance runs – but the ball was a catchable one. A *New York Times* article was headlined: "Ramírez: Big Bat, Blunders." Ramírez had leapt to catch the ball, only to have it land at his feet. He wasn't charged with an error, but he had clearly erred in anticipating the ball's trajectory.

Ramírez drove in 20 more runs (to a total of 165, tied for 14th all-time for single-season RBIs) in 1999. He hit .333 (with a .442 on-base percentage) and scored 131 runs. He homered 44 times. For the fifth year in a row, the Indians made the postseason, but this time lost to the Red Sox in the Division Series. Ramírez got just one base hit in 18 at-bats (.056), but he did draw four bases on balls and scored all five times he got on base. Ramírez placed third in the MVP voting, the highest he ever ranked. (It was a ranking he tied in 2004.)

The year 2000 was Manny's contract year in Cleveland and he got off to a great start, but he was on the disabled list with a serious hamstring injury from May 29 to July 13, missing 39 games. Despite missing a quarter of the season, he still had 122 RBIs and 38 homers. He hit .351 and led the league in slugging (.697) and OPS (1.154). There was no doubt Ramírez was due for a big contract.

Red Sox GM Dan Duquette won the bidding war. Ramírez was a huge fan favorite in Cleveland and the Indians kept upping their offer, but he signed with the Red Sox for a reported $160 million/eight-year deal.[12] Manny had one final condition before signing: that the Red Sox hire Cleveland clubhouse man Frank Mancini, to accompany him to Boston.[13] It was reminiscent of him wanting Charlie Manuel to come with him from Charlotte. It also didn't happen.

Some wondered if Ramírez could handle the intensity of the Boston market. Rhodes and Boburg quoted Macaco as saying that "Manny's lack of anonymity at shopping malls was one of his primary dissatisfactions with life in Boston." Bizarre as that may seem, "Manny always wants to go to shopping malls. Sometimes we'll go two or three times a day." And it wasn't necessarily to buy anything.[14] He just liked going to malls, but quite naturally didn't want to be relentlessly fawned over and followed by fans.

Ramírez was the Red Sox DH into June, when he began to play left field. In late August he reverted to DH. (He was DH for 87 games and left fielder for 55.) He had a career high in strikeouts, with 147, but still achieved a .405 on-base percentage (hitting .306), and drove in 125 runs, 37 more than anyone else on the Red Sox. He had 41 homers, 14 more than Trot Nixon's second-place 27.

Ramírez lost more than a full month in 2002 due to a broken left index finger, fractured on a head-first slide into home plate on May 11 (he was out), and not returning until June 25. In 120 games, he drove in 107 runs, with 33 homers. His .349 average (.450 OBP) won the American League batting title.

It was back to the playoffs in 2003, the first full year under new ownership. Ramírez played in a career-high 154 games, and led the league in on-base percentage (.427). He hit .325, just one point behind the AL batting champion, teammate Bill Mueller. He hit 37 homers, drove in 104 runs (one behind teammate Nomar Garciaparra), and scored 117 runs. Too often, there seemed to be a discordant note. In late August the Yankees came to Boston for what was really a key series. Manny was excused from the game due to throat inflammation – but was discovered in the Ritz-Carlton bar with Enrique Wilson of the Yankees, which didn't go over well with the Red Sox fan base. Neither Ramírez nor David Ortiz hit that well in the Division Series, but the team pulled through and Manny's three-run homer in Game Five made all the difference in the 4-3 win.

Ramírez homered twice and drove in four runs in the ALCS against the Yankees, a series that went to seven games and seemed to be in Boston's hands until manager Grady Little (who'd been the bench coach on the Indians in Manny's last years there) put Pedro Martínez back into the game when he seemed so obviously out of gas. The Yankees rallied and tied the game, then won it on Aaron Boone's home run leading off the bottom of the 11th. Little was fired, and Terry Francona hired as manager for 2004.

Ramírez had more than once expressed a wish to get out of Boston. At the end of October the Red Sox placed him on waivers – they could have called him back if any team had claimed him, but none did. There was, after all, close to $100 million remaining on his contract. Perhaps the Red Sox did it just to make a point with Manny about what a good deal he had – so good no other team was willing to pay the freight to get him.

There was also discussion about trading Ramírez, as part of two trades that would have brought Álex Rodríguez from the Rangers for Manny and Jon Lester, and sent Garciaparra to the White Sox for Magglio Ordóñez. A-Rod wanted to come to Boston and was willing to take a $25 million pay cut to do so, but the Players Association refused to sign off on such a hefty cut.

Early in 2004 Ramírez became an American citizen and, when he took his position before the game on May 11, he ran out to left field carrying a miniature American flag. He then handed it off to a spectator. He later joked, "Now they can't kick me out of the country." Before his first at-bat, the team played the song "Proud to Be an American" on the sound system.[15]

Manny Ramírez was World Series MVP in 2004, the Red Sox this time rolling over Anaheim in the Division Series (he had seven RBIs in three games) and then losing the first three games of the ALCS to the Yankees, only to come back and win an unprecedented final four in a row. Oddly, Ramírez didn't have even one RBI in the ALCS, though he hit .300 and scored three times.

Facing the St. Louis Cardinals in the World Series, Ramírez looked like a stumblebum in left field, committing two errors in Game One. He overran a ball in the top of the eighth, allowing one run to score, and then made an awkward slide to try to catch a ball on the very next play, letting it get past him as another run – the tying run – scored, costing the Red Sox the lead. He was 3-for-5 in the game with two RBIs.

In Game Three, he homered in the first inning and drove in another run later in the game, a 4-1 Red Sox win. Derek Lowe shut out St. Louis in Game Four and the Red Sox swept the Series. It was their first World Series win in 86 years. Any number of Red Sox players might have been voted MVP, but Ramírez (1-for-4 in Game Four, without either an RBI or run scored) got the nod, perhaps in recognition of his having had at least one base hit in every one of the 14 playoff games in which the Red Sox had played.

The Ramírez work ethic was noted earlier. Billy Broadbent, the Red Sox video coordinator, said Manny put in as much time with video as any other player or more, and he added a few twists to his study. Preparing for whomever he might face, if it was a pitcher against whom he'd not previously batted, he'd call up at at-bats of another right-handed slugger, like Miguel Tejada, and look to see how the pitcher had worked Tejada. "It's something he came up with all on his own," said Broadbent. "It's nothing we suggested. He came up to these determinations on his own. He was one of the hardest workers that you'd ever want to see."[16]

Ramírez may have seemed oblivious at times, or just downright goofy, but there were perhaps two unexpected aspects to the approach he took to hitting. First of all, the way he slipped into a kind of zen mode helped to create an almost preternatural focus, slowing down time and allowing all that he had learned to be brought to the fore. He could tune out distractions. Simply put, in the words of Jim Thome, "He's good at not letting things get to him."[17] He was perhaps like the "absent-minded professor, whose mind is so specialized and consumed by his craft that he is as helpless as a lamb outside the lab."[18] There was also craftiness in the way he would try to set up pitchers. Allard Baird reportedly told columnist Joe Posnanski that he believed "Manny will swing and miss at a pitch in April so that the pitcher will throw him the same pitch in September."[19] Álex Rodríguez told the *New York Times*, "When it comes to his craft, his art, his skill, he's as smart as anyone in the American League. And he takes it as seriously as anyone in the game."[20] If he was a savant, he was a studious savant. That doesn't mean he wasn't also a little flaky and a little naïve.

Ramírez never once hit over .300 in 2005, and was as low as .224 more than a quarter of the way through the season (on May 27, after game number 47). One month later, on June 26, he was leading the American League in RBIs (with 66) and he finished the season with career highs in homers (45, matching his 1998 season in Cleveland) and drove in 144 runs, just four behind the league leader, David Ortiz. This was the season when Manny stepped inside the Green Monster during a conference on the mound and didn't come out until after the first pitch after play resumed. He was also marching to his own drummer, when he insisted on taking a scheduled day off despite teammate Trot Nixon having suffered an oblique strain in late July. There was tension in the Red Sox clubhouse, which had a player apparently unwilling to set his personal wishes aside to help out his team in a pennant race. There was a stronger sense of him quitting on the team in 2006, when he reported himself unable to play because of patellar tendinitis and he missed 22 games from late August into September. He still drove in 102 runs but the Red Sox failed to make the postseason (they'd gotten into the ALDS in 2005, but were swept in three games, Ramírez hitting .300).

In 2007 the Red Sox won the World Series again. Ramírez started slow, got hot for a stretch, and then suffered his own oblique strain. His power numbers were down on the year, with only 20 homers and 88 RBIs (the first time he'd been below 100 in a decade, since 1997), but come the playoffs, he contributed. In Game Two of the Division Series, when Angels manager Mike Scioscia had Ortiz walked to get to Ramírez with two outs in the bottom of the ninth, it may have triggered something in Ramírez – he hit a walkoff three-run homer. His fourth-inning homer in Game Three was literally the game-winner, giving Boston a 2-1 edge in a game they won, 9-1.

In the 2007 ALCS, Ramírez was facing his former team, the Indians. He drove in 10 runs, with two more homers and a .409 average. The Red Sox swept the Rockies in the World Series; he hit .250 and drove in two runs, but all in all, he was .348 with 16 RBIs in the 14 postseason games.

The last guaranteed year of Ramírez's Red Sox contract was 2008. It was the year he joined the 500-HR club, homering off Chad Bradford in Baltimore on May 31. June was a tough month for Manny's reputation in Boston. First he got into a fight with Kevin Youkilis in the Red Sox dugout during a game. Then, on June 28, he got in an argument over complimentary tickets with traveling secretary Jack McCormick and shoved the 64-year-old man to the ground.[21] There were a couple of game-play situations where Ramírez seemed not to be giving his all. There were thoughts he was provoking the team into trading him. On July 31, at the trading deadline, two deals were done: Ramírez's contract was transferred to the Los Angeles Dodgers, who agreed to pick up the money remaining on his contract (the Red Sox freed him from the two option years), and Boston acquired left fielder Jason Bay from Pittsburgh to take his place.

If he'd been dogging it, it wasn't entirely self-evident; Ramírez had hit .347 during July. But he'd worn out his welcome in Boston. Once he hit Los Angeles, he became an instant sensation and he reveled in the "Mannywood" moniker given him. In 53 games, he drove in 53 runs, and he hit for a .396 average. The Dodgers won the NLDS (Manny hit .500 with two homers), but lost the NLCS in five games (Manny hit two more homers and drove in seven runs, batting .533).

Come 2009, however, Manny's hitting came back to earth – he was 37 years old, and hit .290 in 104 games, with 63 RBIs. He likely would have played more games, but he tested positive for a banned substance and was suspended for 50 games during the season, from May 7 through July 2.[22]

In 2010 Ramírez got off to a good start with the Dodgers, and was batting .322 through the end of June. But he played in only two games in July and, after a month, returned to play in five late-August games. The Dodgers placed him on waivers and he was selected by the Chicago White Sox on August 30. For the White Sox, he played in 24 September games but hit for only a .261 average, with just one home run and only two

RBIs in 24 games. The White Sox chose not to try to re-sign him. At the end of January the Tampa Bay Rays signed Ramírez on perhaps something of a flyer but he again tested positive for a performance-enhancing drug and thus faced a 100-game suspension. He played in five games (batting .059) but then announced his retirement.[23]

After the 2011 season was over, however, Ramírez struck a deal under which he would accept a 50-game suspension and be permitted to return. He signed with the Oakland Athletics for 2012. He played in 17 games, batting .302 without a home run, for Oakland's Triple-A club in Sacramento, but never played for Oakland itself. The Athletics released him in June.

Ramírez played in Taiwan for the EDA Rhinos, but left at the midpoint of the season. His agent, Barry Praver, said, "The reason he decided not to return for the second half was to free himself to be available to play in the United States. This whole thing with Manny in Taiwan was a phenomenon. He invigorated the league. Attendance went through the roof. It was a very positive experience for both sides."[24]

The Texas Rangers signed Ramírez to a minor-league deal in July 2013, but six weeks later, after he hit .259 for Triple-A Round Rock in 30 games, they released him.

Near the end of May 2014, Ramírez signed with the Chicago Cubs and he was again asked to play in Triple-A, this time for the Iowa Cubs as a player/coach. He claimed he was a new man, that he and his wife, Juliana, had been in church for almost four years. "Now, I realize that I behaved bad in Boston," he said. The *Boston Globe*'s Christopher L. Gasper wrote, "Manny being Manny means something entirely different now if you are to believe Ramírez, who will turn 42 on Friday. Chastened by time, the diminishing of his skills, and his newfound faith, he has finally found a manager he likes – God."[25] Of course, time will tell. The Cubs' president of baseball operations, Theo Epstein, hoped he would become a mentor for Cubs prospects. He played in 24 games and hit .222 with three home runs.

NOTES

1. The 2009 drug was human chorionic gonadotropin, a fertility drug for women. See *New York Times*, May 10, 2009.
2. The best source for much more information about Manny Ramírez and the primary source for this biography is Jean Rhodes and Shawn Boburg, *Becoming Manny: Inside the Life of Baseball's Most Enigmatic Slugger* (New York: Scribner, 2009). The quotation noted here is from page 3.
3. Rhodes and Boburg, 5.
4. The "Ramírez family settled in one of New York City's most dangerous and drug-infested neighborhoods (between 1987 and 1991 there were 462 homicides, 58 percent of them drug-related, in Washington Heights' police precinct)." Rhodes and Boburg, 49.
5. Rhodes and Boburg, 9, 10.
6. Sara Rimer, *New York Times*, April 26, 2011. Rimer's lengthy profile of Ramírez, someone she had met and observed since his high school years is recommended to readers.
7. Rhodes and Boburg, 84, 85, 96.
8. Rhodes and Boburg, 111, 118.
9. Rhodes and Boburg, 147.
10. Rhodes and Boburg, 152, 153.
11. Rimer, *New York Times*.
12. *New York Times*, December 12, 2000.
13. Rhodes and Boburg, 193.
14. Rhodes and Boburg, 128, 143.
15. *Boston Globe*, May 12, 2004.
16. Author interview with Billy Broadbent on June 28, 2013.
17. *New York Times*, July 22, 1999.
18. Rhodes and Boburg, 290.
19. Rhodes and Boburg, 292.
20. *New York Times*, April 17, 2008.
21. It wasn't the first time Ramírez had struck a team employee. In 1998 he slapped Cleveland clubhouse assistant Tom Foster. See *New York Times*, March 30, 1998.
22. For a full report on the suspension, see the May 8, 2009, *New York Times*.
23. *New York Times*, April 9, 2011.
24. "Manny Ramírez Leaving Taiwan," ESPN.com, June 19, 2013. espn.go.com/mlb/story/_/id/9403816/manny-Ramirez-parts-ways-eda-rhinos-taiwan-league. Posted June 20, 2013.
25. *Boston Globe*, May 29, 2014.

POKEY REESE

BY BOB LEMOINE

"That was the most exciting thing I ever accomplished in baseball, and to do it with those guys was great."
Pokey Reese, on being a member of the 2004 Boston Red Sox.[1]

Pokey Reese didn't have many things when he was a kid, including a baseball glove. He chucked a tennis ball against the wall to learn how to field. "Just used my hands," he said.[2] He borrowed a glove from his Little League coach, and finally owned one in high school. He was already a dazzling fielder by then. When he was 17, the Cincinnati Reds' scouting report described Reese as "agile, good athlete, [who] reacts well, fluid, first-step quickness, great range, good arm from the hole."[3] Pokey Reese's glove took him from a South Carolina shack with no running water to an eight-year major-league career. He received two Gold Glove Awards and recorded the last out as the Boston Red Sox won the 2004 American League Championship Series. The Red Sox walked off the field with their first World Series championship in 86 years, and Reese walked off the field a champion after a lifetime of hardship, poverty, and tragedy. "Most of us walk miles to get where we want to be," wrote Paul Daugherty in the *Cincinnati Enquirer*. "Reese had walked more than that."[4]

Calvin Reese Jr. was born on June 10, 1973, in Arthurtown, an unincorporated part of Columbia, South Carolina, to Calvin Reese Sr. and Clara (Barnes) Reese. Calvin Sr. was a truck driver who was in and out of the family's life over the years, a victim of alcohol and drugs. Clara was a nurse's assistant. They divorced, remarried, then divorced again when Calvin Jr. was in high school.[5] He was nicknamed Pokey by his grandmother, who was actually saying "porky" in her Southern accent. "I was a little chubby guy," Reese said. "I had a hernia, so, my navel stuck out. Everybody poked me in my navel."[6]

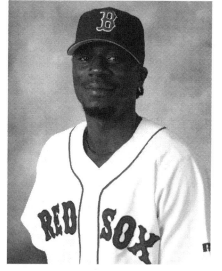

Arthurtown, founded by freed slaves after the Civil War, resembled more the 1870s, not the 1970s. With no public sewer or water, the Reeses had an outhouse. Pokey and his brothers, Tony, and Angelo Wilson (who had a different father), and two sisters, Alissia (Peaches) and Candy, would carry water in jugs from their grandfather's well a half-mile down their dirt road called Sugar Hill Lane. They heated water on the stove for baths and washed clothes on a washboard. "It was crazy, but we got by," Reese said. They did have electricity, and Pokey listened to Braves games on the radio, and watched the *Game of the Week* on television at his great-grandfather's house down the hill.[7]

Pokey once stole a bag of Clara's flour to create foul lines and batter's boxes in the side yard where he played baseball. Pokey saw a perfect ball field, but Clara, horrified, saw lost biscuits and cornbread. She had to feed her family of nine (including grandma and cousins Randy and Gerald) in a two-bedroom house. Pokey used soda cans for bases and the doghouse for the center-field wall.[8]

When Pokey was 9, they moved to the Starlight low-income community in Columbia. "I used to run on the concrete with no shoes on, scraping my toes up, chasing balls," he remembered. His Little League uniform was yellow and black, making Pokey an instant fan of the Pittsburgh Pirates.[9]

Calvin Sr. played semipro baseball with both the all-Black Arthurtown Buccaneers and the integrated Columbia Bulls. Pokey was the team batboy and legend has it that he snared a foul line drive while adults ducked.[10] Calvin Sr. was known as Slick for his fielding at shortstop, and Pokey played shortstop modeling his dad.[11]

Reese began his high-school career at A.C. Flora High School but transferred to Lower Richland High School, which also produced Richard Seymour of the NFL and Stanley Roberts of the NBA. As a sophomore, Reese batted .329 with 11 stolen bases. "He's by far the best glove man at his position I've seen in a long time," his coach, Henry Mixon, said. "He is so smooth."[12] Reese learned a lot from Mixon, whom he depended on for rides.

Reese batted .426 with 15 steals as a junior and made the state's AAAA-AAA All-Area Team.[13] As a senior he batted .446 with 5 home runs and 20 stolen bases as Lower Richland (25-5) won the Region 4-AAAA title. Reese drew attention during a playoff game against Lancaster. "I made a diving catch up the middle," Reese said, "and I made a backhanded play in the hole and threw a batter out. A scout came up to me after the game and said, 'Your stock is rising.' I said, 'Oh gosh.'"[14]

Paul Faulk of the Cincinnati Reds scouted Reese, who was also a phenomenal football player, starring as a quarterback, wide receiver, and free safety. In his senior year, he rushed for

154 yards and one touchdown, threw for 1,066 yards, caught one touchdown pass, made 36 solo tackles, and ran 281 yards in kickoff returns.[15] "He's probably the best defensive back who's ever played here," his coach, Bill Kimrey, said. "He can score on defense as quick as he can on offense and covers a lot of ground."[16] Reese signed a letter of intent to play football at Arizona State but was not academically eligible.

Baseball America rated Reese prospect number 37 out of 100 players nationally. He was drafted in the first round (20th overall) in the June 1991 amateur draft by the Cincinnati Reds. "I was so excited the world champions picked me," an elated Reese said. "It's been a dream ever since I was small to play major league baseball." Reese received a $200,000 signing bonus.[17] He was assigned to Princeton (West Virginia) of the short-season Appalachian League. In 62 games he batted .238 with 3 home runs and 10 stolen bases. He committed 31 errors at shortstop in 270 chances for an .885 fielding percentage.

In 1992 Reese advanced to Charleston (West Virginia) of the low Class-A South Atlantic League. He batted .268 in 106 games. "He's a very exciting player to watch," commented Reds minor-league coordinator Jim Tracy, saying Reese had "the makeup and the build to remind you a heck of a lot of Ozzie Smith." Reese improved his fielding percentage (.932) and played in the South Atlantic League All-Star Game.[18]

In 1993 Reese made the jump to Chattanooga of the Double-A Southern League. He struggled, batting .212 in 102 games. The scoreboard operator at Engel Stadium was instructed not to post his batting average until Reese reached .200 near season's end. "I'm glad," Reese said. "It was that bad. I was not patient at all."[19] Reese cut his errors at shortstop to 25 in 506 chances (.951). Reese was sent to the Florida Instructional League after the season for practice at second base "to make him a little more versatile," said Reds player development director Sheldon "Chief" Bender."[20]

Reese spent 1994 at Chattanooga and batted .269 with 12 home runs with an increased on-base percentage (.336 vs .258 in 1993). "I've surprised myself sometimes," he said. "I've been on fire. I hope it keeps going." "He's showed me a lot," coach Ray Knight said, "especially his instincts, baseball knowledge and reading situations." Reese committed 38 errors in 621 chances at shortstop, but manager Pat Kelly blamed it on poor field conditions. "You watch. He'll make an Ozzie Smith-type play tonight. It's a nightly occurrence." Rival Birmingham manager Terry Francona said, "We've graded him higher than any player in this league at any position. That's how highly we think of him."[21]

Reese spent the next two seasons at Triple-A Indianapolis, being groomed as Barry Larkin's possible replacement if the Reds future Hall of Famer left via free agency.[22] Reese hit a home run in his first Triple-A at-bat in 1995 and batted .368 in early May but missed a month with an ankle sprain.[23] He batted .239 for the season with 10 home runs (.316 OBP) and spent the winter in the Arizona Fall League.[24]

Reese missed action in 1996 with a strained medial collateral ligament in his left knee after being upended on a hard slide into second base. The same sore knee forced him to miss September.[25] He batted .232 in 79 games with Indianapolis, with a .948 fielding percentage (19 errors in 367 chances at shortstop).

Cincinnati experimented with Reese in the outfield in an attempt to get him on the major-league roster. Larkin and Bret Boone at shortstop and second base meant Reese had nowhere to play. Bowden still considered Reese "untouchable" and wouldn't trade him.[26] Reese batted .373 with three home runs in spring training 1997 and made the club, for one day. He made his major-league debut on April 1 as a defensive replacement for Larkin with his mother and grandmother sitting behind home plate. Reese was immediately sent back to Indianapolis. "They gotta do what they gotta do," he said. "There's a lot of ups and downs in this game."[27] He was soon recalled when Larkin had a bad heel. He started at shortstop on April 12, grounding out in his first at-bat against Kevin Brown. The game was 1-1 into the bottom of the 10th. With Eric Owens on second, Reese blooped a single to right off Rick Helling, Owens scored, and Reese's first major-league hit was a walk-off, snapping a Reds five-game losing streak. The ball went to Pokey's mother. "I'm so happy right now, I can't express it," Reese said. "It's a dream come true. My first hit is the game-winning hit."[28]

Reese's first home run, a three-run shot, came the next day against the Marlins' Al Leiter in a 6-4 Reds victory. He briefly returned to Indianapolis before returning for good on May 6. He started 92 games at shortstop for the injured Larkin. Reese made only 15 errors in 447 chances (.966) and just one error in his first 60 games (April 1-July 15) with a solid .995 fielding percentage. He finished the season batting .219 but was second on the team behind Deion Sanders with 25 stolen bases. The Reds were a disappointing 76-86.

Reese had a forgettable 1998 Opening Day against San Diego, making four errors, three in the third inning and two on one play. Manager Jack McKeon joked that Reese should go for the record of errors by a shortstop on Opening Day. Reese tied the Cubs' Lou Stringer, who had four miscues at shortstop in his debut in 1941. Stringer had more success selling cars, putting Elvis Presley into a shiny new Corvette. Reese was not all shook up, however, about the infamous record. "I just want to put it behind me and go out and get them tomorrow," he said.[29]

When Larkin returned, Reese started just 14 of 31 games and batted a paltry .143. The 30-43 Reds were already 14 games behind in the NL Central Division when McKeon moved Reese to third base. He batted .321 in 24 games and the Reds went 17-11 over that span. Reese's only home run of the season, on June 25, snapped an 11-game losing streak. Reese belted a three-run home run off Keith Foulke of the White Sox in a 7-5 interleague victory. The Reds won 15 of their next 16 games. Reese dived for a Javy López grounder on July 30 and tore a ligament in his thumb, ending his season early.[30] The Reds (77-85) finished in fourth place.

Bret Boone's trade to Atlanta gave Reese a chance to start at second base, and he excelled. He posted career highs in batting average (.285), RBIs (52), stolen bases (38, tied for fifth in the

NL), and OPS (.747). But it was Reese's defense that truly shined as he won a Gold Glove Award at second base. His Defensive WAR (3.2) trailed only Rey Ordóñez and Andruw Jones in the National League. Reese ranked second among second basemen in putouts (325), tied for third in assists (409), first in total zone fielding runs above average (27), fourth in double plays turned (91), second in range factor per nine innings (5.40), and third in fielding percentage (.991), committing just seven errors in 741 chances.

The 1999 Reds surprised the baseball world by making a playoff run. Reese had a four-hit game in an 8-1 win over Florida on May 29 and a five-hit game on June 22 at Arizona in an 8-7 victory. He had a 10-game hitting streak August 13-22, and hit safely in 16 of 17 games August 13-29. On September 4 Reese hit one of the Reds' nine home runs that day against Philadelphia, still a National League record as of 2022. His 12th-inning walk-off three-run home run off Ricky Bottalico in the last week of the season beat the Cardinals, 7-5. The win, combined with a Mets loss, put the Reds ahead in the wild-card race by one game with seven to go. "In the game of baseball," Reese reflected, "you can't give up. I don't think I've ever had a hit like that one. Maybe in Little League or A-ball. It's the biggest RBI of my career. I'm going to write that on the ball and I'm going to give it to my mom."[31]

The Reds moved one game ahead of Houston in the NL Central but lost four of their next five games. Houston passed them in the Central, and the Mets rallied to tie them for the wild card. In a one-game playoff, Al Leiter shut out the Reds on two hits in a 5-0 victory.

In the offseason, the Reds sought to acquire future Hall of Famer and Cincinnati native Ken Griffey Jr. The trade couldn't happen because Bowden refused to include Reese as part of the deal. Even the humble Reese was surprised. "To get Ken home to Cincinnati, I'd have made the deal," he said honestly. "I'm honored my name was used in the same sentence as his."[32] Bowden eventually acquired Griffey anyway, without giving up Reese.

Reese had another defensively stellar season in 2000. His Defensive WAR ranked fourth in the NL, Total Zone Fielding Runs above average as a second baseman ranked first, and his range factor per game was tied for second. He walked away with his second Gold Glove in as many years. Reese started strong offensively, batting .366 through April, but batted only .235 in the second half. He matched his career high with five hits against the Giants on April 20 and had a career-high six triples. He stole 29 bases and was caught just three times (a NL-best 90.63 percentage). Reese missed time in July (a strained left groin), in August (a strained left hamstring), and the last nine games of the season (a bruised left hand).[33] The Reds finished 85-77-1 and missed the playoffs.

In 2000 Pokey Reese's life went under the spotlight, but not Pokey the Gold Glove winner. In the June 12 issue of *Sports Illustrated*, Michael Bamberger wrote an article, "Fast and Loose," delving into Reese's family issues and tragedies. Reese and his girlfriend, Tieronay Duckett, had a baby girl, LaBresha, born in November 1992. Reese and Duckett were engaged to be married. After a brief breakup the year before, Reese had a son, Naquwan, born two months before LaBresha, through a one-night stand with Rhonda Richardson. Duckett was killed in a car accident in 1993, just before Reese went to spring training. LaBresha was raised by her great-grandmother.

The tragedy no doubt contributed to Reese's poor 1993 season at Chattanooga in which he started 0-for-30. He called his mother. "I'm comin' home," he said, despondently. "I can't concentrate. It isn't worth it." His mother persuaded him to not give up.[34]

Rhonda was eight months pregnant with a child who was not Reese's. In 1996 she died from an illness, losing the baby as well. Naquwan was raised by his grandmother, Patricia Richardson, and great-grandmother, Nellie Green. The unthinkable happened on December 23, 1997, when Patricia's live-in boyfriend murdered her and Nellie in their home. Naquwan was found near their bodies.

"It's new every time," Reese said about the tragedies he experienced. "I don't want anyone to die on me. I hate that stuff. It's scary. People you love here one day, then gone the next. It's hard, but I try not to think about it. It's always going to be in the back of my head, of course, but I just try to go out and have my fun on the field."[35]

Also in 1997, Reese fathered a girl, McKayla, with Christy Jones, whom he had met while in Indianapolis. Reese and Jones broke off an engagement. Reese also has a son Cameron from another relationship.

Scott MacGregor of the *Cincinnati Enquirer* called Reese's family life "a world he cannot escape, where death touches him or his family with the arbitrary stroke of an artist's brush, painting his life black when it should be nothing but bright."[36] Brighter days would one day come.

With Larkin injured most of 2001, Reese made 70 starts at shortstop and 46 at second base, disrupting his chance at a third straight Gold Glove. Reese himself missed 43 starts with numerous injuries, including a bad shoulder.[37] He still managed a .980 fielding percentage at second, committing only five errors in 247 chances. At the plate, Reese dropped to .224 with 9 home runs and had the highest stolen-base percentage (86.21) in the NL with 25 steals in 29 attempts.

The 2001 season was disastrous for the 66-96 Reds, and Reese's relationship with the organization soured. Before the season, he withdrew from attending Redsfest because he didn't want to discuss his contract negotiations. The Reds wanted to give him a $900,000 raise; Reese wanted $1.8 million. In April Reese declined the Reds offer of a four-year extension for $21 million. Rumors swirled that Reese sought $10 million a year, which he denied. Other rumors surfaced that Reese was a clubhouse problem. Bowden acquired second baseman Todd Walker before the trading deadline, leaving Reese few options. Teammates denied Reese was a problem, but Pokey felt a change was needed. "Do I really want to be here?" he said. "Not really. There comes a time in your life when you might need a change."[38]

Reese was a year away from free-agent eligibility, and the cost-cutting Reds sought to move him in the offseason. He was making $3.2 million and the Reds were attempting to cut payroll. On December 18, 2001, the Reds traded the once "untouchable" Reese and reliever Dennys Reyes to Colorado for pitcher Gabe White and minor-league pitcher Luke Hudson. "Mentally, Reese was outta here in June," Paul Daugherty wrote in the *Enquirer*. "The trade just sends the rest of him packing."[39]

Rockies GM Dan O'Dowd, also cutting payroll, said the Rockies had no plans for Reese and were prepared to deal him. They found a taker in the Boston Red Sox and a day later traded Reese for catcher Scott Hatteberg. Both players were arbitration-eligible and both clubs had 48 hours to offer a contract to their new player. The Red Sox, after coming to terms with free agent Johnny Damon, declined to tender Reese a contract, knowing he would have received $5 million to $6 million in arbitration. The Red Sox were already paying second baseman José Offerman a similar salary. Reese became a free agent.[40]

Reese signed a two-year deal with the Pittsburgh Pirates for $10 million. "It's a new start," he said. "I'm not one to make excuses. I had the bad year. Jim Bowden wasn't out there playing. Hopefully, last year was my worst. I'm happy to be here."[41] He pulled his batting average up to .264. His fielding percentage (.988) ranked fourth in the NL for second basemen. He made 116 starts at second base. "He makes us 10 or 12 games better when he's out there," Pirates manager Lloyd McClendon said of Reese's defense. Reese missed 30 games with injuries, including a strained hamstring, injured index finger, strained oblique, and a bruised knee.[42] He might have won another Gold Glove if it were not for the injuries. His Range Factor and fielding percentage were far better than those of Gold Glove winner Fernando Viña. Reese was also popular with Pirates fans and had his own Bobblehead night.[43]

Reese tore the ligament in his left thumb and played just 37 games in 2003. The Pirates declined his option at the end of the season and Reese became a free agent. In December he signed a one-year contract with Boston. "He's one of the few players in baseball who can really make an impact with his glove," said Red Sox GM Theo Epstein. "He's an outstanding defensive second baseman and that will make a huge difference for us."[44] "My goal," said Reese, "was to one day play behind Pedro (Martínez), and I got that opportunity, and I couldn't turn it down."[45]

Reese was expected to be the starting second baseman, but instead started the season at shortstop when Nomar Garciaparra began the season on the disabled list. Reese played 53 games at shortstop (50 starts) until Garciaparra returned June 9. He batted a respectable .250, but it was his solid defense that was the biggest asset. Reese had a .975 fielding percentage and made just six errors in that span. He became an instant fan favorite in Boston with his acrobatic defense, cheery smile, and grit.

Reese sparkled in a memorable moment at Fenway Park on May 8. The Red Sox and Kansas City Royals were tied, 1-1, in the bottom of the fifth. Reese blooped a fly ball down the right-field line off Jimmy Gobble. The ball bounced along Fenway's nooks and crannies of the right-field wall and scooted past right fielder Juan González. It rolled toward the Red Sox bullpen as Reese sprinted around the bases and beat the throw to the plate by Desi Relaford. It was an inside-the-park home run, the only one of Reese's career. He followed in the sixth inning by launching a home run to left field off Jason Grimsley. It was the only multi-home-run game in Reese's career and the fans gave him a standing ovation. "Pokey Reese is the first official folk hero of the 2004 baseball season," wrote Bob Ryan in the *Boston Globe*.[46]

After Garciaparra returned, Reese started only 17 games in a utility role through July 19. He batted a weak .172 over that time. Reese injured himself taking swings in the batting cage and suffered an oblique muscle tear. He was placed on the disabled list and did not return until September.[47] By then Garciaparra was gone, traded to the Cubs, and Orlando Cabrera had been acquired as the new shortstop. Mark Bellhorn established himself at second base as the Red Sox drove on to clinch the wild card. Manager Terry Francona had a spot for Reese in the postseason, replacing Bellhorn defensively in the late innings when the Red Sox had a lead.

Reese ran for Bellhorn in the 10th inning of Game Three of the American League Division Series. He walked home on David Ortiz's game-winning home run. In the Championship Series, Reese replaced Bellhorn in Games Four, Six, and Seven as the Red Sox made their remarkable comeback after trailing the Yankees three games to none in the series. Reese threw out Ruben Sierra on a grounder with two out in the ninth in Game Seven to clinch the pennant for the Red Sox.

In the World Series, Reese finished all four games at second base as the Red Sox swept the Cardinals. A photographer captured him leaping onto the pile of his celebratory teammates. Reese sent one of his World Series jerseys to coach Mixon, the man who drove him to practice in high school.[48] His lasting memory of the 2004 season was the opportunity to be a teammate of Pedro Martínez, who Reese said "was just awesome." Reese also cherished his time with Manny Ramírez and Dave McCarty, who like him were drafted in 1991. "It was such a great time," he said.[49]

This was Reese's final time on a major-league field as a player. A free agent after the season, he signed a one-year contract with a team option with Seattle, having a chance to play every day. It was a gamble for Seattle, noting that Reese missed an average of 55 games per year. He injured his shoulder in the spring and underwent surgery, missing the 2005 season.

After the season the Mariners declined Reese's option and he signed a contract with the Florida Marlins for 2006.[50] He suddenly departed spring training. The Marlins, not hearing from him, terminated his contract. The situation involved another complicated family issue. "I was a single parent; I was missing my daughter. Things weren't going right," he said. "I love my family, and I wanted to do better for her. I wasn't feeling right. I didn't have the love for the game anymore. I did it wrong, yes, but it was the decision I made."⁵¹ In a way, Reese followed the advice he had heard when he was a boy: "Don't be like your father." Reese was there for his family even though it may have cost him another year or more of his career.⁵²

In 2008 the Washington Nationals signed Reese to a minor-league contract, but he retired after playing a few minor-league games.

Reese returned to South Carolina and joined his brother Angelo in running a trucking business. In 2015 he returned to Lower Richland to coach the baseball team for a couple of seasons. In 2017 he became the assistant coach of the South Carolina State softball team. The head coach was Cheretta Stevenson, a former softball player at North Carolina A&T. They met when Pokey was in the stands watching one of her games. In 2018 the head coach and assistant coach were married. Their wedding took place at Spirit Communications Park, home of the Columbia Fireflies. Groomsmen and bridegrooms were dressed in baseball uniforms, and instead of a first dance, his new bride threw Pokey a first pitch.⁵³ One member of the wedding party was "Slick," Pokey's dad, with whom he had reconciled.⁵⁴

As of 2022, the Reeses were devoting their time to a South Carolina youth travel baseball team.⁵⁵

Reese's comment about his marriage and newfound love also rings true of his life:

"It's amazing how God works," he said. "It took a while, but it finally came to fruition."⁵⁶

SOURCES

Thank you to Cassidy Lent, reference librarian at the A. Bartlett Giamatti Research Center at the Baseball Hall of Fame for providing their file on Pokey Reese, and to Pokey Reese, for speaking with the author after reviewing this biography. Besides the sources cited in the Notes, the author also utilized the following:

Baseball-reference.com

Retrosheet.org

NOTES

1. David Cloninger, "The Search for Pokey," *Columbia* (South Carolina) *State*, November 16, 2014: C6.
2. Chuck Finder, "Reese's Pieces: Poverty and Crime Have Made Life Complicated for the Pirates' Second Baseman, but on the Field Things Are Sweet," *Pittsburgh Post-Gazette*, June 14, 2002: B1.
3. John Erardi, "Between Freshly Painted Lines," *Cincinnati Enquirer*, August 19, 1997: D1.
4. Paul Daugherty, "Triple A Won't Tarnish Pokey's Day at the Top," *Cincinnati Enquirer*, April 2, 1997: D1.
5. "Marriages and Divorces," *The State*, June 15, 1989: 82.
6. Finder, "Reese's Pieces."
7. Finder, "Reese's Pieces"; Erardi, "Between Freshly Painted Lines," D5; Michael Bamberger, "Fast and Loose," *Sports Illustrated* Vol. 92 (24), June 12, 2000: 92.
8. Erardi, "Between Freshly Painted Lines," D5.
9. Finder, "Reese's Pieces."
10. Erardi, "Between Freshly Painted Lines," D5.
11. Bamberger, "Fast and Loose," 90-91; Several articles mention Calvin Sr. playing minor-league ball for the Pittsburgh Pirates. However, no minor-league record of a Calvin Reese can be found, and this author is skeptical of its accuracy. Perhaps he was only there in spring training.
12. Neil White, "Diamonds' Pitching, Defense Shaping Up," *The State*, March 1, 1990: 73.
13. Bertram Rantin, "13 Players Make AAAA-AAA Team," *The State*, June 7, 1990: 31; Amanda Mays, "Renovated Diamonds Reach Lower State Finals," *The State*, May 24, 1990: 86.
14. Neil White, "Reds Make LR Shortstop Reese First State Selection," *The State*, June 4, 1991: 1C.
15. "The Boys in Red," *Myrtle Beach* (South Carolina) *Sun-News*, December 12, 1990: 22.
16. Amanda Mays, "From the Beginning," *The State*, October 4, 1990: 109.
17. Neil White, "Reese Leads List of State Players in Amateur Draft," *The State*, June 3, 1991: 1C.
18. Neil White, "Ex-LR Star Reese Making Pro Mark," *The State*, May 27, 1992: 1C, 5C; Neil White, "Garcia's Single Decisive," *The State*, June 23, 1992: 1C.
19. Jeff Horrigan, "Reds' Top Pick of '91 Begins to Find Swing," *Cincinnati Post*, August 22, 1994: 1C.
20. Bill Peterson, "Major Prospects," *Cincinnati Post*, October 23, 1993: 5C.
21. Horrigan, "Reds' Top Pick of '91," 1C, 3C.
22. Many articles refer to this from 1994-1995. Two specifically are Hal McCoy's "Money Has Changed Game, Reds' Larkin Says," *Dayton Daily News*, April 16, 1995: 8D, and Andy Furman's "Reds Grooming Shortstop at Indianapolis," *Cincinnati Post*, May 26, 1995: 5C.
23. Jeff Horrigan, "Brantley Shelves Slider," *Cincinnati Post*, May 3, 1995: 3D; Furman, "Reds Grooming Shortstop"; Bill Benner, "Tribe's Reese Senses His Luck Is About to Turn," *Indianapolis Star*, May 30, 1996: E1.
24. Chris Haft and Rory Glynn, "Reds Try to Reach Out to Rijo," *Cincinnati Enquirer*, October 7, 1995: C2.
25. Kim Rogers, "Reese Suffers Knee Injury, But No Surgery Expected," *Indianapolis Star*, April 8, 1996: D3; Benner, "Tribe's Reese Senses His Luck Is About to Turn"; Kim Rogers, "Trimmed Tribe, 89ers Not Expected in Finale," *Indianapolis Star*, September 12, 1996: G8.
26. Tim Brown, "Is Grass Greener in the Outfield?" *Cincinnati Enquirer*, March 7, 1997: D9; Tim Brown, "Won't Trade Him; Won't Play Him," *Cincinnati Enquirer*, March 23, 1997: C12.
27. Daugherty, "Triple A Won't Tarnish."
28. Tim Sullivan, "Key Hit Helps Reese Feel at Home," *Cincinnati Enquirer*, April 13, 1997: C5.
29. Scott MacGregor, "Just One of Those (Opening) Days," *Cincinnati Enquirer*, April 1, 1998: C7; Bill Nowlin, "Lou Stringer," SABR BioProject. Retrieved July 4, 2022. sabr.org/bioproj/person/lou-stringer/.
30. Scott MacGregor, "Thumb Tear Ends Reese's Season," *Cincinnati Enquirer*, July 31, 1998: B5.

31 Tim Sullivan, "Reese Gives Reds a Powerful Stroke," *Cincinnati Enquirer*, September 27, 1999: D7.
32 "Baseball Insiders Realize Value of Reese to Reds," *Cincinnati Post*, December 15, 1999: 2B.
33 *2004 Red Sox Media Guide*, 239.
34 Erardi, "Between Freshly Painted Lines," D5.
35 Scott MacGregor, "Pokey Dealing With Life," *Cincinnati Enquirer*, March 8, 1998: D13.
36 MacGregor, "Pokey Dealing With Life."
37 *2004 Red Sox Media Guide*, 239.
38 John Erardi, "Can Reese Rise Again?" *Cincinnati Enquirer*, August 26, 2001: C10; Tony Jackson, "Tucker's Two-Year Extension Nearly Done," *Cincinnati Post*, January 24, 2001: 3B; John Fay, "Reds Finally Dump Pokey," *Cincinnati Enquirer*, December 19, 2001: D2; Tim Sullivan, "Pokey Reese: Moving Him May Not Be the Answer," *Cincinnati Enquirer*, July 29, 2001: C1.
39 Paul Daugherty, "Reds Baseball Is Wasting Away into 'Pirateville,'" *Cincinnati Enquirer*, December 19, 2001: D1.
40 Tom Kensler, "Rockies Acquire Reyes, Reese, White and Hudson in Trade," *Denver Post*, December 19, 2001: D3; Bob Hohler, "Reese Doesn't Get Offer," *Boston Globe*, December 22, 2001: G10.
41 Robert Dvorchak, "Reese, Pirates Good Fit; Second Baseman Says He Wants a 'New Start,'" *Pittsburgh Post-Gazette*, January 31, 2002: F1.
42 *2004 Red Sox Media Guide*, 238-239.
43 Ron Cook, "Reese's Play Gets the Fans in a Head-Bobbing Mood," *Pittsburgh Post-Gazette*, July 19, 2002: B1.
44 David Heuschkel, "Sox Safer at Second," *Hartford Courant*, December 24, 2003: C6.
45 Gordon Edes, "Reese Is Nice Grab for Sox," *Boston Globe*, December 24, 2003: D2.
46 Bob Ryan, "The Catch on This Day: His Increased Power," *Boston Globe*, May 9, 2004: C8.
47 Michael Silverman, "Gutierrez in for Reese," *Boston Herald*, July 22, 2004: 92.
48 White, "The Search for Pokey," C7.
49 Pokey Reese, interview with the author, July 25, 2022.
50 John Levesque, "Mariners' Gamble on Reese a Good One," *Seattle Post-Intelligencer*, January 6, 2005: D1; Associated Press, "M's Decline Options on Hasegawa, Reese," *Vancouver* (Washington) *Columbian*, November 2, 2005: B5.
51 White, "The Search for Pokey," C7.
52 Bamberger, "Fast and Loose," 92.
53 Chris Clark, "Wedding on a Diamond," *Orangeburg* (South Carolina) *Times & Democrat*, June 24, 2018: C1, C8.
54 "Cheretta & Calvin," Zola Wedding website. Retrieved July 1, 2022. zola.com/wedding/cherettaandcalvin2018/wedding_party
55 Pokey Reese, interview with the author.
56 Clark, "Wedding on a Diamond," C8.

Photo by Bill Nowlin.

DAVE ROBERTS

BY RICHARD BOGOVICH

"Dave Roberts is a novice manager, but he seems born to the task," longtime San Francisco sportswriter Bruce Jenkins wrote about the offseason Dodgers hire in mid-2016. "He took a disjointed clubhouse and made it whole, instilling a good-times brand of confidence and telling SI.com, 'I put my hand on each player every single day – literally.'"[1] Roberts was named NL Manager of the Year three months later, guided LA in 2017 to their first World Series since 1988, and won the 2020 World Series with them. Roberts apparently can be quite the spark, given that he is revered by Red Sox fans for a stolen base in 2004 that was crucial to the least likely postseason comeback ever. As an unusual indication of how memorable his stimulus for Boston was, more than a decade later general manager Daryl Morey of the NBA's Houston Rockets posted a video of Roberts' theft on social media as those basketballers also faced a deep playoff deficit.[2]

David Ray Roberts was born on May 31, 1972, in the city of Naha on the Japanese island of Okinawa to Eiko Ikehara and Waymon Dewitt Roberts. His mother was born in Japan on August 25, 1948, four days after his father was born in Liberty, Texas. Waymon Roberts was stationed at Okinawa during a long career in the United States Marines, during which he reached the rank of master gunnery sergeant.[3]

Dave's sister, Melissa, was born in California in the summer of 1973.[4] During their childhood the family moved from one military base to another a considerable distance away. The family's first move was from Okinawa to California, and they had later stints in North Carolina and Hawaii before finally settling in the San Diego area in 1984.[5]

Dave Roberts received periodic attention on local sports pages while attending Washington Middle School in Vista,[6] which is in San Diego County about 40 miles north of San Diego. His earliest mentions by sportswriters, as both Dave and David, might have been during the winter of 1984-1985 while playing in the Vista Parks & Recreation Junior Basketball Association with a team called the Traveling Panthers (or vice versa).[7] Not much later, David Roberts of Washington Middle School won the 100-meter race among boys born in 1972 during the Vista City Track Meet held on April 13.[8] Three more months later, Roberts was a member of the Vista Pony League "13-year-old All-Stars" as they won a district championship and competed in sectionals.[9]

On May 3, 1986, David Roberts again won a 100-meter dash among boys born in 1972, with a time of 12.06 seconds. This time the event was the San Diego County Track and Field Championships. Meanwhile, Melissa Roberts placed fourth among girls born in 1973.[10] About four years later, she was on their high-school track team as a short sprinter.[11]

In June 1986 Dave Roberts was instrumental in his Sport About team's Pony League championship finale, with a home run and a save in relief.[12] That fall he was a freshman at Vista High School. In a lengthy 1989 interview for the *San Diego Tribune*, about midway through his senior year of high school, Roberts said he was promoted to Vista's varsity football team as a freshman but couldn't play because he was only 15 years old. "I told Coach [Dick] Haines it would be a good idea if I didn't suit up," Roberts recalled. "I didn't want to just stand there and do nothing. So I sat up in the stands. I knew I had three more years."[13] In the spring of 1987 he played baseball for Vista High as a freshman, and was named the Most Valuable Player of the junior varsity team, which won 19 out of 22 games.[14]

For his sophomore year, Roberts switched to the brand-new Rancho Buena Vista High School. A *Los Angeles Times* sportswriter in an article on the difficulties of launching an athletic program at such a new institution, quoted the varsity football team's sophomore quarterback. "It's a challenge. We're the underdogs. We want to take advantage of that," Roberts said. "We want to be ourselves. We want to build our own tradition."[15] Soon enough, Roberts was doing his utmost to build those traditions as a basketball player[16] and then as a baseball player as well. No RBV baseball player was named to the Avocado League's First Team after the 1988 season and only one was named to the Second Team, but Roberts was one of two teammates to receive Honorable Mention.[17]

As the Longhorns prepared for the 1988 football season, Roberts suffered a knee injury in spring practice so serious that it was known well in advance of the regular season that he wouldn't play at all. Coach Craig Bell described the uncommon characteristic he hoped for in a replacement for Roberts at that time. "A bomb could go off beside him and he'd just smile and go on," said Bell. "That kind of leadership is invaluable on the field, especially from a quarterback."[18] That positive, unflappable attitude was likely important during Roberts' very gradual recovery, because at some point he was told by at least one doctor that he'd never play any sports again.[19]

Roberts' injury was to his right knee's anterior cruciate ligament and required major reconstructive knee surgery. He stood with his teammates during games, wearing a cast that encased his leg from thigh to ankle. When Roberts returned to the team as a senior, Bell's praise shifted from his quarterback's poise as a sophomore to his intelligence. "He's like having another coach on the field," Bell said, which now seems like foreshadowing. "He makes life easy for me. If he were a coach, I'd probably be out of a job."[20]

It was estimated that Roberts played most of the football season of his senior year at 85 percent of his capability, but the Longhorns won the California Interscholastic Federation Division I title, setting a record for total yards of offense in the process. "David was the single biggest reason we won the CIF title," said Bell. "He wouldn't allow the team to lose. He drove that team every hour, every minute, every day of the season."[21]

Roberts lettered in football, basketball, and baseball at Rancho Buena Vista.[22] His high-school baseball career ended on a personal high note in mid-1990 when he was the only RBV player named to the CIF All-Section team.[23] Still, because his severe knee injury also caused him to miss his junior year of baseball, his chance to be recruited by colleges had been undercut considerably. As it was, his only offer for collegiate football came from the Air Force Academy. Though football was his first love, he reasoned that baseball was the more promising option after high school. He was a walk-on at UCLA and became a scholarship recipient his sophomore year there.[24]

Roberts was named to the All-Pac-10 Team in 1992 and 1994, and lettered each season from 1991 through 1994.[25] By the time he graduated in 1995, he'd set a university record for most stolen bases. That resulted in large part from setting a record for stolen bases as a senior. When he left UCLA, he ranked second all-time in runs scored, third in triples, fifth in hits, and fifth in walks. He earned a degree in history; he also developed a shoulder so sore that it required surgery.[26]

Through mid-1994, Roberts considered his greatest thrill in baseball to have occurred in 1992, which was playing in an NCAA regional championship game in Starkville, Mississippi, on the cusp of the College World Series.[27] The game was played on May 24, the same day UCLA eliminated Mississippi State. Though UCLA was shut out by Oklahoma, Roberts led off and had two hits in four at-bats.[28]

Roberts was selected in baseball's June 1993 amateur draft by the Cleveland Indians, though not until the 47th round.[29] His UCLA coach, Gary Adams, said Roberts seemed acutely aware that seven of his UCLA teammates who were also juniors were drafted much higher. "He came into my office after the draft was held feeling really down in the dumps," Adams recalled. "I didn't see him that way really often." Roberts, who decided not to sign with Cleveland, quickly requested advice from Adams on how to get drafted higher the next year, and Adams theorized that scouts were looking for stronger throws from an outfielder. Adams and fellow coaches Don Tamburro and Vince Beringhele helped Roberts with that the following season, and Roberts led UCLA outfielders in assists.[30] All that effort did come at a cost. "I wasn't used to all that throwing," Roberts said, because he'd mostly been a designated hitter during his first three seasons at UCLA. "So I hurt my shoulder, and it required surgery."[31]

Nevertheless, the Detroit Tigers selected Roberts in the 28th round of the June 1994 draft, and he accepted a bonus of $1,000.[32] He also secured a guarantee from Detroit that the club would help finance the remainder of his undergraduate education.[33] Roberts signed his first pro contract on June 9, 1994. Dennis Lieberthal was the scout who arranged that.[34]

Roberts was assigned to the Jamestown Jammers of the Class-A New York-Penn League. The club began its season on June 16,[35] but when Roberts signed, he informed the Tigers that he wouldn't report to Jamestown until he was done at UCLA that semester, and thus his arrival was delayed about two weeks. It took another week for him to crack the starting lineup.[36] His name didn't appear in Jamestown stats printed by the *Detroit Free Press* on June 29, which covered their New York affiliate's first 10 games.[37]

Roberts made his professional debut on June 28, 1994, in Jamestown. In hindsight decades later, it was fitting that he took part only as a pinch-runner. He didn't steal a base off the Welland Pirates, but did score a run in what turned out to be a 17-inning marathon, won by Jamestown, 8-7.[38] Jamestown's scheduled game the next day was rained out, so his next chance to play was in a doubleheader on June 30.[39] He led off the first game as the DH and went 0-for-4.[40] After the team's first 22 games, Roberts was just 6-for-34 (.176).[41] He overcame this very slow start to hit .292 by the end of the short 1994 season.

For the remainder of the decade, Roberts advanced steadily toward the majors. After hitting .303 in 1995, he reached Double-A partway into 1996, the first of several seasons he split at two different levels. His combined total of stolen bases for 1996 was 65, which led minor leaguers at all levels.[42]

Roberts played a full season at Double A in 1997 and had a .296 batting average. On November 8 of that year, he married his high-school sweetheart, Tricia Schempp. Their relationship dated back to the spring of 1988, around the time he suffered the serious knee injury that cost him his junior season of football.[43]

On June 24, 1998, Roberts was involved in a trade for the first time, when Detroit packaged him and pitcher Tim Worrell to Cleveland in exchange for outfielder/DH Geronimo Berroa.[44] He hit .326 at Double-A Jacksonville before the trade, and hit .361 for Double-A Akron afterward. He tied an Akron record with a 22-game hitting streak.[45] He also played his first Triple-A ball in 1998, for Cleveland's affiliate in Buffalo, though he played in just five games.

In mid-1999, Roberts had a big thrill when he was named to Team USA for that summer's Pan Am Games.[46] His manager at Buffalo, Jeff Datz, advised him that missing up to three weeks of high-level pro ball in favor of amateur competition might have a negative effect after his return, but Roberts was eager to take that risk. "I figured you have a limited chance to play for your country so you might as well take it," he said. His father's time in the Marine Corps was also a motivation. "He represented this country for three decades; the least I could do was two weeks."[47] Roberts helped Team USA earn a spot in the 2000 Olympics by hitting .308 in the leadoff spot and swiping four bases. "It was incredible – the best experience of my life," Roberts declared. He then returned to Buffalo for just two games before even more exciting news: Cleveland had called him up to the majors to sub for injured superstar Kenny Lofton.[48]

Roberts made his major-league debut with the Indians on August 7, 1999, in Tampa Bay. He was put atop Cleveland's batting order and assigned to patrol center field. More than 38,000 fans watched him thrive beginning in the second inning. To begin the game, he grounded out to pitcher Bobby Witt after a first-pitch strike, but in the next inning he worked the count to 3-and-1. He then lined a two-out double toward the left power alley for his first hit in the majors, though the following batter's out left him there. All told, Roberts went 3-for-5 with a walk, a stolen base, and three runs scored as his team won a 15-10 slugfest. Regardless, the game was of considerable historical significance because Wade Boggs homered with his hometown team for the 3,000th hit of his Hall of Fame career.[49]

Roberts hit his first home run in the majors at home on August 30, against Anaheim. He was in the leadoff spot and went 3-for-4 with four runs scored. The homer was off Ramon Ortiz in the second inning, with two outs and two men on base.

He stayed with Cleveland for the remainder of the regular season, and in 41 games had a .238 batting average. He capped his rookie season by appearing in two American League Divisional Series games against the Red Sox; he was 0-for-3 with two strikeouts. Roberts also spent some time the next two seasons with Cleveland, but the 41 games he played for them in 1999 were his maximum.

Dave and Tricia's life together took a new turn shortly after the 2000 season, when their first child was born on October 9, son Cole. He ultimately graduated from Santa Fe Christian School in Solana Beach, California. In June of 2019, Cole was chosen by the San Diego Padres in the 38th round of the amateur draft and as of the summer of 2023 was still listed on the roster of LA's Loyola Marymount University.[50]

On December 22, 2001, Cleveland traded Roberts to the Dodgers for minor-league pitchers Christian Bridenbaugh and Nial Hughes. Roberts had expected Cleveland to offload him that offseason. "I didn't know where I might end up, but it couldn't have worked out any better than it did," he said. "Cleveland is a great organization, but the opportunities there were hard to come by."[51]

Roberts' optimism was rewarded. He became a regular as he was turning 30, and continued as a starter the following five seasons, playing a minimum of 107 games in each from 2002 through 2007. Over those six years his 226 stolen bases ranked fourth among all major leaguers.[52]

In 2002 Roberts played in 127 games for the Dodgers, almost exclusively in center field, and had a solid .277 batting average. He reached base by hit or walk in 80 percent of his games. Some statistician took the time to determine that Roberts, Vladimir Guerrero, and Luis Castillo were the only three major leaguers that season to pair at least 40 walks with 40 or more stolen bases.[53]

Roberts' 2003 season represented a step backward, with a .250 batting average in 20 fewer games, but the hamstring soreness that contributed to that didn't prevent him from stealing 40 bases again. Only two other National League players stole that many.[54] It was business as usual for him with the Dodgers into the 2004 season, though better in at least one way: Through July, he'd swiped 33 bases and was caught stealing only once. On July 31 the Dodgers traded Roberts to the Red Sox for fellow outfielder Henri Stanley (whose pro career peaked at Triple A). Not surprisingly, it was reported that Boston wanted to obtain Roberts to improve their fielding and add speed. Though Roberts had missed three weeks on May after pulling a hamstring, he was expected to allow for some healing of starting center fielder Johnny Damon's nagging injuries. "It's great to have Dave around so this old, broken-down body can get a day off every now and then," Damon said, adding that they'd played together "on Team Florida years ago. He's a good player with speed who makes things happen on the basepaths."[55]

Before 2005's regular season began, Roberts revealed how he and Tricia reacted upon learning by phone that he had been traded by the Dodgers. "It was a bad day," she said. "At the time we thought it was the worst thing that could have happened." Complicating matters was the fact that Tricia was in the final weeks of pregnancy with their second child.[56] Emmerson Roberts, who often goes by Emme for short, was born at a Boston hospital on September 19. Her father skipped that afternoon's game in New York and was in time to witness the birth.[57]

Roberts played his first game for Boston on August 3, and over the next two months got into 45 games. His batting average was little better than in 2003, though his slugging percentage of .442 over those two months was his highest in the majors. He was on Boston's roster for the ALDS against the Anaheim Angels, but only entered the second of those three games, solely as a pinch-runner, and was forced out at second base on a grounder to short by Damon.

That set the scene for the American League Championship Series against the Yankees. On October 17, 2004, the Red Sox began play trailing three games to none, and entering the bottom of the ninth inning the score was Yankees 4, Red Sox 3. Future Hall of Famer Mariano Rivera was on the pitcher's mound, charged with preserving that lead. The first Boston batter he faced was Kevin Millar. Red Sox manager Terry Francona maintains that moments earlier he went down in the tunnel to tell Roberts that "Millar is going to get on and you're going to steal."[58] After Millar drew a walk, he immediately headed to the dugout and exchanged a quick gesture while passing

Roberts. "No words were necessary," Millar said. "It's not like I was about to give him baserunning advice."[59]

Even a decade later, for the book *Don't Let Us Win Tonight: An Oral History of the 2004 Boston Red Sox's Impossible Playoff Run* (from which Francona's and Millar's quotes above are excerpted), Roberts found it difficult to describe how he felt in that moment. "I can't tell you how many emotions went through me," he said. "To be honest, the fear of being the goat definitely went through my mind because I hadn't played in 10 days and didn't feel fresh."[60] One specific thought was a conversation on a Florida field in 2002. "Maury Wills told me that at some point in my career there will be an opportunity for me to steal a base, a big base, and everyone in the ballpark knows I'm going to steal, and I can't be afraid to steal that base," Roberts added.[61]

Roberts recalled feeling "really calmed" after Rivera's second pickoff attempt, and was glad Rivera hadn't begun with a quick-pitch to batter Bill Mueller. First-base coach Lynn Jones and Roberts seemed of like mind. "There was no doubt the pickoff throws heightened his senses," said Jones, who added, "They helped take those jitters away. He kept moving out there a little bit further, and we're talking about inches, but when you're out there that far, holy smokes. He's *way out there*."[62] After Rivera's third consecutive throw over to first, Roberts decided to go at the next sign of any meaningful movement by the pitcher. Roberts said the chest-high, outside pitch to Mueller wasn't a pitchout but functioned as one for catcher Jorge Posada.[63] One sportswriter succinctly summarized what happened next that night and in the days afterward:

> Mueller would single up the middle past a sprawling Rivera to score Roberts and tie the game. [David] Ortiz would hit a game-winning home run in the 12th inning. Less than 24 hours later, Millar again would walk and Roberts again would pinch run, this time participating in a less-remembered hit-and-run to reach third base and eventually score a Game 5-tying run on [Jason] Varitek's sacrifice fly off Rivera. And Ortiz would hit a game-winning single in the 14th inning.
>
> The Red Sox inconceivably would become the first team to climb out of an 0-3 playoff-series hole, would end the franchise's 86-year championship drought, would become an exemplary sum of unconquerable parts large and small.[64]

Roberts didn't get to play in the 2004 World Series against the St. Louis Cardinals, but that apparently made no difference to the legend he'd become. "For his singular contribution, Dave Roberts has been practically canonized in this town," Bob Ryan of the *Boston Globe* wrote seven years later. "No comparable Boston sports hero stakes his claim to eternal fan gratitude on the basis of one act that compassed about four seconds, give or take."[65]

On December 20, 2004, Roberts was sent to the team that played where he grew up. The Red Sox dealt him to the San Diego Padres for fellow major leaguers Jay Payton and Ramón Vázquez, future major leaguer David Pauley, and cash. Roberts responded by having his best two-year stint in the majors in 2005 and 2006. He hit .275 in 2005 and then followed that up by batting .293, easily his highest mark during any of his full seasons in the majors. In 2006 he tied Tony Gwynn for most triples in a season by a Padre, with 13.[66]

After both of those regular seasons Roberts experienced a National League Division Series against the Cardinals. He played in all three of the 2005 games and all four of the 2006 games. Though he hit only .222 in the Padres' 2005 NLDS, he did swat a homer at home, in the seventh inning of the final game. In the Padres' 2006 NLDS, he went 7-for-16 for an impressive .438 batting average. That concluded his postseason experience as a player.

On December 2, 2006, Roberts took advantage of free agency by signing a three-year, $18 million contract with the San Francisco Giants.[67] He batted .260 in 114 games for the Giants in 2007 but plunged to .224 in just 52 games the next season. Barely a week into April, he went on the disabled list, and didn't play for the Giants again until July 23, because he ultimately needed knee surgery, this time on his left knee.[68] The final game of his career as a player was on September 28, 2008, which was the season finale for the Giants, hosting the Dodgers. He singled as a pinch-hitter, and soon scored what turned out to be the winning run. On March 5, 2009, Roberts was released by the Giants.[69]

Within two months, Roberts was hired by the New England Sports Network as an in-studio analyst for Red Sox broadcasts.[70] Late that same year, one *Boston Globe* sportswriter summed up Roberts' performance across the season. "Roberts was almost too friendly, to the point where he was either reluctant to or incapable of criticizing players who had recently been his peers," Chad Finn wrote. "And he maintained many of the same verbal tics at the end that he had at the beginning, such as the habit of saying 'right there' or 'great' when analyzing a replay. In the end, he proved how difficult the transition to television really is."[71]

On December 7, 2009, Roberts was hired by the Padres as a special assistant for baseball operations.[72] One of his assignments during the subsequent spring training was to advise players how to read pitchers and get better jumps on stolen-base attempts.[73] About a week into May the Padres were leading the National League in steals, with a success rate above 80 percent, and Roberts received some of the credit.[74]

In May of 2010, Roberts announced that he had been diagnosed with Hodgkin's lymphoma, a kind of cancer. By the time he went public, he'd already had two rounds of chemotherapy.[75] In September he was found to be cancer-free, and on June 20, 2011, that was confirmed by the Dana-Farber Cancer Institute. He happened to be in town with the visiting Padres, for whom he'd switched to first-base coach shortly after the 2010 season. Fans at Fenway Park gave him a rousing ovation.[76]

After three seasons as first-base coach, on November 18, 2013, Roberts was promoted to bench coach for Padres manager Bud Black. He served in that secondary role for the 2014 and 2015 seasons, and even managed the Padres one game, on June

15, 2015, after Black left that role.⁷⁷ The Padres lost at home to Oakland, 9-1.

Around Halloween of 2015, Roberts was interviewed by the Dodgers to fill their managerial vacancy, and he "aced" it, according to *Los Angeles Times* sportswriter Bill Plaschke, who added that Roberts had apparently become the front-runner for the position. Plaschke endorsed that course of action fervently.⁷⁸ David Ray Roberts was announced as the Dodgers' new manager on November 23, 2015,⁷⁹ and he still held that job through 2023.

It wouldn't be difficult to double the length of this biography by cataloging the many insightful comments Roberts has offered in that high-profile role and by describing the countless ways he made and makes a difference as Dodgers manager, game to game, month to month, and season to season. Much more challenging is paring down a list of his highlights as a manager, but that's one of the assets of franchise media guides.

Roberts became the 32nd manager in the history of the franchise and just the 10th since the move from Brooklyn to Los Angeles for the 1958 season. He also became the Dodgers' first minority manager and the fourth to have both played for and later managed Los Angeles. His first Opening Day as manager was against the Padres on April 4, 2016, and the Dodgers' 15-0 cakewalk was the largest margin of victory in any Opening Day shutout in major-league history. After winning the NL's West Division in 2016, he was named NL Manager of the Year. The award, which was initiated in 1983, had gone to a first-year manager only five times before Roberts. During his second season, the Dodgers had a stretch where they won a staggering 43 of 50 games, which hadn't happened since the 1912 New York Giants. His 195 wins across the 2016 and 2017 regular seasons are the fifth most by any manager in his first two years.⁸⁰

When the Dodgers qualified for the playoffs in 2021, Roberts became the first major-league manager to lead his team to the postseason in his first six full seasons with that franchise. He extended that record in 2022 when the Dodgers won 111 games, a franchise record, In establishing that, he exceeded his own record of 106 wins, which he set in 2019 and tied in 2021. The Dodgers have captured three NL pennants under Roberts and won the 2020 World Series. Despite the Dodgers' frequent successes in recent decades, it can be easy for even the oldest fans to forget that Roberts became only the third manager in franchise history to achieve that ultimate championship.⁸¹

Roberts' father only lived long enough to experience his son's 2016 successes. Waymon Roberts died shortly before Opening Day 2017, on March 17, at the age of 68.⁸² He is buried at Eternal Hills Memorial Park in Oceanside, California. His gravestone notes that he received the Good Conduct Medal during his time in the Marine Corps.⁸³

About half a year later, Dave Roberts admitted that his father talked him out of quitting baseball after the 1995 season, his second in the minor leagues. Though he had made the Florida State League all-star team, for 1996 the Tigers sent him to yet another Class-A team, the Visalia Oaks, which was considered a destination for marginal prospects. It helped that Waymon was less than six hours away by car.⁸⁴ Fans of the Boston Red Sox and Los Angeles Dodgers, among innumerable other baseball enthusiasts, certainly remain very glad Dave Roberts didn't choose a different career before the turn of the century.

SOURCES

Except where otherwise noted, information about Roberts' personal life and managerial accomplishments is from the *2022 Los Angeles Dodgers Media Guide* (see Note 81). The primary source for his statistics and individual game information as a player, including during postseasons, is baseball-reference.com.

NOTES

1   Bruce Jenkins, "Bochy's Crew Has the Edge over L.A.," *San Francisco Chronicle*, August 14, 2016: B1, B3.

2   Diamond Leung, "Warriors One Win away from NBA Finals," *Sacramento Bee*, May 25, 2015: B6, B10.

3   Dave Roberts' completed Howe Sportsdata International questionnaire dated September 1, 1994 (accessible via ancestry.com). See also Eiko Roberts' 1991 naturalization paperwork and the Texas Birth Index, 1903-1997, accessible via genealogical websites, plus Waymon's findagrave.com entry, especially the gravestone photograph.

4   California Birth Index, 1905-1995, accessible via genealogical websites. A distinguishing detail in this index is the mother's maiden name.

5   Billy Witz, "Dodgers' New Manager Reflects on Team's Ties to Breaking Barriers," *New York Times*, December 2, 2015: B13. Andy McCullough, "Unifying Dodgers Is His Purpose," *Los Angeles Times*, February 14, 2016: A1, A16, A17.

6   Bill and Jean Rath, "Sports Letters," *North County Times* (Oceanside, California), April 9, 2003: C-4.

7   For example, see "Youth Basketball," *Escondido* (California) *Times-Advocate,* January 24: 1985: C6. One of Roberts' teammates was Junior Moi, with whom he would later play Pony League baseball and high-school sports.

8   "Youth Track and Field," *Escondido Times-Advocate*, April 14, 1985: D4.

9   "Vista Stars Stopped in Ramona," *Escondido Times-Advocate*, July 25, 1985: D4. Junior Moi was also on this team, which adds credence to the presumption that it was the same David Roberts on those teams.

10 "Track and Field," *Escondido Times-Advocate*, May 15, 1986: D4.

11 John Schlegel, "Rivalry to Replace Jorgensen Will Have to Wait," *Solana Beach* (California) *Blade-Citizen,* March 15, 1990: C-4.

12 "Sport About Wins Vista Pony," *Escondido Times-Advocate*, June 26, 1986: D4.

13 Jeff Savage, "The Long Wait Is Almost Over for Quarterback of Longhorns," *San Diego Tribune*, December 7, 1989: D-6.

14 J.P. Hoornstra, "How New Dodgers Manager Dave Roberts Emerged as a Leader at Every Stop," *Los Angeles Daily News*, November 25, 2015, accessible at https://www.dailynews.com/2015/11/25/how-new-dodgers-manager-dave-roberts-emerged-as-a-leader-at-every-stop/.

15 Steve Beatty, "Home on the Ranch," *Los Angeles Times:* September 10, 1987: Part III, 11, 13.

16 For example, see "Pollard Leads Torrey Pines to Rout," *Los Angeles Times*, December 6, 1987: III, 12.

17 "1988 Spring All-League Selections," *Escondido Times-Advocate*, June 5, 1988: D2.

18 Terry Monahan, "Longhorns Seek Winning Tradition," *Escondido Times-Advocate*, September 3, 1988: Football 1988 section, 8, 14.

19 John Maffei, "Racing Through Adversity," *North County Times* (Escondido, California), May 13, 1996: C-1. Andy McCullough, "Unifying Dodgers Is His Purpose," *Los Angeles Times*, February 14, 2016: A1, A16, A17.

20 Hoornstra.

21 Maffei, C-1.

22 Dave Roberts' completed Howe Sportsdata International questionnaire dated September 1, 1994 (accessible via ancestry.com).

23 "San Diego Day in Sports," *Los Angeles Times*, June 21, 1990: C13A.

24 Andy McCullough," Unifying Dodgers Is His Purpose."

25 Mike Leary, *UCLA Baseball 2014 Media Guide*: 99, accessible at https://ucla_ftp.sidearmsports.com/pdf/2014BaseballFullGuide.pdf. See page 73 for Roberts' seasonal stats with UCLA. His UCLA stolen-base records hadn't been eclipsed through at least 2013, as indicated on page 104.

26 Maffei, C-6. On this page, UCLA coach Gary Adams said Roberts wasn't drafted in 1993, at the end of his third year, but Adams apparently meant that Roberts didn't *sign* then. See other text herein quoting Adams about the June 1993 amateur draft.

27 Dave Roberts' Howe Sportsdata International questionnaire.

28 "NCAA Tournament," *Jackson* (Mississippi) *Clarion-Ledger,* May 25, 1992: 2C.

29 Chris Assenheimer, "Managers Reminisce about Their Playing Time in Cleveland," *Elyria* (Ohio) *Chronicle-Telegram,* July 10, 2019: B4.

30 Hoornstra. Though this article provided several insightful quotations, it incorrectly added that Roberts was drafted by Cleveland in the 28th round of the 1994 draft, but that second time he was drafted by Detroit.

31 Maffei, C-6.

32 McCullough, A17.

33 Steve Scholfield, "David Roberts Has His Priorities Straight," *Solana Beach Blade-Citizen*, September 9, 1994: C-1, C-2. In contrast to many other sources, Scholfield reported Roberts' bonus as $1,500 rather than $1,000.

34 Dave Roberts' Howe Sportsdata International questionnaire.

35 "Minor Leagues," *Philadelphia Daily News*, June 17, 1994: 134.

36 Scholfield, C-2.

37 "Tigers' Affiliates," *Detroit Free Press*, June 29, 1994: 9C.

38 Jim Riggs, "'After Midnight' Was Theme of Jammers' 17-Inning Win," *Jamestown* (New York) *Post Journal,* June 29, 1994: 21. It wasn't clear from the box score when Roberts might've entered the game, but Riggs did allude to a pinch-runner helping to propel a crucial four-run rally in the eighth inning.

39 "Pittsfield Mets Rained Out, Will Play 2 Games Tonight," *Berkshire Eagle* (Pittsfield, Massachusetts), June 30, 1994: C1.

40 "Mets, 6-1," *Berkshire Eagle*, July 1, 1994: C2.

41 "Tigers' Minor League Affiliates," *Detroit Free Press*, July 13, 1994: 7C.

42 See the back of Roberts' 1999 Bowman baseball card, number 392.

43 Scholfield, C-2. This article provided her surname, and in it Roberts indicated how long they'd been in a relationship. Their wedding date was specified by the same sportswriter late that decade. See Steve Scholfield, "Roberts to Make His Point," *North County Times*, November 7, 1999: C-1.

44 Gene Guidi, "Worrell for Berroa; Anderson Coming," *Detroit Free Press*, June 25, 1988: 7C.

45 Scholfield, "Roberts to Make His Point."

46 "Aeros Notes," *Akron* (Ohio) *Beacon Journal*, July 5, 1999: C6.

47 Steve Scholfield, "Roberts' Great Year Continues," *North County Times*, August 10,1999: C-1, C-5.

48 "Roberts' Great Year Continues." Roberts was not on the Team USA roster in the 2000 Olympics – see https://www.baseball-reference.com/bullpen/2000_Olympics_(Rosters)#United_States.

49 Bill Chastain, "Worth the Wade," *Tampa Tribune*, August 8, 1999: sports, 1, 14. This article incorrectly stated that Roberts' first hit in the majors was in the fourth inning; that was when he logged his second hit of the game. For detailed stats about this game, see https://www.baseball-reference.com/boxes/TBA/TBA199908070.shtml.

50 See https://www.baseball-reference.com/register/player.fcgi?id=roberto01col and https://lmulions.com/sports/baseball/roster/cole-roberts/12072.

51 "RBV Grad Roberts Traded to Dodgers," *North County Times*, December 22, 2001: C-5.

52 San Diego Padres Communications Department, *2011 San Diego Padres Media Guide*, 35.

53 See the back of Roberts' 2003 Topps baseball card, number 544.

54 See the back of Roberts' 2004 Topps Heritage baseball card, number 368.

55 Nick Cafardo, "Glove at First Sight: Newcomers Can Field," *Boston Globe*, August 1, 2004: C7. For information about Stanley's minor-league career, see https://www.baseball-reference.com/register/player.fcgi?id=stanleo01hen.

56 Chuck Culpepper, "Stolen Moment," *Newsday* (Long Island, New York), March 6, 2005: B8.

57 Peter May, "Wife's Surgery Sends Cabrera on Home Run," *Boston Globe*, September 21, 2004: F5.

58 *Four Days in October* (ESPN Films 30 for 30), Major League Baseball Productions, 2010.

59 Allan Wood and Bill Nowlin, *Don't Let Us Win Tonight: An Oral History of the 2004 Boston Red Sox's Impossible Playoff Run* (Chicago: Triumph Books, 2014), 126.

60 Wood and Nowlin, 127.

61 Wood and Nowlin, 127.

62 Wood and Nowlin, 128.

63 Wood and Nowlin, 129.

64 Culpepper, B13.

65 Bob Ryan, "Stolen Glory in '04," *Boston Globe*, October 14, 2011: C1.

66 San Diego Padres Communications Department, *2011 San Diego Padres Media Guide*, 35.

67 Andrew Baggarly, "Giants Fill a Need for Speed, Adding Roberts," *Oakland Tribune*, December 2, 2006: Sports, 8.

68 "Giants Place Roberts on DL," *San Francisco Examiner*, April 9, 2008: A24. Janie McCauley, "Giants Still Alive in NL West," *San Francisco Examiner*, July 17, 2008: A39.

69 Andrew Baggarly, "Giants Swallow Pride, Roberts' $6.5M Contract," *Oakland Tribune*, March 5, 2009: Sports, 1-2.

70 Chad Finn, "NESN's Edwards Man of His Words," *Boston Globe*, May 1, 2009: C9.

71 Chad Finn, "Hitting the Ground Running," *Boston Globe*, December 11, 2009: C3.

72 Peter Abraham, "Relationship No Longer Dicey," *Boston Globe*, December 8, 2009: C6.

73 Manny Navarro, "Question of the Week," *Miami Herald*, April 25, 2010: 6D.

74 John Shea, "Padres Finally a Fit for Petco," *San Francisco Chronicle*, May 9, 2010: B6.

75 Nick Cafardo, "Roberts Won't Run from This," *Boston Globe*, May 4, 2010: C2.

76 Michael Vega, "Rizzo Finally Makes His Debut at Fenway," *Boston Globe*, June 21, 2011: C2. See also San Diego Padres Communications Department, *2011 San Diego Padres Media Guide*, 35.

77 San Diego Padres Communications Department, *2011 San Diego Padres Media Guide*, 35. *2018 Los Angeles Dodgers Guide*, 16.

78 Bill Plaschke, "Authority Figures," *Los Angeles Times*, November 4, 2015: D1, D7.

79 Dylan Hernandez, "Roberts' Story Is Human Interest," *Los Angeles Times*, November 24, 2015: D1, D7.

80 *2018 Los Angeles Dodgers Guide*, 16.

81 *2022 Los Angeles Dodgers Media Guide*, 24.

82 Andy McCullough, "Kershaw Takes Long View after Three-Homer Outing," *Los Angeles Times*, March 18, 2017: D10.

83 See https://www.findagrave.com/memorial/182341718/waymon-dewitt-roberts.

84 Steve Wulf, "Roberts' return to L.A. 'was meant to be,'" ESPN.com, October 9, 2017, accessible at https://www.espn.com/mlb/story/_/id/20914762/los-angeles-dodgers-manager-dave-roberts-took-long-road-back-home-la. This article offered several familial anecdotes.

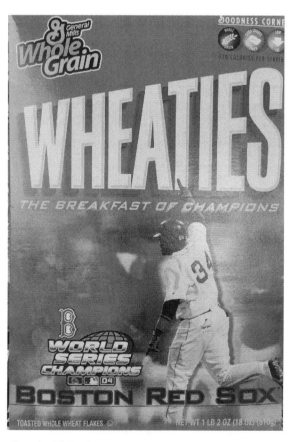

Photo by Bill Nowlin.

CURT SCHILLING

BY BILL NOWLIN

Curt Schilling's father, Cliff, served in the United States Army for 22 years, a master sergeant with the 101st Airborne Division who was stationed at Elmendorf Air Force Base adjacent to Anchorage, Alaska, when his son Curtis Montague Schilling was born on November 14, 1966. Curt was the middle child of Cliff and Mary Schilling.

Sgt. Schilling introduced his son to baseball early; a biographical entry on ESPN says, "When Curt was brought home from the hospital, there was a baseball glove in the crib that Cliff had placed there."[1] The same bio continued, "The family moved to Kentucky, Illinois and Missouri before finally settling in Phoenix, Ariz. Curt's father was a Pirates fan, and the first baseball game Curt ever attended was Roberto Clemente's last."

A power-pitching right-hander, Curt Schilling struck out 3,116 major-league batters, one of only 16 pitchers to join the 3,000 Strikeout Club. Schilling and Roger Clemens are the only two "members" of this exclusive club not yet inducted into the National Baseball Hall of Fame.

With a postseason record of 11-2, Schilling holds another distinction: No one with 10 or more postseason decisions has a better winning percentage (.846).[2] He has won World Series games for three different franchises – the Phillies, Diamondbacks, and Red Sox. With Randy Johnson, he was co-MVP of the 2001 World Series.[3] When pitching for the Red Sox, he won game in each of the three rounds of the playoffs in 2004 and again in 2007, his most courageous performance being his famous "bloody sock" win over the Yankees in the 2004 American League Championship Series, one that he reprised against the Cardinals in that year's World Series just five days later. He was told by the surgeon who sutured his tendons in place that it was a procedure that probably couldn't be done a third time.

Ryan Spaeder has pointed out that there were five games Schilling started when his team was facing elimination. In those five games, he pitched to a 1.37 ERA, and his team won all five games. There were three games in which he was given starts when his team had the opportunity to clinch. In those three games, he pitched to a 1.16 ERA, and his team won all three games.[4]

Schilling struck out 120 and walked 25 in postseason play.

In the regular season, his 3,116 strikeouts are balanced against only 711 walks, 4.38 K's for every BB. As of 2015 that is the best strikeouts-to-walks ratio of any pitcher to ever play in the majors since 1900 who struck out at least 1,000. Pedro Martínez ranks second with 4.15.

Spaeder pointed out that Schilling threw 64 games in which he struck out at least seven opponents and walked no one. That's the most of any pitcher in history. Randy Johnson ranks second with 54 and Greg Maddux is third, with 44. He also wrote, "No pitcher in baseball history has both a higher strikeout percentage and a lower walk percentage than Schilling had in his career."[5]

Three times – 1997, 1998, and 2002 – Schilling recorded more than 300 strikeouts. Speaking of walks and strikeouts, he set another record in 2002 that dates back to at least 1946 and perhaps to 1900: From May 13 to June 8, he didn't walk a batter for a stretch that embraced 56 strikeouts. Second and third on the list is Greg Maddux, who had a 53-strikeouts-without-a-walk streak in 2001 and Pedro Martínez, at 49 in 2000.[6]

Schilling is a six-time All-Star, and finished second in Cy Young Award voting in 2001, 2002, and 2004. He won 216 major-league games, and lost 146.

By the time Curt was in high school, at Shadow Mountain High School in Phoenix, he was playing baseball, but he didn't make the varsity until his senior year. There had been talks with scouts, but they were shelved after Schilling suffered a broken left elbow on a hit-by-pitch during the summertime. He enrolled at Yavapai Junior College in Prescott, Arizona, a school that has produced 15 major leaguers through 2014. In 1986 he went to the Junior College World Series, the fifth time a Yavapai team had reached the series. The right-hander was drafted by the Boston Red Sox as their choice in the second round of the January 1986 draft; he signed on May 30.

The Red Sox assigned Schilling to the Elmira Pioneers in the New York-Penn League, where he had a 7-3 record with a 2.59 ERA, 75 strikeouts, and 30 walks in 93 innings. It was a good first start in professional baseball.

In 1987 he maintained a strong strikeouts-to-walks ratio, with 189 K's and 65 BB's for the South Atlantic League's Greensboro Hornets. The team's record was 55-85, and Schilling's 8-15 came close to reflecting that. His 3.82 ERA indicates a more difficult season.

Schilling began 1988 at Double A, pitching for Boston's New Britain Red Sox (8-5, 2.97 in 21 games) but was traded (along with outfielder Brady Anderson) to the Baltimore Orioles for pitcher Mike Boddicker as the Red Sox prepared to make a run for the pennant. He was 5-2 (3.18) for Charlotte, before the Orioles called him to the big leagues in time to make his first appearance on September 7. The Red Sox were visiting Baltimore and Schilling was given the start. The home-plate umpire was Steve Palermo. Curt's father, Cliff, had died eight months earlier, in January, of brain cancer at age 52.[7] Curt later said, "My father was the glue that held us together. When he died, I kind of lost my family." Curt was said to be "estranged from his mother and older sister."[8]

"I saw a scared kid," Palermo told writer Joe Posnanski years later. He said he saw how nervous Schilling was and told him, "You get that first pitch close, I'll call it a strike. And we'll get this game going." Looking at the play-by-play of the game, it seems Schilling did quite a good job, but the reality on the field was that he had forgotten the signs and was throwing unexpected pitches. He worked seven innings and gave up three runs on six hits, but he walked five. He hadn't thrown a wild pitch, but the way Posnanski told it, he kept hitting Palermo with pitches. Finally, Palermo said, he went out to the mound with a ball and said, "You're OK, kid. Just relax. You're going to make it in this game. You've got what it takes. It's all going to be OK. Just relax and throw strikes."[9] The 4-3 game was won by the Orioles in the bottom of the ninth, but Schilling was gone by then. For the Orioles in September 1988, he lost his next three starts and was 0-3 with a 9.82 ERA.

He was still just 21. It took him a little more time to truly be ready for big-league pitching.

Schilling was a September pitcher again in 1989. After a 13-11 season with Rochester with a good 3.21 earned-run average, he got the call back to Baltimore and was 0-1 with a 6.23 ERA in five appearances. He began the 1990 season with Rochester again, but was brought up near the end of July and got his first extended taste of major-league pitching, working exclusively in relief, working 46 innings in 35 games, with an excellent 2.54 ERA. He did book his first win, but was tagged with two more losses. On January 10, 1991, he was traded to the Houston Astros (with Steve Finley and Pete Harnisch) for Glenn Davis.

Now in the National League, Schilling worked 56 games in relief in 1991, with a 3-5 record and a 3.82 ERA. Just before the 1992 season began, he was traded to the Philadelphia Phillies straight up for Jason Grimsley on April 2.

With the Phillies, Schilling settled in. His first year was also manager Jim Fregosi's first. Schilling pitched nine seasons with the Phillies and won 101 games. His first year, 1992, was one of the best – a 2.35 earned-run average and a league-leading WHIP (walks and hits per inning pitched) of 0.990. With 26 starts (and 16 relief appearances), Schilling won 14 games, losing 11 for a sixth-place team. He threw 10 complete games.

It was also the year Schilling married Shonda Michelle Brewer, a graduate of Towson State University in Maryland whom he met when she was moonlighting at Foot Locker. She came from a blue-collar family in Baltimore.[10]

The 1993 Phillies went all the way to the World Series. Schilling (16-7) and Tommy Greene (16-4) tied for the team lead in wins. Schilling was named MVP of the NLCS against Atlanta. In the World Series, against the Toronto Blue Jays, he was tagged for seven runs (six earned) in Game One, and bore the loss. In Game Five, when a Jays win would have given them the championship, Schilling threw a five-hit, 2-0 shutout. Toronto won Game Six and the Series.

The Phillies didn't have another season that even got them to .500 until 2001, at which point Schilling was gone.

Schilling had two really rough years in 1994 and 1995. Starting the 1994 season with a subpar spring training and then going 0-7 made it clear that something was wrong. Though among the losses were a 2-1 one-hit effort through seven and a 1-0 loss, his earned-run average climbed to 5.40 during the stretch through May 16, after which he didn't pitch for two months because of surgery to remove bone spurs on his right elbow. Then the player strike brought about an end to the season; Schilling looked back on a 2-8 year. In 1995 he suffered a torn labrum and after July 18 needed season-ending surgery. He came back on May 14, 1996, with seven innings of no-run ball and was clearly back on track. In 1996 Schilling started 26 games and led the league with eight complete games. His won-lost record reflected the team; he was 9-10, but he pitched with a 3.19 ERA, ranking him seventh.

Schilling's first All-Star Game was in 1997; he pitched two innings, striking out three and not allowing a run. By year's end, he had 319 strikeouts, leading the league, and he had a record of 17-11 (2.97). He was named to the All-Star team in both '98 and '99. He didn't appear in 1998, but started the 1999 game (at Fenway Park) and bore the loss, giving up two runs in two innings. He struck out an even 300 opponents in 1998 and led the majors with 15 complete games. In both 1998 and 1999, Schilling won 15 games. From July 23, 1999, when he had to leave a game due to right biceps and shoulder issues, to September 3, he appeared in only one game, giving up eight runs.

In 2000 there was a change of scene. Schilling had a middling 6-6 (3.91) record as the trade deadline approached; on July 23, the Arizona Diamondbacks traded four players so they could add Schilling to their rotation: The Phillies got Omar Daal, Nelson Figueroa, Travis Lee, and Vicente Padilla. Schilling more or less continued as he had been, 5-6 with a 3.69 ERA the remainder of the season.

But in 2001 the Diamondbacks got everything they had been hoping for, and maybe more. Schilling had a dominant 22-6 season, with a 2.93 earned-run average, leading the league in wins and coming in second only to teammate Randy Johnson in ERA.

Come the postseason, Schilling shone. He threw a three-hit shutout in Game One of the Division Series against the Cardinals. He won the clinching Game Five with a 2-1 complete game. In the League Championship Series, he pitched once, again throwing a complete game and again giving up just one run. This put Schilling in position to start Game One of the World Series against the New York Yankees. He allowed three hits and one run in seven innings, winning the game and improving his record to 4-0 in the 2001 postseason. At this point he had a 0.79 ERA. He started two more games in the World Series, Game Four (again seven innings, three hits, one run) and Game Seven (7⅓ innings, with six hits and two runs.) Both Games Four and Seven were closely contested games, the Yankees winning Game Four in the 10th inning and the Diamondbacks winning the deciding Game Seven with two runs in a come-from-behind bottom of the ninth.

Schilling's final record in the 2001 postseason was 4-0 (1.12) and he was named co-MVP of the World Series with Randy Johnson. Johnson had been 21-6 in the regular season, and was 5-1 (1.52) in the postseason, 3-0 in the World Series itself, winning the final Game Seven when he threw the final inning and a third in hitless relief.

The next season, 2002, was very similar to 2001. Schilling won one more game and lost one more, for a still very enviable 23-7. His ERA nudged up to 3.23, a figure most pitchers could only aspire to get down to. His 0.968 WHIP led the league and was the best of his career. For the second year in a row, Schilling placed second in Cy Young voting. (Both times Randy Johnson was first.) Schilling started the All-Star Game again, giving up one hit and no runs in the first two innings. When it came to the postseason, he couldn't have pitched much better – one run in seven innings of Game Two of the Division Series against St. Louis, but the Cardinals swept.

Schilling's 2003 season saw him have an appendectomy and then, on May 30, he was struck twice on his right hand by batted balls and broke the hand. He battled through the season and emerged with a 2.95 ERA but a record of 8-9. (No pitcher on Arizona had more than 10 wins.)

After the 2003 season, with an excruciating last-minute loss to the Yankees in the ALCS, the Boston Red Sox were ready to make some dramatic moves. The team was in the first couple of years of new ownership and with a new GM on board in Theo Epstein. They wanted to get Curt Schilling and they wanted to get a new closer. Epstein made a later-celebrated trip to the Schilling household in Scottsdale, and he came prepared with just the sort of data that would show he'd done his homework and impressed the detail-oriented Schilling. Gracious hosts, the Schillings even invited Epstein and assistant GM, Jed Hoyer, to have Thanksgiving dinner at their home. Some of the data showed that Fenway Park was by no means necessarily a bad park for a right-handed power pitcher.

Schilling broke the mold in a number of ways, and one of them was in acting as his own agent. He talked turkey with the Sox emissaries and said he'd be on board if they could pull off a deal with the Diamondbacks. In a November 28, 2003, deal, the D'backs got four players for Schilling – Casey Fossum, Brandon Lyon, Jorge de la Rosa, and minor-leaguer Mike Goss. In January, Boston got its closer in Keith Foulke.

Curt Schilling was back with the team that first drafted him. On signing, he famously said, "I guess I hate the Yankees now." Not that he hadn't already helped defeat them in the 2001 World Series. He also filmed a Ford commercial that ran in New England saying he was coming to Boston to win a championship. That's exactly what he helped do, with some unwanted but very real drama come playoff time.[11] He was also reunited with Terry Francona as his manager, Francona having managed the Phillies from 1997 through 2000 and having been hired by the Red Sox not that long after Schilling had signed.

Schilling was legendary for his preparation, and maintained a number of notebooks which he was sometimes seen to consult on the bench between innings. He was a good fit for catcher Jason Varitek, who kept equally well informed. Schilling praised his catcher on many occasions; one comment summarized it all: "He's one of the few catchers I have ever played with who I feel places 10 times more emphasis on his job behind the player than he does at the plate."[12]

Schilling led the American League with 21 wins; he lost six times, and worked to a 3.26 ERA. Johan Santana won the Cy Young; Schilling again finished second. The Red Sox and Yankees met again in the ALCS. Schilling won Game One in the Division Series against the Angels, but at a cost that appeared evident when it happened; he seemed to come up lame after making a play by the first-base line in the seventh inning. "I felt the tendon tear," he said later.[13] The Red Sox swept, so Schilling wasn't called on again until the ALCS. There he also pitched the first game, but right from the start it was clear he was hampered. Schilling gave up six runs in three innings and it looked probable that his season was done, and the Red Sox hopes would be dashed yet again.

The Yankees took the first three games, the third one a 19-8 beatdown in Boston. No team in history had ever come back from a three-games-to-none deficit and won a playoff series. But this year's Red Sox team was resilient. Dave Roberts stole a base; the Red Sox tied Game Four in the bottom of the ninth. In the bottom of the 12th, David Ortiz won it on a walkoff homer. In Game Five, Ortiz won another one in extras, a walkoff single in the bottom of the 14th. The two teams traveled to Yankee Stadium to play Game Six, and Curt Schilling had a medical procedure done by Dr. Bill Morgan on his damaged ankle to temporarily stitch his tendons back into place.[14]

There was some seepage of blood from the procedure and it shows through Schilling's white sanitary stockings while he was on the mound; the 4-2 win was built on Schilling's seven innings of one-run, four-hit pitching and a surprise three-run homer hit by Red Sox second baseman Mark Bellhorn. The Red Sox won Game Seven, a game that wasn't even close, over a now-demoralized New York team.

The Red Sox had won four in a row, and went on to make that eight consecutive wins, sweeping St. Louis in the World Series. Schilling pitched Game Two, at Fenway Park, allowing just an unearned run on four hits in six innings, again pitching on a sutured ankle, one that Dr. Morgan said could not have been rigged up for a third time. He got the win.

The Game Two victory made Curt Schilling the only pitcher to win a World Series game for three different teams. He'd won for the Phillies, Diamondbacks, and now the Red Sox.

After offseason surgery, Schilling was back in 2005 but his three starts in April were all poor ones and other injuries kept him from pitching again until July 14. "I came back way too early," he told ESPN's Bill Simmons after the season.[15] He worked exclusively in relief, primarily as the closer, until August 25, when he resumed starting. His record was 8-8 (with nine saves) and a 5.69 ERA. The Red Sox won the wild card again, but were swept by the White Sox in the Division Series and Schilling was not used.

In 2006 Schilling improved to a sub-4.00 ERA (3.97), with a record of 15-7 in 31 starts. He reached 3,000 strikeouts on August 30 in Oakland.

Schilling's final year on the mound was 2007, and he went out with glory, winning one game each in the Division Series (Game Three in Anaheim, seven innings, no runs), Game Six in the League Championship Series against Cleveland (seven innings, two runs), and Game Two in the World Series against the Colorado Rockies (5⅓ innings, one run). There had also been an unsuccessful start but a no-decision in ALCS Game Two.

On June 7 Schilling threw 8⅔ innings of no-hit ball against Oakland, only to yield a single. He was 9-8 for the season (3.87). He signed to come back for one last year in 2008, but was physically unable to perform, so – though anti-climactically – his last work from a major-league mound was his win in Game Two of the 2007 World Series.

Never one to shy from interaction with the public or the media, Schilling had been active on the Internet and with his own blog from at least the start of his time in Boston, and he was an inveterate gamer who had launched his own company in 2006, called 38 Studios, and who was determined to develop and launch a role-playing video game, *Kingdoms of Amalur: Reckoning*, which was indeed launched in February 2012. 38 Studios had relocated to Rhode Island, thanks to the state's Economic Development Corporation, which had wooed the company away from Massachusetts with a $75 million loan. The game was well received at first and reportedly sold well over 300,000 copies in its first month. But it had been very expensive to develop, and sales were not sufficient to cover costs as well as ongoing development of a new massively multiplayer game under the working title *Project Copernicus*. The studio was unable to meet a scheduled repayment, and unable to meet payroll. It ultimately went bankrupt, amid mutual recriminations including the studio's charge that the state had failed to come through on promises to fund the completion of the second game, which might have proved sufficiently successful.

For its part, the State of Rhode Island has sued Schilling and officials of its own Economic Development Corporation, alleging fraud and other acts that misled the state into granting 38 Studios the $75 million loan, which Rhode Island's taxpayers are obliged to repay.[16] (The loan and its consequences became the subject of a long-running battle in the state's political circles. Some have suggested that it soured the state on providing financial assistance that might have helped keep the Pawtucket Red Sox in Rhode Island rather than moving to Worcester, Massachusetts.)

A writer for *Forbes* once said, "Schilling overdoses on confidence."[17] Perhaps believing too strongly in his vision, in the product, and in himself, Schilling had pledged personal guarantees, and that came back to bite him as the company was forced into bankruptcy. This cost Schilling much of what he had been able to save from his earnings as a pitcher.

Working on the game took a toll, one that Schilling never mentioned during all the controversy over the financial problems and collapse of 38 Studios. In November 2011, he suffered a serious heart attack. The story only emerged two years later.[18]

The Schilling family name has long been associated with charitable causes. They became active in the fight against ALS (Lou Gehrig's disease) when Pennsylvania computer consultant Dick Bergeron was stricken with the disease in 1992. Beginning in 1993, Curt and his wife, Shonda, launched Curt's Pitch for ALS, which raised money for every strikeout he threw, the money to be used to help provide better quality of life for victims of the disease.[19] Within the first 15 years, they had raised over $10 million. The Schillings' oldest child, of four, is named Gehrig. Gabriella, Grant, and Garrison are the couple's three other children.

After Shonda Schilling was diagnosed with malignant melanoma in 2000. She had to undergo five surgeries to rid herself of the cancer. Part of the Schillings' response involved the founding of the Shade Foundation in 2002, described as "the only national children's foundation devoted to skin cancer education and prevention."[20]

Then in February 2014, Curt himself was diagnosed with cancer. The information was kept private for months but he had mouth cancer, squamous cell carcinoma, "which he believes was caused by a 30-year smokeless tobacco habit. He underwent radiation and chemotherapy, lost 70 pounds, had two bouts with pneumonia and a painful staph infection."[21] Stan Grossfeld wrote a lengthy feature on his addiction.[22] On June 25, 2014, Schilling announced on Twitter that his cancer was in remission and wrote, "Start the 5 year clock!"

The *Sports Illustrated* article briefly noted other challenges the Schilling family has faced: "Gehrig battled an eating disorder during his pre-teen years. Gabby has had some issues with her hearing. Grant has Asperger Syndrome, a form of autism."

That same article noted how Schilling had defended his daughter against cyber-bullies, quoting Gabby herself, "I didn't really like all the attention it got. But I began to see what he was doing wasn't just for me, but it was putting a spotlight on Internet bullying. I think he ended up getting a really good message out there."[23]

Shonda Schilling had sent messages of her own over the years, including becoming a marathoner after her cancer diagnosis, her 2005 run in the Boston Marathon alone raising over $50,000 for the Shade Foundation.[24] In March 2010, William

Morrow published her book, *The Best Kind of Different: Our Family's Journey with Asperger's Syndrome*.[25]

Asked in 2006 what he saw himself doing 10 years in the future, he replied, "Being a dad. I can't wait to pay back my wife and kids for the time they have sacrificed for my career. I owe them that."[26]

Schilling has received a number of recognitions for his charitable efforts, such as the 2001 Hutch Award (named after Fred Hutchinson) and the Roberto Clemente Award. In December 2002 *Worth* magazine named him its "Young Benefactor of the Year."[27] He later received the 2004 "Good Guy" award from *The Sporting News*. In 1996, *USA Today's Weekend* magazine had named him "Baseball's Most Caring Athlete."

In 2010 Curt Schilling was honored with inclusion in the Arizona Sports Hall of Fame, and in 2012 he was inducted into the Boston Red Sox Hall of Fame.

Any candidate for the National Baseball Hall of Fame needs 75 percent of the votes from the members of the Baseball Writers Association of America who participate in the election. Schilling received 39.2 percent in the totals announced in January 2015, a significant 10 percent increase from the previous year (down itself from the 38.8 percent he had received in 2013.) Asked for comment afterward, he made some good points about John Smoltz (who had quite similar stats) getting elected (with 82.9 percent of the votes) primarily because of Smoltz's association with the Atlanta Braves team that had won 14 consecutive trips to the postseason (ignoring 1994, when there was no postseason play). Smoltz has a 213-155 record (3.33 ERA) in the regular season and an exceptional 15-4 (2.67) record in the postseason. As noted above, Schilling's record in the regular season was 216-146 (3.46) with an 11-2 (2.23) record in the postseason.

Schilling suggested that his outspoken support of Republicans running for political office may have cost him 100 or more votes in his first years of eligibility. He later said he'd been joking. But Schilling has always been outspoken (*Boston Globe* columnist Dan Shaughnessy dubbed him a "blowhard" and wrote that he was incapable of saying, "No comment.") Tom Verducci wrote, "Schilling has always been a man without a mute button."[28] That has often rubbed people the wrong way. The subjective opinions of sportswriters have often been evident in MVP, Cy Young, and Hall of Fame voting. Schilling himself has said that he doesn't like doing interviews but always viewed it as a responsibility that comes with the job.[29]

Suffolk University marketing professor Daniel Ladik looked at it this way: "Schilling is a proven winner, a workhorse who wears his passion on his sleeve."[30] Red Sox GM Theo Epstein had his thoughts about Schilling's self-motivation. "One of the things people didn't realize about Schilling is that he was really motivated by fear, fear of failure," Epstein said. "He really did not want to fail, and he was very cognizant of his fear of failure. So he worked himself up through his nerves to go out and dominate to the best of his ability every time he had the ball. That was where some of the 'clutchness' came from, the realization that he had about how much he hated failure, and how much he feared failure."[31]

In 2010 ESPN hired Schilling as a studio analyst for *Baseball Tonight*, and in December 2013 he was given a multiyear contract extension, which included his joining the network's *Sunday Night Baseball* broadcast team.[32] Even that achievement had its potholes. In August of 2015, Schilling was yanked from ESPN telecasts of the Little League World Series after a tweet on Twitter in which he compared Muslim extremists to Nazis in Germany. A contrite Schilling said: "Bad choices have bad consequences and this was a bad decision in every way on my part." But after other inflammatory tweets, ESPN in September removed Schilling from its *Sunday Night Baseball* telecasts for the remainder of the season.[33]

Over the years, he seemed to become more vocal politically, and controversially so, perhaps intentionally. In 2021, he fell short of the number of votes necessary to be elected to the Hall of Fame, receiving 71 percent of the writers' vote (285 of 401), prompting headlines such as Politico's "Baseball Hall of Fame rejects politically outspoken star Curt Schilling."[34] *Boston Globe* columnist Dan Shaughnessy, no stranger to needling himself, wrote a column calling out Schilling for his support of the January 6, 2021 insurrection, among other things.[35] Schilling asked to be removed him from consideration on the ballot for 2022. He was not, and his percentage dropped to 58.6%.

SOURCES

In addition to the sources noted in this biography, the author also accessed Schilling's player file from the National Baseball Hall of Fame, Retrosheet.org, Baseball-Reference.com, and the SABR Minor Leagues Database, accessed online at Baseball-Reference.com. Thanks to Rob Neyer and Tom Ruane for assistance.

NOTES

1. espn.go.com/mlb/player/bio/_/id/2112/curt-schilling.
2. Mariano Rivera had a record of 8-1, and a much better 0.70 ERA, but lacked the one decision that would vault him to the (admittedly arbitrary) 10-decision level. One should note Lefty Gomez at 6-0 and Orlando Hernandez at 9-3. John Smoltz, a 2015 Hall of Fame inductee, stands at 15-4.
3. A good feature on the Johnson/Schilling duo at the time is Tom Verducci's "The Power of Two," *Sports Illustrated*, December 17, 2001. Interestingly, Schilling won a World Series game for the Phillies while he was in his 20s, for the Diamondbacks while he was in his 30s, and for the Red Sox while he was in his 40s.
4. Ryan Spaeder, "Curt Schilling Should Be in the Hall of Fame, and It's Not Close," *The Sporting News*, January 21, 2015.
5. Spaeder.
6. Data courtesy of Tom Ruane of Retrosheet, email to author July 26, 2015.
7. The ESPN profile (see note 1) reported that Schilling arranged to leave a ticket for his departed father at each game he pitched.

8   Bob Carter, "Pitching Ace Deals Best Under Pressure," ESPN.com, undated. Retrieved on October 8, 2015, from espn.go.com/classic/biography/s/Curt%20Schilling.html.
9   Joe Posnanski, "Schilling paying back Palermo's kindness," KansasCity.com, February 8, 2003.
10 Bella English, "Heading for Home; Baseball Brings Glory to the Schillings, But Their Philanthropy Makes Them Value Players in the Community," *Boston Globe*, February 17, 2004: F1.
11 Gordon Edes wrote a lengthy feature which shows Schilling's mindset at the time. See "New Sox Seem to Fit; Why Schilling See Boston as the Right Move," *Boston Globe*, December 3, 2003.
12 Lisa Olson, "Spilling Guts & Blood," *USA Today*, July 17, 2005: 52.
13 Author interview with Curt Schilling, April 18, 2013.
14 The full story of the procedure is told through interviews with Dr. Morgan and Curt Schilling and appears with a photograph of Schilling's ankle in Allan Wood and Bill Nowlin, *Don't Let Us Win Tonight: An Oral History of the 2004 Boston Red Sox's Impossible Playoff Run* (Chicago: Triumph Books, 2014).
15 Bill Simmons, "Curious Guy: Curt Schilling," Page 2, ESPN.com, January 25, 2006.
16 Associated Press, "Curt Schilling Sued Over Loan," October 1, 2012.
17 David Armstrong, "Shilling Schilling," *Forbes*, September 3, 2007.
18 Stan Grossfeld, "New Lease on Life," *Boston Globe*, August 11, 2103: C1.
19 The work continues today through The ALS Association. See alsa.org/.
20 shadefoundation.org.
21 Jeff Bradley, "In Defending Daughter, Curt Schilling Becomes Powerful Antibullying Voice," si.com/mlb/2015/06/19/curt-schilling-daughter-twitter-gabby. Retrieved July 31, 2015.
22 Stan Grossfeld, "Schilling Fights His Toughest Battle – Trying To Quit a Long-Standing Addiction," Boston Globe, July 6, 2004: C1.
23 Jeff Bradley, SI.com, op. cit.
24 Joan Freedman, "Role Reversal," SI.com, April 17, 2005.
25 For a nice story on the genesis of the book, see Stan Hochman, "Shonda Schilling, On Handling Life's Curveballs," *New York Daily News*, April 6, 2010.
26 Lisa Olson, "Spilling Guts & Blood," *USA Today*, July 17, 2005: 53.
27 *Worth*, December 2002: 68.
28 Tom Verducci, "The Power of Two," *Sports Illustrated*, December 17, 2001.
29 Lisa Olson, "Spilling Guts & Blood."
30 Naomi Aoki, "On, Off the Mound, Schilling Makes His Pitch," *Boston Globe*, June 13, 2004: A1.
31 Adam Kilgore, "Schilling Puts It in Writing," *Boston Globe*, March 24, 2009: C1.
32 Chad Finn, "ESPN Adds Curt Schilling to Sunday Night TV Booth," *Boston Globe*, December 9, 2013.
33 Bob Raissman, "ESPN Suspends Curt Schilling for Rest of MLB Regular Season, Wild Card Game," *New York Daily News*, September 3, 2015.
34 David Cohen, "Baseball Hall of Fame rejects politically outspoken star Curt Schilling," *Politico*, January 26, 2021. https://www.politico.com/news/2021/01/26/curt-schilling-baseball-hall-fame-462801.
35 Dan Shaughnessy, "Curt Schilling falls short of Baseball Hall of Fame induction, and that's a good thing," *Boston Globe*, January 26, 2021. https://www.bostonglobe.com/2021/01/27/sports/curt-schilling-falls-short-baseball-hall-fame-induction-thats-good-thing/

PHIL SEIBEL

BY GREG D. TRANTER

Phil Seibel was a career minor leaguer, playing eight seasons with eight different teams in six leagues. He had one brief moment in the big leagues, playing two games for the 2004 curse-breaking World Series champion Boston Red Sox and that garnered him a World Series ring.

Philip Matthew Seibel was born on January 28, 1979, in Louisville, Kentucky, to Ronald and Leslie (Woodward) Seibel. They had two sons, Philip and Geoffrey. A job change took Ron and the family to California. For many years the couple ran a family-owned insurance agency.

"I loved baseball from a young age and had a natural gift for it. I also loved the art of it," Seibel said in a 2023 interview.[1] The young boy began taking pitching lessons at 10 years old from former major-league pitcher Frank Pastore. And he started throwing curveballs at 12.

Phil attended Cypress (California) High School. He was the star pitcher on the school's baseball team in his junior and senior seasons. Seibel finished his junior year with a 10-2 record, a 1.82 ERA, and 93 strikeouts. He threw two no-hitters and was one of Orange County's strikeout leaders. He was named to the All-County second team by the *Los Angeles Times*. His first loss of the season was a heartbreaking 2-0 defeat to Katella High School because with a victory Cypress would have won the school's first-ever Empire League title.

As a senior the 6-foot-1 175-pounder received several baseball scholarship offers and chose the University of Texas. He verbally committed to the Longhorns on November 12, 1996, and signed his official letter of intent in the spring of 1997, prior to the start of his senior season.

Seibel had a solid senior campaign, but the team, having lost some solid players to graduation, was not quite as good as in the previous year. Despite that, Seibel was 6-2 with a 2.30 ERA. His coach, Mark Steinert, said of Seibel after a 13-strikeout performance in Cypress's opening game of the season, "He stays in good shape and he knows how to pitch. He's just a bulldog. You can't get the ball out of his hand."[2] On May 9 in a two-hit shutout win over Century, Seibel struck out a school-record nine consecutive batters. But the highlight of his senior season was a 2-0 one-hitter he pitched against Empire League champion El Dorado.

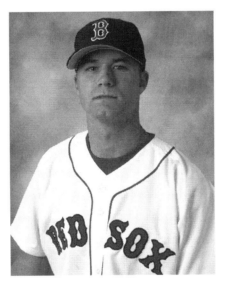

Seibel was named first-team All-County Southern Division II. He was also selected to the California Baseball Coaches Association All Star series as a member of the South team and he played for the North in the Kiwanis All-Star game.

As a University of Texas freshman in 1998, Seibel made the varsity baseball squad as a starting pitcher and was given jersey No. 32. But after struggling to a 1-3 record in five starts with a 6.30 ERA, he was relegated to the bullpen. His first four career starts were at the University of Southern California (they won the 1998 National Championship), LSU, Stanford, and at Miami, all college baseball powerhouses. In his Miami start he faced a lineup with future major leaguers Jason Michaels, Pat Burrell, and Audrey Huff. "I throw Huff a really good pitch, down and away, and he hits a laser beam out of the ballpark for a home run. I come into the dugout and pitching coach Burt Hooton says to me, 'Good pitch. He is just better than you,'" Seibel recalled.[3] The left-hander pitched mostly out of the bullpen for the remainder of the season, with a couple of spot starts. He finished with a 3-3 record.

The Longhorns did not have a good season, finishing with the school's first losing record in 42 years (23-32-1) and an eighth-place finish in the Big-12 Conference (11-18). Seibel said of losing, "Instead of going to sleep, I'll stay awake, wondering what went wrong during the day."[4] He recalled that he felt overwhelmed at times and struggled with some self-doubt.

To hone his pitching skills, Seibel played in Alaskan summer baseball with the Anchorage Glacier Pilots between his freshman and sophomore seasons.

Texas was much improved in 1999. Early in the season the Longhorns stunned top-ranked USC, sweeping the Trojans in a three-game series. Seibel had become the team's closer and was the winner in the 8-7 ninth-inning victory that secured the sweep. Afterward he said, "This team is a lot more confident than we were last year. Last year we were pretty good and we knew we had some talent but we weren't quite sure what to expect. … As far as confidence goes, we weren't really confident in what we were doing."[5] (Seibel earned saves in the other two victories over USC.)

In one of the Longhorns' bigger moments of the season, Texas led 10th-ranked Baylor 4-2 in the bottom of the ninth on April 10 and Seibel was summoned with the tying runs on base. He hit a batter to load the bases but retired the final three

Bears, striking out Anthony Hensley on a 3-and-2 pitch to end the game. "This is probably the most important game we've played all year," Seibel said in the joyous locker room. "If we lose, it would have put us in a big hole as far as the conference title goes."[6]

The Longhorns compiled a 35-24 record and a sixth-place finish in the tough Big-12 (17-13) but their overall record was good enough to garner an NCAA Tournament berth. They were placed in the Houston Regional and won one of three games but were eliminated by the University of Houston in an 8-5 loss. In the Longhorns' only victory, a 7-5 affair over Southwest Texas State, Seibel pitched two scoreless innings to notch the save.

Seibel improved significantly throughout his sophomore season. He posted a 5-2 record with a team-leading five saves. He was named honorable mention All-Big-12 and was a first team All-Academic Big-12 selection. He was one of two Texas players invited to the US National baseball tryouts in Tucson in June, and was named to the final roster of the 22-player squad. The highlight of their season was a trip to Japan June 22-July 1 to play the Japan Collegiate All Star team.

Seibel got off to a great start in his junior season at Texas. He moved out of the closer role and became the Sunday starter. He compiled a 4-1 record with a 1.99 ERA, highlighted by being named Big-12 player of the week on February 9, 2000. He was honored after pitching 12 innings while allowing only one run for a 0.75 ERA and winning two games. But on March 5 in a start against Missouri, he strained a ligament in his elbow and missed the next 2½ months of the season. Seibel did not realize it at the time but he had torn his ulnar collateral ligament. He followed a very tight exercise and diet regimen that allowed him to recover and pitch effectively. He returned in time for the Big-12 tournament.

Before he was injured, Texas had moved up to the number-2-rated team in the country. Though the team did not keep that pace with Seibel out, they finished with a 40-18 record and received an NCAA tournament bid to the Tempe Regional hosted by Arizona State. The Longhorns won two of their first three games in the regional but faced an elimination game against Arizona State. Seibel was called on to make the start and threw 6⅓ solid innings, allowing five hits and one earned run as the Longhorns defeated the Sun Devils, 6-4. Seibel said he "probably isn't 100 percent yet, but this is close enough." He added, "I threw everything … fastball, slider, changeup … and they all worked and there was no pain."[7] The next day Texas again defeated Arizona State and moved onto the Super Regionals for a three-game series with Penn State. Texas coach Augie Garrido paid tribute to Seibel, saying, "In Tempe, the whole pitching staff was awesome, and Phil's return just highlighted it."[8] Seibel made the All-Regional Tournament Team.

Texas defeated Penn State in back-to-back games in Austin, 7-3 and 10-8, to win the Super Regional and qualify for its first College World Series since 1993. Meanwhile the baseball amateur draft was being held, and Seibel was selected on June 5 in the eighth round by the Montreal Expos with selection No. 225. He was disappointed that he was not drafted higher. "I think my injury had something to do with that," he said. "I felt a little shortchanged by having to miss as much of the season as I did. But I thought it went well when I was healthy and able to pitch."[9]

The Longhorns opened the World Series on June 10 and lost to eventual national champion LSU, 13-5. Seibel pitched the second game, against Florida State, making only his third start since his injury. He pitched five innings and allowed four runs to keep Texas in the game, but the Longhorns lost 6-2 and were eliminated. It was Seibel's last college game.

In the postgame locker room, reflecting on his time at Texas, Seibel said, "This is a big step for the program. My first three years here were terrible. Now we finally feel like we did something. We got to the World Series. Now I feel like my career here was worthwhile. We can say we got Texas back on track to be one of the best teams in the nation."[10] Texas finished the season ranked number 7 in the USA Today/ESPN poll.

Seibel, despite missing time, finished his junior season with a 5-2 record and a 2.42 ERA. He lettered all three seasons at Texas and ended his career with an overall 12-7 record. He said his two greatest thrills in baseball before becoming a professional were playing in the College World Series and pitching on the Fourth of July for Team USA. For more than a month, he pondered whether to sign and forgo his senior season. "I thought if I go back to school and I injure myself, I will never forgive myself and I can always go back to school to finish my degree," he said.[11] Seibel signed with the Expos on August 7 and passed up his senior season with the Longhorns.

Seibel began his Expos career in the Class-A Florida State League as a starter with the Jupiter Hammerheads. He had a solid season with a 10-7 record and a 3.95 ERA. His season was punctuated by nine consecutive starts in which he allowed two runs or fewer. His 10 wins led the team.

Seibel's strengths as a pitcher were his breaking balls. He could throw a curve, slider, and cutter. His 86-88-MPH fastball complemented his arsenal of breaking pitches. He had a good feel with the ball and his location was usually excellent. Seibel was an analytical pitcher, always looking for an edge before that was in vogue.

Seibel was scheduled to play for the Harrisburg Senators in the Double-A Eastern League in 2002. However, on April 5 he and two other players were traded by the Expos to the New York Mets in exchange for four players. Seibel was assigned to the Eastern League's Binghamton Mets, and put up almost identical numbers to the previous season with a 10-8 record and a 3.97 ERA. He pitched a career-high 149⅔ innings for the North Division third-place Mets and his 10 wins led the team. Seibel flirted with a no-hitter on May 31 against his former Harrisburg mates. He went into the seventh inning without allowing a hit, but a home run ended the bid in a 2-1 loss for Seibel. "It kind of stings losing 2-1, and it really stings losing to those guys," Seibel said.[12] He had a season-high 12 strikeouts in seven innings in a 5-1 win over Trenton later that season.

On November 21 Seibel was added to the Mets' 40-man roster. He went to spring training with the Mets in the spring of 2003, then was assigned to Triple-A Norfolk. He enjoyed his first major-league camp, rubbing elbows with Tom Glavine (his childhood idol) and Al Leiter. "It was awesome," he said, "The first day I was working on my bunting with the other guys, and Glavine was pitching and Mike Piazza was catching. I couldn't even concentrate. I just kept thinking, 'Please don't foul one off and hit Piazza in the head.'"[13]

Seibel did not last long in Norfolk. New York acquired David Cone and some cascading moves sent Seibel back to Binghamton on April 9. He was with Binghamton for most of the season, but spent a month back in Norfolk as the Mets tried him out as a reliever and spot starter. In Binghamton he had a 5-5 record and 3.59 ERA in 17 starts. But he faltered in Norfolk: In 11 games he had a 6.03 ERA and a 2-3 record. After the season the Mets placed him on waivers.

The Red Sox claimed Seibel on November 20, 2003, and placed him on the 40-man roster. Seibel signed a one-year contract with Boston on March 4 and began spring training with the Red Sox in Winter Haven, Florida. He was optioned to the Pawtucket Red Sox on March 20 and began the season with the Triple-A club. He pitched the Pawsox' opening game and hurled five scoreless innings.

Shortly after, on April 15, Seibel was called up to Boston. He replaced left-hander Bobby Jones, who had been optioned to Pawtucket. Seibel recalled his call-up: "I get a call on my cell phone, but I did not recognize the number, so I didn't answer it. My hotel phone then rings and it is manager Buddy Bailey. He says, 'You have to get to the field (at the time the Pawsox were in Rochester for a series with the Red Wings) to go to Boston,' and hangs up the phone. I am uncertain if I am getting called up because he was not very clear. I arrive at the ballpark and yes, I am going to the big leagues."[14] He recalled his excitement, but then his flight was delayed over six hours for weather. He was flying to Providence so he could pick up a suit and they had not informed Jones yet of his demotion and did not want Seibel arriving in Boston too soon. Seibel then waited several more hours in Pawtucket before hearing from the Red Sox to finally come to Boston.

Seibel made his major-league debut that night against the Baltimore Orioles at Fenway Park. He relieved Bronson Arroyo in the 11th inning with the Red Sox trailing 9-7 and the bases loaded. The first batter Seibel faced was left fielder Larry Bigbee. He induced Bigbee to hit a groundball to first baseman Kevin Millar but Millar misplayed it, resulting in a run scoring and leaving the bases loaded. Seibel then faced Brian Roberts and walked him, allowing another run to score. Seibel was then replaced by Frank Castillo, but the damage was done and the Red Sox lost 12-7.

The New York Yankees were the next opponent to come to Fenway Park for a key early-season four-game series. Seibel was excited to be part of a Yankees vs. Red Sox showdown at Fenway. The Red Sox won the first two games. In the third game, on Sunday, April 18, the Yankees jumped to a quick 7-3 lead over Boston after three innings as Derek Lowe had a bad outing for the Red Sox. Seibel, with the Red Sox still trailing by four runs, entered the game in the sixth inning. He hit the first batter he faced, Jason Giambi. But after his nerves settled down, the young left-hander pitched 3⅔ innings of hitless, scoreless relief. (He walked four batters.) The highlight of his 59-pitch outing was retiring Álex Rodríguez on a groundball with two on and two out in the seventh inning. The Red Sox could not mount a rally and, though Seibel held the Yankees at bay, Boston lost 7-3.

After the game the bright-eyed youngster said, "My parents were here and got to see the game. I'm sure my dad will probably say to me, 'Do you realize what just happened?'"[15] Seibel added, "I'm sitting in Fenway Park about to face the Yankees, and I'm thinking, 'Holy Cow, that's Derek Jeter, that's Álex Rodríguez.' My first real series was Red Sox-Yankees at Fenway, and being a baseball fan all my life, I couldn't have imagined being part of that."[16] Asked if the major leagues were everything they were cracked up to be, he responded, "And then some."[17]

Seibel then traveled with the Red Sox to Toronto and New York as Boston won two of three from the Blue Jays and swept a three-game series with the Yankees. He did not make an appearance in any of those games but was with the club when they returned home to face the Tampa Bay Devil Rays. The Red Sox won the first game of the series, but the next day Seibel was optioned to Double-A Portland to make room for Byung-Hyun Kim.

During Seibel's stay on the roster, the Red Sox were 9-3 and stood atop the AL East Division with a 13-6 record. His final line with Boston was 3⅔ innings pitched, 66 pitches thrown, no hits, no runs, five walks, one hit batter, one strikeout, and a 0.00 ERA. Seibel was a student of the game and commented, "I marveled at how Curt Schilling used video to prepare for a game and used that information to determine how he would pitch to individual hitters."[18] After that, Seibel began using video in his preparation.

Seibel was not in Portland long – one start – before being recalled to Pawtucket on May 4. He landed on the disabled list on June 12 with elbow soreness. Seibel was 1-2 with a 3.02 ERA in eight games with Pawtucket before the injury. He returned in August, pitching three rehab outings in the Gulf Coast League, and then moved to Portland where he finished the season pitching in three games with an 0-1 record and a 7.50 ERA in six innings pitched.

The Red Sox released Seibel on September 28 and then re-signed him on October 12. Seibel did not pitch in 2005 as he underwent Tommy John surgery as the torn UCL had finally caught up to him. While recovering from the surgery, he went back to the University of Texas that fall to finish his degree. "When the Sox made the run to win the World Series, I was home on my couch, studying and staying up late watching the games," Seibel recalled with a chuckle.[19] Though he was on the disabled list throughout 2005, he came to the Opening Day celebration at Fenway Park honoring the 2004 World Series champions and received his World Series ring.

Seibel was back in the Red Sox minor-league system to begin the 2006 season and he started with the Greenville (South Carolina) Drive in the Class-A South Atlantic League. He opened the season for the Drive in their brand-new West End Field in front of a sold-out crowd of 5,700. He made the first pitch in the ballpark's history, got its first strikeout, and his five innings of one-hit ball with seven strikeouts earned him its first victory as the Drive won 6-1. "It felt great to be out there opening night in a beautiful ballpark," said Seibel. "I was excited, the whole city was. But I just tried to concentrate and get ready. None of us have opened a ballpark before. That's something I'll always take with me."[20]

After four starts in Greenville, Seibel was promoted to Portland, where he made nine starts, and finished the season in Pawtucket coming out of the bullpen. His overall record was 6-3 with a 1.24 ERA in 22 games. He set the team record for the Portland Sea Dogs with 21⅓ consecutive scoreless innings. His Red Sox career appeared to be looking up again, but on December 15 Boston traded him to the California Angels for pitcher Brendan Donnelly.

Seibel made two starts for the Triple-A Salt Lake Bees in 2007, compiling an 0-1 record and 11.25 ERA before he received his unconditional release on May 28. His baseball-playing career was over.

Seibel joined the Arizona Diamondbacks organization as an assistant in the scouting and player development departments in June of 2007 and served until January 2009. He then embarked on a career in insurance, beginning as a risk management adviser and then a producer. In 2023, working with his father, he was president of Advanced Benefit Solutions, near Austin, Texas, an insurance brokerage catering to small and medium-sized businesses. Seibel recalled that baseball really helped him build his insurance career. "The World Series ring is a conversation starter and people open up to me because of it. And that really helped open doors early in my insurance career," he said.[21]

Seibel and his wife, Charity, were married in 2009 and have two daughters, Madeline, born in 2014, and Shelby, born in 2016.

SOURCES

In addition to the sources cited in the Notes, the author consulted Ancestry.com, Baseball-Reference.com, LinkedIn, Retrosheet.org, the *Boston Red Sox Media Guides* for 2004 and 2005, and the *Texas 2022 Baseball Fact Book*, https://texassports.com/documents/2022/2/14//22_fact_book_full_web.pdf?id=16368

NOTES

1 Interview by author with Phil Seibel, February 23, 2023. (Hereafter Seibel interview).

2 "Seibel Leads the Way Again for Cypress," *Los Angeles Times*, March 19, 1997: C6.

3 Seibel interview.

4 Rick Cantu, "Bright Spots Can't Eliminate Dark Cloud of Another UT Loss," *Austin American-Statesman*, May 3, 1998: C5.

5 Rick Cantu, "Longhorns Sweep Trojans," *Austin American-Statesman*, February 8, 1999: C7.

6 Rick Cantu, "Seibel Seals the Deal as Texas Turns Tables, Beats Baylor," *Austin American-Statesman*, April 10, 1999: C1.

7 Whit Canning, "Call to Arms," *Fort Worth Star-Telegram*, June 2, 2000: 9D.

8 Canning.

9 Lon Eubanks, "Taipei Hitters Find Titans' Saarloos Is a Type-A Pitcher," *Los Angeles Times*, July 25, 2000: D11.

10 Rick Cantu, "Horns Driven Home," *Austin American-Statesman*, June 13, 2000: C1.

11 Seibel interview.

12 Scott Lauber, "A Hard-Luck Loss for B-Mets' Seibel," *Press and Sun-Bulletin* (Binghamton, New York), June 1, 2002: 5D.

13 Scott Lauber, "Seibel Stays Focused Despite Demotion." *Press and Sun-Bulletin*, April 10, 2003: 5D.

14 Seibel interview.

15 Gordon Edes, "Thrills for Newcomer Even During a Loss," *Boston Globe*, April 19, 2004: D6.

16 Scott Lauber, "Connolly Hopes Numbers Game Adds Up to a Pirates' promotion," *Press and Sun-Bulletin*, April 27, 2004: 4D.

17 "Connolly Hopes Numbers Game Adds Up to a Pirates' Promotion."

18 Seibel interview.

19 Seibel interview.

20 Bart Wright, "A Place That Takes You Back in Time," *Greenville (South Carolina) News*, April 7, 2006: 5C.

21 Seibel interview.

EARL SNYDER

BY BUDD BAILEY

Earl Snyder was a professional baseball player for 10 years, and he did it well by almost any definition. It's unusual, then, that the highlight of his career came when he played one generally unmemorable game for the Boston Red Sox during the 2004 season. It earned him that most cherished of baseball possessions: a championship ring.

Earl Clifford Snyder was born on May 6, 1976, in New Britain, Connecticut. He stayed close by as he attended Plainville High School, which is just west of New Britain. Earl followed in his father's footsteps at Plainville, as his dad, Earl Jr., developed a love of softball during this time at that school. He served in the Army in Vietnam and was an engineer in the manufacturing industry. Earl Jr. died in 2014. Earl's mother, Rovena, and grandfather Earl Sr. (he went by "Grandpa Tickey" in the family) both died around 2003. Rovena Snyder was only 51.[1]

At Plainville, Snyder was part of something of a high-school dynasty. The Blue Devils had split two state championship baseball games in 1992 and 1993, and they didn't miss a beat in Snyder's senior year in 1994. Earl was a very good player, but not a great one. Plainville won the Connecticut title game over Holy Cross-Waterbury, 10-6 in 10 innings, as the infielder hit a huge home run early in the game. It's a blast that is still remembered, as it soared over the fence in Middletown's Palmer Field and ripped through some trees before finally reaching the ground. It was his fifth homer of the season, during which he hit .378. It was a small step up from a .361 average as a junior in 1993.[2] In 2012 Snyder eventually was honored for his baseball achievements with his induction into the Plainville Sports Hall of Fame.[3]

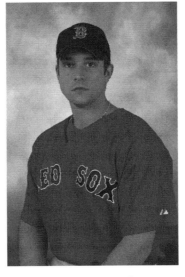

Snyder took his baseball talents to the University of Hartford. It's fair to say that the relationship worked out well for both sides. "I stopped being lazy, and began to work out," he said much later.[4] Snyder is called "the most productive offensive performer in the history of the baseball program" in his biography for the school's athletic Hall of Fame.[5] He was the team's most valuable player three times, and was all-Northeast, all-New England, and all-conference in those 1996-98 seasons. Snyder broke many of the school records set by Jeff Bagwell – a future Baseball Hall of Famer – by hitting 53 home runs (18 as a senior), scoring 146 runs, and driving in 173 runs. He's second on the Hawks' all-time list with 222 hits, and third in program history in batting average (.374). That set up some comparisons between Snyder and Bagwell, who admittedly was a hard act to follow. "If it was Joe Schmo and we had the same numbers, it wouldn't be a big deal," Snyder said as a junior. "It's nice, I guess."[6]

While Snyder found personal success at Hartford, the team didn't do as well. Jim Bretz coached the team for Earl's first three seasons, and he averaged about 16 wins a season. Bob Nenna took over as coach in 1998, and Hartford went 13-32. The Hawks' regular seasons weren't enough baseball for Snyder. During the summers, he played with Middletown and Danbury in the New England Collegiate Baseball League and the Wareham Gatemen of the Cape Cod Baseball League.

Snyder, who stood an even 6 feet tall, graduated in 1998 with a degree in criminal justice, and he no doubt spent part of the summer wondering if he had done enough in college to be drafted by a professional team. The first round saw the selection of such players as Mark Mulder, J.D. Drew, Brad Lidge, and CC Sabathia. Snyder was selected on the second day by the New York Mets in the 36th round – "the nosebleed section," as he put it later.[7] Snyder was one of three players in that round who made it to the majors; the others were Erick Eckenstahler and Tim Olson. Snyder signed with the Mets a couple of days later for $1,000, and started a pro career that mostly saw him at first and third base although also included work at shortstop and the outfield, and as designated hitter.

Snyder's first professional home was Pittsfield in the New York-Penn League. He led the team in home runs (11) and RBIs (40) while hitting .262 in a team-best 71 games. The Pittsfield Mets went 35-41 in the short-season Class-A league; the only other future major leaguer on the roster was Ty Wigginton. One of the season's personal highlights for Snyder came when his grandfather came up the Interstate from Connecticut to see Earl play. "We took my father up there," said Lawrence Snyder, Earl's uncle. "That's when he hit a home run. My father beamed about him. Somebody actually shagged the ball and gave it to my father. It was like the most glorious moment in my father's life."[8]

The 1999 season was even better for Snyder, who spent the season with the Capital City Bombers (Columbia, South Carolina) in the South Atlantic League. Snyder was the top Bomber in homers with 28 and in RBIs with 97. He hit .268 for a team that went 83-58 and won the Central Division title. Snyder's play demanded that the Mets take a closer look at him.

"The bigger prospect guys are prioritized in the beginning, and rightly so," he said years later. "I had a couple of good seasons in the beginning when I first got into pro ball to kick the door in a little bit, to be pushed along a little further than the Mets envisioned for me."[9]

In 2000 Snyder moved up another notch to High Class-A ball with the St. Lucie Mets of the Florida State League. His batting average improved to .282, and he had 93 RBIs to go with 25 homers. Snyder might be remembered in St. Petersburg for a particularly odd reason. Whenever he made an out there for St. Lucie, he was serenaded over the public-address system by the song "Goodbye Earl," made popular by the Dixie Chicks.[10]

Snyder wasn't serenaded very often that season, helping his team to the division title as the Mets went 81-58. He was awarded the Mets' Nelson Doubleday Award as his team's Most Valuable Player for the second straight season. At the age of 25, Snyder finally reached Double-A ball in 2001, pounding out what had become another typically good year: .282/20 homers/75 RBIs. That was good for another Doubleday Award – the first Met to win such an honor three straight times. The infielder even spent six games at Triple A with the Norfolk of the International League, hitting .474. But he was 25 years old at that point, and it was easy to wonder what the future held for him.

Snyder found out on December 13. Two days earlier, the Mets had traded Alex Escobar, Matt Lawton, Jerrod Riggan, and two players to be named later to the Cleveland Indians for future Hall of Famer Roberto Alomar, Mike Bacsik, and Danny Peoples. On December 13, Snyder and pitcher Billy Traber were formally included in the transaction. Years later, Indians general manager Mark Shapiro called it the worst trade of his time in that position.[11]

The change of scenery didn't change Snyder's offensive profile, as he posted good numbers again while playing for Buffalo in the Triple-A International League. He even won a home-run contest when the Indians came to Buffalo for an exhibition game. That Bisons team had a bundle of talent, including such players as Cliff Lee, Brandon Phillips, Jake Westbrook, Chris Coste, Jolbert Cabrera, and Josh Bard, but Snyder was the team's top slugger. Buffalo went 87-57 but fell four games short of winning the division despite having the second-best record in the league.

Along the way, Snyder was called up to "The Show." He had just struck out three times in a game in late April when Buffalo manager Eric Wedge called him into his office and told him he had been called up. At first he thought it was a joke, and he kept his cell phone off until he was within sight of the stadium in Cleveland just in case someone tried to call and tell him there was a mistake.[12]

Snyder debuted in the major leagues in Texas on April 28, hitting a single in the ninth inning in his first at-bat. He thus entered the major-league record book. "I look back at it now and wish I had a little more fun when I did it," Snyder said 20 years later. "I took it as a job … and you grind away at it. You don't smell the roses while you are there. Looking back at it now, I did it the right way, I did it my way. I worked hard. I was never the best athlete, but I wanted to be there."[13]

Snyder stayed with the Indians for another six games through May 5, and then returned to the Cleveland roster for a six-game stay in July and another six in September. Since he had grown up as a Boston Red Sox fan, it must have been meaningful for him to play in Fenway Park on September 16 and 18. Snyder saved the best for last, hitting a home run on September 29 in a 7-3 win over Kansas City in Cleveland. "Victor Martinez and I went back-to-back," Snyder remembered. "I don't remember what the count was. I wanted so badly to hit a home run in Jacobs Field. It was to left-center field about 8 or 10 rows back."[14] An usher retrieved the ball for him.

In 18 games for the Indians, Snyder hit .200 with the home run and 4 RBIs. A trip to the majors is something to which everyone who has played baseball aspires. Still, it was a difficult year, thanks to the Buffalo-Cleveland shuttle. "I was up and down the whole year," Snyder said. "By the time the year was over, I was just spent. This offseason was good for me to kind of reflect on everything."[15]

Snyder finished 2002 with 19 homers and 66 RBIs for Buffalo, and set a franchise record by driving eight runs on June 13, 2002, in Syracuse. He tried playing winter ball in the Dominican Republic, but felt rather fried mentally after the long season and cut short his trip to the Caribbean after a month. "I was bad," said Snyder, who hit .088 with the team playing in Aguilas. "It was a long season with everything going on. I was ready to get home. … My mind really wasn't in it."[16]

The Boston Red Sox were coming off a good (93-69) but not great 2002 season. Theo Epstein had been hired as the new general manager, and he thought the Red Sox needed to upgrade at first base. Boston had used Tony Clark, Brian Daubach, and José Offerman at the position in 2002 and Daubach had left as a free agent to sign with the Chicago White Sox. Epstein was looking for talent anywhere he could find it, and he noticed that the Indians had put Snyder on waivers on January 15, 2003. The Red Sox claimed him two days later, figuring someone with a proven minor-league bat could prove a wise investment in their search for a new first baseman.

"We claimed [Snyder] because we had roster space at the time," Epstein said in a February 2003 interview. "We thought he would be a good addition, provide some depth. We don't have a lot of upper level prospects. Then it turned out we had a rash of moves the next week where we needed a roster spot."[17]

Less than a week after the signing, Boston dropped Snyder from the 40-man roster to make room for pitcher Héctor Almonte. The Red Sox assigned Snyder to Triple-A Pawtucket. Boston continued its search for a bargain option at first base. By the end of the spring the team had acquired Jeremy Giambi, Kevin Millar, Dave Nilsson, and a free agent from the Twins named David Ortiz.

In Pawtucket, Snyder started slowly. "Let's be honest, he's had a tough year offensively – the offensive numbers aren't what he's accustomed to, but he's helped us win games with his glove at third base," PawSox manager Buddy Bailey said in midseason.[18] A consolation was that he had plenty of family and friends who made the drive from Connecticut to Rhode Island to see him play. For the season, Snyder hit .255 with 22 homers and 71 RBIs.

Snyder knew he had to do better in 2004 to make the last step up to the majors. He lit up the International League to the tune of 36 homers (tying a franchise record) and 104 RBIs to go with a .273 average. The home run and RBI totals led the league, and he was an All-Star that season in the International League. It was considered to be one of the great seasons in the history of the Pawtucket franchise. His reward along the way was to be called up … for one game. Kevin Youkilis was on the disabled list with a bone bruise in his right ankle, and Boston needed a third baseman.

"It wasn't really expected," Snyder said that day about the recall. "It's just a great feeling. … Being a New England guy, playing for the Red Sox is a dream. To play for the team you've rooted for your whole life, it's a thrill to be here."[19] Buddy Bailey added, "He had a tremendous second half last year and he's been consistent all year with his home runs, base hits and RBI. He plays a couple of positions, first and third, and with (Boston's) injuries, he's going to get an opportunity to help that ballclub as well."[20]

The date was August 18, and the Red Sox hosted the Blue Jays. It took a little time for Snyder to figure out how to navigate the streets of Boston to arrive at Fenway Park. Once he got there, he had one major goal even before the game started. "The only thing I wanted to do in batting practice was hit the ball over the Green Monster," said Snyder, who in his youth had designed a replica of Fenway Park for Wiffle ball in a friend's backyard.[21]

Snyder, wearing uniform number 37, started at third base, and handled five chances flawlessly (two putouts and three assists). At the plate, he batted ninth and had his first at-bat in a Boston uniform in the bottom of the second inning. He struck out swinging against Miguel Batista. In the fourth, Snyder hit into a double play, and he followed that in the sixth with a fly out to deep center.

Finally in the bottom of the eighth, Snyder fulfilled the dream of every youngster who grew up a Red Sox fan: he singled to left with two outs. Sadly, he didn't get to enjoy the view from first, as teammate Bill Mueller was thrown out trying to score from second base on the play ("By about 60 feet," Snyder said with a laugh.) That ended the inning. Boston took a 6-4 victory. "I wanted to get the kid an RBI in Boston," Red Sox third-base coach Dale Sveum said later about the play.[22]

That was it for Snyder's major-league career. Mark Bellhorn was ready to play again, so Boston activated the infielder. Snyder was on his way back to Pawtucket and the minor leagues. He stayed there for the rest of the season, as his hopes for a September call-up were dashed. Snyder watched like everyone else as the Red Sox went on to end an 86-year drought by winning the World Series in October. That meant he had earned a championship ring for his efforts. There were 16 other players who played no more than 21 games for Boston that season, but Snyder and pitcher Abe Alvarez were the only two who participated in just one game. None of the 17 players on the list played in the major leagues after 2004.[23]

"I stole it," Snyder said about the ring years later. "I can say I stole it, because the statute of limitations has run out now. I got a call from the front office after the season, and asking, 'What ring size are you?' I'm thinking – this is a joke. But whatever, 'Here's my ring size.'"[24]

Snyder became a free agent after the 2004 season, and – after talking with the Indians about a return – signed with Tampa Bay. Along the way in 2005, a package came to his house back home. Wife Kristen called her husband and said, "Did you order any sneakers? It's something from Boston." She opened it up, and it was the ring. "I was glad she was home," Snyder said, with the ring securely in a safe at home as of 2022. "I appreciate the ring now more than I did at the time."[25]

In 2005 Snyder had another good season for Durham of the IL, with 29 homers and 92 RBIs. Then it was on to the Cincinnati Reds, hoping for a chance at big-league fame. "It's just a matter of being in the right place at the right time – getting that opportunity, and maybe that hasn't happened yet," he said during spring training in 2006.[26] Alas, Snyder ended up in Louisville that season, and he had 17 homers and 77 RBIs there. He stayed in the Kentucky city for the opening of the 2007 season but lost some of his batting stroke. After a slow start, he was released on June 8. He moved on to Charlotte in the Chicago White Sox chain a week later, but couldn't do much better. He was a 31-year-old who hit a combined .215 with 13 homers and 53 RBIs. That turned out to be his last season in Organized Baseball.

Along the way, Snyder figured out his major-league dreams weren't going to come true. "(It was) right around that 2005 season, where I just hit as good as I could have – I couldn't put up better numbers," he said. "In '05, Lou Piniella was the manager of the Rays, but I had three at-bats in spring training and was sent down. At that point, there's nothing else I can do aside from hitting 75 home runs – and that's not going to happen – to get over that hump."[27]

Snyder moved on to the rest of his life after leaving baseball, knowing he had given the sport his best shot. "I thought I ran my time out," he said. "I played 10 years after college. I did everything I could. I did it my way. I can look back at it and be proud."[28] As of 2022, he lived in Glastonbury, Connecticut, and worked as a police officer in nearby East Hampton. He and Kristen had three children – Rayah, Peighton, and Sage.[29]

Snyder played 10 seasons in the minors, finishing with a .262 batting average with 220 homers and 771 RBIs. He had 59 at-bats in the majors, with 12 hits, one homer, 4 RBIs, and 22 strikeouts. And a ring.

SOURCES

In addition to the sources cited in the Notes, the author consulted Baseball-reference.com and Retrosheet.org.

NOTES

1 "Earl C. Snyder Jr." Bailey Family Funeral Homes, 2014. https://www.bcbailey.com/obituary/Earl-Snyder.

2 Ryan Chichester and Matt Hornick, "Plenty of Options to Choose From for Most Memorable Baseball Teams in Area History," *New Britain Herald*; April 19, 2020. http://www.newbritainherald.com/NBH-Berlin+Sports/370511/plenty-of-options-to-choose-from-for-most-memorable-baseball-teams-in-area-history.

3 "Hall of Fame Inductees 2012." Plainville Sports Hall of Fame. https://plainvillesports.com/inductees/2012-inductees.

4 Woody Anderson, "With Snyder, There Are Powerful Similarities." *Hartford Courant*; March 5, 1997. https://archive.ph/Bhrca#selection-2613.0-2613.116.

5 "Earl Snyder." Alumni Athletics Hall of Fame. https://hartfordhawks.com/honors/alumni-athletics-hall-of-fame/earl-snyder/85.

6 Anderson.

7 "Episode 68: Moonlight Graham," Fanbase; March 28, 2022. https://www.youtube.com/watch?v=l7eZyYEHRQk.

8 David Heuschkel, "Painful Year for Snyder," *Hartford Courant*, February 25, 2003. https://www.courant.com/connecticut/hc-xpm-2003-02-25-0302251477-story.html.

9 "Episode 68: Moonlight Graham."

10 "Playing Music for the Visiting Team." SportsAnnouncing.com; September 5, 2015. http://www.sportsannouncing.com/playing-music-for-the-visiting-team/.

11 Vince Grzegorek, "Mark Shapiro's Self-Proclaimed Biggest Mistake: That Robbie Alomar for Matt Lawton Deal." Scene; June 7, 2010. https://www.clevescene.com/news/mark-shapiros-self-proclaimed-biggest-mistake-that-robbie-alomar-for-matt-lawton-deal-1926166.

12 C.L. Brown, "Snyder in a League of His Own," *Louisville Courier-Journal*; March 28, 2007. https://www.redszone.com/forums/archive/index.php/t-56003.html.

13 "Episode 68: Moonlight Graham."

14 "Episode 68: Moonlight Graham."

15 Heuschkel.

16 Heuschkel.

17 Heuschkel.

18 Angel Verdejo, "Snyder Figures Out Ways to Help," *Buffalo News*; August 5, 2003. https://buffalonews.com/news/snyder-figures-out-ways-to-help/article_429281fe-236b-59b4-9a78-2f154574offc.html.

19 David Borges, "Red Sox Bring Up Snyder," *Middletown (Connecticut) Press*; August 19, 2004. https://www.middletownpress.com/news/article/Red-Sox-bring-up-Snyder-11924495.php.

20 Borges.

21 Associated Press, "Sox fan starts at 3rd," *Cape Cod Times* (Hyannis, Massachusetts), August 19, 2004. https://www.capecodtimes.com/story/sports/2004/08/19/sox-fan-starts-at-3rd/50924954007/.

22 Bill Simmons, "SGW Quote of the Day Archive," ESPN.com. http://www.espn.com/espn/page2/story?page=simmons/quotes/archive/vol1&num=0.

23 Bill Nowlin and Matthew Silverman, *Red Sox by the Numbers* (Champagne, Illinois: Sports Publishing LLC, 2016).

24 "Episode 68: Moonlight Graham."

25 "Episode 68: Moonlight Graham."

26 "HRs Don't Give Snyder a Major Boost," *Sarasota* (Florida) *Herald-Tribune*; March 11, 2006. https://www.heraldtribune.com/story/news/2006/03/12/hrs-dont-give-snyder-a-major-boost/28466363007/.

27 "Episode 68: Moonlight Graham."

28 "Episode 68: Moonlight Graham."

29 "Episode 68: Moonlight Graham."

A RED SOX MEMORY

Late in Game Six of the 1986 World Series, my wife and I woke up our 3½-year-old son Dave to watch the Red Sox finally become champs, but they couldn't quite do it. Eighteen years later, while our younger son Andy was spending an "Official Visit" with the UMass/Amherst baseball team, my wife and I endured a 19-8 crushing by the "Evil Empire" in the third game of the A.L. Championship Series. Things could not have gotten worse.

And as we all now know—THEY DIDN'T! THEY ONLY GOT BETTER!!

SKIP TUETKEN

MIKE TIMLIN

BY BILL NOWLIN

Right-handed reliever Mike Timlin pitched in more than 1,000 major-league games and has four World Championship rings. His 1,058 games rank him eighth all-time among pitchers. He played postseason baseball with 11 teams during his 18 years in the major leagues.[1] The World Series wins were with the Toronto Blue Jays in 1992 and 1993 and the Boston Red Sox in 2004 and 2007.

In a big-league career that ran from 1991 through 2008, Timlin started four games and relieved in 1,054, thus averaging more than 58 appearances per season and facing a total of 5,082 batters in 1,024⅓ innings. His career ERA was 3.63, with a won-lost record of 75-73.

Timlin's best pitches were described as "a sinking fastball that is regularly clocked at around 94 mph and a vicious, biting slider. … he keeps the ball low and induces groundouts."[2]

Michael August Timlin was born in Midland, Texas, on March 10, 1966, and graduated from Midland High School, moving on to Southwestern University in Georgetown, Texas.[3] After his junior year, he was a fifth-round selection of the Blue Jays in the June 1987 draft. Timlin was 6-feet-4 and listed at 205 pounds.

"Coming out of West Texas, all you know is oil fields and football," he said in 2000. "Baseball wasn't a real big thing. But it was a God-given ability for me to play baseball. I grew fast, but I grew skinny. I wasn't a football player. It wasn't for me."[4]

Timlin's parents were Jerome Francis Timlin Sr. and Nancy Sharon Beyer, known in the family as Sharon. "I never knew my father," Mike Timlin said in a December 2021 interview. "He was gone before I was born. My mom raised me and my three older sisters alone. Her mom and dad helped out. We lived on our own but they lived in the same town. Basically, my father was her father. His name was Sylvester August Beyer – 'Jake.'"[5]

Mike's sisters were Jeri, Tracy, and Sherri. As of 2022, two lived near Austin, Texas, and Sherri lived in Maine. Their mother, Sharon, "worked for Exxon for 27 years," Mike said. She worked in Midland, where Exxon had a headquarters office overseeing the exploration and drilling work done in the region. "She worked in the operations file room. She had a high-school education, but she had precedence over every well or operation that was in that area. All you had to do was mention the name of an operation – exploration or drilling – and she could locate the file and tell you what was in it."

Jerome Timlin had been a truck driver. The first time Mike met him was when he was perhaps 11 or 12 years old, at a truck stop. There were two other times they met, once when Mike was in college and once when Mike was a major leaguer playing with the Red Sox in Texas.[6]

Of his mother, Mike said, "It wasn't real easy with four kids, but she did a hell of a job."[7]

Her parents, Jake and Opal Beyer, helped. After elementary school, Mike would walk over to their house until his mother returned home from work. His grandmother had a home sewing shop where she worked on alterations and clothing and made quilts. Grandfather Jake, interestingly, worked for a different oil company, Gulf Oil.

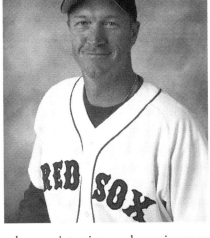

It was at Midland High School that Mike began to blossom at baseball. Most of the time he played outfield. But one day when he was on the junior varsity team, playing against the varsity, his coach beckoned him to the mound. Mike told the coach he didn't really want to pitch, but the coach – times were different – told him, quietly, "You'll pitch because I'll tell you to pitch. Otherwise, you can walk off the field." As he tells it, Mike said, "'OK,' and I turned around and pitched. And I turned out to be a pitcher."

When others were pitching, Timlin returned to center field, though he put in a bit of time as backup catcher and first baseman. His pitching earned him a half-scholarship to Southwestern University in Georgetown, Texas. Before beginning his freshman year, becoming an architect had appealed to him, but the school didn't offer appropriate programs. Instead, he majored in physical education. It was while pitching in college that he was spotted by pro scouts.

"The dream for most of the kids in Texas was to play for the University of Texas or A&M or a Division I school. At Southwestern, since we were just north of Austin, we played against University of Texas. The scouts were watching the games there. I pitched the first game of a doubleheader; I was facing off against Calvin Schiraldi. I lost that game, 1-0. I gave up three hits. He gave up one hit. I think that was the first time I was on somebody's radar."

Scout Jim Hughes contacted Timlin on behalf of the Toronto Blue Jays, leading to his being drafted, and ultimately came to Mike's house to sign him for what was in 1987 a significant bonus.[8]

Timlin's first assignment took him far from Texas – to Medicine Hat, Alberta, where he pitched in rookie ball in the Pioneer League. He started 12 of 13 games, and was 4-8 with a 5.14 ERA for the 26-43 Medicine Hat Blue Jays, who finished last in the North Division.

He showed far better in his first full season of pro ball, starting in 22 of his 35 appearances in the South Atlantic League's Single-A Myrtle Beach Blue Jays and producing a 1988 record of 10-6 with a strong 2.86 ERA.

Timlin was asked to put in another year at Single A, in 1989 for the Dunedin Blue Jays in the Florida State League, and to begin to work primarily in relief (26 of his 33 games). He was 5-8 (3.25).

Over those first three years, Timlin essentially been converted to become a reliever. Pitching coach Bill Monbouquette had counseled him at Myrtle Beach that he was "only a step or two away from the big leagues." Timlin didn't necessarily believe it at the time, but it essentially proved to be true.

The 1989 Dunedin team, though a Single-A team, had 15 players make it to the majors.

Most of 1990 was at Dunedin as well, working exclusively in relief. In 42 games, closing 40 of them, he recorded a 1.43 ERA. Timlin also got substantial work in Double A for the Knoxville Blue Jays (Southern League); after arriving in late July, he was 1-2 in 17 games with a 1.73 ERA. He played winter ball for Lara in Venezuela.

The next year, 1991, Timlin made the majors. He debuted on April 8 and after pitching a total of 5⅓ innings, he was 2-0. His first two innings were at SkyDome against the visiting Red Sox. He faced six batters and didn't let the ball out of the infield, though he did walk two. His first win came two days later, also against Boston. Working the top of the eighth, he struck out the first two batters and got a groundout from the third, then saw teammate Pat Tabler hit a three-run homer to boost the Jays to a 5-3 lead they maintained as Tom Henke closed the game.

Two days after that, on April 12, Timlin faced the Brewers and pitched the 9th, 10th, and 11th innings, allowing just a single. The Jays tied the game in the bottom of the ninth and won it on Mark Whiten's leadoff homer in the 11th. Manager Cito Gaston was no doubt pleased. Pitching coach Galen Cisco was certainly pleased with Timlin's first start, in Cleveland on June 12. Timlin worked six innings, allowing one hit, a high bouncer that was the only ball to leave the infield.[9] "Impressive? He was nearly impeccable, and there's a word I've always wanted to use."[10] Timlin was OK with starting, but he really appreciated the value he could bring out of the bullpen. "'I don't mind starting because I'm all for the team concept and that overrules what I want,' Timlin said. He went on to suggest, though, that he sees himself as a stopper, saying 'I've had success at it.'"[11]

In a game on August 1, Timlin went on the disabled list with tendinitis in his right elbow. A very effective set-up man, Timlin was 11-6 (3.16) by season's end. His 63 appearances were topped only by Duane Ward's 81, but Timlin pitched one more inning than Ward. During the last stretch of the season, he became less effective.[12]

Timlin appeared in four postseason games, the four games the Jays lost to the Minnesota Twins in the 1991 ALCS. His ERA was 3.18 but he bore the loss in Game Three, when pinch-hitter Mike Pagliarulo homered off him in the top of the 10th. "It was a horrible pitch," Timlin said afterward, "Right down the middle."[13] There was a reason he'd been less effective; after the season, he underwent arthroscopic surgery to remove a bone spur and a chip from his right elbow.

The next year, 1992, the Blue Jays went all the way and won the World Series. Timlin didn't join the team until June, as it took time to rebuild arm strength after the surgery.[14] He pitched in six games in Dunedin and then in seven games for Triple-A Syracuse as part of his rehab, a total of 21⅓ innings. His first game with Toronto was on June 13. Of the first 11 batters he faced after rejoining Toronto, only one got a hit, a single. He bore a loss on June 18, giving up four runs (two earned) in two innings against the Tigers. His only two decisions in 1992 were both losses, the other one coming on July 29. By the end of the year, Timlin had worked in 26 games for a total of 43⅔ innings, with an ERA of 4.12, just marginally above the team ERA of 3.91.

Timlin pitched in the ALCS, with a hold in Game Three against Oakland and a scoreless eighth inning in Game Four. In the World Series, against the Atlanta Braves, he pitched a perfect seventh inning in Game Five and then earned a save in the final, triumphant Game Six. With a 4-3 lead in the 11th inning, two outs, and a runner on third base, Timlin took over from Jimmy Key. The speedy Otis Nixon thought to perhaps take advantage of a reliever who had worked only one inning in the past 13 days. On an 0-and-1 count, Nixon laid down a squeeze bunt. Timlin "fielded it cleanly and then threw what [fellow pitcher and teammate David] Cone called 'an Olympic shot-put.' To Blue Jays fans, it was the longest throw in club history. But when it finally arrived, it was true."[15] Timlin hadn't been caught unaware. First baseman Joe Carter had advised Timlin, "This guy will lay it down. You got to bounce off the mound." Timlin said he was "surprised that he was able to remain calm. 'It's just a Single-A game,' he said he told himself. 'Just relax and throw strikes.'" Fielding the bunt, he said, "I wanted to tag him but he was already past me. Then I wanted to make sure I didn't throw it over Joe's head."[16] The Blue Jays had won the World Series. During the clubhouse celebration, the Jays chanted, "Pee-eff-pee! Pee-eff-pee!"[17] The initials p.f.p. stood for pitchers' fielding practice. Clearly, they appreciated Timlin's work.

The Jays became repeat champions, winning it all again in 1993, beating the White Sox in the ALCS and the Phillies in the World Series. With 71 appearances, closer Duane Ward ranked first but set-up men Mark Eichhorn and Timlin were tied for second-most with 54 apiece – and Timlin did close 27 games. Timlin's regular-season record was 4-2 with a 4.69 ERA, one of the higher ERAs in his career. It had been 5.64 as of August 12 and he was sent to Dunedin to work with coach

Bill Monbouquette on his mechanics and control. That strategy seemed to work. He had a strong stretch-run drive in September, shaving off nearly a full run from his ERA. In the postseason, Timlin worked 2⅓ innings in the ALCS, allowing just one run, and 2⅓ scoreless innings in the World Series, appearing in Games Two and Four.

The Jays fell to third place in the strike-shortened 1994 season and fifth (last) in 1995, with the bullpen workload being spread more evenly among several. He missed 15 days in late May and early June with a right-shoulder issue. He wasn't used as much in pressure situations. Timlin's ERA climbed to 5.18 in '94, the highest of his career until his final season in 2008.[18]

Timlin very successfully brought the ERA down to a career-best 2.14 in 1995. Again there was a mixture of set-up and closing work, and a brief trip to the disabled list. The Blue Jays finished in last place, 30 games out. His own record was 4-3.

In 1996 Timlin became the Jays' closer, in 56 of his 59 appearances. His won-lost record was 1-6 but his ERA was good at 3.65, and he racked up 31 saves, including eight in September alone. After the season, the Jays signed him to a two-year contract – but he was swapped to Seattle on the last day of July 1997.

The season hadn't started well. The very first pitch Timlin threw was on Opening Day at SkyDome, with the Blue Jays holding a 5-4 lead heading into the top of the ninth. Norberto Martin homered to left-center. The game was tied. Dan Plesac coughed up the winning run to the White Sox in the 10th. Timlin pitched quite well after that, and as July ended he was 3-2, 2.87, closing 26 of 38 appearances. Toronto traded for José Cruz Jr., sending both Timlin and Paul Spoljaric to the Mariners for a player who was believed could be a budding star. Timlin worked as set-up man for closer Heathcliff Slocumb. Timlin's ERA was 3.86 (3-2).

Seattle won the AL West but lost the Division Series to Baltimore in four games. Timlin appeared just once, in Game One at Kingdome. The Orioles already had a 5-1 lead when he came in to pitch the sixth. Chris Hoiles hit a leadoff home run. Timlin was charged with three more runs, departing with just two outs.

Timlin worked the full 1998 season for Seattle. The team finished in the middle of the pack in the AL West. The closer's role was shared by four pitchers, though Timlin's 40 games finished ranked first, as did his overall 70 appearances. His 2.95 ERA was tops, better by more than two full runs than any other reliever on the staff. From May 26 to July 15, he allowed just one (inconsequential) earned run in 19 appearances. September was particularly strong, with seven saves and one win. He was an example of what a *Chicago Tribune* writer called an unsung workhorse.[19]

Entering free agency for the first time, Timlin signed a four-year deal with the Baltimore Orioles beginning in 1999. He was seen as a "proven closer," something the O's needed.[20] He truly looked forward to the role, saying, "Any relief pitcher prefers to pitch the ninth. It's nice to be out there to win the game and have everybody come out to shake your hand."[21] He was with them for a year and a half. The '99 team finished in fourth place, 20 games behind the Yankees. The season started roughly, with a 6.45 ERA through June 8. Through the All-Star break, Timlin had 10 blown saves or losses. He began to settle down and 10 of his 27 saves came in September as he finished strong again. Timlin's season record was 3-9, but with a solid 3.57 ERA that was more than a run better than the 4.77 team ERA.[22]

The Orioles, though, were less than satisfied and reportedly willing to eat a significant portion of Timlin's salary if there was a deal to be made. Beginning 2000 on the DL with an abdominal strain, he had a dismal start to the season but got progressively better as the weeks went on. He brought his ERA under 5.00 in late July, but was traded on the 29th to the St. Louis Cardinals for a minor leaguer, first baseman Chris Richard, and cash.[23] In the National League, the Cardinals used him less frequently to close games. He shaved a run and a half off his earned-run average, while working in 25 games.[24]

Timlin helped stabilize the bullpen and the Cardinals finished first in the NL Central. He worked in five more postseason games. The only one in which he surrendered an earned run (two of them) was in NLDS Game Two, which the Cardinals won, 10-4. They swept the Braves in the NLDS but lost the NLCS to the Mets, four games to one. Timlin bore the loss in Game Two in the ninth inning, 6-5, after his first baseman committed an error, followed by a sacrifice bunt and then a single.

In 2001 the Cards reached the postseason again, but lost out in the NLDS to Arizona. During the regular season, Timlin had worked in 67 games, closing 19, but the 67 games ranked him only tied for third in relief appearances by a frequently-used staff. He would have worked more but for arthroscopic surgery at the end of July to fix torn cartilage in his left knee. His 4.09 ERA was the highest among the five top relievers. His one appearance in the playoffs was in Game Three, when he got four groundouts, giving up just one single.

In 2002 Timlin was traded again at the end of July, this time to the last-place Phillies.[25] He'd pitched very well for St. Louis – with a 2.51 ERA in 42 games (closing 10). In the mix was one solitary start – on April 19 in Milwaukee. It was his first start since the three he had in 1991, and also the last of his career. It didn't go well; he gave up four runs in 4⅓ innings. For the Phillies, he was 3.79 in 30 games. The team improved and finished in third place. For the season as a whole, Timlin gave up 15 homers. Never before had he topped nine.

A free agent once more, Timlin signed in January 2003 with the Boston Red Sox. He was with them for the final six seasons of his career, a team that made the postseason in five of those six years.

The original idea was to have Alan Embree, Ramiro Mendoza, and Timlin constitute a "three-headed closer committee."[26] As spring training progressed, the idea transformed into a "committee in short relief."[27] As it turned out, Timlin's 72 appearances led the pitching staff, but only 13 of them were as closer. Byung-Hyun Kim and Brandon Lyon closed most of the games. Timlin was 6-4 (3.55) with 17 holds and two saves.[28] He had a very impressive 7.22 strikeout-to-walk ratio (65 K to 9 BB) in 83⅔ innings. It was by far his best year in that department; for his career, Timlin's K/BB ratio was 2.31.[29]

The 2003 Red Sox finished second to the Yankees in the AL East, beat Oakland in a five-game Division Series, and then lost to the Yankees in the 11th inning of Game Seven of the ALCS. Timlin pitched in eight of the 12 playoff games, a total of 9⅔ innings with an ERA of 1.38. In five of the eight games, he earned a hold. His longest stint was in Game Three of the ALDS, which ran to 11 innings, with Timlin working a perfect 8th through 10th. In Game Seven of the ALCS, when Boston manager Grady Little famously sent spent starter Pedro Martínez back out to pitch in the eighth – at which point Martínez coughed up three runs and brought New York into a 5-5 tie, Alan Embree faced one batter and got him out. Timlin finished that inning and pitched a scoreless ninth. Tim Wakefield took over and Aaron Boone homered off him to win the game, and the series, on his first pitch in the 11th. Had Little replaced Martínez after the seventh, it likely would have been Timlin who replaced him.[30]

In 2004 Timlin added 11 more postseason games to his growing total. He also earned another World Championship ring – despite a postseason ERA of 6.17. Terry Francona was Boston's new manager. Timlin was back under a new two-year deal. Curt Schilling (21-6) was the new ace. Timlin (5-4, 4.13) led the team in appearances with 76 (and a nearly-identical 76⅓ innings pitched). Though he finished 12 games, the closer was Keith Foulke with 61 (in 72 appearances).

The Red Sox swept the Division Series from the Angels in three games, surviving Vladimir Guerrero's grand slam off Timlin that tied the game 6-6. David Ortiz hit a two-run homer in the bottom of the 10th to win it. The grand slam was the only home run Timlin surrendered in 28 playoff games with Boston.[31]

In an understatement, Timlin said before the ALCS got underway, "The Red Sox have a long history of not quite getting there."[32] The Yankees got to him for two runs in Game One of the ALCS, and caused him to blow a save in Game Four – though the Red Sox famously won that game, kicking off an eight-game winning streak that catapulted them over the Yankees and into sweeping the World Series from St. Louis. Timlin pitched in Games One, Two, and Three of the World Series. The Red Sox had won it all for the first time in 86 years.

The year 2005 saw the Red Sox reach the Division Series but they were swept there by the ultimate World Series-winning Chicago White Sox. Timlin had led the entire American League in appearances, with 81 – exactly half of the 162-game schedule. He was 7-3 (his 13 saves were only two fewer than closer Foulke's) with a 2.24 ERA. He allowed only two home runs all year long, and had a 2.95 K/BB ratio (59-20). He appeared in the postseason, pitching the final top of the ninth in Game Three, giving up one run as the White Sox prevailed, 5-3. Red Sox fans voted him the "10th Player Award."

In the offseason, Timlin and catcher Jason Varitek were on the US team in the inaugural 2006 World Baseball Classic.

The 2006 season was an off-year for the Red Sox, who finished third. Timlin was back on a new contract, one he negotiated himself without an agent, part of an ongoing series of one-year deals that took him through 2008. He was 6-6 in a club-leading 68 games, gave up seven homers, and had a 4.36 ERA. He struck out 30 and walked 16. He battled injury during the season, missing games between May 25 and June 13 with a strained right shoulder and another week in the latter half of September.

Though missing more than five weeks with tendinitis – including all of May after May 2 – Timlin still appeared in 50 games, and picked up his fourth World Series ring, in 2007. His regular-season record was a modest winning one (2-1). Jonathan Papelbon was the closer. Hideki Okajima had the most relief appearances (66). Javy López worked in 61 games (for Papelbon it was 59), but Timlin's 55⅓ innings pitched were third on the bullpen staff, despite the long stretch on the DL. His 3.42 ERA was better than the team's 3.87.

The 2007 Red Sox finished first in the division, two games ahead of the Yankees. On August 31 Timlin made his 1,000th major-league appearance. The Red Sox swept the Division Series (against the Angels) and the World Series (against the Colorado Rockies), but the ALCS was a hard-fought seven games against Cleveland – Boston winning the first one, then losing three in a row before coming back with the three wins necessary to prevail. Timlin wasn't used in the ALDS. He pitched in the first three games of the ALCS, without giving up a run and he pitched a perfect eighth inning in Game One of the World Series. In Game Three, he got the final two outs in the sixth, then gave up singles to the first two batters in the seventh. Okajima replaced him and Matt Holliday homered, narrowing Boston's lead to 6-5. The Red Sox added four more runs and won, Timlin credited with a hold. In Game Four, he struck out the only two batters he faced, to finish the seventh and earn another hold.[33] The Red Sox won the game, 4-3, and thus the Series.

Timlin's last season in the majors was in 2008. He was 42 years old, and when he and Tim Wakefield (41) combined on a shutout of the Tigers on May 6, it was said to be the first time in the modern era that two pitchers over 40 had done so.[34] Though the other four relievers each worked more games, Timlin still got into 47. Papelbon closed 62, but Timlin was second with 26. His season ERA was elevated – 5.66. There was one more run at the postseason, Boston beating the Angels three games to one in the Division Series. Timlin again sat out the ALDS but when playing Tampa Bay in the ALCS, he pitched in Games Two and Four. He was saddled with the loss in Game Two, coming into an 8-8 tie game to pitch the bottom of the 11th at Tropicana Field. After walking the first two batters, then seeing both runners advance on a groundout that went third to first, he intentionally walked the next batter, but lost the game on a sacrifice fly by B.J. Upton. In Game Four, he entered in the top of the eighth in a game the Rays were winning, 11-2. A walk, groundout, triple, and single added two more runs before he induced a 4-6-3 double play. He had thrown his last pitch in the majors.

Timlin's 46 postseason appearances place him sixth all-time, through the 2021 season.

Giving it one last shot, after something of a chance conversation with Colorado Rockies GM Dan O'Dowd early in the season, Timlin worked out for a month and then signed a minor-league deal in July 2009. He was sent to Casper, Wyoming, to pitch for the rookie-league Casper Ghosts – interestingly, a team in the same Pioneer League where he had first begun. He pitched well in two games there, and was promoted to the Triple-A Colorado Springs Sky Sox, for whom he worked 4⅔ innings in four games (six strikeouts, seven hits, two runs). When the Sky Sox left for a road trip and his status has not been clarified, he chose to officially retire, leaving on his own terms.

After a lengthy career, Timlin was financially secure enough that he could pursue what interested him. He had married Dawn Wood in 1992 and the couple had two children – Jacob, born in 1996, and Mykayla, born in 2000. He became pitching coach for Valor Christian High School in Highlands Ranch, Colorado, and served in that role for nine years, until both children had graduated. "Luckily, we won three state championships while I was there. I worked with some awesome kids. It was a great time. As soon as my daughter graduated, we decided I'm going to stop there, we'll travel and go watch her play volleyball. She doesn't play anymore but that's what we do now. We just kind of travel and go and have fun."

While in Boston, Dawn Timlin was known for her charitable efforts and running the Boston Marathon, which she did five times. Husband Mike said, "She does a lot of charity work. We're involved with the Angel Fund there; we help Dr. Robert Brown at Mass General. We raise money for research for ALS. She does a lot of stuff helping raise money."

SOURCES

In addition to the sources cited in the Notes, the author consulted Baseball-Reference.com, Retrosheet.org, and SABR.org.

NOTES

1. It could have been 12, in that he started the 2002 season with a Cardinals team that made it to the NLCS, but in late July he had been traded to the Phillies, who were not a contender.
2. Richard Justice, "Orioles' Timlin Savors Closer Role," *Washington Post*, February 28, 1999: D8.
3. Mike Stanton was a teammate of Timlin's at both Midland High and Southwestern. Al Pickett, "Abilenian Pulls for Blue Jays, and Other Notes," *Abilene Reporter-News*, October 3, 1991: 21. Stanton enjoyed a 19-year major-league career. His 1,178 appearances rank second all-time, following only Jesse Orosco's 1,252. Timlin primarily played outfield at Midland High.
4. Mike Eisenbath, "Oft-traveled Timlin Is Relieved to Have Landed with the Cards," *St. Louis Post-Dispatch*, August 18, 2000: D1.
5. Author interview with Mike Timlin on December 10, 2021. Unless otherwise indicated, all direct quotations attributed to Timlin come from this interview.
6. His father had two sons with him that latter time. See Gordon Edes, "Timlin Stands Tall off and on Mound," *Boston Globe*, March 24, 2005: C1, C3.
7. Eisenbath.
8. It was only some years later, when visiting Midland and talking with his former high-school coach that the coach let Timlin know a letter of interest had come to the school from Stanford. "You got a letter from Stanford when you were in high school but I didn't give it to you because I didn't think you could make the grades." Interview December 10, 2021.
9. Associated Press, "Rookie Timlin acts like old pro," *Globe and Mail* (Toronto), June 13, 1991: D12.
10. Neil MacCarl, "Toronto Blue Jays, "*The Sporting News*, June 24, 1991: 19.
11. Neil A. Campbell, "Jays Rotation Keeps Spinning," *Globe and Mail*, June 19, 1991: C12.
12. In fact, the *Globe and Mail's* Neil Campbell wrote that Timlin had become "dreadful recently as the setup man." Neil Campbell, "What It Takes to Win a Pennant," *Globe and Mail*, October 8, 1991: D11.
13. Jerome Holtzman, "Pagliarulo Pulls His Weight … and Biggest HR," *Chicago Tribune*, October 12, 1991: A5. The *Globe and Mail* called him "one of the weaker links in the Blue Jay 'pen." Neil Campbell, *Globe and Mail*, October 12, 1991: A14.
14. Larry Millson, "Timlin Armed and Ready," *Globe and Mail*, June 13, 1992: A20.
15. Mark Newman, "What's Past Is Past," *The Sporting News*, November 2, 1992: 14.
16. Murray Chass, "Winfield and Carter: History Doesn't Repeat," *New York Times*, October 26, 1992: C1. Catcher Pat Borders agreed that they'd talked about the possibility of a bunt during a meeting on the mound. See Bill Plaschke, *Los Angeles Times*, October 25, 1992: C1. Timlin also said, "I was hoping he'd pop it up to me or it would come right to me so I wouldn't have to run over there and field it because I was afraid I was going to fall down." Neil A. Campbell and Larry Millson, "Timlin Last on Scene That Cone Helped Create," *Globe and Mail*, October 26, 1992: D5.
17. Chass. Timlin said he was one of the few pitchers who actually enjoyed pitchers' fielding practice.
18. At one point, Larry Millson wrote, "You have to wonder how many more chances Mike Timlin will get in meaningful situations." And that was early in the season. Larry Millson, "Blue Jays Bail Out Timlin," *Globe and Mail*, April 21, 1994: E10.
19. Phil Rogers mentioned Timlin, Terry Mulholland, Jeff Montgomery, and a few others. "Attention, Shoppers: Stock Up on Durable Arms," *Chicago Tribune*, October 25, 1998: 135.
20. Richard Justice, "For Orioles, Opening Move Is Signing Closer Timlin," *Washington Post*, November 13, 1998: C1.
21. Justice, "Orioles' Timlin Savors Closer Role."
22. There was some suggestion that manager Ray Miller may have "misused his relievers" in 1999. See Dave Sheinin, "Comfortable and Effective? Timlin Hopes He Is Closer," *Washington Post*, February 28, 2000: C6.
23. It was thought the Orioles might have paid as much as 50 percent of the remaining money on Timlin's $16 million, four-year contract.

Rick Hummel, "Jocketty Lands Bullpen Help in Trade for Orioles' Timlin," *St. Louis Post-Dispatch*, July 30, 2000: D10. It was thought Timlin's role was to set up closer Dave Veres.

24 Hummel summarized his time with St. Louis in 2000, grading him with a C+: "Timlin has well above average stuff but was less consistent than the club would have liked. He was among the most durable relievers, though, after coming from Baltimore." Rick Hummel, "Cardinals Charge into Playoffs Earns High Grades," *St. Louis Post-Dispatch*, October 22, 2000: D11.

25 He was part of a five-player swap that also involved some cash. Accompanied by Placido Polanco and Bud Smith, he went to Philadelphia for Scott Rolen, Doug Nickle, and cash.

26 Michael Silverman, "Boston Red Sox," *The Sporting News*, January 27, 2003: 57.

27 David Srinivasan, "RotoRap," *The Sporting News*, March 3, 2003: 61.

28 He was deemed "one of the most dependable arms in Boston's often-erratic bullpen." Bob Hohler, "Francona on Deck for Sox," *Boston Globe*, November 5, 2003: F56.

29 Though it was Kevin Millar who used the year's team slogan phrase "Cowboy up!" most often, it was reportedly Mike Timlin who introduced it. Nick Cafardo, "Thrills Were in Season," *Boston Globe*, October 8, 2003: 67.

30 Bob Ryan, "His Appearance May Have Provided Relief," *Boston Globe*, March 5, 2004: C6. Ryan wrote that Timlin had been "just about unhittable" in October 2003.

31 "I threw a not-so-great pitch to a really great hitter," Timlin said. He felt he'd let his teammates down, but in the end the Red Sox won. Nick Cafardo, "Pick-Me-Ups Were a Relief to Timlin," *Boston Globe*, October 9, 2004: E4.

32 John Powers, "A Clashing Combination," *Boston Globe*, October 12, 2004: C2.

33 In the six 2007 postseason games, Timlin struck out seven of the 20 batters he faced, and walked nobody. The two runs that were charged to him came in on the homer hit after he had departed.

34 Associated Press, "Veteran Bosox Pitchers Share Historic Shutout," *Globe and Mail*, May 8, 2008: S6.

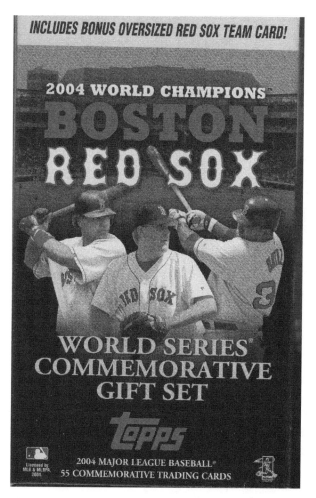

Photo by Bill Nowlin.

JASON VARITEK

BY CHAD HAGAN

Jason Andrew Varitek (nickname: Tek) was a major-league baseball catcher who played all 15 seasons of his major-league career for the Boston Red Sox (1997-2011), a switch-hitter who threw right-handed. Varitek was a member of two World Series winners for Boston, in 2004 and 2007. After retiring as a player, he continued to work for the team and, as of 2023, served as game planning coordinator for the Red Sox.

Varitek was born on April 11, 1972, in Rochester, Michigan, the second oldest son of Joe and Donna Varitek. His family moved to Longwood, Florida, when he was 7. He has three brothers, Justin, Joe, and Jared.

Jason's parents and extended family were highly supportive of his sporting endeavors, and he credited growing up in such an atmosphere as a pivotal foundation to his success. The entire family, extended family, and family friends, helped with carpooling to games and practices. Jason played multiple sports as a youngster, but settled primarily on baseball at around age 6 or 7.

Varitek is one of only three men to have played in a championship game of the Little League World Series, the College World Series, and the Major League World Series. (Ed Vosberg and Michael Conforto are the others.)[1] In 2020 he was inducted into the National College Baseball Hall of Fame.[2]

At 12, Jason played in the 1984 Little League World Series for the Altamonte Springs, Florida, team, and helped lead his team to victory in the US Championship bracket, beating a team from Southport, Indiana. His team made it to the international championships, ultimately losing to a team from Seoul, South Korea.

In a 2023 interview, he said: "For a 12-year-old boy, this was about as great an experience as you can go through. I was extremely fortunate for the coaching staff that taught these young men the fundamentals of baseball. Two-a-day practices. This carried me through life. Fun and hard work. We lost in the finals, and it was on national television. A special time for that age group."[3]

In high school Varitek was a third baseman and catcher for the Lake Brantley High School baseball team in Altamonte Springs. He was also a catcher on the 1992 US Olympic team.[4]

In college Varitek helped lead the Georgia Tech baseball team to the 1994 College World Series championships (along with teammates Nomar Garciaparra and Jay Payton).

He was named *Baseball America's* 1993 College Player of the Year. In 1994, he won the *Baseball America* College Player of the Year Award and the Dick Howser Trophy for National Collegiate Player of the Year.

Varitek was an all-American in 1992, 1993, and 1994, earned first-team all-Atlantic Coast Conference honors each of those years and was named Atlantic Coast Conference Player of the Year in 1993. In 1994 he won the Golden Spikes Award, honoring the nation's top amateur baseball player, and was the national collegiate player of the year.

Varitek is the only Georgia Tech player to have his jersey number (33) retired. He holds the Georgia Tech records for career home runs (57), runs scored (261), hits (351), doubles (82), RBIs (251), and total bases (610). His career batting average of .384 is fifth-best in Georgia Tech history.[5] He graduated with a degree in management.

The Houston Astros offered Varitek a six-figure deal out of Lake Brantley High School, but he turned down the deal and committed to Georgia Tech.[6] In 1991 and 1993 (in 1992 Varitek was a member of the US Olympic team), he played in the Cape Cod Baseball League with the Hyannis Mets, winning both the league batting championship (.371) and the 1993 MVP Award. He was drafted 21st overall in the first round by the Minnesota Twins in 1993, but the deal fell through, and he returned for his senior year of college.

After college graduation, Varitek signed with agent Scott Boras and was drafted by the Seattle Mariners in the first round of the June 1994 amateur draft (14th pick overall). The Mariners sent him to their Port City Roosters (Wilmington, North Carolina) in the Double-A Southern League and played for them in 1995 and 1996. In 1997 he was promoted to the Tacoma Rainiers of the Triple-A Pacific Coast League and batted .254 with 15 homers and 48 RBIs in 87 games.

On July 31, 1997, Varitek and pitcher Derek Lowe were traded to the Red Sox for reliever Heathcliff Slocumb, a trade that would go down as one of the most important in recent Red Sox history[7] and one of the worst in Mariners history. Varitek later said that both he and Lowe were quite untested: "He was a one-pitch pitcher, and I couldn't catch, hit, or throw."[8]

Varitek played in 20 games for the Triple-A Pawtucket Red Sox in 1997 and made his major-league debut on September 24 in Detroit and collecting his first big-league base hit. The Red Sox held a 9-2 lead over the Tigers after eight innings. With a man on first and one out, manager Jimy Williams had Varitek pinch-hit for catcher Scott Hatteberg, facing Detroit's Kevin Jarvis; on the second pitch, he singled to left field. He caught the bottom of the ninth.

Varitek spent the 1998 as Hatteberg's backup, playing in 86 games and batting .253 with 7 home runs.

The 1999 season brought changes to the lineup; starting catcher Hatteberg was injured and out of action for three months. Varitek played in 144 games and batted .269 with 20 home runs and 76 RBIs. In 2000 Varitek supplanted Hatteberg as the Red Sox starting catcher, playing 139 games, batting .248/10/65.

Varitek got off to a strong start in 2001, and was batting .293 through 51 games, but his season ended after June 7, when he broke his right elbow. He was already seen as a key member of the team, dubbed by *Boston Globe* columnist Dan Shaughnessy as the team's "True North."[9] Hatteberg returned as starting catcher. In December 2001, Hatteberg was traded to the Colorado Rockies for infielder Pokey Reese. Varitek's future as Boston's starting catcher was solidified. Over the following eight seasons, he averaged 127 games per season.

By the 2003 season it was clear that Varitek was a team leader, with a strong influence over the baseball club and team. That season was a career best for Varitek, and he was named an All-Star for the first of three times. He became a fan favorite as well. He finished the season with a .273 batting average, 25 home runs, and 85 RBIs. The Red Sox played deep into the postseason, losing to the New York Yankees in Game Seven of the League Championship Series. The 2004 season began with a new manager (Terry Francona) and a new team that it was hoped would carry them further.

The season started well, but by midseason the Red Sox were struggling from numerous issues (including injuries and defensive woes). In the top of the third inning of a nationally televised game against the Yankees on July 24, Red Sox pitcher Bronson Arroyo hit Álex Rodríguez with a pitch. An argument ensued and Varitek shoved his glove in Rodríguez's face, attempting to hold Rodríguez back; Rodríguez reacted aggressively, and a scuffle broke out with both teams running out on the field. Both Varitek and Rodríguez were ejected. The Yankees built a 9-4 lead, but the Red Sox scored an 11-10 comeback victory. This is often regarded as the turning point in the Red Sox' season; they posted the best record in the majors after the incident. It's worth noting that the photograph of the tussle between Varitek and Rodríguez became one of the most iconic images in modern day Red Sox iconography.

Varitek finished the regular season with a career-high .296 batting average, with 18 home runs and 73 RBIs.

The 2004 American League Championship Series saw the Red Sox and Yankees meet again in postseason play. The Red Sox had fallen behind their rivals, three games to zero, including a devastating 19-8 loss in Game Three at Fenway Park, but the Red Sox rallied and won the last four games of the series. It was the stuff of legends – the first time a team had rallied from an 0-3 deficit to win a playoff series. Varitek drove in seven runs in the seven games.

The Red Sox swept the St. Louis Cardinals in the World Series to win their first World Series in 86 years. Varitek's two-run triple in the first inning of Game Two help set the Red Sox on the path to a 6-2 win.

In December of 2004, the Red Sox honored Varitek by naming him just their third captain since 1923 after signingin him to a $40 million, four-year deal. Varitek was unaware of the honor until he was presented with home and road jerseys bearing a red "C." Varitek's strong work ethic, hard-driving devotion and substantial influence led to the designation. (The role of team captain is now honorary, but in the past it came with management and coaching responsibilities.)

The 2005 sason was another banner year for Varitek, with the *Bleacher Report* calling it "the best all-around year in Varitek's career." He batted .281 with 22 home runs and 70 RBIs. Varitek made his second All-Star team and won a Gold Glove Award and a Silver Slugger Award. "It is worth noting that 'Tek had not previously, or since, won another Gold Glove or Silver Slugger Award," *Bleacher Report* said.[10] The team fell short in the postseason, losing to the Chicago White Sox.

Before the start of the 2006 season, Varitek appeared in three games for the US team in the 2006 World Baseball Classic. On July 18 he played in his 991st game for the Red Sox, eclipsing catcher Carlton Fisk's Red Sox record. The crown gave Varitek a standing ovation. In his 1,000th game, on July 31, he was injured, requiring surgery to repair torn cartilage in his left knee. He was out until September 4.

The 2007 season saw Varitek reach his 1,000th career hit. The Red Sox returned to the World Series and again swept their National League opponent, the Colorado Rockies. Varitek had 5 RBIs in the four games.

The 2008 season saw Varitek play 131 games, with 43 RBIs, 13 home runs, and a .220 batting average..

By calling Jon Lester's no-hitter on May 19, 2008, Varitek became the first major-league catcher to have caught four no-hitters. In 2015 Carlos Ruiz of the Philadelphia Phillies caught his fourth no-hitter, matching Varitek's total. Had it not been for a 1991 rule change in the definition of a no-hitter, Varitek would be credited with five. On the final day of the 2006 season, he caught Boston's Devern Hansack, who allowed no hits in a 9-0 win over the Baltimore Orioles. The game was called after five innings, however, and the 1991 criteria required nine. As had been noted, "It's in the books as a complete game, a shutout, and there were no hits by the Baltimore batters."[11]

Varitek's batting numbers fell off in the 2009 through 2011 seasons, and he retired as a player after the 2011 season, having appeared in 1,546 games over his 15-year playing career with a .256 batting average and 193 home runs.

As a switch-hitter, he batted .247 against right-handed pitching, but .278 against left-handers. Varitek, one observer wrote, holds an "impressive place in Red Sox history, placing 10th in games played and doubles, 10th in runs batted in, 11th in home runs and at-bats, 14th in walks, 17th in hits, and 17th in runs scored."[12]

Perhaps most important, according to another writer, "his on-field actions helped lead a generation of Red Sox fans to believe that beating the Yankees was possible."[13]

From the playing ranks, Varitek moved into the Red Sox front office as a special assistant to the head of baseball operations and catching instructor. His influential presence and hard work ethic was a natural fit for team management. His responsibilities included "major league personnel choices, evaluations, and mentoring and training of young players."[14]

In 2018 Varitek was listed as special assistant to the president of baseball operations, and in 2020 as special assistant/catching coach. In November of 2020, he was designated as game planning coordinator on manager Alex Cora's coaching staff, and in 2021 was named player information coach.

The position of game planning coordinator largely deals with the analysis of player analytics, in conjunction with implementing strategies between the Red Sox starting pitcher and the catcher; catching coach entails game planning regarding pitching and catching. As Alex Speier of the *Boston Globe* wrote about Varitek: "[T]he role of game planning coordinator was a natural outgrowth of a combination of his skills, his role in recent years, and the explosion of information in the game."[15]

Red Sox manager Cora has publicly acknowledged Varitek's coaching talent, going as far as saying in 2021 that Varitek "will manage in the big leagues. He will. But it's a process, and we talk about it. I think, with time, somebody's going to give him a chance and he's going to kill it. He's going to be great. I have so much respect for him. We've got a friendship and we like each other and he has been amazing to me through the whole process. He was there for me."[16]

In November of 2022, the Red Sox signed Varitek to a multiyear contract extension, a team source confirmed to the *Globe*'s Speier. Varitek's wife, Catherine, first broke the news on Twitter, noting that the former captain had signed up to remain with the Red Sox for the next three years. "You're officially stuck with him!" she tweeted.

As of 2023, Varitek was listed as the Red Sox game planning coordinator/catching coach.[17]

Varitek has been married twice and has four children: three daughters from his first marriage to Karen Mullinax, Ally, Kendall, and Caroline, and one daughter, Liv, from his marriage to Catherine Panagiotopoulos. Catherine frequently updates followers on social media about Varitek and his career.

As of 2023 the Variteks reside in Hingham, Massachusetts, having previously lived in Suwanee, Georgia, northeast of Atlanta.

When Varitek retired after 15 seasons as a player, he was the fifth-longest tenured player in Red Sox history behind Carl Yastrzemski (23 seasons), Ted Williams (19), Dwight Evans (19), and Tim Wakefield (17).[18]

In the 2023 interview, Varitek was very matter-of-fact. There was no mincing of words. He offered a perspective on helping the 2004 Red Sox finally win a World Series after an 86-year drought: "Anyone who knows anything about Boston, it wasn't easy. It took the entire organization, and generations from the past. Ted Williams, Dwight Evans. Took everyone, took everything. Toe the line. Rivals. The stepping stones were laid by the greats. One of the most surreal moments of my life. Wasn't easy getting there."[19]

SOURCES

In addition to the sources cited in the Notes, the author consulted Baseball-Reference.com.

NOTES

1. Vosberg pitched for the 1997 Florida Marlins and Conforto was an outfielder with the 2015 New York Mets. Varitek (who was with the Red Sox in both the 2004 and 2007 World Series) and Vosberg were on the winning team in their respective World Series.

2. "Jason Varitek Becomes First Little League Baseball World Series Graduate Inducted into the National College Baseball Hall of Fame," LittleLeague.org, September 9, 2020. Jason Varitek Becomes First Little League Baseball® World Series Graduate Inducted into the National College Baseball Hall of Fame – Little League. Accessed September 29, 2023.

3. Author interview with Jason Varitek, February 17, 2023.

4. The US team was eliminated in the semifinals by Cuba, the ultimate winner.

5. "Varitek, Garciaparra Highlight Tech Hall of Fame Class," RamblinWreck.com, July 30, 2004. Georgia Tech Athletics – https://ramblinwreck.com/varitek-garciaparra-highlight-tech-hall-of-fame-class/.

6. Brian McTaggart, "How the Astros Missed Out on Tek Support," MLB.com, May 25, 2018. https://www.mlb.com/news/astros-missed-on-jason-varitek-in-1990-c278343114.

7. Peter Abraham, "Duquette Recalls Bringing Jason Varitek to Boston," *Boston Globe*, February 28, 2012. https://www.bostonglobe.com/sports/2012/02/28/duquette-recalls-bringing-jason-varitek-boston/Xh27MPWuirtn1OuSQ4UJHP/story.html.

8. Tony Massarotti, "'Tek Support," *Boston Herald*, April 28, 2002: B24.

9. Dan Shaughnessy, "Team Caught Short by Varitek's Injury," *Boston Globe*, June 9, 2001: G1. Shaughnessy wrote, "Varitek has emerged as the True North of this baseball team. He's tough and he's clutch. … Only Manny Ramirez is a more valuable everyday presence on the active roster. Pitchers love throwing to Varitek." He added that "a switch-hitter catcher is every manager's dream."

10. Christopher Benvie, "Boston Red Sox: Top 10 Greatest Moments of Captain Jason Varitek's Career," *Bleacher Report*, February 16, 2012. https://bleacherreport.com/articles/1066338-jason-varitek-ranking-10-greatest-moments-of-red-sox-captains-career.

11. Bill Nowlin, "Devern Hansack," SABR BioProject. https://sabr.org/bioproj/person/devern-hansack/.

12 Lewis M. Brooks III, "Blog #76: Red Sox News: Jason Varitek Retires," lmb3.net, March 7, 2012. https://lmb3.net/2012/03/07/blog-76-red-sox-news-jason-varitek-retires/. Accessed September 28, 2023.

13 Jake Devereaux, "All-Time Red Sox Roster: Jason Varitek," Over the Monster.com, April 21, 2020. https://www.overthemonster.com/2020/4/21/21229251/boston-red-sox-all-time-roster-jason-varitek-no-hitters.

14 Lee Schecter, "Breaking Down Jason Varitek's Past, Present and Future Impact on Boston Red Sox," Bleacher Report.com, February 25, 2013. https://bleacherreport.com/articles/1543205-breaking-down-jason-variteks-past-present-and-future-impact-on-red-sox,%20February%2025,%202013.

15 Alex Speier, "What Exactly Does Jason Varitek Do as the Red Sox 'Game Planning Coordinator'?" *Boston Globe*, March 18, 2021. https://www.bostonglobe.com/2021/03/18/sports/what-exactly-does-jason-varitek-do-red-sox-game-planning-coordinator/?p1=BGSearch_Advanced_Results.

16 Chris Cotillo, "Jason Varitek Has Increased Presence for Boston Red Sox in New Coaching Role: 'He Will Manage in the Big Leagues, Alex Cora Says," MassLive.com, February 26, 2021. https://www.masslive.com/redsox/2021/02/jason-varitek-has-increased-presence-for-boston-red-sox-in-new-coaching-role-he-will-manage-in-the-big-leagues-alex-cora-says.html.

17 https://www.mlb.com/redsox/roster/coaches.

18 David Dorsey, "Jason Varitek on Retirement: 'My Decision Wasn't One I Took Lightly," *Fort Myers* (Florida) *News-Press*, March 1, 2012. https://www.masslive.com/redsox/2012/03/post_13.html.

19 Varitek interview, February 17, 2023.

Photo by Bill Nowlin.

TIM WAKEFIELD

BY BILL NOWLIN

Unfortunately, Tim Wakefield just kind of ran out of time. The knuckleballer spent 17 seasons with the Boston Red Sox, recording 186 of his 200 career victories with the franchise – just six short of the team record held by Cy Young and Roger Clemens.[1]

He was also a member of two World Series champions, including the memorable 2004 team that ended an 86-year drought. Wakefield pitched until he was 45 years old, an age at which various "butterfly" specialists have remained productive. Wakefield might have tried to hook on with another team, but he said, "I never wanted to pitch for another team."[2]

Just over a decade after his retirement from the Red Sox, he died from brain cancer at 57 years old.

It's not as though Wakefield was ever shooting for the Red Sox wins record in the first place. In fact, he wasn't even a pitcher to begin with. When he started his career in the Pittsburgh Pirates organization, he was an infielder.

Timothy Stephen Wakefield was born in Melbourne, Florida on August 2, 1966. He grew up in Melbourne and attended the public schools there, graduating from Eau Gallie High School in Melbourne.

His father, Steve, actually taught him the knuckleball early, at age 7 or 8. Steve was an active softball player who worked the morning shift (3 A.M. – 11 A.M.) at the Harris Corporation, an electronics company for which he designed circuits. Steve's wife, Judy, had one other child, a daughter named Kelly. In time, Judy Wakefield also worked for Harris as a purchaser and professional assistant.[3]

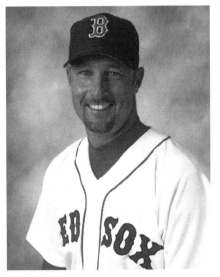

Steve started throwing a knuckler to his son. "I robbed my son of a lot of things because I was so dedicated to softball," he said. "So if he asked me to go out in the yard and play catch, I always said yes. But then he'd want to play and play and play, so I started throwing knuckleballs at him. He didn't like it. Eventually, he's say, 'OK, I've had enough.'"[4] So Tim learned early on how confounding the knuckleball could be, difficult to catch and difficult to hit. But, he admitted later, he hadn't seen it as a serious tool. It was more like a "magic trick or a party stunt."[5]

Tim went through T-ball and Little League, and as a Floridian, he could play baseball every day. The Atlanta Braves were his favorite team and Dale Murphy his favorite player. Tim won a baseball scholarship to Brevard Community College, but the other players were so good he quit the team before he ever got into a game. Head coach Les Hall of the Florida Institute of Technology saw potential in him and recruited him. Wakefield played first base for Florida Tech and did well enough, hitting 22 homers in one season, that in June 1988 he was selected by the Pittsburgh Pirates in the eighth round of the draft. He signed for a bonus of $15,000 and the commitment by the Pirates to pay for the remainder of his college tuition when he went back to school.

The Pirates placed Wakefield with their Watertown (New York) affiliate in the New York-Penn League. He played first base, appearing in 54 games. In 192 plate appearances, he managed only a .189 batting average with three homers and 20 RBIs, and he struck out 57 times. He was overmatched, but he showed good enough plate discipline to draw 25 walks, bumping up on his on-base percentage to .328.

In 1989, he played for two teams – a few games for the Augusta Pirates in the South Atlantic League, a Class A team, and then for the Welland (Ontario) Pirates back in the NYPL. His manager in extended spring training, Woody Huyke, had seen him fooling around with the knuckleball while playing catch with a teammate and saw how difficult it was to catch. At Welland, Wakefield was told to bring out the knuckler and he split his time between the infield and pitching (in 18 games). He won one and lost one and recorded a 3.40 ERA, and was sent to Instructional League in the fall. He knew he wasn't going to make it as a hitter, so developing the unusual pitch seemed his only possible road – however unlikely it might be – to making the major leagues. Wakefield wasn't thrilled about it, though, saying, "When they put an infielder on the mound, it's like they're putting you out to pasture. They're saying you don't have what it takes to get to the big leagues."[6]

In 1990, his first season playing exclusively as a pitcher, his ERA was 4.73, and his record for the last-place Salem (Virginia) Buccaneers was 10-14 (hey had the worst record in the Carolina League.) In 1991, the Pirates advanced him to Double-A ball, pitching in Raleigh for the Carolina Mudcats in the Southern League. He had a very good year, 15-8 with a 2.90 ERA in 25 starts. He pitched in one game for Triple-A Buffalo and lost it.

In 1992, halfway through the season, Wakefield was called up to the major leagues. He'd been 10-3 (3.06) with Buffalo. The Pirates were truly in need of pitching.

He made his debut on July 31, 1992 for manager Jim Leyland. The Pirates couldn't have hoped for a much better start, a complete-game win at Three Rivers Stadium against the visiting St. Louis Cardinals. He allowed six hits and walked five, but he struck out 10. Although he allowed two runs, neither of them was earned. It was a close 3-2 victory. "Really, I wasn't nervous except for the first pitch," he told reporters afterward. "I just stepped off the mound and looked around and saw Andy Van Slyke in center and Barry Bonds in left and Chico Lind at second…that always makes a pitcher feel better."[7]

Wakefield's next three starts were superb, too. Over his first four starts, he allowed just five earned runs and he was 3-0 with a 1.32 ERA. He lost one, 6-5 to the Giants in San Francisco, but didn't give up more than three runs a game for the rest of the season, finishing 8-1 with a 2.15 ERA. In 92 innings, he'd given up only 76 base hits. Knuckleballers are rare. When Wakefield matched up against the Dodgers' Tom Candiotti on August 26, it was the first time National League knuckleball pitchers had met since September 13, 1982 (when Phil Niekro faced his brother Joe).[8] Wakefield threw a six-hit, 2-0 shutout.

Despite the late start, he came in third in Rookie of the Year voting – which was done before the postseason, in which Wakefield continued to shine. The Pirates made it to the National League Championship Series and Pirates GM Ted Simmons said his rotation was going to be "Doug Drabek, Danny Jackson, and the Miracle. That's what Timmy has been for us since he came up."[9] Wakefield had two decisions, both complete-game wins, in Games Three (3-2) and Six (13-4). The Braves beat the Pirates in Game Seven. Wakefield's postseason ERA was 3.00.

The magical first year was followed by a disappointing 1993 season. Wakefield was given the honor of being the Opening Day pitcher, and won the game, but he walked nine batters. He was 6-11 with a 5.61 ERA with the Pirates, "a model of inconsistency – looking sharp in one outing and struggling in the next."[10]

That inconsistency reflected the unpredictability of the pitch he threw. A couple of years later, Wakefield said, "I have no idea where it's going, the hitter doesn't know where it's going, and the catcher doesn't know where it's going. I just try to throw it down the middle of the plate."[11] At one point, Wakefield was sent down two levels in midseason, back to Raleigh and the Double-A Mudcats for a couple of months. He put a good face on it, choosing not to take it as a demotion, but as something akin to a "rehabilitation assignment."[12] Even in Double A, however, he was 3-5 with a 6.99 ERA.

And in 1994, back in Buffalo at Triple A for the full year, he struggled even more; his ERA was 5.84 with a 5-15 record. It was mystifying at the time, but in some senses his performance simply reflected the most unpredictable to pitches: one really never knew when it would be "on" or "off." Phil Niekro, the masterful knuckleball pitcher who made it to the Hall of Fame, said, "Tim was so successful early, and then he just lost it. That's when it becomes tough mentally to throw a pitch everybody knows is coming. I've told him that he's got to keep learning, he's got to eat, sleep, walk, and talk the knuckleball until it floats in his bloodstream like a spirit inside him."[13]

Wakefield also benefited from advice from other members of the knuckleball fraternity, including Charlie Hough and Candiotti, who taught him how to change speeds, pick spots with hitters, and be patient when it didn't work. Wakefield "paid it forward" to knuckleballers who came after him, notably R.A. Dickey.[14]

On April 20, just as the 1995 major-league season was to begin (after the players' strike which had prematurely ended 1994), the Pirates released Wakefield. Six days later, the Boston Red Sox took a flyer and signed him to a Triple-A contract. Red Sox GM Dan Duquette had seen Wakefield pitch when Duquette was GM for the Montreal Expos. He had a pitching staff in Boston that needed renewal and bolstering. Duquette's appeal to Wakefield was based in part on an arrangement to hire Phil Niekro as a consultant and offer to set the young pitcher up with him. Wakefield said, "Boston was the only team to make me a decent offer."[15]

Called up in time to pitch on May 27, he made back-to-back starts on May 27 and, on two days' rest, May 30. Wakefield had one of his best years with the Red Sox in 1995. He finished the season with a 2.98 earned run average. He won his first four starts – two of them complete games, allowing just two earned runs over 34 innings. And he kept on winning – even taking a no-hitter into the eighth inning twice, on June 9 and July 9 – until the point he was 14-1 (1.65) in mid-August.

But the knuckleball teaches humility. August 18 was a horrific game in which he was so wild the Mariners took the first 18 pitches he threw, and then – on his second swing – Mike Blowers hit a grand slam. Knuckleballers are prone to giving up homers, though; in his career, Wakefield surrendered 418, or one every 7.7 innings.

Including that outing, he was 2-7 over the rest of the season, losing the last four games he started. Despite the ups and downs, The *Wall Street Journal* wrote in late September that Wakefield was having "one of the best knuckleball seasons of all time."[16] The Red Sox finished first in the AL East, but were swept in the Division Series by the Cleveland Indians. Wakefield lost Game Three, 8-2. His key contribution to getting the team to the postseason was recognized; he placed third in voting for the Cy Young Award. He had been 16-8 (2.95), leading the team in victories.

There followed a couple of so-so years. In 1996 he was 14-13 (5.14). He then went to arbitration over salary differences with the Red Sox, and prevailed. In 1997, after a swollen elbow put him on the 15-day disabled list in April, he was 12-15, despite an improved 4.25 ERA. His 15 losses were the most in the AL.

Clearly, the team around any pitcher matters a great deal. In 1998, the Red Sox reached the postseason again. Wakefield's ERA was 4.58, but in wins and losses he was 17-8. Boston faced the Indians again in the Division Series. This time, Wakefield pitched in Game Two. He lasted only 1 1/3 innings, was bombed for five runs, and took the loss.

Closer Tom Gordon was injured in 1999, so the Sox used Wakefield as a swingman. He started in stretches and relieved in others. As a closer, he saved 15 games in 18 opportunities. There was one remarkable inning on August 10 in Kansas City when he managed to tie a major-league record by striking out four batters in one inning (the 10th); he also blew a save in the game.

Was the knuckleball just one pitch in his repertoire? He'd answered that question years earlier, talking to Jerome Holtzman of the *Chicago Tribune*: "No, basically, I'm a one-pitch pitcher. Here it is. If they hit it, they hit it."[17]

One of the lessons he had learned, he said, was "Don't pitch to the names."[18] In other words, don't worry about the strengths and weaknesses of whoever might be in the batter's box. Just try and get the ball over the plate and let the knuckler's unpredictable movement perform its magic. As much as anything Phil Niekro taught him, it was that throwing the knuckleball required a degree of psychological fortitude, to be able to maintain self-confidence and faith. No one knew how the ball was going to flutter; "use that uncertainty to your advantage."[19] When he was pressing, sometimes it meant he was throwing the ball too hard. Teammate Mike Greenwell noticed this once and told him, "Ease up a little. Don't put so much pressure on yourself. You're trying too hard…Try taking a little off."[20]

The Red Sox made it to the postseason yet again in 1999, and Wakefield worked in two games in the Division Series, for a total of two innings, giving up three earned runs.

Wakefield wasn't pleased about being assigned to the bullpen in 2000, at almost the last minute. "It's hard to swallow two days before the season starts and all the work I've put in. I don't see any reasoning for it."[21] In some key respects, Wakefield's record in 2000 (6-10, 5.48) was almost a carbon copy of 1999's (6-11, 5.08). In 2000, however, Derek Lowe became Boston's full-time closer. Wakefield received only one save opportunity and failed to convert it.

Wakefield started 17 games for the third straight year in 2001. He brought his ERA down to 3.90; his record was 9-12. He'd seen a few managers come and go in Boston, and felt that Jimy Williams was made a scapegoat for a dysfunctional clubhouse in 2001. Replacing Williams with pitching coach Joe Kerrigan was, unfortunately, a short-term move that saw the club get worse.

Wakefield's autobiography (published in 2011) is an exceptionally honest one, admitting to uncertainty and vulnerability. The Red Sox took advantage of his versatility, sometimes perhaps a bit too much. Ballplayers in general tend to benefit from routines, and particularly with regard to certainty as to their role. Wakefield went through numerous changes, of managers and of roles, and even of ownership when the Henry/Werner/Lucchino group purchased the ballclub in early 2002. In some ways, he felt, "My whole career has been in a state of flux."[22]

In 2002, under new manager Grady Little, Wakefield started the season being told he would be working in the bullpen. "I'm not upset about it. I accept it," he said. "That's the way things are around here."[23] When it came down to it, though, his first two appearances were starts. By season's end, he had started 15 games and relieved in 30 others, with three saves in five chances. Despite the three different roles, his ERA in 2002 was 2.81 and he posted an 11-5 record. His mixed roles in the years 1999 to 2002 may have cost him as many as 20 or more wins, which would have secured his standing as the winningest pitcher in Red Sox history.

In November 2002, Wakefield married Stacy Stover, whom he had met in Massachusetts. The couple has two children, Trevor and Brianna. Stacy has been an active supporter of the Jimmy Fund. She also worked with Wakefield's Warriors, a group associated with the Franciscan Hospital for Children in Boston which gave children the opportunity to come to Fenway Park, watch batting practice, and meet some of the players.

In 2003, Wakefield returned to starting, almost exclusively. With rare exception, and a bump in 2010, he remained a starter for the remainder of his career. He never achieved better than his 4.09 ERA in 2003 over those final nine years. He was 11-7 during the 2003 regular season, nine of the wins coming while starting.

After a three-year gap, Boston got back to the postseason once more in 2003. Wakefield started and lost Game One of the Division Series, but then blossomed in the ALCS against the Yankees. He won Game One, 5-2, working six innings as the starter. He also started and won Game Four, 3-2, giving up just one run in six innings.

Game Seven took place three days later. It pitted Pedro Martinez (Boston) against Roger Clemens (Yankees); the score was tied, 5-5, after eight. Mike Timlin got the Yankees 1-2-3 in the bottom of the ninth. Manager Little called on Wakefield to pitch the bottom of the 10th and he got them 1-2-3. Wakefield threw just one pitch in the 11th, and it was the one he would most like to get back. Third baseman Aaron Boone hit a game-winning home run which sent the Yankees to the World Series and sent the Red Sox home for the winter. "It wasn't supposed to end like this," Wakefield said. "It's difficult, period. We are brothers in here. We have been family going on nine months and it hurts."[24]

Alluding to the team's stunning loss in Game Six of the 1986 World Series, Wakefield also told Red Sox clubbie Joe Cochran, "I just became Bill Buckner."[25] Though he apologized to Red Sox fans afterward, hardly anyone blamed Wakefield or thought poorly of him. Indeed, at the Boston Baseball Writers dinner over the winter, Wakefield received a standing ovation from the thousand or more fans in attendance.

This was – almost – the nadir for Boston in the long rivalry between the Red Sox and the Yankees, right up there with the "Bucky Dent" single-game playoff loss for the AL East title in 1978. Here it was 25 years later, and the Sox had still never beaten the Yankees in a high-stakes matchup.

The true nadir came a year later in the 2004 League Championship Series, after the Yankees took the first three games, trouncing Boston in Game Three, 19-8. Wakefield had been 12-10 during the regular season, eating innings again. In Game Three, after New York had already scored nine times, he volunteered to relieve even though he had been slated to start Game Four. He pitched 3 1/3 innings midgame, more than any other Boston pitcher that day, and was touched for five runs. In doing so, he took one for the team, foregoing his start. Doug Mirabelli, Wakefield's "personal catcher," said, "You don't want your bullpen to get blown out....For him to be able to go out there and suck up some innings for us, that was a huge help."[26]

When it came to Game Four, the Red Sox pulled out a win with some magic in the ninth and then more magic in the 12th. Game Five ran even longer, and Wakefield pitched the 12th, 13th, and 14th innings. He was the winner when David Ortiz – for the second night in a row – delivered the game-ending hit.

The Red Sox won the next two games and the series; that team is still the only one in MLB history to climb back from a 0-3 deficit in the playoffs. One moment Wakefield treasured the most came not long after the Red Sox had won Game Seven and eliminated the Yankees. As the celebration in the clubhouse was winding down, he was told he had a phone call. It was the Yankees' manager calling. "He said, 'Wake, this is Joe Torre. I just wanted to congratulate you. You're one of the guys over there that I respect. Just remember to have fun. You guys deserve it.' Afterward I wrote him a note and told him how much that meant to me. That's one of the highest compliments you ever get from an opposing manager at that point…It really touched me deeply for him to call me."[27]

Boston then swept the World Series over the St. Louis Cardinals, breaking an 86-year-old "curse." Wakefield appeared only in Game One. He started, and though the Red Sox supported him with seven runs, he gave up five in 3 2/3 innings and got no decision. It was the last time he pitched in 2004.

Wakefield was 16-12 (4.15) in the 2005 regular season, the winningest pitcher on the staff. His best game was a complete-game 1-0 loss to the Yankees on September 11, a three-hitter in which he struck out a career-high 12 New Yorkers. Boston returned, briefly, to postseason play, getting swept in the Division Series by the eventual World Series winners, the Chicago White Sox. After the Red Sox lost the first two games on the road, Game Three was at Fenway Park. Wakefield was the starter and loser; in the top of the sixth, Paul Konerko hit a two-run homer off him to give Chicago a 4-2 lead. The final score was 5-3.

Experience had proven that it takes a certain talent to be able to corral the knuckleball – some handled Wakefield's better than others. Boston's first-string catcher, Jason Varitek, experienced considerable difficulty with the knuckler. Other catchers caught Wakefield over the course of his career, and it was always a challenge. Doug Mirabelli used an outside softball catcher's glove. Victor Martinez wound up using a first baseman's mitt, the better to help him snare the ball.

Nonetheless, that December, the Red Sox traded Mirabelli to the San Diego Padres for Mark Loretta. After Wakefield started the 2006 season 1-4, the Sox reacquired Mirabelli on May 1. Thanks to a State Police escort from Logan Airport – Mirabelli changed into his catcher's gear in the back seat of a car – the catcher arrived at Fenway just in time to handle Wakefield for a start against the Yankees. The Sox won the game, but with four runs in the bottom of the eighth, just after Wakefield had left the game. He won his next two starts, but lost two months in the second half of the season to a stress fracture in his rib cage. He finished the season losing his last three decisions and was 7-11 (4.63).

Though his ERA edged up to 4.76 in 2007, once again the team around a pitcher truly helps. Wakefield was 17-12 that year, second in wins on the Red Sox only to Josh Beckett (20-7). He became a World Champion again, as the Red Sox rolled over the Colorado Rockies with a sweep in the World Series.

Recurring problems in the back of his shoulder problems kept Wakefield inactive for nearly two weeks in August. As a result, he was kept off the roster for the Division Series and the World Series.[28] His only appearance during the postseason was a start in Game Four of the ALCS against Cleveland. He gave up five runs, and bore the defeat. Maybe he could have pitched once in the World Series, but he asked, "Are you going to get 100 percent out of Tim Wakefield? I don't know that…It's not fair for the rest of the 24 guys in that clubhouse for me to put them through that."[29]

He pitched in just one more postseason game. In the 2008 regular season, though he brought his ERA down to 4.13, his won/loss record was 10-11, fourth in wins among the Red Sox starters behind Daisuke Matsuzaka, Jon Lester, and Beckett. (That August, another Wakefield knuckleball disciple, Charlie Zink, pitched his lone major-league game for Boston. Ironically, it came because Wakefield was on the DL again with a stiff shoulder.[30]) Wakefield's one appearance in the playoffs was in Game Four of the ALCS against the Tampa Bay Rays. He gave up five runs in 2 2/3 innings and lost the 13-4 game. Including his two wins for the Pirates, this left him with a postseason record of 5-7 (6.75).

In 2009, once again Wakefield won in double digits for the Red Sox in the regular season, 11-5 (4.58). Only Beckett and Lester won more. That year, Wakefield was named by Tampa Bay's Joe Maddon to the American League All-Star team, the only year in which he earned the distinction. He didn't appear in the game, a 4-2 AL win.

Wakefield was below .500 in his final two seasons: 4-10 in 2010 and 7-8 in 2011. Both years, his ERA was over 5 (5.34 and 5.12). After winning his 199th career game on August 24, it took eight more starts until he won #200, his last, on September 13.

Wakefield was just six wins short of the franchise record for wins, and during the final week of the season, he told Fox Sports that the fans "deserved" to see him break it. However, the team's new general manager, Ben Cherington, said that while he respected the veteran, he had to be honest with him about his chances of making the team.[31] Wakefield decided it was time to call it a career, saying, "I'm still a competitor. But ultimately I think this is what was best for the Red Sox and I think this is what's best for my family and, to be honest with you, seven wins isn't going to make me a different person or a better man.[32] His total of 3,006 innings pitched for the Red Sox ranked first, 230 innings more than second-place Clemens.

Longevity of tenure had a lot to do with Wakefield racking up 186 wins for the Red Sox. When he finished his career, he'd pitched 17 seasons for Boston. He was one of only 19 pitchers in major-league history to have spent 15 or more seasons with a single franchise.[33]

There had been some other honors along the way. In 2010, Wakefield won baseball's Roberto Clemente Award, given to the player who "best exemplifies the game of baseball, sportsmanship, community involvement and the individual's contribution to his team."

From June 2012, Wakefield worked as a studio analyst for the New England Sports Network (NESN) broadcasts of Red Sox games, frequently offering pregame and postgame commentary. He served as the Honorary Chairman of the Red Sox Foundation and hosts a number of events such as the foundation's annual celebrity golf tournament. He also continued to help other knuckleballers develop their craft, notably Steven Wright, who became an AL All-Star in 2016 for Boston.[34]

Tim Wakefield died of brain cancer on October 1, 2023, at just 57 years old. Red Sox Charman Tom Werner was among many who offered tributes to the man who had spent 29 years in the organization as a player, special assistant, and broadcaster. "It's one thing to be an outstanding athlete; it's another to be an extraordinary human being. Tim was both. He was a role model on and off the field, giving endlessly to the Red Sox Foundation and being a force for good for everyone he encountered."[35]

SOURCES

A major source for this biography was Tim Wakefield's autobiography, *Knuckler: My Life with Baseball's Most Confounding Pitch*. In addition to the sources noted in this biography, the author also accessed Retrosheet.org, Baseball-Reference.com, and the SABR Minor Leagues Database, accessed online at Baseball-Reference.com.

NOTES

1. The 200 wins represent a milestone that only six other knuckleballers have reached. Ahead of him (as of 2023) were Phil Niekro (318), Ted Lyons (260), Joe Niekro (221), Charlie Hough (216), Jesse Haines (210), and Eddie Cicotte (208).
2. "Knuckleballer Tim Wakefield retires," ESPNBoston.com, February 18, 2012. http://www.espn.com/mlb/story/_/id/7585718/tim-wakefield-retires-17-seasons-boston-red-sox
3. Tim Wakefield with Tony Massarotti, *Knuckler: My Life with Baseball's Most Confounding Pitch Knuckler* (Boston and New York: Houghton Mifflin Harcourt, 2011), 37.
4. *Knuckler*, 37.
5. *Knuckler*, 37.
6. "A First Baseman Takes the Mound," *New York Times*, May 4, 1992: C2.
7. Associated Press, "Pirates Rookie Doesn't Knuckle Under in Debut," *Evansville Courier and Press*, August 1, 1992: 17.
8. Mike Hiserman, "Pirates' Wakefield Wins Game of the Decade," *Los Angeles Times*, August 27, 1992: C1.
9. Jack O'Connell, "Rookie Knuckler is Pirates' Hope," *Daily Advocate* (Stamford, Connecticut), October 9, 1992: 17. Already Wakefield was attracting attention in Boston. See Michael Madden, "He Thrived During White-Knuckle Time," *Boston Globe*, October 10, 1992: 72.
10. Associated Press photo caption, *Marietta Journal*, May 28, 1993: 23.
11. Danny Gallagher, "Tim Wakefield Floats Like A Butterfly to Cy Young Award," *St. Albans* (Vermont) *Daily Messenger*, August 23, 1995: 23.
12. "Around the Majors," *Washington Post*, July 10, 1993: C4.
13. Quoted in *Knuckler*, 73.
14. Jeremy Repanich, "R.A. Dickey, Tim Wakefield, Charlie Hough and the Art of the Knuckleball," *Sports Illustrated Kids*, September 27, 2012. http://www.sikids.com/node/11953316
15. Danny Gallagher. Wakefield was initially placed with Boston's Fort Myers team in the Gulf Coast League; Phil Niekro was working there at the time managing the Colorado Silver Bullets.
16. Stefan Fatsis, "Gnarly Knuckleball Enjoys Overdue Season in the Sun," *Wall Street Journal*, September 29, 1995: B9.
17. Jerome Holtzman, "Wakefield Resists Knuckling Under to Pressure," *Chicago Tribune*, October 13, 1992: B5.
18. *Knuckler*, 62.
19. *Knuckler*, 81-83.
20. *Knuckler*, 109.
21. "For Demoted Wakefield, Bullpen Isn't A Relief," *Washington Post*, April 4, 2000: D4.
22. *Knuckler*, 148.
23. Bill Ballou, "Wakefield Accepts Bullpen Role," *Worcester Telegram & Gazette*, February 26, 2002: D4.
24. Bill Finley, "From Brink of Pennant to Brink of Despair," *New York Times*, October 17, 2003: D4.
25. *Knuckler*, 178.
26. Author interview with Doug Mirabelli, May 17, 2013.
27. Author interview with Tim Wakefield, May 8, 2013. Wakefield's memories of the 2004 season appear throughout the book by Allan Wood and Bill Nowlin, *Don't Let Us Win Tonight: An Oral History of the 2004 Boston Red Sox's Impossible Playoff Run* (Chicago: Triumph Books, 2014). This particular quotation is on page 202.
28. Amalie Benjamin, "He's Left Off the Roster Because of Ailing Shoulder," *Boston Globe*, October 24, 2007: D4.
29. Benjamin.
30. "Fellow Knuckleballer Zink to Start for Wakefield," *USA Today*, August 11, 2008.
31. Peter Abraham, "Sox' Wakefield Announces Retirement," *Boston Globe*, February 18, 2012: C1.
32. Ian Browne, "Emotional Wakefield Announces his Retirement," MLB.com, February 17, 2012. http://m.mlb.com/news/article/26730038//
33. *Knuckler*, 7.
34. Michael Hurley, "Steven Wright Credits Tim Wakefield For Much Of Success With Red Sox," CBS Boston, July 6, 2016. http://boston.

TOO LONG AT THE FAIR, TOO SHORT AT THE GRAVEYARD

My father, Don, died just before noon on the first day of winter in 1999. He was an unskilled laborer and veteran of the Korean War, and his body had broken down from years of unloading steel from trucks and breathing toxic fumes while serving as a fireman on a Navy destroyer.

He passed with our entire family by his side. A well-known figure throughout our small Massachusetts community, he had served as umpire-in-chief for many years in our county, earning a reputation as being fair, quick-witted, and someone who never mailed a game in –regardless of quality of play on the field or weather conditions in the air.

Shortly after he passed, there was somehow a moment where he and I were alone together in his hospital room. My mom and siblings were down the hall, making arrangements with the funeral home that was located a block away from the house I grew up in. At that moment, I could have said anything in the world to him that I wanted to. An entire lifetime together had led to this. It felt like a scene from a movie where it was time for me to say something profound – something incredibly noteworthy. Get busy living or get busy dying, right?

And do you know what I said?

"Well, Dad – it looks like that Lewis kid you like is probably going to lead off again. Offerman is going to bat second and play second base. And then Nomar!!! What a year Nomar had, huh?"

And so on.

It seems ridiculous now in many ways, but the most natural thing I could say to my just-deceased father – with his spirit likely still in the room – was to talk about the Red Sox lineup for the coming season. It was how we had spent days in the summer sun and nights in the winter's cold for my entire life. Why not now?

So, nearly five full years later – at 3:30 in the morning of October 28, 2004 – I stood soaked from head to toe and shivering in the cold air at Brookside Cemetery in Easthampton, Massachusetts. I had just completed my shift at the local barroom, serving hundreds of deliriously happy individuals. I was covered in a combination of my own sweat, champagne, a couple of beers that friends had dumped on my head during the celebration. I've been told that the roar from the bar when Keith Foulke shoveled the ball to Doug Mientkiewicz for the final out could be heard the next town over. To this day, I don't think I can honestly say that I saw any of the ballgame, as I was so busy with pouring drinks for what felt like half of the town.

Photo by Eric Poulin.

As I approached my father's grave marker, I could see a glow emanating from about 100 yards away. I correctly guessed that I wasn't the first member of my family to visit the site, as my brother had been there earlier, lighting a candle for our dad almost immediately after the final out. As I looked around, I noticed there were several other candles that had been lit that evening at various gravesites by brothers and sons, mothers and daughters – all of whom wanted to share the moment with their loved ones who had gone before us.

So, there I was – once again – alone with my father. I knew this shouldn't be a long visit, as the fear of catching pneumonia in the cold autumn air went hand-in-hand with my knowledge that it wouldn't be terribly long until the sun started coming up. Once again – but this time in the cold, in the dark, and while the rest of the world was sleeping – I could say anything in the world.

And do you know what I said this time?

"Well, Dad – this should be interesting. Schilling is probably going to need surgery in the offseason. And Pedro is going to be a free agent – they need to sign him up to finish his career here. Then after that – who knows? They'll probably need to get some pitching help. ..."

As tears ran down my face, it occurred to me that, while this was the happiest night of my life to that point, time inevitably moves on. Kids will grow up, friends will move away, parents will eventually grow older and move on from this world, and there will always be another baseball season to worry about. And like that morning in 1999 – as I stared at the grim reality of my first Red Sox season without my father – I knew there was a certain emptiness to this championship that I would have to reconcile with for the rest of my life.

ERIC T. POULIN

SCOTT WILLIAMSON

BY MARK SCHREMMER

When Scott Williamson joined the Cincinnati Reds at spring training in 1999, he was a nonroster invitee with long odds of making the team. Before the year was over, however, the hard-throwing right-hander was an All-Star and the National League Rookie of the Year.

Although injuries prevented Williamson from replicating the success of his rookie season, he enjoyed a nine-year major-league career that included three saves in the 2003 American League Championship Series and a World Series ring with the Boston Red Sox in 2004.

Williamson was born February 17, 1976, in Fort Polk, Louisiana. At the age of 4, he was adopted by Ray and Ann Williamson, a chemical engineer and kindergarten teacher, respectively. In a 1999 interview, Williamson said he declined attempts to find his biological parents, because "God gave me two great parents," and that it "would be betraying them."[1]

Scott was coached by his father in multiple sports growing up, and his baseball talents were evident early. At age 10, he was throwing 70 mph and playing in a league for 12-year-olds. The Williamson family moved from Louisiana to Texas when Scott was 14.[2]

At Friendswood High School in Friendswood, Texas, Williamson quickly emerged as one of the top pitchers in his area. He was named first-team all-district as a junior,[3] before leading his Mustangs to the Class 4A regional finals as a senior.[4] Williamson finished his senior season with a 12-4 record and a 0.66 ERA, earning designation as the *Galveston Daily News*' 1994 All-County Baseball Player of the Year.[5]

Williamson's success in high school led to a scholarship at Tulane University. There, he sparred with coach Rick Jones and grew homesick for Texas.[6] Seeking a better fit for his personality, Williamson transferred to play for Tom Holliday's Oklahoma State Cowboys for the 1997 season, when he was 7-3 and earned first-team All-Big 12 honors.[7]

"Holliday gave me back my love for the game," Williamson said. "I lost my love at Tulane."[8]

The Cincinnati Reds selected Williamson in the ninth round of the 1997 amateur draft and sent him to pitch at the Rookie level for the Billings (Montana) Mustangs, where he was 8-2 with a 1.78 ERA in 13 starts.

In 1998 Williamson bypassed Single A and was assigned to play for the Double-A Chattanooga (Tennessee) Lookouts. In his first start for the Lookouts, Williamson faced Atlanta Braves veteran pitcher John Smoltz, who was down with the Greenville Braves on a rehabilitation assignment. Williamson allowed two runs in six innings of the 6-5 loss, but Chattanooga manager Mark Berry walked away impressed. "I expected him to be more erratic because of Smoltz, the big crowd and the whole situation," Berry said. "It's something he can build on."[9]

Williamson started 18 games at Double A before being promoted to the Triple-A Indianapolis Indians toward the end of the season. Cincinnati planned to call him up in September, but his season ended when he stretched a tendon in the middle finger of his pitching hand during a game for Indianapolis.[10]

Arriving at 1999 spring training as a nonroster invitee, Williamson was a long shot to make the Reds out of camp. However, he arrived with a fastball that was now topping out at 98 mph, giving the team reason to consider moving him to the bullpen.[11]

The 23-year-old broke camp with the Reds as a reliever and made his major-league debut in an 11-8 Opening Day loss to the San Francisco Giants. Williamson entered in the top of the ninth and opened by allowing a line-drive single to Ellis Burks. He rebounded to strike out Brent Mayne, and then got Rich Aurilia to hit into a double play, ending the inning.

It was a solid start to a dream rookie season for the hard-throwing righty. On April 25, he earned his first major-league save by striking out Jeff Bagwell in a 7-6 win over the Houston Astros, which was Williamson's favorite team as a youngster.[12]

A good April turned into a great May. Williamson opened the month with a 3.95 ERA and shrank it to 1.69 to start June. In May he was 2-0 with five saves, no runs allowed, and 24 strikeouts in 18⅓ innings. In a 4-3 win over the Los Angeles Dodgers on May 27, he struck out all six batters he faced.

"I'm throwing harder now," Williamson said. "When you're a closer, you can just go out there and let it go." He also utilized a split-finger that he learned from future Hall of Famer Bruce Sutter when he played with Bruce's son, Chad, at Tulane.[13]

Reds manager Jack McKeon soon had Williamson splitting closer duties with Danny Graves. Both were subject to heavy use as Williamson and Graves pitched 93⅓ and 111 innings respectively in 1999. In a 2-0 Reds win over the Brewers on June 17, Williamson recorded a rare four-inning save.

Williamson was named to the National League All-Star team after earning a 7-4 record with a 1.66 ERA in the first half of the season. However, the rookie did not enter the midsummer classic at Fenway Park that ended with a 4-1 win by the American League.

He tired some in the second half of the season and missed a week from shoulder tendinitis as the Reds made a postseason push.[14] Cincinnati finished the regular season with a 96-66 record, tied with the New York Mets for the wild card. The Mets beat the Reds 5-0 in a play-in game at Cincinnati. Williamson didn't enter the game.

Finishing the season with a 12-7 record, a 2.41 ERA, 19 saves, and 107 strikeouts in 93⅓ innings, Williamson earned 17 first-place votes to win the National League Rookie of the Year. He became the seventh Reds player to win Rookie of the Year, following Frank Robinson (1956), Pete Rose (1963), Tommy Helms (1966), Johnny Bench (1968), Pat Zachry (co-winner 1976), and Chris Sabo (1988).[15]

Williamson said the award didn't even cross his mind when he arrived at spring training.

"My biggest goal at that time was just make the big-league team … coming in there, with no chance at all," he said.[16]

As the Reds looked to acquire star outfielder Ken Griffey Jr. from the Seattle Mariners before the 2000 season, Williamson's name was floated among Seattle's trade targets.[17] However, the Reds were able to obtain Griffey without having to give up Williamson or second baseman Pokey Reese. Instead, Cincinnati acquired the future Hall of Famer for pitcher Brett Tomko, outfielder Mike Cameron, and minor leaguers Jake Meyer and Antonio Pérez.

Williamson struggled with control early in the 2000 season, throwing 12 wild pitches in his first 28 outings. Much of the wildness was attributed to his split-finger fastball, which he was releasing too low and seeing it end up in the dirt.[18] He finished the season with 21 wild pitches, second most in the National League.

On July 9, Williamson moved into the starting rotation, lasting into the sixth inning of a 5-3 loss to the Cleveland Indians. He earned his first win as a major-league starter six days later in a 7-4 win over the Colorado Rockies in Coors Field.

Williamson said in 2000 that the move to the rotation was a welcomed one. "When I was a little kid, I dreamed about being a starting pitcher in the big leagues," he said. "There's a lot more pressure in relieving than in starting. If you give up one or two runs (when you start), your team still has a chance. If you give up a run when you relieve, it's (usually) a blown save or loss. Relieving is not easy. I've learned that the last season and a half."[19]

His most successful start of the season came in a 3-0 win over the Chicago Cubs on August 12. Williamson allowed only four hits and struck out seven over seven innings.[20]

The progress Williamson was a making as a starter was derailed when his season ended in September after he broke two toes in his right foot.[21] He made all 10 starts of his major-league career in 2000.

With Bob Boone taking over as Reds manager in 2001, Williamson was moved back to the bullpen. The young pitcher took the decision in stride. "I need to help the team out of the bullpen," he said. "I've had success in the bullpen. I like the bullpen. We both agreed that it's not a demotion."[22]

However, a torn ligament in his throwing elbow forced Williamson to miss the rest of the 2001 season after only two appearances.[23] The injury, which some blamed on Williamson's delivery and the way the Reds used him, required Tommy John surgery. "I was surprised it took that long for Williamson to get hurt, the way the Reds used him," said Astros general manager Gerry Hunsicker.[24]

A healthy Williamson returned in 2002, enjoying a 2.92 ERA and 8 saves in 63 appearances.

His 2003 season opened with a bizarre incident during spring training. Williamson said a ghost woke him up from a sound sleep while staying at the Renaissance Vinoy Hotel in St. Petersburg, Florida.

"I was laying on my stomach and all of a sudden, I couldn't breathe," Williamson said in 2004. "It was like something was pushing down on me. I turned around, when there was this guy dressed in 1920s, '30s-style staring at me. I never believed in ghosts before, but, like I said, I couldn't breathe. I told somebody about it the next day in the clubhouse, and then it was all over the news."[25]

The encounter has been featured in several books about paranormal activity, including 2007's *Haunted Baseball*, 2008's *Haunted Florida*, 2014's *Ghosts of Florida's Gulf Coast*, and 2022's *Haunted Hotels*.[26]

The incident was the start to a successful but turbulent 2003 season for Williamson.

He remained effective to begin the 2003 season but was traded to the Boston Red Sox on July 30 as part of a "salary dump." The trade came less than a week after his first child, Scott Reese Williamson, was born and only one day after his wife, Lisa, was admitted to the emergency room with high blood pressure. "This is really stressful on my family," Williamson said. "But it's a business. You have to do what you have to do."[27]

For the Red Sox, acquiring Williamson was a win over the rival New York Yankees, who were also bidding to trade for the former All-Star.[28]

The trade, however, was not an instant success. Williamson, who was coping with a new environment as well as concerns about the health of his wife and newborn son,[29] struggled with a 6.20 ERA through 24 regular-season appearances with the Red Sox. Lisa required hospitalization for hemorrhaging four times after giving birth, and Scott Reese battled a high fever and rash that led to a spinal tap and intravenous injections.[30]

After working with Red Sox pitching coach Tony Cloninger and after his wife and child recovered, a rejuvenated Williamson took the mound in the 2003 postseason.[31]

He appeared in all five games of the American League Division Series, helping the Red Sox beat the Oakland Athletics. Williamson was 2-0, allowing only two hits and no runs over five innings. In Game Three, he pitched a perfect top of the 11th before Red Sox outfielder Trot Nixon hit a walk-off home run in the bottom half to give Boston a 3-1 victory.

Williamson's success followed him into the American League Championship Series against the Yankees. He recorded saves in Games One, Four, and Six. He helped extend the Series to seven games by pitching a perfect ninth inning – striking out Jason Giambi before getting Bernie Williams and Jorge Posada to fly out – in a 9-6 win.

Williamson was available to pitch a day later in Game Seven, but Red Sox manager Grady Little controversially opted to bring Pedro Martínez back for the eighth inning with a 5-2 lead.[32] A fatigued Martínez allowed a double to Derek Jeter, a single to Williams, and doubles to Hideki Matsui and Posada that helped the Yankees tie the game 5-5. In the bottom of the 11th, New York's Aaron Boone hit a game-winning home run off Boston's Tim Wakefield. Williamson did not enter the game.

His postseason success led to a one-year, $3.175 million deal from the Red Sox for the 2004 season.[33] Williamson picked the contending Red Sox, who acquired All-Star closer Keith Foulke in the offseason, over opportunities to be traded to a team that would give him the ninth inning.[34]

"I'm the closer in the eighth inning now. That's the way I look at it," Williamson said in 2004. "But for me to be a part of what happened last year, that's what I want to do again. That was so much fun."[35]

Williamson started the 2004 season strong with a perfect earned-run average through his first eight outings. He continued to pitch well, but injuries to his ankle and elbow forced him to miss games from May 19 through June 11 and July 1 through September 9. On June 30 Williamson removed himself from a game against the Yankees. New York won 4-2, and Red Sox pitcher Curt Schilling reportedly questioned Williamson's manhood after the game.[36] Schilling later called the report an example of unethical journalism and said that he had spoken with Williamson but that he never questioned whether he was hurt.[37]

Either way, Williamson was hurt. After the June 30 game, it was discovered that he suffered an impingement of the radial nerve of his right elbow.[38] Williamson returned September 10 and made seven appearances in September and October, allowing only four hits and one earned run over seven innings.

He finished the 2004 season with a 1.26 ERA and 28 strikeouts over 28⅔ innings, but the still-injured Williamson was left off the postseason roster. Instead, he spent Boston's championship run recovering from his second Tommy John surgery.[39]

When Dr. Tim Kremchek got inside Williamson's right elbow with an arthroscope, he learned the injury was much worse than previously thought. "I couldn't believe what I saw," said Kremchek, who was the Cincinnati Reds team physician. "It looked like a grenade had gone off in there. The damage was far worse than the MRIs or any examination alluded to."[40]

Williamson apparently pitched the final month of the regular season with a completely torn ulnar collateral ligament, mangled cartilage ripped from the bone on the other part of the elbow and several bone chips and loose bodies within the cavity of the joint.[41]

Calling it a "solid gamble," Chicago Cubs general manager Jim Hendry, in 2005, signed the 28-year-old Williamson to a minor-league deal for a minimum salary of $316,000 that would increase to $500,000 if he was called up to the majors.[42]

However, the former Rookie of the Year was never the same after his second Tommy John surgery. Williamson made 17 appearances for the Cubs in 2005 but recorded a 5.65 ERA. Despite the underwhelming season, the Cubs picked up Williamson's $2 million option for the 2006 season.[43]

Williamson struggled again in 2006, posting a 5.08 ERA in 31 appearances with the Cubs before being traded to the San Diego Padres for minor leaguers Fabian Jimenez Angulo and Joel Santo on July 22. In 11 outings for the Padres, he was 0-1 with a 7.36 ERA.

San Diego released Williamson after the season, and the Baltimore Orioles signed him to a $900,000 contract for 2007. The veteran reliever started strong with a 1.13 ERA through May. However, Williamson dealt with tightness in his right triceps and a bruised foot,[44] and his ERA ballooned to 4.40 after seven appearances in June. The Orioles released Williamson in July after what turned out to be his final major-league appearance on June 29, 2007.

He continued to pitch professionally for the next several seasons, competing in the minors for the New York Yankees in 2007, the Seattle Mariners and Atlanta Braves in 2008, the Detroit Tigers and Florida Marlins in 2009, and multiple independent teams into 2011.

With his pro baseball career over, Williamson chose to auction off his 2004 World Series ring in 2011 to "ease the strain of an overbuilt home that sapped his family's cash reserves" and to help pay for a youth indoor baseball facility on the Indiana-Ohio line.[45]

Williamson's World Series ring sold for $89,000 in October 2011.[46]

According to Jim Prime's book on the 2004 Red Sox, Williamson was the pitching coach for the 15-and-under Cincinnati Tribe baseball club in 2014.[47] He participated in Reds alumni events, attending Opening Day ceremonies as recently as 2023.[48]

SOURCES

All statistics and box scores were taken from baseball-reference.com, except where otherwise indicated. The articles cited in several of the Notes come from photocopies of articles from Scott Williamson's file at the National Baseball Hall of Fame, and were provided to the author by library staff.

NOTES

1. Sean Keeler, "Williamson Savoring Reds' Run," ESPN.com (Scripps Howard News Service), August 25, 1999. http://espn.go.com/mlb/features/01413113.html. This article is found in Williamson's player file at the Hall of Fame, but as of summer 2023 was no longer available online.
2. "Williamson Savoring Reds' Run."
3. "All-District Baseball Teams," *Galveston* (Texas) *Daily News*, May 27, 1993: 18.
4. Michael Peters, "Cubs Rain on Mustang parade, 8-2," *Galveston Daily News*, June 3, 1994: 17.
5. Glenn McLaren, "Mustangs Lead All-County Team," *Galveston Daily News*, June 15, 1994: 16.
6. "Williamson Savoring Reds' Run."
7. "Sports Briefs," *New Braunfels* (Texas) *Herald-Zeitung*, May 14, 1997: 14.
8. Keeler, "Williamson Savoring Reds' Run."
9. Larry W. Fleming, "Smoltz Mows Down Lookouts," *Chattanooga Times*, April 3, 1998: E1.
10. Hal McCoy, "Williamson's on DL," *Dayton Daily News*, August 26, 1998: 5D.
11. "Scorecard: Young Gun … Byung Gun," *Sports Illustrated*, June 7, 1999: 31.
12. Joey D. Richards, "Williamson Lighting Up Big Leagues," *Galveston Daily News*, July 2, 1999: 13.
13. "Scorecard: Young Gun … Byung Gun."
14. Chris Haft, "Cincinnati Reds Notebook," *The Sporting News*, October 4, 1999: 60.
15. Associated Press, "Williamson Named NL Rookie of the Year," ESPN.com, November 8, 1999. http://a.espncdn.com/mlb/news/1999/1108/159246.html
16. "Williamson Named NL Rookie of the Year."
17. Joe Kay (Associated Press), "Williamson Facing Uncertainty in Second Year," Fastball.com, November 10, 1999.
18. Mark Schmetzer, "Cincinnati Reds Notebook," *The Sporting News*, June 12, 2000: 52.
19. Stephen Cannella, "Inside Baseball," VaultSI.com (*Sports Illustrated*), July 24, 2000. https://vault.si.com/vault/2000/07/24/inside-baseball.
20. Mark Schmetzer, "Cincinnati Reds Notebook," *The Sporting News*, August 28, 2000: 27.
21. "Cincinnati 6, Houston 4," ESPN.com, September 23, 2000. https://www.espn.com/mlb/2000/20000923/recap/houcin.html.
22. Joe Kay (Associated Press), "Pitching Rotation for Reds Is Ready," *Greenville* (Ohio) *Daily Advocate*, March 28, 2001: 7.
23. Chris Haft, "Reds Lose Williamson for Season," Cincinnati.com (*Cincinnati Enquirer*), April 5, 2001.
24. Stephen Cannella, "Inside Baseball," Vault.SI.com (*Sports Illustrated*), April 23, 2001. https://vault.si.com/vault/2001/04/23/inside-baseball.
25. Dan Shaughnessy, *Reversing the Curse: Inside the 2004 Boston Red Sox* (Boston: Houghton Mifflin Company, 2005).
26. Mickey Bradley and Dan Gordon, *Haunted Baseball* (Essex, Connecticut: Lyons Press, 2007); Cynthia Thuma and Catherine Lower, *Haunted Florida* (Lanham, Maryland: Stackpole Books, 2008); Alan Brown, *Ghosts of Florida's Gulf Coast* (Lanham, Maryland: Pineapple Press, 2014); Tom Ogden, *Haunted Hotels* (Lanham, Maryland: Globe Pequot, 2022).
27. Kyle Nagel, "Reds Trade Williamson to Red Sox," Daytondailynews.com, July 30, 2003.
28. Hal Bodley, "Red Sox's Epstein Has Wisdom Beyond His Years," USAToday.com, August 1, 2003.
29. Jackie MacMullan, "This Is One Pair That Has Beaten Odds," *Boston Globe*, October 5, 2003: C2.
30. Bob Hersom, "Scott Williamson: Injury-Filled Career," Oklahoman.com, July 26, 2005. https://www.oklahoman.com/story/news/2005/07/26/scott-williamson-injury-filled-careerbrlife-the-real-worldbrex-osu-standout-knows-the-value-family/61933141007/.
31. "This Is One Pair That Has Beaten Odds."
32. Brendan Cartwright, "What's Scott Williamson Up To?" RedReporter.com (SBNation), December 10, 2012.
33. Ronald Blum (Associated Press), "Sasaki Quits Mariners," *Indiana* (Pennsylvania) *Gazette*, January 20, 2004: 15.
34. Howard Ulman (Associated Press), "Williamson Chooses Team Over Closer Role," CapeCodTimes.com, March 16, 2004.
35. "Williamson Chooses Team Over Closer Role."
36. Sean McAdam, "Sox Try to Sweep Series under the Rug," ESPN.com, July 2, 2004. https://www.espn.com/mlb/columns/story?id=1833306.
37. "Being Curt: The Schilling Interview," Boston.com, October 27, 2004. https://bostondirtdogs.boston.com/Headline_Archives/2004/10/the_schilling_i.html.
38. "Sox Try to Sweep Series under the Rug."
39. Jeff Horrigan, "Williamson Has Tommy John Surgery," BostonHerald.com, October 13, 2004.
40. "Williamson Has Tommy John Surgery."
41. "Williamson Has Tommy John Surgery."
42. Paul Sullivan, "Cubs Reward Barrett with 3-Year Contract," ChicagoSports.com (*Chicago Tribune*), January 18, 2005.
43. Bruce Miles, "Cubs Begin Off-Season Moves," DailyHerald.com, October 29, 2005.
44. Adam Kilgore, "Reliever Williamson Is Let Go," WashingtonPost.com, July 5, 2007.
45. John Tomase, "Ex-Sox Hurler to Auction '04 Series Ring," BostonHerald.com, October 15, 2011. https://www.bostonherald.com/2011/10/15/ex-sox-hurler-to-auction-04-series-ring/#:~:text=Former%20Sox%20reliever%20Scott%20Williamson,on%20the%20Indiana%2DOhio%20line.
46. Peter Abraham, "A Red Sox 2004 Series Ring Up For Grabs," Boston.com (*Boston Globe*), August 15, 2013. https://www.boston.com/sports/extra-bases/2013/08/15/a_red_sox_2004_series_ring_up_for_grabs/.
47. Jim Prime, *Amazing Tales from the 2004 Boston Red Sox Dugout* (Chicago: Sports Publishing, 2014), 83-84.
48. Molly Schramm, "Reds Opening Day 2023: Bronson Arroyo, Danny Graves to Be Grand Marshals of Parade," SpringfieldNewsSun.com, March 8, 2023. https://www.wcpo.com/sports/baseball/reds/reds-opening-day-2023-bronson-arroyo-danny-graves-to-be-grand-marshals-of-parade.

KEVIN YOUKILIS

BY DAVE DIONISIO

You've seen him on television and in movies. You've perhaps enjoyed his beer or seen him on his web series.

Oh yeah, he was a pretty good baseball player too.

Kevin Edmund Youkilis was born on Thursday, March 15, 1979, in Cincinnati to Carolyn (Weekley) and Mike "Bear" Youkilis, who was himself a "well known third baseman in the Jewish Community Center fast-pitch softball league."[1] Mike came from a Jewish family, while Carolyn converted to Judaism upon marriage, and they owned Midwest Diamond Distributors, where Kevin and his older brother, Scott, worked during their childhood.[2]

A right-handed-hitting and -throwing third baseman, Kevin began playing baseball at Cincinnati's Sycamore High School. According to his coach, Chris Shrimpton, the freshman Youkilis needed time to develop his body, but had "raw talent with a lot of potential."[3]

Kevin found quick success, winning the varsity starting third-base job his sophomore year, as well as an AAU championship, in 1994.

He was elected team captain both his junior and senior years, and he led the Sycamore Aviators to a pair of sectional championships, and one district championship while also being named team MVP his senior year.[4]

Despite this dominance, Kevin was not getting attention from scouts. Knowing what he had, Coach Shrimpton took the initiative. He began talking to college coaches regarding Kevin playing at the next level and found a coach, Brian Cleary, who was interested.

Cleary had been hired recently as the head coach at the University of Cincinnati, which had cleaned house after a 5-34 season in 1996.[5] Cleary had been interested in Kevin since he spotted him at a University of Cincinnati baseball camp that Youkilis had been attending every year from childhood through his senior year of high school.[6]

Youkilis had an affinity for the school because his father, Mike, was a 1971 graduate. After Youkilis went undrafted in the 1997 major-league draft, he accepted a baseball scholarship to the University of Cincinnati beginning in the 1998 season.

He had some big shoes to fill. The university already touted a pair of Baseball Hall of Famers among its alumni: New York Yankees manager Miller Huggins and Los Angeles Dodgers pitching great Sandy Koufax.

Once at the university it emerged quickly that Youkilis was going to be a special player and the coaches started noticing his batting eye. "It was really readily apparent, he had the best feel for the strike zone of anybody that I had ever coached," Cleary said.[7]

Youkilis's fielding also went under the radar of scouts, which Coach Cleary attributed to style. "He wasn't a flashy defender. But when you got to see him play defense every day … he was capable of both highlight plays and was incredibly consistent."[8]

Between his junior and senior years, Youkilis played in the Cape Cod Baseball League, the premier collegiate summer league based on Cape Cod, Massachusetts. Just getting into the league in the first place took some work.

Mike Rikard, coach of the Bourne Braves in the summer of 2000, kept getting voice messages from the unrecruited Youkilis. As Youkilis kept calling and calling, more players began dropping off Cape League rosters to join the US Olympic team that summer. "I offered him an opportunity to come on as a temporary player," Rikard said. "And he tore it up from day one."[9]

Youkilis started his Cape Cod League career in dramatic fashion on June 12, 2000, by hitting a home run in his first at-bat, a feat also achieved by former Red Sox great Carlton Fisk for the Orleans Firebirds in the summer of 1966.[10]

According to Matt Haas, a Red Sox scout who signed Youkilis in 2001, during his time on Cape Cod, Youkilis "got his name on the map and made the rest of us pay a little more attention to him the next year."[11]

Youkilis had been again passed over in the 2000 draft. Back for his senior year at Cincinnati, he had what the university record book called "the top offensive career in school history," and finished his collegiate career "owning or sharing 10 school records."[12]

But Youkilis was still not garnering a lot of interest from major-league scouts, and Cleary pushed hard for Haas to draft him.[13] Haas sent Youkilis's name to Red Sox scouting director Wayne Britton. The team selected him with the 17th pick (243rd overall) in the eighth round of the 2001 draft, which made A's general manager Billy Beane livid to the point that he fired his entire scouting department afterward[14] and led to Youkilis's later being a featured character in one of the most important sports books of the twenty-first century, Michael Lewis's seminal book *Moneyball*.[15]

The Red Sox offered to sign Youkilis for a mere $12,000.[16] According to his father, Mike, "Kevin would have played for a six-pack of beer."[17]

Beginning his professional baseball career with the Lowell Spinners, the Red Sox' affiliate in the short-season Class-A New York Penn League, Youkilis put up an astonishing league-leading .512 on-base percentage.

He was named the Spinners' Player of the Year and earned a late-season five-game call-up to the low Class-A Augusta GreenJackets. His combined on-base percentage mark of .504 for the 2001 season was second only to San Francisco Giant Barry Bonds' .515 in Organized Baseball.

Youkilis started the 2002 season with the GreenJackets but was only there for 15 games,[18] and spent the bulk of the season with the Sarasota Red Sox of the high Class-A Florida State League. There he earned another late-season call-up, this time to the Double-A Trenton Thunder, and for his performance with the three teams, Youkilis was named the Red Sox 2002 Minor League Player of the Year.[19]

While the Red Sox were sold at this point on his plate discipline and fielding, they wanted to see a more athletic and explosive version of Youkilis. Assistant GM Theo Epstein recommended that Youkilis attend the Athletes Performance Institute in Arizona over the offseason with the goal of transforming his body and unlocking his power and agility.[20]

Youkilis began the 2003 season with the Portland Sea Dogs of the Double-A Eastern League, and was selected to both the midseason and postseason all-star squads (the postseason honor despite that fact that he was promoted out of the league at the end of July.[21]

When Youkilis was called up to the Triple-A Pawtucket Red Sox, he was on a franchise-record run of reaching base in 62 straight games. He extended that streak by reaching base in each of his first nine games in Pawtucket, tying the minor-league record of 71 held by future teammate Kevin Millar.[22]

In the offseason Youkilis returned to the Athletes Performance Institute and played south of the border for Mayos de Navojoa in the Mexican Pacific League. He began the 2004 season back in Pawtucket.

He was having a perfectly respectable season there through 38 games when he got that dream call. It was in Charlotte, North Carolina, when Pawtucket manager Buddy Bailey asked Youkilis, "Do you have a passport?"[23] Youkilis was on his way to becoming a member of one of the seminal teams in Boston Red Sox history.

The Red Sox were in Toronto to face the Toronto Blue Jays. After it was determined that starting third baseman Bill Mueller would be unable to play because of an injury, Youkilis was in.[24]

On May 15, 2004, at SkyDome, his parents, Mike and Carolyn, were seated two rows behind the Red Sox dugout.[25] On the mound was 1996 AL Cy Young winner Pat Hentgen.

In his second big-league at-bat, Youkilis deposited a 2-and-1 Hentgen changeup into the left-field bleachers.[26]

He was just the seventh Red Sox player to hit a homer in his first major-league game, but once he rounded the bases and got to the dugout … nothing. Crickets. Nobody congratulated him. It was a "silent treatment" prank organized by teammate Pedro Martínez. Youkilis was left to mime some high fives with imaginary teammates while his parents celebrated joyfully in the stands. It wasn't until Red Sox manager Terry Francona hugged Youkilis that they pulled the plug on the rookie's silent treatment.[27]

Playing third base almost every day in May, Youkilis was named AL Rookie of the Month. He continued to play regularly through June, but was mostly used as a late-game replacement for Mueller the rest of the season.

When he put the Division Series roster together, Francona, impressed with Youkilis's performance, chose the rookie for the last available spot rather than add another pitcher.[28] His only postseason appearance in 2004 was in Game Two of the ALDS. He was 0-for-2 at the plate. He was on the roster for the World Series as well, though he did not appear.

While Youkilis didn't make an impact in the playoffs, playing in 72 regular-season games he finished eighth on the team in bWAR, better than Bill Mueller, the player he was backing up.

On March 3, 2005, Youkilis agreed to a one-year contract for $323,125 with the Red Sox and began the season on the Opening Day roster. As is the lot of a young ballplayer, he was optioned and recalled four times over the course of the 2005 season.

Playing for the Red Sox, Youkilis entered a game on August 8 in the ninth inning and took the field along with teammates Adam Stern and Gabe Kapler. This set a record for the most Jewish players on the field at one time in an American League game.[29]

When veteran third baseman Mike Lowell arrived in Boston as part of a trade for Marlins starting pitcher Josh Beckett, plans for Youkilis to succeed Mueller at third base were altered.[30] Moved across the diamond, Youkilis establish himself as the Red Sox' everyday first baseman.

The third-place 2006 Red Sox fell one short of tying the 2003 Seattle Mariners' major-league record for the fewest team errors in a season , 65. An innocuous error by Youkilis on a pickoff throw to first base on July 4 preceded a record-breaking streak of defensive consistency as a first baseman, and he finished the 2006 season, and all of 2007, without another error. In doing so,

he broke Stuffy McInnis's team record of 119 errorless games at first base and bested Mike Hegan's American League mark of 178 games.[31]

At the end of 2007 Youkilis had achieved the only errorless season for a major-league first baseman[32] and received his first American League Gold Glove Award.

In 14 postseason games, Youkilis homered four times and drove in 10 runs, seven against Cleveland in the American League Championship Series as Boston came back from a 3-1 deficit to win the Series. If not for the brilliant Series pitching of Beckett, Youkilis might have been named MVP.

Youkilis's bat cooled off a bit in the World Series but Boston still made tidy work of the Colorado Rockies. Winning in a four-game sweep, the Red Sox captured their seventh championship overall and second in four years, placing Youkilis in the rare group of living Red Sox players with multiple championship rings alongside David Ortiz, Manny Ramírez, and Curt Schilling.

After avoiding arbitration and agreeing to a one-year contract, Youkilis entered the 2008 season a two-time champion and on an unprecedented unblemished defensive streak at first base, having not committed an error at the position since July of 2006.

On April 2, 2008, he scooped up a groundball by Jack Cust of the Oakland A's and recorded an unassisted out at first base to wrap up a 5-0 Red Sox victory. With this, Youkilis completed his 194th straight errorless game at first base and passed the bar set by Steve Garvey for the San Diego Padres from 1983 to 1985.[33]

Youkilis played another 44 games at first base without a fielding miscue. His streak ended during a Fenway Park game in which he started at third base and moved to first in the eighth inning. On June 7, 2008, against the Seattle Mariners, he had trouble handling a throw from second baseman (and later Red Sox manager) Alex Cora in the ninth and the streak was over.[34] He had fielded a record 2,379 consecutive chances in 238 games without an error.[35]

Baseball and its fans took notice. Youkilis was voted the starting American League first baseman in the 2008 All-Star Game, his first of three selections.

The Baseball Writers Association of America also took notice. Youkilis finished third in the 2008 MVP voting (behind teammate Dustin Pedroia and former MVP Justin Morneau), garnering two first-place votes. He also received the Hank Aaron Award, given annually to the best hitter in each league.

With career bests of 29 homers and 115 RBIs (both tops on the team), Youkilis helped the Red Sox to a second-place finish in the AL East in 2008, two games behind Tampa Bay, and made his third playoff appearance, with the Red Sox ultimately falling to the Tampa Bay Rays in the ALCS.

Team goals may not have been met but things were looking up for Youkilis. In the offseason he and the Red Sox hammered out a contract befitting a Gold Glover, All-Star, team leader, and fan favorite, agreeing to a four-year, $41.25 million contract with a fifth-year option.[36] Before the regular season, Youkilis joined the US team in the World Baseball Classic.

His WBC journey ended in the second round when he was sidelined by Achilles tendinitis. Youkilis returned to Red Sox spring training, but a string of injuries limited him to 136 games for the 2009 season and hampered him the rest of his career.

Youkilis gritted out his second All-Star nod in 2009, this time as a reserve, and set career marks in on-base percentage (.413) and OPS (.961), both of which were second in the American League behind Minnesota Twins catcher Joe Mauer. He finished sixth in the MVP voting.

The offseason brought some more accolades for Youkilis. An organization called the Jewish Major Leaguers held an online vote to determine the "Best Jewish Player of the Decade." Competing against fellow Jewish players Shawn Green and Ryan Braun, Youkilis won the honor.[37]

In December 2009, Youkilis was given the Dick Berardino Distinguished Alumni Award by his former minor-league team, the Lowell Spinners. A few weeks later, at the Boston Baseball Writers Dinner, he was honored with the Thomas A. Yawkey Award as the 2009 team's most valuable player.[38]

Battling nagging injuries early in the 2010 season, Youkilis was actually having his best year at the plate through early August. After being removed from a game with a torn thumb muscle, he required season-ending surgery.[39] In 2011 he was limited to 120 games with a litany of injuries but still managed to be a highly effective middle-of-the-order bat and was selected as a reserve to his third and final All-Star team.

Youkilis had founded a charity, Youk's Kids, in 2007. In August 2011 it sponsored a baseball camp for about 200 youngsters at Northeastern University.[40]

The 2011 Red Sox finished third in the AL East and saw significant managerial upheaval. Manager Francona was fired in September. GM Epstein followed him out the door and agreed to a five-year, $18.5 million deal to be president of the Chicago Cubs.[41]

The 2012 season brought a number of transitions into Youkilis's life as well, both personally and professionally. There was a new manager, Bobby Valentine, who had a dearth of popularity in the clubhouse.[42] And now on the downhill side of age 30 and with injuries piling up, he was perhaps starting to feel that his time with the Red Sox might be short.

In the midst of this diamond drama, Youkilis and his fiancée Julie Brady, sister of legendary NFL quarterback Tom Brady, were married in April of 2012 in a private ceremony.[43]

"It was definitely the greatest offday of my life. It was a lot of fun, good times," Youkilis said of the wedding.[44]

Julie brought Jordan, her daughter from a previous marriage, into the family, and the couple went on to have two other children, Zachary and Jeremy.[45]

Back on the diamond, being hampered by injuries the past few years and feuding with the manager on a second-division team led to trade whispers. Add an emerging third-base prospect (Will Middlebrooks), and Youkilis was on the trade block. And on June 24, 2012, Youkilis was traded to the Chicago White Sox.[46]

Suiting up in the Fenway Park clubhouse to face the Atlanta Braves that evening, he didn't know it would be his last game in a Red Sox uniform. He strode to the plate and proceeded to stroke a triple to deep right-center.[47]

Removed for a pinch-runner, Youkilis blew a kiss to the crowd. They serenaded him with a long standing ovation and a shower of appreciation in recognition of what he had given them: a Gold Glove, three All-Star appearances and two World

Series rings. The move left David Ortiz as the last remaining player on the roster who was a member of the 2004 Red Sox.

On the eve of his homecoming to Fenway 22 days later, Youkilis posted a letter online thanking the Boston fans, coaching staff, and his family for the support and great times he had over his 8½ years in a Red Sox uniform.[48]

Youkilis agreed to play for Team Israel in the World Baseball Classic if the squad made it past the qualifying round. It was personally important for him to contribute to baseball-building efforts in Israel. But the team was eliminated in the opening round.[49]

In the offseason the White Sox declined the $13 million option on his contract for the 2013 season and he became a free agent.[50] Boston fans were a bit aghast at where he wound up next: On December 14, 2012, Youkilis signed a one-year, $12 million contract with the New York Yankees.[51]

Opening the 2013 season at Yankee Stadium, Youkilis's first game with the Yankees would be, fittingly, against the Red Sox. In the three-game series (the Red Sox won two), he was 4-for-12 with two doubles. His early season was compounded by a return of his back issues, and he sat out all but one day of May.

While on the injured list, Youkilis went to Hollywood. He played a bit part as Chuck in the film *Once Upon a Time in Brooklyn*. The film, in which his former Red Sox teammate Bronson Arroyo acted alongside him, was actually the second movie Youkilis had appeared in; he had a brief part in the 1994 film *Milk Money*.[52]

Youkilis's back issues persisted. He was removed from the lineup in mid-June and had season-ending back surgery after playing in only 28 games. His playing career was over. Youkilis's last big-league game, at Oakland on June 13, went 18 innings, all of which he played. He didn't have any hits in eight plate appearances; his last hit being a single off 2005 AL Cy Young winner Bartolo Colon two days earlier.

Youkilis had opportunities to remain in the majors but felt the best move for him and his family was to agree to a one-year, $4 million contract with the Tohoku Rakuten Golden Eagles of the Nippon Professional Baseball League in Japan.[53]

The injury bug followed Youkilis across the Pacific and he opted out of his contract with the Golden Eagles after 21 games due to his struggles with plantar fasciitis.[54] When the malady did not respond to treatment, on October 30, 2014, Youkilis announced his retirement as a player.[55]

In February 2015 Youkilis took a consulting job with the Chicago Cubs under his old boss Theo Epstein.[56] And the floodgates opened to allow accolades to rush in over the next few years.

In May 2015 Youkilis's number 36 was retired by the University of Cincinnati.[57]

In March of 2017 Sycamore High School retired his number 13. (He was already a member of their Hall of Fame.) The ceremony was held alongside the inaugural Kevin Youkilis Youth Baseball Camp.[58]

> Like many Jewish families across the world, the Youkilis family has a proud and complicated history. The most commonly accepted version of their journey begins in modern-day Romania with a great-great-great-great grandfather named Weiner who fled south to Greece to escape persecution at the hands of the Cossacks.[71]
>
> In Greece Weiner had a family friend who had the last name Youkilis. Looking to conceal himself upon his return to Romania years later, he assumed the Youkilis moniker for himself. Weiner/Youkilis eventually married in Romania and eventually moved with his wife and 10 children, including Kevin's grandfather, to America, where the family settled in Cincinnati.[72]
>
> Kevin's familial roots came back into play regarding the University of Cincinnati's new baseball facility, which opened in 2004. In 2006, after a $2 million donation to the athletic department from the Schott Foundation, it was renamed Marge Schott Stadium, and the school approached Youkilis about having his name on the facility as well.[73]
>
> Having been asked to provide a donation to the school that would have resulted in the name being Kevin Youkilis Field at Marge Schott Stadium, he declined due to the antisemitism expressed by Schott consistently over the course of her life.
>
> "Kevin, that is a tremendous honor that they would think of doing this," his father said to him. "The only problem is that … I will never let our family name be next to someone that was filled with such hatred of our Jewish community."[74]
>
> Youkilis stayed connected to this cause, supporting UC pitcher Nathan Moore in 2020 when he called for the school to change the name of the stadium.[75]

Later the Red Sox announced that Youkilis was part of their 2018 Hall of Fame class alongside former teammates Derek Lowe and Mike Lowell, as well as former player Buck Freeman and nonuniformed inductee Al Green.[59]

Throughout his baseball career while traversing the nation, Youkilis had taken advantage of the opportunity to visit as many breweries as he could. "I was researching and studying and saying, Hey, when I finally take off the jersey and the spikes, I'm gonna look into owning my own," he said in 2019.[60]

Within two years of the end of his baseball career Youkilis had opened Loma Brewing Company, a gastropub in Los Gatos, California, with the help of his brother Scott, a restaurateur.[61]

Located in Los Gatos, California, the restaurant serves food and Youkilis' own sudsy concoctions, such as the Greek God of Hops.[62] With these creations he won California Commercial Beer Brewery of the Year at the 2017 state fair.[63]

Like many businesses, the coronavirus pandemic hit Loma Brewing Company hard and there was fear about its future,[64] but as of 2023 it continued to thrive and has expanded into merchandise.⁶⁵ Youkilis's Happy Hour with Youk is an internet series that takes place live at Loma and focuses on craft beer discussions.⁶⁶

Having a successful restaurant on top of a successful baseball career might satisfy some men, but Youkilis looked to get back into the game and in 2021 he joined the studio analyst rotation for New England Sports Network (NESN) broadcasts of Red Sox games.⁶⁷ Subsequently the network slotted him to be in the broadcast booth as an analyst for 50 games in 2022.⁶⁸

When full-time analyst Dennis Eckersley retired after the 2022 season, Youkilis was bumped up to the primary in-game color commentary role and was slated to do about half of all Red Sox games.⁶⁹

When he was not in the booth for the Red Sox, he would be back in Los Gatos, focusing on family and work. He took time out from running Loma to, as he put it, take Little League coaching "to another level." He also had his eye on opening a second brewpub, as well as a production facility in nearby Manteca, California.⁷⁰

NOTES

1 Mark Bechtel, "Making a Name for Himself: Kevin Youkilis Has Become a Folk Hero in Boston," SI.com, October 19, 2007. https://web.archive.org/web/20121026072304/http://sportsillustrated.cnn.com/2007/writers/the_bonus/10/19/bonus.youkilis/, accessed September 9, 2023.

2 Dave Clark, "Mike Youkilis, Former Knothole Coach and Father of Sycamore HS/UC star Kevin, Dies at 71," Cincinnati.com, July 23, 2020. https://www.cincinnati.com/story/sports/college/university-of-cincinnati/2020/07/14/mike-youkilis-obituary-scholarship-help-future-uc-bearcats-player/5433156002/, accessed September 9, 2023.

3 Chris Shrimpton, email correspondence with author, November 22, 2022.

4 Mike Dyer, "Sycamore High School to Retire Jersey Number of Former MLB Star Kevin Youkilis," WCPO.com, March 31, 2017. https://www.wcpo.com/sports/high-school-sports/ohio-high-school-sports/sycamore-to-retire-high-school-jersey-number-of-former-mlb-star-kevin-youkilis, accessed September 9, 2023.

5 Chaz Scoggins, "Youkilis Didn't Take the Easy Way to the Top," LowellSun.com, December 27, 2009, updated July 13, 2019. https://www.lowellsun.com/2009/12/27/youkilis-didnt-take-the-easy-way-to-the-top/, accessed September 9, 2023. For Bearcats statistics, see https://www.thebaseballcube.com/content/college_history/20357/ . Accessed December 6, 2023.

6 Keith Jenkins, "UC Alum Kevin Youkilis Wins 2007 World Series Ring," Magazine.UC.edu, https://magazine.uc.edu/issues/0408/sports.html, accessed September 9, 2023.

7 Brian Cleary, telephone interview with author, August 22, 2022.

8 Cleary.

9 Jen McCaffrey, "Talent and Promise in 'Baseball Heaven': Behind the Scenes With a Scout at the Cape Cod League," TheAthletic.com, August 9, 2021. https://theathletic.com/2750669/2021/08/09/talent-and-promise-in-baseball-heaven-behind-the-scenes-with-a-cape-league-scout/, accessed September 9, 2023.

10 CCBL Public Relations Office. "Kevin Youkilis Joins Cubs as a Special Assistant," CapeCodBaseball.org, February 20, 2015. https://www.capecodbaseball.org/news/league-news/index.html?article_id=2010, accessed September 9, 2023.

11 Matt Haas, telephone interview with author, September 9, 2022. Upon his return to UC, Coach Cleary noticed a difference. "I think most guys head to the Cape, and think, 'Oh geez, I hope I can belong,' and I think Youkilis went there knowing that … this was his chance to let everybody know he belonged. And he came back … more confident." Cleary interview.

12 University of Cincinnati 2022-23 Baseball Record Book GoBearcats.com, https://gobearcats.com/documents/2022/9/22/2022-23_Baseball_Record_Book.pdf, accessed September 9, 2023. Youkilis was honored for his collegiate career in 2004 when he was elected to the University of Cincinnati Hall of Fame, and again in 2015 when the school retired his number 36. Youkilis was similarly honored by Conference-USA, as he was named to their All-Decade team in 2007, and inducted into their Hall of Fame in 2019. See WKRC. "Huggins, Martin, Youkilis Named to First Conference USA Hall of Fame Class," Local12.com, July 8, 2019. https://local12.com/sports/uc-bearcats/huggins-martin-youkilis-named-to-first-conference-usa-hall-of-fame-class-cincinnati-bearcats-bob-kenyon-kevin-college-basketball-baseball-boston-red-sox-new-jersey-nets-nba, accessed September 9, 2023.

13 Cleary.

14 Scoggins. Beane thought the A's should have drafted Youkilis themselves, much higher in thedraft.

15 Michael Lewis, *Moneyball* (New York: W.W. Norton), 2004.

16 Alex Speier, "The Transformation of Kevin Youkilis," WEEI.com, March 18, 2009. https://web.archive.org/web/20110716024440/http://www.weei.com/sports/boston/red-sox/alex-speier/transformation-kevin-youkilis, accessed September 9, 2023.

17 Scoggins.

18 Combined with his five from the previous season, he played in only 20 games for the GreenJackets. However, due to the remarkable nature of his baseball career in general, Youkilis was inducted into their Hall of Fame in 2018. Larry Taylor, "Greenjackets Induct Youkilis Into Hall of Fame," AugustaChronicle.com, August 10, 2018. https://www.augustachronicle.com/story/sports/2018/08/11/former-red-sox-great-kevin-youkilis-inducted-into-augusta-greenjackets-hall-of-fame/6499792007/, accessed September 9, 2023.

19 Jenkins, "UC Alum Kevin Youkilis Wins 2007 World Series Ring."

20 Speier.

21 MILB.com, "Kevin Youkilis Inducted Into Sea Dogs Hall of Fame," MILB.com, August 30, 2013. https://www.milb.com/news/gcs-59012604, accessed September 9, 2023.

22 He was later rewarded for his accomplishments he was elected to the Unum Portland Sea Dogs Hall of Fame in 2013 and was named as the third baseman on the 20th Season All-Time Team. "Kevin Youkilis Inducted into Sea Dogs Hall of Fame."

23 Bob Hohler, "Youkilis Was Flying Before – And After – Game," Boston.com, May 16, 2004. http://archive.boston.com/sports/baseball/redsox/articles/2004/05/16/youkilis_was_flying_before____and_after____game/, accessed September 9, 2023.

24 Hohler.

25 Hohler. See also Brian MacPherson, "Remembering The Beginning of the Kevin Youkilis Era," ProvidenceJournal.com, June 25, 2012. https://www.providencejournal.com/story/sports/mlb/2012/06/25/20120625-remembering-the-beginning-of-the-kevin-youkilis-era-ece/35427067007/, accessed September 9, 2023.

26 MacPherson.

27 Dan Shaughnessy, "He Walks Away With a Dreamlike Debut," Boston.com, May 16, 2004. http://archive.boston.com/sports/baseball/redsox/articles/2004/05/16/he_walks_away_with_a_dreamlike_debut/, accessed September 9, 2023. One can see the home run and aftermath on YouTube at https://www.youtube.com/watch?v=ri5XpTaLEOs.

28 "We thought having the position player may come in handy," Francona said. "It will allow us to use Dave Roberts in a pinch-running situation a little bit more aggressively and gives us a couple of more options." Allan Wood and Bill Nowlin, *Don't Let Us Win Tonight: An Oral History of the 2004 Boston Red Sox's Impossible Playoff Run* (Chicago: Triumph Books, 2014), 29.

29 Four Jewish players had taken the field for the New York Giants in 1941. Jewish Virtual Library, https://www.jewishvirtuallibrary.org/kevin-youkilis, accessed September 9, 2023.

30 Lowell was a three-time All-Star, Gold Glove, and World Series–winning third baseman.

31 Fenway Fanatics, "Youkilis Sets New Consecutive Error-Free Games Record," FenwayFanatics.com, April 2, 2008. https://www.fenwayfanatics.com/content/2008/04/02/youkilis-sets-new-consecutive-error-free-games-record/, accessed September 9, 2023.

32 Gordon Edes, "Youkilis: 'I'll play anywhere,'" ESPN.com, September 13, 2010. https://www.espn.com/blog/boston/red-sox/post/_/id/6008/youkilis-ill-play-anywhere, accessed September 9, 2023.

33 Fenway Fanatics. "Youkilis Sets New Consecutive Error-Free Games Record."

34 Gordon Edes, "Youk Muffs Throw, Errorless Streak Ends," Boston.com, June 7, 2008. https://www.boston.com/sports/extra-bases/2008/06/07/youk_muffs_thro/, accessed September 10, 2023.

35 *2023 Boston Red Sox Media Guide*, 318.

36 Ian Browne, "Youkilis, Sox Agree to Four-Year Deal," MLB.com, January 16, 2009. https://web.archive.org/web/20090121175636/http://mlb.mlb.com:80/news/article.jsp?ymd=20090115&content_id=3745442&vkey=hotstove2008&fext=.jsp, accessed September 10, 2023.

37 Jewish Virtual Library.

38 Scoggins.

39 Associated Press, "Youkilis to Miss Remainder Of Season," NYTimes.com, August 5, 2010. https://www.nytimes.com/2010/08/06/sports/baseball/06bats.html, accessed September 10, 2023.

40 Evan Drellich, "Youkilis Lends His Time, Expertise to Clinic," MLB.com, https://www.mlb.com/news/youkilis-lends-his-time-expertise-to-clinic-c22738144, accessed September 10, 2023.

41 Eric Bowman, "Theo Epstein Agrees to Join Chicago Cubs, Leaving Boston Red Sox in a Bind," BleacherReport.com, October 12, 2011. https://bleacherreport.com/articles/890464-theo-epstein-agrees-to-join-chicago-cubs-leaving-boston-red-sox-in-a-bind#:~:text=Chicago%20Cubs-,Theo%20Epstein%20Agrees%20to%20Join%20Chicago%20Cubs%2C%20Leaving,Red%20Sox%20in%20a%20Bind&text=Former%20Boston%20Red%20Sox%20general,to%20John%20Dennis%20of%20WEEI., accessed September 10, 2023.

42 Sean McAdam, "Red Sox a House Divided?" NBCSportsBoston.com, June 21, 2012, updated January 15, 2013. https://www.nbcsportsboston.com/mlb/boston-red-sox/mcadam-red-sox-a-house-divided/321842/?blockID=728034&feedID=3352, accessed September 10, 2023.

43 Gabe Zaldivar, "Kevin Youkilis and Julie Brady Get Married at Private Wedding Ceremony," BleacherReport.com, April 24, 2012. https://bleacherreport.com/articles/1157978-kevin-youkilis-and-julie-brady-get-married-at-private-wedding-ceremony, accessed September 10, 2023. Youkilis first met Julie in 2004 when he bumped into the Super Bowl–winning quarterback and his three sisters at Boston's Avalon nightclub. While interested, Kevin was wary. He was merely a Red Sox backup while Brady had already cemented his status as a Boston sports legend with three Super Bowl victories under his belt. According to Julie, "[Kevin] was intimidated to ask for my phone number because he didn't want to step on any toes with Tommy." Kirsten Fleming, "Pulse," *New York Post*, June 14, 2013. Julie reminded Kevin of this when they ran into each other again in 2010 and the road to marriage was paved.

44 "Report: Youkilis Marries Brady's Sister," FoxSports.com, April 24, 2012. https://www.foxsports.com/stories/mlb/report-youkilis-marries-bradys-sister, accessed September 10, 2023.

45 Karl Rasmussen, "Julie Brady, Tom Brady's Sister, Is Married to Another New England Sports Legend," FanBuzz.com, February 24, 2023. https://fanbuzz.com/nfl/kevin-youkilis-wife/, accessed September 10, 2023.

46 Tony Lee, "Kevin Youkilis Sent to White Sox," ESPN.com, June 24, 2012. https://www.espn.com/mlb/story/_/id/8091584/kevin-youkilis-traded-boston-red-sox-chicago-white-sox, accessed September 10, 2023.

47 Lee.

48 Scott Boeck, "Youkilis' Letter to Red Sox Fans: 'I Am Forever Grateful.'" *USA Today*, July 15, 2012.

49 JTA and Steve Klein, "Baseball World Classic, Youkilis Says He Will Play for Israel, if It Qualifies for Tournament," Haaretz.com, August 24, 2012. https://www.haaretz.com/2012-08-24/ty-article/mlb-star-youkilis-ready-to-play-for-israel/0000017f-dbb3-db22-a17f-ffb3ec8b0000?v=1694363172880, accessed September 10, 2023.

50 Legacy User, "White Sox Decline $13m option on Kevin Youkilis, Sign Jake Peavy for Two Years," Boston.com, October 31, 2012. https://www.boston.com/sports/boston-red-sox/2012/10/31/white-sox-decline-13m-option-on-kevin-youkilis-sign-jake-peavy-for-two-years/, accessed September 10, 2023.

51 Andrew Marchand, "Sources: Kevin Youkilis to Yankees," ESPN.com, December 11, 2012. https://www.espn.com/new-york/mlb/story/_/id/8737974/kevin-youkilis-agrees-deal-new-york-yankees-sources, accessed September 10, 2023.

52 See the Kevin Youkilis IMBD page: https://www.imdb.com/name/nm1753938/?ref_=nv_sr_srsg_0_tt_0_nm_1_q_Kevin%2520Youkilis.

53 Jerry Crasnick, "Japan Champs to Sign Kevin Youkilis," ESPN.com, December 20, 2013. https://www.espn.com/mlb/story/_/id/10172824/kevin-youkilis-play-japan-tohoku-rakuten-golden-eagles, accessed September 10, 2023.

54 Jen McCaffrey, "Kevin Youkilis Back From Japan Recovering From Plantar Fasciitis, Hoping to Still Play," MassLive.com, May 29, 2014.

55 https://www.masslive.com/redsox/2014/05/kevin_youkilis_back_from_japan.html, accessed September 10, 2023.

55 Associated Press, "Kevin Youkilis Walking Away," ESPN.com, October 30, 2014. https://www.espn.com/boston/mlb/story/_/id/11791585/former-boston-red-sox-infielder-kevin-youkilis-retires, accessed September 10, 2023.

56 Jesse Rogers, "Ramirez, Youkilis to Consult Cubs," ESPN.com, February 24, 2015. https://www.espn.co.uk/mlb/story/_/id/12374325/chicago-cubs-hire-manny-ramirez-kevin-youkilis-consultant-positions, accessed September 10, 2023.

57 GoBearcats.com, "Youkilis Celebration, Senior Day Slated for Final American Series," GoBearcats.com, May 13, 2015. https://gobearcats.com/news/2015/5/13/Youkilis_Celebration_Senior_Day_Slated_for_Final_American_Series.aspx, accessed September 10, 2023. See also: https://www.youtube.com/watch?v=Kl6AKSZuvWA.

58 Dyer.

59 Dave Clark, "Kevin Youkilis, Former Sycamore HS and UC Bearcats Star, Elected to Boston Red Sox Hall of Fame," Cincinnati.com, December 1, 2017. https://www.cincinnati.com/story/sports/high-school/ohio-high-school/2017/12/01/kevin-youkilis-former-sycamore-hs-and-uc-bearcats-star-elected-boston-red-sox-hall-fame/912425001/, accessed September 10, 2023.

60 Mark Bechtel, "Former Red Sox Great Kevin Youkilis Crafting a New Path with California Brewery," SI.com, June 25, 2019. https://www.si.com/mlb/2019/06/25/kevin-youkilis-boston-red-sox-loma-brewing-company, accessed September 10, 2023.

61 Sarah Fritsche, "Youkilis Brothers Open Loma Brewing Company in Los Gatos," SFGate.com, August 18, 2016. https://www.sfgate.com/restaurants/article/Youkilis-brothers-open-Loma-Brewing-Company-in-9171305.php, accessed September 10, 2023.

62 Lomabrew.com.

63 Bechtel, "Former Red Sox Great Kevin Youkilis Crafting a New Path With California Brewery."

64 Mike Rosenstein, "Where Are They Now? Ex-Yankee Kevin Youkilis Struggling as the Greek God of Hops," NJ.com, June 3, 2020. https://www.nj.com/yankees/2020/06/where-are-they-now-ex-yankee-kevin-youkilis-struggling-as-the-greek-god-of-hops.html, accessed September 10, 2023.

65 See, for instance, https://www.redbubble.com/i/t-shirt/Kevin-Youkilis-The-Greek-God-of-Walks-by-bridge2oblivion/35131463.6ATOD.

66 John Metcalfe, "Kevin Youkilis' Journey from Baseball to Brewing," MercuryNews.com, April 20, 2022. https://www.mercurynews.com/2022/04/20/kevin-youkilis-journey-from-baseball-to-brewing/, accessed September 10, 2023.

67 Chad Finn, "NESN to Add Ellis Burks, Mo Vaughn and Kevin Youkilis to Red Sox Broadcasts," BostonGlobe.com, March 19, 2021. https://www.bostonglobe.com/2021/03/19/sports/nesn-add-ellis-burks-mo-vaughn-kevin-youkilis-red-sox-broadcast/, accessed September 10, 2023.

68 Dave Clark, "Kevin Youkilis Joins NESN Broadcast Booth for 50 Boston Red Sox Games," Cincinnati.com, March 15, 2022, updated April 20, 2022. https://www.cincinnati.com/story/sports/mlb/2022/03/15/kevin-youkilis-joins-nesn-broadcast-booth-50-boston-red-sox-games-2022-season-sycamore-hs-bearcats/7054392001/, accessed September 10, 2023.

69 Chad Finn, "Kevin Youkilis Will Be NESN's Primary Color Analyst for Red Sox Games in 2023, Lou Merloni Set to Join," Boston.com, January 21, 2023. https://www.boston.com/sports/boston-red-sox/2023/01/21/nesn-red-sox-booth-announcers-2023-kevin-youkilis-lou-merloni-will-middlebrooks-kevin-millar-time-wakefield-dave-obrien/, accessed September 10, 2023.

70 John Metcalfe, "Kevin Youkilis' Journey from Baseball to Brewing."

71 Richard Sandomir, "Fascination With a New Yankee's Jewish Roots," NYTimes.com, December 12, 2012. https://www.nytimes.com/2012/12/13/sports/baseball/fascination-with-a-new-yankees-jewish-roots.html, accessed September 9, 2023.

72 Sandomir.

73 Dan Gartland, "University of Cincinnati Baseball Players Want Racist Ex-Reds Owner's Name Taken Off Stadium," June 8, 2020. SI.com, https://www.si.com/extra-mustard/2020/06/08/cincinnati-bearcats-baseball-stadium-name-marge-schott-reds, accessed September 9, 2023.

74 Gartland.

75 Keith Jenkins, "Kevin Youkilis Joins UC Baseball Player in Calling for Name Change to Marge Schott Stadium," Cincinnati.com, June 7, 2020. https://www.cincinnati.com/story/sports/2020/06/07/uc-pitcher-kevin-youkilis-want-marge-schotts-name-removed-stadium/3170386001/, accessed September 9, 2023.

A RED SOX MEMORY

Red Sox flags

On graves rest

After World Series win.

Nuff Ced

Rest in Peace!

BELT HIGH HALLISEY

TERRY FRANCONA

BY ROBERT EMERSON

Terrence Jon Francona, colloquially Terry, has seen baseball from just about all of its vantage points. From that of a highly touted first-round pick. As the last man to make a 25-man roster. And then during a lengthy but mostly successful managerial career, including two championships in Boston. It has not come easy for Tito, the nickname he inherited from his former major-league All-Star father, but his managerial accolades over the years have shown that he's learned a thing or two in a lifetime of professional baseball.

Born in Aberdeen, South Dakota, on April 22, 1959, to John Patsy "Tito" and Roberta "Birdie" Francona, the family relocated to Tito's hometown of New Brighton, Pennsylvania, where Terry's younger sister was born two years later. When Terry was born, Tito Francona was a 25-year-old utilityman and pinch-hitter traded twice in the past calendar year, looking for a role to settle into in the bigs. Later that year he found that role in Cleveland, playing center field and first base, hitting .363 in 122 games (missing the plate appearance per game qualifier for the American League by 34 plate appearances) and finishing fifth in the MVP voting.

Young Terry ended up spending the better part of his tweens in the clubhouses of the Cardinals, Phillies, Braves, Athletics, and Brewers, seeing the inner workings and learning the weight of responsibility that players, coaches, managers, and executive can carry on their shoulders.

When he wasn't on the road with his father, Terry was home in New Brighton, playing baseball. As a sophomore at New Brighton High School, he hit .545 in 1975 and a whopping .769 in his junior season. He also played golf in the fall and basketball in the winter.

In his 1977 senior season, Francona separated his shoulder and accumulated only 10 at-bats (although he got hits in seven of them). But he had presented enough of a body of work to attract the interest of scouts. In a stacked 1977 draft, Francona was picked in the second round (38th overall) by the Chicago Cubs. Jim Brock, head coach of the powerhouse Arizona State University, was also on the line.[1]

Terry got what he felt was a disappointing offer of $18,000 (the Cubs were willing to go up $1,000),[2] and Francona had shined in high school and never had once received a call from Brock until after the draft. He declined both offers and made the decision to play at the University of Arizona in the fall of 1977.[3]

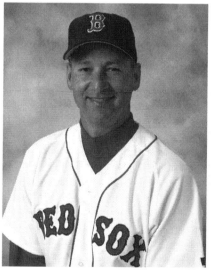

It was at Arizona that Francona met Brad Mills, the Wildcats' third baseman, who would become Francona's eventual baseball consigliere. In 1979 both were named all-stars in the Southern Division of the PAC 10, as Francona batted .378 and led the team in RBIs (81 in 67 games), getting a conference all-star nod, and being voted team MVP by his teammates.

In 1980 Francona won the Golden Spikes Award, given annually to the best amateur baseball player in the nation, after leading Arizona to a top ranking and second straight College World Series appearance. Francona was named Most Outstanding Player after Arizona won the tournament, and following the CWS, coach Jerry Kindall – who'd played with Terry's father with the Indians – told Francona, "Time for you to move on,"[4] and on June 3, 1980, he was picked 22nd overall by the Montreal Expos, the lone first-round pick of the seven Wildcats drafted.

The Montreal Expos, coming off their first season over .500 and finishing two games out of the NL East crown in 1979, entered the 1980s full of promise, with a roster that included future Hall of Famers Gary Carter and Andre Dawson, with pitcher Tim Wallach, who had won the Golden Spikes and was the Expos' first-round pick the year before Francona did both, in Triple A.

Francona began his minor-league career in Memphis (Double-A Southern League) the same day he signed his contract, June 16, hitting .300 in 60 games for the Chicks. After postseason correspondence with John McHale and Class-A manager Bob Bailey, Francona spent the winter in the Florida Instructional League.

After 41 games with Memphis in 1981, he was promoted to Triple-A Denver. He didn't stay there long, though, being sent to join the Expos in Houston on August 19, potentially facing Astros gunslinger Nolan Ryan in his major-league debut.

Francona didn't arrive at the Astrodome until the fourth inning. Ryan, the day's starter, was about to go through Montreal's lineup for the second time, accruing six strikeouts and no hits. By the time Francona got into the clubhouse to drop his baggage and change into his uniform, reliever Dave Smith was in for Ryan, who lost his no-hit bid in the top of the sixth with a Bobby Ramos base hit. No sooner had Francona stepped into the dugout than Expos manager Dick Williams called him to lead off the eighth inning as a pinch-hitter for

Elias Sosa. He grounded out to first baseman César Cedeño, who took it unassisted.[5]

Francona got his first big-league hit on August 22 in the second game of a doubleheader, a pinch-hit single off Braves starter John Montefusco. Francona was used by Williams mostly as a pinch-hitter, but after Williams was fired on September 8 and Tim Raines was injured in a September 13 game against the Cubs, Francona got an opportunity, and started in left field in 18 of the Expos' last 19 games. In that span, the Expos went 13-6, clinching a playoff spot and winning the NL East championship in the second half of the strike-interrupted season.[6] They faced the first-half leaders, the Philadelphia Phillies, in the first playoff series outside the United States.

Francona played in all five games of the Division Series against the Phillies, starting three, as the Expos won their only playoff series in Montreal. But he had only one at-bat in the NL Championship Series against the Los Angeles Dodgers, who had a largely left-handed pitching staff. Manager Jim Fanning employed switch-hitting Jerry White in all five games. White hit .313, second on the team for the series, but the Expos lost in five games to the eventual World Series champions.

In the 1981-82 offseason, Francona had surgery on a disc in his neck, and he began the 1982 season a backup in the outfield and at first base, batting .286 in spot starts and pinch-hit appearances.[7] But Tim Raines made the move from left field to second base, and on May 17, 1982, Francona became an everyday starter for Montreal, manning left field.

For the next month, Francona, mostly hitting behind Raines, raised his batting average to .321. On June 16, playing the St. Louis Cardinals, he showed situational awareness in the second inning with a two-out bases-loaded bunt, and was later driven in by a bases-clearing double by Andre Dawson. But in the seventh inning, protecting the lead he established, while fielding a Julio González fly ball, Francona crashed into the center-field wall of Busch Memorial Stadium, tearing his anterior cruciate ligament and meniscus.

Francona was placed on the disabled list and underwent his first (of many to come) knee surgery. Two days later, the Expos announced that Francona would be out the rest of the season. He spent his time traveling with the team rehabbing with team trainer Ron McClain, only leaving in early September for the funeral of his grandfather.

After the 1982 season Francona traveled to West Germany with manager Fanning and Expos announcer Dave Van Horne to Canadian Armed Forces bases to conduct baseball clinics.[8] In 1983 spring training, new manager Bill Virdon, not wanting to rush his rehabilitation, kept him out of the first 10 exhibition games "for his own good."

The cautionary path paid off for Francona, who received a $5,000 bonus for not going on the DL before the All-Star break, but the Expos finished 82-80, eight games back of the first-place Phillies. Francona, coming off the bench in defensive situations and pinch-hitting most of the season, finished the year with a .257 batting average.

After winning MVP of the Caribbean Series (Winter League) and improving his swing in 1984 spring training, Francona began the season starting at first base and was hitting .367 in the first two months of the season. But on June 14, in the third inning of a game against the Pittsburgh Pirates, while avoiding a tag by Pittsburgh pitcher John Tudor on a groundball up the line, Francona tore a ligament in his left knee, and was carried off the field on a stretcher. Two days later, on the second anniversary of his right-knee injury, he underwent surgery to repair the torn ligament and remove cartilage. His season was over thereafter. Montreal finished 78-83, firing Virdon at the end of August; Fanning finished the season as manager.

Francona came back in 1985 with his left knee almost as strong as his right, but was reduced to a bench role after the Expos signed power hitter Dan Driessen. Francona wasn't playing every day, and a potential trade partner was hard to find. The situation frustrated Francona, who voiced displeasure with it, saying, "It's like I told my father, this year has been a real character builder. But I've got enough character to play."[9]

After Driessen was traded in July, Francona began playing more. He was told by the Expos not to play winter ball, and had arthroscopic knee surgery after slipping in his garage in February. He made it to spring training but was released on April 1, 1986. Two days later he signed a minor-league deal with the Chicago Cubs, reporting to their Triple-A affiliate Iowa.[10] He was called up to Chicago on May 2, and was mainly used as a backup. In November the Cubs optioned him back to Iowa.

In early 1987 the Cincinnati Reds invited free agent Francona to spring training, where he battled Nick Esasky and Dave Concepción for the first-base position. He signed a one-year deal after landing the starting role. A free agent in 1988, Francona signed a minor-league contract with Cleveland's Triple-A affiliate Colorado Springs Sky Sox. He hit .432 in spring training but was sent back to Colorado Springs.[11]

Riding a .323 batting average and a 20-game hitting streak in Triple A at the Fourth of July, Francona was called up to Cleveland as a reserve at first base and left field, later getting more starts at DH. He finished with a .311 average in 62 games, hitting .310 in 47 starts. A free agent once more, he was invited to Brewers spring training in February 1989 and, after batting .310, earned a roster spot.

Platooning at first with Greg Brock and Dave Engle, Francona batted .232 in 89 games, including his first and only major-league pitching appearance, on May 15. (He recorded the only strikeout by the Brewers in a 12-2 loss to that year's eventual World Series champs, the Oakland A's, striking out center fielder Stan Javier looking on a knuckleball.)

Francona signed a contract with the Brewers in December 1989 and made the roster for the 1990 season. He subbed in three games before being placed on waivers at the end of April to make room for Paul Molitor coming off the disabled list.

Signing a minor-league contract in May 1990 with the Cardinals affiliate Louisville Redbirds, he hit .263 in 86 games. He signed another minor-league contract for 1991, but the

Cardinals released him before the start of the season. Francona's playing career, once promising from the onset, marred by injuries, ended with a .274 batting average in 707 games in a 10-year career.

Francona stayed in baseball, signing on as a hitting instructor for the Chicago White Sox' rookie-level Gulf Coast League team. He spent the rest of 1991 teaching young draftees the ins and outs of major-league pitching. He was named the manager of the White Sox' affiliate in South Bend (Class-A Midwest League) for 1992. Francona went 73-64 in his first year managing, and was promoted to manage the Double-A Birmingham Barons for the '93 season. The White Sox thrust Francona and the Barons into the national spotlight when Michael Jordan made his move from basketball to baseball.

Jordan worked hard to transfer his athleticism from a basketball mindset to a baseball mindset, and it paid off at the end of the year with the White Sox petitioning Jordan to play in the Arizona Fall League. Jordan himself admitted in October of '94 that he couldn't have done that without Francona.[12]

But Jordan soon returned to basketball,[13] and the Barons went 80-64 in 1995, earning Francona an opportunity to join Detroit manager Buddy Bell's staff at the third-base coach. It was a bleak year in Detroit, but Francona seemed to escape real blame.

Francona was identified as a possible candidate to replace Pirates manager Jim Leyland, but on October 31, 1996, he was named the manager of the Philadelphia Phillies, who were coming off three consecutive losing seasons, losing 95 games in 1996.

Francona did everything he could to tinker with a consistently losing roster, but the Phillies lost 15 of 17 heading into July, and at the All-Star break 1997, they held the worst record in the majors at 24-61, 30 games behind their nearest competitor. After that they played above .500 ball and finished the season 67-95.

Francona used his young stars Scott Rolen and Bobby Abreu and ace Curt Schilling to improve the Phillies to 75-87 in 1998. The next season they were 61-48 on August 6, but injuries to Rolen and Schilling took a toll, and the Phillies finished the season 77-85.

Things went worse in 2000. Schilling was still recovering from shoulder surgery that prematurely ended his '99 season and didn't return until late April. He and the Phillies struggled early. Schilling was dealt to Arizona on July 26, with the Phillies at 44-55. They went 21-42 afterward and on October 1 Francona was fired. The team finished the year 65-97, and Francona's four-season tenure in Philadelphia resulted in a 285-363 record.

Two days after being fired, Francona was mentioned again as the potential Pirates manager, this time succeeding Gene Lamont. Instead, on November 22 he was named a special assistant for baseball operations for the Cleveland Indians, under GM John Hart and assistant GM Mark Shapiro. It was a learning experience for Francona and would lead to the formation of important relationships in his managing career.[14]

Francona was not in a front office for long. On November 14, 2001, he was hired as bench coach for Texas Rangers manager Jerry Narron (but not before managing the US National Team to a Silver Medal in the 2001 Baseball World Cup). Narron was fired after the 2002 season, and Francona was on the shortlist to replace him. He was also considered in Seattle and for the New York Mets.

In October Francona had surgery to relieve staph infections in both knees, which had led to pulmonary embolisms in each lung. Buck Showalter was hired in Texas on October 11; Francona was not retained. A month later Francona joined the Oakland A's staff as bench coach. Former Montreal teammate Ken Macha was replacing Art Howe, who took the New York Mets job.

Francona recovered from his surgeries as the 2003 season went on, and he was Macha's right-hand man as they led Oakland to an AL West title, going 96-66. Francona was in the dugout for the playoffs for the first time since 1981, going up against the wild-card Boston Red Sox, led by manager Grady Little, in the Division Series.

The A's went up 2-0 against Boston, but then lost three straight to end their season. The Red Sox, in turn, fell to the New York Yankees in seven games in the ALCS. The series is best remembered for its 12-inning Game Seven, which went to extra innings after an exhausted Pedro Martinez gave up three runs in the eighth inning. Aaron Boone's home run in the 12th inning won the game, and Little's decision to leave Martinez in the game was widely criticized. He was fired two days after the World Series ended.

Francona, coming off interviews with the White Sox and division opponent Orioles, became a candidate for Little's job. The meeting between Francona and Red Sox GM Theo Epstein and assistant GM Josh Byrnes lasted six hours and left both parties with a good impression. On December 4 Francona was introduced as the 44th manager of the Red Sox.[15] He was seen as the man who could meld a statistical and traditionalist approach to managing, in contrast to Little's old-school intuitive style that won them that many games but not their biggest one of the season.

Neck and neck with the Yankees for the first two months of the 2004 season, Boston was seven games back at the All-Star break. At the trade deadline, the Red Sox acquired first baseman Doug Mientkiewicz and shortstop Orlando Cabrera while trading franchise cornerstone Nomar Garciaparra.

With the addition of utility outfielder Dave Roberts in a separate trade, Francona had all of his tools nearly finalized for a playoff run. The Red Sox finished three games behind the Yankees, earning a wild-card berth. They beat the Angels in the ALDS, and once again, the Yankees loomed in the ALCS.

The Yankees were poised for a sweep after winning the first three games, but Francona kept the ship tight, and admitted, "It starts looking a little daunting if you start looking at too big of a picture."[16] A comeback win in Game Four to stave off elimination lit a fire.[17]

Winning the next three games was a lot more daunting – not to mention unprecedented – and the fact that they were all decided by two runs or less was a testament to how well

Francona knew his team and the right time to pull the proper strings. The 10-3 win in Game Seven gave the Red Sox all the momentum they needed going into the World Series.

"It's just not time to have the final celebration," Francona would say between series, "We're excited to be doing what we're doing, but we're not done yet."[18]

The Red Sox faced the Cardinals, beating them 11-9 in Game One on the way to a decisive sweep. Francona had helped do the impossible and ended the 86-year championship drought in Boston baseball.

The next season the Red Sox won 95 games, but lost in the ALDS to the eventual World Series champion Chicago White Sox, themselves ending a lengthy World Series drought. The Red Sox won 86 games in 2006, finishing third in the division and missing the playoffs. But the 2007 Red Sox came back swinging, winning 96 games and tying with Cleveland for the best record in baseball. This team was almost completely remade from 2004.

After a 3-0 ALDS sweep of the California Angels, the Red Sox faced the Indians in the 2007 ALCS. Once again the team overcame a three-games-to-one deficit to win the series. Francona seemed to do fantastic work with his back against the wall. The Red Sox swept the Colorado Rockies. After going 86 years between World Series wins, the team had won two in four years.

On February 28, 2008, Francona was given a three-year contract extension, with club options for 2014 and 2015. "The ballclub showed a lot of trust in me, which I don't take lightly," he said.[19]

In 2008, a 95-win season got the Red Sox a wild-card berth behind the 97-win Tampa Bay Rays. After dispatching the Angels in the ALDS, the Red Sox were once again down three games to one in the ALCS to the Rays. Boston forced a seventh game, but there was no comeback this time, as they lost the game.

The Red Sox advanced to the playoffs in 2009, losing in the ALDS to the Angels, and in 2011 were 83-52 heading into September. But that month they went 7-20, falling from first to third place. After losing out on a playoff spot on the final day of the season, the club announced that Francona's last two contract years wouldn't be picked up. His 744 victories as Red Sox manager rank second only to Joe Cronin (1,071).

Francona made the shortlist of potential candidates to replace Tony La Russa in St. Louis in 2012,[20] but after Mike Matheny was named manager, Francona found work at ESPN as a baseball analyst for the 2012 season.

On October 6, 2012, Francona was named the manager of the Cleveland Indians. The 2012 Indians finished with 68 wins under manager Manny Acta and interim Sandy Alomar Jr.[21] Under Francona in 2013 they improved by 24 wins, earning a wild-card spot. At that time the wild-card "series" was a single game, and the Indians lost to the Tampa Bay Rays, 4-0. Still, Francona was named AL Manager of the Year.

The Indians turned in winning seasons in 2014 and 2015, but didn't make the playoffs. But they began building their arsenal of young talent, developing José Ramírez, Corey Kluber, and Francisco Lindor.

In 2016 the Indians won 94 games and their first AL Central Division title since 2007. Francona worked his old postseason magic in a 7-1 record in the first two rounds of the playoffs, with a sweep of the Red Sox in the Division Series and a 4-1 Championship Series win over the Toronto Blue Jays. It was Cleveland's first appearance in the World Series since 1997, and they were looking to win their first Series since 1948. They faced the Chicago Cubs, who were in their own pursuit of breaking a 108-year championship drought.

Cleveland went up three games to one, but Chicago won the next three games, two of them by one run, including the 10-inning Game Seven. Still, Francona won his second AL Manager of the Year award.

The Indians won AL Central titles in 2017 and 2018 but lost in the Division Series in both years. The 2017 team posted the second-longest major-league winning streak ever, 22 games in a row in a 102-win season. The Indians won 93 games in 2019 but missed the playoffs.

In the pandemic-shortened season of 2020, Francona's own season was further shortened when he underwent a procedure in August to relieve a blood clotting issue, with Sandy Alomar Jr. filling in.

Francona took the rest of the year and postseason to recover, looking to come back in 2021 more healthy after a Cleveland wild-card loss to the Yankees. In 2021, with Cleveland at 50-49 heading into August, Francona stepped away again to deal with health issues, leaving coach DeMarlo Hale as acting manager for the rest of the year. Cleveland finished with an 80-82 record.

In 2022 a recovered Francona returned to guide the renamed Cleveland Guardians to a 92-win season. With franchise cornerstone José Ramírez and young pitching power in Shane Bieber, Triston McKenzie, and Emmanuel Clase, the Guardians won the Central Division title and beat the Rays in the wild-card series before falling to the Yankees in five games in the Division Series. Francona was recognized for his capability by winning his third Manager of the Year Award.

The Guardians faltered in 2023, and in August Francona started hinting at retirement, saying before a game, "I've talked to (President) Chris (Antonetti) and (general manager Mike Chernoff) at length about the future and everything, because I don't want to put them in any kind of a predicament. We've had a lot of talks about moving forward."[22]

Francona got a de-facto farewell tour in the final month of the season, and stepped down after the season. The Guardians hired Stephen Vogt as his replacement. Francona won 921 games as Cleveland manager, tops in team history.

Francona's 1,950 wins place him 13th all-time in managerial wins, just ahead of Hall of Famer Casey Stengel and behind Hall of Famer Leo Durocher's 2,008 wins. Francona's success as manager in Boston and Cleveland will likely get him his place in baseball eternity as one of baseball's men of constant success.

ACKNOWLEDGMENT

Thanks to Vince Guerrieri for working on and improving this biography.

NOTES

1. Joe Noga, "At 18 Years Old, Terry Francona Spurned His Dream College and Enrolled at Its Biggest Rival, Telling the Coach 'I'm Going to Kick Your (Behind),'" Cleveland.com, March 9, 2020. https://www.cleveland.com/tribe/2020/03/at-18-years-old-terry-francona-spurned-his-dream-college-and-enrolled-at-its-biggest-rival-telling-the-coach-im-going-to-kick-your-behind.html.

2. John Perrotto, "MLB Draft: Money Made It Easy for New Brighton's Francona to Choose College," *Beaver County Times* (Aliquippa, Pennsylvania), June 4, 2014. https://www.timesonline.com/story/sports/mlb/2014/06/04/mlb-draft-money-made-it/18499608007/.

3. [3] Joe Noga, "At 18 Years Old, Terry Francona Spurned His Dream College and Enrolled at Its Biggest Rival, Telling the Coach 'I'm Going to Kick Your (Behind),'" Cleveland.Com, March 9, 2020. www.cleveland.com/tribe/2020/03/at-18-years-old-terry-francona-spurned-his-dream-college-and-enrolled-at-its-biggest-rival-telling-the-coach-im-going-to-kick-your-behind.html.

4. Zack Meisel, "A Trip Down Memory Lane with Cleveland Indians Manager Terry Francona: From Star High Schooler to 1st-Round Draft Pick," Cleveland.com, June 2, 2014. https://www.cleveland.com/tribe/2014/06/a_trip_down_memory_lane_with_t.html.

5. Zack Meisel, "Terry Francona Shares Tale of His Chaotic MLB Debut." Cleveland.Com, May 17, 2017. www.cleveland.com/tribe/2017/05/terry_francona_recalls_his_maj.html.

6. That year, a players strike split the season in half, leading to the first Division Series, where the first-half winners played the second-half winners in each division. The Cincinnati Reds finished with baseball's best record, but couldn't participate in the postseason because they didn't finish either half in first place.

7. Charlie Feeney, "Oliver Is Shooting for World Series," *The Sporting News*, April 24, 1982: 16-17.

8. Ian MacDonald, "Francona Big Hit at Army Bases," *The Sporting News*, February 21, 1983: 32.

9. Ian MacDonald, "Francona Angry Over Bench Role," *The Sporting News*, July 8, 1985: 19.

10. Ian MacDonald, "Webster Feels He's Proven Self," *The Sporting News*, December 9, 1985: 54-57.

11. Sheldon Ocker, "Change of Scenery May Get Upshaw 'Whacking Again,'" *The Sporting News*, April 11, 1988: 32.

12. Paul Newberry, "Barons Open Tonight With a Celebrity in Right Field," *Indiana* (Pennsylvania) *Gazette*, April 8, 1994: 15.

13. In the 2020 documentary *The Last Dance*, Francona said that if Jordan kept at it, he could have gotten to the major leagues. Nick Selbe, "Terry Francona: Michael Jordan Would Have Made Majors 'With 1500 At-Bats,'" si.com, May 10, 2020. https://www.si.com/extra-mustard/2020/05/11/michael-jordan-terry-francona-mlb-baseball-career.

14. Zack Meisel, "Terry Francona Has Been One of MLB's Most Influential Managers. What if This Is It?" *The Athletic*, August 23, 2023. https://theathletic.com/4799824/2023/08/23/terry-francona-guardians-retirement/.

15. Jim McCabe, "For Terry Francona, Pressure Rolls Right Off His Back," *Boston Globe*, November 4, 2007. https://www.bostonglobe.com/sports/2007/11/04/for-terry-francona-pressure-rolls-right-off-his-back/wfj1WOwWdOiHXnBMMzrNVK/story.html . Francona himself collaborated with Dan Shaughnessy of the *Boston Globe* on a full-length autobiography devoted to his years with the Red Sox. Terry Francona and Dan Shaughnessy, *Francona: The Red Sox Years* (Boston: Houghton Mifflin Harcourt, 2013).

16. Associated Press, "Middle of Order Powers Yankees," ESPN.com, October 17, 2004. https://www.espn.com/mlb/recap/_/gameId/241016102.

17. Ronald Blum (Associated Press), "Yanks Pummel Red Sox 19-8," *Indiana Gazette*, October 17, 2004: C5.

18. Howard Ulman (Associated Press), "Francona Wants Title," *Greenwood* (South Carolina) *Index-Journal*, October 22, 2004: 4B.

19. Howard Ulman (Associated Press), "3-year Extension for Francona," *Quincy* (Massachusetts) *Patriot-Ledger*, February 24, 2004. https://www.patriotledger.com/story/sports/pro/2008/02/24/3-year-extension-for-francona/40256603007/.

20. "Source: Terry Francona Interviews With Cardinals," WBZ Radio, November 8, 2011. https://www.cbsnews.com/boston/news/terry-francona-could-interview-with-cardinals-as-early-as-tuesday/.

21. Tyler Kepner, "Francona's Approach Draws Raves In Cleveland," *New York Times*, September 18, 2013. www.nytimes.com/2013/09/19/sports/baseball/act-2-in-cleveland-is-working-out-well-for-francona.html.

22. Chris Assenheimer, "Guardians Manager Terry Francona Hints at Retirement, *Medina* (Ohio) *Gazette*, August 22, 2023. https://medina-gazette.com/news/362859/guardians-manager-terry-francona-hints-at-retirement/.

INO GUERRERO

BY BILL PRUDEN

As the unofficial but recognized spiritual adviser to the ever-mercurial Manny Ramírez, Ino Guerrero had a distinctive role on the 2004 World Series champion Red Sox.[1] Given the nature of the team's offensive prowess, his official role as batting-practice pitcher would seem to be enough for most people, and yet his role as the attendant to Ramírez's spiritual needs gave Guerrero added luster while adding another dimension to a team fondly remembered, in the words of Johnny Damon, as the "Idiots."[2] Who knows? Perhaps it was the spiritual connection upon which Ramírez drew in winning the World Series MVP Award and leading the team that laughed at both history and the odds as they ended the franchise's eight-decade-plus championship drought. Regardless, on a team that defied history, Ino Guerrero had a distinctive role.

Inocencio Guerrero was born on December 28, 1960, in Higueral in the Dominican Republic. He attended Escuela Primaria High School but beyond that little is known about his youth in the Dominican Republic.[3] At the same time, given that he began his minor-league career as an 18-year-old, it is safe to assume that like so many Dominican youngsters from an early age, he harbored dreams of playing major-league baseball in the United States.

Guerrero's professional baseball career started in 1979 when he appeared in 23 games for the Atlanta Braves team in the Gulf Coast (Rookie) League. While he hit only .225, he showed a good eye for the ball, working pitchers for 10 walks in his 92 plate appearances. He also spent the following season with the GCL Braves, this time hitting only .195, although he did raise his on-base percentage to .312.

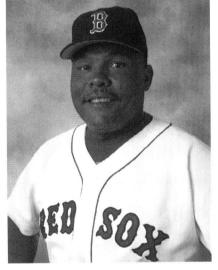

Such was the beginning of a professional odyssey that saw Guerrero spend 10 seasons in the minor leagues, crafting a career that saw parts of two seasons spent in Triple A, parts of six in Double A, parts of four in Single A, and two in the Rookie League. As he pursued his major-league dreams, Guerrero compiled a decade-long career that led one observer to say that he was the real Crash Davis, the minor leaguer at the heart of the baseball classic *Bull Durham*, the movie whose 1988 release coincided, ironically, with Ino Guerrero's third stint with the real-life Durham Bulls, and his final season as a minor-league player.[4]

Over the course of his time in the minors, on rosters from the rookie leagues to Triple A, Guerrero played in the Gulf Coast, South Atlantic, Carolina, International, and Southern Leagues. Making stops in towns ranging from the capital of Virginia, Richmond, to the site of the Shoeless Joe Jackson Museum in Greenville, South Carolina, Guerrero spent a decade in the heart of minor-league baseball, but finally, after a 1988 split between Greenville and Durham, Guerrero, who most often played first base but also did stints in the outfield and behind the plate, retired as a player.

It is hard to say which season was Guerrero's best, so often was his time split between two different teams, but in 1982, in 131 games with the Anderson Braves in the Class-A South Atlantic League, Guerrero hit .288, with an on-base percentage of .399 and a slugging average of .458. His numbers placed him among the leaders in numerous offensive categories for Braves minor leaguers. He followed that up with a strong first half in 1983, hitting .332 with the Durham Bulls, before being called up to the Double-A Savannah Braves. Unhappily, he was unable to maintain that pace. In the end, he fell short of his big-league dream. But over the course of 10 years and 955 games in the minors, Guerrero compiled a career batting average of .265. He had 813 hits, 90 of which were home runs, and he drove in 500 runs. Yet while he never got the proverbial cup of coffee, his retirement as a player after the end of the 1988 season did not represent the end of his baseball days.

In fact, in the eyes of his colleagues and experienced baseball observers, as his career wound down and he enjoyed his final stint with the Bulls, in addition to being seen as a Crash Davis-like character, he was also, in the words of one writer, "auditioning for the role of Organization Man."[5] In that role, one befitting, or at least most likely to be played by, one of the team's elder statesmen, the Organization Man looks after the young players, sets an example in the clubhouse, and serves as a mentor. Ideally, they are a "stabilizing influence" in the clubhouse and if the audition goes well, they will be able to keep their baseball career alive as a hitting instructor or a coach. For a Dominican Republic native like Guerrero, there was also the added role of helping young native Dominican players adjust to both American baseball and American society and culture.[6] As Guerrero played out the string, his Bulls manager,

Grady Little, with whom he would subsequently be reunited on the Red Sox, recognized and appreciated the role. Indeed, having already managed almost 900 minor-league games, the 38-year-old Little observed, "I've got aspirations of being a big-league coach or manager. There's dues to pay."[7] Guerrero clearly understood that code and was getting a head start.

In fact, the major leagues, albeit in a capacity more akin to the Organization Man he was preparing to become, still beckoned, but not before he paid a few more dues in the minors. Indeed, following his retirement as a player, Guerrero began an odyssey not unlike his minor-league playing career, serving in a number of different roles for a number of different teams, for the most part in the Braves organization. He started as a coach with the Durham Bulls in 1989.[8] But over the course of the next decade and a half he held a number of positions in the Braves and Red Sox organizations, including coaching the Braves' Dominican Republic summer team, working as a hitting instructor for the Red Sox' short-season Lowell Spinners (New York-Penn League) and the advanced Class-A Sarasota Red Sox, where in 1999 he filled in briefly as manager when manager and former Red Sox skipper Butch Hobson was ill.[9]

For all the uncertainties and the circuitous path Guerrero had taken to the Red Sox, his efforts in the minors had an impact on the young players who were so very much like what he had once been. Indeed, one of his players from the 1999 Sarasota Red Sox, Morgan Burkhart, who was an independent league legend before joining the Sarasota Red Sox and subsequently going on to serve as a hitting coach for the San Diego Padres minor-league affiliate Fort Wayne Tin Caps, recalled that "Ino Guerrero was my first hitting coach in the (Red Sox) organization. I learned a lot from him because he didn't say a whole lot. You know you're looking for these guys to get on you all the time, but he'd watch you over and over and then he'd be able to find out when something went a little different."[10]

The 2003 season saw Guerrero reunited on the Red Sox with former manager Grady Little. While Little was a familiar face, variously described as a "staffer" or "coach," he was often seen with David Ortiz and Manny Ramirez, and by many accounts Ino's arrival was based in his status as a "Friend of Manny (FOM)."[11] His closeness to Ramírez was recognized and acknowledged by all. Indeed, whether it was as staff assistant or simply as "major league staff," Guerrero's usual official title, one that most often translated into batting-practice pitcher, or through his socializing with Ramírez and Ortiz away from the field, a role that often included cooking the slugging duo their Dominican favorites, Guerrero had a distinctive tie to Ramírez.[12] And yet he remained with the team well beyond the end of the Ramírez era. However, the strength of his ties to the enigmatic Ramírez, for whom he had served as coach, cheerleader, hitting coach, and confidant, were evident for all to see when Ramírez returned to Fenway Park for the first time after having been traded to the Dodgers. The 2004 World Series MVP gave his buddy a huge hug, and the image, captured by a wire-service photographer and often accompanying an article reporting on the "many reactions" to Manny's return, appeared in papers across the country.[13]

At the same time, over the years the FOM endeared himself to the Red Sox community, establishing a bond that transcended his relationship with Ramírez. Through his personality, the experience-based knowledge he brought to his responsibilities, and his willingness to do whatever seemed to be needed, he carved a niche for himself on the Red Sox, although his most consistent and official role was as the team's batting-practice pitcher, a role he performed so well that some Red Sox said he threw the best BP in baseball.[14] Indeed, it was his efforts in that role that led to his being selected to serve as David Ortiz's designated pitcher in the 2004 Home Run Derby at the All-Star Game.[15] Unhappily, with only three home runs in the first round, Ortiz did not advance and the Red Sox slugger switched to Red Sox third-base coach Dale Sveum for 2005.[16] In the aftermath of Ortiz's disappointing effort, Guerrero, whose pitching had been erratic, acknowledged the difference in performing on the big stage, admitting that he had felt a kind of pressure that was unlike anything that daily batting practice offered. After the contest, he commented, "Yes, I was a little nervous. It was the first time I did that. It was a nice experience, but it's like the first time you're in the major leagues. You feel a little nervous."[17]

That same kind of humanity, as well as the distinctive if multifaceted role that Guerrero played on the Red Sox, was evident in numerous incidents over the years. Typical was the 2009 preseason game between the Red Sox and Boston College. As *Boston Globe* columnist Dan Shaughnessy put it, the game took on a "circus-like feel" when the "ancient Ino Guerrero came up to hit for Ortiz."[18] After noting that Guerrero was best known as the caddy for Manny Ramírez, Shaughnessy commented that while he was listed as "major league staff" and was reported to be 48 years old, no one really knew what he did or how old he was. Nevertheless, his stature as a beloved figure on the team was evident when, as he strode to the plate carrying a bat and wearing number 80, the dugout came alive. He walked on five pitches and after a pinch-runner was sent out to take his place, Guerrero's return to the dugout reminded observers of the response Kirk Gibson got after his World Series home run, no small feat for the single spring-training at-bat that had become something of a team tradition.[19] Meanwhile, manager Terry Francona commented that he liked the way Guerrero flipped his bat after the walk as though he had hit a home run, adding that he might he might get another chance in the coming game against Northeastern University.[20]

Another incident that pushed Guerrero suddenly and unhappily into the spotlight took place on February 28, 2011, when he was involved in a freak accident during spring training that left Red Sox pitcher Josh Beckett with a concussion. In the midst of hitting shagged balls back from the outfield to the infield, Guerrero's misguided attempt to use a fungo bat to hit a ball into the bucket stationed behind second base instead hit Beckett, shagging balls in the outfield, in the left temple. The incident was picked up by the wire services and suddenly Ino Guerrero, the Red Sox' major-league staff assistant, found himself with a much higher public profile. Fortunately, Beckett, the team's ace right-hander, was able to walk off under his own power (accompanied by the team's trainers) and was diagnosed with mild concussion symptoms. He rested the next day (Tuesday), rode a stationary bike on Wednesday, and pitched a simulated game on Friday.[21] In an alleged effort to overcome a lack of right-handed hitters, Beckett tried to get Guerrero to be a part of the opposing lineup but the staffer deferred, ruining any opportunity for good-natured revenge that Beckett might have been entertaining.[22]

Equally entertaining, but not as much of a threat to the team's well-being, was the time in in spring training 2013 when during a baserunning drill, the ever-helpful Guerrero, serving as the third-base coach, was observed waving his arm counterclockwise as the runners came by, prompting Red Sox second baseman Dustin Pedroia to call out, "Wrong way, Ino."[23]

Later that same year Guerrero underwent spinal surgery. It was originally announced that he would be sidelined while he recovered, but in fact, it seems that the surgery marked the end of his days with the Red Sox, if not all of professional baseball.[24] Indeed, after almost 3½ decades in professional baseball in the United States, it appears that Ino Guerrero has retired to a home in his native Dominican Republic. But efforts to confirm that yielded little in the way of confirmation. Indeed, efforts to contact him through the SABR Dominican Republic network were singularly unsuccessful.[25] Meanwhile, inquiries of the Red Sox were no more helpful with Sarah C. Coffin, the team's alumni relations manager and team curator, writing that she was "not able to disclose that" when asked if she knew if Guerrero was "back in the Dominican Republic, having returned there after his career ended."[26] And so the mystery of Ino Guerrero remains.

SOURCES

In addition to the source cited in the Notes, the author consulted Baseball-Reference.com and a number of other sources.

NOTES

1. Mark Blaudschun, "Ramirez Picked His Spot," *Boston Globe*, October 7, 2003.
2. Ian Browne, "Genius Moniker: Origin of '04 Sox 'Idiots,'" MLB.com, February 5, 2021; https://www.mlb.com/news/2004-red-sox-idiots-nickname-explained.
3. Inocencio Guerrero Baseball Card, 1989, Durham Bulls, *Durham Sun/Durham Morning Herald*; https://www.tcdb.com/GalleryP.cfm/pid/74411/Inocencio-Guerrero.
4. Thomas Ferraro (United Press International), "Durham Bulls: Art Imitates Baseball – The Real-Life Durham Bulls," July 3, 1988; https://www.upi.com/Archives/1988/07/03/Durham-Bulls-Art-imitates-baseball-The-real-life-Durham-Bulls/3701583905600/.
5. Jim Naughton, "Durham Bulls," *Washington Post*, July 24, 1988.
6. Naughton, "Durham Bulls."
7. Naughton, "Durham Bulls."
8. "Durham Bulls '89," *Durham Sun*, April 7, 1989.
9. Carroll Rogers, "Braves Appoint Runge as New Macon Manager," *Macon Telegraph*, December 8, 1995; "Red Sox Named Guerrero the Hitting Coach of the Lowell Spinners of the New York-Penn League (A)," Transactions, *National Post*, December 17, 1998; Steve Megargee, "Dodgers Come Up One Rally Short," *Vero Beach (Florida) Press Journal*, April 14, 1999.
10. John Nolan, "From Construction to Curveballs: Morgan Burkhart Handles It All," Holding Down the Fort, May 23, 2013; https://tincaps.mlblogs.com/from-construction-to-curveballs-morgan-burkhart-handles-it-all-4e253452e5ba.
11. Gordon Edes, "Slugger Is Bringing Out the Best," *Boston Globe*, September 4, 2003; Dan Shaughnessy, "Nice Try, but They Cannot Give Him Away," *Boston Globe*, October 31, 2003.
12. Bob Hohler, "Clouds Around Ramirez Seem to Have Lifted," *Meriden (Connecticut) Record-Journal*, March 30, 2003; Edes, "Slugger Is Bringing Out the Best"; Bob Hohler, "Ramirez Snaps Out of It with Pop," *Boston Globe*, April 3, 2004.
13. Jimmy Golen (Associated Press), "Many Reactions to Manny's Return." *Honolulu Star-Advertiser*, June 19, 2010.
14. Ron Borges, "Ino Guerrero Captivates with His Own BP," *Boston Herald*, March 4, 2010.
15. John Shea, "Big Hitter Only as Good as Cookie-Tossing Pitcher," SFGate.com, July 9, 2007; https://www.sfgate.com/sports/shea/article/Big-hitter-only-as-good-as-cookie-tossing-pitcher-2582454.php.
16. Shea, "Big Hitter Only as Good as Cookie-Tossing Pitcher."
17. "Big Hitter Only as Good as Cookie-Tossing Pitcher."
18. Dan Shaughnessy, "Lasting Images for BC," *Boston Globe*, February 26, 2009.
19. "Lasting Images for BC"; "A Monster Day, Saturday, February 26, 2011 – City of Palms Park, Ft. Myers," RedSoxDiehard.com; http://redsoxdiehard.com/wordpress/2011/02/26/a-monster-day/.
20. Amalie Benjamin, "Nothing Floats Past Bard," *Boston Globe*, February 26, 2009.
21. Joe McDonald, "Beckett Cleared to Have Normal Day," ESPN.com: Red Sox Report, March 3, 2011; https://www.espn.com/blog/boston/red-sox/post/_/id/8424/beckett-cleared-to-have-normal-day.
22. Maureen Mullen, "Beckett: 'I'm pretty Much Back to Normal,'" NBC Sports, March 4, 2011; https://www.nbcsports.com/boston/boston-red-sox/beckett-im-pretty-much-back-normal.
23. "Red Sox Spring Training Report, Thumbs Down," *Boston Globe*, February 16, 2013.
24. Peter Abrahams, "Middlebrooks Returns but Iglesias Will Stick," *Boston Globe*, June 11, 2013.
25. Email, Julio M. Rodriguez G. to Bill Pruden, March 4, 2023.
26. Email, Sarah C. Coffin to Bill Pruden, March 13, 2023.

BILL HASELMAN

BY DAVID MOORE

With a professional playing career that spanned 1987 to 2003, Bill Haselman spent 13 major-league seasons as a backup catcher for four different teams. He first reached the majors in 1990 with the Texas Rangers, a team he had three stints with, and appeared in a career-high 77 games in 1996 with the Red Sox. He played in one postseason game, during the 1995 American League Division Series with Boston, and was a fill-in first-base coach for the 2004 Red Sox team that went on to win the World Series. He later served as a minor-league manager, and returned to the major leagues as catching coach for the Los Angeles Angels in 2022.

William Joseph Haselman was born in Long Branch, New Jersey, on May 25, 1966, the youngest child of Albert and Bernice (Martin) Haselman. His father, who saw Babe Ruth play, grew up in New Jersey, worked in New York, and would play catch and throw batting practice to Bill.[1] Albert Haselman had an engineering degree and worked as an executive for a communications company.[2] He had three children with his first wife, Thelma (née White), who died in 1962. After he remarried in 1964, a daughter was born in 1965, followed by Bill the next year. In the fall of 1966, the Haselmans sold their house in Rumson, New Jersey, and moved to Saratoga, California.

In high school in Saratoga, Bill Haselman played baseball and was the starting quarterback and a defensive back in football.[3] As a senior in 1984, he batted .457 and played shortstop.[4] Haselman was offered a football scholarship at the University of Nevada-Reno, but not knowing if he wanted to pursue baseball or football, he went to UCLA for a walk-on opportunity with the baseball team.[5] He made the team and redshirted as freshman, then also made the football team as a walk-on.[6] He spent half a season as a member of the football team, and while some sources refer to him as having been Troy Aikman's backup, Haselman points out that their stints with the Bruins did not overlap and the two didn't meet until years later.[7]

In the spring of 1986, despite not having previously caught, Haselman became UCLA's backup catcher, and saw his first playing time when starter Todd Zeile injured his ankle.[8] Haselman made the most of his opportunity, and ended up as the team's starting right fielder.[9] The next season the Bruins compiled a 40-25-1 record with a roster that included multiple future major-league players including Haselman, Jeff Conine, Bob Hamelin, Eric Karros, and Torey Lovullo. The team fell a game short of qualifying for the 1987 College World Series, losing to Arizona State in the NCAA tournament.[10] Haselman batted .304 as the team's starting catcher, driving in 57 runs in 65 games.

Baseball America ranked Haselman 20th in its annual Top 30 list; Ken Griffey Jr. was ranked first and Craig Biggio was ranked 22nd.[11] In the 1987 amateur draft, the Rangers used their first pick (No. 19) on pitcher Brian Bohanon, then selected Haselman four picks later, having received the Yankees' first-round pick (No. 23) for the signing of free-agent outfielder Gary Ward.[12]

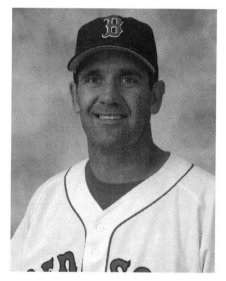

Haselman's first professional team was the 1987 Gastonia Rangers, a Class-A team in the South Atlantic League that included Juan González and Sammy Sosa. Primarily used as a designated hitter, he recorded 72 hits in 61 games, finishing with a .306 batting average and 8 home runs. During the offseason, Haselman underwent rotator cuff surgery,[13] needed to repair a partial tear that he blamed on throwing too hard before he was loose during a workout.[14] The *Fort Worth Star-Telegram* ranked Haselman as the team's fourth-best prospect, behind González and pitchers Kevin Brown and Bohanon, and just ahead of Sosa.[15]

For the 1988 season, Haselman was again in Class A, with the Port Charlotte Rangers of the Florida State League. He began the season as designated hitter as he completed recovery from his surgery.[16] Still learning the ins and outs of catching, he noted, "Trying to learn with this injury has been especially tough."[17] He went on to catch in 48 of the 122 games he played in, while posting a .245 batting average.

After being a nonroster invitee to the 1989 Rangers' spring training, Haselman spent his first of two seasons with the Tulsa Drillers, a Double-A team in the Texas League. He played 107 games, 104 as catcher, while batting .270 with 7 home runs. He was also a selection to the league's midseason all-star game. After the season, the *Star-Telegram* opined that Haselman was the Rangers' "most immediate catching prospect," but his defense needed improvement for him to play in the majors.[18] In mid-November, in advance of the Rule 5 draft, he was added to the Rangers major-league roster.

Although he was now on the 40-man roster entering the 1990 season, the Rangers optioned Haselman back to Tulsa at the end of March. In July Haselman was again named to the league's all-star game. He noted that the honor meant "you're putting up good numbers," but "my goal is to move up."[19] In late July, Haselman had a power surge, hitting six home runs in five games.[20] He finished the minor-league season with 18 homers in 120 games, while batting .319 with 80 RBIs. In August the *Star-Telegram* saw Haselman as closer to a call-up than the 18-year-old Iván "Pudge" Rodríguez.[21] Accurately, Haselman was called up at the beginning of September, while Rodríguez had his major-league debut the following June. Haselman's time with the Rangers in September 1990 was limited to three pinch-hitting appearances, four innings at catcher, and three starts as designated hitter. He collected two hits in 13 at bats (.154), with his first major-league hit coming on September 27 off left-hander Joe Klink of the Oakland Athletics.

Haselman had to wait before returning to the majors, as he spent all of the 1991 season in Triple A with the Oklahoma City 89ers of the American Association. Batting .256 with 9 home runs and 60 RBIs in 126 games, he caught 109 games. Meanwhile, Pudge Rodríguez made the jump from Double A, and was the starting catcher for half of the Rangers' games.

In February 1992 the Rangers signed Haselman to a one-year contract, at the major-league minimum of $109,000.[22] During spring training, he suffered a severely bruised rib cage and began the season on the disabled list.[23] He came off the DL in early May, but was designated for assignment later that month. On May 29 the Seattle Mariners claimed Haselman and optioned him to the Calgary Cannons of the Pacific Coast League. He welcomed the change in scenery, stating, "I don't miss Texas and I'm happy to have a fresh start here. … I never really felt I got an opportunity there at all."[24] In his first 44 games with Calgary, he hit 13 home runs.[25] He commented, "Now I'm just trying to focus on one game at a time and not try to figure out what they are thinking."[26] In 105 Triple-A games (88 with Calgary and 17 with Oklahoma City), he batted an overall .253 with 20 home runs, the most homers during any season of his career. In early September, he was called up by the Mariners, for whom he appeared in eight games and batted 5-for-19 (.263).

Haselman and the Mariners agreed to a contract in March 1993; at $117,500, it was slightly above the minimum.[27] Under new manager Lou Piniella, the team began the season with Dave Valle as the starting catcher and Haselman as backup. Haselman was hitting .238 with one home run when he got his 10th start of the season on June 6, a notable game of his career.

Facing the Orioles at Camden Yards, Haselman hit a solo home run in the fifth inning off Baltimore starter Mike Mussina. Meanwhile, Seattle starter Chris Bosio allowed home runs in the fourth and fifth innings, and threw behind batters in the fifth and sixth innings. Thus, when Haselman faced Mussina again with two outs and the bases empty in the top of the seventh, it wasn't surprising that the first pitch hit Haselman, on the shoulder. What was surprising was the intensity of the brawl that ensued after Haselman charged the mound. It delayed the game for 20 minutes with both benches and bullpens emptying;

video of the fight shows significant grappling, some punches thrown, and several outbreaks following lulls in the action. Bosio also reinjured his collarbone, which he had broken earlier in the season.[28] After the umpiring crew decided to eject seven players – four Mariners including Haselman and Bosio, and three Orioles but not Mussina – Piniella took exception and was tossed for the first time as Seattle manager. Cal Ripken Jr., still 340 games from breaking Lou Gehrig's consecutive-game record, strained a knee ligament and almost missed the next day's game.[29] Commentary was negative. One writer called the fight "a $50-million free-for-all, instigated because a journeyman catcher named Bill Haselman was peeved over a pitch."[30] He grew tired of questions about the brawl, commenting in 1997, "I've been hearing about it for four years and it's getting old."[31] The fracas is still well remembered by Mariners fans, appearing at the top of a list of Seattle sports fights compiled by the *Seattle Times* in 2022.[32]

Haselman finished at .255 for the 1993 season, hitting 5 home runs in 58 games and catching in 49 games.

In February 1994 Haselman agreed to terms with Seattle on a one-year contract at $175,000. After Valle left as a free agent, the Mariners acquired Dan Wilson to be their new starter via a trade with the Cincinnati Reds. As a backup, Haselman hit only .193 in 38 games through mid-July. The Mariners then purchased the contract of Chris Howard from Triple A, and outrighted Haselman there. On being back in Calgary, Haselman said, "It was a little bit of a surprise to me, you know, I was only playing once a week and I wasn't really doing the job."[33] While the major-league season ended in August due to a players strike, Haselman played through the end of the minor-league season, batting .331 with 15 home runs in 44 games with Calgary. On October 15 Haselman became a free agent for the first time.

Boston signed Haselman on November 7 for $200,000 to be a backup, while Mike Macfarlane was signed on April 8 for $1.7 million to be the starter.[34] For the 1995 Red Sox, Haselman batted .243 with 5 home runs and 23 RBIs in 64 games. The Red Sox won the AL East, finishing seven games ahead of the Yankees, and faced Cleveland in the ALDS. In a 13-inning Game One at Jacobs Field, Haselman made the only postseason appearance of his major-league career, entering the game at catcher in the bottom of the ninth, after Matt Stairs had pinch-hit for Macfarlane. He grounded out to the pitcher in both of his plate appearances, as Cleveland won on Tony Peña's walk-off homer and then swept the series.

In December Boston re-signed Haselman for the 1996 season for $300,000. The team also signed free-agent catcher Mike Stanley at $2.3 million.[35] For the season, Stanley started 98 games behind the plate; his season ended in early September due to a herniated disk in his neck.[36] Haselman started 60 games, including 25 of 26 to end the season.[37] One of his starts came on September 18 at Tiger Stadium, when he caught the second 20-strikeout game of Roger Clemens' career. Haselman commented, "This game is number one with me as far as catching."[38] He appeared in a career-high 77 major-league games while batting .274 with 8 home runs.

In January 1997 the Red Sox signed Haselman to a one-year contract at $650,000. Stanley, who exercised his $2.1 million option to remain with Boston,[39] had his role set as part-time DH by new manager Jimy Williams,[40] who named Haselman the starting catcher with rookie Scott Hatteberg as his backup.[41] On April 27 Haselman had a career day at the plate against the Orioles, hitting a home run and three doubles while driving in four runs. His batting average was hovering around .300 before he went the first half of May without a home run or RBI, and his batting average fell by almost 30 points. With Hatteberg hitting .316, Williams announced a platoon at catcher.[42] In the second half of June, Haselman missed nine games after Carl Everett of the New York Mets crashed into him on a play at the plate.[43] In his second game back, a wild pitch from Red Sox starter Jeff Suppan broke his right thumb.[44] Haselman was out of action until early August.[45] Williams continued to have his two catchers platoon, and Haselman said, "There is no one to blame but me. I'm not mad at anybody else – just myself."[46] The team finished 20 games out in the AL East, and Haselman finished the season with a .236 average and 6 home runs in 67 games with Boston. In November Haselman was traded back to Texas as part of a five-player deal.

In his second stint with the Rangers, on a one-year contract at $625,000, Haselman was batting .333 in limited action through late May and noted, "It's always nice to contribute offensively ... [but] what I really concentrate on is my defense and trying to call a good game."[47] In September Rick Herrin of the *Fort Worth Star-Telegram* deemed Haselman the best backup catcher to play under Rangers manager Johnny Oates,[48] who had arrived in 1995. The Rangers went on to finish first in the AL West, but were swept in three games by the Yankees in the ALDS, without Haselman making an appearance. For the season, Haselman played in 40 games and batted a career-high .314 with 6 home runs and 17 RBIs. In the second half of October, he filed for free agency.

In mid-December of 1998, Haselman signed a two-year contract with the Detroit Tigers, worth $650,000 in 1999 and $1.1 million in 2000. An opportunity for Haselman to be the Tigers' starting catcher faded in mid-January 1999 when the team acquired Brad Ausmus from the Houston Astros. In mid-June, after seeing limited action while batting around .300, Haselman asked to be traded, remarking "I gave it a few months. I didn't sign to sit and be a backup."[49] A trade did not materialize during the season, as Haselman batted .273 with 4 home runs and 14 RBIs in 48 games.

In November 1999 Detroit sent Haselman to Texas as part of a nine-player deal that returned Juan González to the Tigers. Haselman was brought in for his third stint with the Rangers to again back up Pudge Rodríguez, at salaries of $1.1 million and $8 million, respectively.[50] Oates said Rodríguez, if healthy, would catch 140 games during the 2000 season.[51] Haselman was used sparingly until two weeks after the All-Star Game, when Rodríguez broke his right thumb and was lost for the year.[52] Haselman took over as the starter, with Oates later noting, "[I]f you've got to have a guy sitting behind Pudge, Bill Haselman is as good a guy as there is in the game."[53] In August the Rangers signed Haselman to a two-year contract extension, at $800,000 per season plus a club option for a third season.[54] He missed the season's final 12 games after rotator cuff surgery on his right shoulder.[55] He played in a total of 62 games, batting .275 with 6 home runs and 26 RBIs.

Entering the 2001 season recovering from his shoulder surgery, Haselman initially thought he might be ready to play in mid-March.[56] However, a bone spur in his elbow required another surgical procedure.[57] A strained forearm during rehab further delayed his return.[58] He was finally activated on June 22, and became the sixth catcher the Rangers used during the season.[59] In September Rodríguez was again lost to surgery, and Haselman became the team's primary catcher for the final weeks of the season.[60] Haselman batted .285 with 3 home runs and 25 RBIs while appearing in 47 major-league games.

During the 2002 season, Rodríguez was limited to 97 starts at catcher, with Haselman making 49 starts while appearing in 69 games, the second-highest of his major-league career. The team finished last in the four-team AL West, while Haselman batted .246 with 3 home runs and 18 RBIs. After the season, the Rangers opted to pay him a $150,000 buyout rather than bringing him back for another year.[61]

Before the 2003 season, Haselman signed a minor-league contract with Detroit. With Brandon Inge as the starting catcher, the Tigers opted to start the season with Matt Walbeck, who had significantly outhit Haselman during spring training, as Inge's backup.[62] Haselman was reassigned to minor-league camp, but he requested and was granted his release.[63] In early April, he signed a minor-league contract with Boston. He played 79 games in Triple A with the Pawtucket Red Sox, batting .225 with 6 home runs and 24 RBIs. At the start of September, he was added to Boston's major-league roster, as the Red Sox made a push to reach the postseason. Haselman appeared in four games, each as a defensive replacement, going 0-for-3 at the plate. He was not included on Boston's playoff roster, as the wild-card team advanced to the ALCS before falling to the Yankees in seven games.

After the 2003 season Haselman indicated he might retire,[64] although he did file for free agency at the end of October.[65] He and Roger Clemens discussed playing for Team USA in the 2004 Summer Olympics, but their plan was dashed when the American team, rostered with collegiate players during qualification, failed to advance to the main competition in Greece.[66] Haselman was a nonroster invitee at Orioles spring training, stating that he would retire if he didn't make the team.[67] After seeing action in just four games during spring training, he was released by the Orioles on March 25.[68] New manager Lee Mazzilli called Haselman a class individual and said he had agonized for two days over the decision.[69]

In early May of 2004, the first-base coach of the Red Sox, Lynn Jones, sustained a serious eye injury while at his home in Pennsylvania, requiring multiple surgeries.[70] The Red Sox turned to Haselman, who had joined the organization as a special-assignment scout, to act as interim first-base coach.[71] He served in that role from May 6 through July 21. When Jones rejoined the team, Haselman remained with the organization, working with catchers as an instructor and consultant.[72] The team went on to finish the season at 98-64 (.605), qualifying for the postseason as the AL wild card. With playoff series victories over the Anaheim Angels, New York Yankees, and finally the St. Louis Cardinals, the team captured the Red Sox' first World Series championship since 1918.

For the 2005 season, the Red Sox named Haselman their new bullpen coach. Manager Terry Francona said Haselman had done "an unbelievable job" filling in for Jones, thus was added as a full-time coach.[73] The Red Sox again finished as the AL wild card, but were swept in the ALDS by the White Sox.

The Red Sox made multiple coaching changes for the 2006 season, with Haselman becoming the first-base coach, succeeding Jones. The Red Sox finished the season in third place in the AL East, missing the postseason for the first time since 2002. The *Boston Globe* reported that Haselman was offered but declined the job as manager of the Lowell Spinners,[74] a Class-A Short Season team located about 30 miles from Boston.

For the next two years, Haselman was out of baseball, with the *Globe* noting that he was employed with Merrill Lynch and obtaining a broker's license, while also hosting a postgame radio show for the Seattle Mariners.[75] In February 2008 his father died in the Metro Atlanta area, aged 95.[76] In August 2009 Haselman joined the Washington Huskies college baseball staff as a volunteer assistant coach.[77] In January 2010 the Rangers hired Haselman to manage the Bakersfield Blaze of the Class A-Advanced California League.[78] The following season, Haselman worked for the Red Sox, assisting their minor-league catching instructor.[79]

From 2012 through 2018, Haselman managed several different minor-league teams. In 2012 he joined the Inland Empire 66ers,[80] a California League farm team of the Los Angeles Angels, and guided them to a league title in 2013.[81] Moving to the Los Angeles Dodgers organization in 2014, he first managed the Great Lakes Loons of the Class-A Midwest League.[82] The next season he returned to the California League and managed the Rancho Cucamonga Quakes,[83] leading them to the league title.[84] From 2016 through 2018, he managed the Oklahoma City Dodgers[85] of the Triple-A Pacific Coast League, helping them reach the PCL championship series in his first season.[86]

Haselman next spent two seasons mentoring managers in the Dodgers organization, then rejoined Oklahoma City in 2021 as the team's bench and third-base coach.[87] In 2022 Haselman returned to the Angels organization, with the major-league team as catching coach.[88] He served as the Angels' interim manager for two games in July, due to suspensions of other members of the coaching staff.[89] For the 2023 season, he was named the Angels' third-base coach.[90]

Overall during his 13-season major-league playing career, Haselman batted .259 with 47 home runs and 210 RBIs in 589 games. Defensively, he played in 524 games as a catcher (410 starts) and posted a .991 fielding percentage. Additionally, he played parts of 10 seasons in minor-league baseball, batting .269 while appearing in 783 games. He and his wife, Tracy, have two children, the first of whom – a son, Ty – was born in March 1998 while Haselman was playing with the Mariners.[91] In a 1996 *Boston Globe* story about the wives of Red Sox players, Tracy noted that the couple had already moved 20 times during their first six years of marriage.[92] Ty briefly followed in his father's footsteps, playing college baseball in 2018 as a catcher with the UCLA Bruins. After spending almost every season since 1987 in a professional league as a player, coach, or manager, Haselman remained active as of 2023. Reflecting on the 2004 Red Sox more than a decade after their championship, he said, "It's something I'll never forget. Those guys had a great chemistry on that team." And he added, "They believed in themselves."[93]

SOURCES

In addition to the sources cited in the Notes, the author relied on Baseball-Reference.com, TheBaseballCube.com, and retrosheet.org.

NOTES

1   Jacob Unruh, "Collected Wisdom: Bill Haselman," *Daily Oklahoman* (Oklahoma City), April 17, 2016: 8B.

2   "New Rotarian," *Red Bank* (New Jersey) *Daily Register,* July 12, 1962: 10.

3   Paul Salvoni, "St. Francis Has Three Finalists," *Peninsula Times Tribune* (Palo Alto, California), June 7, 1984: D-3.

4   Paul Salvoni, "Boys' Athlete of the Year," *Peninsula Times Tribune*, June 10, 1984: E-3.

5   Unruh, "Collected Wisdom: Bill Haselman."

6   "Collected Wisdom: Bill Haselman."

7   Jacob Unruh, "Haselman Introduced as New Manager for OKC Dodgers," *Daily Oklahoman*, February 10, 2016: 5B.

8   Bob Cuomo, "UCLA Gets Hot, Takes Lead in Pac-10 Southern Division," *Los Angeles Times*, April 17, 1986: III-15.

9   "Collected Wisdom: Bill Haselman."

10 "Arizona St. 14, UCLA 4," *Macon* (Georgia) *Telegraph and News,* May 26, 1987: 3C.

11 "Baseball America's Top 30," *Fort Worth Star-Telegram*, May 31, 1987: 2-8.

12 Tony DeMarco, "Rangers' Draft Follows the Plan," *Fort Worth Star-Telegram*, June 3, 1987: 3-3.

13 T.R. Sullivan, "Intangibles," *Fort Worth Star-Telegram*, April 23, 1988: 3-5.

14 Paul Harris, "Rangers' Haselman Adjusting This Season," *Fort Myers* (Florida) *News-Press,* May 28, 1988: 1C.

15 "Rating the Rangers' prospects," *Fort Worth Star-Telegram*, November 22, 1987: 2-22.

16 Sullivan, "Intangibles."

17 Harris, "Rangers' Haselman Adjusting This Season."

18 T.R. Sullivan, "Baseball," *Fort Worth Star-Telegram*, October 1, 1989: 2-7.

19 Joe Powell, "McCray, Drillers Sweat Out 4-2 Win Over JaxMets," *Jackson* (Mississippi) *Clarion-Ledger*, July 4, 1990: 4C.

20 Gannett News Service, "Texas League Notes," *El Paso Times*, July 29, 1990: 7C.

21 Simon Gonzalez, "Solid Catcher Prospects on Rangers' Horizon," *Fort Worth Star-Telegram*, August 19, 1990: 3-5.

22 Tony DeMarco, "Texas Rangers Notebook: '92 Payroll," *Fort Worth Star-Telegram*, March 6, 1992: C5.

23 Bob Hersom, "89ers Hope 'V' Is for Victory," *Daily Oklahoman*, April 5, 1992: B6.

24 Daryl Slade, "Calgary Catches a Good Prospect," *Calgary Herald*, June 11, 1992: F2.

25 Daryl Slade, "Haselman Switches On Power," *Calgary Herald*, July 23, 1992: E2.

26 "Haselman Switches On Power."

27 "Baseball Salaries: Seattle Mariners," *Dayton Daily News*, April 8, 1993: 5D.

28 Associated Press, "M's Bosio Out 2-3 weeks," *Longview* (Washington) *Daily News*, June 8, 1993: D3.

29 John Eisenberg, *The Streak: Lou Gehrig, Cal Ripken Jr., and Baseball's Most Historic Record* (New York: Houghton Mifflin Harcourt, 2017), 174-175.

30 John McGrath (McClatchy News Service), "Chorus of Boos Deserved for Money-Wasting Brawl," *Tri-City Herald* (Pasco, Washington), June 7, 1993: B2.

31 David Ginsburg (Associated Press), "Haselman Helps BoSox Blast Orioles," *North Adams* (Massachusetts) *Transcript*, April 28, 1997: B1.

32 Bob Condotta (Seattle Times), "These Seattle Sports Skirmishes Live Forever," *Spokane* (Washington) *Spokesman-Review*, June 29, 2022: Sports 1.

33 Mike Board, "Cannons Look to Regain Rhythm," *Calgary Herald*, July 18, 1994: D3.

34 Nick Cafardo, "Red Sox Notebook," *Boston Globe*, August 28, 1995: 41.

35 "The Numbers Game: Red Sox," *Boston Globe*, April 7, 1996: 50.

36 "Bad Disk Threatens Career of Stanley," *Minneapolis Star Tribune*, September 12, 1996: C6.

37 Gordon Edes, "Stanley Wants to Keep Job, but There Might Be a Catch," *Boston Globe*, January 29, 1997: F7.

38 Larry Whiteside, "Something Amiss," *Boston Globe*, September 19, 1996: D5.

39 Edes, , "Stanley Wants to Keep Job, but There Might Be a Catch."

40 Gordon Edes, "Haselman Looks Set to Receive Job," *Boston Globe*, March 9, 1997: D11.

41 Kris Dufour, "Sox Set to Swing into Summer '97," *North Adams Transcript*, March 29, 1997: A10.

42 Gordon Edes, "Red Sox Notebook: Hatteberg Platoon Member," *Boston Globe*, March 19, 1997: D3.

43 Michael Vega, "Red Sox Notebook," *Boston Globe*, June 17, 1997: E7.

44 Larry Whiteside, "Red Sox Win One, Could Lose One," *Boston Globe*, June 30, 1997: D3.

45 Marvin Pave, "Red Sox Notebook: Thumbs Up," *Boston Globe*, August 9, 1997: G3.

46 Lee Jenkins, "He's Been Playing Catch-Up," *Boston Globe*, August 16, 1997: E3.

47 Andy Friedlander, "Haselman Makes the Most of Few Opportunities He Gets," *Fort Worth Star-Telegram*, May 24, 1998: C4.

48 Rick Herrin, "A 3-Stage Success for Haselman," *Fort Worth Star-Telegram*, September 8, 1998: D4.

49 John Lowe, "M's Rodriguez Praises Weaver," *Detroit Free Press*, June 19, 1999: 7B.

50 "Signed and Delivered," *Fort Worth Star-Telegram*, December 30, 1999: 3D.

51 "Pudge Goes on Offensive for Rangers," *Marshall* (Texas) *News Messenger*, February 27, 2000: 5C.

52 Johnny Paul, "Haselman Takes Spotlight," *Fort Worth Star-Telegram*, July 25, 2000: 4D.

53 "Rangers Report: Haselman Picks Up Where Pudge Left Off," *Austin American-Statesman*, August 4, 2000: C5.

54 T.R. Sullivan, "Short Hops: Haselman Gets Extension," *Fort Worth Star-Telegram*, August 20, 2000: 5C.

55 Tim Price, "Short Hops: Haselman to Have Surgery," *Fort Worth Star-Telegram*, September 13, 2000: 4D.

56 "Spring Training: Texas Rangers," *Orlando Sentinel*, March 6, 2001: C5.

57 T.R. Sullivan, "Breaking Down the Rangers' Roster," *Fort Worth Star-Telegram*, April 1, 2001: 14N.

58 T.R. Sullivan, "Short Hops: Haselman Suffers Setback," *Fort Worth Star-Telegram*, May 19, 2001: 4D.

59 T.R. Sullivan, "Short Hops," *Fort Worth Star-Telegram*, June 24, 2001: 6C.

60 "Rangers Report," *Austin American-Statesman*, September 6, 2001: D5.

61 T.R. Sullivan, "Rocker Cut by Rangers: Haselman Also Gone as Shake-Up Continues," *Fort Worth Star-Telegram*, October 4, 2002: 6D.

62 John Lowe, "Tigers Corner," *Detroit Free Press*, March 27, 2003: 4G.

63 Associated Press, "Baseball Roundup," *Lansing* (Michigan) *State Journal*, March 28, 2003: 8C.

64 Bob Hohler, "Red Sox Notebook," *Boston Globe*, October 28, 2003: D11.

65 Associated Press, "Jones, Haselman File for Free Agency," *North Adams Transcript*, October 31, 2003: B3.

66 Nick Cafardo, "Baseball Notes: Dreams Dashed," *Boston Globe*, November 23, 2003: C2.

67 Roch Kubatko, "Spring Training: Fort Lauderdale, Fla.," *Baltimore Sun*, March 8, 2004: 4E.

68 David Ginsburg (Associated Press), "Mazzilli, Haselman Have Miserable Day," *Salisbury* (Maryland) *Daily Times*, March 28, 2004: 33.

69 "Mazzilli, Haselman Have Miserable Day."

70 Bob Hohler, "Red Sox Notebook," *Boston Globe*, May 7, 2004: E6.
71 Hohler, "Red Sox Notebook."
72 Bob Hohler, "Red Sox Notebook," *Boston Globe*, July 25, 2004: D6.
73 "Coaching Staff," *Boston Globe*, April 1, 2005: F13.
74 Nick Cafardo, "Baseball notes: Decision-making process," *Boston Globe*, October 29, 2006: D13.
75 Gordon Edes, "Pitching Change Logical," *Boston Globe*, June 26, 2007: D6.
76 Albert Haselman obituary, February 2008 (https://www.mckoon.com/obituaries/Albert-Haselman/#!/Obituary).
77 "Briefs: Baseball," *Tri-City Herald* (Pasco, Washington), August 13, 2009: C3.
78 Associated Press, "Texas Rangers," *Pensacola* (Florida) *News Journal*, January 8, 2010: 8C.
79 Nick Cafardo, "Baseball Notes: Updates on Nine," *Boston Globe*, May 1, 2011: C11.
80 "Transactions: Baseball," *White Plains* (New York) *Journal News*, January 14, 2012: 6C.
81 Jacob Unruh, "Haselman's Playoff Success," *Daily Oklahoman*, September 13, 2016: 4B.
82 "Haselman's Playoff Success."
83 "Haselman's Playoff Success."
84 Jacob Unruh, "OKC Dodgers Bring Back Staff," *Daily Oklahoman*, December 22, 2016: 5B.
85 Jacob Unruh, "Dodgers Announce New Hitting, Pitching Coaches," *Daily Oklahoman*, January 9, 2018: 2B.
86 "OKC Dodgers Bring Back Staff."
87 Jacob Unruh, "Westmoore's Wright Named OKC Dodgers Pitching Coach," *Daily Oklahoman*, February 9, 2021: B7.
88 Jack Baer, "Angels Promote Catching Coach Bill Haselman to Interim Interim Interim Manager," Yahoo Sports, July 1, 2022. https://sports.yahoo.com/angels-promote-catching-coach-bill-haselman-interim-interim-interim-manager-234111347.html.
89 Baer, "Angels Promote Catching Coach Bill Haselman to Interim Interim Interim Manager."
90 Jeff J. Snider, "Angels News: Phil Nevin Names New Third-Base Coach for 2023 Season," SI.com, November 22, 2022. https://www.si.com/mlb/angels/news/angels-news-phil-nevin-names-new-third-base-coach-for-2023-season-js77.
91 T.R. Sullivan, "Rangers Report," *Fort Worth Star-Telegram*, March 26, 1998: D8.
92 Dick Lehr, "The Wives of Summer," *Boston Globe*, September 5, 1996: E1, E6.
93 Unruh, "Collected Wisdom: Bill Haselman."

A RED SOX MEMORY

From 1998-2005, I was part of the crew that operated the manual scoreboard at Busch Stadium II. I was behind the board when the Red Sox finished their sweep of the Cardinals in Game Four. After Edgar Renteria made the last out of the game (Renteria played for the Scarlet Hose the next year), I noticed that fans were jumping out on the field. I thought that was CRAZY because Boston was the road team. Fast forward three years and I was watching the movie Fever Pitch and reliving, as a Cardinal fan, that moment of agony. Upon seeing Jimmy Fallon and Drew Barrymore trespassing on our home turf, a light bulb went off. I later researched the film clip and found out it was staged for the movie!!

To add salt in the wound after leaving that night with a co-worker heading to our cars, we ran into a Red Sox fan and a Cubs fan walking towards us and giving us grief. Needless to say, it was a tough night being a Cardinal fan!!

MARK STANGL
A BAD DAY AT THE BALLPARK IS BETTER THAN A GOOD DAY OF WORK

RON "PAPA JACK" JACKSON

BY TONY OLIVER

Thirty men registered plate appearances for the 2004 Boston Red Sox, but one of the biggest contributors to the offensive juggernaut did not face a single pitch. Had it not been for the December 27, 2002, announcement of Ron "Papa Jack" Jackson as the team's new hitting coach, Boston's stunning rise to the zenith of the baseball world may have never happened.[1]

Ron (Ronnie) Jackson was born on May 9, 1953, in Birmingham, Alabama. He bore a strong resemblance to his brick-mason father, Thomas. The elder Jackson and his wife, Mary, had 14 children (nine girls and five boys), including Lawrence (Kenny) who played in the Chicago White Sox farm system in 1968 and 1969.[2] Both parents played an integral role in Ronnie's character: "My dad always taught me to show respect for everyone. Our family has always been close. … We never did without. Mom always saw to that. She kept us well-fed and clean. My father made sure we got to play sports and he often bought us the equipment to play with."[3]

Ron, as he became known, joined the Powderly Hill (Cooper Green) Little League team at 7 years old. He soon progressed to other levels and starred on the Wenonah High School team, always as a third baseman, and idolized fellow Alabamians Willie Mays, Hank Aaron, and Cleon Jones.

The California Angels drafted Jackson in the second round of the 1971 June amateur draft (37th overall). Although he also excelled in football, Jackson opted to pursue a baseball career: "I always wanted to be a major league baseball player, so when I got to high school … and the California Angels told me, 'We're going to draft you high,' I had a tough decision to make – baseball or football."[4] Years later he confirmed having received "200 scholarship offers, and I could have gone to any major school I wanted to … Alabama, Stanford, USC. All my brothers … played football. … (I) wanted to do something different than them."[5] Despite the decision, Jackson did not have second thoughts: "First of all, I guess I really liked baseball better. But also I considered one other point. Had I decided to go to Alabama, for instance, I didn't figure to get much playing time until I was a junior."[6]

Angels scout Bob Reasonover, a 1950s minor-league infielder for the Dodgers, signed Jackson to his first professional contract, and the Angels assigned Jackson to Idaho Falls of the rookie-level Pioneer League. He struggled against his peers (.208/.312/.250) in 70 games. In 1972 he moved to the Class-A Midwest League with the Quad Cities affiliate of the Angels. His numbers improved (126 games, 541 PAs, .274/.336/.436), and he enjoyed an early professional highlight on May 12 as he connected for two singles, a double, and a triple during a 12-2 victory over Cedar Rapids.[7] He finished the year with the Arizona Instructional League, where he won the batting title, though it was later rescinded due to insufficient plate appearances.[8]

Jackson matured as a player in two campaigns with the El Paso Sun Kings of the Double-A Texas League. He settled nicely with the club in 1973 and connected for a grand slam on July 2, though Amarillo walloped El Paso, 17-6.[9] He won the Gene Lolling Award for his off-the-field contributions,[10] but his on-the-field performance was not always impeccable. According to his manager, Norm Sherry, "[O]ne day in Memphis

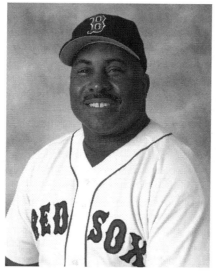

… his whole family came to see him play for the first time as a professional. And I have never seen a ballplayer have a worse day. He made five errors and did everything else wrong."[11]

A sterling .328 average in 1974 was second in the league – but also second in the now-renamed Diablos club to teammate Jerry Remy.[12] Offseason press articles about the Angels, winners of the Topps Award for best minor-league organization, touted the prospect.[13] Nevertheless, the club assigned Jackson to the Salt Lake City Gulls of the Triple-A Pacific Coast League for more seasoning in 1975. In 144 games, he hit .281 with 85 RBIs, 20 stolen bases, and roughly as many walks as strikeouts, earning a nod to the league's all-star game.[14] While still a third sacker, Jackson played 16 games in the outfield and 13 at first base, as the Angels "called in the last month of the season and they wanted me to play more than one position. … You have to rotate. When you get to the big leagues, we're going to want you to play more than one position. … it really helped me as once I got to the big leagues, Carney Lansford got to the big leagues. … (John) McNamara said, 'We need your bat in the lineup.'"[15] His stock rose even higher thanks to a lengthy article in *The Sporting News*; farm director Tom Sommers pegged the "line-drive hitter … (as) the type who, when he matures, will learn to lift the ball more and get his drives over the fences."[16]

The Angels called up Jackson once the rosters expended in September. Hitting sixth on September 12, 1975, in Kansas

274

City, Jackson contributed a pair of the Angels' four hits in a 7-2 loss. His first major-league safety was memorable: "My first time up I got a base hit up the middle, stole second, and scored all in one at-bat. In the two-game series against the Royals, I think I went 4-for-5, so I broke in the right way."[17] His performance – four hits in seven plate appearances, a pair of runs scored and two driven in – prompted the Angels to give the rookie ample playing time down the stretch. He finished the season with a .231/.268/.282 slash line and 10 strikeouts in 43 plate appearances, proof that despite his potential, he needed to adjust to big-league pitching.

Although Jackson made the Angels' 1976 Opening Day roster, he had only two pinch-hit plate appearances in California's first six contests. The Angels optioned him to Salt Lake City so he could get more playing time. Jackson's scorching .364/.476/.606 explosion in his first 10 games left no doubt he had little to prove in Triple A. His first career round-tripper in the majors, on June 4 against Boston, was a tonic for the power-challenged Angels, who had labored through 18 games without a home run. The sixth-inning blast tied the score before California won in extra innings.[18] A banner Independence Day doubleheader (4-for-7, two home runs, eight runs driven in) would pique the interest of the opposition Minnesota Twins, a harbinger of future events. Jackson's season totals (127 games, 454 PAs, 40 RBIs, 141 total bases) cemented the franchise's faith in his ability to perform at the big-league level.

Jackson's flexibility and humility earned him fans on the coaching staff, including skipper Sherry: "He may have bad days, but he never lets them drown him. He was voted the Most Popular Player in the Texas League in 1973. The whole league voted for him. I guess the reason is he talks to the other guys, he doesn't pop off, he's not a hot dog, and he plays hard."[19]

In January 1977, Sherry felt "the only spots open this spring are at third base and center field. ... We'll let Dave Chalk and Ron Jackson fight it out at third base."[20] Both youngsters had solid credentials from the prior year: Chalk played 45 games and Jackson started 103 contests at the hot corner. Newly acquired free agent Bobby Grich, a four-time Gold Glove winner with the Orioles, would take over at shortstop. Injuries limited Grich to 52 games, drastically altering the plans. Jackson improved his OPS from .633 to .691 in 106 games and drove in the winning run in consecutive games on June 25 and 26.[21] However, the Angels spun their wheels and finished in fifth place in the AL West Division (74-88). As the season neared its conclusion, they were no-hit by Bert Blyleven on September 22. Jackson reached in the third inning on an error by Bert Campaneris. He was the sole Anaheim baserunner until Carlos May drew a walk in the ninth.[22]

California finally took the anticipated step forward in 1978 behind Don Baylor's potent bat and the one-two unch of Frank Tanana and Nolan Ryan atop the rotation. Jackson shared playing time with Ron Fairly at first base, but the former's defensive flexibility opened spots in the lineup. He started the season on a tear, batting .524 in the first two weeks, tops in the junior circuit: "This is just the beginning. ... I'd like to look there in September and see that my name is leading."[23] A profile in *The Sporting News* featured his now famous nickname, "Papa Jack," though it did not cite its origin: Ryan coined the sobriquet upon hearing Jackson was now the proud father of a baby boy. Manager Dave García lauded Jackson's offensive prowess, noting, "I'm not saying he is the best first baseman in the league, but he is playing the position as well as anyone."[24] Among those impressed was Minnesota manager Gene Mauch, whose path would cross with Jackson's in the offseason. After watching Jackson hit consistent line drives in batting practice, Mauch told reporters, "He should be playing some place."[25]

Jackson wore down during June and July (48-for-192, .250) and missed August with a wrist injury. Nevertheless, he finished strongly in September and October (.290/.305/.430). The Angels climbed to second place and Jackson reached new heights in RBIs, slugging percentage, and on-base average. His .297 batting average paced the club while his 116 OPS+ trailed only Baylor, though neither Angel made the All-Star Team. The Citizens Savings Athletic Foundation Awards Board named Jackson the Southern California Athlete of the Month for May.[26] Things appeared to look up for both the franchise and its young hitter, but the offseason dealt a curveball.

Angels GM Buzzie Bavasi sought outfield help and dealt Jackson and Danny Goodwin to Minnesota for Dan Ford. Jackson anticipated a position switch since the Twins featured seven-time batting champion Rod Carew at first base. Jackson said he would gladly "play anywhere because I want to hit in that park," a reference to his .364 career average at the Twins' Metropolitan Stadium.[27] However, Minnesota traded Carew to the Angels in early 1979, freeing up first base for Jackson. Mauch warmly welcomed Jackson to the club, telling his new acquisition he had been "trying to get you for three years."[28]

Jackson provided a spark during the Twins' 16-6 drubbing of the Blue Jays on May 8, 1979. Hit by a Mike Willis pitch, Jackson confronted the hurler on the way to first base. Jackson argued with Toronto coach Don Leppert while the dugouts emptied and the umpire tossed Jackson from the game. Jackson hit safely in 20 of his next 23 contests, lifting his batting average by 38 points. His defense also impressed and he made only five errors in the first half of the season. The Angels had criticized his fielding, frustrating Jackson, who remarked, "I don't know why, but baseball players receive labels quickly. They're hard to lose, too. I've always liked to play defense. I knew I was a good first baseman when I came here."[29]

The AL West race was close throughout the year, but the Angels (88-74) finished six games ahead of the Twins (82-80, fourth place) to win their first division title. Jackson enjoyed his finest year in the major leagues: 159 games, 40 doubles, 68 RBIs, 85 runs, 51 walks, 14 home runs, and a .429 slugging average. But only three of his round trippers came in the second half of the season.

On October 10, 1979, Jackson underwent surgery to remove bone fragments from his left wrist.[30] The ailment, caused by a collision with Gorman Thomas, had dislodged "bone chips in the palm of that hand … and they affected my swing."[31] Despite the success of his first season in Minnesota, Jackson was unhappy with the front office and went to arbitration. He sought $150,000 but the panel opted for the Twins' $115,000 offer.[32] Jackson regressed at the plate (.265/.316/.391) in 131 games as the Twins fell to 77-84, 19½ games behind the eventual AL champion Kansas City Royals.

The 1981 season began on the right foot for Jackson, who won his second arbitration showdown with the Twins. His $200,000 request was a significant increase from the club's $130,525 offer.[33] Though the decision was binding, the franchise was likely upset about the result, which saw rookie Mark Funderbunk as a potential cheaper replacement. Although new manager Johnny Goryl supported Jackson, others in the organization were less sanguine. Mickey Hatcher started at first base on Opening Day in front of 42,658 fans, by far the largest crowd the Twins would draw to their ballpark that year. Hoping to shake off his slow start, Jackson turned to hypnosis. He lifted his batting average to .275, but as the players strike threatened the season, his free agency at the end of the year hung in the balance. Jackson and the Twins, parties in a strained relationship, could not officialize their divorce. To demonstrate his commitment to the game, Jackson organized a baseball clinic, but the fans were less than enamored with the underachieving club.

Two weeks after the strike ended and the season restarted, the Twins traded Jackson to the Tigers for Tim Corcoran. He played in 31 games for Detroit (115 OPS+) and 54 for the Twins (93 OPS+). Officially a free agent at the season's end, Jackson was unclaimed in the free agent reentry draft. His agent, Abdul Jalil, continued to negotiate with Detroit (the team was reputed to have offered a five-year, $2.5 million contract, but it was a three-year, $750,000 deal.[34]) Jalil said, "As far as I'm concerned, the whole thing is dead in Detroit."[35] The imbroglio turned ugly; Tigers manager Sparky Anderson was rumored to have convinced management, unwilling to bid against itself, to withdraw its offer, though Anderson denied the allegations, saying, "I like Ron Jackson. … Only time will tell whether he was right or wrong."[36] Jackson ultimately fired Jalil, whose smokescreen comments about other teams offering more money proved a failed tactic.[37]

Unsigned through the winter, Jackson returned to the Angels after agreeing to terms on April 11, 1982, and reported to their minor-league complex in Mesa, Arizona, to get into playing shape.[38] He backed up Carew and Doug DeCinces at the infield corner spots and was a common pinch-hitter for manager Mauch. He took advantage of Carew's summer injury, hitting .420 (21-for-50) in 15 games after the All-Star Game.[39]

Jackson reached career highs in batting average (.331) and on-base percentage (.381) in 159 plate appearances. More significantly, he played meaningful October baseball for the first time as the Angels won the AL West championship. Seemingly destined to reach the World Series after winning the first two games, California lost the last three to the Milwaukee Brewers. Jackson had a sole at-bat, as a pinch-hitter for Tim Foli in the ninth inning of the final game. He led off the ninth with the Angels down by one run and laced the first pitch from Bob McClure to center field for a single. Speedy Rob Wilfong replaced Jackson as a pinch-runner but the Angels failed to hit the ball out of the infield and lost the game, 4-3.

Jackson traveled to Venezuela to play in the 1982-1983 winter league. In 39 games for La Guaira Tiburones (Sharks), he hit .265 and slugged .429 (statistics are incomplete, but he is credited with 147 at-bats, 39 hits, and 29 runs batted in.[40]) His team won the national championship and the country hosted the 1983 Caribbean Series. Although the Arecibo Lobos (Wolves) from Puerto Rico won the four-country tournament, five players from Venezuela made the All-Star team, including Jackson. He won the second game of the round-robin with a dramatic walk-off three-run home run in the bottom of the ninth inning against Mexico.[41] A photo captured the contrast between the ebullient Jackson and the losing pitcher, Luis Enrique Aponte, the former high-fiving a teammate while the latter walked dejectedly off the field, under the caption "Ron Jackson viró la tortilla" ("flipped the omelet," the equivalent of "flips the script.")

Jackson returned to the Angels in 1983 and played both the corner infield and corner outfield positions along with an occasional designated-hitter stint. Although he played in 102 games and garnered 379 plate appearances, his average dropped to .230. His offensive contributions further regressed in 1984 (.193 in 45 games) before the underperforming Angels released him on August 2 to make room for Dick Schofield, activated from the disabled list. Baltimore signed him 12 days later and he played in 12 games (8-for-28) for the fifth-place Orioles. The club released him on December 17.

The St. Louis Cardinals gave Jackson a look in 1984 and despite solid hitting during spring training, he was optioned to Louisville. The veteran played in 62 games and hit .238/.295/.359 but the coveted call-up to the majors never came. He attempted a comeback in 1988 with the Vancouver Canadians (Triple-A affiliate of the Chicago White Sox) but hit only .177 in 18 games.

In 10 seasons of major-league baseball, Jackson played in 926 games and collected 774 hits, good for a .259 batting average and a 94 OPS+. He was a better hitter against southpaws (.284) and slightly better in the second half (.264).

He coached the Double-A Birmingham Barons in 1989. The club finished the regular season with the league's best record (88-55), beat the Huntsville Stars in the playoffs (3-1), and swept the Greenville Braves in the finals (3-0). The squad became known as the "Runaway Train" for its dominating performance.

Like many former major leaguers, Jackson still felt he could play competitively. Unlike most, he was given the opportunity in 1989, thanks to the Senior Professional Baseball League, brainchild of former minor leaguer Jim Morley.[42] The league was open to those 35 and older (32 for catchers) and fielded eight clubs for a 72-game campaign. The recently concluded major-league season had more than 70 players who would have qualified, though understandably none chose to trade the big leagues for the novelty circuit.

Curiosity did not extend to the turnstiles as poor attendance plagued the Florida-based franchises. As the Fort Myers Sun Sox' starting third baseman, Jackson hit a robust .344, eighth-best during the league's maiden season. He remained with the team until it folded on December 26, 1990, an action that triggered the circuit's demise. He recalled the competitive juices: "I remember guys pulling muscles. Some of the older guys tried running the bases like they used to. Just seeing some old friends. ... Some of them are a little heavier, a little thicker, but it was a lot of fun."[43]

During his professional career, Jackson had demonstrated an uncanny ability to absorb the game. On the way to the big leagues, he explained his approach as "no(t) ... try to pull everything. I usually go with the pitch. If the defense sees you trying to pull all the pitches, they'll gang up on you."[44] He had not wasted his time on the bench, choosing to absorb the action from that vantage: "Most of your good coaches, they didn't play every day. My biggest thing was, I watched the hitter. I always wanted to be a major league hitting coach. I watched the bad hitters. ... I started preparing myself before my career was over."[45]

Many young players would benefit from this advice in the coming decades. Jackson was the Milwaukee Brewers' minor-league hitting coordinator in 1991 and 1992, monitoring the progress of future big leaguers John Jaha, Dave Nilsson, Jeff Cirillo, and José Valentín. Prior to the 1993 season, he became the batting coach for the Triple-A New Orleans Zephyrs, the Brewers' top minor-league affiliate. During his three years tutoring the prospects, the team was competitive, setting the stage for future big-league call-ups.

In the dark, World Series-less 1994 offseason, Milwaukee passed over Jackson for hitting coach in favor of his former high-school teammate Lamar Johnson, skipper of Class-A Stockton. Jackson returned to New Orleans but the White Sox hired him in June of 1995 for their first-base coaching vacancy.[46] In five years with Chicago, Jackson alternated between first-base and hitting coach roles and oversaw a potent offense with Frank Thomas, Robin Ventura, and Albert Belle. Shortly after replacing Bill Buckner as the White Sox' hitting coach, he shared his methods with the *Chicago Tribune*: "If you're going to help hitters, you have to know what you're looking for. I feel like it's a gift from God for me. I've been watching hitters my whole life. I've talked about hitting with guys like Tony Muser, Don Baylor, Dave Parker, and Lamar Johnson."[47]

The team was unable to repeat its 1993 postseason trip and manager Jerry Manuel fired Jackson early in 1998 as the White Sox struggled at the plate. The Brewers rehired him for the 1999 season as the first-base coach, though he would also counsel the hitters once batting coach Jim Lefebvre replaced fired skipper Phil Garner in August.

Jackson joined the Triple-A Albuquerque Dukes as the hitting coach for the 2000 season and remained with the Dodgers organization as the franchise switched its affiliation to the Las Vegas 51's. The 2002 team, piloted by Brad Mills, lost in the postseason semifinals. Though neither suspected it, both Mills and Jackson would be on their way to Boston.

After missing the postseason in 2002 despite a 93-69 record, the Red Sox franchise suffered through a roller-coaster offseason. After enticing coveted GM Billy Beane from the Oakland Athletics, the Red Sox were shocked when cold feet kept Beane with Oakland. A pivot to fresh-faced 28-year-old Theo Epstein filled the vacancy but blockbuster free agents nevertheless jilted Boston.

The Red Sox – runners-up to the Yankees in the AL East five straight years – raised eyebrows by firing longtime player Dwight Evans as their hitting coach shortly after the 2002 season ended. Offense was not the Boston weakness; the team placed second in batting average and third in the suddenly-in-vogue on-base percentage. However, the shift was not occurring fast enough to overcome the lack of solid hurlers behind Pedro Martínez. After his dismissal, Evans opined, "The only way that's going to change is if (the team) gives incentives for guys to finish with a higher on-base percentage. You have to start at the root of the problem, the low minors."[48] *Moneyball*, soon to be published, spread the gospel of the walk across the sport, but Jackson had the exact experience Evans highlighted: a history with young talent in the organization's lower levels.[49] Under new GM Epstein, the Red Sox searched for overlooked players, but once they wore the uniform, Jackson ensured their discipline: "We had four or five guys who had long swings and didn't load up early enough ... and we had guys who didn't do the small things, like move over runners or get the sacrifice fly when the runner was on third. It was the small things."[50]

In the 2003-2005 seasons combined, Boston led the major leagues in batting average, slugging average, and on-base percentage. It ranked first each year, except for slugging in 2005 (second place, behind the Texas Rangers).[51] The Red Sox boasted superb offensive talent and many players enjoyed career highs in OPS+ during the era, among them Trot Nixon (149, 2003); Bill Mueller (140, 2003); and Jason Varitek (successive highs in 2003, 2004, and 2005). Ever humble, Jackson downplayed his role: "Most of the time, it's nothing major the guys do. It's just small things, making adjustments here and there. Just being there for them."[52] Jackson noted that the resilient team "fed off each other" throughout the 2004 season.

Although the January 22, 2003, David Ortíz free-agent acquisition is now seen as a turning point for the team's fortunes, at the time Ortiz was deemed as a spare piece, not as a lineup anchor. While Ortiz had shown promising power with the Twins, the Minnesota front office felt his defensive shortcomings were too drastic to justify this presence in the roster. Under Jackson, Ortiz matured from a dangerous hitter into a lethal one: "He got to know me, I got to know him. When he'd get into a little funk, he'd come to me. ... I wouldn't go to him. He'd come to me and say, 'What do you see?'"[53] After breaking Jimmie Foxx's single-season home-run record in 2006, Ortiz gave Jackson the bat as a memento. Only a few years earlier, Ortiz's swing was even throughout its motion, his hands level. Jackson noticed and suggested a mechanical adjustment; the rest is Red Sox history.[54]

"My four years with the Red Sox, we broke all kinds of records. ... We had an outstanding hitting team, I was just blessed to have those players. ... It made me look good."[55] Jackson took advantage of the national platform to record an instructional video, *Ron Jackson's Hitting Factory: Becoming a Champion Hitter*, a natural foray given his jovial personality.[56] He cherished the 2004 World Series victory: "This is my 33rd season in professional baseball and this is the best feeling I've had when it comes to baseball."[57]

Uncharacteristically, the Red Sox struggled at the plate in 2006. Despite a .351 OBP (second in baseball, trailing only the Yankees), the club finished with a pedestrian .269 batting average, exactly the league norm. As it did with Evans four years earlier, the club fired Jackson, though he was powerless to address the main reason for the drop in performance: injuries. Varitek (58 games), Manny Ramírez (30), Coco Crisp (57), Nixon (48), and shortstop Álex González (51) missed considerable playing time.

Jackson's contract expired at the end of the 2006 season and Boston pursued a different direction. The team hired Dave Magadan, who had previously coached the San Diego Padres. According to press reports, Epstein had been in contact with Magadan during the season and offered him a role.[58] With Jackson's departure, every member of Francona's 2004 staff had turned over.

Jackson was thankful for the opportunity. He released a five-paragraph statement to the press to express his gratitude: "I want to thank the Red Sox and all the fans of this great team. I will always cherish being a part of Boston's long road back to the World Series and I loved watching the development and the hard work of the players during my time here in Boston."[59]

Red Sox broadcaster Joe Castiglione called Jackson "the guy who really turned David Ortiz into a home-run-hitting superstar in '03. David used to have trouble hitting the inside fastball. Papa Jack got him to adjust, and he took off from that point. Jackson was an excellent hitting instructor."[60] Fellow commentator (and former Jackson colleague) Jerry Remy called the '03 club "an outstanding offensive team ... really the start of the Golden Era of Red Sox baseball. Ron 'Papa Jack' Jackson was the hitting coach and he did a great job with the hitters."[61]

Through the 2022 season, Birmingham has produced 87 major-league baseball players, but the city's connection to the sport is much deeper. With little interruption, teams by the Barons name have played in the minor leagues for over 100 years. In 2023 the Barons were a member of the Double-A Southern League as a Chicago White Sox affiliate.[62]

The Black Barons, first organized in 1920, under the "Stars" nickname, were one of the Negro Leagues' premier franchises. The club alternated between the Negro Southern League and the Negro National League with a roster that included Satchel Paige, George "Mule" Suttles, and a young Willie Mays on his way to the New York Giants.[63]

Birmingham is also home to the nation's oldest ballpark, Rickwood Field. While no longer the home of the Barons, it still hosts exhibition games. Since its doors opened in 1910 (almost two years before Fenway Park and four prior to Wrigley Field), it has hosted thousands of minor-league, exhibition, and Negro League games. As a child, Jackson attended Atlanta Braves exhibitions: "They used to pack it in. ... I used to get excited to see the lights. I played in Rickwood Field in high school all-star teams."[64]

These three elements explain Jackson's commitment to his hometown, where baseball has been dropped from some elementary- and middle-school athletic programs. After three seasons with the Round Rock Express, Papa Jack chose to continue his coaching career but with younger charges. In 2014 he managed the Willie Mays Youth baseball team (11- and 12-year olds) to the Reviving Baseball in Inner Cities (RBI) championship.[65] A year later, the city built Cooper Green Park to promote the sport to its youth, and the "Papa Jack Youth Baseball Classic" highlighted local talent to entice MLB's RBI program to open an academy in Birmingham. Jackson reiterated the importance of "making sure ... they are student-athletes instead of athletes, making sure they do their homework, making sure they learn how to read ... because that's going to take them a long way in life."[66] Citing the importance of a strong foundation, he compared the sport and life: "You are going to have a lot of ups, and a lot of downs, you're going to have to accept both and move on. ... Work ethic is very important."[67]

Jackson started the Ron "Papa Jack" Baseball Foundation to train young players and aspiring coaches and enhance the quality of life of the Birmingham community.[68] Asked about his legacy, Jackson simply stated "Freddy Kennedy, Leo Dawson, and my dad all helped me out when I was little, so I felt like it was my duty to come back and give back. ... in June, when school is out, to have an organization where the kids can go play baseball and sharpen their skills. If I can make a difference in someone's life, I think I've done my job."[69]

Jackson has three children with his former wife Marva Turner, two stepchildren, and five grandchildren. In his 70th year, he notes "we teach kids more than just play baseball...to go into the real world and be decent citizens. This will prepare them for what they're going to be in life."[70] This commitment continues with his son Ronnie, who coached Ramsay High School to the 2022 Staten Football Championship, and high school basketball player Nyah Hardy, the granddaughter of his life partner, Beverly Thomas.

ACKNOWLEDGMENTS

Thanks to Valyncia M. Johnson for connecting the author to Ron Jackson for a telephone interview.

SOURCES

Unless otherwise noted, quotes stem from the author's interview with Ron Jackson on May 26, 2023.

NOTES

1. "Red Sox Hire Ron Jackson as Batting Coach," *Edwardsville (California) Intelligencer,* December 30, 2022. https://www.theintelligencer.com/news/article/Red-Sox-Hire-Ron-Jackson-As-Batting-Coach-10554362.php.
2. "About Us," Papa Jack's Gap to Gap Hitting Mat, https://ism3.infinityprosports.com/ismdata/2008102700/std-sitebuilder/sites/200801/www/en/aboutus/aboutpapajack/.
3. Ray Herbat, "One Footballer Who Got Away, Jackson Climbing Angel Ladder," *The Sporting News,* June 28, 1975: 35.
4. "Where Are They Now?" YouTube.com, recorded 2011, https://www.youtube.com/watch?v=qpYLlaVpBog.
5. Dick Miller, "Jackson Spreads Wings at Angel Plate," *The Sporting News,* July 3, 1976: 16.
6. Herbat.
7. "Class A Leagues," *The Sporting News,* May 27, 1972: 47.
8. Ed Prell, "Cactus Loop Picks 16 Man All-Star Squad," *The Sporting News,* December 2, 1972: 53.
9. "Texas League," *The Sporting News,* July 21, 1973: 41.
10. Dick Miller, "Angels Saw Energy Crisis in September," *The Sporting News,* December 1, 1973: 40.
11. Herbat.
12. Dick Miller, "Kiddie Crop Brightening Angels' Outlook," *The Sporting News,* October 19, 1974: 26.
13. Dick Miller, "Scouts Rate More Cheers – Wiencek," *The Sporting News,* February 1, 1975: 32.
14. "Albuquerque Has Seven PCL All-Star Selections," *The Sporting News,* July 26, 1975: 32.
15. Author's telephone interview with Ron "Papa Jack" Jackson, May 26, 2023.
16. Herbat.
17. "Where Are They Now?"
18. Dick Miller, "T. Davis Pumps Up Feeble Angel Attack," *The Sporting News,* June 26, 1976: 16.
19. Miller, "Jackson Spreads Wings at Angel Plate."
20. Dick Miller, "Lineup Is Least of Sherry's Worries," *The Sporting News,* January 15, 1977: 54.
21. "AL Flashes," *The Sporting News,* July 16, 1977: 44.
22. Randy Galloway, "Aching Blyleven Hands Angels No-Hit Pain," *The Sporting News,* October 8, 1977: 17.
23. Dick Miller, "Poppa Jack Makes Folks Cry Uncle," *The Sporting News,* May 13, 1978: 12.
24. Miller, "Poppa Jack Makes Folks Cry Uncle."
25. Miller, "Poppa Jack Makes Folks Cry Uncle."
26. Dick Miller, "Angels Rue Huge Free-Agent Tab," *The Sporting News,* July 8, 1978: 10.
27. Bob Fowler, "Twins' Park a Hit Haven for Jackson," *The Sporting News,* January 6, 1979: 41.
28. Fowler, "Twins' Park a Hit Haven for Jackson."
29. Bob Fowler, "Twins' Jackson Succeeding as First Baseman," *The Sporting News,* August 4, 1979: 21.
30. "Caught on the Fly," *The Sporting News,* October 27, 1979: 30.
31. Bob Fowler, "Twins Look to Jackson," *The Sporting News,* January 19, 1980: 35.
32. Murray Chass, "Finley 0-for-5 in Salary Hearings," *The Sporting News,* March 15, 1980: 36.
33. Murray Chass, "$600,000 for Kemp is Arbitration Champ," *The Sporting News,* March 14, 1981: 34.
34. Tom Gage, "Jackson Offered Generous Contract," *The Sporting News,* November 28, 1981: 55.
35. Tom Gage, "Kemp Price Too High for Tigers," *The Sporting News,* December 12, 1981: 44.
36. Stan Isle, "Caught on the Fly," *The Sporting News,* April 3, 1982: 38.
37. Joe Falls, "Gripes on TV, Agents, NBA Rookie Voting," *The Sporting News,* May 3, 1982: 8.
38. John Strege, "AL West: Forsch to Join Free Agent Club," *The Sporting News,* April 24, 1982: 30.
39. John Strege, "DeCinces Joins an Elite Circle," *The Sporting News,* August 23, 1982: 27.
40. "Ron Jackson," Registro Histórico Estadístico del Béisbol Profesional Venezolano, https://www.pelotabinaria.com.ve/beisbol/mostrar.php?ID=jackron001.
41. Tweet dated February 4, 2020, by @Tiburonmusiu, https://twitter.com/tiburonmusiu/status/1224670206380990466/photo/1.
42. William Schneider, "One Last Season in the Sun: The Saga of the Senior Professional Baseball Association," originally published in Society for American Baseball Research, *The National Pastime: Baseball in the Sunshine State,* Miami, 2016, https://sabr.org/journal/article/one-last-season-in-the-sun-the-saga-of-the-senior-professional-baseball-association/.
43. Glenn Miller, "Papa Jack Generates Hits at Plate," *Fort Myers (Florida) News-Press,* March 9, 2004, http://www.greatest21days.com/2021/12/ron-jackson-watched-hitters-his-whole.html, https://www.newspapers.com/article/90777111/ron-jackson-march-9-2004/.
44. Herbat.
45. Bill Nowlin, "'Papa Jack' Ron Jackson, Red Sox Hitting Coach," *Diehard Magazine,* 2005.
46. United Press International, "ChiSox Fire Lamont, Promote Bevington," June 2, 1995, https://www.upi.com/Archives/1995/06/02/Chisox-fire-Lamont-promote-Bevington/8960802065600/.
47. Phil Rogers, "Coach a Smash Hit in New Job," *Chicago Tribune,* September 1, 1997: 48, http://www.greatest21days.com/2021/12/ron-jackson-watched-hitters-his-whole.html, https://www.newspapers.com/article/90774900/ron-jackson-sept-1-1997/.
48. Lenny Megliola, "Evans Not Surprised by Dismissal," *Milford (Massachusetts) Daily News,* October 5, 2002. https://www.milforddailynews.com/story/sports/2002/10/05/evans-not-surprised-by-dismissal/41297849007/.
49. Michael Lewis, *Moneyball* (New York: W.W. Norton, 2003).
50. Dennis Tuttle, "Baseball: The Power of Nine," *The Sporting News,* August 31, 2003: 10-12.

51 The Red Sox and the Angels tied in 2004 with an identical .282 batting average, but the Angels were no match for the Red Sox in the three-game ALCS sweep.

52 Glenn Miller, "Papa Jack Generates Hits At Plate."

53 "David Ortiz's Hitting Coach Ron 'Papa Jack' Jackson," Action Unlimited, originally broadcast on CBS 42 Birmingham, 2022. Accessed via https://www.youtube.com/watch?v=T7ek_Kwe-tk.

54 Benjamin Chase, "Boston Red Sox: The David Ortiz Origin Story," Call to the Pen, originally published in 2017, https://calltothepen.com/2016/08/29/boston-red-sox-david-ortiz-origin-story/3/.

55 "Where Are They Now?"

56 "Ron Jackson's Hitting Factory: Becoming a Champion Hitter," Championship Productions, https://www.championshipproductions.com/cgi-bin/champ/p/Baseball/Ron-Jacksons-Hitting-Factory-Becoming-a-Champion-Hitter_LD-02394B.html.

57 William C. Rhoden, "Red Sox Hitters Found a Mentor in Papa Jack," *New York Times*, October 31, 2004, Section 8, 3.

58 Associated Press, "Magadan Attempts to Enhance Offense," October 21, 2006, *Worcester* (Massachusetts) *Telegram & Gazette*, https://www.telegram.com/story/news/local/north/2006/10/21/magadan-attempts-to-enhance-offense/53033468007/.

59 Nick Cafardo, "Papa Jack Thanks Boston Fans," Boston.com, October 3, 2006, https://www.boston.com/sports/extra-bases/2006/10/03/papa_jack_thank/.

60 Joe Castiglione and Douglas B. Lyons, *Can You Believe It? 30 Years of Insider Stories with the Boston Red Sox* (Chicago: Triumph Books, 2021), 176-7.

61 Jerry Remy, Nick Cafardo, and Sean McDonough, *If These Walls Could Talk: Boston Red Sox* (Chicago: Triumph Books, 2019), 141.

62 The current Birmingham Barons moved from Montgomery prior to the 1981 season. The Birmingham Sports Pro web site details the city's sports lineage, http://www.birminghamprosports.com/.

63 "The Birmingham Black Barons," Negro Southern League Museum, Birmingham, Alabama, https://www.birminghamnslm.org/the-birmingham-black-barons/.

64 Author's telephone interview with Ron "Papa Jack" Jackson, May 26, 2023.

65 "Birmingham Boys Returning Home as Baseball Champions as City Officials Work to Recruit Annual Major League Event," Alabama.com, July 16, 2024, https://www.al.com/news/birmingham/2014/07/birmingham_boys_returning_home.html.

66 "Inaugural 'Pappa Jack' [sic] Classic Draws Huge Crowd & 'Sportskid of the Year' Mona Davis, City Council of Birmingham, 2016, https://www.youtube.com/watch?v=n05x0P3h7f0.

67 Ron "Papa Jack" Jackson interview, Sideline show, originally published 2009, https://www.youtube.com/watch?v=7YiuEj2n_vM.

68 Papa Jack's Baseball Website, https://papajackbaseball.org/.

69 "Where Are They Now?"

70 Willie Mays RBI League, YouTube, originally published on April 19, 2015, https://www.youtube.com/watch?v=qasGY9YfSOA

LYNN JONES

BY PAUL HOFMANN

A career backup outfielder, Lynn Jones had nearly a 35-year career in professional baseball as a player and well-traveled coach and manager. Jones played eight seasons in the majors – five with the Detroit Tigers and three with the Kansas City Royals – before embarking on a coaching career that touched the lives of thousands of players. While his career totals are modest (a .252 average with 7 home runs and 91 RBIs), they do not accurately reflect the value he brought to his teams. Jones was a steady outfielder with a strong arm, often used as a late-inning defensive replacement, who had the ability to come up with timely, clutch hits.

Lynn Morris Jones was born on January 1, 1953, in Meadville, Pennsylvania, and grew up on the outskirts of the small town of Harmonsburg, a village of about 300 people about 10 miles east of Meadville. Meadville is about 40 miles south of Erie and 90 miles north of Pittsburgh. It is the county seat of Crawford County. In the 1950s the city had a population of about 19,000.

Lynn was the youngest of four sons of Paul Hairston and Valeria Marcella (Sterling) Jones (nicknamed Sue). Lynn's father played semipro football with the Meadville Zippers and later worked for Talon Zippers for 35 years before retiring for health reasons.[1] He was instrumental in establishing the local Little League and coaching his four sons. Valeria, the valedictorian of her high-school class, cleaned houses, worked in restaurants, and held other jobs as she raised her boys and pursued a degree to become a licensed practical nurse. Valeria was employed for 15 years as an LPN at the Meadville City Hospital and for 15 years as an office nurse in private practice.[2] Lynn's parents were both twins.

The Jones brothers grew up in a religious home. He and his brothers attended Harmonsburg United Methodist Church every Sunday morning with their parents. Valeria was a member of the church for over 75 years and served in all phases of the church, including youth groups, board member, United Methodist Women, community vacation Bible school, and Wednesday Bible study.[3] Looking back on his upbringing and his parents' influence on his faith, Jones said, "My parents were not religious zealots, or anything like that, but they were strong in their faith."[4]

All the Jones boys (Paul, Leslie, Darryl, and Lynn) were all-around athletes, all excelling in basketball and baseball. Leslie, Lynn's second oldest brother, died of a heart condition soon after he graduated from high school in 1962. Lynn believes he was the "best athlete of all of us."[5] Darryl Jones, Lynn's third oldest brother, was also an outfielder who played in the major leagues. He played in 18 games for the New York Yankees in 1979. He hit .255 and drove in 6 runs.

Lynn attended Linesville Conneaut Summit High School in Linesville, Pennsylvania, where he played basketball, baseball, and volleyball, and ran cross-country. He ran cross-country for the purpose of getting in shape for the basketball season. Basketball was his primary sport in high school.

After high school, Jones decided to attend Thiel College, an independent liberal-arts college in Greenville in western Pennsylvania. Jones decided to attend college largely because of the military draft. "I went to school because my draft number was 150 and I needed to do something. I was a borderline student in the beginning but gradually got better. My last semester I was on the Dean's List."[6] Jones earned a bachelor's degree in sociology, a degree he said helped him through his baseball career. "My degree helped me understand people. I was never surprised by who I encountered."[7]

Jones was a three-sport athlete at Thiel College, earning three letters each in baseball and basketball and two in soccer. He was a two-year captain on the basketball team and was named an All-Lutheran Honorable Mention selection his senior year.[8]

While Jones went to Thiel to play basketball, he also made a name for himself on the baseball diamond. A two-year team captain on the baseball team, Jones was a standout outfielder. During his junior year, Jones batted .360 and was an All-Presidents' Athletic Conference First Team selection. As a senior, Jones established a since-broken school record by hitting .440. For the second consecutive year he was selected to the All-PAC First Team.[9] Jones said the Thiel baseball teams were not very good when he played there, and he didn't garner much attention. "We didn't play many games back then and I caught the attention of scouts during the summers," Jones recalled.[10]

It was during the summer between his junior and senior years that Jones met Tom Brookens, an infielder from Chambersburg, Pennsylvania, who was attending Mansfield University of Pennsylvania. Both were playing in the Shenandoah Valley League. The two were teammates with the Detroit Tigers for five years and the friendship they developed is the longest of Jones's baseball career. "We still talk to this day," Jones said in 2023.[11]

Reflecting on his childhood and days at Thiel, Jones said there were three movies that summarized his life up to that time: *The Sandlot*, *A Christmas Story*, and *Animal House*. *The Sandlot* referred to his childhood of growing up playing baseball on the playgrounds of western Pennsylvania. *A Christmas Story* was representative of the nurturing environment his parents created: "We weren't rich, but my parents always found a way to give us what we wanted."[12] And finally, *Animal House* referred to his years at Thiel where he was a member of the Alpha Chi Rho fraternity.

A 5-foot 9-inch 21-year-old, Jones was selected in the 10th round (239th overall) of the 1974 free-agent draft by the Cincinnati Reds. He was only the second player ever drafted from Thiel. A year earlier, right-handed pitcher Kevin Meistickle was drafted in the 34th round (691st overall) by the New York Mets. Jones is the only Tomcat to play in the majors.[13]

Jones was signed by award-winning scout Elmer Gray, who is credited with signing Barry Bonds, Ken Griffey Sr., Moises Alou, and many others. Jones received a $1,000 bonus and a plane ticket to Billings, Montana, in return for his signature on his initial contract.

Jones began his professional career in 1974 with the Seattle Rainiers of the short-season Class-A Northwest League. He played in 76 games and hit .262 with 2 home runs, 37 RBIs, and 22 stolen bases. The Rainiers were managed by first-year skipper Greg Riddoch, whom Jones credits with making him a ballplayer. "He put my career on track. I owe a lot to him," Jones said.[14]

For the next season Jones was advanced to the Trois-Rivieres (Quebec) Aigles of the Doube-A Eastern League. The move was more of an experiment than an actual promotion. The Aigles did not have a shortstop and Jones was given the chance to see if he could make it as an infielder. He did not enjoy the same success as he did in Seattle. He was hitting just .206 with one home run and 14 RBIs in 53 games played when he was sent back to the Northwest League. (The franchise was now in Eugene, Oregon.)

At Eugene, Jones was reunited with Riddoch. Jones enjoyed a breakout season in low-A ball at Eugene. In 62 games with the Emeralds, the right-handed batter and thrower hit .337 with 13 home runs (his career-high in Organized Baseball), 63 RBIs, and a team-leading 1.044 OPS. The Emeralds won the Northwest League's Southern Division title and beat the Portland Mavericks two games to none in the best-of-three championship series.

As reported in *The Sporting News*, Jones played a key role in Eugene's series win:

> "Eugene (Northwest) outfielder Lynn Jones waved the big stick as the Emeralds swept a doubleheader from Portland, 1-0 and 4-3. Jones hit a solo home run in the sixth inning to win the opener, then delivered a two-run triple in the seventh inning, when Eugene rallied for four runs to take the nightcap."[15]

The home run was off former major leaguer Jim Bouton, who was attempting a comeback as a knuckleballer.

At the end of the 1975 season, Jones was selected to *The Sporting News* Class-A All-Star Team.

Jones returned to Trois-Rivieres as an outfielder in 1976. His second season with the Aigles was better. In 131 games he hit .251 with 2 home runs and 36 RBIs. However, the young outfielder was questioning his ability. "I didn't think I was going to get out of Double-A. The lights were bad, and the pitching was very good."[16] Jones also recalled "lots of long bus rides that really wore me down."[17]

The Aigles won the Eastern League Northern Division championship with a record of 83-55 and faced the West Haven Yankees, the Southern Division winners. The best-of-five championship series marked the only time the Jones brothers played against each other in professional ranks. The Yankees beat the Aigles three games to none, giving older brother Darryl family bragging rights for the winter.

Jones returned to Trois-Rivieres in 1977 and played in 94 games as he shared outfield duties with four other outfielders who played in 40 or more games. Jones hit .269 with 5 home runs, 32 RBIs, and 15 stolen bases as the Aigles repeated as division champions. West Haven also repeated, albeit without Darryl, who was now with Syracuse of the International League. The result of the Eastern League's championship series was identical to the previous year, a three-game sweep by West Haven.

Jones made only one error that season and was awarded a Rawlings Silver Glove, the minor-league equivalent to the Gold Glove Award. "That award reinforced who I was as a player, I was a good defensive player," Jones said.[18]

Prior to the 1978 season, Jones decided it would be his last in professional baseball. He came to spring training with the Indianapolis Indians as one of five outfield candidates who included Champ Summers, Ed Armbrister, Arturo DeFreites, and John Valle. However, an injury to Reds third baseman Ray Knight led to Mike Grace being called up by the Reds, which had a ripple effect that opened additional playing time. Jones took advantage of the opportunity.[19]

"By the time Grace returned from the big leagues, I had cemented my position as the team's center fielder," Jones said.[20] In 126 games he hit .328 with 9 home runs, 62 RBIs, and 20 stolen bases. Despite his offensive production, Jones was not called up to the Reds when the rosters expanded in September.

On December 4 the Detroit Tigers selected Jones in the Rule 5 Draft. He was chosen fourth behind outfielder Bobby Brown, catcher Bob Davis, and utilityman Ken Macha. The move assured Jones a spot on the Tigers' 1979 roster, assuming the Tigers did not want to return Jones to the Reds organization and forfeit the $25,000 paid for Jones. The Tigers also selected infielder Dave Machemer from California in the same draft.

Jones made his major-league debut on April 13, 1979, in Arlington, Texas. Starting in center field, he went 2-for-3 with a walk and a stolen base in the Tigers' 5-4 loss to the Texas Rangers. His first major-league hit was a fifth-inning leadoff single to left field off right-hander Dock Ellis. He also had an infield single off Jim Kern to lead off the seventh inning. Despite going 2-for-5 against Kern during his career, Jones said Kern was among the three most difficult pitchers he faced. The other two were Bert Blyleven and Ron Guidry.[21]

On April 26, in the second game of a doubleheader at Milwaukee's County Stadium, Jones hit his first major-league home run, a fifth-inning solo shot to left off Brewers left-hander Jerry Augustine. The home run tied the score at 1-1, but the Brewers went on to win the game, 7-5. John Wockenfuss, the Tigers' backup catcher and first baseman, was in the bullpen that night and traded five bullpen balls to the Brewers' relievers for the home-run ball, which he presented to Jones.[22] The Tigers outfielder hit only six more home runs during his career.

Jones finished his rookie campaign with a .296 batting average, with career highs in home runs (4), RBIs (26), stolen bases (9), and OPS (.739). The fifth-place Tigers were 54-41 (.568) in games Jones played. The effort earned Jones Tiger Rookie of the Year honors. At 26 years old, he figured to factor into the Tigers future as a fourth outfielder under new manager Sparky Anderson, who had replaced Les Moss a third of the way into the 1979 season. The change wasn't the best for the rookie outfielder.

Jones described Moss, with whom he got along well, as "a man of few words."[23] By comparison Jones wasn't a favorite of Sparky's. "I could have played more, instead I became a pine brother." Jones continued, "Sparky liked to pencil in the same lineup day after day."[24] Jones said he would have become a better hitter if he had been given more playing time.

The Tigers broke camp in the spring of 1980 with Jones as the team's fourth outfielder. He appeared in nine games in April and was hitting .294 when he suffered a right knee injury (wear on articular cartilage) that required arthroscopic surgery. When he was cleared to begin playing, he was sent to the Triple-A Evansville Triplets on a rehabilitation stint. In Evansville he was invited to live with Mark Fidrych, who was trying to find his way back to the major leagues after suffering a series of injuries following his memorable 1976 season. Jones remembered Fidrych as a "super nice guy who was always enthusiastic about going to the ballpark and watching the game."[25]

Jones played in 34 games for the Triplets and batted .273 with 11 RBIs before being called back up to the Tigers when rosters expanded in September. He played in 21 games and batted .237 after his recall, finishing the year with a .255 average and 6 RBIs.

The strike-interrupted split-season of 1981 was a tale of two seasons for Jones as the young Tigers began to show hints that they were on the verge of contending. Jones got off to a slow start and was batting just .189 at the start of play on May 25. That day he had a career-high four hits that started a nine-game hitting streak. He had another four-hit performance on June 1.

He hit .462 during the streak. When the strike interrupted the play Jones was batting .307 with one home run and 15 RBIs as the fourth-place Tigers were 31-26.

Given the uncertainty of how long the strike would last, Jones decided to remain in Detroit. "I did lots of fishing on Lake St. Clair, the Detroit River, and Lake Erie," he said as he recalled how he passed the summer days usually occupied by baseball.[26]

When play resumed, the young Tigers surged into contention largely due to the contributions of a group modestly called the Riders of the Lonesome Pine, or the Pine Brothers for short. The group comprised Mick Kelleher, Champ Summers, Bill Fahey, Rick Leach, Stan Papi, Wockenfuss, and Jones. Kelleher was referred to as "El Capitan" and Jones was "King Pine." In an August 1981 *Sports Illustrated* article, regular left fielder Steve Kemp credited the Pine Brothers for the Tigers' recent nine-game winning streak. "The Pine Bros. have been more instrumental in this streak than the regulars," Kemp said as the Tigers remained in contention until the final weekend of the season.[27] The Pine Brothers became their own brand in Detroit that summer, complete with T-shirts and other memorabilia.

Jones's batting average remained above .300 through the end of the Tigers' streak. He cooled off considerably afterward. From August 24 until the end of the season, he hit .133 (6-for-45) and the young Tigers finished 29-23 in the second half, tied for second place with the Boston Red Sox, a game and a half behind the Milwaukee Brewers.

In 1982 Jones served primarily as the Tigers' fourth outfielder and was often a late-inning defensive replacement. From July 2 to 9, he enjoyed an eight-game hitting streak (13-for-31, .419), raising his season average from .182 to .280 when he filled in for Chet Lemon who missed several games due to nagging injuries,[28] including a sore left hand.[29] He cooled off again when his playing time diminished and finished the season with a .223 average and 14 RBIs.

Jones's playing time continue to diminish in 1983. He played in only one of the team's first 26 games and appeared in only 49 games and had 64 at-bats for the entire season. Again, he demonstrated that when he had the chance to play, he could produce. During a seven-game hitting streak between August 6

Photo by Bill Nowlin.

and 20 he was 8-for-22, .364. He finished the season with a .266 average.

Jones became a free agent at the end of the 1983 season. On December 6 he signed a two-year contract with the Kansas City Royals. A favorite of many Tigers fans, he had played in 303 games for Detroit and hit .264 with 6 home runs and 71 RBIs.

Royals executive vice president and general manager John Schuerholz spoke of the club's rationale behind signing the outfielder. "Jones was available and based on our scouting reports and (manager) Dick Howser's feeling, we believe he can help us," Schuerholz said. "He provides us with some added depth in the outfield."[30] Howser added that Jones was "a good outfielder with a strong arm."[31]

Jones's 1984 season was derailed in spring training when he was hit by a pitch from Braves right-hander Jeff Dedmon, suffering a broken left hand. The Royals' newly acquired outfielder missed the rest of the spring training and started the season at Triple-A Omaha.

On September 24 Jones hit his first home run in three years, a solo shot off left-hander Geoff Zahn of the California Angels in the sixth inning of the first game of a doubleheader at Royals Stadium. It was the seventh and last home run of his major-league career. He finished the year with a career-high .301 batting average, albeit in 47 games, helping the team capture the American League West title, the reward for which was a date with Jones's former club, the Detroit Tigers, in the 1984 ALCS.

Jones pinch-hit for right fielder Pat Sheridan in all three games of the series and went 1-for-5 in the series. With the Royals trailing 3-2 in Game Two, he had an eighth-inning leadoff pinch-hit single off 1984 AL Cy Young and MVP Award winner Willie Hernández. He came around to score the tying run on a double by Hal McRae, which forced the game into extra innings. Jones remained in the game, playing right field, and had two additional at-bats – both deep fly balls. The Tigers eventually won the game, 5-3 in 11 innings, and went on to sweep the Royals in three games.

"I had a strong sense of satisfaction," Jones said as he reflected on watching the Tigers celebrate. "I loved those guys, and I was okay. It was well deserved."[32]

On January 19, 1985, Jones married Lisa Cicarella of Detroit in a ceremony held in Jamaica. Alan Trammell, with whom Jones is particularly close, was the best man. They have three daughters, Lynsey, Alexis, and Skylar, and, as of 2023, one grandchild.

The Royals started the 1985 season on the road and their second series was in Detroit against the Tigers. Jones took some good-natured ribbing from his former teammates. Milt Wilcox, the Tigers' right-handed junkballer, shouted across the field, "Hey, Jonesy! You missed out on a ring."[33] The needling continued at lunch with friends Kirk Gibson, Tom Brookens, and Trammell. When Jones sat down at the table the three Tigers intentionally placed their hands on the table to prominently display their newly received World Series rings. Jones said he ultimately got the last laugh with his 1985 World Series ring. "Our rings trumped their rings by so much."[34]

Jones played in a career-high 110 games in 1985. His primary role was as a late-inning defensive replacement in the outfield. In 152 at-bats, he hit .211 and drove in 9 runs as the Royals went 91-71 to capture the AL West Division title for the second consecutive season. Reflecting on his career, Jones said he feels very fortunate: "I had a playing career longer than the average and enjoyed a long career in the game."[35]

"I cringe whenever somebody asks me about our reserve strength because you hope you don't have to use them," Royals manager Howser said in 1985. "But it's impossible to win pennants without guys like that who can contribute," referring to Jones, Sheridan, and other members of The Scrapheap.[36] The Scrapheap was the nickname given to a group of veteran players the Royals brought in to fortify their bench. In addition to Jones and Sheridan, The Scrapheap included Jorge Orta, Omar Moreno, and Dane Iorg.

The Royals faced the Toronto Blue Jays in the ALCS. After falling behind three games to one, the Royals rallied to win the series in seven games. Jones appeared in five games during the series, but had no plate appearances.

Jones played a larger role in the Royals' World Series seven-game victory over the St. Louis Cardinals. He played in six games during the Series and went 2-for-3 at the plate. In Game One, Jones had a pinch-hit triple off left-hander John Tudor. Though the Royals loaded the bases, Jones was stranded at third and the Royals lost 3-1. In Game Four Jones pinch-hit for pitcher Joe Beckwith and had a leadoff double off Tudor. Once again, the Royals failed to drive him home and lost 3-0, falling behind three games to one in the Series. Jones's final at-bat in the Series came in the Royals' 11-0 Series-clinching blowout victory. After replacing Lonnie Smith in left field in the top of the sixth, he faced left-handed Ken Dayley in the bottom of the seventh and flied out to right field.

During the celebration in the clubhouse after the game, Dick Howser approached Jones and apologized for not allowing him to pinch-hit for Smith as opposed to inserting him in the lineup as a defensive replacement. Unbeknownst to Howser at the time, Jones would have had a chance to establish a World Series record of three pinch hits in a Series. "That showed you what kind of guy Dick Howser was," Jones said.

After the Royals' World Series victory, Jones filed for free agency. That December he signed a nonguaranteed contract to return to the Royals for $185,000 in 1986, which gave him the opportunity to come to spring training and complete for a job.

The following spring, Jones, who had been a role player for his entire seven-year career to this point, was once again battling for a roster spot. He humbly told *The Sporting News*, "People come up to me and tell me all of the time, 'You should be playing more.' I tell them, 'No, I shouldn't.'" Jones said being a defensive replacement is "an unheralded job by all means. Sometimes it's boring, and you sit and talk to yourself. You're not going to get your name splattered in the paper. And, certainly, it's not a job you are going to get rich at. But to me it's a job that's very self-rewarding."[37]

The 1986 season was Jones's last. He played in 67 games. In 47 at-bats, he hit just .128 and the Royals finished third in the AL West with a record of 76-86. Now 33 years old, he played in the 527th and final game of his major-league career on October 4, the second-to-last game of the season. He was a ninth-inning defensive replacement for Rudy Law in left field. After the season Schuerholz informed Jones the Royals would not offer him a contract for 1987. After receiving no other offers, Jones retired as a player. However, his baseball career was far from over.

Jones began working as an investment broker with DSR Financial Services, a firm he founded. The former outfielder worked in this capacity until 1990, when an opportunity arose to coach with the Kansas City Royals. Jones was visiting Kansas City on business and was meeting with former teammate and Royals manager John Wathan. Wathan was looking for a first-base coach and encouraged Jones to interview for the position. The next morning Jones interviewed with general manager Herk Robinson. "I was more worried about catching my flight home than I was with how I answered the interview questions," Jones recalled. As fate would have it, Jones was offered the job and returned to the Royals organization as the team's first-base coach in 1991.

Jones was the first-base coach in 1991 and 1992. He was coaching first base on September 30, 1992, when George Brett recorded his 3,000th hit in Anaheim, only to be picked off first by Angels rookie left-hander Tim Fortugno. "Boy were the fans on me," Jones recalled.[38]

After the 1992 season, Jones and Adrian Garrett, the Royals third-base coach and hitting coach, were fired. John Boles, who was the farm director for the new Florida Marlins franchise, hired both.

Jones spent the next nine seasons as the manager of several minor-league clubs in the Marlins organization. He began his minor-league managerial career in 1993 with the Elmira (New York) Pioneers of the short-season Class-A New York-Pennsylvania League. Jones guided the Pioneers to a 31-44 record and third place in the NYPL's Pinckney Division.

From 1994 to 1997, Jones managed the Kane County (Geneva, Illinois) Cougars of the Class-A Midwest League. With the Cougars, Jones complied a record of 275-273, reaching the postseason in both 1995 and 1997. During his tenure with Kane County, Jones managed more than 20 players who eventually made it to the major leagues, including Antonio Alfonseca, Kevin Millar, Luis Castillo, Randy Winn, Álex González, Mark Kotsay, Ryan Dempster, and Scott Podsednik.

In 1998 Jones managed the Portland (Maine) Sea Dogs of the Double-A Eastern League. He guided the team to a third-place finish with a record of 66-75. This was followed by a two-year stint (1999-2000) as manager of the Calgary Cannons of the Triple-A Pacific Coast League. The Cannons finished in last place both years and had a combined record of 117-164.

Jones returned to the big leagues in 2001, joining the Florida Marlins as their first-base coach. When Tony Pérez was hired in midseason, replacing John Boles as manager, Jones was moved to third-base coach. After the season, Jones and the entire staff were fired.

In 2002 Jones managed the Macon Braves, the Class-A South Atlantic League affiliate of the Atlanta Braves. Macon had a record of 66-74 and finished fifth in the eight-team Southern Division.

In 2003 Jones joined the Boston Red Sox coaching staff as an outfield and baserunning coach. He returned to the NYPL circuit, a decade after he started his minor-league managerial career at Elmira, when he replaced John Deeble, who had to return to his native Australia. In his final managerial stint, Jones managed the Lowell (Massachusetts) Spinners for eight games. The Spinners (39-35) were 3-5 under Jones and finished in third place in the NYPL Stedler Division.

Jones finished his managerial career with a record of 558-635 (.468).

Jones rejoined the Red Sox coaching staff in 2004 and served as the team's first-base coach the year the Red Sox broke the Curse of the Bambino and won the World Series for the first time in 86 years. Recalling the Red Sox' epic comeback from a three-games-to-none deficit, Jones said, "With each win there was a mounting desperation on the part of the Yankees. We played perfect. The right guys were up at the right time during each of the last four games."[39]

Jones returned as first-base coach of the Red Sox in 2005 and was the first-base coach for the American League All-Star team. The All-Star Game was a special experience for Jones for many reasons. The game was held in Detroit, which allowed him to share the event with friends and family. The All-Star ring he received is one of his most cherished rings because of the Tiger that adorns it. The game had added significance because good friend Alan Trammell was the American League's honorary captain for the game. Finally, two players whom Jones managed at Kane County were on the All-Star rosters. Scott Podsednik, an outfielder with the Chicago White Sox and Luis Castillo of the Florida Marlins.

In 2006 Jones rejoined the team that drafted him out of Thiel in 1974, the Cincinnati Reds. He served as an outfield-baserunning roving instructor during the 2006 and 2007 seasons. "I loved that job. It gave me a chance to work with the kids and I was home one week every month," Jones said.[40] He then spent the next four years with the Atlanta Braves organization in a similar capacity.

In 2012 Jones became a volunteer coach for the Thiel College baseball team. "Lynn brings a wealth of big-league experience and baseball knowledge not only to our team, but our coaching staff as well," head baseball coach Joe Schaly said.[41]

Speaking about his role with the Tomcats, Jones said, "I offer some instruction, but instruction in college is different than instruction in the professional ranks. I basically try to help the coaching staff out and if they need things, I help obtain them."[42]

Jones resides in rural Pennsylvania, outside of Conneautville, with his wife, Lisa. The Joneses enjoy spending time at home, visiting with their granddaughter, and RVing.

SOURCES

In addition to the sources cited in the Notes, the author relied on Baseball-reference.com and Retrosheet.org.

ACKNOWLEDGMENTS

The author would like to thank Lynn Jones for his generosity with his time and openness to share his life story.

NOTES

1. The Talon Zipper company was the first zipper manufacturing company. It was founded in 1893 as the Universal Fastener Company, manufacturing hookless fasteners for shoes, but a move to Meadville, Pennsylvania, led to its becoming the first manufacturer of zippers. The company flourished through the 1960s when it is estimated that seven out of every 10 zippers were Talon zippers.
2. 2 Valeria M. Jones," Retrieved on April 10, 2023, from www.waidcolemanfh.com/obituary/Valeria-Jones.
3. "Valeria M. Jones."
4. Lynn Jones, interview, April 24, 2023.
5. Lynn Jones, interview, April 24, 2023.
6. Lynn Jones, interview, June 6, 2023.
7. Lynn Jones, interview, June 6, 2023.
8. "Hall of Fame: Lynn Jones." Retrieved on April 17, 2023, from https://thielathletics.com/honors/hall-of-fame/lynn-m-jones/69.
9. "Hall of Fame: Lynn Jones."
10. Lynn Jones, interview, June 6, 2023.
11. Lynn Jones, interview, June 6, 2023.
12. Lynn Jones, interview, June 6, 2023.
13. Meistickle played seven seasons in the minor leagues and finished with 12-14 with 9 saves and a 5.90 ERA.
14. Lynn Jones, interview, April 24, 2023.
15. "Class A Leagues," *The Sporting News*, August 23, 1975: 39.
16. Lynn Jones, interview, June 6, 2023.
17. Lynn Jones, interview, June 6, 2023.
18. Lynn Jones, interview, September 1, 2023.
19. First baseman Harry Spilman moved to third base and DeFrietes moved from the outfield to first base.
20. Lynn Jones, personal correspondence, August 28, 2023.
21. Lynn Jones, interview, June 6, 2023.
22. Lynn Jones, interview, April 24, 2023.
23. Lynn Jones, interview, April 24, 2023.
24. Lynn Jones, interview, April 24, 2023.
25. Lynn Jones, interview, August 29, 2023.
26. Lynn Jones, interview, June 6, 2023.
27. Steve Wulf, "Let's Give the Tigers a Great Big Hand: Take a Couple of Gridiron Greats, Throw in the Peerless Pine Bros., Ladle on Hot Sauce – And You Have a Nine-Game Detroit Winning Streak," *Sports Illustrated*, August 31, 1981. Retrieved on June 7, 2023, from https://vault.si.com/vault/1981/08/31/lets-give-the-tigers-a-great-big-hand-take-a-couple-of-gridiron-greats-throw-in-the-peerless-pine-bros-ladle-on-hot-sauce-and-you-have-a-nine-game-detroit-winning-streak.
28. "Lemon #1 Culprit in Tigers' Swoon," *The Sporting News*, July 5, 1982: 21-22.
29. "Forkball Turns Tobik into Bullpen 'King,'" *The Sporting News*, June 28, 1982: 31.
30. "Royals Sign Outfielder," *Iola* (Kansas) *Register*, December 7, 1983: 8.
31. "Royals Sign Outfielder."
32. Lynn Jones, interview, April 24, 2023.
33. Lynn Jones, interview, April 24, 2023.
34. Lynn Jones, interview, April 24, 2023.
35. Lynn Jones, interview, April 24, 2023.
36. Ben Walker, "Royals End Losing Skid," *Gettysburg* (Pennsylvania) *Times*, September 3, 1985: 15.
37. "Baseball: Royals," *The Sporting News*, March 31, 1986: 36.
38. Lynn Jones, interview, August 28, 2023.
39. Lynn Jones, interview, June 6, 2023.
40. Lynn Jones, interview, August 28, 2023.
41. "Lynn Jones," Retrieved on May 31, 2023, from https://thielathletics.com/sports/baseball/roster/coaches/lynn-jones-74/2180.
42. Lynn Jones, interview, June 6, 2023.

DANA LEVANGIE

BY SAUL WISNIA

It was as much a psychological move as a baseball one. Game Five of the 2004 American League Championship Series at Fenway Park was tied, 4-4, heading into the bottom of the ninth. Red Sox pitchers Curt Schilling, Derek Lowe, and Tim Wakefield, gloves in hand, began walking from the team's first-base dugout out to the bullpen. Fans noticed them making the trek and gave the trio a standing ovation, which was the desired effect.

Despite a dramatic extra-innings win against the Yankees in Game Four less than 24 hours earlier, the Red Sox still faced elimination in the best-of-seven series. They needed to beat New York three more times to reach the World Series, and while Schilling, Lowe, and Wakefield were not scheduled to pitch in this contest, the meaning of the moment was clear. In order to pull out this game, and then two on the road at Yankee Stadium, Boston would need all hands on deck – and all arms loose. Most of those looking on likely thought the architect of the decision was Boston manager Terry Francona, but it was in fact an individual far less known to those at Fenway and throughout Red Sox Nation.

Bullpen catcher Dana LeVangie.

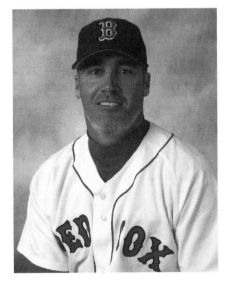

"I called from the bullpen and said, 'Hey, listen. Tell those guys to get their gloves and have them walk across the field,'" LeVangie would reflect later. "It was incredible, the intensity it brought to the park. It also sent a message to the Yankees: We're not going down without a fight, no matter what."[1]

In the end, LeVangie's move proved to be more than just good theater. The game went 14 innings, and Wakefield pitched one-hit ball for the last three to get the 5-4 win. Boston then punched its World Series ticket with two victories in New York, becoming the first major-league team ever to win a best-of-seven playoff series after being down 3-0.[2] These events, in a way, sum up LeVangie's unparalleled career. For nearly 30 years before he became pitching coach for one of the winningest teams in Red Sox history, LeVangie served his hometown club in numerous behind-the-scenes ways he could never have imagined when drafted as a player by the Boston organization in 1991. While earning World Series rings in four different roles with the Red Sox – bullpen catcher (2004), advance scout (2007), bullpen coach (2013), and pitching coach (2018) – he proved himself an indispensable part of the organization time and again, garnering the praise and ear of everyone from Francona to Hall of Fame pitcher Pedro Martínez for his baseball acumen.

"His understanding of the game, how to attack hitters, is second to none," Red Sox reliever Matt Barnes said of LeVangie in 2018, a consensus held by players and coaches across the decades. "He knows everybody from every team that's ever played. It's unbelievable."[3]

Before becoming a revered coach and scout, LeVangie started out like countless other New England kids who envisioned *playing* for the Boston Red Sox. The daughter of Jeanne and Alan LeVangie, he was born on August 11, 1969, in Brockton, Massachusetts, and was a three-sport athlete (football, wrestling, baseball) at Whitman-Hanson High School in nearby Hanson.[4] "I went to Fenway Park as much as I could," LeVangie said of his childhood. "I didn't watch as many games as I'd like because I was playing. When we played Wiffle ball, we pretended we were in Fenway Park. I always loved Carlton Fisk."[5]

When LeVangie graduated from Whitman-Hanson in 1987, his big-league dreams appeared behind him. He enrolled at Cape Cod Community College to study hotel and restaurant management that fall, and was not even known to the school's baseball coaching staff. "I was an OK player, but when I graduated from high school, I wasn't necessarily looking to keep playing ball," he said. "Once I got to [Cape Cod CC], I saw the team and wanted to get involved."[6]

LeVangie had changed his mind; he was not yet ready to put baseball completely in his rear-view mirror. He decided to try out for the Cape Cod CC team as a catcher, more out of necessity than a desire to be the next Pudge Fisk. Although he had barely played the position previously, LeVangie felt it offered him his best chance to make the squad and get playing time. The strategy worked, and he found he enjoyed being in the thick of the action behind the plate. "Deciding to play catcher was one of the best choices I ever made," he later said. "Playing catcher really made me a better communicator and it gave a better understanding of the game."[7]

LeVangie's play for Cape Cod CC during the next two seasons attracted interest from pro scouts as well as four-year colleges offering scholarships and two more years of eligibility. He chose to attend American International College, a Division II school in Springfield, Massachusetts, from which a handful of players had previously been drafted by major-league teams.[8]

And as LeVangie would prove time and again in his long career to come, it proved the right move at the right time.

LeVangie shined at American International (AIC). After a strong junior season for the Yellow Jackets in 1990, the right-handed hitter posted off-the-charts numbers as a senior: a .473 average, 13 homers, and 87 RBIs in less than 50 games.[9] He paced the Northeast-10 Conference in all three categories, led AIC to a 32-12 record, and helped the team to its first-ever berth in the College World Series. The performance earned LeVangie both Northeast-10 Player of the Year and Division II All-American first-team accolades, and he would later be inducted into the AIC Hall of Fame (in 2005) as well as the Northeast-10 Hall of Fame (in 2011).[10]

Although AIC was quickly eliminated from the College World Series, LeVangie's star was now in full ascent – leading to a most memorable day on June 6, 1991. That afternoon the 21-year-old prospect took part in the annual New England Collegiate All-Star Game at Fenway Park, collecting an RBI single in his first time playing on the hallowed ground where he had watched Fisk and the rest of his boyhood heroes perform. Then, after returning home that night, he learned by phone that the Red Sox had selected him in the 14th round of the 1991 major-league draft. "It was a dream come true," recalled LeVangie, who signed with legendary Boston scout Bill Enos shortly thereafter.[11]

LeVangie's professional playing career, which began later that same month with Elmira in the short-season Class-A New York-Penn League, wound up encompassing six years, seven teams, and four levels. While his defensive play and strong throwing arm were praised at each stop, he struggled when at the plate rather than behind it. He batted .149 at Elmira in 1991, .192 at Class-A Winter Haven in '92, and .188 at Class-A Fort Lauderdale in '93 – notching just one home run in a combined 191 games and 589 at-bats. "It was a mind thing," he later said of this period. "I got it set in my head that I couldn't hit professional pitching."[12]

Despite these struggles, the Red Sox felt strongly enough about LeVangie's catching skills and work ethic to promote him to Double-A Lynchburg in 1994. There he seemed to turn the corner offensively; given the chance to start, he had a .234 average and 3 homers in 79 games. "The organization wants LeVangie to catch more," Louisville manager Mark Meleski explained after one stretch in which LeVangie went 10-for-22. "He's definitely our best defensive catcher. And it just so happens right now he's swinging the bat very, very well. So that's helped his cause out too."[13]

Asked then what he thought was responsible for the improvement, LeVangie said, "I used to have a little loop in my swing, kind of a long swing, and now I'm throwing my hands directly at the ball." Meleski credited LeVangie's willingness to listen and learn from Red Sox minor-league batting instructor Steve Braun, who had worked with him to cut down his swing – leading to better contact and more line drives.[14]

Not surprisingly, given this development, LeVangie was bumped up the ladder yet again in 1995 to Double-A Trenton and Triple-A Pawtucket, the two top clubs in the Boston farm system. His average was back down to a combined .185 between the two spots, but again he seemed to adjust; although a broken hamate bone in his left wrist limited LeVangie to 25 games split between Trenton and Pawtucket in 1996, he hit a combined .220 in 75 at-bats with the highest OPS (.720) of his career.

He was, however, about to reach a crossroads in his professional life. "I talked to the Red Sox about my future in the offseason," he later recalled. "I was told that they planned on my catching at the Double-A or Triple-A level [in 1997] and I was feeling pretty good about the situation."[15] Two weeks later, however, another situation presented itself when Bob Schaefer, minor-league coordinator for the Red Sox, asked him if he wanted to put his playing career behind and go up to the majors as Boston's bullpen coach. "It was a full-time gig and I would be traveling with the team," LeVangie said of the offer. "It was the push that eventually led me in the direction of scouting and coaching."[16]

As bullpen catcher for the next eight seasons (1997-2004), LeVangie was with the Red Sox in uniform – home and away – from the start of spring training to the final game each year. In addition to loosening up starting pitchers on their offdays, he spent each game in the bullpen waiting for word from the manager or pitching coach to warm relievers up. The job was one of near-anonymity. Apart from those seated directly behind the Boston bullpen at Fenway Park and other big-league venues, most fans never saw LeVangie's face; even fewer heard his name.

The team, however, appreciated his work immensely. By providing daily scouting reports to the pitchers and coaching staff, and in discussing the best ways to approach each opposing hitter, he quickly earned the respect of both those in uniform and the front office. "Dana has a great eye for baseball," said Red Sox reliever Mike Timlin. "Catching in the bullpen, he could tell you something you were doing wrong while you were doing it. He had that kind of eye. He's a very learned baseball man. Awesome."[17]

One sign of the high regard players had for LeVangie came in 1998, when he was voted a full share of playoff bonus money after the Red Sox reached the postseason as a wild-card team.[18] At the time, LeVangie was still spending the offseason working as a bar manager, while his wife, Traci, taught sixth grade.[19] The couple would eventually have two children, a son, Liam, and a daughter, Avery, both of whom also excelled athletically.[20] Pedro Martínez, Boston's ace starter and arguably the best pitcher in the majors during this period, was another big LeVangie fan. Martínez suffered a variety of injuries to his priceless right arm, and throwing sessions with LeVangie – often under the scrutiny of coaches and media members – was a standard step in his rehab routine.[21] When reliever-turned-starter Derek Lowe was having trouble with his mechanics, working with LeVangie helped turn things around.

As an area native who was living with his young family in East Bridgewater, Massachusetts, year-round, LeVangie had the time of his life when Boston broke through and finally won the World Series in 2004.[22] "It was incredible," he said of that season. "Not only getting to where we had to be in the playoffs, but we had a great group of guys who came in expecting to win every day and have fun doing it. Then beating the Yankees (after being) down 3-0 was like winning the World Series itself. I probably didn't sleep for 12 days straight."[23]

Helping end Boston's 86-year title drought earned LeVangie a promotion to a new role in the organization: major-league scout. First as a pro scout (in 2005), and then as an advance scout (2006-2012), he now spent the majority of his time traveling away from the team rather than with it. As Bill Nowlin described the role in a SABR essay "Dana LeVangie: Every Game Is a Road Game," the advance scout "typically travels four to eight days ahead of the team, scouting a team the Sox will face a couple of series later. … LeVangie never sees his own team play. Every game is a road game, and he never gets to enjoy the companionship of his colleagues."[24]

Even though he was no longer around the team regularly, LeVangie remained a favorite of Boston's veteran players. Schilling was among the pitchers who praised the work of the team's advance scouts as vital to helping him put together an effective game plan, and catcher Jason Varitek said, "Having been with Dana and having developed a great deal of trust in him and his knowledge of the game … he observes the game so much there's probably nobody in the advance-scouting world that I would trust as much as him."[25]

There were certain times in particular that the skills of LeVangie and his fellow advance scouts were especially appreciated. When Boston closer Jonathan Papelbon picked off Colorado's Matt Holliday at first base in the eighth inning of Game Two of the 2007 World Series, it was advance scout Todd Claus' report on Holliday's running tendencies – passed on through Red Sox bench coach Brad Mills – that helped Papelbon gain the edge needed to make the play.[26]

A few days later, after the Red Sox completed their four-game sweep of the Rockies to clinch their second World Series championship in four years, rookie second baseman Dustin Pedroia took a moment during Boston's champagne-soaked celebration to praise the team's scouting staff. "Our scouts were unbelievable," Pedroia told reporters. "They're the best in baseball. You've got so much confidence because they give you so much information."[27]

USA Today writer Bob Nightengale was so impressed with Boston's dominance of Colorado that he devoted an entire story to the team's preparation. "Chief advance scouts Todd Claus and Dana LeVangie provided reports so precise the Red Sox players thought they were going into the field with cheat sheets," Nightengale wrote.[28] The statistics bore this out: Boston batters hit .333 during the Series, the second-best team average in World Series history, while the hard-hitting Rockies were held to a .218 mark.

It took back-to-back disappointing seasons by the Red Sox – the "chicken and beer" collapse of September 2011 that cost manager Terry Francona his job, and the last-place finish of 2012 that resulted in Francona's successor Bobby Valentine losing his – to bring LeVangie back in from the road. Valentine's replacement as manager was John Farrell, who as pitching coach with the team from 2007 to 2010 had benefited from LeVangie's wise counsel. Farrell reached out to LeVangie and offered him a position as bullpen coach.

"I got a phone call from John Farrell two weeks before spring training and he asked how interested I was," LeVangie said. "It was kind of a no-brainer."[29] Part of the appeal to LeVangie was the chance to have more time at home with his wife and kids in East Bridgewater; he estimated for reporters that he had spent an average of 270 days on the road each of the past seven years.

For Farrell, his new coach checked several boxes. Like longtime catcher and team captain Varitek, with whom he had a close relationship, LeVangie was already very familiar with Boston's pitchers and catchers. His own experience as a top-notch defender meant he could serve in a dual role as a catching instructor, and he could continue to assist in advance scouting as well. "He has been a valuable asset to the Red Sox in a variety of roles," Farrell said. "His vast knowledge of the major leagues, particularly the American League, will enable him to make an impact with our staff and with our bullpen."[30]

The impact Farrell was hoping for came immediately. After compiling a 4.70 ERA as a staff in 2012 (12th in the AL), Red Sox pitchers improved to a 3.79 ERA (sixth) with LeVangie preparing game plans with pitching coach Juan Nieves. Among position players, one of the season's brightest stories was the defensive progress made by heavy-hitting catcher Jarrod Saltalamacchia – thanks in part to extensive work put in with LeVangie.[31] Not coincidentally, Boston's record changed dramatically as well – from 69-93 to 97-65 – and after a worst-to-first finish in the competitive AL East, the Red Sox went on to beat the St Louis Cardinals in the 2013 World Series.[32]

As the fortunes of the team varied during the next four seasons, LeVangie's value remained impactful. Red Sox catchers ranked second in the major leagues by throwing out 31.6 percent of opposing baserunners from 2014 to 2017, and the 3.15 ERA compiled by Boston relievers in 2017 was second-best in the majors as well. LeVangie was lauded for his work mixing and matching relievers for different game situations. When Saltalamacchia left as a free agent, LeVangie helped mentor young catchers Blake Swihart and Christian Vázquez. The latter would emerge as one of the league's most respected young receivers.

Late in the 2015 season, management showed its respect for and faith in LeVangie once again. When Farrell was forced to take a leave of absence from the team to undergo lymphoma treatment, and bench coach Torey Lovullo was named interim manager, he elevated LeVangie to interim bench coach for the remainder of the campaign.[33] "To have that bench coach there to challenge some of my thoughts, to endorse some of my thoughts, is going to be nice to have, especially given Dana's background," Lovullo said. "There's immediate trust there."[34]

Yet another promotion for LeVangie, this time without an interim label, was to come. After Boston lost in the divisional round of the AL playoffs for the second straight season in 2017, Farrell was fired and replaced by former Boston utility player Alex Cora. Then, in a surprising move, Cora named LeVangie his pitching coach. LeVangie was the first nonpitcher to hold this role on the Red Sox since Mike Roarke in 1994, as well as the only pitching coach in the majors in 2018 to claim that distinction.[35] But Cora, who had gotten to know LeVangie while an infielder with Boston from 2005 to 2008, defended his selection.

"I was very impressed with Dana when I played here," Cora said. "He understands the game, and it seems like we talk the same language. When everybody started talking about me being a manager, he was a guy that I always considered was going to be part of my staff. He's well-prepared, and versatile enough that he can work with catchers and be a pitching coach. I'm very comfortable with Dana being in this role. He knows the guys, and he's going to be someone that I'm going to really rely on and I'm going to trust."[36]

Pedro Martínez was similarly enthused. Arriving at spring training in 2018 for his sixth season as a special instructor with Boston, Martínez told reporters he planned to be more hands-on with current Red Sox pitchers than in the past due to his friendship with and respect for LeVangie. "Every year I do enjoy it. This year, it's special," Martínez said. "I'm committed to helping out my friend Dana and the organization, and I have a little bit more leverage so I'm using it."[37]

Cora agreed, adding that "Pedro connecting with Dana, and for us to understand he's not stepping on anybody's toes is great. It's a great situation not only for us as a staff, but also the players."[38]

For one year, at least, the arrangement worked beautifully. Red Sox pitchers ranked third in the American League in 2018 with a 3.75 ERA, and held opponents to a .237 batting average against – the lowest mark by a Boston staff in the Live Ball Era (post-1920).[39] Partnering with Cora, LeVangie carefully monitored the workload of top starters Chris Sale, David Price, and Rick Porcello – not allowing them to go too deep into games too often – with a goal that all would remain healthy and strong for the stretch drive.

This was particularly important with Sale, the ace of the staff, who had struggled in September of the previous season. When, despite these precautions, Sale's velocity diminished in October 2018, LeVangie worked with him on his mechanics and encouraged him to "save his bullets" and not throw too many fastballs.[40] And after romping to the American League East title with a 108-54 record, the Red Sox went on to win 11 of 14 postseason games. Sale, who was briefly hospitalized with a stomach ailment in the playoffs, wound up closing out Game Five of the World Series against the Los Angeles Dodgers – clinching the title for Boston.[41]

Players and coaches heaped praise on LeVangie during and after the 2018 season. "Dana definitely goes about it the right way," said Price. "He puts in the work and the time. Whenever he says something, I may not know it at the time, but as soon as he says it, I'm like, 'That is what's going on, and that's something I can fix.'" Matt Barnes credited LeVangie for helping him adapt to the majors and relief pitching, stating that "he had this passion for the game, and for knowing each guy on their own level." Varitek, who had worked with LeVangie for 20 years as a player and coach, cited his "unbelievable game vision" and "ability to see the game through different lenses."[42]

Despite such support, and his long list of accomplishments, LeVangie eventually met the fate that befalls almost all coaches and managers after things go sour. When the defending World Series champion Red Sox failed in 2019 to even reach the postseason, finishing third in the AL East with an 84-78 record, the club's team ERA of 4.70 (19th in the majors) stood out as a major cause.[43] Sale, beset by injuries, saw his ERA balloon from 2.11 to 4.40, and fellow starters Price and Nathan Eovaldi were also hurt. Boston's relief pitching – a key to the previous year's success – stumbled to rebound from the loss of closer Craig Kimbrel to free agency.

Just after turning 50, and completing his 29th year in the Red Sox organization, LeVangie was out as pitching coach – reassigned in October 2019 to a position as a pro scout for the team.[44] Because of his respect around the game, there was some thought that LeVangie might be offered a coaching job with another club. Peter Abraham of the *Boston Globe* speculated that it could be as a bench, pitching, or bullpen coach for the Pittsburgh Pirates, who had just hired former Red Sox general manager Ben Cherington as their GM.[45]

As of the end of the 2023 season, however, LeVangie remained with Boston in a pro scouting role. He was no longer in uniform, and no longer interacting with players on a daily basis. But there was certainly no doubt in anybody's mind within the organization that after 33 years and four World Series titles with the Red Sox, he was still finding ways to help his hometown team.

SOURCES

In addition to the sources cited in the Notes, the author consulted Baseball-Reference.com, the Baseball Cube, and the *2019 Boston Red Sox Media Guide*.

NOTES

1   Allan Wood and Bill Nowlin: *Don't Let Us Win Tonight: An Oral History of the 2004 Boston Red Sox's Impossible Playoff Run* (Chicago: Triumph Books, 2014), 146-147.

2   Prior to 2004, there had been 25 teams to trail a best-of-seven series 3-0. Of these 25, 20 lost the fourth game, 3 lost the fifth, and 2 lost the sixth. None had reached a Game Seven.

3   Julian McWilliams, "LeVangie Out as Sox Pitching Coach," *Boston Globe*, October 9, 2019: C4.

4   LeVangie's mother remarried after his father's death and became Jeanne Fenton.

5   Howard Herman, "2 Sox Fans Live a Dream in NY-Penn," *Berkshire Eagle* (Pittsfield, Massachusetts), August 4, 1991: 21.

6   Mike Kehoe, "Dana LeVangie: Journey to the Big Leagues," *Main Sheet* (Cape Cod Community College school paper), April 9, 2019: online edition. https://mainsheetcapecod.wordpress.com/2019/04/09/dana-levangie-journey-to-the-big-leagues/.

7   Kehoe.

8   AIC draft picks prior to LeVangie, per The Baseball Cube: Robert Carlson (1965), Charles Paglierani (1969), Tom Farias (1972-73), Paul Stockley (1979), Jim Van Houten (1983-84), and David Brown (1989).

9   LeVangie's senior statistics vary depending on the source; these are from the *2019 Red Sox Media Guide*. The Northeast-10 record book has him leading the conference in 1991 with a .473 average, 10 homers, and 66 RBIs, but it's unclear if those numbers are only from conference games.

10 List of Northeast 10 Hall of Famers, found on conference's official website: https://www.northeast10.org/halloffame/Complete_HOF_List.

11 Paul Harber, "Former Prospect Makes It to the Bigs as Sox Bullpen Catcher," *Boston Globe*, September 26, 1999: 33.

12 Harber.

13 Gary Crockett, "LeVangie Keeps L-Sox Winning," *Lynchburg* (Virginia) *News and Advance*, May 14, 1994: 13.

14 Crockett.

15 Marvin Pave, "Sox Scout Takes Role as Bullpen Coach," *Boston Globe*, March 10, 2013 (online edition). https://www.bostonglobe.com/metro/regionals/south/2013/03/10/former-whitman-hanson-standout-dana-levangie-back-field-for-red-sox/lt9O5JuBCldJIQxHxDhwfP/story.ht.

16 Pave.

17 Bill Nowlin, "Dana LeVangie: Every Game Is a Road Game," in Jim Sandoval and Bill Nowlin, eds., *Can He Play? A Look at Baseball Scouts and Their Profession* (Phoenix: SABR, 2011), 160.

18 Harber.

19 Harber.

20 Both LeVangie kids played Division I college sports; Liam was a right-handed pitcher at Bryant University, and Avery a forward on the Northeastern University women's soccer team.

21 Gordon Edes, "Martinez to Skip Start; Williams Out of Loop," *Boston Globe*, June 13, 2001: 83.

22 In the official 2004 Red Sox team photograph that hangs in bars and rec rooms throughout New England to this day, LeVangie is in uniform and fifth from the right in the second row, just to the right of rookie pitcher Lenny DiNardo.

23 Erin Shannon, "Whitman Native Dana Levangie Settles In as Red Sox Bullpen Coach," *Brockton Enterprise*, April 8, 2013 (online edition). https://www.enterprisenews.com/story/sports/pro/2013/04/08/whitman-native-dana-levangie-settles/40055357007/.

24 Nowlin.

25 Nowlin.

26 Gordon Edes, "Sox' Scouts' Honor: Attention to Detail," *Boston Globe*, October 28, 2007: 33.

27 Bob Nightengale, "Scouts Play Critical Role in Series Sweep," *USA Today*, October 30, 2007, reprinted in *Mansfield* (Ohio) *News Journal*: 15.

28 Nightengale.

29 Shannon.

30 Nick Cafardo, "LeVangie Gets the Nod," *Boston Globe*, February 6, 2013: C5.

31 Nick Cafardo, "Catcher Handling This," *Boston Globe*, May 21, 2013: C2.

32 After the 2013 season, LeVangie was part of the Red Sox three-day holiday caravan that brought the team's three World Series trophies to local schools, businesses, and hospitals.

33 As a result of these moves, Class-A pitching coach Bob Kipper was elevated to interim bullpen coach. The Red Sox went 28-20 under this arrangement, although Baseball-Reference credits Farrell as manager for the entire 78-84 season. Farrell returned as manager at the start of the 2016 season.

34 Peter Abraham, "Coaching Staff Gets Makeover," *Boston Globe*, August 17, 2015: C3.

35 Like LeVangie, Roarke was a catcher with New England roots (born in West Warwick, Rhode Island), whose success as a college player led to his being signed by a Boston team – although in Roarke's case it was the Boston Braves who signed him out of Boston College in 1952. After nearly a decade in the minors, Roarke hit .230 as a backup catcher for the Detroit Tigers from 1961 to 1964 before stints as a major-league bullpen catcher and later a pitching coach for several clubs including the Red Sox.

36 Audio from interview with Cora upon LeVangie's hiring, archived on MLB.com "Film Room." https://www.mlb.com/video/LeVangie-on-joining-sox-staff-c1866646883.

37 Ian Browne, "Pitching Staff Getting Tips from Pedro," MLB.com, February 16, 2018. https://www.mlb.com/news/red-sox-staff-getting-tips-from-pedro-martinez-c266612762.

38 Browne.

39 The previous lowest batting average compiled against a Boston pitching staff post-1920 came against the 1967 "Impossible Dream" Red Sox that also reached the World Series. (LeVangie bio, *2019 Red Sox Media Guide*).

40 Alex Speier, "Coach: Chris Sale Is Fine," *Boston Globe* (appeared in *Hartford Courant*, October 15, 2018: C3.

41 LeVangie's knowledge of major league pitchers was crucial at the 2018 trade deadline, when he identified Nathan Eovaldi of Tampa Bay as someone who could help Boston with some small tweaks to his delivery. Once he was picked up, Eovaldi worked with LeVangie and assistant coach Brian Bannister to make the adjustments and recorded a 3.33 ERA in the rest of the regular season – then lowered it to 1.61 in 22⅓ dominant postseason innings.

42 Chad Jennings, "Dana LeVangie Is a Red Sox Institution," *The Athletic*, October 2, 2019.

43 The ERA for Boston's starters was even worse – 4.95 – than the team's overall total.

44 LeVangie's replacement as Red Sox pitching coach, former big-league pitcher Dave Bush, held the position for four seasons. Bush was fired after a last-place finish in 2023 during which Boston's starting pitchers averaged 4.8 innings per start, 27th in the majors.

45 Peter Abraham, "Red Sox Rotation Fix? A Few Ways It Could Go," *Boston Globe*, November 24, 2019: C6.

BRAD MILLS

BY WILL HYLAND

James Bradley "Brad" Mills was born on January 19, 1957, in Exeter, California, in the state's Central Valley. As a young boy, he and his three brothers took frequent trips with their father, a cattle rancher and orange farmer, to San Francisco or Oakland to see the Giants or Athletics. The car rides were often filled with discussions about baseball, which Mills credits with developing his love for the game.[1]

Being a baseball-obsessed kid during his youth led Mills to idolize Giants superstar Willie Mays during his Little League years. However, his father encouraged him to play infield rather than outfield, and young Brad acquiesced.

He played baseball at Exeter Union High School, which also produced baseball players Satoshi Hirayama, Adam Pettyjohn, and Jeriome Robertson. Mills played third base, and as a big leaguer measured 6-feet and 196 pounds. He batted left-handed. In 2010 his number 7 was retired at Exeter Union.

After high school, Mills went to the College of the Sequoias (COS), a junior college in nearby Visalia. While playing for the COS Giants for two seasons, Mills was named First Team All-Conference and the team's Most Valuable Player in 1976. The following season, he was named team captain.

This recognition propelled Mills to continue his college career at the Division I level at the University of Arizona, even though he was drafted in 1977 in the 16th round by the Minnesota Twins. In 1978, his first year at Arizona as a junior, Mills batted .435 with 51 RBIs and only 9 strikeouts in 54 games. His senior year, he batted .361 with 8 home runs and 58 RBIs. Exposure as a significant prospect wasn't the only thing Mills experienced at Arizona. A teammate helped him immensely in his career and became one of his best friends in baseball. The teammate was Terry Francona, son of former big-leaguer Tito Francona and a blue-collar corner infielder and outfielder with a sky-high ceiling.[2]

Terry Francona led Arizona to the 1980 College World Series championship. He was named the tournament's Most Outstanding Player and won the Golden Spikes Award as the best amateur player in the United States. Mills had moved on to pro ball by that time; the two saved their moments of fame together for the big leagues.

After college ball, Mills was taken 426th overall in the 17th round of the 1979 draft by the Montréal Expos, 14 picks ahead of Orel Hershiser and 67 ahead of Don Mattingly. All three ended up coaching after their careers.

Mills made his professional debut in the summer of 1979 for the West Palm Beach Expos, the Expos' advanced Class-A affiliate. In 78 games he batted .271 with 5 home runs and a .402 on-base percentage. His high OBP was aided primarily by the 58 walks he received. Plate discipline and the ability to get on base remained one of Mills' best assets throughout his minor-league career.

The next season, 1980, Mills made the jump to Double-A Memphis, where in 55 games he batted .295 with 44 RBIs. That performance earned him a promotion to Triple-A Denver. For the Bears, Mills had 201 at-bats as an everyday player in 52 games. During his time with Denver he batted .289 and earned the most coveted call-up of them all.

On June 8, 1980, Mills made his major league debut with Montréal during a doubleheader against the St. Louis Cardinals at Olympic Stadium. In game two of the twin bill, Mills got the start at third base and went 1-for-3 with a single and a walk. However, his time with the Expos in 1980 was short-lived, and he finished the season with 18 hits in 21 games.

In 1981 Mills returned to Denver and had arguably his best minor-league season yet at Triple A. He played in 118 games, the first time in his career that he exceeded 300 at-bats in a season with a single club. (He ended his time in Denver with 477 plate appearances.) He hit .314 with 12 home runs and 66 RBIs, and while his walks were down, he finished with an .850 OPS. This performance earned him a late-season call-up in August to Montréal, where he had another "cup of coffee," going 5-for-21 in 17 games.

Mills spent 1982 as a bench player for the Expos, with a brief spell at Wichita, Montréal's new Triple-A affiliate. With the Expos he had only 73 plate appearances, batting .224, the first time he hit less than .250 for his primary team. Mills was teammates that season with Andre Dawson, a 2010 inductee in the National Baseball Hall of Fame, and Bill Lee, a member of the Boston Red Sox Hall of Fame.

In 1983 Mills played mostly with Wichita, with two stints with the Expos, in the spring and in September. In 81 games at

Wichita, he batted .317 with 46 RBIs. One of his three strikeouts with Montréal was at the hands of Nolan Ryan on April 27, and it was Ryan's 3,509th, exceeding Walter Johnson's then current record of 3,508. As it turned out, it was Mills' last year with an appearance in a major-league game; his at-bat against Ryan etched him in history as part of a baseball trivia question.[3]

Injuries began to plague Mills' career in the final three seasons of his professional tenure. And while he still produced modestly when healthy, his quest to return to the major leagues ran dry by 1986 as a result. He batted a healthy .315 for Indianapolis in 1984 but was traded in July to Houston, which sent him to its Tucson affiliate. After reaching free agency in the Fall of 1985, Mills joined the Triple-A Iowa Cubs in 1986 but unfortunately experienced a devastating knee injury while baserunning that season all but ended his playing career. He suffered a torn ACL, MCL, and cartilage after his cleat was caught in second base.[4] Though as his playing days closed, the next rewarding chapter of his baseball life opened.

Following his playing career, Mills was named the manager of the Rookie-level Wytheville Cubs (Appalachian League). The team finished out of the postseason but the Cubs were impressed by Mills' performance, and for the next five seasons he moved up the organization's managerial ladder. His best seasons came with Peoria of the Midwest League in 1989 and Winston-Salem of the Carolina League in 1990-91: 80 or more victories in each season. In 1992 the Cubs rewarded Mills with a promotion to the Triple-A Iowa Cubs. In 5½ years, Mills had gone from an injured player looking for his next big-league call-up to a seasoned minor-league skipper just one step away from coaching in the majors.

Mills had an underperforming 1992 season at Iowa: a 51-92 slate. And in 1993 he found himself in a new organization, managing the Colorado Rockies' Triple-A affiliate in Colorado Springs. Mills' team struggled and finished 16 games behind in their division, missing the playoffs. In his second season, 1994, the Sky Sox made it to the postseason where they lost in the semifinals. (This was also the season of the player strike in the major leagues.)

In 1995, the major-league season resumed and the Pacific Coast League carried on as usual too. Despite a modest 77-66 regular-season record, Colorado Springs qualified for the postseason and went on to win the league championship, beating Salt Lake three games to two. It was Mills' first championship as a skipper.

The 1996 season was Mills' last with the Rockies organization. Colorado Springs plunged to 10th place in the PCL and failed to repeat as champions. However, that season Mills still had the opportunity to manage future major-league skipper Craig Counsell and future Hall of Famer Larry Walker. Around the same time, his old college teammate Terry Francona was named manager of the Philadelphia Phillies. Francona hired Mills to be his first-base coach, marking their reunification and starting a new chapter of their friendship in the dugout. Mills later reflected fondly on his journey through the minor leagues and its impact on his career during a 2004 interview with SABR's Bill Nowlin.

"There's things that you learn in the minor leagues, either as a coach or a manager in the minor leagues," Mills recalled. "You learn how to teach. You learn how to talk to people. You just kind of mature and grow in your profession, which is a professional baseball coach. That's kind of like your developing ground or whatever. There's things that you can learn, but it's just so much different at the major league level. It's so much different but that can help season you and get you ready for the major leagues."[5]

But despite reaching the major leagues, working with Francona, and having future World Series champions in Scott Rolen and Curt Schilling as part of the roster, the Phillies never finished above .500 during the four years that Mills and Francona spent in Philadelphia.

At the end of the 2000 season, 20 years since their days in Arizona, Francona was fired by the Phillies and Mills left with him, as was customary for positional coaches when a manager was fired. They went separate ways for a few years. Francona moved on to Cleveland as a scout, then to Texas and Oakland as a bench coach. Mills went back to the minors in 2002 to manage the Las Vegas 51s, the Triple-A affiliate of the Los Angeles Dodgers. Knowing he was managing in one of the most distracting cities in America, Mills told his players early in the season that he would only "get them out of jail" if it happened during the first few days of the season.[6] His tough love worked, as the 51s qualified for the postseason with Mills' leadership, but lost to the eventual champions, the Edmonton Trappers, in the semifinals.

Photo by Bill Nowlin.

Mills left Las Vegas after one season to return to the Expos organization, spending the next to last year of the club's existence in Canada as their bench coach. This was a post that Mills spent a lot of time in throughout his career, most notably under Francona.

After only one season back in Montréal, Mills was invited into the Red Sox coaching staff to serve as Francona's bench coach starting in 2004. This tenure was arguably the most successful in Mills' career in the dugout. The 2004 Red Sox team, led by Francona and Mills, became one of the most storied teams in the history of the sport. Boston had gone 86 years without winning a World Series title, and even went to Game Seven of the American League Championship Series the year before, losing to the New York Yankees. But despite the lofty expectations, the team performed exceptionally well at the beginning of the 2004 season, and even better during the months of August and September, ultimately finishing with a 98-64 record. In October, they completed a three-game sweep of the Anaheim Angels, setting up a rematch with New York. And when the team went down three games to none in the series, they were practically left for dead, only to complete the greatest postseason series comeback in major-league history, punching their ticket to the World Series, in which they dispatched St. Louis in a sweep. It was Boston's first championship since 1918 and the first of Mills' career as well.

After disappointing finishes in 2005 and 2006, the Red Sox once again flourished in 2007 under the leadership of Mills and Francona. From start to finish, Boston played like the best team in the league, led not only by returning champs Curt Schilling, David Ortiz, Jason Varitek, and Manny Ramírez, but also by a new young core of players that included Dustin Pedroia, Jon Lester, Jonathan Papelbon, and Jacoby Ellsbury. The Red Sox won their first division crown since 1995 and entered the postseason as a favorite to win another World Series championship. After disposing once more of the Angels, they rallied from another deficit in the ALCS to top the Cleveland Indians, boosted by masterful pitching from Josh Beckett and timely hitting from the offense. In the World Series, Mills coached against his former team, the Rockies, who had just won 21 of 22 games to reach the fall classic. However, Colorado was no match for the ruthless Red Sox, who completed their second four-game sweep in four years to win their second title of the decade. At that point, it seemed that Mills and Francona belonged in Boston together forever. Tony Massarotti, a longtime Boston baseball commentator and writer, told a story in his book *This Is Our City* of a time shortly after this season when the two of them were applauded by guests at a Boston restaurant.[7]

But of course, not all baseball dynasties last forever. At the end of the 2009 season, Mills was given the opportunity to interview for the Houston Astros vacant managerial position. Mills won the job and Astros general manager Ed Wade rewarded him with a two-year deal and a one-year club option for 2012. Wade had worked with Francona in Philadelphia and respected his endorsement of Mills.

"This organization and this city, as I have said many times in this process, has a very good name in major league baseball," said Mills at his opening press conference. "I'm thrilled and excited to be involved in it and get on board and help keeping us going in the right direction. The experience is going to aid mightily in helping this organization move forward and become winners as well."[8]

Wade added, "The big separator in this thing is the chair he's sat in in Boston for the last several years. He's coached in 45 postseason games and two World Series and has more World Series rings than anybody in this room."[9] It was clear that Mills' success with Boston as the number two man and his close relationship with Francona were factors in his landing the Houston job; Wade also lauded Mills' experience as a communicator and his ability to properly organize a team.[10]

The Astros though, were nearing their lowest point from a competitive standpoint, four long years past their 2005 World Series berth. Unfortunately for Mills, he caught the franchise development curve just before Houston became a perennial powerhouse in the late 2010s after moving to the American League.

In 2010, Houston had some well-known names in Mills' first season as a big-league skipper, including Roy Oswalt, Carlos Lee, and Lance Berkman as well as younger players like Jason Castro and Hunter Pence. Mills also managed catcher Kevin Cash, who went on to manage a big-league team of his own, just as Counsell did. But despite the talented names, Houston underperformed, going 76-86 and missing the playoffs. Faces-of-the-franchise Berkman and Oswalt were eventually dealt in midseason.

By 2011, largely the same squad remained, but the results regressed to a point where the Astros lost over 100 games. The franchise was clearly in a rebuild. Mills had his 2012 option picked up for the following season, but he was fired on August 18, 2012.

Mills took his talents to the Cleveland Indians in 2013, reuniting again with Francona, who had been named manager after his dismissal from Boston, and serving as his third-base coach. That iteration of the Indians included a number of talented players, but the team had disappointing finishes in 2014 and 2015, finishing over .500 in both seasons but failing to make the postseason. The Indians stuck with Francona and his staff. By this point, Mills had been promoted to bench coach.

As in Boston, this was a recipe for success in Cleveland for the next two seasons. In 2016 the Indians marched toward an American League pennant and marched through October, sweeping Mills' former club the Red Sox. However, in the World Series, Cleveland fell in a dramatic Game Seven to the Chicago Cubs, a team of destiny put together by general manager Theo Epstein, the man who hired Mills and Francona in Boston. Chicago, as Boston did in 2004, broke a "curse" of massive proportions, winning their first title in 108 years.

Even with the letdown of losing the World Series, the Indians stayed resilient in 2017 and put together their best regular season since 1954. Led by basically the same core of players, Cleveland scorched through the second half of the season, winning 22 games in a row at one point to set an American League record. But a few weeks before that happened, bench coach Mills was forced to take over the Indians on an interim basis while Francona underwent a heart procedure. The situation lasted five games, but with Cleveland being the defending league champion, Francona was to manage the American League team in the 2017 All-Star Game. He ended up not participating due to the operation, allowing Mills to manage the All-Star squad along with the rest of the Indians staff. Tampa Bay Rays manager Kevin Cash, who played under Mills in Boston and Houston, was the bench coach. The American League team won 2-1 on a go-ahead home run by Robinson Canó in the 10th inning.

Cleveland failed to win a postseason round in both 2017 and 2018, losing to the Yankees and Astros respectively. By 2019, much of the Indians' young core had aged. Mills and Francona spent their last year together in the dugout in 2019; however even with an impressive 93-69 record, the Indians missed the playoffs.

When the COVID-19 pandemic unfolded in early 2020, the major-league season was in jeopardy as spring training was stopped. Just before that time, Brad Mills suffered the loss by drowning of his grandson, Beau.[11] Beau was also the name of Mills' only son, who was drafted in 2007 by the Indians but retired in 2012 from professional baseball. Mills and his wife of 45 years, Rhonda, also have two daughters, Taylor and Rochelle.[12] His grandson was just 18 months old at the time of his death. Mills did not coach in 2020 or beyond, opting out of that season in order to spend more time with his family in the wake of the tragedy and the ongoing pandemic.[13]

The support Mills received at the end of his career and during that horrible time was a testament to the strong relationships he had built over four decades in baseball. Cleveland pitcher Mike Clevinger once commented of Mills, "You trust what he's saying because you know there's a lot of time and effort and there's real love and want in what he's doing with his work."[14] There may not be a better compliment of a coach, leader, or mentor than that. Brad Mills is a steadfast disciple of the game and a devoted family man. His adoration for baseball began in the shadows of Candlestick Park, and his time in the game spanned generations, taking his career from coast to coast.

SOURCES

In addition to the sources cited in the Notes, the author consulted numerous websites including Baseball-Reference.com, MiLB.com, and TheBaseballCube.com.

NOTES

1. Pat McManamon, "Brad Mills: A Baseball Life That Forged an Unshakeable Friendship with Terry Francona," *The Athletic*, February 5, 2020. Accessed February 18, 2023. https://theathletic.com/1583141/2020/02/05/brad-mills-a-baseball-life-that-forged-an-unshakeable-friendship-with-terry-francona-cleveland-indians.
2. McManamon.
3. McManamon.
4. McManamon.
5. Bill Nowlin interview with Brad Mills, June 9, 2004.
6. McManamon.
7. Tony Massarotti, *This Is Our City: Four Teams, Twelve Championships, and How Boston Became the Most Dominant Sports City in the World* (New York: Abrams Press, 2022), 176.
8. Brian McTaggart, "Mills Named Astros Manager." MLB.com, October 27, 2009. Accessed February 18, 2023. https://web.archive.org/web/20121003064545/http://houston.astros.mlb.com/news/article.jsp?ymd=20091027&content_id=7558016.
9. McTaggart.
10. McTaggart.
11. Paul Hoynes, "Cleveland Indians' Coaching Staff, Front Office Attend Funeral of Brad Mills' Grandson," Cleveland.com, February 22, 2020. Accessed March 7, 2023. https://www.cleveland.com/tribe/2020/02/cleveland-indians-coaching-staff-front-office-attend-funeral-of-brad-mills-grandson.html.
12. McManamon.
13. Mandy Bell, "Mills Won't Return as Tribe's Bench Coach." MLB.Com, October 31, 2020. Accessed April 8, 2023. https://www.mlb.com/guardians/news/brad-mills-will-not-return-as-indians-bench-coach.
14. McManamon.

EUCLIDES "EUKY" ROJAS

BY TONY S. OLIVER

Ninety miles. To most baseball fans, the term refers to fastball speed, a pitch whose "standard" for major-league success hinges on such baseline velocity. A ball thrown at such speed can cross home plate in little more than a second. By contrast, it takes much longer to travel the 90 miles that separate Cuba and Florida, especially when the voyager attempts to cross the treacherous waters in a jerry-rigged boat. Some reach the mainland while others languish at sea, much as aspiring players can remain mired in the minor leagues while others make the big show.

Pirates (the real kind, not those who play in Pittsburgh) once roamed the strait, but they took far sturdier ships than the one that took Euclides Rojas. He spent five days adrift, enough to have read Hemingway's *Old Man and the Sea* countless times, but unlike the book's protagonists, who discussed baseball while waiting for the fish to bite, Rojas and his 12 companions dreamed of freedom.

Euclides was born on August 25, 1967, in Havana, eight years after Fidel Castro's revolution took over Cuba. "Nené," his single mother, raised seven children and instilled an early passion for baseball; years later, she would become a fixture in Euclides' games.[1] He grew up in La Timba, home to many government institutions and the Plaza de la Revolución (Revolution Square). As a child, he told his mother he would like to be a musician, a doctor, or a baseball player. Much like baseball, one out of three ain't bad.

Although he always liked the pitching mound, Euclides' earlier coaches suggested that he play the infield to avoid putting undue stress on his arm. In his midteens, he was finally allowed to pitch, and he quickly made the National Series team with Guira and, a year later, with Industriales, the club that would forge his identity. He credited his coaches, Mario Muñiz, Boricua Jiménez, Yosvani Gallego, and Isidoro León, for his development, which began at age 11 from José Luis Acuña School. He modeled his preparation after Agustín Marquetti, Armando Capiró, and Pedro Medina, Industriales' big three. Medina, a catcher, would impart sage advice to his young pupil about how to attack batters. Gallego imparted a zest for control upon his young charge, highlighting the relevance of pitch location and displaying the importance of placing pitches where needed. Much like his namesake, the father of geometry, Euclides' aptitude with angles helped him on the mound.

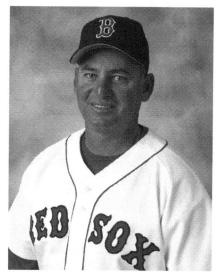

At age 14, Euclides was asked to face the fearsome slugger Antonio Muñoz with the caveat that the hitter should not win the game. Rojas promptly hit Muñoz in the back, awarding him first base, and then induced an out from the next batter. The matchup pitted the prospects of Industriales with the Cuban club traveling to Canada for the 1981 Intercontinental Cup, ultimately won by the United States. The act of bravado won Rojas a spot with the Industriales parent (senior) club.

Rojas was left off the Cuban youth team in 1982 due to concerns about his brother's political opinions, although Rojas himself noted that it would have been a great honor to represent his nation.[2] According to Rojas, the sibling was jailed for four years because of his unwillingness to work for the government, and his parents' business was seized by the government during his childhood.[3] The episode would prove to be harbinger of future events that would ultimately make Rojas question his government.

At the urging of a coach, his manager slotted Rojas in the fireman's role, not yet popularized in the major leagues. Rojas was puzzled, asking point-blank if that was "pitching, right?"[4] He found the opportunity a good fit with his competitive nature and his willingness to pitch every day.

Rojas debuted in the Serie Nacional at 16 and competed against some peers twice his age. He appeared in nine games for the Industriales, five of them starts, and while he won two and lost two, his 4.91 ERA was his career worst. He became a full-time reliever two years later and never looked back, dominating the league in 1992-1993 with a minuscule 0.58 ERA (two runs allowed, 25 strikeouts, 7 walks in 31 innings). Not blessed with a blazing fastball, he instead relied on off-speed pitches and had a penchant for taking his time on the mound, often taking his cap off and touching his uniform in an often successful attempt to unnerve his foes. Almost three decades after wearing the team's blue uniform, he proudly recalled, "It's the capital city's team. My mom was a big fan (of the club), and I became a fan since I was a boy. It was an honor to play for them. I'm very thankful for that experience."[5]

Not yet 19 years old, Rojas was thrust into the hero role in a game remembered as among the Cuban league's greatest contests. Staked to a one-run lead, he allowed a game-tying single to Iván Davis but was saved from infamy by a walk-off home run. So ended the 1985-1986 Cuban National Series, with the Industriales besting the Vegueros, 6-5. As of 2023, it remained the sole occasion a final series ended on a swing.[6]

Rojas saved 90 games and won 59 others during his Cuban career, totals that would have likely been loftier had the government not pursued a draconian punishment for Rojas' "transgressions." His 2.92 ERA in 13 years in the Cuban Serie Nacional (National Series, the post-Revolutionary name of the Cuban league) relied on guile and control throughout his 847⅔ innings pitched.[7] He led the leagues in saves in seven out of his 13 Cuban Serie Nacional campaigns.[8] His 90 saves stood as the Cuban league record until broken by Orestes González, José A. García, Duniel Ibarra, Danny Aguilera, and Yolexis Ulacia, as the stopper role became a necessity rather than a luxury in team rosters.[9] Rojas, like the major-league relievers of the 1970s, often came into the game in the middle innings when the situation demanded it, rather than only when staked with a ninth-inning lead.

As a member of the formidable Cuban national baseball team, Rojas understood the expectation that only a gold medal would be acceptable in foreign competition. The island's superiority in the sport was at stake, but more importantly for the government, the tacit proof of the advantages of the Socialist system. Rojas traveled to Indianapolis for the 1987 Pan-American Games as part of the powerful squad, though he pitched only four innings. Years later, he would recall that the opportunity began to change his attitude toward the government: "[H]anging out with the other athletes and the US people made me realize we were treated with respect and kindness. ... The regime's propaganda was full of lies."[10]

Rojas was part of the teams that won the 1988 (Rome) and 1990 (Edmonton) Baseball World Cup and the 1990 (Seattle) Goodwill Games. He stood out among his peers for his preparation and poise against the US squad, focusing on the execution of his chosen pitch. He won four contests for the unbeaten 1988 Cuban team, defeating the United States twice (once in the regular tournament and again in the finals). Years later, Rojas explained his poise on the mound: "The pressure is a privilege. No matter the situation in the game, you must execute your pitches well to obtain a favorable result. You don't need extraordinary conditions but you must recognize each situation to know what to do in it."[11] The Rome tournament juxtaposed the pressure he felt on the mound with the oppression off it. He sold his uniform to a fan for $200; noting that "the state had given us a total of forty dollars to last the entire trip."[12]

Rojas's greatest international success came right at home, as part of the 1991 Pan American Games in his hometown. Cuba defeated the United States, 3-2, in the preliminary rounds and both squads were widely expected to meet again in the finals. However, Puerto Rico surprised the United States and instead faced Cuba in the Gold Medal game. An 18-3 final score left no doubt of the superiority of Cuban baseball.

Rojas's international exposure prompted him to learn English, using Rafael Gómez Mena's *Basic English* book. Without access to a Xerox machine, Rojas copied the book by hand and by his own admission, "[O]nce I was done, I practically knew the entire book."[13]

However, the 1990s proved to be a difficult decade for the island, as the decades-old patronage from the Soviet Union abruptly ended. The euphemistic "special period" espoused by the government produced a heavy dose of belt-tightening across the island, and even sports icons were not immune to its difficulties. Rojas would launder his own uniform at home and ride his bicycle to the ballpark. His sixth-floor apartment lacked an elevator, so even after pitching, he would carry his bicycle up the stairs to prevent its theft.

Rojas recalled, "I never thought about staying. ... Things started to happen that made me very unhappy in my own homeland and I decided to leave on a homemade raft with my wife, child, and some neighborhood friends."[14] His decision was influenced by René Arocha, the first high-profile deserter, who decamped in 1991. Rojas recalled, "This was a personal decision of René's. ... It worked out for him, and he always told me he was deserting as someone seeing freedom. ... Whether he played baseball or not was not his concern. He wanted to be a free man; it worked out for him, and I am thankful he confided in me. He did not make a mistake. Mistakes were made by those who arrived in 1959."[15] Cuban officials, recalled Rojas, were unwilling to face reality: "They kept saying that maybe he had been drugged or kidnapped or something. They didn't want to accept the truth."[16]

Arocha's actions stunned the Cuban authorities. Since the Castro regime took over, only two major leaguers had deserted the island, Rogelio Álvarez and Bárbaro Garbey. Álvarez left in 1963, at the height of Cold War tensions, while Garbey departed in 1980 when the government allowed more than 100,000 of its subjects to leave for Miami. However, Arocha was a bona fide star, and his decision shook the system. The government routinely interviewed players returning from foreign competitions to intimidate and prevent any future "issues."

The government took punitive actions, ordering Rojas to pitch nine innings on three days' rest in the 1991-1992 tournament, regardless of pitch count, "under threat of suspension."[17] The toll on the mound, coupled with the physical and emotional tax of ongoing blackouts and other difficulties of 1990s Cuba, cemented his decision to depart the island: "The wool was pulled from my eyes. I realized our enemies were at home, not abroad."[18]

Although Rojas and his wife, Marta, welcomed son Euclides Jr. on December 23, 1991, the government was quick to diminish the family's joy. The government did not select Rojas for the 1992 Olympic team, as it suspected he had known of Arocha's plans to defect. Wistfully, Rojas pondered: "It was my mistake not to desert with him."[19] The omission opened a spot for Rolando Arrojo to make the Gold Medal-winning squad.[20] Arrojo himself defected in 1996 while in Atlanta for the next Olympic Games.

On Rojas's return from a tournament in Colombia in 1993, two police officers harassed him, demanded to check his luggage, and took him in custody. After his release, Rojas's mother pleaded with her son to leave the island at his next opportunity.[21]

The Cuban economy's collapse led to riots in the summer of 1994. The government had previously detained anyone seeking to leave the island by sea, but it temporarily lifted the restriction to relieve some of the pressure. An estimated 35,000 Cubans departed, mostly on handmade and jerry-rigged vessels.[22] Although no official tally exists, the US Coast Guard estimates that 8,000 perished trying to reach the United States.[23]

The American policy of "dry foot, wet foot" proved a heavy obstacle. Under such guidelines, Cubans intercepted at sea would be returned, while those lucky to land on American soil would be rewarded with immediate asylum. Rojas, his wife, and their young son set sail on August 19 aboard a raft that carried 10 others. Words fail to accurately capture the ordeal: "We navigated by the stars and the rising and setting of the sun. … We did not speak of it, but we became gripped by fear. … We ran out of water but managed to swap food for water with other boat people."[24] Although Rojas was hesitant to bring his family, his wife, Marta, said, "We're going with you. … If we die, we die together as a family."[25]

Rojas had saved his meager salary for a year to afford the wood; his fisherman friend built the boat.[26] The engine stopped working after only five hours. After five days alternating between manual rowing and the whims of the ocean's current, the US Coast Guard intercepted the boat and its voyagers were sent to Guantánamo Bay.[27] To Americans, this would be the equivalent of almost reaching Park Place on the Monopoly board but instead being sent back to home.

An episode of *Nuestra Historia*, a documentary series produced by US-government funded (and heavily anti-Castro) Radio Televisión Martí, shows a shirtless Rojas, surrounded by other boat people, stating, "My name is Euclides Rojas, and I was a former member of the Cuban baseball team. We'd rather lose our lives at sea than to live under such a hostile regime."[28] Another scene shows Rojas, holding his young son in his arms, talking to José Canseco during the latter's visit to Guantánamo.

The government tried to equate Rojas to Lucifer, a fallen angel who renounced heaven, but to Rojas and countless other Cubans who had risked their own lives to seek freedom, it was the opposite. Rojas was clear-cut in his assessment: "I left Cuba just like any other Cuban, dreaming of freedom."[29]

After six months at the US Navy Base in Guantánamo Bay, Rojas and his family were allowed to enter the United States. Arocha himself sponsored his old friend for the necessary visa.

Photo by Bill Nowlin.

On February 15, 1995, Rojas reached the mainland, and began cutting grass and doing handyman jobs to earn a living. At the recommendation of Arocha, he and fellow defector Ariel Prieto signed with the Palm Springs Suns of the Western League, an independent eight-team circuit. Rojas started five games, winning one and losing four. Although being thrust into an unfamiliar role may have affected his performance, his 3.34 ERA was considerably better than the 4.33 league average.

His audition prompted the Florida Marlins to select Rojas in the 30th round of the 1995 amateur draft. The franchise's only Cuban-born player, Orestes Destrade, had struggled in South Florida, leaving former big leaguer and then-pitching coach Cookie Rojas as the biggest draw for Cuban fans. The prospect of a former Cuban national hero proved to be irresistible for the team that would later boast Miami-born Alex Fernández and playoff sensation Liván Hernández in the Marlins' 1997 World Series-winning rotation.

Ten productive innings with the Rookie League Gulf Coast Marlins in 1995 (one run, six hits, one walk, seven strikeouts, two wins) earned Rojas a quick promotion to Double-A Portland, where he struggled against more robust competition. A 7.77 ERA, his worst as a professional, was attributed to a lack of command (13 walks) and the league's power-friendly ballparks (three home runs in 22 innings). Nevertheless, Rojas progressed to Triple-A Charlotte for a three-inning showing (one run, two hits, two walks, two strikeouts).

Rojas's arm, already strained by a punitive workload in Cuba, was further injured by the hours of constant rowing during his escape. A nine-inning stint with Charlotte in 1996 confirmed the worst fears: While the eight strikeouts were emboldening, the pain was too much to ignore. The organization was nevertheless impressed by Rojas's devotion to the young hurlers and offered him successive coaching opportunities. Though he grudgingly accepted while he figured his arm would heal, the 27-year-old Rojas found the chance for a second career to be a beguiling option. An arm operation as a coach sealed his future: "What I lacked was being younger and having my health. … I arrived with an injured arm. … Back then, in Cuba, pitchers were used differently."[30]

Rojas rejoined the Gulf Coast Marlins at the pitching coach, leading them to the playoffs in his third year (bowing in the semifinals to the Devil Rays' rookie squad). He cheered Liván Hernández and his mates as they won the 1997 World Series, becoming the toast of Miami, and likely of Havana as well, despite the government's disapproval. After a year off, Rojas coached the Florida Summer League Brevard County Manatees team in 2001, then returned to the GCL Marlins. Among his charges, Brad Penny and A.J. Burnett found the big-league success that eluded him. Rojas left the organization to join the

Pittsburgh Pirates in 2001 as a roving instructor. His mother died in 1999, and given the conditions surrounding his departure from Cuba, the government did not allow Rojas to return to the island for her funeral.

Rojas joined the Boston Red Sox organization as its bullpen coach prior to the 2003 season. GM Theo Epstein noted his experience with the Cuban national team as a deciding factor, given the franchise's bullpen struggles in the 2001 and 2002 campaigns. The move garnered scant attention during the offseason, but Epstein was confident he had landed a prized asset: "Every time we asked someone about him, they said, Wwhy isn't he in the big leagues?"[31] Manager Grady Little was also impressed by Rojas during the interview: "We were overwhelmed with what he brought to the table. It didn't take us long to decide he was our man."[32]

Despite the animosity between the Red Sox and the Yankees, Rojas could not help but wax nostalgic about the 2004 ALCS: "We were down 3-0 ... 'El Duque' jumped the fence from the Yankees bullpen, shook my hand, hugged me, and congratulated me. It was an incredible experience, to win that way and then to play against St. Louis. That team played with a lot of confidence and determination."[33] Orlando "El Duque" Hernández had been his teammate with the Industriales and the national team, giving the pair another chapter in their baseball lives. Rojas recalled the 2004 team as "unflappable. They would never give up. ... Schilling, Pedro, Wakefield, Lowe ... They would challenge each other, it was incredible."[34]

Orlando Hernández was not the only compatriot wearing pinstripes; José Contreras, whose signing gave birth to Larry Lucchino's "[T]he evil empire extends its tentacles even into Latin America" statement, played for New York until he was traded to the Chicago White Sox. Rojas knew Contreras' wife and daughters had been attempting to escape the island, finally succeeding on June 21, 2004, aboard a powerboat. The Contreras family had been separated since the hurler abandoned the national team in Mexico on October 1, 2002. "To feel what he did you have to have experienced what he did, and I didn't. I thought about leaving Cuba alone but with the idea of bringing (my family) along. I'm glad my wife said, 'We make it together, or we sink together.'" Nevertheless, Rojas added, "If we face him, I'd like to win but beat him 3-2 ... Even though I'm a coach on the Red Sox, I wish him well."[35]

Rojas left the organization after the World Series triumph, an under-the-radar move during an offseason that saw Pedro Martínez and Derek Lowe depart Boston. According to press reports, he was offered another role within the franchise, but he opted to seek other opportunities.[36] He fondly recalled his time with the Red Sox: "Being with Manny Ramírez, with David Ortiz, with Pedro Martínez and that group of ballplayers and coaches will always be a great accomplishment. ... Fenway Park reminded me of the Estadio Latinoamericano. ... That love for the game, that passion, the energy in that stadium is just like in Havana. It was like being back home."[37]

Rojas returned to the Pirates as the Latin American field coordinator and eventually the franchise's bullpen coach. The long-suffering franchise steadily improved and reached the postseason in three straight seasons (2013-2015). Rojas left Pittsburgh in 2019; in his nine years, the Pirates bullpen mirrored the fortunes of the franchise, swinging from 3.7 WAR in 2015 to -3.5 WAR in 2019. Rojas took great pride in his work with the relievers, noting that "pitching coach Ray Searage and I have been working together for a long time, since we met with the Marlins. We're like brothers and trust each other. ... The first thing is to learn the routine of every reliever. ... We communicate a lot and work hard, so they trust me."[38] His pupils raved about his work: José Veras called him "an unbelievable person" and Daniel Moskos added, "He's a great guy to be around on a daily basis. He's done wonders for me."[39]

Rojas was thankful for the opportunity to work with the Pirates, stating, "It's a privilege to work for such a long time with the organization, especially with the young bullpen arms. My job is a lot of fun and I am motivated every day."[40] As a coordinator, he took great pride in the creation of the Pirates' Dominican Republic academy, which not only developed the athletic promise of the young prospects but also assisted in the critical transition to American life: "I can see their confidence when they come to the country, so it's not a big change. ... They're comfortable, they speak English."[41] Rojas again recalled his experience with the Marlins, especially with then-assistant GM Dave Littlefield: "The support they gave me, I wasn't expecting it. It was awesome. It was something that will stick with me for the rest of my life. That's something I try to pass on."[42]

Rojas also coached the pitching staff of 2011-2012 Navegantes de Magallanes club in the Venezuelan league and the Aceros (Steel Workers) of Monclova's pitching staff during the 2021 Mexican League's summer season.[43] He joined the Detroit Tigers organization in 2021 as its director of Latin American player development, a position he still held in 2023.[44]

While some players have called for a unified Cuban team in international competition, Rojas is steadfast on his stance. As an outspoken proponent of political freedom for his homeland, he maintains, "If I were to get a call asking me to be the pitching coach of a unified Cuban team, I wouldn't do it until there is democracy in my country."[45] Amid rumors of a Cuban boycott of the 2023 World Baseball Classic, an organization calling itself the Association of Professional Cuban Baseball Players touted its willingness to field a team of expatriates with Rojas and former big leaguers Garbey, Contreras, Arocha, and the Hernández brothers as part of the coaching staff.[46]

Should Cuban baseball ever elect a "Team of the Century," as Major League Baseball did in 1999, Rojas would be a worthy candidate as the team's closer. He is regarded as "one of the highest examples of the art of relief pitching in the 50 years of post-professional baseball. Though he was not blessed with the astronomical velocity of the classic stopper, he based his dominance on perfect control. He was a tireless student of the opposition and sought to display an unnerving calm from the mound, employing a hard-to-hit curve that found its target in the bottom and corners of the strike zone."[47] Asked by Orlando Hernández about the most important traits for a closer, Rojas was unequivocal: "Having faith in oneself, knowing how to warm up in the bullpen so as not to waste pitches … and observing the game while it is in progress."[48]

Rojas exhorts aspiring Latin coaches "to learn, listen, respect the game and the opponent, and to focus on how to help the players," noting that "being patient is the hardest part."[49]

NOTES

The referenced links were accessed on January 8, 2023.

1. "El Duque entrevista a Euclides Rojas-Azules de corazón," Cubanplay, originally broadcast in "La estrella invitada." https://www.youtube.com/watch?v=a6oBLZWkKE8.
2. "Euclídes Rojas cuente por qué lo dejaron fuera del equipo de Cuba a La Olimpiada de Barcelona 92," TU Miami TV. https://www.youtube.com/watch?v=WE5O5X0Z7AI.
3. Michael Silverman, "The Greatest Relief: Freedom," *Boston Herald*, April 27, 2003.
4. "Euclides Rojas: aventura y triunfo de un balsero y pelotero cubano," *Playoff Magazine*, August 10, 2020. https://playoffmagazine.com/euclides-rojas-aventura-y-triunfo-de-un-balsero-y-pelotero-cubano/.
5. "Euclídes Rojas, de Industriales a coach de Grandes Ligas," *Periódico Cubano*, April 14, 2018, https://www.periodicocubano.com/euclides-rojas-industriales-coach-grandes-ligas/.
6. Yirsandy Rodríguez, "Momentos memorables en el béisbol cubano: ¡36 años después del mítico jonrón de Marquetti!," *Baseball de Cuba*, January 19, 2022, https://www.baseballdecuba.com/post/momentos-memorables-en-el-b%C3%A9isbol-cubano-36-a%C3%B1os-despu%C3%A9s-del-m%C3%ADtico-jonr%C3%B3n-de-marquetti.
7. Rogério Manzano, "Euclídes Rojas," Desde mi palco de fanático, https://desdemipalcodefanatico.wordpress.com/jugadores/euclides-rojas-1/.
8. Cuban Serie Nacional is the post-Revolutionary name of the Cuban league.
9. Dilberto Camagüey, "José Ángel García primero con 200 salvados em Series Nacionales," *Béisbol en Cuba*, March 28, 2016, https://www.cubaencuentro.com/fernando-vila/blogs/palmar-de-junco/entrevista-a-euclides-rojas-ii.
10. "Euclídes Rojas cuente por qué lo dejaron fuera del equipo de Cuba a La Olimpiada de Barcelona 92."
11. Emilio Sosa Martín, "Euclídes Rojas: 'Espero regresar el día que mi Cuba sea libre,'" *Pelota Cubana USA*, May 10, 2019, https://pelotacubanausa.com/2019/05/10/euclides-rojas-espero-regresar-el-dia-que-mi-cuba-sea-libre/16/13/49/.
12. Steve Fainaru and Ray Sanchez, *The Duke of Havana: Baseball, Cuba, and the Search for the American Dream* (New York: Random House, 2001), 45.
13. "Euclídes Rojas: aventura y triunfo de un balsero y pelotero cubano."
14. "Euclídes Rojas: aventura y triunfo de un balsero y pelotero cubano."
15. "Nuestra historia: Euclídes Rojas." Radio Televisión Martí, https://www.youtube.com/watch?v=pmA7d6IU100.
16. *The Duke of Havana: Baseball, Cuba, and the Search for the American Dream*, 51.
17. "Nuestra historia: Euclídes Rojas." Radio Televisión Martí, https://www.youtube.com/watch?v=pmA7d6IU100.
18. "Nuestra historia: Euclídes Rojas."
19. "Euclides Rojas: aventura y triunfo de un balsero y pelotero cubano."
20. "El Duque entrevista a Euclides Rojas-Azules de corazón," Cubanplay. Originally broadcast in "La estrella invitada." https://www.youtube.com/watch?v=a6oBLZWkKE8.
21. Daniel de Malas, "El jefe de la estación le dijo al policía si no le daba pena lo que estaba haciendo." *Swing Completo*, June 2, 2020, https://swingcompleto.com/choque-euclides-rojas-policia-cuba-pedido-su-madre/
22. University of Miami, "The Cuban Rafter Phenomenon." http://balseros.miami.edu/.
23. John Grupp, "Pirates Bullpen Coach Rafted to U.S. from Cuba Seeking Freedom." *Pittsburgh Tribune*, June 26, 2011.
24. Matthew Syed, "'Glorious Amateurs' Risk Lives in Attempt to Flee Castro," *London Times*, March 5, 2007: 64.
25. *The Duke of Havana: Baseball, Cuba, and the Search for the American Dream*, 54.
26. "Pirates Bullpen Coach Rafted to U.S. from Cuba Seeking Freedom."
27. Different accounts state he was detained 5, 15, and 19 miles from Key West.
28. "Nuestra historia: Euclídes Rojas."
29. Emilio Sosa Martín, "Euclídes Rojas: 'Espero regresar el día que mi Cuba sea libre.'".
30. Francys Romero, "Euclídes Rojas: Llegué de Cuba con mi brazo lastimado," *Cibercuba*. June 17, 2019, https://www.cibercuba.com/noticias/2019-06-17-u194102-e194102-s27066-euclides-rojas-llegue-cuba-mi-brazo-lastimado.
31. Greg Sukiennik, "Sox Sign Rojas to Save Bullpen – New Coach Replaces Kipper," *Worcester* (Massachusetts) *Telegram & Gazette*, December 3, 2002: D1.
32. "Sox Sign Rojas to Save Bullpen."
33. "Euclídes Rojas: aventura y triunfo de un balsero y pelotero cubano."
34. "El Duque entrevista a Euclides Rojas-Azules de corazón," *Cubanplay*. Originally broadcast in "La estrella invitada." https://www.youtube.com/watch?v=a6oBLZWkKE8.
35. Rafael Hermoso, "Reunited, and It Feels So Good," *USA Today*, June 2, 2004.
36. "Red Sox Notes," *Worcester Telegram & Gazette*, November 23, 2004: D4.
37. Fernando Vilá, "Palmar de Junco: Blog de Fernando Vilá Chao," *Cuba Encuentro*, August 18, 2009, https://www.cubaencuentro.com/fernando-vila/blogs/palmar-de-junco/entrevista-a-euclides-rojas-i.
38. Jorge Ebro, "Euclídes Rojas: Al béisbol le ha pasado lo mismo que a todo en Cuba," *Playoff Magazine*, May 1, 2017, https://playoffmagazine.com/euclides-rojas-al-beisbol-le-ha-pasado-lo-mismo-que-a-todo-en-cuba/
39. "Pirates Bullpen Coach Rafted to U.S. from Cuba Seeking Freedom."
40. "Euclídes Rojas, de Industriales a coach de las Grandes Ligas."

41 Roger Castillo, "Detroit Tigers Hire a New Director of Latin American Player Development," *Motor City Bengals,* October 17, 2021. https://motorcitybengals.com/2021/10/17/detroit-tigers-latin-player-development-euclides-rojas/.

42 Bill Briknk,???? Spelling? "MLB Has a Diversity Problem, and It Goes Beyond the Rosters," *Pittsburgh Post-Gazette,* August 21, 2017.

43 "Euclides Rojas retorna al desarrollo de las grandes ligas." Acereros Website, October 9, 2021, http://acereros.com.mx/euclides-rojas-retorna-al-desarrollo-de-las-grandes-ligas/. ?fbclid=IwAR1g VWX5h7eB6YLxr3CxFXpRHQAJlXO7qGDrnaJIcUVN9t-uuBv6zHNas8A.

44 "Detroit Tigers Hire a New Director of Latin American Player Development."

45 Daniel de Malas, "El jefe de la estación le dijo al policía si no le daba pena lo que estaba haciendo."

46 "Conforman cuerpo técnico de la Asociación de Peloteros Cubanos Profesionales." *Diario Las Américas,* September 13, 2022, https://www.diariolasamericas.com/deportes/conforman-cuerpo-tecnico-la-asociacion-peloteros-cubanos-profesionales-n4256723.

47 Desde Mi Palco de Fanático: Memorias y reflexiones del baseball cubano."

48 "El Duque entrevista a Euclides Rojas-Azules de corazón."

49 "Euclídes Rojas, de Industriales a coach de las Grandes Ligas."

DALE SVEUM

BY BILL PRUDEN

As the third-base coach on the 2004 Red Sox, Dale Sveum earned the first of two World Series rings that were the high points of a lengthy and multifaceted career in professional baseball. Through his efforts as a player, coach, and manager, the former high-school football star earned a reputation as a savvy, classy baseball man, one who had seen and done pretty much all one can do in the professional game, all the while weathering the ups and downs central to the game. Out of it he earned the respect of the peers and colleagues with whom he had shared the experiences of his almost four decades in professional baseball.

Dale Curtis Sveum was born November on 23, 1963 in Richmond, California. He was the younger of two boys born to Sandrea Kay and George Sveum. After a stint in the Marines, George Sveum worked as an independent trucker. He later drove for a couple of different companies before becoming involved with the Teamsters. He eventually rose to become secretary-treasurer, which according to Dale, was the true position of power in the local Teamsters Union.[1]

Dale Sveum was a local athletic legend in high school. A standout three-sport (football, basketball, baseball) star at Pinole Valley High School in Pinole, California, he was also reputed to be the best golfer in the school; and the track and swimming coaches were known to covet his services. Football, in which he had completed an 80-yard touchdown-pass play as a sophomore in leading Pinole Valley to an upset victory in the sectional playoffs, was reportedly his favorite sport. However, the offer of a scholarship from Arizona State could not compare to the $100,000 signing bonus he received from the Milwaukee Brewers after scout Harry Smith identified him as a top-flight talent and the Brewers made him the 25th overall pick in the 1982 amateur draft.[2]

Sveum began his professional career in the summer of 1982 with the Pikeville Brewers in the Brewers Rookie-level entry in the Appalachian League. Always playing infield, from there he advanced to the Stockton Ports in the Class-A California League in 1983, the El Paso Diablos in the Double-A Texas League in 1984, and the Vancouver Canadians in the Triple-A Pacific Coast League in 1985 and into the start of the 1986 season. His performance for El Paso (.329, 84 RBIs) offered the best evidence of his major-league readiness. That readiness became a reality when, on May 12, 1986, just about the time he would have been graduating from Arizona State (probable redshirt year aside), Sveum made his major-league debut, starting at third base and going 2-for-3 in the Brewers' 6-0 loss to the Mariners in Seattle.

Once he got to the big leagues, Sveum worked hard to stay there. He finished the 1986 season hitting .246 in 91 games. He had 317 at-bats, hit 7 home runs, and drove in 35 runs. The next season, 1987, was his most complete and successful season. Appearing in 153 games and logging 586 plate appearances, he hit .252 while recording career highs in every meaningful hitting category, including, most impressively, 95 runs batted in, second on the team only to Robin Yount's 103. Sveum got 135 hits, 27 of which were doubles and 25 were home runs. It was one of two double-figure home-run seasons he had. Sveum also had his career high in strikeouts with 133. Little did he know that 1987 would prove to be his career year.

In 1988 Sveum played in 129 games, hitting .242 but he experienced major drop-offs in every other area. More importantly, on September 3, 1988, while playing shortstop, Sveum broke his left tibia in a collision with left fielder Darryl Hamilton while he was chasing and catching a fly ball in left field, near the foul line. Sveum was taken from the field on a stretcher.[3] To complicate matters, the bone did not heal properly and on November 18 Sveum underwent surgery. In what doctors said was a not uncommon procedure, another smaller bone next to the tibia needed to be broken in order to facilitate and speed the healing process of the larger bone. The natural process had been taking longer than it normally should and if it was allowed to proceed there was little chance that Sveum would be ready for spring training. With the surgery the Brewers felt that their shortstop would be back.[4]

But in fact, Sveum was never again the same player. In the immediate aftermath of the surgery, he struggled just to play. Despite the initial optimism, he did not bounce back from the surgery as hoped. In fact, he did not play a single game in the major leagues in 1989 and appeared in only 17 in the minors, splitting time between Class-A teams Stockton and Beloit.

The 1990 season was not much better. Sveum split time between the Denver Zephyrs of the Triple-A American Association and the Brewers. But after hitting .289 in 57 games with Denver, he hit only .197 in 48 games with the Brewers.

After hitting .241 in 90 games for the Brewers during the 1991 season, Sveum was traded after the season to the Philadelphia Phillies for Bruce Ruffin. It was the start of an eight-season baseball odyssey that saw the former first-round draft choice struggle to stay in the big leagues.

Beginning with the Phillies in 1992, over the course of the next eight seasons, Sveum played for six different major-league teams and four in the minors with his longest stint being almost three full seasons (1994-96) with the Calgary Cannons of the Pacific Coast League, interrupted only by a six-week period from April 27 to June 5, 1994 during which he got into 10 games after being called up by the Seattle Mariners. But that ended when he finished the 1996 season with the Pirates. Over the course of his odyssey, he played with the Phillies, the Chicago White Sox, the Oakland A's, the Seattle Mariners, the Pittsburgh Pirates, and the New York Yankees, before finishing up in a return stop with the Pirates. His playing career came to an end on October 3, 1999, when, in the top of the eighth with one out, pinch-hitting for pitcher Kris Benson and facing New York Mets hurler Turk Wendell, he flied out to left-center field.

While he went to spring training in 2000 intent on winning a spot on the Pirates' roster, the effort was unsuccessful and Sveum's playing days were over. His professional playing career spanned 18 seasons. He spent parts of 12 seasons in the major leagues (862 games). He had a career batting average of .236 with 597 hits, 69 home runs, and 340 RBIs. He also spent parts of 12 seasons in the minors, appearing in 976 games and finishing with a .281 batting average.

After a year away from the game, in 2001, Sveum managed the Pirates' Double-A team in Altoona, Pennsylvania. As manager, he also coached third base, an experience that was new to him but which would come in handy down the road. In preparation for the new role, he pumped the brains of numerous former teammates, with former Pirates roommate Tommy Sandt being a particularly valuable resource.[5] Sveum's efforts in Altoona were well received and in 2003 *Baseball America* called Sveum the best potential major-league manager in the Eastern League.[6] His climb up the managerial ladder took a detour when in January 2004, just weeks after Terry Francona had been hired as manager of the Boston Red Sox, Sveum's former Brewers teammate awakened him from a deep sleep – Francona apparently had forgotten about the time zone difference – to ask him if he wanted to be the Red Sox third-base coach. After getting over the surprise, discussing the job in depth with Francona and then being interviewed by Red Sox general manager Theo Epstein, Sveum joined the Red Sox in February 2004, a team hungry for a championship after 86 years without a World Series crown and especially after a near-miss in the playoffs the previous season.[7]

While Sveum's contributions to the team were many, he also became a somewhat controversial figure as he violated a central rule of coaching – he became noticed. His unwanted high profile stemmed from the fact that a number of Red Sox runners he waved home from his perch in the third-base coaching box were cut down at the plate – results that invited second-guessing. Indeed, in early August 2004, after a game in which Tampa Devil Rays center fielder Rocco Baldelli threw out Red Sox runners at home plate on successive at-bats – the second and third home-plate-bound Red Sox runners that Baldelli had cut down that month – Sveum's decision-making was the subject of a *Boston Globe* article.[8] The runners themselves, not to mention manager Terry Francona, defended Sveum while recognizing the challenges involved in the process.[9] Sveum himself acknowledged in an interview with the author that it was a no-win situation, noting that a coach did not get plaudits when a runner he sent home was safe, while each out offered a chance for second-guessing. He recognized that not getting publicity as a third-base coach was a good thing and that his recent spate of attention was not something to be desired.[10] In the end, given his years of experience in the game, Sveum knew it was part of the job, although he would later admit that after Dave Roberts stole second in Game Four of the ALCS against the Yankees, the possibility that he might have to wave him home flashed through his mind.[11] Of course, in fact, he did – and the rest was history.

While most of his nonplaying career still lay ahead of him, Sveum remembered the last out of the Red Sox victory over the Yankees in Game Seven of the American League Championship Series at Yankee Stadium as "probably the most exhilarating moment" of his career.[12] Indeed, so improbable and momentous was the team's unprecedented comeback, Sveum said, that the subsequent World Series win over the St. Louis Cardinals was "almost anticlimactic."[13]

One of Sveum's most vivid memories of the Red Sox' improbable comeback win was the impact of Kevin Millar in the Red Sox clubhouse. Sveum recalled that seemingly everybody outside the team saw the outlook as "dismal," a sentiment he said he fully understood in the aftermath of the Red Sox' devastating 19-8 loss in Game Three of the ALCS. However, it was different for the team in the locker room where, he recalled, things just picked up when Millar walked in. While acknowledging the strength and determination of the whole team, Sveum said Millar played a "big part," recalling the special way that Millar, almost by dint of his own personality "got the clubhouse in a different state of mind," warning anyone who would listen that they had better not let the Sox win tonight.[14] As everyone knows that prediction proved prescient. With Dave Roberts stealing second, Big Papi coming up big, Curt Schilling bravely pitching the "Bloody Sock" game, and countless others stepping up, the Red Sox made history.

After again serving as the third-base coach in 2005, Sveum left the Red Sox, taking a job as bench coach of the Milwaukee Brewers under manager Ned Yost.[15] The team finished 2006 in fourth place in the National League's Central Division and moved up to second in 2007. While they continued to improve in 2008, with only 12 games left in the season Yost was fired and Sveum, who had assumed the role of third-base coach in 2007, was tapped to replace him, serving as interim manager for the final dozen games of the regular season.[16] When the team won seven of those remaining 12 under Sveum's leadership, they snuck into the postseason for the first time since 1982. But the fairy tale ended when they lost to the Philadelphia Phillies in the NLDS in four games.[17] When Ken Macha was named manager for the 2009 season, Sveum remained with the club as the hitting coach, overseeing one of baseball's more potent offenses and in the process establishing himself as a hot managerial prospect.[18]

Indeed, after the 2011 season Sveum engaged in extended conversations with both the Red Sox and the Cubs about their managerial openings. He was seen as the front-runner for the Red Sox job, and subsequent reports revealed that while general manager Ben Cherington preferred Sveum for the position, he had been overruled by the team's ownership, with the Red Sox ultimately opting for former Mets skipper Bobby Valentine.[19] Instead, on November 17, 2011, with a three-year contract in hand, Sveum accepted the job as manager of the rebuilding Chicago Cubs.[20]

Sveum served in that post for two seasons as the team struggled while beginning to build a roster that would ultimately win the 2016 World Series. Perhaps his Cubs fate was foretold when in the offseason after the 2012 campaign, Sveum was the unwitting victim of a hunting accident. While shooting quail with friend and Milwaukee Brewers legend Robin Yount, Sveum was accidentally hit in the right ear and the back by Yount's errant shot. While there were reports of blood splattering all around, they were able to laugh it off, relieved that there were no serious injuries.[21] Indeed, Sveum would later say that he was surprised by all the attention the incident received, adding that such incidents were not totally uncommon.[22]

In fact, the Cubs did improve in 2013, winning five more games than the year before, but it was not enough. His three-year contract notwithstanding, the day after the 2013 season ended, Sveum, who acknowledged his disappointment for the Cubs' 127-197 record over two seasons, was fired as manager.[23]

In the aftermath of the firing, questions were raised about the slow development of prized prospects Starlin Castro and first baseman Anthony Rizzo.[24] At the same time, Sveum was given credit for the way he connected with his young roster. It was clear that despite the lack of success the players respected him and worked hard under his tutelage.[25] Indeed, the Cubs organization, recognizing the important role Sveum played in developing many of the players on the championship team as well as helping build the foundation of that club, awarded him a World Series ring.[26]

While his time in Chicago ended in disappointment, Sveum said he "loved every minute of managing the Cubs."[27] Despite "being behind the eight ball every night," he relished the challenge and the opportunity to try to apply everything he had learned in his big-league career.[28] In each of the many positions he held, Sveum was constantly drawing upon the lessons he had learned previously. In particular, he saw his time with the Brewers and the lessons he learned from Paul Molitor, and especially his best friend Robin Yount, as being tremendously important to his career. Sveum was a dedicated student of the game, saying that "if you are not learning in baseball every day, you are not paying attention."[29] He said he was always trying to learn and especially as a young player he would often just sit back and "be a sponge," taking it all in.[30] He learned early on that a player "needs to be locked in and focused on every pitch."[31]

The major-league veteran was not without a job for long. Soon after his release by the Cubs, the Kansas City Royals hired him as a coach and infield instructor, a job that reunited him with manager Ned Yost, his former Brewers mentor.[32] Sveum was promoted to hitting coach in early 2014 as the Royals advanced from third to second in the American League's Central Division, snagging a wild-card spot in the postseason lineup.[33] To the surprise of the baseball world, the Royals took full advantage of their postseason opportunity, defeating the Oakland A's, the Anaheim Angels, and the Baltimore Orioles on the way to winning the American League flag and a chance to meet the San Francisco Giants in the World Series. While their loss to the Giants in the seventh game of the Series was disappointing, for Sveum it represented a tremendous contrast with his previous two seasons with the Cubs. It also left him and the Royals primed for another run at the championship. And in 2015, with Sveum as hitting coach, the offense scored over 70 more runs than the year before, powering the Royals to the AL Central Division crown. They then defeated the Houston Astros in the AL Division Series before winning the pennant in six games over the Toronto Blue Jays. The Royals then capped the season with a victory in five games over the New York Mets in the World Series to end the magical run.

Not unlike the Red Sox in 2004, that experience too was a distinctive and special one for Sveum. The Royals, having come in 2014 as close as a team can come before falling short, were determined to turn things around in 2015 and that is exactly what they did. Sveum called 2015 a "magical season" while also noting that it was a team that was focused and motivated from day one.[34] The Royals were a good hitting team, with a strong veteran core, and as hitting coach Sveum sought to capitalize on the talent they had. He emphasized the need to "just keep the line moving."[35] It was a focus based in who they were and what were the factors central to the team. They were not, he recalled, a team that was going to walk a lot and Kauffman Stadium did not lend itself to lots of home runs. but if they put the ball in play, they would – as they did – win games.[36]

For Sveum as a coach, it was an approach that reflected his belief that it was very important that one "thinks outside the box," and that a coach "needs to coach the players in the way that brings out the best in them."[37] It was an approach brought home to a young Sveum early in his time with the Brewers when sessions with the baseball veteran and one-time batting champion Harvey Kuenn helped the struggling youngster get on track and stay in the game.[38] Indeed, it all came together those many years later when the Royals' 2015 title validated his "keep the line moving," situation-based approach. At the same time, in looking back, Sveum also recalled how the Royals, like the

Red Sox in 2004, also had that little bit of the luck that Sveum called an inevitable part of almost any victorious venture.[39]

In 2017 Sveum was promoted to bench coach.[40] He remained on the Royals coaching staff through the 2019 season, after which Yost retired. Sveum was seen as a leader among the inside candidates to be Yost's successor, but in the end the Royals opted for former Cardinals manager Mike Matheny. Sveum remained with the organization, serving for two years as a special assistant to the general manager, before retiring after the 2021 season.[41]

Sveum and his wife, Darlene, who have two adult children, live in Scottsdale, Arizona.

SOURCES

In addition to the sources cited in the Notes, the author consulted Baseball-Reference.com and a number of additional sources.

NOTES

1. "Kansas City Royals Win Series, With a Serious Assist From a Pinole Valley Spartan," Pinole Valley High School website; https://www.wccusd.net/site/Default.aspx?PageType=3&DomainID=689&PageID=2428&ViewID=047e6be3-6d87-4130-8424-d8e4e9ed6c2a&FlexDataID=9736; author interview with Dale Sveum, May 21, 2023.
2. "Kansas City Royals Win Series, With a Serious Assist From a Pinole Valley Spartan."
3. United Press International, "Baseball Central," September 4, 1988; https://www.upi.com/Archives/1988/09/04/Baseball-Central/2090589348800/.
4. United Press International, "Milwaukee Brewers Shortstop Dale Sveum Will Be Operated On," November 18, 1988; https://www.upi.com/Archives/1988/11/18/Milwaukee-Brewers-shortstop-Dale-Sveum-will-be-operated-on/5234595832400/.
5. Daniel McGinn, "He's Safe … for Now," *Boston Globe*, May 15, 2005.
6. "Brewers Hire Dale Sveum as Third Base Coach," onMilwaukee, October 19, 2005; https://onmilwaukee.com/articles/sveumreturns.
7. McGinn; Sveum interview.
8. Marc Craig, "Sveum Feeling Heat at Corner," *Boston Globe*, August 13, 2004.
9. Craig.
10. Craig.
11. McGinn; Sveum interview.
12. Sveum interview.
13. Sveum interview.
14. Sveum interview.
15. Tim Williams, "Dale Sveum Becomes the 6th Candidate to Interview," *Pirates Prospects*, October 13, 2010; https://www.piratesprospects.com/2010/10/dale-sveum-becomes-the-6th-candidate-to-interview.html.
16. Reuters, "Brewers Rule Out Sveum for Permanent Coaching Job," October 18, 2008; https://www.reuters.com/article/us-baseball-brewers/brewers-rule-out-sveum-for-permanent-coaching-job-idUSTRE49H0IT20081018.
17. "Brewers Rule Out Sveum for Permanent Coaching Job."
18. Colin Fly (Associated Press), "Macha Hired to Manage Brewers," *Peoria* (Illinois) *Journal-Star*, October 30, 2008; https://www.pjstar.com/story/sports/2008/10/30/macha-hired-to-manage-brewers/42493735007/; "Brewers Confirm Manager Macha Being Let Go," Fox News, November 20, 2014; https://www.foxnews.com/sports/brewers-confirm-manager-macha-being-let-go.amp.
19. David Waldstein and Zach Schonbrun, "Valentine Fired by Red Sox After One Trying Season," *New York Times*, October 4, 2012.
20. Jeremy Reid, "Dale Sveum: Hitting Coach Offered Golden Ticket with Chicago Cubs Gig," *Bleacher Report*, November 17, 2011; https://bleacherreport.com/articles/945096-dale-sveum-third-base-coach-offered-golden-ticket-with-cubs-gig.
21. Ryan Rudnansky, "Dale Sveum: Cubs Manager Accidentally Shot by Brewers Legend Robin Yount," *Bleacher Report*, December 5, 2012; https://bleacherreport.com/articles/1434465-dale-sveum-cubs-manager-accidentally-shot-by-brewers-legend-robin-yount.
22. Sveum interview.
23. "Cubs Fire Manager Dale Sveum," ESPN, September 30, 2013; https://www.espn.com/chicago/mlb/story/_/id/9748610/chicago-cubs-fire-manager-dale-sveum-two-years.
24. "Cubs Fire Manager Dale Sveum."
25. "Cubs Fire Manager Dale Sveum."
26. Chris Kuc, "Cubs Gave World Series Ring to White Sox Manager Rick Renteria, Says Jerry Reinsdorf," *Chicago Tribune*, August 16, 2017; https://www.chicagotribune.com/sports/white-sox/ct-rick-renteria-cubs-world-series-ring-20170816-story.html.
27. Sveum interview.
28. Sveum interview.
29. Sveum interview.
30. Sveum interview.
31. Sveum interview.
32. "Royals Add Dale Sveum to Coaching Staff," October 3, 2013; Mlb.com/blogs; https://royals.mlblogs.com/royals-add-dale-sveum-to-coaching-staff-b6a72877eca6.
33. Andy McCullough, "Hitting Coach Sveum Keeps Royals' Line Moving During KC's Second Straight World Series," *Kansas City Star*, October 29, 2015.
34. Sveum interview.
35. Sveum interview.
36. Sveum interview.
37. Sveum interview.
38. Sveum interview.
39. Sveum interview.
40. Nicholas Sullivan, "Kansas City Royals Announce Dale Sveum to Become Bench Coach," *Fansided*, October 2017; https://kingsofkauffman.com/2017/10/18/kansas-city-royals-dale-sveum-bench-coach/.
41. Noah Yingling, "The Top 100 Coaches Most Likely to Become MLB Managers," Call to the Pen, *Fansided.com*; https://callltothepen.com/2022/01/31/the-top-100-coaches-most-likely-to-become-mlb-managers/20/; text, Dale Sveum to author, May 21, 2023.

DAVE WALLACE

BY BILL PRUDEN

On June 9, 2003 with pitching coach Tony Cloninger taking a leave of absence to fight cancer, the Boston Red Sox named former Mets and Dodgers pitching coach Dave Wallace to fill the void.[1] For Wallace, a Connecticut native with over three decades of professional baseball experience, it was not only a chance to go home to New England, but he was joining a team that was then sitting at 35-26, a half-game ahead of the New York Yankees in the American League East. But with that standing based far more on the club's offensive production than on its pitching, Wallace was taking on no small challenge. Despite boasting multiple Cy Young Award winner Pedro Martínez as its ace, the staff that Wallace inherited had a team earned-run average of 5.26, the second worst in the American League. Less than 18 months later, with the interim tag removed, Wallace had helped transform the staff into one whose ERA in 2004, his first full season with the club, was not only third-best in the American League, but which, led by Martínez and Curt Schilling, made history as the Red Sox won the 2004 World Series, the team's first title since 1918.

It was the high point in Wallace's baseball career, one that added a special sheen to his other accomplishments, but it was by no means an isolated achievement. Indeed, over the course of just under 50 years in professional baseball, Dave Wallace established himself as one of the most accomplished and respected pitching coaches and baseball men in the game. It was no accident that in 2012 *Bleacher Report* included him on a list of baseball's top 50 all-time pitching coaches.[2]

David William Wallace was born on September 7, 1947, in Waterbury, Connecticut. He grew up in the city about equidistant – 2 hours and 15 minutes in either direction – from New York City and Boston, and he starred in football, basketball, and baseball at Waterbury's Sacred Heart High School.[3] Focusing on his real passion, he played baseball at the University of New Haven. There the 5-foot-10 right-handed pitcher compiled a record of 24-7 with a 2.18 earned-run average and 311 strikeouts over his four-year career, one that saw him lead the team into the National Association of Intercollegiate Athletics (NAIA) national tournament in 1966 and earned him induction into the university's Hall of Fame in 2000.[4] After graduating, the undrafted Wallace signed as a free agent with the Philadelphia Phillies in the fall of 1969.

Wallace began his professional career with the Spartanburg Phillies in the Class-A Western Carolina League in the summer

of 1970. There he went 8-8 with a 5.16 ERA in 24 games, all starts. He threw seven complete games and pitched 150 innings.

The 1971 season saw Wallace improve those numbers significantly. Moved to the bullpen, and pitching for the Peninsula Phillies in the advanced Class-A Carolina League, he lowered his ERA to 1.24. He compiled a record of 6-1 while giving up only 30 hits in 58 innings. That performance earned him a promotion to the Triple-A Pacific Coast League Eugene Emeralds. Wallace was called upon for an occasional spot start, but 41 of his 47 appearances for Eugene were in relief as he went 8-5 with an ERA of 4.55. He started the 1973 season back in Eugene but after 43 appearances was sent down to the Reading Phillies in the Double-A Eastern League. There he shined, boasting a 1.59 ERA in 11 relief appearances and earning a call-up to the Phillies.

Wallace made his major-league debut on July 18, 1973, against the Cincinnati Reds at Cincinnati. Two months shy of his 26th birthday, he began the bottom of the eighth inning, relieving future Hall of Famer Steve Carlton, who had given up five runs in his seven innings of work. For Wallace it was something of a baptism by fire: Three of the first four batters he faced were future Hall of Famers. Wallace walked Joe Morgan to start the inning and then gave up a run-scoring double to Dave Concepción. That was followed by a single by Johnny Bench that put runners at first and third. Wallace then struck out Tony Pérez. However, the relief was only temporary as Wallace next gave up a double to Andy Kosco, which drove in Concepción. With the score now 7-0, Bucky Brandon replaced Wallace, who exited his debut with an ERA of 54.00.[5] Wallace made three more appearance with the Phillies that season, totaling 3⅔ innings while giving up 13 hits for an ERA of 22.09.

While he appeared in three games with the Phillies in 1974 and six with the Toronto Blue Jays in 1978, from 1974 through the end of 1979, Wallace spent most of his time in the minors, playing for the Toledo Mud Hens, the Oklahoma City 89ers, the Syracuse Chiefs, and finally the Pawtucket Red Sox. He retired as a player after the 1979 season never having earned a major-league win; his major-league record was 0-1 with an ERA of 7.84 in 13 appearances and 20⅔ innings pitched. Not auspicious numbers to be sure, but the lessons Wallace learned and his ability to impart them to younger pitchers would make for an impressive second career in professional baseball.

After a year away from professional baseball, in 1981 Wallace returned to the game, joining the Los Angeles Dodgers organization. For two seasons he coached for the Vero Beach Dodgers. From there he moved to the San Antonio Dodgers for the 1983 campaign before doing a three-season stint with the Albuquerque Dukes from 1984 to 1986. He was the organization's minor-league pitching coordinator from 1987 to 1994, then the Dodgers' pitching coach from 1995 to 1997. Over the course of his time in the Dodger organization he played a role in the development of a number of great pitchers, including most prominently Pedro Martínez and Orel Hershiser.

In 1999 Wallace switched gears, joining the New York Mets, for whom he was the pitching coach for two seasons, 1999 and 2000. During his time in New York, Wallace helped the Mets reach the NL Championship Series in 1999 and the World Series in 2000, with strong pitching being central to their success – the 1999 team was fifth in the league in ERA while the 2000 team was third. Despite the success, Wallace and Mets manager Bobby Valentine never developed a close relationship and Wallace opted to return to the Dodgers after the 2000 season.[6] There he worked as a special assistant to the general manager before assuming the role of interim general manager for the 2001 season and had the title of senior vice president for baseball operations in 2002. In the latter role he oversaw the team's minor-league operations and was a consultant to Dodgers GM Dan Evans.

Wallace's hiring by the Red Sox in 2003 was not a total surprise, for while the move to replace Cloninger came in midseason, the Red Sox had long coveted him, contacting the Dodgers during the previous offseason about the possibility of Wallace's moving east. While it was just an inquiry, the Dodgers made clear that they valued Wallace, telling the Red Sox that they would want compensation if such a move occurred. Of course, given that he had spent 20 years spread out over two different stints with the Dodgers, it was not a surprise that they were reluctant to see him go. At the same time, the prospect of going to the Red Sox represented something of a homecoming for the Connecticut native. When Cloninger was forced to go on indefinite medical leave, the Red Sox became more aggressive in their pursuit of Wallace, with a member of the Red Sox ownership contacting Dodgers chair Bob Daly seeking permission to talk with the pitching guru, an inquiry not the norm for a pitching-coach candidate. And yet while the Dodgers relented, and Wallace joined the team in June, many expected that his coaching days would be limited with a return to the front office a likely future move. In fact, Wallace was attracted to the idea of returning to the field and to working directly with players as well as returning to New England, where he had grown up, and while he was initially an "interim" when he began in June, he expected to be there for the long haul.[7]

And so it was that while Cloninger successfully beat the cancer and subsequently remained with the Red Sox for almost 15 years as a player development consultant, Wallace quickly made the post his own, while setting out to gain the trust of a struggling rotation, one that behind ace Martínez included starters Derek Lowe, Tim Wakefield, and John Burkett, with closer Byung-Hyun Kim and Mike Timlin and Alan Embree, anchoring the bullpen. The veteran coach had done his homework and he knew what they had to offer, but especially coming in midseason, Wallace said that nothing was more important than "building a bond with the players" and demonstrating that he was "sensitive to their needs."[8] Wallace acknowledged that the whole process was made easier by his previous work with Martínez, who could attest to what his old coach had to offer.[9] The results of Wallace's tutelage soon became apparent. As the season unfolded and under Wallace's steady hand, the staff came together, showing substantive improvement. By season's end, the team ERA had dropped to 4.48, which ranked eighth in the American League.

As the Red Sox headed into 2004, with the partial 2003 season having given Wallace a sense of what the pitching staff could do, the team was ready to take the final step toward its long-sought championship. The near-miss against the Yankees in the previous year's American League Championship Series had led GM Theo Epstein to strengthen the pitching staff, securing the services of All-Star right-hander Curt Schilling as well as Bronson Arroyo. The team also acquired Keith Foulke to be the closer after Byung-Hyun Kim had struggled down the stretch in 2003, dogged by a series of injuries that that never allowed him to return to his peak form. Wallace was particularly pleased with the addition of Schilling and Foulke, a pair he believed did much to "firm up a solid rotation."[10]

This group under the new manager, Terry Francona, and with Wallace overseeing the staff from the start, helped the Red Sox win 98 games to finish second behind the Yankees. The pitching staff, featuring starters Schilling, and Martínez at the top, complemented by Derek Lowe, Tim Wakefield, and Bronson Arroyo, with Timlin and Embree handling most of the middle-inning work and Foulke the closer, continued the improvement that had occurred under Wallace in 2003, further lowering the staff's ERA to 4.18, third-best in the American League.

The postseason was memorable and historic as the Red Sox made an unprecedented comeback, erasing the Yankees' three-games-to-none lead in the League Championship Series to take the American League pennant, before sweeping the St. Louis Cardinals to win the franchise's first World Series in 86 years. While heroes abounded, the honor roll certainly included Wallace's pitching staff, especially Schilling, Martínez, Lowe, and Foulke.

Wallace has called the season the "peak" of his career, saying that "words can't describe the satisfaction" he felt as the team came back against the Yankees before ultimately winning the World Series.[11] He remembers the team fondly, saying it was "quite a conglomerate of personalities."[12] It was, he recalled, an extraordinary experience as the team methodically put together the comeback for the ages. As "crazy" as the team was,

Wallace remembered their focus. Down three games to none, they knew they had to win one game at a time. And to do that, he remembered, they determined to take it one step at a time, focusing on "winning the at-bat," "winning the situation," and ultimately winning the game en route to mounting a comeback for the ages.[13] The team's determination was mixed with a toughness embodied in Schilling's "Bloody Sock" game, an effort that did not surprise Wallace, who had no doubts about the hard-throwing right-hander making the start.[14]

While the Red Sox again finished second to the Yankees in 2005, Wallace faced many new crises on a pitching staff that had been so important to the success of the 2004 World Series team. Pedro Martínez and Derek Lowe signed as free agents with the New York Mets and Los Angeles Dodgers respectively, and Curt Schilling suffered a series of injuries that limited the right-handed workhorse to fewer than 100 innings pitched.[15] That left only Tim Wakefield and Bronson Arroyo from the championship starting staff, and while the middle relievers and closer remained, Wallace had to work hard to put together a staff that could compete. Ultimately the Red Sox lost to the White Sox in the American League Division Series, ending their quest for a repeat championship.

The 2006 season was a nightmare for Wallace. Driving to spring training in February, he was in South Carolina when he experienced a searing pain in his hip, which had been previously replaced. He called the team doctor, who told him to drive to the nearest hospital. Unable to continue, Wallace was picked up by an ambulance at the side of the road in Spartanburg, South Carolina.[16] He went into septic shock caused by salmonella attacking the artificial hip. He spent three days in intensive care before he was transferred to a hospital in Massachusetts. Released after three weeks in the hospital, he was forced to return after two days. The artificial hip was removed and replaced and Wallace was on crutches for just short of six months.[17] He returned to the Red Sox by midsummer but the team had essentially moved on and he resigned at the end of the season.

But Wallace was not ready to leave the game, and although weak and with his weight down to 150, 35 pounds under his playing weight, he accepted an offer to join the Houston Astros as their pitching coach.[18] It did not turn out well, and at the end of the 2007 season, Wallace headed back to the West Coast, accepting a job as special assistant to the Mariners' executive VP, pitching development. At the end of the 2008 season he was named the team's minor-league pitching coordinator.

Wallace returned to the East the following year, joining the Atlanta Braves, for whom he was the minor-league pitching coordinator from 2010 to 2013. That stint was interrupted briefly in 2011 when he filled in for Braves pitching coach Roger McDowell who was placed on administrative leave while the team investigated allegations of homophobic slurs and threatening behavior. However, after 2013, differences between Wallace and the front office led to a parting of the ways.

From Atlanta Wallace moved north and back to the American League, becoming the pitching coach for the Baltimore Orioles. In three seasons working with manager Buck Showalter, he helped with a team renaissance. During that time the Orioles won the AL East in 2014 while winning 96 games as well as securing the wild-card spot in 2016. It was to Wallace's credit that despite the fact that the Orioles had no true ace, they were still able to finish with the third-best ERA in the American League in 2014. Things did not get any easier in the next two years. In fact, in 2016, the Orioles had only a single starter who won more than 10 games on a staff that saw 27 pitchers make at least one appearance. It was challenging, to be sure.

In the aftermath of the 2016 season, the Orioles announced that Wallace had decided to retire as the team's pitching coach after his three-year stint. According to Baltimore manager Showalter, Wallace hoped to stay involved with the game as a part-time pitching instructor in the major leagues, but at the time of the announcement he had no definite plan.[19] Not long afterward, he returned to the Braves, signing on as a pitching consultant. It was seen as a more passive role for the then 69-year-old Wallace, and was ultimately one he filled for three years until February 2020, when it was announced that he and the team had mutually agree to part ways, a move likely resulting from some substantive changes in the way the new front-office leadership sought to proceed.[20]

Wallace's departure from the Braves appeared to mark the end of his professional career, one that dated back to his first season of minor-league ball in the Phillies organization. And yet while he sat out the COVID pandemic of 2020, in April of 2021 Wallace was named the pitching coach for the United States national baseball team, which at that point still needed to participate in a final qualifying tournament to earn a spot in the delayed 2020 Olympics taking place in Tokyo at summer's end.[21] Led by former Angels manager Mike Scioscia, the team qualified for the trip to Tokyo and with Wallace continuing as pitching coach for the Olympics, the US earned a Silver Medal, falling to the home-team Japanese in the championship game in a 2-0 pitchers' duel.[22]

In many ways, the Olympic assignment was an appropriate end to the second half of Dave Wallace's career. His time with Red Sox had marked a return to dealing directly with players, particularly pitchers, and it was an experience he realized brought him his greatest satisfaction. Likening what he did to being a teacher, in looking back, he said he realized that it was that interaction with the players that he really enjoyed and found the most rewarding. Working with a mix of players, each with their different backgrounds and cultures, Wallace relished "the chance to have an impact on their lives." That, he said, was what really appealed to him. He said the Olympics and the chance to represent their country brought out another side to the players, one he observed again during the 2023 World Baseball Classic.[23]

In the aftermath of the Olympics, Wallace returned to Waterbury, where he was honored by his former hometown, which gave him the key to the city. Expressing his surprise and appreciation at the turnout, Wallace called Waterbury a "baseball crazy town" and the place where he had gotten the foundation for the almost half-century-long career that had culminated in the Olympic Silver Medal-winning effort.[24]

While he had expected the Olympics to be his last assignment, as spring training 2023 approached, an old friend, Miami Marlins general manager Kim Ng signed Wallace as a consultant, a post that allowed him to bring his years of experience to the young Marlins staff, one headed by 2022 Cy Young Award winner Sandy Alcantara. Wallace said it was an ideal assignment, another one that allowed him to work and mentor young hurlers in the Marlins organization, traveling periodically to different sites during the season from his summer home in the Boston area.[25]

Wallace has been married to the former Joyce Shellman since January 4, 1997.[26] The couple split their time between Florida in the winter and the Boston area during the baseball season.[27]

SOURCES

In addition to the sources cited in the Notes, the author consulted baseball-almanac.com and Baseball-Reference.com.

NOTES

1. Jimmy Golen, "Red Sox Tab Wallace to Replace Ailing Cloninger," *New Bedford* (Massachusetts) *Standard Times,* June 10, 2003; https://www.southcoasttoday.com/story/sports/2003/06/10/red-sox-tab-wallace-to/50392644007/.
2. Doug Mead, "The 50 Best MLB Pitching Coaches of All Time," *Bleacher Report,* February 1, 2012; https://bleacherreport.com/articles/1047146-the-50-best-mlb-pitching-coaches-of-all-time.
3. David W. Wallace, 1947, Bronson Library; http://www.bronsonlibrary.org/filestorage/1521/1545/HOF_2014_Wallace_David_W.pdf.
4. "Dave Wallace," University of New Haven Athletic Hall of Fame; https://newhavenchargers.com/honors/hall-of-fame/dave-wallace/92.
5. Matt Veasey, "Phillies 50: Forgotten 1973 – Ron Diorio and Dave Wallace," July 18, 2020; https://mattveasey.com/2020/07/18/philadelphia-phillies-50-forgotten-1973-ron-diorio-and-dave-wallace/.
6. "Dave Wallace Stats," Baseball Almanac; Dave Wallace: 2000 N.L. Champion Mets Pitching Coach (1998-2000)," centerfieldmaz, September 06, 2022; http://www.centerfieldmaz.com/2018/09/2000-nl-champion-mets-pitching-coach.html.
7. Dave Wallace, telephone interview, February 27, 2023.
8. Wallace interview, February 27, 2023.
9. Dave Wallace, telephone interview, April 13, 2023.
10. Wallace interview, February 27, 2023.
11. Wallace interview, April 13, 2023.
12. Wallace interview, April 13, 2023.
13. Wallace interview, February 27, 2023.
14. Wallace interview, February 27, 2023.
15. "2005 Boston Red Sox Statistics," Baseball Reference; https://www.baseball-reference.com/teams/BOS/2005.shtml.
16. Tyler Kepner, "A Mentor Whose Experience Goes Far Beyond Pitching," *New York Times*, September 22, 2014.
17. Kepner.
18. Kepner.
19. "Former Red Sox Coach Dave Wallace Retiring," Boston25 News, October 6, 2016; https://www.boston25news.com/sports/former-red-sox-coach-dave-wallace-retiring/454309756/.
20. "Braves, Dave Wallace Mutually Part Ways," ATL, Atlanta Sports Talk, February 28, 2020; https://www.sportstalkatl.com/braves-dave-wallace-mutually-part-ways/.
21. "Former Orioles Pitching Coach Dave Wallace to Be Mike Scioscia's Olympic Pitching Coach," *Baltimore Sun*, April 23, 2021; https://www.baltimoresun.com/sports/orioles/bs-sp-dave-wallace-olympic-pitching-coach-20210423-v4c5uyyxuvg3nop2alf4qdik4e-story.html.
22. "Team USA Brings Home Silver From Olympic Games Tokyo 2020," *USA Baseball,* August 7, 2021; https://www.usabaseball.com/news/topic/general/team-usa-brings-home-silver-from-olympic-games-tokyo-2020.
23. Wallace interview, April 13, 2023.
24. "Waterbury Walkabout: Former Baseball Pro Receives Keys to the City," *Waterbury Republican American,* September 25, 2021; https://archives.rep-am.com/2021/09/25/waterbury-walkabout-former-baseball-pro-receives-keys-to-the-city/.
25. Wallace interview, February 27, 2023.
26. "Dave Wallace," IMDb; https://www.imdb.com/name/nm1991613/bio.
27. Wallace interview, February 27, 2023.

HOW THE 2004 RED SOX TEAM WAS PUT TOGETHER

BY BILL NOWLIN

The team that finally won the World Series for Boston, for the first time in 86 years, was not a homegrown team, a product of a robust Red Sox farm system.

Of the 25 players on the postseason roster, only two had come up in the system – Trot Nixon and Kevin Youkilis.

Five were players who had been released or placed on waivers by other teams.

Six were free-agent signings.

And the other 12 were players for whom the Red Sox traded. Of course, in making those trades the Red Sox included a number of players who had been developed in their own farm system.

These trades and acquisitions were made by GMs Dan Duquette and Theo Epstein. The following chart chronicles the moves to build the 2004 Red Sox, as to the players on the final postseason roster. There were other players who contributed earlier in the season who for one reason or another did not make the roster.

Players drafted and developed by the Red Sox

Trot Nixon – selected by the Red Sox in the first round (the seventh overall pick) of the June 1993 amateur draft, from high school in Wilmington, North Carolina. GM = Lou Gorman. Debut September 21, 1996.

Kevin Youkilis – selected by the Red Sox in the eighth round of the June 2001 amateur draft, from the University of Cincinnati. GM = Dan Duquette. Debut May 15, 2004.

Signed as free agents by the Red Sox

Manny Ramirez – December 19, 2000. GM = Dan Duquette. Ramirez was signed to an eight-year deal. He played with the Red Sox until he was traded on July 31, 2008.

Johnny Damon – December 21, 2001. GM = Dan Duquette. Damon was signed to a four-year deal. After the term was complete, he signed with the New York Yankees in January 2006.

Mike Timlin – January 6, 2003. GM = Theo Epstein. Timlin signed again after the season, on November 17, and pitched for the Red Sox through the 2008 season, his last in the majors.

Bill Mueller – January 10, 2003. GM = Theo Epstein. A veteran of seven seasons with the Giants and Cubs, Mueller played three seasons for the Red Sox.

Pokey Reese – December 23, 2003. GM = Theo Epstein. The year 2004 was his eighth and final major-league season, after seasons with Cincinnati and Pittsburgh.

Keith Foulke – January 7, 2004. GM = Theo Epstein. After pitching for the Giants, six years with the White Sox, and 2003 for Oakland, Foulke signed with the Red Sox and pitched for Boston from 2004 through 2006.

Players signed who had been released or placed on waivers by other teams

Tim Wakefield – Originally drafted by the Pittsburgh Pirates in 1998, he was released by the Pirates on April 20, 1995, and signed by the Red Sox six days later. GM = Dan Duquette. Red Sox debut May 27, 1995. After six seasons with the Red Sox, he became a free agent and then signed again, once more by Dan Duquette, in December 2000.

David Ortiz – Originally signed by the Seattle Mariners, he was traded to the Minnesota Twins in September 1996 but after playing parts of six seasons for the Twins was released by them on December 16, 2002. On January 22, 2003, he was signed by the Red Sox. GM = Theo Epstein. Red Sox debut April 1, 2003.

Bronson Arroyo – Originally signed by the Pirates, he pitched parts of three seasons for them (2000-2002), but on February 4, 2003, he was claimed off waivers by the Red Sox. GM = Theo Epstein. Red Sox debut August 25, 2003.

Gabe Kapler – Kapler played in the majors for the Detroit Tigers, Texas Rangers, and Colorado Rockies from 1998 into 2003. He was purchased by the Red Sox from the Rockies on June 28, 2003. GM = Theo Epstein. Red Sox debut June 28, 2003.

Curtis Leskanic – Leskanic began his career with Colorado and pitched for the, Rockies, the Milwaukee Brewers, and the Kansas City Royals from 1993 into June 2004. The Royals released him on June 18, 2004, and he was signed by the Red Sox on June 22. GM = Theo Epstein. Red Sox debut June 25, 2004.

Players acquired by trades or waivers

Derek Lowe – July 31, 1997. GM = Dan Duquette. The Red Sox traded reliever Heathcliff Slocumb to the Seattle Mariners for Derek Lowe and Jason Varitek.

Jason Varitek – July 31, 1997. GM = Dan Duquette. In the same straight-up trade involving Derek Lowe, the Red Sox acquired two future All-Stars and World Champions.

Pedro Martinez – November 18, 1997. GM = Dan Duquette. The Montreal Expos traded the 1997 Cy Young Award winner to the Red Sox for Carl Pavano and a player to be named later (Tony Armas).

Doug Mirabelli – June 12, 2001. GM = Dan Duquette. The Red Sox traded pitching prospect Justin Duchsherer to the Texas Rangers for catcher Mirabelli. Duchsherer was 1-1 for Texas and later was 32-24 for Oakland.

Alan Embree – June 23, 2002. Interim GM = Mike Port. In another midseason trade the Red Sox sent minor-league pitchers Brad Baker and Dan Giese (who reached the majors in September 2007) for minor-league reliever Andy Shibilo and veteran lefty reliever Embree.

Kevin Millar – February 15, 2003. GM = Theo Epstein. The Red Sox sent cash to the Florida Marlins for Kevin Millar, who had hit over .300 each of the prior two seasons.

Curt Schilling – November 28, 2003. GM = Theo Epstein. Schilling had originally been drafted by the Red Sox in January 1986, then traded in midyear of 1988 to Baltimore. After time with the Phillies and a World Series championship with the Diamondbacks, he was traded by Arizona to the Red Sox for pitchers Casey Fossum, Brandon Lyon, and Jorge De La Rosa, and minor-league outfielder Mike Goss.

Mark Bellhorn – December 16, 2003. GM = Theo Epstein. Bellhorn was sent to the Boston Red Sox by the Colorado Rockies for $125,000, a straight-up cash deal, per a September 13, 2022, email from Sarah Coffin of the Red Sox to Jason Scheller.

Orlando Cabrera – July 31, 2004. GM = Theo Epstein. The Red Sox acquired Cabrera as part of a four-team trade-deadline deal. He came from the Montreal Expos, who received pitcher Francis Beltran, infielders Alex Gonzalez and Brendan Harris from the Chicago Cubs. The Cubs also sent minor-leaguer Justin Jones to the Minnesota Twins, who sent Doug Mientkiewicz to the Red Sox. The Cubs received Nomar Garciaparra and Matt Murton from the Red Sox.

Doug Mientkiewicz – July 31, 2004. GM = Theo Epstein. As noted in the above summary, Mientkiewicz came from the Twins to the Red Sox as part of the four-team trade.

Dave Roberts – July 31, 2004. GM = Theo Epstein. On the same day as the Red Sox acquired Cabrera and Mientkiewicz, they added Dave Roberts in a separate trade, sending minor-league outfielder Henri Stanley to the Los Angeles Dodgers.

Mike Myers – August 6, 2004. GM = Theo Epstein. Myers was placed on waivers by the Seattle Mariners on August 6, and was claimed by the Red Sox in a cash transaction.

Red Sox GMs:
Theo N. Epstein	2002-2005
Michael D. Port (interim)	2002
Daniel F. Duquette	1994-2002
James "Lou" Gorman	1984-1993

Theo Epstein
Senior Vice President/ General Manager

Tom Werner
Chairman

Larry Lucchino
President/Chief Executive Officer

John W. Henry
Principal Owner

RED SOX RESERVES IN THE PLAYOFFS

BY BILL NOWLIN

Before Game One of the 2004 World Series, the Red Sox team and staff were introduced individually, coming out from the dugout and standing along the Fenway Park first-base line. This included the batboys – Andrew Crosby and Chris Cundiff – the trainers, the clubhouse staff, and – as a bonus, "Mr. Red Sox" Johnny Pesky.[1]

Five of the players on the 25-man World Series roster had not been on the team on Opening Day: Orlando Cabrera, Curtis Leskanic, Doug Mientkiewicz, Mike Myers, and Dave Roberts.

There were a number of players introduced who were not on the 25-man roster, but who had made contributions to the team during the course of the season.

There were also players introduced who were on the roster but, as events transpired, did not see action in the World Series, which lasted only four games since the Red Sox swept the Cardinals. These included Terry Adams, Ellis Burks, Curtis Leskanic, Sandy Martinez, Dave McCarty, Ramiro Mendoza, Mike Myers, Dave Roberts, and Kevin Youkilis.

Others introduced before the game who were not on the roster were Lenny DiNardo, Ricky Gutierrez, and Adam Hyzdu.

It was quite gracious of the Red Sox to recognize the players in this fashion, players who had been readied as possible reserves should they have been needed. Adam Hyzdu said, "Theo was nice to do that. It would have been a fluke [had either Lenny or I been needed], but once the Series started you can't really do anything with your roster. A couple of days there working, doing some hitting, to be kind of fresh – just in case."[2] His understanding was at first pitch, the rosters were locked.

Lenny DiNardo said, "I was fortunate enough to be on the team — 22 games that season — and they allowed to line up with the team at home, in uniform." Though he did not travel with

Lenny DiNardo being transported by Bill Janovitz and Pete Caldes. Courtesy of Lenny DiNardo.

the team to St. Louis, he was at the first two games, at Fenway Park. "I was either in the clubhouse or the dugout, traveling back and forth. I do remember meeting Steven Tyler in the clubhouse. He came in and got a cup of coffee and I talked to him for a minute. James Taylor, maybe, at some point? Most of the time, I was in the clubhouse taking it in on the couch. Ortiz would come in every now and then – he was DH-ing. He would come in and hang out.

"I think they did their best to let me be a part of the festivities and whatnot. Obviously I was on the duckboat parade.

"A 24-year-old kid who wasn't going to be on the postseason roster. There were a lot of veterans on that club—a lot of dirt on their spikes. I don't look back on it with any regret."[3]

Adam Hyzdu did travel with the team to St. Louis as well. "In uniform, in the dugout. It was really cool gesture to fly us back. Obviously appreciated, because it was an experience that very few get. You got a room. You got your meal money. Everything was normal. You're just not an active player. It was a really good seat, for sure. A good seat." And at the end, doused with champagne.

NOTES

1. Full coverage of the introductions can be seen on this YouTube video: https://www.youtube.com/watch?v=sYCweQS5nVo&t=1494s
2. Interview with Adam Hyzdu on June 13, 2023.
3. When the Red Sox won the final game of the World Series, DiNardo said, "I was at a bar with a lot of my friends who were musicians – Flat Top Johnny's [Kendall Square.] Bill Janovitz, who was in a band called Buffalo Tom, and Pete Caldes, Ed Valauskas, and Juliana Hatfield, and a bunch of other musicians that I became friends with and am 'til today – ended up picking me up and crowd-surfing me from one side of the bar to the other. I think I landed on a pool table." Interview with Lenny DiNardo on August 27, 2023.

THE VIEW FROM ABOVE THE CROWDS

BY BILL BALLOU

For reporters covering the Red Sox, the 2004 baseball season started in the earliest hours of October 17, 2003.

That was when Boston suffered another in four-score and five years of excruciating defeats, a 6-5 loss to the Yankees on Aaron Boone's game-ending and series-ending – Game Seven at that – home run in the American League Championship Series.

In our business, news is like cash. There is no such thing as too much. This time there was, though, considering how much happened in such a short span and past deadline for that matter. For some of us, what happened after Boone's home run was more important than what happened before, an event that spoke to a future none of us could envision.

There were two elevators from the press box to the basement in the old Yankee Stadium. One was for VIPs and if some unfortunate and unaware person blundered into it by mistake, something bad happened. We didn't know what, since nobody ever came back.

Our elevator was small and slow. On this night we had to wait in line as shift after shift of writers was ferried to the respective clubhouses. About 25 of us were in the third wave, crammed in and barely able to inhale – all things considered, a blessing – when the door finally began to close.

Suddenly an arm came through the door from out of the waiting area. A heavyset figure backed into the elevator to the groans of its occupants, squeezing things even more uncomfortably. From the hairstyle it was easy to see who it was – Donald Trump.

Rather than wait for the VIP elevator, he encroached on ours. With him in there, the door wouldn't close no matter how often the elevator operator tried and that must have been five, maybe six times. We were overweight, too, and the alarm started going off.

Meanwhile, the interviews of players and managers were beginning in the question-and-answer room. We were all missing some of it, probably the most important parts. Still the elevator stayed at the top of Yankee Stadium, alarms ringing, the door opening and closing futilely.

Eventually the operator said, "If this elevator is gonna move, somebody's gotta get off."

Somebody did – a baseball writer, maybe two – but not Trump. He just didn't care about anyone else, care about how his actions might affect a bigger picture than his own personal one.

Some things never change.

When everyone finally reached the interview room, manager Grady Little was about to leave. We had no idea at that time that it was his last press conference as Red Sox manager. Little was fired before the month was over, then replaced by Terry Francona.

At the time, it seemed like just another nonsensical Boston managerial move. Like Joe Kerrigan replacing Jimy Williams, Butch Hobson replacing Joe Morgan, Mike Higgins replacing Billy Jurges, who had previously replaced Higgins.

Little had been good to deal with and hardly anybody was happy to see him go. If he had been a radio station, his format was Soft Rock. Little had tried cotton farming in between two stints with pro baseball, and baseball turned out to be better even if you could get fired.

Francona was coming off a disastrous four years managing the Phillies.

He was, it turned out, the perfect pick. Francona was a study in contrasts. He was approachable, but mercurial. It was easy to get a rise out of him, but he would eventually calm down and sue for peace. Most big-league managers hate being called "coach." With Francona, that sin bordered on mortal.

There was a radio lightweight in Chicago who invariably referred to him as "Coach Tony Francona," not even getting the first name right, and Francona could barely restrain himself from coming across his desk and throttling the dweeb.

In group settings Francona was careful to the point of boring. With reporters he knew and trusted, he was available, candid, and insightful.

One of the first things he said after taking over the team was prophetic, although nobody knew it at the time. "I will never," he said, "tell one of my players – 'Back when I was a player, we did it this way.'"

Little known fact at the time – Francona hated to drive. He was the guy going 50 on the Mass Pike, although always in the slow lane. Francona was not rude, just cautious. His years in Philadelphia were mostly miserable and he told us that after he was fired – he deserved to be fired, he said – he did not think he ever wanted to manage again. His attitude changed, as did the fortunes of the Red Sox.

The 2004 Sox were a fairly easy team to cover. They were good, which makes everybody happier and more approachable. General manager Theo Epstein was also cautious in public but candid with trusted reporters, a good source for on-the-record contributions and valuable background.

The new owners were approachable, too, especially Larry Lucchino. He enjoyed the give-and-take with reporters more than John Henry but Henry would talk to us, albeit softly. He could be candid, too, if caught at the right time and place.

One of those times and places was October 26 at Busch Stadium in St. Louis, where the Red Sox had a two-games-to-none lead in the World Series. Henry was in the Boston dugout before the game doing some baseball chit-chatting when Associated Press reporter Jimmy Golen asked him, out of the blue, "Are you a billionaire?"

Henry shook his head and grimaced a bit, answering, "Oh, no. No, no, no, no." At least he answered.

Boston had several players who enjoyed talking to the news media. That had not always been the case in years past. In fact, it was rarely the case. The '04 Sox, though, had Kevin Millar, Johnny Damon, Derek Lowe, and Bronson Arroyo. David Ortiz was in the early stages of his Hall of Fame career and was approachable. Trot Nixon was a serious interviewee, thoughtful and candid even if he ruffled feathers along the way. Jason Varitek was professional, approachable, and available – but essentially colorless.

Then there were Curt Schilling and Nomar Garciaparra.

In 2004 Schilling was standing at the edge of reason but had not yet gone over it. All we needed to know about him happened on the first day of spring training when Red Sox public relations scheduled, at Schilling's request, a group interview at 12:15 at the minor-league complex in Fort Myers.

We waited and waited and waited for Schilling to show up. He finally did at 3 P.M. and that was just the way it was going to be with him. Schilling's nickname throughout baseball, by the way, was "Table for One."

Garciaparra became difficult as his years in Boston accumulated. It got to the point where he had the team create a red line in the carpet of the clubhouse floor, in front of the lockers. Reporters were not supposed to venture beyond it in visiting with players. According to the Major League Baseball rules governing access, the red line was absolutely unenforceable and Boston was the only clubhouse with one. Still, the message was clear: Keep Out.

As often happens where there is a new manager, the team got off to a very strong start. Boston was 31-19 after 50 games and was in first place by a half-game on the morning of May 31.

Then the Sox slipped into mediocrity. They were 24-26 in their next 50 games, the end of that stretch coinciding with the trade deadline of July 31. By that time, Garciaparra's misery was palpable and destructive. Finally, right at the last hour of the deadline, Epstein dealt him to the Cubs as part of a complex four-team trade.

The Red Sox were in Minneapolis at the time, the Twins still in the dreary Metrodome. Reporters had had a very long wait in its sterile tunnels before Garciaparra finally emerged from the Boston clubhouse. He stopped to talk about the deal, then tried to go out on a high note. He shook hands with everyone in the media contingent encircling him, then kept going for another round.

The All-Star shortstop realized what was happening, stopped, and said sheepishly, "I wanted to thank every one of you, and some people more than once."

The deal brought shortstop Orlando Cabrera and first baseman Doug Mientkiewicz to Boston but was not an immediate season-changer. The Sox went 4-4 in their first eight games after it, but then began to put things together. Starting with August 16, Boston went 22-3 in its next 25 games, reestablishing itself as one of the best teams in baseball.

The Sox clinched a playoff berth on September 27 in Tampa Bay. The next day Damon was asked to compare the 2004 team with the previous season's. The '04 clinching celebration was much subdued than the one in '03. The reason, Damon said, "We're a bunch of idiots, but we're grownup idiots now."

The playoffs started on October 5 in Anaheim. The day before was a workout day, an easy one for reporters. I got to the ballpark early. Anaheim Stadium was surrounded by acres of parking lots. They were empty that afternoon save for a solitary human orbiting the fringes of the ballpark.

Upon closer inspection it turned out to be Manny Ramírez.

"Hey, man," was his standard greeting and that's how he called out to me. "How do you get into this place?" I told him I was not sure either, but follow me and we'll find a way in, which we did. I always wondered whether if I had not happened upon Manny in the parking lot he would have wound up at Disneyland or Knott's Berry Farm and missed the Division Series.

Boston swept that series, setting up a rematch with the Yankees in another ALCS. We know how that turned out. I was very friendly with two former Red Sox players wearing Yankees uniforms, catcher John Flaherty and reliever Paul Quantrill, and talked with them whenever possible. Clubhouse access is limited during the postseason, though, so the conversations were relatively short.

They did give me a sense of what was going on with the Yankees, though. After their overwhelming Game Three victory at Fenway Park, the team was in a bubble of invincibility. Even after Ortiz's dramatic home run to win Game Four – I had mixed feelings about it because Quantrill, one of the most standup guys ever to wear a Boston uniform – was the New York pitcher.

After the Sox won Game Five, though, the Yankees' team demeanor changed a bit. They sensed that they had a real chance to be the first team in baseball history to lose a series after leading three games to none.

Which is exactly what happened.

Game Seven at Yankee Stadium ended on Ruben Sierra's groundball to second baseman Pokey Reese with Alan Embree on the mound. This time there was no Donald Trump to deal with, only champagne. That was easy. In the press box postgame, it was apparent that there were still a lot of Red Sox fans in the ballpark, some still cheering, most just taking it all in.

The Yankees essentially let them stay for as long as they wanted, a very classy act.

The World Series was not anticlimactic, but it was the hot fudge on the coffee ice cream of 2004. Game Four was on October 27, a damp night in St. Louis. Busch Stadium was on its way to abandonment and the press box roof leaked, forcing us writers to find a dry spot wherever we could.

The bottom of the ninth arrived with Boston leading, 3-0. It had an eerie feel to it. We understood that this Red Sox team was a different creature from previous ones and would likely be celebrating a World Series title in a matter of minutes. Still, there had been 1946, '67, '75, '86, 2003, and etc.

My wife, Debbie, was in town with me but not at the game. She was watching it from our hotel bar, cheering for the Sox as the game progressed. When the ninth inning finally arrived, a Cardinals fan sitting with her asked, "Why aren't you celebrating?"

Debbie responded, "You don't know much about the Red Sox, do you?"

When Edgar Renteria came up, I called my wife. If she could not be at the ballpark to see the Red Sox win the World Series, she could at least hear the moment.

The first thing I said was, "I wanted you to be able to hear...." and at that moment, Edgar Renteria bounced a groundball to Keith Foulke. There was a brief moment of suspended animation, then it was official.

"My God," I said, "the Red Sox just won the World Series. I have to write."

Before I headed to the clubhouses, I called my daughter – Abigail Brinkman – in Chicago. Her husband, Charles, had grown up a White Sox fan and actually worked as an usher at the original Comiskey Park. The White Sox had not won a World Series since 1906. Between husband and wife there were 184 seasons of baseball misery watching the TV.

Abby was literally delirious. She was making noise but none of it made sense, so I finally just said goodbye. Who would ever have imagined that one year later the White Sox would end their World Series drought? What were the odds of that? But aren't things like that the reason baseball is the world's most compelling game?

At the time, almost all of us in the press box were glad the drought was over. It had become tiresome answering the same old questions every year. None of us, though, had any inkling this would be merely the first of four such championships in 15 years.

Would the next three have happened without 2004? Probably, but we all knew that from there on out, covering the Red Sox would never be the same.

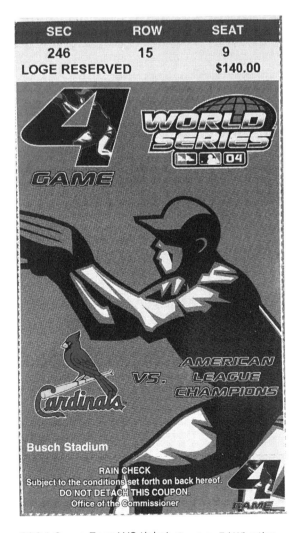

2004 Game Four WS ticket. Courtesy Ed Wheatley

DOWN ON THE FARM: THE STORY OF THE 2004 SARASOTA RED SOX

BY CHRISTOPHER CHAVIS

Jon Lester, Jonathan Papelbon, Hanley Ramirez, and Dustin Pedroia – names you likely would not expect to read about in a book about the 2004 Boston Red Sox. After all, these men were key players in the 2007 World Series championship. Lester, Papelbon, and Pedroia were on the team, while Ramirez was traded to the Florida Marlins for Josh Beckett and 2007 World Series MVP Mike Lowell. However, it is difficult to fully tell the story of the 2004 Red Sox without understanding the moves that were being made to secure a future championship. Not because the Red Sox were destined to win a World Series in 2004 but because if "the curse" had reared its ugly head again, this was the core that would continue the fight to bring a World Series championship back to Boston.

All four men would appear at varying points in the season down in Sarasota, Florida, for the Sarasota Red Sox, the Red Sox Advanced-A affiliate in the Florida State League.

Jon Lester

Jon Lester almost started 2004 in the Texas Rangers farm system. If all had gone according to plan, he would have been a part of a trade that brought Alex Rodriguez to Boston. In 2003 he had gone 6-9 and posted a 3.65 ERA with the Augusta (South Carolina) Greenjackets, the Red Sox Low-A affiliate, and entered minor-league camp projected to end up in Sarasota.[1]

Lester battled injuries in the late spring and early summer, which temporarily sidelined him.[2] However, the injuries did not stop his momentum as he continued progressing up the ladder in the Red Sox organization. By the late summer, the team was thinking about moving him up to the Double-A Portland (Maine) Sea Dogs in 2005. He became a consistent strikeout threat with a fastball reaching 96 MPH.[3]

Lester ended 2004 ranked by *Baseball America* as the fourth-best prospect in the Red Sox system.[4]

Projected to join him in the 2005 Portland rotation was future closer Jonathan Papelbon …

Jonathan Papelbon

Jonathan Papelbon, a 2003 draft pick, entered 2004 as a starter for the Sarasota Red Sox. The idea of Papelbon as a starter is likely foreign to most Red Sox fans, but before transitioning to closer, he worked his way through the Red Sox minor-league system as a starter. And frankly, he was not terrible. During their time together in Sarasota, Papelbon kept pace with and sometimes outperformed Lester. By May 9, Papelbon was 3-1 with a 2.86 ERA in 28⅓ innings pitched, outpacing Lester, who was 1-2 with a 5.48 ERA in 21⅓ innings pitched.[5] While Lester improved throughout May and ultimately ended the month with a 4-3 record with a 4.14 ERA in 45⅔ innings pitched, Papelbon kept up his pace and ended the month with a 4-3 record with a 3.16 ERA in 51⅓ innings pitched.[6] A direct comparison between the two became more difficult after May as Lester struggled with injuries and spent time on the disabled list.[7]

Papelbon's success even sparked calls to have him promoted to Portland in mid-2004, prompting Red Sox general manager Theo Epstein to shoot down these calls by saying that Papelbon needed to stay in Sarasota to work on his offspeed stuff.[8] Luckily for Papelbon, the Red Sox eventually embraced his firepower and moved him into the closer role in 2007.

Papelbon ended 2004 ranked by *Baseball America* as the third-best prospect in the Red Sox organization, just ahead of Jon Lester.[9]

Papelbon was ultimately selected to the Florida State League All-Star Game, an honor he shared with Hanley Ramirez …

Hanley Ramirez

Hanley Ramirez entered 2004 as the top prospect in the Red Sox system and the top prospect in all of baseball.[10] He even started the year playing with the Red Sox in spring training, and there were talks of his starting the year in Portland, not Sarasota.[11] Despite these predictions, Ramirez joined the squad in Sarasota.[12]

Ramirez started strong, batting over .300 through April and May. However, despite his best efforts to play through it, a wrist injury sidelined him for a month at the end of May.[13] Despite being named to the All-Star team, Ramirez could not play.[14]

When he returned from injury, he picked up from where he left off, hitting .362 in his first 14 games in July.[15] His performance with Sarasota earned him recognition as the best defensive shortstop in the Florida State League and a promotion to Double-A Portland.[16] At the end of the season, Ramirez retained his spot as the top prospect in the Red Sox system.[17]

Ramirez's promotion opened the door for new draft pick Dustin Pedroia …

Dustin Pedroia

Dustin Pedroia started in 2004, not in Boston, but at Arizona State University. In June he was selected by the Red Sox in the second round (65th overall) of the amateur draft.[18] He was the Red Sox' first pick in the draft. The team had lost its prior pick as compensation to the Oakland A's for signing Keith Foulke.

Pedroia had excelled at Arizona State, having been named the best collegiate defensive player in the nation in 2003 and batting .384 with a .466 on-base percentage during his three years there.[19] *Baseball America* ranked him as the second-best defensive player in the draft.[20] Given his résumé, the Red Sox had actually expected him to go higher in the draft.[21] Luckily for the Red Sox, Pedroia ultimately ended up in Boston.

After he signed with the Red Sox in July, the team assigned him to the Single-A Augusta GreenJackets.[22] The Red Sox planned for him to spend a couple of weeks in Augusta and then move to Sarasota.[23] After 12 games in Augusta, Pedroia moved to Sarasota, where he batted .307 batting with a .382 on-base percentage in his first 24 games without committing an error.[24] It was a strong start, and it only got stronger. Pedroia ultimately played 30 games in Sarasota, posting a .336 batting average.[25]

Pedroia visited Fenway Park on September 20, and took batting practice with the team. It was his first time in Boston.[26] He ended the season ranked by *Baseball America* as the sixth-best prospect in the Red Sox organization.[27]

The 2004 Sarasota Red Sox

How did the team itself actually do? Despite its wealth of future stars, the Sarasota Red Sox finished 37-30, third in the Western Division of the Florida State League and out of the playoffs.[28] At the end of the season, the team opted to leave the Florida State League in favor of the Carolina League. Starting in 2005, the Wilmington Blue Rocks replaced the Sarasota Red Sox as the Advanced Class-A affiliate of the Boston Red Sox.[29]

The legacy of the 2004 Sarasota Red Sox extends beyond its on-field performance. It incubated future stars and pieces for a Red Sox World Series team. It was also unusual for the number of future stars it had. There were more future pieces in Sarasota than in either Portland or Pawtucket. By the end of the season, six of the Red Sox' top 10 prospects had spent time there.[30] Aside from Pedroia, Papelbon, and Lester, Manny DelCarmen and Brandon Moss also spent time with Sarasota and, ultimately, with the 2007 Boston Red Sox. However, DelCarmen was the only one of the two actually to appear with the team in the playoffs. While Hanley Ramirez was not a part of the 2007 team, he was a crucial part of the trade that brought vital pieces of that team to Boston.

In 2004, the future of the Boston Red Sox was in Sarasota.

NOTES

1 Gordon Edes, "He's Dealing With It Just Fine," *Boston Globe*, February 27, 2004: E6.
2 Bob Hohler, "Youthful Farm Hands Making Hay," *Boston Globe*, June 20, 2004: E10.
3 Gordon Edes, "Baseball Notes," *Boston Globe*, August 8, 2004: C12.
4 Gordon Edes, "Checking on Short Subjects," *Boston Globe*, November 14, 2004: D10.
5 "Minor League Red Sox Statistics," *Boston Globe*, May 9, 2004: C10.
6 "Red Sox Minor League Averages," *Boston Globe*, May 30, 2004: C9.
7 Bob Hohler, "Youthful Farm Hands Making Hay," *Boston Globe*, June 20, 2004: E10.
8 "Youthful Farm Hands Making Hay."
9 Gordon Edes, "Checking on Short Subjects."
10 "Gordon Edes, "Selig Denies Playing Favorites," *Boston Globe*, January 11, 2004: D2.
11 Nick Cafardo, "In-Depth Look at Injuries," *Boston Globe*, March 20, 2004: D2.
12 Chris Umpierre, "Sarasota Collects 6-4 Win Against Sloppy Fort Myers," *Fort Myers* (Florida) *News-Press*, April 10, 2004: C7.
13 Nick Cafardo, "Garciaparra to Play for PawSox Tonight," *Boston Globe*, May 30, 2004: C8.
14 Bob Hohler, "West Going in the Right Direction," *Boston Globe*, June 6, 2004: C9.
15 Nick Cafardo, "He's Short on Patience," *Boston Globe*, July 18, 2004: D10.
16 Gordon Edes, "Baseball Notes," *Boston Globe*, August 8, 2004: C12.
17 Gordon Edes, "Checking on Short Subjects," *Boston Globe*, November 14, 2004: D10.
18 "Red Sox Draft Picks," *Boston Globe*, June 8, 2004: F5.
19 Bob Hohler, "It's Reunion Time For Padres Alumni," *Boston Globe*, June 8, 2004: F5.
20 Gordon Edes, "Age Hasn't Caught Up Yet," *Boston Globe*, June 13, 2004: C12.
21 Bob Hohler, "It's Reunion Time For Padres Alumni," *Boston Globe*, June 8, 2004: F5.
22 "Boston Signs Top Draft Pick," *North Adams (Massachusetts) Transcript*, July 14, 2004: B3.
23 Nick Cafardo, "He's Short on Patience," *Boston Globe*, July 18, 2004: D10
24 Bob Hohler, "Only a few will realize big dreams," *Boston Globe*, August 29, 2004: F11
25 Peter May, "Wife's surgery sends Cabrera on Home Run," *Boston Globe*, September 21, 2004: F5
26 Peter May, "Wife's surgery sends Cabrera on Home Run," *Boston Globe*, September 21, 2004: F5
27 Gordon Edes, "Checking on Short Subjects," *Boston Globe*, November 14, 2004: D10.
28 "Minor League Beat," *Orlando Sentinel*, September 6, 2004: D12.
29 "Sox Leave Sarasota," *(Fort Myers) News-Press*, September 23, 2004: C2.
30 Gordon Edes, "Checking on Short Subjects," *Boston Globe*, November 14, 2004: D10.

A YANKEE FAN'S PERSPECTIVE ON THE 2004 AMERICAN LEAGUE CHAMPIONSHIP SERIES

BY JEB STEWART

Even for a confident Yankees fan (are there any other kind?), the 2003 offseason began with troubling signs. True, Brian Cashman found a way to obtain Alex Rodriguez, who had seemed destined to bolster Boston's already impressive lineup just days earlier.

However, the losses of starting pitchers Roger Clemens and Andy Pettitte, both of whom signed with Houston, damaged the pitching staff. Their replacements, Javier Vázquez and Jon Lieber, were above-average starters, but neither had pitched in the playoffs before, let alone in Fenway Park or Yankee Stadium in the cool air of October. By contrast, Boston had two aces in Pedro Martinez and Curt Schilling, both of whom had already turned in dominant performances against the Yankees in the postseason.

And all season, there was no good statistical reason for anyone to believe New York was better than Boston. True, the 2004 Yankees had a team OPS+ of 111, which was essentially the same as the Red Sox' collective OPS+ of 110.[1] However, there was a marked difference in the quality of the teams' pitching staffs, as the Yankees posted a below-average team ERA+ of 96, while Boston had a superior team ERA+ of 116.

Boston's record of 98-64 was slightly better than its expected record (96-66), considering the team's +181 run differential, so there is no evidence that the Red Sox underachieved during the season. However, the Yankees' 101-61 record far exceeded its expected record (89-73), as revealed by the team's more modest +89 run differential. The real surprise in 2004 was that New York won the AL East championship by three games over Boston. But if anyone believed the Yankees should have been favored over the Red Sox in the 2004 ALCS, such an idea was fool's gold.[2]

Ticket purchase receipt to Game Five of the 2004 World Series — had it been played at Yankee Stadium. Photo by Jeb Stewart.

In hindsight, Boston's advantages seem obvious. But on October 16, 2004, I had a ticket to see my beloved Yankees in Game Five of the World Series in St. Louis. With a three-games-to-none lead over the Red Sox in the ALCS, there was no need to think I didn't need to pack. My only real concern at the time was that Houston, with Carlos Beltran playing out of his mind, was going to beat the Cardinals to ruin my trip. To believe that Boston might come back and overcome such a large deficit was not only unthinkable but unprecedented, at least in major-league baseball. When it mattered, the Yankees had *always* beaten the Red Sox.

I'll never forget that wonderful October day in 1978 when I sprinted home from school to watch Game 163 – in effect, an AL East playoff game[3] – on a 13-inch black-and-white TV with snowy reception. Bucky Dent's name will always be infamous in Boston because of that game. And while Aaron Boone's home run in Game Seven of the 2003 ALCS was still fresh in every fan's mind, the 2004 ALCS now seemed destined to be decided in just four or five games.

But Games Four and Five became recurring nightmares for Yankees fans. I could not bring myself to watch either game in its entirety in writing this essay. I remember enough as it is.

In Game Four, with the Yankees leading in the bottom of the ninth, Kevin Millar worked a walk. Pinch-runner Dave Roberts stole second, Mariano Rivera then blew the save, and David Ortiz homered to win the game for Boston in the 12th inning. The following morning, I dragged myself out of bed and drove to my office. One of our secretaries walked up to my door and shouted, "How'd you like that Red Sox game?!" I glared and closed my door without responding.

Game Five was nearly six hours of identical torture. Once again, Rivera blew a save and the Yankees lost, this time in 14 innings. I walked into work even more exhausted and grumpier, only this time with the sickening feeling that the Yankees were going to blow the ALCS. Deep down, I knew I would be selling my World Series ticket.

Of course, everyone remembers Game Six as the "bloody sock" game because of Schilling's heroics. My enduring memory of that game was Yankee reliever Tom "Flash" Gordon throwing up in the bullpen with the Yankees trailing, 4-2.[4] Gordon knew too. And the Yankees lost.

I rationalized some hope for Game Seven. After all, the Yanks had won two games over the Red Sox to clinch the pennant in '49, had beaten Boston in that playoff back in '78, and had won Game Seven in 2003. But I knew the Red Sox were the better team. They destroyed Kevin Brown and Vázquez in short order, which sucked the energy out of the crowd at Yankee Stadium, and the series was over.

I did have the brief fortune of selling my World Series ticket at a profit to a Red Sox fan in my office, but that proved to be fool's gold too as the baseball gods weren't finished having fun with me. There was no Game Five because Boston swept St. Louis, so it turned into a phantom ticket, and I had to return his money. The Cardinals then made me return the actual ticket to get my money back. With a nonrefundable fee of $10 per ticket, it ended up costing just that much. I still have my ticket receipt, which has a World Series logo on it, though I'm not sure why I haven't burned it. I suppose it's to remember Bart Giamatti's rueful words about the game of baseball being "designed to break your heart," which is really what makes it the best game there is. Baseball broke mine creatively in October 2004.[5]

ACKNOWLEDGMENTS

Thanks to Bill Nowlin for encouraging me to write this essay. Aside from reliving my suffering, my biggest concern was being viewed as a heretic by Yankee fans everywhere for even considering contributing to a book about the 2004 Red Sox. Of course, I quickly realized that Yankees fans are unlikely to find out, so please don't tell on me. Thanks also to Miles Millon, who is probably the youngest Red Sox fan I know. Like most fans, he inherited the memories of Boston's long history of suffering from his father. And while he experienced a taste of that himself in 2003, he has shared four World Series championships with his father since then. Finally, I would be remiss if I did not mention that part of my motivation for writing this essay was to disprove Bill Chapman's theory that I am incapable of saying anything positive about the Red Sox. My wife and I traveled to Boston a few years ago and Bill C was a great guide.

Although the 2004 ALCS made me miserable, I do take great comfort in knowing that having the Red Sox defeat the Yankees, win the World Series, and end the Curse of the Bambino was probably the best year of Bill N's, Miles', and Bill C's baseball fandom. So, I'm glad about that. Well, almost.

NOTES

1 All statistics and team records were taken from Baseball-Reference.com.

2 My own belief that the Yankees would win the series was completely rooted in the history between the teams, as well as New York's success during Joe Torre's tenure. However, the glaring statistical disparity between the pitching staffs, as well as the Yankees' improbable regular-season record, exaggerated the strengths of New York relative to Boston. Not surprisingly, the Red Sox had won the teams' regular-season matchups, 11-8. With all these warning signs, if there was ever a team that was primed to blow a 3-games-to-none lead it was the 2004 New York Yankees. Similarly, if there was ever a team that was built to overcome such a deficit it was the 2004 Boston Red Sox. Even so, the fact that the greatest closer in the history of baseball had the opportunity to send the Yankees to the World Series twice, but blew saves in back-to-back games, is not something anyone can explain.

3 Both Keith Jackson of ABC Sports and Frank Messer of WPIX described the game as being a playoff in their broadcasts, which are available on YouTube at https://www.youtube.com/watch?v=C47bgmpLmPk and https://www.youtube.com/watch?v=IowgfzVsXGA.

4 Memory is a funny thing. Before I started this project, I was positive that Gordon got sick in the bullpen during Game Four or Game Five, and I had seen it on the TV broadcast. Since I could not find evidence that this happened by watching Gordon warm up in either game in the portions of the broadcasts I watched on YouTube, I turned to newspapers.com and found an article confirming that Gordon got sick during Game Six. Bob Klapisch, "Lack of Heart, Bad Ideas, Too Much for Yankees' Dollars to Overcome," *Hackensack (New Jersey) Record*: October 22, 2004: S-1. I am speculating, but I assume that I read this report shortly after the series ended and confabulated the memory because I still cannot find video evidence that it ever happened.

5 I was tempted to write that I finally understood Giamatti's essay on a visceral level after the Yankees collapsed in 2004. However, most baseball fans get their hearts broken every season, and some years are worse than others. The 2001 World Series – not the 2004 collapse – remains the worst defeat of this Yankee fan's baseball life.

GRAVEYARD VISIT IN OCTOBER 2004

Christopher Collins was a lifelong Red Sox who died of cancer in 1995 at just 41 years old. As the *Cape Cod Times* told it, "Weeks before succumbing to the disease, Collins insisted his family etch the phrase 'Never lived long enough to see the Red Sox win it all!' into his headstone."[1]

Collins had been a police officer in Harwich, and a Little League coach.

His son, Chris Jr., visited his grave at the Brewster cemetery on Cape Cod just hours after the 2004 Red Sox finally won it all. Chris Jr. was 23 at the time. He said, "He had such a great spirit. He wanted to put something on his tombstone that would make people chuckle a bit as they walked by."

He told the reporter of the 2004 graveside visit: "I was like a little boy who rushes to show his parents what Santa brought for Christmas. To be able to share this incredible win with him was one of the best experiences of my life." In a whisper, he told his dad, "They finally did it."

Collins's wife, Jane, had visited the grave a week earlier, after the Red Sox beat the Yankees in the League Championship Series. She and the family had decorated the grave with "Red Sox balloons, banners, a Sox cap and a miniature scarecrow doll with a Red Sox batting helmet."

She said, "I wish he was still here to enjoy this great moment with all of us, especially his kids whom he loved very much. But I know he's partying with Babe Ruth now and smiling."

ACKNOWLEDGMENT

Thanks to SABR member Paul Doutrich and his wife, Cynthia Doutrich, who took the photograph in June 2023. This article was written by Bill Nowlin.

NOTES

1 Jason Kolnos, "Departed Sox Fans Can Rest in Peace," *Cape Cod Times* (Hyannis, Massachusetts), October 30, 2004. Updated January 6, 2011. https://www.capecodtimes.com/story/news/2004/10/30/departed-sox-fans-can-rest/50927108007/. Accessed June 14, 2023. All quotations come from this article.

THE RED SOX AND THE YANKEES: FATHER AND SON

BY PAUL SEMENDINGER

There is the story that when the British surrendered to the colonial forces at Yorktown to end the Revolutionary War, that their band played a song titled "The World Turned Upside Down."

As a Yankees fan, I felt that a similar song should have been played when the Red Sox defeated the Yankees and then went on to win the 2004 World Series. What happened to the eternal Curse of the Bambino? There was a part of me that hoped the Yankees would never lose to the Red Sox…

I'll never forget the feelings I had during those four games when the Red Sox came roaring back to defeat the Yankees after going down 3-0 in the American League Championship Series. The Yankees had dominated the Red Sox in Game Three, 19-8. It was all but certain, to me, and most Yankees fans, that another World Series for our team was on the horizon.

That was the way it was supposed to be. That was the natural order. The Yankees should win. The Red Sox need to lose. It was a formula that worked well.

And then it all fell apart – suddenly and completely.

All these years later, I don't remember any specific games, just moments from the games, moments when the impossible happened time and time and time again.

The mighty Yankees fell. It didn't seem logical. It didn't seem real. But it was.

The memories I have of those games, the moments when everything changed, are scattered. I don't recall when these events happened, and I'll never go back and watch those contests again. I simply remember being in total shock game-after-game as these things took place:

Dave Roberts stealing second base.

Mariano Rivera blowing a save. And then blowing another game.

David Ortiz hitting a walk-off homer.

Johnny Damon circling the bases.

Flash Gordon giving up run after run after run.

Derek Jeter going 1-for-7 in an extra-inning game.

The bloody sock.

Kevin Brown failing to get through the second inning in the decisive Game Seven.

The looks of confusion on Joe Torre's face.

What was happening?

Some of it, most of it, still doesn't seem real.

Did the Red Sox really clinch their victory on the field at Yankee Stadium? It can't be!

I was in complete disbelief as this all played out.

In the end, I turned off the television and sat in silence.

The Red Sox were the champions?

***

Most might think that I was angry when the Yankees lost, or, said differently, when the Red Sox won. But, although I was stupefied, I wasn't upset. In fact, part of – a small part at first – but part of me found some solace and even a degree of happiness because I knew that Red Sox victory brought with it an unbelievable amount of joy to a very Red Sox fan.

Once, a long time ago, in 1946, in the town of Norwood, New Jersey, a little boy named Paul fell in love with the game of baseball. He loved the sport and the players. In his youthful exuberance, he gravitated toward a team far from home and to a player who he felt was the greatest ever. As an 8-year-old kid, my father Paul connected with Ted Williams and the Red Sox and he has loved that player and that team with all his heart, ever since.

I don't think there has ever been a bigger Red Sox fan than my dad. And, although I was permitted to choose my own team to root for, and I chose the Yankees, I was also brought up knowing that Teddy Ballgame, Yaz, and so many others were players to be respected and looked up to.

In my home, alongside the names of Gehrig, Mantle, Jackson, and others, there was also an untold affinity for Bobby Doerr, Johnny Pesky, Vern Stevens, Rico Petrocelli and so many others. Yeah, the Yankees had the Great DiMaggio, but the DiMaggio on the Red Sox wasn't so bad either. I knew early on that Babe Ruth had first been a Red Sox and a World Champion before he ever came to New York.

As I look back, it must have been difficult for my father to see the Sox fail year after year and decade after decade – especially living in an area filled with Yankees fans and in a historical period dominated by the Yankees. The Impossible Dream of 1967 ended with a loss. Fisk's homer in 1975 only led to eventual heartbreak. Bucky Dent's homer in 1978, as my dad's 10-year-old son leapt for joy, must have been a bitter pill to swallow. And 1986, with that groundball, it must have been the worst of all. I think that groundball was the bitterest pill to swallow.

My dad never expected me to become a Red Sox fan. On some level, he may have even taken joy that his son got to enjoy seeing his team win so many championships… Maybe?

Still, my dad had to wonder what it was like to see one's favorite team, the team he rooted for over a lifetime, win it all. I am sure my father wondered if the Red Sox would, or could, ever win a championship.

And then, there they were… Millar and Mueller, Ortiz and Damon, Pedro, Lowe, and Schilling, Varitek. And the rest. They were the champions. The Red Sox had defeated the Yankees and were on their way to being baseball's best team.

The Red Sox as a franchise struggled for 86 long years, but for 58 of those years, my dad suffered along with them. It was a long and tiring road, one filled with heartbreak time and again, but then it was all over. A magical new story was written; a story that ended with baseball's ultimate glory. A story that concluded with the Red Sox on the top of baseball.

The world had indeed turned upside down.

I wasn't happy that the Yankees lost. But the joy that my father felt, and still enjoys today, made it okay.

I'm not happy that the Yankees lost. I didn't enjoy any of it. But in a way, I am very glad the Red Sox won.

Paul Semendinger and Paul Semendinger, 2023. Photo by Janet Semendinger.

THE TROPHY TOUR: TOUCH 'EM ALL ACROSS RED SOX NATION

BY CECILIA M. TAN

It's not unusual for a championship team to show off some hard-won hardware. The Stanley Cup of the National Hockey League famously travels from player to player in the offseason, making public appearances along the way. Championship trophies often make the rounds of the local statehouse or city hall, and may even be displayed in a victory parade.

That the 2004 World Series trophy would tour at least *some* places was a given, but Red Sox team President Larry Lucchino had prior experience in the power of a trophy to capture hearts and minds. He had overseen the tour of the National League trophy around San Diego after the Padres' pennant win in 1998. Until 2017, the National League's Warren C. Giles Trophy was passed from one winning team to the next like the Stanley Cup. At the time the Padres were politicking for a new ballpark, and Lucchino saw firsthand the impact of letting people actually touch the hallowed object. The stadium referendum passed and a seed was planted in Lucchino's mind.[1]

An epic, historic championship run – like the one had by the Red Sox in 2004 – required an epic, historic trophy tour. The pledge to take the trophy to all 351 cities and towns in the commonwealth of Massachusetts was announced by Lucchino – in what he later termed a fit of "irrational exuberance"[2] – after the trophy had already made many appearances, including onstage at a Tim McGraw concert in Connecticut, and even a stop in the Dominican Republic for a "social visit"[3] with star pitcher Pedro Martínez (who was then about to begin contract negotiations with the team) and at the new Red Sox baseball academy in El Toro. The trophy made trips to Atlanta, to the headquarters of Red Sox sponsors Delta and Coca-Cola, and to some outposts of Red Sox Nation in other parts of the country, like Fat Face Fenner's Fishack in Hermosa Beach, California.[4] But as the anecdotes continued to roll in from every appearance about staunch New Englanders who had waited their whole lives for a championship breaking down in tears upon seeing – and sometimes hugging – the trophy, it seemed only fair to give as many of them as possible a chance to see it in person. Thus, the "Mass 351" challenge was on.

Red Sox front-office employee Colin Burch was given the task of booking the logistics of the tour, and it quickly became clear that he was going to need to schedule stops every day, often as many as six in a day, if the Red Sox didn't want the tour to take another 86 years. The tour was also going to need financial support to cover the cost of transporting the trophy and accompanying personnel. The Mass State Lottery was brought on as tour sponsor, reportedly pledging $250,000 toward transportation, publicity, and security.[5] "Like the Red Sox, the Massachusetts State Lottery is synonymous with success," read the announcement from Massachusetts State Treasurer Tim Cahill about the lottery partnership. "We have one of the most successful lotteries in the country, and … [t]he more successful the Lottery, the more money that can be returned to cities and towns across Massachusetts. We feel it makes perfect sense for us to hit the road with the Red Sox as they begin their World Series Trophy Tour across the state."

Cahill's measured announcement belied his personal excitement. "In the two years I've been treasurer, there's been a lot of exciting things," he told the Associated Press. "[B]ut I haven't been nervous except in the presence of this trophy."[6]

The Commissioner's Trophy itself carried a $15,000 price tag at the time, but of course the significance is priceless.[7] Each year, Tiffany & Co. makes a new trophy from sterling silver, which stands about 2½ feet high, and reportedly weighs 30 to 35 pounds.[8] For the tour, a rolling road case that looked as if it belonged with Aerosmith was custom-built for the hardware, which traveled to many tour stops in a dedicated vehicle. Fully decked out with the Red Sox and Mass Lottery logos and emblazoned with the words "World Championship Trophy Tour," the snazzy sport utility vehicle was a Volvo – a Red Sox sponsor.[9]

The trophy also traveled by plane, ferry, helicopter, and train. "At one point we took it to New York City," longtime Red Sox front-office official Dr. Charles Steinberg gleefully recounted, "to a Red Sox bar down there called 'The Riv,' and we took it by Amtrak. We put the trophy into the luggage area at the back of the car and the case took up basically the whole area. A conductor came along and barked, 'You can't put that thing here!' But then [he] recognized us and all of a sudden he goes, 'Is that what I think it is? Can I see it?'"[10] The conductor soon had a photo with the trophy, as did everyone else on that train.

The trophy traveled with people who were dubbed "Fenway Ambassadors," who were very occasionally Red Sox players, leading to incidents such as the time when Johnny Damon handed the trophy to a group of fans to pass around at a Patriots football game, resulting in two of the flagpoles being damaged.[11] Former Red Sox such as Jerry Remy, Luis Tiant, and others also made some appearances.[12] But the trophy itself, not players, was the draw. "It's a very visible representation of the fact that we won the Series, that's why," Red Sox vice president Chuck Steedman told the *Globe*. "[O]ur players have come and gone over the years. This is the commissioner's trophy. It's here for keeps."[13]

The trophy's usual travel companions were Burch, Steedman, and a security guard or two, sometimes including Remy's son Jared.[14] As the *Globe* reported, "Steedman kept it at his house one night and recalled, 'My wife slept on the couch and I had the trophy.'"[15]

Another frequent member of the entourage was Joe McDermott, a supervisor of Red Sox security. "At that point, the trophy was like seeing God. It was something they never thought they would see in their lifetimes," he said. "Every place we visited, we'd be seeing more than a thousand people in the course of a couple of hours. And a large number of them had pictures of loved ones who had died and had never seen it."[16] One of the oldsters who had her chance to touch the trophy was Rose Bolger, 100, who was honored alongside the trophy in Fall River, Massachusetts, with five generations of her family in attendance.[17]

By December 4, 2004, the day of a victory rally in Fort Myers, the Red Sox longtime spring-training home, the trophy had already made over 100 stops with "about 400 more scheduled."[18] While getting to all 351 towns in Massachusetts was a priority, many sites throughout the other five New England states also petitioned for a visit. A minority owner of the Red Sox, Les Otten, arranged for the trophy to stop in Maine at his Phoenix House and Well restaurant, near the Sunday River ski resort. "The place was so packed," the *Globe* reported Otten as saying, "they had to pass the trophy in through a window."[19]

Of course, with so much handling, there were many opportunities for damage. As when a flying full beer can struck it during the "Rolling Rally" victory parade, the damaged trophy had to be sent back to its maker – in New York City – for refurbishment and repair.[20] In a post on the Boston Dirt Dogs website in 2004, a Tiffany's employee wrote to lay to rest the idea that there must have been multiple copies of the trophy making the rounds in order to get to all 351 stops. The trophy was singular, he attested, adding, "We are a New York based company filled with Yankee fans. So it must have killed the guys who worked on it that the Sox won."[21]

By January the trophy had gained a sidekick: the ball from the final out of the 2004 World Series. After making the putout, first baseman Doug Mientkiewicz had held onto the ball and asserted ownership, a claim the Sox disputed. Both parties agreed to set aside the question of ownership to let the ball join the festivities.[22]

Photo by Bill Nowlin.

Some school districts bused their students to see the trophy, and many local politicians took the opportunity to do some glad-handing as well. As representative Daniel E. Bosley (D-North Adams) said when he accompanied the tour around North County in the farthest western reaches of Massachusetts, "People here identify so much with this team, and the Red Sox haven't forgotten us. They've let it be known it isn't just their trophy – it belongs to everyone."[23]

The tour included stops in towns like Aquinnah (population 439), Nahant, Phillipston, Petersham, and Mattapoisett.[24] Schools, senior centers, town halls, public libraries, and hospitals were frequent destinations, as well as college campuses, like a February 2005 visit to a college basketball game at UMass Amherst on February 23, 2005. "As part of the celebration, all fans are encouraged to wear Red Sox apparel," read the announcement from UMass Athletics. "One lucky fan wearing Red Sox gear will be selected randomly to have their photo taken with the World Series Trophy at halftime."[25] The town of Holliston – the site of the Mudville neighborhood that some believe inspired the poem "Casey at the Bat" – hoped to have the trophy visit for the inauguration of its newly lighted baseball fields, but had to settle for the local high school since the lights wouldn't be installed until after the tour's end.[26] At the time of the Holliston event, 329 out of 351 towns had been visited, not counting additional stops outside New England, like the Pentagon and Walter Reed Medical Center.[27]

The tour's final stop came midway through the 2005 season, on June 25, in the tiny town of Gosnold, with its numerologically resonant 86 residents. Gosnold comprises nine small islands southwest of Falmouth on Cape Cod, with the tour touching down on Cuttyhunk Island, described by the *Globe* as "a breezy island where the innkeeper is also the police chief, and [which] boasts a healthy population of deer, coyote, and rabbit, but if you want a gin and tonic, you better bring your own, and if you want pizza, you best know which unmarked, weathered cottage sells slices out of the basement."[28] The trophy traveled there by helicopter with Larry Lucchino handling the hardware himself. When asked before takeoff to comment on the trophy tour, he quipped, "It seemed like a good idea at the time."29

Gosnold might have been the official last stop of the Mass 351, but it was far from the final appearance for the 2004 trophy. With three more trophies since added to the collection – in 2007, 2013, and 2018 – all four continue to make public appearances, and Colin Burch, the Red Sox vice president of marketing and broadcasting, is still involved with arranging their appearances. "Any time we win, we want to celebrate with as many fans as possible," Burch told the *Improper Bostonian*. "In 2004, when we went around, I'm not sure there was a dry eye. And you still see a similar joy in 2007, 2013, and 2018. There's an intergenerational aspect to baseball, and I think that spirit lives among the four trophies in a unique way."30

NOTES

1. Personal interview, Dr. Charles Steinberg, September 4, 2023, via Zoom.
2. Karen Testa, "Sox Trophy to Tour," Associated Press/*South Coast Today*, January 4, 2005. This story appeared on Page C1 of the New Bedford *Standard-Times* on January 5, 2005.
3. Joseph P. Kahn, "Circling the Bases: World Series Trophy Goes on Odyssey to Touch 'Em All in Red Sox Nation," *Boston Globe*, December 9, 2004. https://www.proquest.com/newspapers/circling-bases-world-series-trophy-goes-on/docview/404930985/se-2.
4. Kahn, "Circling the Bases."
5. "Red Sox, Massachusetts Lottery Join Forces in 'Trophy Tour,'" *Boston Business Journal*, January 4, 2005. https://www.bizjournals.com/boston/stories/2005/01/03/daily22.html.
6. Testa, "Sox Trophy to Tour."
7. "Red Sox World Series Trophy Tour," June 27, 2005. https://bostonspastime.com/trophy.html.
8. Meredith Goldstein, "Weight? 35 lbs. Value? $15,000. Peek? Priceless," *Boston Globe*, January 30, 2005. https://www.proquest.com/newspapers/weight-35-lbs-value-15-000-peek-priceless/docview/404936056/se-2.
9. "Volvo Signs Red Sox Sponsorship Deal," *Boston Business Journal*, July 11, 2002. https://www.bizjournals.com/boston/stories/2002/07/08/daily32.html.
10. Personal interview, Dr. Charles Steinberg, September 4, 2023, via Zoom.
11. Dan Shaughnessy, "On This Night, the Star," *Boston Globe*, January 14, 2005. https://www.proquest.com/newspapers/on-this-night-star/docview/404940821/se-2.
12. Glenn Drohan, "Thousands Throng Red Sox Trophy Tour," iBerkshires.com, February 2, 2005. https://www.iberkshires.com/story/16685/Thousands-throng-Red-Sox-trophy-tour.html.
13. Kahn, "Circling the Bases."
14. Jared Remy, son of beloved Sox icon Jerry Remy, was ordered by a lenient judge to seek gainful employment after a domestic violence arrest, and had taken a position with the Red Sox in 2004. Eric Hoskowitz, "For Jared Remy, Leniency Was the Rule Until One Lethal Night," *Boston Globe*, March 23, 2014.
15. Dan Shaughnessy, "On This Night, the Star."
16. Matt Martinelli, "Trophy Life: An Inside Look at the Red Sox Trophy Tour," *The Improper Bostonian*, March 22, 2019. https://www.improper.com/life-style/trophy-life/.
17. Beth Krudys, "The World Series Trophy Tour: Well Worth the Wait," *Red Sox Magazine*: First Edition 2005: 63.
18. Patrick Whittle, "Victory Tour Hits Florida," *Boston Globe*, December 7, 2004. E7. https://www.proquest.com/newspapers/victory-tour-hits-florida/docview/404931472/se-2.
19. Marty Basch, "Snowmaking Heats Up; Mother Nature Adds Her 2 Cents," *Boston Globe*, December 23, 2004. Accessed August 25, 2023: https://www.proquest.com/newspapers/snowmaking-heats-up-mother-nature-adds-her-2/docview/404937235/se-2.
20. "A beer can thrown by excited Red Sox fans during the team's World Series celebration in Boston slammed into some of the flags on the World Series trophy." The report states that it is a "tradition" in Boston to throw full cans of beer to the players in the parade, but that this practice is dangerous to players as well as the trophy. "Red Sox Fans Damage World Series Trophy," *ABC News/Good Morning America*, November 1, 2018. https://abcnews.go.com/GMA/Culture/.
21. Kahn, "Circling the Bases."
22. Gordon Edes, "Ball Will Make Rounds; Mientkiewicz, Sox Come to Agreement," *Boston Globe*, January 29, 2005.
23. Drohan, "Thousands Throng Red Sox Trophy Tour."
24. Tom Trainque, "Red Sox Trophy Comes to Narragansett," *Gardner* (Massachusetts) *News*, January 18, 2005. https://www.thegardnernews.com/story/news/2005/01/19/red-sox-trophy-comes-to/11282958007/; Beth David, "Red Sox Trophy Will Visit Thursday," *New Bedford Standard-Times*, May 2, 2005: A9. https://www.southcoasttoday.com/story/news/2005/05/02/red-sox-trophy-will-visit/50345894007/; "Red Sox Nation Alert: World Series Trophy Pays Visit," *Vineyard Gazette*, June 9, 2005. https://vineyardgazette.com/news/2005/06/10/red-sox-nation-alert-world-series-trophy-pays-visit.
25. "RED SOX APPRECIATION DAY: Come Out to See the World Series Trophy on Feb. 23 at Mullins," February 10, 2005, UMassAthletics.com. https://umassathletics.com/news/2005/2/10/RED_SOX_APPRECIATION_DAY_Come_Out_To_See_The_World_Series_Trophy_On_Feb_23_At_Mullins.
26. Emily Shartin, "Tour Nearing End," *Boston Globe*, June 5, 2005. Accessed October 14, 2023: https://www.proquest.com/newspapers/tiffanys-tribute-red-sox-nearing-end-road-trip/docview/404957159/se-2.
27. "Red Sox World Series Trophy Visits Pentagon," Defense Visual Information Distribution Service, DVIDSHub.net, January 6, 2005. https://www.dvidshub.net/image/2969/red-sox-world-series-trophy-visits-pentagon.
28. Jackie MacMullan, "Guest Took Years to Arrive/Guest Makes Trip," *Boston Globe*, June 25, 2005. https://www.proquest.com/newspapers/guest-took-years-arrive-makes-trip/docview/404962491/se-2.
29. MacMullan, "Guest Took Years to Arrive."
30. Martinelli, "Trophy Life."

KATHRYN GEMME FINALLY SAW THE RED SOX WIN THE WORLD SERIES, AT AGE 109

BY BILL NOWLIN

Not all fans attend the ballpark on a regular basis, but that doesn't diminish their fandom. Take Kathryn Gemme, interviewed by this author at age 109. The paragraphs that follow were written in midsummer 2003 and are, in places, obviously dated — given the fact of the 2004 and 2007 World Championships.

Red Sox fans are renowned for their loyalty and longevity (as in "long-suffering Red Sox fan"). While it's a commonplace to cite the number of years since the Sox last won a World Series, and the "19-18" taunt is often heard during Boston visits to Yankee Stadium, there really aren't that many people still living who recall that 1918 World Series. What about someone who recalls the 1903 World Series — the first World Series ever held?

Kathryn Gemme turned 108 years old in November 2002. She was born on November 9, 1894 and was almost nine years old when Jimmy Collins, Cy Young, Bill Dinneen and others won the 1903 World Series for Boston. And in 2003, she is more of a Red Sox rooter than ever before, a knowledgeable and dedicated fan who loves to put her Sox on.

Mid-season 2002, Ms. Gemme entered the Atrium Nursing Center in Middleboro, Massachusetts and soon encountered Sharon Gosling, the center's activities director who claims for herself the title of the "second biggest Red Sox fan" in the facility.

Kathryn has a Red Sox beanie baby that she holds while watching games. Registered nurse Jan Risgin says of Kathryn, "She pops popcorn and watches the game. She watched that game last night [August 27] and was spitting nails," Risgin said [referring to a 6-0 shutout at the hands of the New York Yankees]. "She's always talking about Braves Field. She saw Lou Gehrig play and thought he was amazing. Babe Ruth, she saw him play…but then he went to *that team*."

That team. She's no Yankees fan. Don't get her started. "The Yankees, they were always our enemy. I hate them. You know who I was glad to see out of the Yankees? Paul O'Neill. He was crabby. And that Clemens. I wish they'd string him up. The way he holds that ball and looks at it. What does he think he's seeing?"

"Kate" Gemme is a diehard Sox fan — and not ready to expire just yet. Once the Sox were eliminated in 2002, she said, "I must just be waiting for them to win another one." She's healthy — the only medicine she takes, reports nurse Risgin, are "baby aspirin and a vitamin."

Photo by Bill Nowlin.

She's followed baseball for years and years. And years. If there's a game on, it's a priority. "Something gets ahold of you. The radio, the announcing…you could picture yourself at the game. Even when I was at home in my 80s, if people came calling, I'd have to tell them, 'There's a game on, you know.' I'd be listening to the game, not listening to what they were saying."

She has her favorite Red Sox players these days and she shows a real understanding of the game. Two favorites of today are Nomar Garciaparra and Jason Varitek. Of Nomar, she says "Nomar — that's MY exercise! Heel and toe. Heel to toe! Nomar. We have accepted Nomar. He is everybody's favorite, he's a natural at what he does, he doesn't thump his chest, and he makes watching baseball thrilling."

Catchers have always fascinated her. Sharon Gosling explains that Kathryn admires them for the role they play in the game, "calling the throws, the continuous movement, well, just the responsibility in general. She admires Jason Varitek for his confidence, the way he portrays himself, his positive attitude, and the fact he is always ready." Sharon and Kathryn share a private joke about Varitek and the way he squats behind the plate, a bit of private humor shared between two women. "Varitek. I just like him," Kathryn says. "When he squats. He seems so confident. I like the way he calls the pitches. They don't shake him off very often."

That's perceptive, and accurate. Pitchers rarely do shake off Jason Varitek. She's observant about other matters, too. "Did you notice what Daubach does before he hits? Takes his hat off and rubs his head three times." This is a woman who's tuned in to the Red Sox.

How long has she been a Red Sox fan? At first, she followed the Boston Braves. "Since I knew anything about baseball, I've followed it. Since I was 14 years old. It was the Braves, the Braves. I was born in Chicopee Falls, my home town. I went to school with Rabbit Maranville. He went to Springfield High School and I was in Chicopee just on the border. We got to know each other. He was a cute little guy. And he had that vest pocket catch!

"Back then, baseball was just a game to me. Hitting the ball and running. It wasn't until I got older that I realized why they would pass anybody [give an intentional walk]. I used say to myself, 'The damn fool put him on base for nothing.'"

Kathryn does recall the first World Series, though only dimly. "Rah-rah-rah. I knew about it. When you're nine years old… until I was 14, you don't pay attention." She has similarly vague memories of the Red Sox triumphs in 1912, 1915 & 1916 — and if she's right about being 18 at the time, she attended her first game the year after Fenway Park opened. "We were young kids. 18 years old. We went on a trolley car. I just know they won a lot of them — but they haven't won for a long time. In 1918, I was 23 and I was raising my children, but I listened to the game on the radio when my husband tuned in. I never forgot the Red Sox. We saw Babe Ruth play. He was a pitcher. I remember him in knickers, and the little steps running to first base. It's a vivid memory. If Babe Ruth was alive today, he'd be my age.

"My mother was just a plain ordinary woman. She died very young at age 39. My dad was a mechanic. He was a Stevens-Duryea mechanic, the automobile. No college graduate, but he had a lot of logic. That's my father. My dad got remarried again, which was a no-no then. There were only two children, myself and my sister.

"My husband was a machinist. Ovella Gemme. During the war, he made guns. Stocks. In Springfield. He had to stay home. We had the two children. Stevens Arms and Tools. Gemme — French. Mine was a French name, too — Moreau, although my mother was Irish.

"I was just plain common Lizzie. I'll tell you, though, I did my share during the war. I helped to assemble parachutes. World War II. They didn't have parachutes in the first World War. They wanted married women to work. You know how big a parachute is. We had to string them and be sure they were strung right, because if they weren't perfect, they wouldn't open. The only time I ever left the house was during the war, to do those parachutes at the Shawmut Woolen Mills."

Though more interested in the Braves than the Red Sox, Kathryn switched loyalties about five years before the Braves left town. Those were some great Red Sox years, starting in 1946, but it was a catcher who caught her eye. "I've been interested in the Red Sox since Birdie Tebbetts."

Today, baseball plays an important role in Kathryn's life. "I watch as often as I can. I would say every game. I've lost some of my eyesight — the corners are cut off — but I still watch every game. Sometimes I can lose track of the ball, lose the flight of the ball, but my eyes are glued to it. I love baseball."

Her family pays for NESN so she needn't miss a single game. At the nursing home, she'll follow every play — though she has to be respectful of her roommate. "But when she's out, I turn it up." What about those late night West Coast road trip games that don't even start until after 10 PM Boston time? "I don't take a nap, but I stay with it. I wait till it's over."

Baseball has taken on more significance since she turned 100. "The last 8 years, I can't read. Baseball always thrilled me. Now it's the only pleasure I have. It's what I like to do. I don't care if other people like it or not. I love it. When I was growing up, I didn't realize [all the strategy]. I just knew I always liked it. I liked the Red Sox. I went to games way back when I didn't know my ear from my elbow. I won't live long enough to learn all there is to know about baseball!"

What about off days during the season? "No game tonight? I'll watch a ball game, though. The National League. Once in a while, I'll watch Maddux pitch. I'll watch something. As long as there's action. I'm ashamed to say, but I like boxing, too."

Does Kathryn have other interests besides sports? "To tell you the truth, there not much. I had to leave the organ. My son-in-law gave me an organ. I played the organ until about 6 months ago. I'm stuck here. The Red Sox are my Godsend."

Some capsule comments from Kate:

Ted Williams: Ted Williams? That's a foregone conclusion. He was the Splendid Splinter. I'd just have to say he was the best ever. I saw him play. I can see that tall, lanky running kid. He kind of loped. I'd never leave my seat, even to go to the bathroom. You had to admire Ted for what he did. I guess he wasn't very sociable, but he was marvelous with no question.

You know who stands out in my memory? The guy who ran backwards to first base. Jimmy Piersall. I always admired him.

Also, another one — I can picture him pushing his home run. Carlton Fisk. I liked him. Big square jaw. Determination right there.

Varitek is right up there with Nomar, but with half the recognition.

Roger Clemens — He registers nil with me because of his poor personality, but he is an excellent pitcher.

Jim Rice — I absolutely loved him. Besides being a handsome man, he was a handsome player. He was a lot of fun to watch.

Wade Boggs — When he got up, I was sure he was going to get a hit.

Mo. I liked Mo Vaughn.

Canseco, he was a crybaby.

Johnny Pesky. From Doerr to Pesky, I remember that. And he played the hot corner, too.

I liked that nice pitcher for the Red Sox, Luis Tiant.

Even now, I try to remember the replacements on the Red Sox. If you remember your own name at 108, you're doing good.

Sharon Gosling wrote a letter to the Red Sox about Kathryn Gemme and they responded with a package containing a letter (unsigned) and photos of Nomar Garciaparra (signed), Jason Varitek and Brian Daubach. "I couldn't believe it — for *me*?" She showed it to all her new friends at Atrium, but they didn't seem that excited. "I thought they'd go ga-ga over it. I love it. There's no doubt about it." Weeks later, Kathryn was still pleased and excited that the Red Sox had sent her these items. They are minor treasures she keeps with her throughout the season.

After the Red Sox won it all in 2004

Kathryn Gemme was invited to a game at Fenway on May 30, 2004 and was rewarded by a visit to the field, a kiss from

Johnny Pesky, and a 9-7 win in 12 innings when Dave McCarty hit a walk-off home run.

After the Red Sox won the 2004 World Series, I reached out to Kathryn the next day and Sharon Gosling wrote me back that day: "She is pleased, and now that her goal is met, she is ready to go. Sad but true, she is now talking about death. She turns 110 on Nov. 9th. She says she hopes to see her 110th, then she's ready."

The trophy came to visit her on May 5, 2005 when State Senator Marc Pacheco made arrangements to bring it to the Nemasket Healthcare Center in Middleborough.[1]

Ms. Gemme died in Middleborough on December 29, 2006, at age 112.

NOTES

This article, save for the last section, originally ran in *Red Sox Magazine* (Fifth Edition, 2003) as "At 108, Kathryn Gemme's Still Putting On Her Sox."

1 Michael Naughton, "At 110, Red Sox fan finds thrill in trophy," *Boston Globe*, May 12, 2005: GlobeSouth 5.

SIGNIFICANT GAMES FROM THE 2004 SEASON

SABR's Games Project gives SABR members the opportunity to write up accounts of games that are of interest, to the author or others. Although most other "team books" – such as *We Are, We Can, We Will – The 1992 World Champion Toronto Blue Jays* (SABR, 2022) contain a number of selected game accounts (that book had 10), our addition of the "memories" section seemed more important to us. Besides, most of the 2004 Red Sox games had already been written by one SABR member.

Those who are reading this book in digital form can access those game writeups through the links presented here. For those who are reading the physical copy of this book, you can go to www.sabr.org and enter the date of the game into the "Search the Research Collection" box. That will call up the game for you.

There are enough games to keep any reader busy for a while – 47 in all, 33 regular-season games and 14 postseason games.

2004 Red Sox games

SABR's Games Project offers members the opportunity to write up accounts of meaningful games or simply those deemed interesting for one reason or another.

Because of the large number of biographies in this book, there was not the room to include the numerous Games Project writeups that could otherwise have been part of this book, but a listing of the 2004 Red Sox games which have written prior to publication is provided here. Each game listing also includes a link to where the game can be found on the SABR website.

Reading through the game accounts offers another way to experience this season as it unfolded.

These games include 33 regular-season games and all 14 postseason games. Normally, a SABR book would enlist a couple of dozen members to offer their takes on these games, but by the time the decision was made to create a book honoring the 2004 team, every one of the postseason games and many of the regular-season games had already been written.

Almost all of the regular-season game accounts benefited from the vetting of John Fredland, chair of SABR's Games Project. Each was fact-checked by Carl Riechers and copy edited by Len Levin.

2004 Red Sox regular-season games

April 4, 2004: Red Sox stumble out of the gate against re-tooled Orioles
Baltimore Orioles 7, Boston Red Sox 2, at Oriole Park at Camden Yards, Baltimore
https://sabr.org/gamesproj/game/april-4-2004-red-sox-stumble-out-of-the-gate-against-retooled-orioles/

April 6, 2004: Red Sox win their first game of a championship season
Boston Red Sox 4, Baltimore Orioles 1, at Oriole Park at Camden Yards
https://sabr.org/gamesproj/game/april-6-2004-red-sox-win-their-first-game-of-a-championship-season/

April 11, 2004: David Ortiz hits game-winning home run for second game in succession
Boston Red Sox 6, Toronto Blue Jays 4 (12 innings), at Fenway Park, Boston
https://sabr.org/gamesproj/game/april-11-2004-david-ortiz-hits-game-winning-home-run-for-second-game-in-succession/

April 16, 2004: Wakefield, Red Sox beat Yankees in first matchup of season
Boston Red Sox 6, New York Yankees 2, at Fenway Park
https://sabr.org/gamesproj/game/april-16-2004-wakefield-red-sox-beat-yankees-in-first-matchup-of-season/

April 17, 2004: New acquisition Curt Schilling beats Yankees for first time in season
Boston Red Sox 5, New York Yankees 2, at Fenway Park
https://sabr.org/gamesproj/game/april-17-2004-new-acquisition-curt-schilling-wins-his-first-game-against-the-yankees-in-2004/

April 19, 2004: Gabe Kapler and Mike Timlin contribute to Red Sox comeback win over Yankees on Patriots Day
Boston Red Sox 5, New York Yankees 4, at Fenway Park
https://sabr.org/gamesproj/game/april-19-2004-gabe-kapler-and-mike-timlin-contribute-to-red-sox-comeback-win-over-yankees-on-patriots-day/

April 24, 2004: 26 Red Sox batters go hitless with runners in scoring position, but beat Yankees in 12th
Boston Red Sox 3, New York Yankees 2 (12 innings), at Yankee Stadium, New York

https://sabr.org/gamesproj/game/april-24-2004-26-red-sox-batters-go-hitless-with-runners-in-scoring-position-but-beat-yankees-in-12th/

April 25, 2004: Pedro Martínez, Scott Williamson blank Yankees as Red Sox complete sweep at Yankee Stadium
Boston Red Sox 2, New York Yankees 0, at Yankee Stadium

https://sabr.org/gamesproj/game/april-25-2004-pedro-martinez-scott-williamson-blank-yankees-as-red-sox-complete-sweep-at-yankee-stadium/

May 7, 2004: Many contributors forge Red Sox rally, walk-off win over Royals
Boston Red Sox 7, Kansas City Royals 6, at Fenway Park

https://sabr.org/gamesproj/game/may-7-2004-many-contributors-forge-red-sox-rally-walk-off-win-over-royals/

May 8, 2004: Pokey Reese hits inside-the-park home run for Red Sox
Boston Red Sox 8, Kansas City Royals 1, at Fenway Park

https://sabr.org/gamesproj/game/may-8-2004-pokey-reese-hits-inside-the-park-home-run-for-red-sox/

May 15, 2004: Bronson Arroyo shuts out Blue Jays; Kevin Youkilis homers in MLB debut
Boston Red Sox 4, Toronto Blue Jays 9, at SkyDome

https://sabr.org/gamesproj/game/may-15-2004-bronson-arroyo-shuts-out-blue-jays-kevin-youkilis-homers-in-mlb-debut/

May 28, 2004: David Ortiz hits 100th career home run as Red Sox beat Mariners
Boston Red Sox 8, Seattle Mariners 4, at Fenway Park, Boston

https://sabr.org/gamesproj/game/may-28-2004-david-ortiz-hits-100th-career-home-run-as-red-sox-beat-mariners/

June 17, 2004: Derek Lowe throws seven shutout innings in his best game of the season
Boston Red Sox 11, Colorado Rockies 0, at Coors Field

https://sabr.org/gamesproj/game/june-17-2004-derek-lowe-throws-seven-shutout-innings-in-his-best-game-of-the-season/

June 25, 2004: Manny Ramírez's 5 RBIs help Red Sox to big win over Phillies
Boston Red Sox 12, Philadelphia Phillies 1, at Fenway Park

https://sabr.org/gamesproj/game/june-25-2004-manny-ramirezs-5-rbis-help-red-sox-to-big-win-over-phillies/

July 6, 2004: Red Sox win their second 11-0 game of the season
Boston Red Sox 11, Oakland Athletics 0, at Fenway Park

https://sabr.org/gamesproj/game/july-6-2004-red-sox-win-their-second-11-0-game-of-the-season/

July 23, 2004: Kevin Millar homers three times, but Red Sox lose to Yankees
New York Yankees 8, Boston Red Sox 7, at Fenway Park

https://sabr.org/gamesproj/game/july-23-2004-kevin-millar-homers-three-times-but-red-sox-lose-to-yankees/

July 24, 2004: Red Sox fired up after walk-off win over Yankees at Fenway
Boston Red Sox 11, New York Yankees 10, at Fenway Park

https://sabr.org/gamesproj/game/july-24-2004-red-sox-fired-up-after-walk-off-win-over-yankees-at-fenway/

August 8, 2004: Boston's Tim Wakefield gives up six home runs to Tigers but wins game
Boston Red Sox 11, Detroit Tigers 8, at Comerica Park, Detroit

https://sabr.org/gamesproj/game/august-8-2004-bostons-tim-wakefield-gives-up-six-home-runs-to-tigers-but-wins-game/

August 12, 2004: Pedro Martínez strikes out 10 Devil Rays batters in shutout
Boston Red Sox 6, Tampa Bay Devil Rays 0, at Fenway Park

https://sabr.org/gamesproj/game/august-12-2004-pedro-martinez-strikes-out-10-devil-rays-batters-in-shutout/

August 16, 2004: Keith Foulke earns 20th save as Red Sox begin summer surge
Boston Red Sox 8, Toronto Blue Jays 4, at Fenway Park

https://sabr.org/gamesproj/game/august-16-2004-keith-foulke-earns-20th-save-of-season-as-red-sox-begin-summer-surge/

September 3, 2004: Two solo homers help Red Sox run win streak to 10 in a row
Boston Red Sox 2, Texas Rangers 0, at Fenway Park

https://sabr.org/gamesproj/game/september-3-2004-two-solo-homers-help-the-red-sox-run-win-streak-to-10-in-a-row/

September 6, 2004: Manny Ramírez and David Ortiz hit back-to-back home runs for the sixth time in season
Boston Red Sox 8, Oakland Athletics 3, at Network Associates Coliseum, Oakland

https://sabr.org/gamesproj/game/september-6-2004-manny-ramirez-and-david-ortiz-hit-back-to-back-home-runs-for-the-sixth-time-in-season/

September 7, 2004: Johnny Damon hits his third leadoff home run of the year for Red Sox
Boston Red Sox 7, Oakland Athletics 1, at Network Associates Coliseum, Oakland
https://sabr.org/gamesproj/game/september-7-2004-johnny-damon-hits-his-third-leadoff-home-run-of-the-year-for-red-sox/

September 8, 2004: Red Sox win gets them as close to first place as they will get in the last four months of season
Boston Red Sox 8, Oakland Athletics 3, at Network Associates Coliseum, Oakland
https://sabr.org/gamesproj/game/september-8-2004-red-sox-win-gets-them-as-close-to-first-place-as-they-will-get-in-the-last-four-months-of-season/

September 10, 2004: Ramírez homers twice, Ortiz once, and Schilling walks no one for fifth consecutive game
Boston Red Sox 13, Seattle Mariners 2, at Safeco Field, Seattle
https://sabr.org/gamesproj/game/september-10-2004-ramirez-homers-twice-ortiz-once-and-schilling-walks-no-one-for-fifth-consecutive-game/

September 16, 2004: Curt Schilling wins his 20th game for Red Sox
Boston Red Sox 11, Tampa Bay Devil Rays 4, at Fenway Park, Boston
https://sabr.org/gamesproj/game/september-16-2004-curt-schilling-wins-his-20th-game-for-red-sox/

September 17, 2004: Mariano Rivera proves mortal, allowing Red Sox a come-from-behind win
Boston Red Sox 3, New York Yankees 2, at Yankee Stadium
https://sabr.org/gamesproj/game/september-17-2004-mariano-rivera-proves-mortal-allowing-red-sox-a-come-from-behind-win/

September 22, 2004: Red Sox win second straight walk-off over Orioles, move closer to clinching wild-card spot
Boston Red Sox 7, Baltimore Orioles 6, at Fenway Park, Boston
https://sabr.org/gamesproj/game/september-22-2004-red-sox-win-second-straight-walk-off-over-orioles-move-closer-to-clinching-wild-card-spot/

September 25, 2004: Red Sox beat Yankees with seven-run eighth inning
Boston Red Sox 12, New York Yankees 5, at Fenway Park, Boston
https://sabr.org/gamesproj/game/september-25-2004-red-sox-beat-yankees-with-seven-run-eighth-inning/

September 26, 2004: Red Sox score early, beat Yankees by 7 runs for the second game in succession
Boston Red Sox 11, New York Yankees 4, at Fenway Park, Boston
https://sabr.org/gamesproj/game/september-26-2004-red-sox-score-early-beat-yankees-by-7-runs-for-the-second-game-in-succession/

September 27, 2004: Bronson Arroyo's 10th win clinches playoff berth for Red Sox
Boston Red Sox 7, Tampa Bay Devil Rays 3, at Tropicana Field, St. Petersburg
https://sabr.org/gamesproj/game/september-27-2004-bronson-arroyos-10th-win-clinches-playoff-berth-for-red-sox/

October 2, 2004: Alan Embree earns hold number 20, with Byun-Hyung Kim getting his second win
Boston Red Sox 7, Baltimore Orioles 5, at Oriole Park at Camden Yards
https://sabr.org/gamesproj/game/october-2-2004-alan-embree-earns-hold-number-20-with-byun-hyung-kim-getting-his-second-win/

October 3, 2004: First baseman Dave McCarty pitches for third time during magical Red Sox season
Baltimore Orioles 3, Boston Red Sox 2, at Oriole Park at Camden Yards, Baltimore
https://sabr.org/gamesproj/game/october-3-2004-first-baseman-dave-mccarty-pitches-for-third-time-during-magical-red-sox-season/

Postseason

American League Division Series

October 5, 2004: Red Sox break Game 1 open with 7 runs in fourth inning
Boston Red Sox 9, Anaheim Angels, 3, at Angels Stadium of Anaheim
https://sabr.org/gamesproj/game/october-5-2004-two-top-teams-face-off-in-the-first-game/

October 6, 2004: Red Sox again run up the score in Game 2 against Angels
Boston Red Sox 8, Anaheim Angels, 3, at Angels Stadium of Anaheim
https://sabr.org/gamesproj/game/october-6-2004-red-sox-again-run-up-the-score-against-the-angels/

October 8, 2004: David Ortiz clinches ALDS sweep in extra innings for Red Sox
Boston Red Sox 8, Anaheim Angels 6 (10 innings), at Fenway Park
https://sabr.org/gamesproj/game/october-8-2004-big-papi-wins-it-in-extra-innings-for-the-red-sox/

American League Championship Series

October 12, 2004: Late Red Sox rally falls short in ALCS Game 1
New York Yankees 10, Boston Red Sox 7, at Yankee Stadium
https://sabr.org/gamesproj/game/october-12-2004-late-red-sox-rally-falls-short-more-of-the-same-sox-lose-again-to-yankees/

October 13, 2004: Yankees win something of a pitching duel in the Bronx
New York Yankees 3, Boston Red Sox 1, at Yankee Stadium
https://sabr.org/gamesproj/game/october-13-2004-yankees-win-something-of-a-pitching-duel-in-the-bronx/

October 16, 2004: Yankees obliterate Red Sox, 19-8, to take commanding lead in ALCS
New York Yankees 19, Boston Red Sox 8, at Fenway Park
https://sabr.org/gamesproj/game/october-16-2004-yankees-obliterate-red-sox-19-8-to-take-commanding-lead-in-alcs/

October 17, 2004: 'Don't Let Us Win Tonight!' Red Sox begin ALCS comeback in Game 4
Boston Red Sox 6, New York Yankees 4 (12 innings), at Fenway Park
https://sabr.org/gamesproj/game/october-17-2004-dont-let-us-win-tonight-red-sox-begin-alcs-comeback-in-game-4/

October 18, 2004: David Ortiz's walk-off single in 14th lifts Red Sox in Game 5
Boston Red Sox 5, New York Yankees 4 (14 innings), at Fenway Park
https://sabr.org/gamesproj/game/october-18-2004-david-ortizs-walk-off-single-in-14th-lifts-red-sox-in-game-5/

October 19, 2004: Curt Schilling keeps Red Sox alive in 'Bloody Sock Game'
Boston Red Sox 4, New York Yankees 2, at Yankee Stadium
https://sabr.org/gamesproj/game/october-19-2004-curt-schilling-keeps-red-sox-alive-in-bloody-sock-game/

October 20, 2004: 'Hell freezes over'; Red Sox complete historic ALCS comeback over Yankees in Game 7
Boston Red Sox 10, New York Yankees 3, at Yankee Stadium
https://sabr.org/gamesproj/game/october-20-2004-hell-freezes-over-red-sox-complete-historic-alcs-comeback-over-yankees-in-game-7/

2004 World Series

October 23, 2004: Red Sox continue momentum with Game 1 win in World Series
Boston Red Sox 11, St. Louis Cardinals 9, at Fenway Park
https://sabr.org/gamesproj/game/october-23-2004-momentum-and-emotion-and-brotherhood-and-everything-else/

October 24, 2004: Stitched up again, Boston's Curt Schilling sticks it to St. Louis in Game 2
Boston Red Sox 6, St. Louis Cardinals 2, at Fenway Park
https://sabr.org/gamesproj/game/october-24-2004-stitched-up-again-schilling-sticks-it-to-st-louis/

October 26, 2004: Red Sox win Game 3 as Cardinals blunder on the basepaths
Boston Red Sox 4, St. Louis Cardinals 1, at Busch Stadium
https://sabr.org/gamesproj/game/october-26-2004-blunder-on-the-basepaths-and-a-failure-to-hit-spell-defeat-for-st-louis/

October 27, 2004: 'Now I Can Die in Peace': Red Sox sweep World Series to win for first time in 86 years
Boston Red Sox 3, St. Louis Cardinals 0, at Busch Stadium
https://sabr.org/gamesproj/game/october-27-2004-now-i-can-die-in-peace/

CONTRIBUTORS

MALCOLM ALLEN lives with his wife and two daughters in Brooklyn, New York, where he manages an event production warehouse. He was one of the 55,338 in attendance at Yankee Stadium on April 25, 2004, when Pedro Martinez hurled seven innings, Manny Ramirez homered with a man aboard, and the Red Sox won, 2-0.

JESSE ASBURY joined SABR in 2017 and is the president of the Oklahoma Chapter. A lifelong Cubs fan, he became a member of Red Sox Nation in the late '90s because he hadn't suffered enough. He still remembers where he was when Edgar Renteria grounded out to Keith Foulke in Game Four of the 2004 World Series. A project manager for the State of Oklahoma, he lives in Norman, Oklahoma, with his wife, Tristianne.

BUDD BAILEY has been part of Buffalo's sports scene for almost 50 years. He spent 23 of those years as a sports reporter and editor for the *Buffalo News*, retiring in 2017. Budd also worked as a reporter and talk-show host for WEBR Radio, and in the communications department for the Buffalo Sabres of the NHL. He has written 15 books. Budd still impresses his friends who are baseball fans by pointing out that he attended the final game of Ted Williams's career in 1960 and Roger Maris's 61st home run in 1961.

KEVIN G. BLEY, a St. Louis native, was present with his wife, Mistie, at Busch Stadium when the Red Sox won the 2004 World Series, but sadly was rooting for the Cardinals. You win some, you lose some (e.g. 1946, 1967, 2004, 2013). Kevin contributes to the SABR Biography and Games Projects. Thanks to Bill Mueller for being a gracious participant in the BioProject. Kevin thanks the Lord for his children, Harry and Evelyn, and countless blessings.

RICHARD BOGOVICH is the author in 2022 of *Frank Grant: The Life of a Black Baseball Pioneer*. His previous books were *Kid Nichols: A Biography of the Hall of Fame Pitcher* and *The Who: A Who's Who*. He has contributed chapters to such SABR books as *The First Negro League Champion: The 1920 Chicago American Giants*. He has degrees from Northern Illinois University, and is office manager of the Wendland Utz law firm in Rochester, Minnesota.

ROBERT BRUSTAD was a professor in the School of Sport and Exercise Science at the University of Northern Colorado with a focus in the social, psychological, and cultural aspects of sport. He had the good fortune of growing up in Southern California where Vin Scully's radio broadcasts provided him with an advanced appreciation of the game during his impressionable youth. He also presented research at the SABR Analytics Conference. Bob died in February 2022.

RALPH CAOLA is from Troy, New York, where he grew up playing baseball and listening to games with his father. After a lack of talent ended his collegiate baseball career, he played softball for 30 years. In 2003 he wrote a series of articles titled "Using Calculus to Relate Runs to Wins," which appeared in SABR's Statistical Analysis Research Committee newsletter, *By The Numbers*. The retired engineer and businessman now spends his summers in Troy and winters in Port Charlotte, Florida, playing tennis and golf.

CHRISTOPHER D. CHAVIS's love affair with the Boston Red Sox began as an undergraduate at Dartmouth College in New Hampshire, where his frequent trips to Fenway Park instilled in him a love of the Olde Towne Team that spawned a deep interest in baseball history. A public-policy researcher and nonprofit leader by day and amateur baseball historian by night, he can usually be found reading a book or watching a documentary about the Sox. He lives in Los Angeles with his wife and two cats, Teddy and Yaz.

KARL CICITTO, a Red Sox fan since 1967, has been a SABR member since 2007. He has contributed articles to the BioProject, Games Project, and SABR books about Mike Sandlock and Jeff Bagwell. He has been a SABR chapter leader since 2014, most recently with the Rabbit Maranville (Springfield, Massachusetts) Chapter of SABR.

ERIC CONRAD is a lifelong Red Sox fan, a SANS Faculty Fellow, and co-owner of Backshore Communications, an internet security consulting company. He is author of several information security books, lives on Peaks Island, Maine, and can be reached at https://ericconrad.com.

DAVE DIONISIO is a writer, musician, and counselor originally from Braintree, Massachusetts. Born the day after the major-league regular season ended in 1974, he holds a Master's degree in Counseling Psychology from Lesley University and enjoys spending time with his dog, Herbie.

ROBERT EMERSON is a lifelong resident of Massachusetts. Red Sox fandom has been a dominant gene in his family; he's been a fan as long as he can remember, his first favorite players being Trot Nixon and Carlton Fisk. He enjoys time spent with his many pets and cooking for his family and/or friends. He has been a SABR member since 2021; this is his first attempt at baseball research.

JEFF ENGLISH is a graduate of Florida State University and resides in Tallahassee, Florida, with his wife, Allison, and twin sons, Elliott and Oscar. He is a lifelong Cubs fan and serves as secretary of the North Florida/Buck O'Neil SABR chapter. He has contributed to multiple SABR projects.

CHAD HAGAN is an entrepreneur and author. His books and articles have been published by *SpringerNature, Palgrave*, Beekman Publications & Audio, *Art News*, SABR, the *Epoch Times, Zero Hedge*, the Huffington Post, and Fox News. He is a lifelong Braves and Red Sox fan.

DONNA L. HALPER is an associate professor of communication and media studies at Lesley University in Massachusetts. She joined SABR in 2011, and her research focuses on women and minorities in baseball, the Negro Leagues, and "firsts" in baseball history. A former radio deejay, credited with having discovered the rock band Rush, Dr. Halper reinvented herself and got her PhD at age 64. In addition to her research into baseball, she is also a media historian with expertise in the history of broadcasting. Among her books is a history of Boston radio. She has also contributed to SABR's Games Project and BioProject, as well as writing several articles for the *Baseball Research Journal*. In 2023 she was inducted into the Massachusetts Broadcasters Hall of Fame.

PAUL HOFMANN has been a SABR member since 2002. He has contributed to more than 25 SABR publications and coedited *The 1883 Philadelphia Athletics: American Association Champions*. Paul is currently the associate vice provost for international affairs at the University of Louisville and teaches in the College of Management at National Changhua University of Education in Taiwan. A native of Detroit, Paul is an avid baseball-card collector and a lifelong Detroit Tigers fan.

JOANNE HULBERT is a Boston Chapter member and SABR Baseball and the Arts Committee cochair, who knows well that although baseball is designed to break your heart, there are moments of great joy that remind us all that waiting for next year will be worth it.

WILLIAM "WILL" HYLAND is a native of Searsmont, Maine, and a graduate of Colby-Sawyer College in New London, New Hampshire. In addition to his work with SABR, William manages an online sports media and podcast network and is working on his first novel. He resides in Lisbon, Maine, with his wife, Summer.

NORM KING (1957-2018) of Ottawa, Ontario, joined SABR in 2010 and became a prolific contributor to the SABR BioProject and Games Project until his untimely death from a rare form of bile duct cancer in 2018. He was the lead editor and author of *Au jeu/Play Ball: The 50 Greatest Games in the History of the Montreal Expos*, published in 2016, and wrote chapters for a number of other SABR books.

BOB LEMOINE is a high-school librarian and adjunct professor at White Mountains Community College and Emporia State University. He lives in New Hampshire and has contributed to several SABR projects. Bob is the author of the book *When the Babe Went Back to Boston: Babe Ruth, Judge Fuchs, and the Hapless Braves of 1935* (McFarland & Co., 2023).

LEN LEVIN is a longtime newspaper editor in New England, now retired. He lives in Providence with his wife, Linda, and an overachieving orange cat. He now (Len, not the cat) is the grammarian for the Rhode Island Supreme Court and edits its decisions. He also copy-edits many SABR books, including this one. He is just down the interstate from Fenway Park, where he has spent many happy hours.

NICK MALIAN lives with his wife, daughter, and son in LaSalle, Ontario, where he was born and raised. Growing up in a border city, he idolized Detroit Tigers greats Cecil Fielder and Alan Trammell. As an impressionable 12-year-old, though, his allegiance shifted to the New York Yankees following their 1996 World Series victory; Nick still attempts the "Derek Jeter jump-throw" (with limited success) at his weekly softball games. Nick is a pharmacist by day and amateur home chef by night.

SCOTT MELESKY has been a sports journalist for over 30 years. He graduated from Syracuse University with a bachelor's degree in history in 1995. Melesky earned his master's degree in education from Pacific Oaks College in May 2021. He has worked as a sports editor and writer for 18 publications and websites including the *Los Angeles Daily News*, the *Quincy (Massachusetts) Patriot Ledger*, and the *Syracuse Herald Journal*. Melesky has also worked in four collegiate sports-information departments highlighted by Marquette University. He has contributed to nine baseball books and is currently co-authoring with Marla McKenna's *Take Back Your Power* and contributing to Nick Del Calzo's *My Baseball Story: The Game's Influence on America*.

DAVID G. MOORE is a New Hampshire native with over 30 years' experience in the computer industry. He joined SABR in 2016 and regularly contributes to baseball articles on Wikipedia. He is a lifelong Red Sox fan, and his favorite Fenway memory is J.D. Drew's grand slam in Game Six of the 2007 ALCS. David lives in the MetroWest area outside of Boston.

MARK MOROWCZYNSKI has been a SABR member since 2019 and, having grown up in Chicago, is a lifelong White Sox fan. He currently lives in Seattle and is an information security professional by day. He can be reached at https://markmorow.com. He has written several information security books; the biographies in this book, with his co-author Eric Conrad, were his first contributions to SABR.

ROBERT NASH is a retired special-collections librarian and professor emeritus at the University of Nebraska at Omaha. A SABR member since 1992 (and a Red Sox fan for much longer), he previously contributed to SABR's *Kansas City Royals: A Royal Tradition; Jackie: Perspectives on 42;* and *The First Negro League Champion: The 1920 Chicago American Giants*. His baseball research has also been published in McFarland's *Rosenblatt Stadium: Essays and Memories of Omaha's Historic Ballpark, 1948-2012* and *The African American Baseball Experience in Nebraska*.

BILL NOWLIN confesses to have left Game Three of the 2004 ALCS before it was over – due to a 13-year-old son at home with a friend. But since the 1950s he has attended countless Red Sox games at a place he often calls his "second home." He waited 59 years to see the Sox win it all. He is one of the founders of Rounder Records; the one Hall of Fame into which he was inducted is the International Bluegrass Music Hall of Fame. He has written and edited many books, mostly on baseball and mostly for SABR, but has not gone far in life – he lives in Cambridge, maybe 10 miles from where he was born in Boston.

TONY S. OLIVER is a native of Puerto Rico currently living in Sacramento, California, with his wife and daughter. While he works as a Six Sigma professional, his true love is baseball and he cheers for both the Red Sox and whoever happens to be playing the Yankees. He is fascinated by baseball cards and is currently researching the evolution of baseball tickets. He believes there is no prettier color than the vibrant green of freshly mown grass on a baseball field.

RYAN PALENCER lives in Clayton, Indiana, with his 5-year-old daughter, Everett. Living his entire life in central Indiana, Ryan graduated from the Indiana University School of Journalism. He has spent the last decade-plus as a minor-league and major-league baseball reporter, mainly covering the Pirates system. As a lifelong fan of the game, he got his start going to minor-league games with his father, and has been for as long as he can remember.

TIM PEELER is a writer who lives in Cary, North Carolina. He has been a SABR member since 2020 and his expertise is in North Carolina sports and history. He attended his first major-league baseball game in 1978, the day after Pete Rose's 44-game hitting streak ended, and saw Tom Seaver pitch a complete-game three-hitter. A 1987 graduate of NC State University with a degree in English/Writing & Editing, he spent more than 20 years writing about sports at newspapers in the Carolinas and has contributed to national newspapers, magazines, and websites. He is a member of the NC State Athletic Hall of Fame Selection Committee and a member of the North Carolina Sports Hall of Fame Board of Directors. He and his wife Elizabeth have two adult sons, Michael and Benjamin.

MATT PERRY is a resident of Holliston, Massachusetts, and has been a SABR member since 2018. A lifelong fan of the Red Sox and the Braves, he enjoys researching and learning about baseball history in New England and has contributed to the SABR Games Project and SABR BioProject as a writer and copy editor. Matthew was published in *Worcester Magazine* about the city's National League history, and posts his other baseball research to his blog, newenglandbaseballhistory.com.

BILL PRUDEN has been a teacher of American history and government for almost 40 years. A SABR member for over two decades, he has contributed to SABR's BioProject and Games Project as well as some book projects. He has also written on a range of American history subjects, an interest undoubtedly fueled by the fact that as a 7-year-old he was at Yankee Stadium to witness Roger Maris's historic 61st home run.

CARL RIECHERS had to work Friday after the Cardinals won the pennant over the Astros on Thursday night. His wife bought him a Cardinals 2004 National League Champions shirt to wear on a trip to visit his Aunt Marie in Albuquerque. Accompanied by his son, he left early Saturday for the 1,000-mile drive just to be in time to watch Game One of the World Series. After the long drive, he stayed awake to watch the Cardinals come back twice to tie the game, only to lose 11-9. The next day, his aunt and son went to the local casino to gamble while he sat in the casino bar and watched Game Two. Everyone else in the bar was rooting for the underdog Red Sox team since they had not won a World Series since 1918. Carl was the only Cardinals fan in the place. There was not much for him to cheer about, and the other patrons gave him plenty of grief while he sat there in his "2004 National League Champions" T-shirt. By Monday evening, he was ready to head home to Wentzville, Missouri, and watch the Cardinals come back and win in six games. They packed up and drove the 1,000 miles back home Monday night and Tuesday morning. He got home in time to grab a nap and get ready for the big comeback! Game Three frustrated Carl and Cardinal Nation with the powerhouse team scratching out just four hits. When the Red Sox took a 3-0 lead in the third inning of Game Four, he changed the channel hoping the worm would turn. Checking back in once in a while confirmed his misery. At the end of the game, he was left with nothing but an old shirt to wear while painting.

Carl has read every player biography and game story while fact-checking this book and cannot understand why anyone would enjoy reading it. The ending is always the same disappointment!

LUCA ROSSI is a public affairs professional living in Bologna, Italy, and a baseball fan since the early '80s. He's been a SABR member since 2004 and is a lifelong Cubs fan.

KELEY RUSSO learned to love baseball and the Red Sox at an early age, thanks to her dad, Babe DeLuca. Many a day was spent in the backyard with her dad playing pickle, pitching, or shagging fly balls, culminating in playing for a winning state championship softball team when she was 12. Babe instilled in Keley a deep love of and devotion to baseball and to the Red Sox, with many fond memories of games at Fenway with her family. Keley is a new SABR member (2022) and this is her first SABR writing experience, collaborating with her sister, Karen DeLuca Stephens. The sisters enjoy discussing in great detail the outcome of every Sox game while keeping an eye on what those Yankees are up to. Keley works for Southern New Hampshire University and resides in Lunenburg, Massachusetts, with her husband and two children.

JASON SCHELLER is a professor of history at Vernon College in Wichita Falls, Texas. His graduate work has been featured in the books *The Empire Strikes Out: How Baseball Sold U.S. Foreign Policy and Promoted the American Way Abroad*, by Robert Elias and *The Boys Who Were Left Behind: The 1944 World Series Between the Hapless St. Louis Browns and the Legendary St. Louis Cardinals*, by John Heidenry and Brett Topel. He joined the Dallas-Fort Worth Banks-Bragan chapter of SABR in 2018. His interests are in World War II baseball, Negro League baseball, the minor leagues and the Boston Red Sox. He enjoys attending minor-league games throughout the country with his wife and daughter each summer. A Red Sox fan since 1986, he follows them every season and relishes the opportunity to attend games at Fenway Park whenever he gets a chance. This is his first publication for SABR.

MARK SCHREMMER is a longtime professional journalist and has written sports articles for such publications as the *Kansas City Star*, the *Topeka Capital-Journal*, and the *Joplin Globe*. He resides in Overland Park, Kansas, with his wife, Colleen. His baseball research interests focus on players from Kansas, the Kansas City Royals, and the Cincinnati Reds.

KAREN DE LUCA STEPHENS grew up in East Boston before girls played Little League ball but thanks to her dad, she was on the diamond for team practices. Karen joined SABR in 2019. After she presented her documentary *One Heck of a Game*, about her father's championship game in Fenway Park in 1937, at a 2019 Boston SABR meeting, the film was included in the 2020 SABR National Convention. For this 2004 Red Sox commemorative book, she and her sister, Keley Russo, decided to work together and would like to dedicate the fun they had on the project to their dad, Amedeo "Babe" DeLuca. Karen is a writer and lives in Mexico City and New York City with her husband. They have five grown children and two granddaughters.

JEB STEWART is a lawyer in Birmingham, Alabama, whose favorite pastime has always been taking his sons, Nolan and Ryan, and his wife, Stephanie, to the Rickwood Classic each year. He has been a SABR member since 2012 and is co-president of the Rickwood Field SABR Chapter. He is an executive committee member on the Board of the Friends of Rickwood Field and is a regular contributor to the *Rickwood Times*. He also edits the Friends' quarterly newsletter, "Rickwood Tales." He has written several biographies for SABR's Baseball Biography Project.

CECILIA M. TAN has been writing about baseball since her fifth-grade book report on *The Reggie Jackson Story*. She has written for Baseball Prospectus, *Yankees Magazine, Gotham Baseball*, and *The National Pastime*. She became publications director for SABR in 2011, and has edited the *Baseball Research Journal* ever since. She also played women's baseball from 2000 to 2007, mostly with the Pawtucket Slaterettes.

GREG TRANTER is a prominent sports historian, curator, and author. He has authored five books on sports history including *The Buffalo Sports Curse, 120 years of Pain, Disappointment, Heartbreak and Eternal Optimism*. Greg has curated multiple sports exhibits and writes for several magazines including *Gridiron Greats* and *NY-PA Collector*. He is the assistant executive director of the Pro Football Researchers Association and the managing editor of *The Coffin Corner*. In 2018 Greg received the PFRA's Bob Carroll Memorial Writing Award and in 2022 its Nelson Ross Award for "outstanding recent achievement in pro football research and historiography." Greg is also a lifelong baseball fan and avid researcher. He is a former executive at Hanover Insurance.

GEORGE "SKIP" TUETKEN has a special interest in Rhode Island-born major leaguers, especially little-known ones, like Art Merewether and Joe Trimble. As a mostly retired safety specialist/consultant, he takes pride in his sons Dave and Andy (who conducted much of the research for this biography and who once doubled between rungs of the Green Monster's ladder during a Beanpot game for UMass/Amherst). Nowadays his biggest enjoyment comes whenever he gets to spend time with any of his three granddaughters or with his grandson.

JOHN VORPERIAN (Johnny V.) hosts *Beyond the Game*, a community syndicated cable television program (www.wpcommunitymedia.org). Since 2002, over 6,500 episodes, with guests such as Robert Kraft, Mo Vaughn, Harry Carson, Loretta Swit, Eddie Money, and Ralph Branca have appeared on *B.T.G.* He contributed to three Professional Football Researchers Association books: *The 1966 Green Bay Packers, The 1958 Baltimore Colts*, and *The 1951 Los Angeles Rams*.

CONTRIBUTORS

BOB WEBSTER grew up in northwest Indiana and has been a Cubs fan since 1963. He worked as a stats stringer on the MLB Gameday app for three years and is a member of the Pacific Northwest Chapter of SABR, the Oregon Sports Hall of Fame, and is on the board of directors of the Old-Timers Baseball Association of Portland.

SAUL WISNIA is the author of numerous books, including *Miracle at Fenway: The Inside Story of the Boston Red Sox 2004 Championship Season; Fenway Park: The Centennial,* and (with Luis Tiant) *Son of Havana.* He has also contributed to various SABR-produced books, publications including the *Washington Post, Boston Globe, Boston Herald,* and *Sports Illustrated,* and has been senior publications editor-writer at Dana-Farber Cancer Institute since 1999 – where he saw up close the tremendous impact the 2004 Red Sox had on the spirits of pediatric and adult cancer patients.

GREGORY H. WOLF was born in Pittsburgh but now resides in the Chicagoland area with his wife, Margaret, and daughter, Gabriela. A professor of German studies and holder of the Dennis and Jean Bauman Endowed Chair in the Humanities at North Central College in Naperville, Illinois, he has edited more than a dozen books for SABR. Since January 2017 he has been co-director of SABR's BioProject, which you can follow on Facebook and X (formerly Twitter).

CONTRIBUTORS TO THE MEMORIES SECTION

A native of Chicopee, Massachusetts, **LAWRENCE BALDASSARO** has authored or edited seven books on baseball, including: *Ted Williams: Reflections on a Splendid Life* (2003) and *Tony Lazzeri: Yankees Legend and Baseball Pioneer* (2021), which received the 2022 SABR Baseball Research Award.

BILL BALLOU has been a SABR member since Cliff Kachline had his office in Cooperstown, and returns there as often as possible even if SABR has moved. A lifelong resident of Whitinsvillle, Massachusetts, he saw his first Red Sox game in 1959 and later covered the team for the *Worcester Telegram* from 1987 through 2018. He covered every game of Boston's playoff run in 2004 (but still considers the Impossible Dream Red Sox of 1967 to be the most exciting team in franchise history). A member of the Boston Chapter, BaseBall Writers Assn. of America, Ballou has been a Hall of Fame voter since 1998.

(FR.) GERALD BEIRNE says, "My memories go back to the days of Rudy York, home-run-hitting first sacker. My wonderful godfather Unc was a Pawtucket [Rhode Island] fireman who took me to weekday afternoon games. I am still disconcerted about the departures of Nomar and Mookie, and am disturbed over the hold this team has over adults who are otherwise sane and rational."

CHARLIE BEVIS is the author of eight books on baseball history. He lives in Chelmsford, Massachusetts.

MIKE BRESCIANI is a lifelong Sox fan from Hopedale, Massachusetts, a retired park and rec director, and first cousin to Red Sox Hall of Famer Dick Bresciani. His first job, in 1978, was at the University of Maryland, where he discovered that radio station WTIC's signal reached parts of Maryland, and "spent way too many nights just driving on the BW Parkway listening to the games." Favorite Sox memory: Carbo Game Six HR. Worst memory: Fisk/Lynn "clerical error."

WALT CHERNIAK was born and raised in Meriden, Connecticut, and has been a Red Sox fan since 1967. He spent seven seasons as a sportswriter covering the Double-A Bristol/New Britain Red Sox before changing careers. He lives in Woodbine, Maryland, and is the longtime editor of *The Squibber,* the quarterly newsletter of the Bob Davids SABR chapter.

KIT CRISSEY is a past president of SABR and for many years coordinated the annual meeting of the Philadelphia chapter of SABR. His primary research interest is World War II baseball.

ANNE ENOS was born and raised on the South Shore of Massachusetts and has nineteenth-century ancestors who were Boston baseball fans. She joined Arizona's Hemond-Delhi Chapter in 2013 and serves as national co-chair of SABR's Baseball Memories Chartered Community, which provides baseball reminiscence programs for people living with memory loss or other chronic health issues. Her experience as a nursing executive and as the daughter of longtime Red Sox scout Bill Enos allows her to combine her health-care knowledge with a love for baseball to bring fun and joy to those in need. She vividly remembers the excitement of the 1967 Impossible Dream season, when she was a young girl.

M. FRANK has been a SABR member since the 1970s, but a Cleveland fan in New York much longer. His interests include collecting, ballparks, and books.

NORM GINSBERG is a retired software engineer and a SABR member since 2007. Although a loyal Red Sox fan, dismayed by his team's last-place finish, he says he considers 2023 as a successful season (Yankees missed the playoffs).

BELT HIGH HALLISEY of Wrentham, Massachusetts, saw his first Red Sox game in 1956 and is a lifelong fan.

BARRY HALPERN was born and raised in Boston but moved away from the area in 1982. During their 51 years of marriage, Barry and his wife, Ellie, moved 26 times, to places within and outside of the US. The Red Sox have always moved along with them. Barry now lives in Sarasota, Florida, and has been a SABR member since 2015.

EVAN KATZ grew up in Brookline, two miles from Fenway Park, in the 1960s and quickly learned the emotional highs and lows of being a Red Sox fan. After a long career in public finance in Massachusetts, he shares his passion for baseball as a high-school coach and through his social media website, Baseball By The Sea Media.

A Native Philadelphian, **SEAMUS KEARNEY** spent 37 years in the Boston area. He became the second moderator of SABR's SABR-L, refounded the Boston Chapter, hosted SABR 32 in 2002, and served on the Boston Red Sox Hall of Fame Selection Committee. He returned home to Philly in 2007, became co-chair of the Connie Mack-Dick Allen Chapter, and co-hosted SABR 43 in 2013. He's a member of SABR's BioProject and Ballparks Committees.

TOM NAHIGIAN grew up in the Boston area and still follows the Red Sox, Celtics, and Bruins. Tom and his wife make their home in Clovis, California. Tom enjoys the Strat-O-Matic Baseball game simulation and reads as many baseball books as he can.

ERIC POULIN is an assistant professor of library and information science at Simmons University and is director of their western Massachusetts-based campus.

Born in Cuba, **JOSÉ RAMÍREZ** joined SABR in 2001. He has contributed to a number of biographies of Cuban-born baseball players, written a book about the last professional baseball season in Cuba in 1961 *Cuba and the "Last" Baseball Season*, and organized the Cuban panel at the 2016 SABR Convention in Miami.

ALEXANDER REARDON is a mechanical engineer in New York City, with a love for baseball stories and statistics. While attending Virginia Tech, he worked as a mascot for the Salem Red Sox.

PAUL SEMENDINGER is the author of numerous books including *The Least Among Them* and *From Compton to the Bronx*. Paul also runs the Yankees website *Start Spreading the News*. A retired principal, Paul stays active running marathons and still playing baseball as a pitcher in a 35-year-old and older wood-bat baseball league.

VIC SON is a lifelong Red Sox fan from Dedham, Massachusetts, who has worked as a tour guide at Fenway Park since 2017, and has been a SABR member since 2019.

A lifelong Red Sox fan, **DAVID SOUTHWICK** has been part of the SABR Boston community since 2001, serving as publicity director from 2003 to 2007. David is on SABR's Deadball Era Committee and studies the writings of Tim Murnane.

MARK STANGL is a St. Louisan and a Cardinals baseball fan since 1964. He was the manual scoreboard operator at Busch Stadium II in 1998-2005 and has been an usher since 2006. Mark has been a SABR member since 1987 (Bob Broeg Chapter); he was president of the chapter 1992-2000, and treasurer from 2019-2022.

A Yankee fan living in Boston who purchased a partial season ticket plan for the Red Sox in 2004, **MARK S. STERNMAN** fully blames himself for the October events that he would prefer to forget. In 2004 Sternman worked for US Sen. John Kerry, who lost the presidential election, and donated a kidney; the Boston World Series win represented by far the most painful of those experiences.

JOHN TIERNEY has been a SABR member for over 30 years. He and his wife have been Red Sox season-ticket holders since 2004.

RICHARD "DIXIE" TOURANGEAU, who lives a mile from Fenway Park, has been a SABR member since 1980. He has contributed to several books and SABR's Deadball and 19th Century Committee newsletters, and authored the "Play Ball!" calendar from 1981 to 2005. Dixie had four full-season tickets behind the third-base dugout from 1988 to 2017 and has witnessed games at 50-plus major-league baseball yards.

ED WHEATLEY is the vice president of the St. Louis SABR chapter and president of the St. Louis Browns Historical Society & Fan Club. He is an award-winning author and producer of multiple baseball books and films on the PBS network. As a Cardinals season-ticket holder, he agonized in the stands during the 2004 and 2013 World Series.

More Books from SABR

ISBN 978-1-933599-97-7
$34.95 pb/$9.99 ebook

'75: The Red Sox Team That Saved Baseball
edited by Bill Nowlin and Cecilia M. Tan

In 1975, the Boston Red Sox played in what was the most-watched World Series in history, an epic seven-game battle with Cincinnati's Big Red Machine that captivated the nation's attention and revived baseball's lagging popularity. '75 tells the life stories of the 37 players who made up the Red Sox roster, from stars like Yaz, Fisk, and El Tiante, to the mop-up men and bench-warmers who were along for the ride.

ISBN 978-1-943816-49-1
$49.95 pb/$9.99 ebook

The 1967 Impossible Dream Red Sox: Pandemonium on the Field
edited by Bill Nowlin and Dan Desrochers

This 500-page book is a tribute to the members of the Impossible Dream team, including biographies of all 39 players that year as well as appreciations of this remarkable season by an all-star lineup featuring Joe Castiglione, Ken Coleman, Gordon Edes, Peter Gammons, Jim Lonborg, and many more. The book also presents over 300 rare photographs and memorabilia, and includes a forward by Jim Lonborg.

Now in ebook!
$9.99 ebook

The Fenway Project
edited by Bill Nowlin and Cecilia M. Tan

Including articles on Red Sox/Boston Braves history and the City Series, The Fenway Project combines historical background as only SABR can deliver it with this fascinating "one night at the ballpark" as recorded by 64 observers all at the same game. From the man who sang the National Anthem (SABR member Joe Mancuso) to the woman who threw out the first pitch (SABR's president Claudia Perry), from a man in the bleachers to a woman in the press box, readers of The Fenway Project will see the game from all angles.

ISBN 978-1-943816-19-0
$39.95 pb/$9.99 ebook

The 1986 Boston Red Sox: There Was More Than Game Six
edited by Bill Nowlin and Leslie Heaphy

One of a two-book set featuring the two teams that went head to head in the 1986 World Series, one book on the Mets, and one on the Red Sox. Every baseball fan knows that Boston was one pitch away from nirvana when it all went wrong, but these Red Sox were full of drama all year, long before Bill Buckner's gaffe. Roger Clemens was young, so was Calvin Schiraldi. The book includes biographies of every player on the 1986 roster, including Oil Can Boyd, Dwight Evans, and Wade Boggs, as well as all the coaches, manager, announcers, and write-ups of several key games from the season as well as the World Series.

ISBN 978-1-933599-97-7
$29.95 pb/$9.99 ebook

Opening Fenway Park in Style: The 1912 Boston Red Sox
edited by Bill Nowlin

With over 300 period photographs and illustrations, this book includes the individual biographies of every player on the team, even Douglass Smith—who appeared in just one game. There are also biographies of owner John I. Taylor and American League founder Ban Johnson. The book also contains a detailed timeline of the full calendar year, with essays on the construction of brand-new Fenway Park and its first renovation, as the team (which won the pennant by 14 games) prepared for Fenway's first World Series.

ISBN 978-1-933599-24-3
$49.95 pb/$9.99 ebook

Red Sox Baseball in the Days of Ike and Elvis: The Red Sox of the 1950s
edited by Mark Armour and Bill Nowlin

The Red Sox spent most of the 1950s far out of pennant contention, winning just enough games to keep their fans' hopes up for the next season. But there can be little doubt that the club was filled with absorbing and fascinating people, and stories that still resonate in New England and beyond. From Harry Agganis and Jimmy Piersall to Jackie Jensen and Pumpsie Green, the names and stories have been the subjects of books and movies. Dominating it all, of course, was Ted Williams, the great star and personality. In this book, members of SABR present biographies of all of these men and many others, 46 in all, along with a season-by-season recap.

ISBN 978-1-933599-58-8
$29.95 pb/$9.99 ebook

New Century, New Team: The 1901 Boston Americans
edited by Bill Nowlin

The team now known as the Boston Red Sox played its first season in 1901, in a new ballpark —the Huntington Avenue Grounds—literally across the railroad tracks from their National League rivals, and out-drew the by more than 2-1, in part because they had enticed some of the most popular players to join them—player/manager Jimmy Collins, pitcher Cy Young, and slugger Buck Freeman. Bios of fans Hi Hi Dixwell and Nuf Ced McGreevy are also included.

ISBN 978-1-943186-29-3
$39.95 pb/$9.99 ebook

Boston's First Nine: The 1871-75 Boston Red Stockings
edited by Bob LeMoine and Bill Nowlin

Before the Red Sox and Braves, there were the Boston Red Stockings. From 1871 through 1875, they won four consecutive pennants in the old National Association, baseball's first major league. The team only fielded 22 players including pitcher Al Spalding, who won more than 50 games in back-to-back seasons of 1874 and 1875. Of the 22 players on the team, five of them are in the Baseball Hall of Fame. Read about George and Harry Wright, Deacon White, Cal McVey, and the South End Grounds in this 400-page volume.

Made in the USA
Middletown, DE
13 April 2024